Napoleon

NAPOLEON

A Political Life

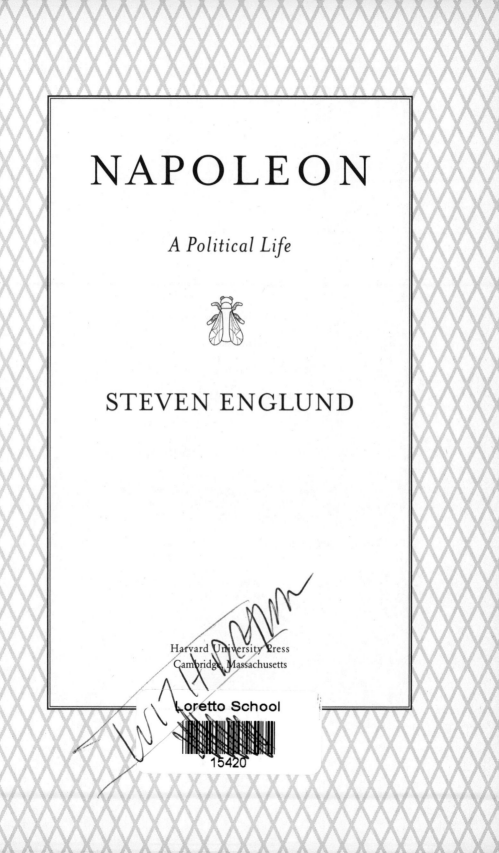

STEVEN ENGLUND

Harvard University Press
Cambridge, Massachusetts

Map and ornaments designed by Andy Beltz

Text set in Berthold Garamond

Printed in the United States of America

Library of Congress Cataloging-in-Publication Data

Englund, Steven.
Napoleon : a political biography / Steven Englund.
p. cm.
Includes bibliographical references and index.
ISBN 0-674-01803-6 (pbk.)
1. Napoleon I, Emperor of the French, 1769–1821. 2. France–Politics and government–
1789–1815. 3. Emperors–France–Biography. I. Title.

DC203.E64 2004
944.05'092–dc22

[B]   2003060371

for Lisa Drew

Contents

Book III: Contre nous, de la tyrannie

207

Book IV: L'Etendard sanglant est levé

357

Map on page   336
Art following page   274

"La Marseillaise"

(The French National Hymn)

Allons enfants de la Patrie
Le jour de gloire est arrivé.
Contre nous, de la tyrannie,
L'Etendard sanglant est levé. [repeated]
Entendez-vous, dans nos campagnes
Mugir ces féroces soldats?
Ils viennent jusque dans vos bras
Egorger vos fils, vos compagnes.
Aux armes, citoyens! Formez vos bataillons;
Marchons, marchons!
Qu'un sang impur abreuve à nos sillons.

Arise children of the motherland
The day of glory has arrived.
Against us, tyranny's
Bloody flag is raised. [repeated]
Don't you hear in our countryside
The roar of their ferocious soldiers?
They are coming into your homes
To butcher your sons and your companions.
To arms, citizens! Form your battalions!
We march, we march!
Let their impure blood water our fields.

The abyss peers back.

Napoleon's Tomb, Hôtel des Invalides, Paris, © Giraudon / Art Resource, NY

Frisson

Go to that chalet in Berchtesgaden, in southern Bavaria. Despite the panoramic *pastorale*, you will feel nothing but revulsion for its most famous Nazi occupant. Go to Red Square. You may have a tremor or two for the October Revolution, but you will feel only hatred for the man who betrayed it with his murderous tyranny over the Soviet empire, 1923–53. If you visit the mausoleum-like memorial for King Louis XVI and Queen Marie-Antoinette in Paris's 8th arrondissement, you may feel reverence for a rich past, but it is one that is irretrievably far away and long ago. As for the Republic's Pantheon for France's "great men," you will find it a place that disappoints you for its spiritual void—surely emptier than the parish church of Sainte Genevieve, which it replaced.

Now go to Les Invalides, which is a veterans' hospital complex, an army museum, and a large church, on Paris's Left Bank. Here lies Napoleon Bonaparte, in a gigantic sarcophagus, emplaced on a high plinth, arising from the lower depths of the Church of Saint-Louis. The tomb lies directly under the grand cupola, towering two hundred feet above. The visitor looks down on it from a marble balustrade.

Visiting Les Invalides is like visiting the Lincoln Memorial: amid all the funereal marble and the airless geometric space, *something is alive*. You revere Abe Lincoln, you long to have known or at least heard him, you feel proud to be part of the republic that spawned him, and if you are born north of the Mason-Dixon line, you feel proud to be a descendant of those who fought for him.

But at *le tombeau de l'Empereur*, something is different. Here the abyss peers back.

The imperial sarcophagus is a costly slab of reddish porphyry—a hard and expensive crystalline rock—that is sculpted like a wave, a shape cut from a continuum: dense and heavy, frozen in stone yet eternally cresting. The stone is unexpectedly, almost shockingly, flesh-colored, not the customary black or white, which would more easily relegate it to a dead past. It is livid and living, the color of a flayed chest in an autopsy, exposing a raw, still-beating heart. The tomb is remarkably modern for an object constructed in the 1850s, quite impersonal and unpictorial, having no story to recount or symbolism to impart. It is not even characteristically French, but is more like the monolith from Stanley Kubrick's *2001*—still and powerful, knowing and alive, overwhelming the impressive ecclesiastical and military setting in which it is placed. You forget you are in a church and a hospital, and despite the presence of all the trophy flags of battle, which the Michelin guide has told you to look for, you even forget that this is a military establishment.

If the large presence is not characterized, it is because the architect of the tomb, Louis-Tullis Visconti (1791–1853), was all too aware of the paltriness of characterization in this case. Unlike historians and writers, the architect was satisfied with seeking to evoke, not to describe or (still less) explain, and in that regard he has succeeded with Nietzschean force: the power, the will, the threat, the thrill are all here. For how to describe or explain this man, though it has been tried and tried—and will be tried again in the pages of this book? As what do you characterize Napoleon? As Hitler? As Prometheus? Both analogies, and even Jesus Christ himself, have been invoked, but the man lying in this tomb was very far from any of them. One might rather say that Napoleon is a character unfinished, like Hamlet; and like Hamlet, a puzzle—full of contradictions, sublime and vulgar. One is pulled in opposing directions.

His tomb evokes no grief or sorrow, as does the Lincoln Memorial. The visitor's throat is not thick with emotion, nor does his heart reflexively fill with high resolve. Rather, his mind is troubled but wide awake, in response to what lurks down there—equally menacing and thrilling, with Sphinx-like qualities of good and evil and mystery. Most present in this place is the awe-evoking sense of human *possibility*, which is a different thing from hope. The wave of this tomb becomes a sleigh that will carry us off into an unknown future, even if only a hundred days' worth.

> *France cannot think of him without trembling, and in her trembling, as much as she regrets it, she is afraid of him, she is afraid of the longing that she still has for him.*
>
> André Suarès*

---

*"De Napoléon," in *Cahiers de la Quinzaine* (1912). Suarès is a French writer who straddles both centuries (1868–1948). His essays and other works are marked by a certain mysticism and cult of artistic creation, and deserve better than the neglect they are currently undergoing.

BOOK I

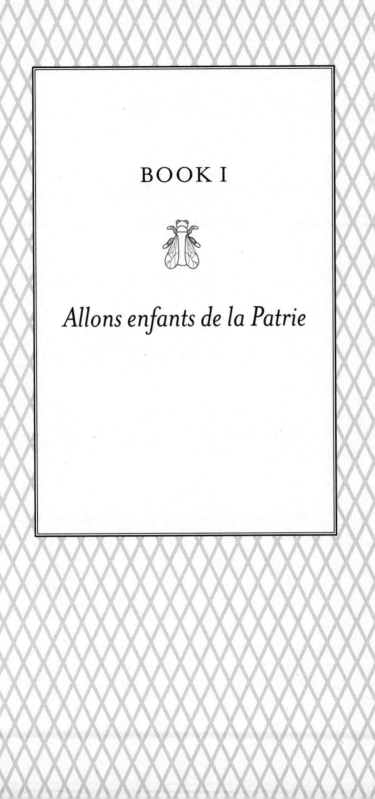

Allons enfants de la Patrie

I

Napoleone di Buonaparte

A man's glory does not flow down to him from the past, it starts with him. The Nile's source is known only by a few Ethiopians, but who is unaware of its mouth?

—Chateaubriand

UNSCEPTERED ISLE:
CORSICA IN THE EIGHTEENTH CENTURY

What, in all the world, is so naked, so abrupt, as this rock?
—Seneca, in exile

There are, in truth, very few things one has to know about the Corsica of Napoleon's infancy and youth. When he departed it in haste, in the summer of 1793, he left it for keeps and never looked back—indeed at the end of his life, he declared Corsica "ruinous for France"—and for this, Corsican nationalists have never forgiven him. Yet Corsican tones broadly suffuse Napoleon and his life the way the famous idée fixe informs the entirety of Hector Berlioz's *Symphonie fantastique,* and if we are to try to know Napoleon, then we must try to sound those chords.

In the eighteenth century (and even today), Corsica was no place for the fainthearted or the indecisive; it frightened the anemic, horrified the otiose, and made the ambivalent, well, unsure. The *île de Corse* demanded of the visitor a degree of tolerance for discomfort unexpected in European venues north of the thirty-fifth parallel. It helped if he was a connoisseur of contrasts, a collector of sights and insights, an amateur of strong emotion and some danger, an admirer of vistas of rough scrub, miles of slow narrow roads punctuated with hairpin turns, bounded by jagged limestone cliffs. The seething morass of the island's scrub retreated only provisionally and defiantly before the human intruder. Parts of Switzerland had the remoteness, quiet, and beauty of Corsica and the same awe-inspiring blend of elemental sky, earth, and water, but the fire was missing.

Corsican fire burned in the eighteenth century, as in the twenty-first. There is no admission fee to the high view from Lion Rock at Roccapina, the only price to be paid being the fear of death one bathes in, in getting there. This natural sculpture, here since neolithic times, is pounded, hundreds of feet below, by the swelling surf of a cobalt Mediterranean; the setting sun may blaze so strongly that for a moment you think it a dying star, and this rock the site Armageddon. The visitor lingers a time; he will not walk away calm and reassured, but pensive and grateful to be alive. In short, he does not readily imagine the white, pampered hand of an Edward Gibbon picking up his pen at a table in a calcium-white stucco villa above the port of Bonifacio, whence to contemplate in equanimity the hyperbolic conflicts of the declining Roman Empire. No, in Seneca's time, as ever after, Corsica is no safe bet for equanimity. Rousseau himself, the great seeker after noble savages, thought hard about moving here, then thought better of it. Try Lausanne, Monsieur Gibbon.

Corsica has always impressed the outsider far more than she is impressed by him. The island calls to mind C. S. Forester's observation about the naval destroyer: "her mission in life was to give and not to receive." So it has been with Corsica. The individuals hailing from the island who have had large impacts on the "mother" societies of Genoa, England, and, above all, France, now in her 236th year of possession, are at the tip of most educated tongues. Of course, a French man or woman will smile if you ask him or her to "name a Corsican who has affected France profoundly," but even if you add quickly, "I mean, other than *that* one," the person can still reel off names: Paoli, Pozzo di Borgo, Sebastiani, Piétri, Pasqua—all political men. Thinking hard, one can adduce a few names in the arts (the philosopher J. T. Desanti; singers Tino Rossi and César Vezzani, the ballerina Pietragalla), yet the balance is clear: Corsica's main export to France has not been olive oil, wine, or chestnuts but politicos, including a vast throng of leading civil servants, nearly always of a distinctly authoritarian flavor. On the other hand, ask a Corsican, educated or not, to name a Frenchman (or, for that matter, an Italian) who has durably affected this island—who has been known and appreciated here in the ways that the above-named have affected France and been received there—and he or she will pause long. "De Gaulle" might come the answer, or if your interlocutor be frank, "Pétain." And that is all. It is a short list for 236 years.

Repeatedly conquered and colonized from classical times onward, Corsica, after the mid–sixteenth century, came under permanent Genoese domination. The republican city-state on the west coast of Italy bestrode the finances of the island, founded a few coastal towns (including Ajaccio), and built those distinctive towers that give the island a certain quaint historical flavor, but by and large the Genoese did not greatly influence the island or its inhabitants. But then Corsica's story has always been the same: it belongs essentially to itself. Its innumerable rebellions never had a happy issue, ending in defeat, imprisonment, execution, and exile. The eighteenth century saw them try again: a rebellion in 1729 evolved into a revolution, the first, it is said by Corsicans, of the "democratic revolutions" that have given the century its fame in modern times. A closer look might see the main role still going to religious traditionalism, feuding clans, and oligarchic powers parading as liberal, but so be it. The next decades saw continuous warfare until, in 1755, the Corsicans managed to adopt a government and elected a head: Pasquale Paoli, the thirty-year-old son of a leader of the 1729 revolution.[1]

That name was far better known in his time than it is in ours, outside of Corsica and a certain town in eastern Pennsylvania. Born in 1725, Paoli spent much of his early life in exile in Naples. He would die in England in 1807, again in exile, but his story in the intervening years is in many ways ours, for the political and intellectual ferment he created proved to be the nursery of the man—also a Corsican, and a sometime patriot—whose name would eclipse Paoli's as completely as in Macedonia, another rocky site, Alexander's eclipsed Philip's. Perhaps as gifted as Bonaparte intellectually, Paoli received a classical education in the kingdom of the Two Sicilies. Like Napoleon, he feasted on Plutarch, the first-century Greek biographer whose *Parallel Lives* memorialized for all time the great figures of classical antiquity. But Paoli did his contemporaries one better: he conscientiously emulated the Olympian hauteur and self-sacrifice of "the noble Greeks and Romans." Even to his adversaries Paoli appeared heroic.

In November 1755, Paoli proclaimed a separate state, which the French and Genoese, distracted by the Seven Years' War, tolerated. During the thirteen years of its luminous existence (1755–68), "the nation of Corsica," or "the realm of Corsica," as it styled itself (it did not call itself a "republic" since the term denominated the hated Genoese), pursued its experiment in self-government. It was led benevolently, but so very firmly, by "the general

of the nation," Paoli. The large peasant majority of the island's 140,000 people called him *Babbù* (meaning "father" in Corsican) and more than likely
found his sophisticated ideas impenetrable, but they liked his strong grip on
the tiller. He *would*, he said, impose a regime on this feuding, assassinating,
divisive, disputatious, and sullen people, but he would also teach them to govern themselves. The Anglo-Scot writer James Boswell, who came for a visit in
1765, fell for the *Babbù*'s austere charms. By then, Paoli had opened a printing press, a newspaper, and a university at Corte, the capital city—all startling
acts of democratic faith and investment in so desperately poor and backward
a country, but not items Paoli regarded as luxuries. Boswell observed truly
when he wrote: "His great object was to form the Corsicans in such a manner they might have a firm constitution, and might be able to subsist without him. Our state, said he, is young, and still requires the leading strings. I
am desirous that the Corsicans should be taught to walk themselves."

This was new. The Corsicans had known rebellion, but the Paolist revolution entailed the concerted political education of a society, the beginning
of the formation of citizens. The island realm and its leader thus generated
high interest among enlightened opinion in Europe and America, from
Voltaire to Ben Franklin. Jean-Jacques Rousseau notes, in his political masterpiece, *The Social Contract:* "I have the feeling this little island will one day
astonish Europe," and he even devoted a small work to laying out a constitution for the little state. Thanks to Paoli's unique blend of the progressive
and the dictatorial, as well as his irreproachable personal morality and total
dedication to the public weal, he gave Corsica one of the more original governments in Europe, and the celebrity status of a much admired nation.
True, he evoked some grumbles for his Caesarian style of rule, yet in the end
he was mainly seen as a figure out of Plutarch, a genuine matinee idol of the
Enlightenment, and, for that matter, of European history since.[2]

What strikes the modern reader is the paradox between, on the one
hand, Corsica's landscape and people, physical vitality and raw primitivity,
and, on the other, her apparent promise as an advanced social experiment.
The contrast seemed intelligible and obvious to Boswell, but then the
twenty-five-year-old writer was hardly more than an adolescent in an enlightened age that defined adolescence: ardent, impetuous, indiscreet, insou-
ciant, curious, capable of scaling heights of optimism and high sentiment,
while sinking into verbosity, malice, and self-occupation unrelieved by
self-awareness.

Despite the fact that French Enlightenment thinkers praised the Corsican
experiment, and many courtiers at Versailles were profoundly impressed by
Paoli's courage and nobility, King Louis XV, for reasons of state, stood with

the Genoese against the Corsican republic. He was well aware of Corsica's critical strategic position in the Mediterranean and the desirability of keeping it out of English hands. The Genoese, for their part, were wholly convinced of the truth of their old proverb "The Corsicans aren't worth the rope it takes to hang them." They eventually got tired of the expense of policing the island and handed over its governance to France. A vastly superior French expeditionary force inflicted an annihilating defeat on the little Corsican "army" in a remote and austere valley of the rocky northeast of the island, at a spot called Ponte Nuovo. Dumouriez, a French officer who was there, remarked with a sigh, "The Corsicans loved liberty; we came to conquer them; they laid traps for us; they were right to do so."[3] With infinite sadness, on June 13, 1769, Paoli embarked on a British frigate to return to the exile he knew too well.

This little-known struggle may be viewed in historical perspective as the rehearsal for the immensely larger conflict looming in 1789, and the Paolist State can be seen as a moment in European, not just Corsican, history.

THE BUONAPARTES OF AJACCIO

Shortly before the final showdown at Ponte Nuovo, a man with a pronounced rhetorical flair gave an address to the Corsican Corta, or national assembly. The peroration—a call for courage and unity—must surely have moved Boswell (or the young Patrick Henry), not to say shaken many at the French court, if they heard about it: "If it be written in the book of destiny that the greatest monarch on earth shall take his measure in battle with the smallest people on earth, then we have reason to be proud, and we are certain to live and die with glory, [for] . . . we fight as men with no hope who are yet resolved to win or die."[4] Napoleon on St. Helena would be so moved by this speech, which he claimed to have known all his life, that he would toss off a paraphrase of equal beauty and considerably greater cogency: "If, to be free, it were only enough to desire freedom, then all people would be free. But history shows that few receive the benefits of freedom because few have the energy, courage, or virtue that it takes."[5]

Bonaparte family legend always held that the original speech before the Corta had been presented by their own Carlo Buonaparte when he was twenty-two. It now appears more likely that it was Paoli himself who gave it. What is undeniable is that the extremely personable, competent, and handsome young Carlo had rapidly drawn close to Paoli and become one of many of his trusted associates, perhaps a secretary. Problems for Carlo's reputation arose, however, after the fall of "the realm of Corsica," when Buon-aparte made the transition to French rule with "shocking" rapidity in the eyes of many. For example, he dined with the brutal French military com-mander of the occupation two months after the battle of Ponte Nuovo. This, coupled with Carlo's well-known ambition, have led some to question his fundamental patriotic sincerity, and to present the short, hardscrabble life (1746–85) of Napoleon's father as an illustration of the social scrambler, not the political revolutionary. It is undeniable that Carlo was a classic frayed-cuff provincial patrician, descended from a long line of similar types, who married into a slightly more successful family. He was a man who, before and after he met Paoli, had few thoughts and took few steps that did not pertain to acquiring something for himself and his family (the terms being redun-dant, in Corsican eyes). But that is not to say he was unable to recognize or be profoundly affected by something else entirely, even long after it was gone. By accenting his youthful role in the Paolist moment—and four years is not so short a time—we place a different emphasis on Carlo's life, and give it a different dignity.

Paoli was a charismatic moralist and teacher as well as politician, whose impact on people far older and cannier than Carlo Buonaparte was leg-endary. Carlo's initial decision to become a *paolisto* perhaps had its self-interested side, but if so, it is not apparent. Surely his own conservative family and his Ramolini in-laws did not see the young man's immersion in revolutionary politics as profitable, but rather, as risky. If they soon came round to it, it must have been due, in part, to the combined effect of their son's (son-in-law's) sincerity, their own patriotism, and the *Babbù*'s inter-national prestige. Then, too, recall: Carlo stuck by Paoli down to the "realm's" bloody end at Ponte Nuovo, where he himself was on hand—something by no means all *paolisti* had the courage to do. The Corta ora-tion—whoever gave it—was no academic exercise but a speech-act in a colonial war, a blow struck for a democratic cause whose time had come. Future events in America and France over the next generation would relent-lessly illustrate the historical impact of variously sincere young men with change on their minds.

What is undeniable is both that Paoli's regime profoundly affected the generation of Corsicans born in the 1740s, and that those effects got passed on to their children. True, the light from the Paolist sun might have been dimmer in Napoleon's generation, *except* that the French Revolution brought Paoli himself back to Corsica. The *Babbù* had armed his hardy simple folk with new concepts and a new vocabulary and had herded them onto his-tory's stage. Once there, they began the process of becoming a public, not just a population. Corsica had become more than an ultimate refuge to the likes of a Carlo Buonaparte; the ancient "patria" was now to be seen as a "nation," in the modern, democratic sense of the term.

Without the Corsican revolution, of which he was the pure product, Carlo Buonaparte would have spent his life as generations of his ancestors had spent theirs: tending the modest family businesses and properties, a task to which he soon returned, but not as the man he had been. Thanks to Paoli, Carlo had become, for a time, a citizen of the new secular order, for which cause he might well have died at Ponte Nuovo. In return for his audacity and courage, Carlo received a *political* education and developed a *political* approach to society. "I am desirous that the Corsicans should be taught to walk themselves," Paoli had told Boswell, and there is every reason to think that Carlo Buonaparte was one of many *paolisti* who appropriated the essentially political expectation that social life is, and should be, made by "citizens" and "patriots" acting as members, and on behalf of "the nation." Carlo never forgot those years; they were what the ancient Greeks called the time of his *kairos*—of ecstasy, of meaning. He never stopped mythifying about them, gilding his own and his wife, Letizia's roles to his children, who in turn gilded their parents' roles—and with good reason. These years were what he knew of the historic. Carlo's personal tragedy would be, as Napoleon understood, that he did not live to participate in the vastly larger, but similar revolution that swept France and Europe after 1789. Carlo lived small and dreamed big. Most of his life after 1769 was undeniably spent in the long forced march of social and economic grubbing. Nevertheless, to stress this is to overvalue the relentless unfolding of *chronos*, of clock-measured time, and to miss what was special. Carlo's *kairos* was his time with Paoli.

Carlo's life was also pregnant with another kind of meaning, no less significant: his wife, Letizia (né Ramolino), was large with child when Paoli embarked on the *Rachel* for England. Two months later, she gave birth to her second son, whom they named for Carlo's uncle Napoleone. The boy, like his brother, was born in the new day. In common with his older brother, Joseph, and his future brothers and sisters, he would have a passion for "the nation" and "equality before the law," and a taste for "the political"—that is, the expectation that being active in the public arena was natural and desirable.

Once in Corsica, the Buonapartes[6] of Saint Charles Street lived a short walk from the sixteenth-century cathedral of Notre-Dame. Ajaccio was then a town of four thousand. Bastia, the new French capital, which replaced

Corte, was the largest town of the island, with a population of five thousand. At the time that Carlo found himself out of his job as revolutionary secretary and part-time orator, he was the father of two sons: Joseph, born in January of the year prior (1768), six months before Genoa ceded Corsica to the French; and Napoleon, born on August 15, 1769, a French citizen from birth. They would be followed by Lucien (1775), Elisa (1777), Louis (1778), Pauline (1780), Caroline (1782), and Jérôme (1784). An attractive couple, Carlo and Letizia were not a match made in heaven. Carlo had loved another, a woman of no importance, whom his family staunchly opposed for marriage. They had lobbied instead for the alliance with the better-off, if far from wealthy, Ramolinis. As for Letizia, who was all of fifteen years old when she married, we know nothing of her feelings, only that they would not have mattered in eighteenth-century Corsica. She was marrying a good catch (Carlo stood a sporting chance to inherit all of the Buonaparte property one day), and that was enough.

For important reasons, however, there was no church wedding. Contrary to legend and to the belief of their own children, the Buonapartes were not joined in holy matrimony on June 1, 1764, in the cathedral. Carlo, resentful at having to give up the woman he loved and marry one he did not, appears to have refused to go through with the hypocrisy of the cathedral wedding that had been planned. The legal union would have to suffice, though for appearances' sake, the family (probably his uncle Lucciano, an archdeacon) altered the church registry, to make it look as if their nuptial mass had taken place. This deficiency never weighed on Carlo; unlike most Corsicans, he was a thoroughly secularized man, Voltairian in his attitude toward religion and the Church.

Soon after his marriage, Carlo committed the one serious indulgence of his life. Leaving a pregnant wife,[7] he skipped off to Italy, theoretically for further education, but in fact to act the part of the spendthrift playboy for several months. This ended when he joined the *paolisti*. That youthful fling, plus a later tendency toward some profligacy of dress, travel, and dining well when he could—which left him occasionally penniless or in debt to relatives—have all but ruined Carlo's historical reputation, including in his children's eyes, unjustly so. Contrary to myth, the family was far from impoverished, even if its cash flow was tight. The Buonapartes and the Ramolinis were both of respectable northern Italian stock whose mercenary forebears had settled in Ajaccio not long after the port's foundation in 1492, and if neither family enjoyed the genealogy it boasted of, they lived comfortably. Carlo's efforts to establish the family's noble status bore fruit under the French administration, and he was able to use it to considerable advantage. In short, if the Buonapartes were small fry compared with the island's rich, the windows of their roomy three-story house were metaphorically lace-curtained.

Something did bind Carlo and Letizia closely: their intense dissatisfaction with their social estate, and the consistency and coherence with which they labored for its improvement. Ambition, not *l'amour*, bound them. Letizia had stood with Carlo from the first moment he joined Paoli, and she stood with him over the long decade and a half following Paoli's defeat—the years that saw Carlo Buonaparte virtually fetter himself and his wife to his career project of improving his family's condition. With the same energy with which he had served the *Babbù*, he pursued the very unromantic tasks of social promotion: landing a civil post for himself, obtaining a certificate of nobility, squeezing a profit from an olive grove, procuring a government subsidy for a draining project, pursuing a lawsuit against a neighbor over a house, winning an appointment in local government, etc. He died at thirty-nine, broken in health, and who can say his labors in these vineyards were not part of the reason? He once wrote a friend that his life could provide the material for a complete romance, but Carlo's life contained only some promising early pages of romance. The story turned abruptly prosaic after Ponte Nuovo.

To serve or not to serve the French overlords was not exactly a tormenting existential question for most Corsicans, even many devoted *paolisti*. The French, after all, dominated, and the Corsicans had a long history of making do with conquerors. A gambler by temperament, a charmer by personality, and a courtier in style, Carlo availed himself of the chance to meet the much older Marbeuf, the French military governor of Corsica. The governor liked Carlo and valued his advice and information about how to govern these prickly, suspicious, vindictive Corsicans. But if Marbeuf took to Carlo, he may have "taken" Letizia. Dorothy Carrington presents a serious case for the old polemical thesis argued by opponents of Napoleon for two centuries that Mme Buonaparte, early in the 1770s, embarked on a decade-long affair with the intendant, a man nearly three times her age.[8] It has even been argued, though this may be pressing things too far, that Marbeuf was the father of Louis, the future king of Holland and father of Napoleon III. In truth, the evidence does indicate that Carlo was roundly delighted at the prestige and benefits procured for the family by their relationship with Marbeuf. Paoli had been, in Carrington's words, "the first great chance of his life,"[9] and undoubtedly the second—of a different, more familiar kind—was the association with Marbeuf.

NAPOLEON'S CHILDHOOD

I was born when the homeland [patrie] *was perishing.*

On St. Helena in exile, Corsica returned. Napoleon talked endlessly, and in loving detail, about his infancy and childhood. This makes for an unfamiliarly modest and attractive picture of our subject, but it is also one we should not peer at too deeply, for if history be a trick we play on the dead, then the sort of autobiography Napoleon was grinding out at St. Helena is the most devious. The St. Helena testimony speaks more accurately to Napoleon's state of mind on the last island in his life than it provides us with sure information about his early years on the first island in his life. In point of fact, little that can be independently confirmed about Napoleon's early years is known, as is so often the case with historical figures before our century.

Nevertheless the statement is worth remembering: "I was born when the *patrie* was perishing." Written in a letter to Paoli in 1789, it sheds light on the lifelong mind-set of this *paolisto* son. The sentence continues, "Thirty thousand Frenchmen spewed onto our coasts, engulfing the throne of liberty in seas of blood: such was the odious sight that first met my eyes." Despite the sternness of such rhetoric, what is important here is not the anti-French sentiment but the diffuse passion underlying it. Napoleon has clearly inherited Carlo's predilection for "the political," as evidenced by his apparently neutral invocation of the "patrie," for the word must not be confused with *the land* or *the people* of Corsica. Neither of these was perishing under the French, despite the high casualties at Ponte Nuovo. What the French had destroyed was "the realm of Corsica"—that is, the republican political experiment of Paoli, whose destruction was well symbolized by their shutting down of the University of Corte. The highly emotional significance of the *Babbù*'s Camelot regime, encased in the hearts of all *paolisti*, must not close our eyes to how much it was a *political* construct. Napoleon on St. Helena, looking back across the arc of his life, has instinctively signaled that his life had a political, not just a patriotic inception in the *patrie*.

Napoleon's early years in Ajaccio were anything but romantic storm and stress. Nuclear families were not the Corsican way. The child Napoleon was part of a large, extended, "functional" family that reached out to include the boy's great-uncle Lucciano, who lived next door. As a ranking priest (archdeacon) at the cathedral, Lucciano was a well-known figure in Ajaccio and he played a large, if contentious role in the family. A pro-Genoese/anti-French believer, Lucciano had his share of arguments with his nephew Carlo, but however irascible or tightfisted the old man was, he was the soul of dependability, and his constant presence was an important element in Napoleon's life. At times, his loans and gifts—not to mention the legacy he left on his death in 1791—enabled the family to cope better.

For the most part, however, Napoleon was surrounded by women—Minana (Letizia's mother), Saveria (Carlo's mother), Geltrude (Carlo's sister), and his nurse, Camilla Ilari. The few among them who survived into the Empire amply enjoyed the Emperor's largesse, in return for the happy childhood he readily granted had been his. The extremely devout Camilla Ilari, in fact—in return for her years spent defusing little Napoleon's temper—would one day enjoy an hour and a half private audience with His Holiness, Pius VII, during which the Supreme Pontiff of the Universal Church did nothing but question her to death about "what was he like as a child."[10]

The center of the young Napoleon's emotional world was his mother, although the boy, perhaps like most boys, would have preferred it to be his father. That was not to be. Certainly, Carlo's two life-ordering convictions—his politicization by Paoli and his quest for social advancement—marked his children, as did the man's intellectual and cultural values. The children grew up in the presence of a library of one thousand volumes (including, of course, a copy of Boswell's *Account of Corsica*), which can only have represented a huge expense and luxury—a *paolisto* sort of investment, indeed. Napoleon, Joseph, and Lucien grew up readers and remained so all their lives. The novelist Stendhal speculated that the young Napoleon was exposed to high-toned, patriotic conversations among the ex-*paolisti* gathered *chez* Carlo.[11]

Carlo was also the indulgent and good-tempered father we would expect him to be, though when seen from his children's memoirs, he becomes something of a weak presence in the family, compared to his wife. Day to day, the patriarch was gone a good deal of the time—to Bastia, for meetings of the Corsican assembly, where he represented the Ajaccio nobility, or to France, on family business. Napoleon's later judgments of Carlo, while not wholly unappreciative, ran to the harsh (e.g., he was "too fond of pleasure"), which leads one to think that the son harbored a degree of permanent grudge or disappointment where the father was concerned. Nevertheless, a profound complicity—of political maturity and the drive for recognition—joined father and son at the root, and Napoleon never forgot it. When he stood in Notre-Dame Cathedral in December 1804, having crowned himself and his wife Emperor and Empress of the French, after being blessed by the Supreme Pontiff of the Universal Church who had never before come to Paris for such an event, Napoleon leaned over to Joseph and whispered, "Si babbù ci vidi!" (If Father could see us now).

Carlo's physical and perhaps psychological absence left Letizia to run the family—a very Corsican state of affairs. She was a formidable woman: young, beautiful, and energetic, frank to a fault, loving but without indulgence; her children loved her but they also feared her. As her second son (who was also her favorite) put it, "Her tenderness was severe. . . . Here was the head of a man on the body of a woman." High praise from a Corsican boy for his mother, but then Napoleon acknowledged that he owed his success to the character formation he received from Letizia—particularly her emphasis on working and suffering without complaint. None of her other children responded to her lessons about self-discipline as well as Napoleon did. As the inimitable Carrington puts it, he "was her masterpiece, fashioned in the nine years' loving intimacy between the proud, spirited, handsome young mother and her intrepid little son."[12]

His siblings would play large roles in his life, but not until later. Only Joseph occupied the stage of Napoleon's childhood, for Lucien, Elisa, and Louis were still babies when the older boys left for school in 1778, while Pauline, Caroline, and Jérôme were not born yet. Joseph was apparently a happy child, of a placid, even serene disposition that stood in sharp contrast with that of his brother. For young Napoleon, the adjectives are usually poured into two categories: on the one hand, "turbulent," "combative," "nervous," and "inattentive" (especially to his appearance; his socks were always down around his shoes); on the other hand, "clever," "quick-witted," "mathematically gifted," "self-confident," and "willful." But one should add, Napoleon was also affectionate and given to feeling guilty, a boy who responded easily to people who responded to him. In his small body were lodged a large intelligence and even larger will, which, if they made him stubborn and headstrong, also rendered him attractive and fascinating. Though Joseph was eighteen months his senior and always physically larger, Napoleon enjoyed complete ascendance over him (forcing him, e.g., to do his homework for him). On the other hand, and this is not a small point: he and Joseph handled things in a way that left them profoundly close to each other, almost as twins can be. The mature Emperor would observe that he "loved very few people," and Joseph was among them.

For want of material to paint a complete portrait of the young Napoleon, one should refrain from speculating that the boy possessed any of the traits assigned him in their extreme form. Child Napoleon stood out in his family for his intellectual talents and willful character, but he was not an apparent genius, megalomaniac, or neurotic. I do not see deep-seated conflict or neurosis lodged in the boy that explains or even sheds much light on his later behavior. Here was not a psychologically hobbled man or a fascinating case of child psychopathology. Napoleon was, overall, I think, a rather bold, brave, and turbulent boy whom it was probably easy to love—and find exasperating.

On the basis of their personalities, Joseph's and Napoleon's careers were determined for them: the Church, for Joseph; the military, for Napoleon. Napoleon had already made it clear this is what he wanted—as a little boy, he played soldier, dressed up like a soldier, made friends with the troops in the nearby garrison, and ate their dark bread with them. Joseph was less certain of his vocation, but an ecclesiastical career seemed a good bet, given that Comte de Marbeuf's brother was the Bishop of Autun and would assure the boy an excellent future. An ecclesiastical career denoted high prestige and was often sought on purely careerist grounds. If the Church of Rome no longer enjoyed the hegemony of bygone days, she yet remained the ideological backbone of the *ancien régime*—France's First Estate; the nobility came second.

But the boys were now at least second-class citizens. They were fortunate indeed, as the time for serious schooling arose, that their father had lobbied so effectively for the family's inscription in the list of the French nobility. This was far more than a question of vanity. Old regime France, unlike Corsica, was a rigidly stratified society that benefited the top two estates. In all, Louis XVI's government integrated seventy-eight Corsican families into the French nobility—useful in forging loyalty to the Crown among many who had lingering *paolisti* or pro-Genoa sentiments. Had Carlo's family not been allowed to add the yearned-for "particle" to their names, signing themselves, "*de* Bonaparte,"[13] then Joseph and Napoleon would have been ineligible to attend French "gentlemen" schools, and could not have aspired to all the other forms of social promotion that were now open to them in the Church and the army. (Nor would Carlo have been permitted to remain deputy of the Ajaccio nobility to the Corsican assembly, a position that gave him some visibility and clout in France, as well as his homeland.)

So, on December 12, 1778, Joseph and Napoleon Bonaparte, accompanied by their parents, departed Ajaccio for Bastia, thence by boat to the French mainland. They were accompanied by their father's young stepbrother, Joseph Fesch, aged fifteen, who would soon receive a scholarship to study for the priesthood at the seminary of Aix-en-Provence. The journey to Bastia took several days—going inland, east, across the plains surrounding their hometown, then north, their route gradually steepening as it came to thick forests of pine and chestnut trees. Eventually, they arrived at

Morosaglia, the birthplace of Paoli; soon they would be skirting rugged, fair-sized mountains, a few with summits of over 7,500 feet, where snow lingered into the summer. On this journey to the capital, the Bonaparte family did two things that were characteristic of their "place" in the Corsican past and present. They stopped off in Corte, the old capital, where they lingered a time with Carlo's and Letizia's *paolisti* comrades, and they made the last lap of the journey with Letizia traveling in the berlin of His Excellency the military governor.

I I

The Making of the Patriot

I know my weakness: a too sincere awareness of the jaded human
heart [although] . . . I still retain that enthusiasm which so often
evaporates under a keen knowledge of men.

                                        —Napoleon Bonaparte, 1788

TO FRANCE (AUTUN AND BRIENNE)

Doubtless, the nine-year-old sailing from Bastia on that mid-December
day did not feel himself lucky to be going to France, the more so as he knew
that his schooling would not permit him to return home anytime soon (for
nearly eight years, as it turned out). Yet lucky he was—historically lucky. Had
Genoa not ceded Corsica to France, he would not be going anywhere at this
point, for the Genoese did not give scholarships to minor Corsican noble
sons. Perhaps, when he had been older, he would have gone to an Italian university, probably Pisa, as his father had done, or maybe Naples, where
Paoli had studied. In one or the other of these ancient, respectable academies,
he would have received a decent education—in letters, probably a finer
education than he actually got at the royal military schools of France—but
then where would he have been? The republic of Genoa had been in
decline for decades; it offered few hopes for promotion for its own young
nobles, let alone for colonial sons. But France was entirely another matter.
With its twenty-two million people, it was the most populous country in
Europe. Moreover, the splendor of its monarchy, the robustness of its economy, the brilliance of its culture all made the kingdom of Louis XVI the cen-

ter of the civilized world. The prospects it could offer an impecunious rustic must have seemed (as indeed they were) incomparable.

In short, it is unlikely that a boy as smart and ambitious as Napoleon Bonaparte did not sense his good fortune and contemplate his future with excitement as he arrived at the *collège* (in French usage) of Autun, one of the oldest and better preparatory schools in France. Here he spent the winter studying French; then, in the spring, he transferred to one of twelve royal military schools situated around France, the one located in Brienne, sixty miles east of Paris, in the Champagne region. He spent five years (1779–84) there, after which he completed his military studies with a year at the Ecole Militaire in Paris. None of this fell automatically into place. This talk of *collèges* and studies should not distract us from the fact that Napoleon was only a boy in these years, a boy who was having to conjure with a foreign language which he spoke (and would always speak) with a strong accent. His inadequate command of French put him at a permanent disadvantage in literature classes, and required him, in general, to work harder than the rest. Then, too, Napoleon was younger than his schoolmates. For example, he was only sixteen when he took his commission in the Royal Artillery in 1785.

For all that they were severe, even draconian institutions, Autun, Brienne, and the Ecole Militaire constituted a fancy education for a provincial impoverished noble. Yet the experience had a dark side for Napoleon. In the registry of Autun, one may find this entry in the neat handwriting of one of the priest-teachers: "*M. Néapoleonne de Bounaparte* pour trois mois vingt jours, cent onze livres, douze sols, huit deniers 111, 12, 8." The words say little: only that the named student has spent three months, twenty days at the college (which he is about to leave) and owes money. Two details stand out. First, the sum of money owed represents, by itself, 10 percent of Carlo Bonaparte's annual salary as county assessor for Ajaccio, his main job. The family had other sources of income, but when the cost of the education of the other children is added to Napoleon's, one gets an idea of the relative enormity of Carlo's investment in his children's education. He never ceased scrounging for the sums to make those payments.

Second, we notice the orthographic crucifixion of Napoleon's name by a teacher who considered him "superb." It is a sign of what went wrong at Autun, and would continue to go wrong at Brienne and the Ecole Militaire. The priest in question, the admiring Father Chardon, may have pronounced Napoleon's name correctly, but the boy's comrades did not. In their ragging, "Napoleone" became the silly "paille au nez" (straw-in-nose). It is hardly surprising. A nine-year-old rustic from a recently conquered territory arrives at an elite boarding school in a kingdom famous for its snobbery and hidebound class system. He may react in one of two general ways to the inevitable teasing that anyone who has attended a boys' boarding school understands. The boy may ingratiate himself or he may isolate himself; blend in and be liked, or stand out and be noticed. Joseph Bonaparte did the first. At Autun, where he spent six years, he was considerate and endeared himself to one and all, although it is clear from his memoirs that the experience cost him something, and he was not as happy there as we are usually told. Napoleon took the second option. He became taciturn, distant, irascible, making himself famously disliked and feared. His way entailed a considerably greater price than Joseph's.

Accounts by Napoleon's contemporaries of his years of schooling in France were all written decades afterwards and reflect their authors' strong feelings on this subject,[1] yet are relevant for their agreement, not only among themselves but also with many of the Emperor's own later observations about Brienne. They concur that Napoleon was unhappy as a student in France, and as a result, he made the people around him unhappy, or tried to. Those describing the adolescent Napoleon trot out the usual adjectives: "unadapted, unsociable, unpopular and aggressive," "gloomy and fierce beyond measure," giving of "piercing, scrutinizing glances," etc. Certainly, one has no difficulty believing that Napoleon was these things. We can easily picture him at Brienne, for example, as he once described himself, gloomily ensconced under his oak tree, feeling desperately sorry for himself, nursing his wounded amour-propre by meditating on how much he hates his French comrades, and they, him (but more on the former than the latter), and what "harm" he will do "you French" one day.

Still, it was not all tumult. No less critical: Napoleon's moods and humors did *not* lead him into a psychological bind in the five years he was at Brienne, nor did they prevent him from making friends (including one genuine confidant, Bourrienne) or studying hard and doing well academically. Napoleon was generous, rarely held grudges, and possessed a powerful imagination. He took pleasure in the learning he accomplished at the several French schools he attended, notably Brienne. The young Napoleon was good at mathematics—he received a prize in it—but he took to ancient history even more. Indeed, one can scarcely overemphasize the illustrational impact of Rome on the political culture of the old regime; it more or less openly replaced Christianity as the storehouse, par excellence of maxims for men in public life. Even the Catholic teaching orders could not stop themselves: their monks were constantly accenting the stories and characters of Plutarch, Nepos (author of *On Illustrious Men*), Livy, Virgil, Cicero, etc., while at the same time ruing that these pre-Christian souls were all consigned to hell or limbo (a contradiction that sufficed to make the adolescent Napoleon lose his faith).

At Brienne, Napoleon probably discovered Caesar, which is hardly a surprise, given the attention Plutarch gives the Roman Empire's founder. Plutarch afforded him models which the eighteenth-century world took gravely seriously. The driving force of Plutarch's narrative, the effect of which is to present his leading figures (Alexander, Caesar, Cicero, Brutus, etc.) as undifferentiated heroes likely made its mark on Napoleon. Napoleon, like Plutarch, admired Brutus as well as Caesar, and did not draw the careful moral or political lines between them that the Romans drew. What mattered was that both were *viri illustres*: great men.

In sum, Brienne was not just a personal or an intellectual ordeal for Napoleon. Much of the challenge he passed with flying colors, and he knew it. As Napoleon noted at St. Helena, "I was the poorest of my mates . . . they had pocket money, I never did. But I was proud and I made every effort to see to it that nobody noticed. . . . I never learned to laugh and play like the others." Most likely, this was not said angrily but with a degree of deserved satisfaction. Midway in his tenure at Brienne, Napoleon had a visit from his father and mother. Letizia found her son "frighteningly thin" and complained of a change in his features. Such mother-displeasing alterations do occur in young adolescents sent off at a young age to a demanding prep school. *Pace* Letizia, they may not be a bad sign.

A habit Napoleon manifested at Brienne that would persevere throughout his life was the expression of concern for his family. It is remarkable to see the degree to which an adolescent with a great many more immediate concerns pressing in on him gives so much time to thinking and worrying about his relatives—and writing to them, too. Only a few of his letters survive and offer insight into the young Napoleon's character. The first, dated July 1784 and addressed to an uncle, is written in the aftermath of Carlo's visit to Brienne. The father came to deliver "Lucciano" (Lucien) to the school's and his brothers' safekeeping. Napoleon's pride in the nine-year-old and his apparent pleasure in having him there are more paternal than fraternal:

My dear Uncle,
    . . . Lucciano is 9 years old, and 3 feet, 4 inches, and 6 lines tall.
    He is in the sixth class for Latin, and is going to learn all the subjects in the curriculum. He shows plenty of good disposition and has good intentions. It is to be hoped he will turn out well. He is in good health, is a big upstanding boy, quick and devil-may-care, and so far, they are

pleased with him. He knows French well and has forgotten his Italian. He will add a message to you at the end of my letter. I shall not tell him what to say, so that you may see for yourself his *savoir-faire*. I hope he will write you more often now than when he was at Autun.[2]

In a second letter, written after he has learned that Joseph will be attending Brienne, Napoleon writes "Mon cher Père" to say, "I will be hugging Joseph before the end of October" and the three brothers will be together—a prospect that brings "consolation" to their hearts. What is agitating Napoleon this time is his worries about his father's health: he hopes that Carlo's return to Corsica will speed his recovery, so that "your health will be as good as my own."[3]

At the end of the academic year of 1783, the inspector of military colleges visited Brienne and is said to have found "Cadet de Buonaparte" to be "docile [*caractère soumis*], gentle [*doux*], honest, grateful [*reconnaissant*], [and] regular in his habits." He judged him ready, though barely fourteen years old, to go to the Ecole Royale Militaire in Paris for final training before his commission. The teachers at Brienne disagreed; they argued strongly he was still too young. Napoleon stayed another year at Brienne, then left for the capital.

Many years later, Napoleon was speeding to Italy on critical business for the Empire. It was April 1804 and the war had recommenced. France was at loggerheads with a formidable host of great powers, yet the Emperor stopped off for two days at Brienne. He walked the grounds of his ruined school, which had not survived the Revolution, received the former employees, examined with the local municipality the possibility of reviving the institution (contributing 12,000 francs to that end), and expressed disappointment that the priest who had given him his first communion was not around. The next day he galloped off on his Arabian horse, riding across the fields surrounding Brienne, gazing at sights he remembered from long past. For three hours, his staff followed him as best they could; then they had lunch. Wrote one of them: "rarely was he so gracious." In his last testament on St. Helena, Napoleon would designate a bequest of a million francs for Brienne. None of this resembles the words or actions of a man beset by unhappy memories of his school days—on the contrary.

GENTLEMAN AND OFFICER

On the evening of October 19, 1784, Napoleon and four schoolmates arrived to take up their admissions in the Ecole Royale Militaire (ERM), on the Left Bank of the Seine. They came by boat but perhaps it took an islander like Napoleon to describe their arrival as "landing" at a "port of call." (Was he aware that Paris is the center of the *île de France*?) The school, designed by one of the era's leading architects, Jacques-Ange Gabriel, was housed in a magnificent set of neoclassical buildings, with imposing façades of Corinthian columns.[4]

Such was the care taken with admission to this institution that each boy had been named to the school by a brevet signed by the king himself, as well as the minister of war. The school was of recent origin (1776), and although it certainly aimed to turn out competent officers, that was not its main goal. Promotion and advancement were not based on achievement or intellect. Instruction, here, ceded place to formation of blue-blooded sons in the love and service of the monarchy and in the ways of the court. Such loyalties were not automatic. They were not dispositions that could be taken for granted; the French nobility was a notoriously independent and divided caste that boasted (there is no other word for it) a long history of insubordination, or indeed rebellion, against the king. Moreover, a prejudice of the leading noble families held that their sons did not, after all, really need training, for they were "born to the military life" and could lead regiments with their pedigrees. Since early in the century royal policy lay in convincing the high aristocratic families to accept alliance with the middle and lower ranks of the nobility in obedience and service to "their" king. This newly unified Second Estate was, at one and the same time, to be properly domesticated in *élégance* for display at Versailles, and trained for the actual leading of troops and conceiving strategy.

Such a setting was not a happy one for a young man whose nobility was recent and "petite." The traditional voice echoing from Napoleonic biographies holds that the young Bonaparte—worker bee extraordinaire suddenly introduced into a hive of drones and queens—reacted with revulsion to his new surroundings. From the limited evidence of Napoleon's views at the time, the new cadet was critical of the ERM from the outset; he reported that he spent a very bad first night there because "the tone was different." At Brienne, run by the monks, the ethos had been Spartan; but on the Champ-de-Mars, in a school run by military officers, one breathed the air of ancient Persepolis. Here, the number of servants, teachers, and sundry factotums (e.g., wigmakers) outnumbered the 215 students two to one. Napoleon loathed this royal cosseting of the nobility and would, one day, effect reforms aimed at making the cadets self-sufficient strivers, not blue-blood snobs.

It was not only a scene of suffering, however, for young Napoleon. The problem with the view that has the cadet completely at odds with the

ERM is that it is "infected" by his late views on St. Helena. All the later postrevolutionary fustian at aristocrats as "the curse of the nation" and "imbeciles who hated all who were not 'hereditary asses' like themselves" gets in the way of telling us what a fifteen-year-old boy may actually have felt when he put on the cadet's blue uniform, with its silver braiding and touches of yellow and scarlet on the cuffs. Late reconstructions indicate nothing of the impact on this Plutarch-intoxicated teenager of seeing for the first time the paintings, plaques, statues, and other memorials of the martial glories of the French monarchy (and one day, of the Empire's glory).

A positive side of the ledger, conceded even by Napoleon, was that the Ecole Militaire, unlike Brienne, boasted some truly fine teachers, including one of the most distinguished scientists and savants in France: the Marquis de Laplace, renowned astronomer and mathematician. At the ERM, unlike at Brienne, Napoleon enjoyed literature. His teacher, Domairon, was the author of a leading language and literature textbook; he instilled in his wards a sure knowledge of the varieties and rules of literary styles (including the genre, "haranguing troops"!), together with the leading examples of each. Napoleon already loved reading; from Domairon he got a sure map of the vast continent of literature to be explored. (Later, he would appoint him inspector general of the Imperial University.) Napoleon also shone in mathematics, and in his prodigious capacity for concentrated work. It paid off: Napoleon was one of the handpicked group of seventeen boys permitted to take the final examination in 1785, after only one year, not the usual two, at the ERM. He was forty-second out of fifty-six in the nation, and became one of the youngest officers to be appointed, the only Corsican lieutenant of artillery. Yet the accent on Napoleon's youth tends to overlook just how "old" the boy was in his personality, how much natural *gravitas* he exuded—"a miniature adult," as Christian Meier says of Caesar.[5] It was just as well for, like Caesar, Napoleon would lose his father at fifteen and from then on, have to grow up even more quickly.

He left the ERM with an ambivalence of the most acute sort. Napoleon's single year at the school showed him the French monarchy in one of its least attractive aspects. As the *ancien régime* approached perdition, matters of "blood" mattered, and never more so than in the military. The Crown's anxious wooing of the high aristocracy had resulted in a promotions system where only the purest and oldest pedigrees could realistically aspire to high rank. The Revolution will come for many reasons, but this matter of sharpening noble caste consciousness—and its effects on the lower castes—was far from last on the list. On the other hand, if young Napoleon was the son of a threadbare nobleman, he was *a nobleman all the same.* The boy, like the father, did not challenge the social bases of French society. The boy, like the father, could not have failed to be proud of his station. As at Brienne, so here, he made a good friend of an aristocrat: Alexandre des Mazis. Like Bourrienne, "the faithful Des Mazis" was a nobleman of old family; he would unhesitatingly side against the Revolution and emigrate with so many of the other royalist officer-graduates of the ERM.[6] In sum, Napoleon emerged from the Ecole Royale a man divided. He was out of place, but nevertheless had become not only something of an officer (he still had lots to learn about artillery), but also something of a gentleman, graced with some of the charm, polish, and eloquence of *ancien régime* society.

FAMILY

Carlo's story often provokes the mockery reserved for a small-town bourgeois trying to rise above his station. . . . [Yet] it must be admitted, his efforts were worth while. If ever a man deserved to have such a son as Napoleon it was he.
                                                            —Dorothy Carrington[7]

Worries over his family constantly troubled, even spoiled Napoleon's later school years. The Emperor put it truly: "They influenced my state of mind and made me grave before my time . . ."[8] The young Napoleon's concern was already clear before he left Brienne, but after he entered the Ecole Royale Militaire, events produced far darker clouds than the small question of Joseph's vocation. Carlo Bonaparte's dreams of making it financially collapsed quickly in the two years before his death, as several of his schemes went bust (notably a project for a mulberry plantation on family-owned land in Corsica). None of this, of course, stopped Carlo from spending money and taking trips he couldn't afford, including one with Letizia to the *very* chic resort of Bourbonne-les-Bains, where they rubbed elbows with the highest nobility—to no benefit. Carlo's pathetic letters to French authorities arguing for and entreating subsidies and payments make for depressing reading. At the same time, another source of patronage contracted: Comte de Marbeuf, recently widowed, remarried in 1783, selecting for his bride the eighteen-year-old daughter of a highborn house. The count remained benevolent toward the Bonapartes, but Carlo and Letizia appeared less often at his various homes.

Worst of all, Carlo's health presently gave way completely. By the turn of 1784–85, with Napoleon settled into classes at the Ecole Militaire, the father heard from the doctors in Montpellier that his stomach illness was terminal. In the face of death, the thirty-eight-year-old skeptic reached out for the Catholicism of his youth. The Napoleon of St. Helena waxed ironical in his appraisal of Carlo's late-found fervor: here, "facing death, there weren't enough priests in all of Montpellier [to allay him]." But his fifteen-year-old self proved less supercilious. Five times in the letter to Uncle Lucciano, penned just after Carlo's demise, Napoleon refers to the "implacable will" of "the Supreme Being" that "deprives us of what we held dearest." In this letter, despite the stylized expressions added to suit the staff of the ERM, which oversaw all cadet correspondence, the young man's emotions speak deeply, if chastely; he does not hide his grief that he and the family have lost someone precious and profoundly important to them. The boy's letter of a fortnight later to Letizia is stiffer, but even it bears witness to stoicism. Napoleon declined the services of a priest when the ERM offered to make one available to him.

Carlo Bonaparte died as he had lived—on credit. The family owed doctors and pharmacists, merchants and undertakers, and, of course, schools—for Joseph, Lucien, and Elisa. Uncle Lucciano now stepped in and assumed a large role in the Bonaparte household, but financial circumstances were, and remained, extremely tight until his death, in 1791, when the archdeacon's fair-sized estate accrued to the family. Napoleon survived entirely on his tiny officer's pay (1,100 francs a year), taking no money from his mother and even trying to send some home when he could. But none of it kept Letizia from having to borrow—a loathsome recourse for any Corsican. She accepted 600 francs from the lieutenant general commanding the French forces in Ajaccio, and sometime later, offered to sell her silver in order to pay him back. The officer gallantly refused.[9]

For all these reasons, then, Napoleon, on leaving the ERM, wanted to return home to attend to family matters. However, this was out of the question, for his military training was not complete. He was assigned to the La Fère regiment stationed in Valence, in the south of France, where he reported at the end of October 1785. His ten months there are among the most important periods, if not the happiest, of his life, though he met almost no one and went out hardly at all: lack of means, lack of interest.

Valence, on the Rhône River, was where Napoleon's mind began to range and his ideas to crystallize. Free from a hidebound curriculum and occasionally mediocre instruction, the born autodidact came into his own. His interests ranged from astronomy and mathematics to geography. He divided his days and nights between practical artillery (e.g., learning how to fire a cannon and command a battery) and reading. (Book-buying was his one vice, at the price of skimping on eating.) He was anything but a passive reader; he tore into these books, took voluminous notes, and thrived on lists, lists of everything, from the parts of speech to the prices of foundry products. He also thought very intensively about what he read, and wrote a little, none of it published. But the thinking had consequences.

What preoccupied the sixteen-year-old "officer" (he always preferred that word to lowly "second lieutenant") was not military topics per se, as one might expect in a soldier, but history and politics–history-as-politics and politics-as-history. War fascinated him, but not nearly so much for strategy and tactics as in the Clausewitzian sense: as an extension of politics by other means. However, the specific concern that focused these disciplines in his mind was Corsica. Why Corsica? Why not France?

ENFANT DE LA PATRIE (PSYCHOLOGY)

The eighteenth century was the nursery of "patriotism"–not the feeling, which is as old as man, but the word.[10] *Patriote* sprouted myriad connotations and enjoyed great significance in the cultural life of the Enlightenment, but while it could often, sometimes intentionally, be vague in its application, it did not mean *anyone* who loved his country. At Brienne and the Ecole Militaire, Napoleon rubbed elbows daily with Frenchmen who loved their native land, yet few of whom styled themselves "patriots"; some, in fact, wrinkled up their noses at the public figures who used a term that struck them instinctively as radical and disloyal to the king. Yet they did their nose-wrinkling largely privately, for "patriot" retained enough of connotation of country-love, of self-sacrificing concern for the commonweal, that one snubbed it at his own risk. There lay the term's uncanny effectiveness.

Corsica, of course, was Napoleon's homeland, his *patrie*–whence the derivatives "patriotism" and "patriot." The island weighed in and on his heart from the moment he arrived at Autun until the moment he returned to Ajaccio in September 1786: "seven years and nine months after my departure," on his exact counting. Loving Corsica was something he did a lot of in his school days. A typical letter from Brienne (1783) had Napoleon begging his father to send him the cherished family copy of "Boswel's [*sic*] *Histoire de Corse.*" In Boswell's day, "patriot" had meant "he who believed in Paoli and fought with him against the Genoese overlords and their French cat's paw." What it meant after France took Corsica was harder to agree upon among Corsicans. It could mean loving and serving France, of whose large kingdom Corsica was now an integral part. That would have been Comte de Marbeuf's viewpoint,

supported fervently or reluctantly by many Corsicans among the newly recognized nobility, including the Bonapartes. However, for another group of
islanders, "patriot" meant hating the French and rising up against them in terrorist and guerrilla action at any opportunity. The 1770s were pockmarked
with desperate rebellion and appalling repression.

No Bonaparte took part in uprisings, however, and if they sympathized
with the rebels, they did not say so publicly, or even privately that we know
of. Rather, Carlo Buonaparte recycled himself as Charles de Bonaparte
and was presented at court in 1779. He became that far-from-strange beast of
two faces who hunted with the hounds and ran with the fox. This could make
for potential conflict both within and without the family.

Memories and statements, unsupported by any evidence from an early
period, contribute only somewhat to summoning an accurate notion of
Carlo's and Napoleon's relationship in the early 1780s, or of Napoleon's
thoughts about his father at the time he died or in the years soon after. And
one strong statement from 1785 goes directly against any conclusion that the
son regarded his father as a traitor. In the letter to Uncle Lucciano on
Carlo's death, Napoleon enumerates the ways that his father will be
mourned. They are personal ways, Carlo's role of brother, father, husband,
etc. But then Napoleon says something more, something he does not strictly
have to say—something that his teachers at the ERM may have frowned
upon even if they let it pass. He writes: "I would even go so far as to say that
the *patrie* has lost, with his death, an enlightened and honest citizen."

Did loving the Corsican *patrie* automatically entail hating the French?[11]
Why didn't Napoleon choose a middle ground—embrace France while yet
guarding a soft spot in his heart for the old Paolist "realm of Corsica," as
Carlo had done? The boy, even by the time he asked for the Boswell volume,
was French-speaking after all. In fact, when he made his first visit home, he
would virtually have to relearn Italian. More to the point, as of January 1786,
he was a commissioned officer in the King Louis XVI's Artillery.

Yet what was not overcome by the relentless process of Frenchification
was the immanent *political* abyss separating Napoleon from the vast majority of his officer mates. The boys he knew at all three of his schools, his
future brother officers, became adversaries of the Revolution. Napoleon was
the only artillery graduate of the ERM to serve the French Republic; his
classmates, together with their families, emigrated or faced the guillotine,
and many of them combated the Revolution tooth and nail. (One of a
handful who stayed was the future Napoleonic marshal Louis-Nicolas
Davout.) In the La Fère regiment, every fellow officer emigrated.

In sum, the likelihood is that Napoleon early on felt himself becoming

French—in language, dress, habits—and in this process, he was both willing and complicit. Whether he said so or whether he shouted the contrary had to do with temper and mood, with the psychology of "reaction formation," where a person's response is indirectly proportional to the attractiveness he or she feels. But in the long run, these humors passed and made no difference to the larger truth of Napoleon's relentless progression to becoming French. His development as a French officer brought him satisfaction except for one problem: the social gap that yawned between *la petite* and *la grande noblesse*. By the end of the century, this had mutated into an inchoate but strong political and ideological dividing line. The *ancien régime* ceded ground to its own "patriot" reformers in many areas as the Enlightenment wore on, as in religious tolerance, but in the sanctum sanctorum of the Royal Army, the absolutist monarchy permitted its high nobility to hold the fort. And they held it in the name of "honor" or "family" or "king," more than in the name of *patrie*.

As the 1780s wore on, this caste exclusiveness in the armed forces got worse, not better—an inflexible, arch-reactionary response to a society in full crisis, as sharp cries for reform were heard everywhere, and heeded everywhere else. On entering the army, young men from minor noble families would retire in the field ranks. At best, one or two might finally attain the grade of colonel or *maréchal de camp,* only long and pointless years after their bluer-blooded confreres had done so. In his reading of ancient history, the young Napoleon cannot have missed the fact that Alexander was born a king's son while Caesar was born into the patriciate and married into the most illustrious social circle of the Republic. Nothing less would have permitted these Plutarchian heroes to move onto the high road of world history. Napoleon, by contrast, had to confront the likelihood that he would not move up the ladder of military promotions despite celebrated talent and hard work. His protests against this social prejudice are what kept him off balance and at odds with his uniformed surroundings at school, even as day to day the boy progressed well in his métier.[12]

Put in psychological terms, the adolescent Napoleon, caught up in a vicious circle of being despised and despising, responded to his tormentors and the system of exclusiveness that sustained them with defiance: he "accepted the Corsican identity thrust on him. Not only accepted it, but gloried in it."[13] The first caricature we have of Napoleon, among the literally hundreds produced, was drawn by a fellow student—no doubt, a boy whose path to becoming general one day was comparatively direct and unencumbered. The cartoon depicts a large figure of young Napoleon braced to defend Paoli, while a professor, depicted as some kind of bug, hangs on to his pigtail and tries to restrain him. The caption reads: "Bonaparte runs, flies to Paoli's aid." Napoleon's "Corsican identity" was a response to a social system he found in place in the French schools he attended, an angry—but fragile and recent—response of emotion and temper. Napoleon is said to have cried out at Brienne: "I shall do these French all the harm I can." We may almost think of this as an "excited utterance," in the legal sense, not more. "The French" he had it in for were not the inhabitants of the kingdom but the gilded bunch of "aristos" at military school. On St. Helena, he reflected: "I am not Corsican. I was brought up in France, therefore I am French, as are my brothers"; "to my way of thinking, Brienne is my *patrie* . . . I am more Champenois than Corsican." The ring of truth in these words should sound as an overtone through all the "noise" of the Corsican patriotism of 1785–93. The young Napoleon became what his father was: an ardent *paolisto* who was, in fact, largely French, but frustrated by the obstacles blocking his progress in French society.

ENFANT DE LA PATRIE (IDEAS)

For Napoleon, the process of becoming a patriot—of furnishing an intellectual foundation for inchoate emotion and deep inner conflict—was arduous. Begun in earnest at Valence in 1785–86, and continuing over the next seven or eight years in Corsica and Auxonne, it required many dark nights of the soul, broken, one gathers, by occasional shimmering flashes of exhilaration. Ultimately, it would issue in promising paths and rationales for political action. In the meantime, however, donning the patriot's mantle entailed a degree of soul-searching, along with the months of close reading, reflection, and impassioned writing.

Deciding which works to concentrate on in his reading was the easy part. The direction and prestige of the era's culture fully consecrated certain styles and bodies of critical thought associated with the Enlightenment and early Romanticism. From 1750 to 1800, writers like Voltaire, Mably, Raynal, Ossian, and a dozen others exercised a famously seductive influence on young minds coming from the whole social spectrum—aristocracy to common-born. Given young Bonaparte's provincial background and his passionate personality and unfettered imagination, however—given, above all, his taste for lockstep reasoning and absolute conclusions—it is not surprising that no author spoke to him as much as the recently deceased (1778) political philosopher Jean-Jacques Rousseau. Works as varied as *The Social Contract* and *The New Eloise* or *The Confessions* straddled the age, exemplifying both critical reason and passionate imagination. Young Napoleon spoke right back, in evocative apostrophes to "Rousseau!" or even, more intimately, "J.-J.," that make one smile to read them.

We are fortunate to have a close picture of Napoleon's thought process as it unfolded in these years. His dozen or so pieces vary in length from an uncompleted paragraph to a formal treatise of fifteen thousand words; in all, they amounted to a slim volume.[14] The style is rarely discursive, but rather evocative and emphatic, sometimes turning to the plaintive and confessional, other times to irony, alternately elegant and heavy-handed. As political thought in its own right, posterity would not read them if not for what their author became; but this said, the essays are, by and large, a remarkable production to come from the pen of a late-teenage artillery officer. The works as a whole touch on three central topics, in ascending order of importance: Napoleon's basic political beliefs, his critique of religion and Church-State relations, and his feelings and thoughts about Corsica. A theme closely related to the last, crystallizing as the prospect of political action rears its head, is the author's will to lay bare what passes in his day for purity of patriotic motive.

Nowhere does the young Napoleon spell out his political thinking in detail—one reason to avoid the term "ideology"—but he says enough in his early writings for us to be able to infer his views. What must be said first is this: notwithstanding young Napoleon's oft-discussed appetite for Rousseau, he does *not* share the Genevan philosophe's beneficent take on human nature. At bottom, writes Napoleon, "the natural spirit of man is the wish to dominate."[15] The Hobbesian view is unmistakable: "Man in nature knows no other law than self-interest: take care of himself, destroy his enemies, these were his daily jobs."[16] The consequence of such a dark view is that the State (a word Napoleon capitalizes, in the French fashion) must be strong.

But not all States. Napoleon, like Rousseau, has harsh things to say about monarchies. In 1788 he wrote the beginning of a "Dissertation on Royal Authority," which views kingly power as essentially a usurpation of society's sovereignty ("there are very few kings who haven't deserved to be dethroned"[17]). Only if the State represents the general will is it a thing of sovereign majesty and grandeur. Napoleon's fascination with the State emerges in unexpected clarity in a curious document he produced in 1788: a draft "constitution" for the society of junior officers (called "la calotte") of his regiment—a task he requested. His colleague lieutenants were amused at the seriousness with which the nineteen-year-old Solon went about the job of "lawgiver" and bemused at the complexity of the structures to be set into place by his 4,500-word document. In accord with Rousseau, Napoleon's constitution would establish the formal equality of its members and their sovereign right to form a group, but then it settles into a most florid portrait of the power and attributes of the "chief" (the senior lieutenant) and his two subordinates (who are called "Infallibles"). The chief is "to each individual member of the group, the organ of public opinion. Night can hold no gloom for him who overlooks nothing that might in any way compromise your rank or your uniform. The penetrating eyes of the eagle and the hundred heads of Argus would barely suffice to fulfill the obligations and duties of his mandate." He can be deposed by nothing less than a unanimous vote of the membership! Thus, despite all its references to "the public weal" and the "prosperity and happiness of our dear Republic," this constitution is a blueprint for very strong leadership.

Napoleon's State is activist, if not indeed invasive. It has the duty to direct the citizenry's consciences, to form and educate the young, and to wring justice where injustice prevails: "The goal of government is to lend a strong hand to the weak against the strong, permitting each person to taste sweet tranquility, to find himself on the road to happiness."[18] But beyond the basic right to State formation, there are no paeans to liberty, freedom, or human rights. His statements presuppose or imply freedom, but none sings of it, none develops it. What takes liberty's place is patriotism, Enlightenment style.

He addresses the question of the State and religion in his challenge to Roustan, a Swiss clergyman who had assailed Rousseau's critique of Christianity in *The Social Contract*. Napoleon's essay is one of his more original pieces. "Refutation of Roustan" was writ all at a go, with virtually no changes, as if for once the author really knows what he has to say and is not distracted by the need to imitate famous authors and established genres. Napoleon does not evince a grain of interest in religion's beliefs and doctrines nor in *homo religiosus* as an anthropological phenomenon. He is concerned with one question only: Does the religion of Christ, in any of its forms, "get in the way of good government?" His answer is a resounding "Yes!" Forget that churches claim to be peacemakers, forget that they claim to preach obedience to authority. They are, at bottom, competitors to government. "Suppose a foreign army asks admission to your city, promising it has no evil intent . . . do you let it in?"

Napoleon's ideal is pre-Christian Rome where religion was a State affair. That "original unity" between religion and politics was ruptured by the arrival of Christianity, with its noxious differentiation between what is owed God and what is owed Caesar. That is lethal, in Napoleon's eyes, the source of fifteen centuries of civil dissent, division, and war, not to mention of the unholy competition between clergy and government. "[T]he priest stands ready to foment rebellion among the people against injustice," he writes, as if that were a bad thing. He reproaches the Roman emperors who converted to Christianity, and he implies that if the West could replace Christianity with State-developed creeds, without great cost and bloodshed, the results might be fruitful. That is no longer possible, he grants; still, one must never forget that where religion flourishes, "it is good-bye [*adieu*] *patrie*."

Again the place that God or liberty occupies in many people's hearts is replaced in the young Napoleon's by his obsession with *la patrie*. And here again we see that strange combination of the Corsican and the Frenchman. Corsica comes in for more attention in his early writings than do political principles or anticlerical thunderings. Two works, *Corsican Novella* and *Letters from Corsica*, are intoxicated threnodies of what their author feels are the constitutive elements of his *patrie*'s history: perfidy, intrigue, assassination, torture, famine, plague, and vengeance—above all, the cry for vengeance ("Citizens, if lightning from on high does not strike these evildoers and avenge the innocent, it is only because the strong and just man is destined to fulfill this noble ministry."[19])

Yet despite the operatic grandiloquence, we have no difficulty penetrating the high emotion to see a political stance. Young Napoleon may have *experienced* patriotism without quotations as the deep call to love and serve his island, yet emerging from his avalanche of inebriated adjectives are pressing political conclusions about Corsica that are not simply emotional exclamations. Napoleon wants to turn Corsica into a kind of Spartan or Roman State. He inveighs against the islanders' softness and cowardice, their corruption by French luxury, their servility and loss of self-mastery, their dearth of heroes and heroic self-sacrifice. They are clearly not heroic enough to deserve the State of his dreams. Our Brutus-author informs us he would fly to Corsica and "plunge the avenging blade into the breast" of the French Caesar, if only the death of one man would suffice to reverse the sorry state of affairs, but it would not. That leaves only few options: "[W]hen the *patrie* no longer exists, the good patriot must die." Absent death, it left writing and political activism.

The last option left the young Napoleon wrestling with purity of motive. Dealing with his own motivations becomes troubling for the young officer. Take, for example, "On the Love of the *Patrie*," a 2,500-word essay, of which we are fortunate in having the lead that he rejected, as well as the one he used. Here is the former:

> I am barely of age, and yet here I am, writing history. I know my weakness: a
> too sincere awareness of the jaded human heart, though for the kind of writ-

ing I am doing now, perhaps that is the best state of mind and soul. I still have
the enthusiasm which so often evaporates under a keen knowledge of men.
The venality that comes with age will not sully this pen. I shall breathe only
truth, and I believe I have the strength to say it. In reading this brief sketch of
our unhappiness, dear compatriots, I can feel your tears flow. We have always
been children of woe. Today, as part of a powerful monarchy, we reap from its
government over us only the vices of its society. We see no relief on the horizon from the evil being done us.[20]

So unrestrained and intimate an appeal cannot sustain the author's shaky
self-confidence; he hastily retreats, trading it in, in the second draft, for a thoroughly prosaic lead wherein, *imitative of Carlo* using French court style, he
addresses not his "dear" and desperately "unhappy" compatriots, but some
"mademoiselle" of literary convention:

> I have barely attained the age where passion dawns, and my heart is still
> agitated with the strong reactions produced by a first knowledge of human
> beings. Yet you, mademoiselle, would have me speak with a profound under-
> standing of the human heart.

The body of the essay examines patriotic motivation under a jeweler's
loupe. Napoleon celebrates the genuineness of ancient patriotism and con-
demns the lust for glory that passes for it among the French. The piece
respires of fervor and sincerity, reminding us of the difficulty that espousing
patriotism must have caused its would-be practitioners. They were constantly
fixated on their own and everybody else's "purity of commitment" to the
public weal. But it was a test one couldn't win, especially a self-proclaimed
Brutus holding views and dispositions closer to those of Caesar. Napoleon
was ready to plunge a dagger into the breast of any French aristocratic version of that would-be king, but what about the Corsican "patriotic" version
of Caesar lurking within himself? Napoleon had to have sensed that his
cause was political and his own motives were dubious, but he responded
with ever shriller assertions of his innocence and zeal, making ever-greater
demands for rigor and purity, for self-sacrifice and heroism—on his own part
and others.

CORSICAN JUNKETS

*Elsewhere they see you rich, noble, or learned, but in Corsica you brag about your
relatives, they are what make a man praiseworthy or feared.*

—Napoleon Bonaparte

Whatever his distractions and preoccupations, Napoleon always stayed in
close touch with his family. At the end of a year at Valence, the young officer received a long furlough that permitted him at last to go home. In September 1786 he made the first of five trips to Corsica; in all he would spend
three of the next seven years on the island of his birth. It was high time he
appeared at *casa* Bonaparte, for there was great need of him. The widowed
Letizia, with four young children to raise, without much money, and without a housekeeper, was swimming hard not to drown. The normally dependable Uncle Lucciano was hors de combat, suffering from severe gout.

Napoleon dove in. Having left home a boy, he returned a responsible and
competent man. One is impressed by the care and the quality of his efforts
for the family. The letter on Uncle Lucciano's behalf to a physician on the
mainland, Dr. Tissot, won no response from the renowned doctor (author
of a well-known treatise repudiating onanism) but it highlights why it was
Napoleon and not the older Joseph on whom devolved the important
work of drafting petitions to schools and seminaries seeking places and scholarships on the children's behalf, or writing memoranda and pursuing the
family's legal and administrative projects in various courts and ministries.

Withal, Napoleon yet took time to think and read and to go on long walks
with his favorite brother. Joseph had been back in Corsica since 1784, but
now, thanks to Napoleon's return, he would be able to leave for the University of Pisa. The times he shared with Napoleon before his departure were
among the best they ever had together.[21] The autumn of 1787 saw Napoleon
briefly in Paris on family business, then he reported back to his regiment, now
stationed at Auxonne, in Burgundy. Here, he resumed his writing, arising at
four in the morning, but if overall, he had less time for himself now than at
Valence, it was because he had his nine-year-old brother, Louis, with him.
Letizia and Napoleon had decided it would make life easier for her and generally be better for the boy if he went to France with his brother. The two of
them lived in close quarters, with barely the means for food, let alone
pleasures. They got on well: Napoleon served as tutor and parent; he even

prepared the boy in his catechism for his first communion. Louis, in turn, helped him correct the proofs of his writing.

Early 1788 found Napoleon back in Corsica—in Bastia, on business for his regiment. He had occasion to dine with several French officers who had been assigned to Corsica. One of them, a devout royalist, wrote of a dinner with him,

> I do not recall his face at all and his personality even less, but his mind was sharp and sententious for a young man his age, a French officer. The idea of making a friend of him did not cross my mind. My knowledge of ancient and modern history was too sparse to argue with him. . . . Our comrades also saw him as slightly ridiculous and pedantic . . . holding forth in a professorial tone . . . arguing strongly for the rights of nations, especially his own [Corsica]. Do you hear that?! [*Stupete gentes!*] One of the officers asked him, "And would you draw your sword against a soldier of the King?" He said nothing. . . . We separated coldly. It was the last time this man did me the honors of dinner.[22]

Joseph, off in Pisa studying law, was also becoming a "patriot," but with less of an edge. He frequented the circles of Paolist exiles where he was well received as a son of Carlo Bonaparte. Of course the talk turned to politics, though Joseph reported in his memoirs that he would not participate if anti-French statements were made, for he had many friends and connections in France, and in some ways considered himself French. Things soon became easier for him, however, because France appeared to one and all, in Pisa, Bastia, or Paris, to be fast on the road to huge change. Joseph wrote, "My enthusiasm knew no bounds."

III

The Unmaking of the Patriot

It is strange that a man naturally possessed of such lively feelings
for humanity, could, in the years to come, have acquired the soul
of a conqueror

—Stendhal[1]

ANNUIT COEPTIS: THE FRENCH REVOLUTION
AND THE EMERGENCE OF "THE POLITICAL"

To try to grasp the power and character of an event of world-historical magnitude, it helps to begin by recalling what writer and reader have known that
is remotely proportional. Like the late eighteenth century, the late twentieth
century is no foreigner to the tremendous and the unexpected: one thinks
of the fall of the Soviet Union (unforeseen by the West's well-stocked intelligence services) or of the reunification of Germany; or the formation of the
European Union. But if we are familiar with the seismic, the surprising, and
the hopeful, we are nevertheless still strangers to the magnitude of hope
generated by the signal event of the late eighteenth century: the Revolution
in France (1789–1815).[2] The sense of that hope—faith, really—is essential to
recover if we are to understand what swept up Napoleon the young man.
This is not easy to do, however, for we have lived through the crash of subsequent great events set in march by 1789—notably, the Bolshevik Revolution of 1917[3] or the first unification of Germany—and we have developed a
carapace of knowingness, both false and real, that insulates us from what we
would call "gullibility." Yet if it protects us from some measure of disappointment and surprise, it also cuts us off from the huge emotional invest-

ment that the late-eighteenth-century "party of hope" (Emerson's phrase) made, and which is captured by the Latin epigraph *Annuit coeptis* (a new beginning is declared)–a phrase imprinted on our money. It was indeed a brave new world, with no irony (or quotations) attached. As Wordsworth famously wrote: "Bliss was it in that dawn to be alive/But to be young was very Heaven!"

The new beginnings wrought or attempted by the French in this, the most unusual quarter century of their unlikely history did not extend just to the abolition of feudalism or the overthrow of Europe's grandest monarchy; it did not stop with the proclamation of the French Republic and the subsequent trial and execution of the French king, nor with the exile of much of the former ruling class; it went beyond the economic rationalization of a country that had more local customs than it had cheeses, beyond the expropriation of France's largest institutional landholder (the Church) and the putting up for sale of its territories (about 20 percent of the country's usable land). These were, after all, measures that one or another of the previous revolutions (English, Dutch, American, or Corsican) had at least seriously studied when not undertaken, so they were not enough for the French once they got going.

No, as 1789 became 1792 and led to the Jacobin Republic and then the measures of 1793 and 1794, the French undertook to refashion the human social and psychological landscape: they changed the way armies were recruited and run, the way wars were fought, the way newspapers were written and published, the way people dressed, and the way they spoke. They even thought to refashion time and space. They made a clean sweep of France's ancient provinces and replaced them with eighty-three roughly equal departments; and they abolished the Gregorian (Christian) calendar and replaced it with a Revolutionary one in an effort to put France's standing religion of thirteen centuries out of business. Catholicism was in some respects the author of France herself–certainly of the monarchy–yet here was the Church of Rome seeing herself replaced by patriotism and State-organized secular cults.

In short, France tendered the world an offer of new secular meaning that was effectively meant to replace the offer of cosmic meaning made by Christ and his apostles in the first century. God was discovered to be nothing more, nothing less, than man himself. *Novus ordo seclorum* replaced *Anno Domini*, but not on the cheap. No less important for our story than the impact of the forces of change and hope was the dialectical response evoked in counterrevolutionary violence and terror, guided by its own variant of the ideologies and politics of *Glaubenskrieg*.[4] As Arno Mayer argues with eloquent urgency, the story of 1789 is ineluctably that of the furies of war–both civil and international–more cruel and savage than wars had been before that time.

The Revolution did something else for which we have a hard time summoning wonder, because we take it for granted: it "discovered politics," as a leading French historian puts it.[5] One could call it "the birth of a nation," where the word "nation" means millions of citizens (no longer royal subjects) who have undergone a rapid apprenticeship into, for them, a new dimension of life: the political. In this dimension, ancient social and economic grievances, perennial panics, famines, and fears were transmuted into new channels that made them the affairs of elections, parties, ideologies, and representatives–above all, a dimension where collective consciousness was refashioned and raised by a widespread diffusion of new symbols (including 60,000 "liberty trees"), and where, finally, in case anyone might miss any point, dozens of "Rousseaus of the gutter press" were churning out hundreds of journalistic articles and popular pamphlets for thousands of common readers–a true intellectual plebe–to remind them of what was politically correct, as we might say. In sum, politics as a phenomenon of mass, not caste.

So the Revolution touched thousands, indeed millions, of lives; it profoundly affected all classes of society throughout Europe (and beyond), but–more than any other group except the liberal bourgeoisie–it touched the small nobility from which Napoleon sprang. More specifically, it dealt a resounding blow to the French officer corps, sending most of them into exile, and opening up nearly limitless possibilities for the few who remained. At a more personal level, the Revolution profoundly touched romantic, turbulent, talented, and ambitious young soldiers (and writers)–men enraptured by Ossian and Plutarch, who mixed politics with literature, "suicide" with patriotism. As for (now) First Lieutenant Napoleon Bonaparte, the Revolution transformed his life no less completely than he, one day, would transform the Revolution's. Of no one else may that be said so securely.

Napoleon's reaction to the tumult of the first hour–what Hannah Arendt calls the violence of revolt before it is yet revolution[6]–was an officer's frown, followed by doubt that these uprisings meant anything of long-range import.[7] But then came assent, as it became clear something major was in the offing. Napoleon Bonaparte was, in one sense, won for the Revolution from the first moment a snot-nosed "aristo" at Autun or Brienne snubbed him. But in another sense–in tolerating popular violence–he was never won. What focused his conscious attention as 1789 dawned was not its promise for him personally (ignoble thought for a patriot) but for the Corsican *patrie*. There was great reason for optimism. The men fast coming into their own in France also styled themselves patriots. In June the Estates-General had brazenly declared itself the National Constituent Assembly, with the self-ordained task of drafting a constitution that would transform the regime into a liberal monarchy. But the speed of events astonished everybody, for within weeks the Assembly was effectively running the country, while Louis XVI and his ministers looked on, gorges rising. As Napoleon put it, not the least "craziness about the French Revolution is that those who once put us to death as rebels are today our protectors, are motivated by our sentiments."

If Frenchified Corsicans like the artillery lieutenant posted at Auxonne found 1789 a heady time, most of his fellow islanders barely looked up from their olive oil presses. It did not occur to them—but then, it did not occur to Napoleon—that the sentiments underlying "patriots" everywhere might cover over deep fault lines in ideas. For a Corsican "patriot," *liberté* meant national autonomy; he said relatively little about democratic ideals. But *liberté* meant something else to the French; patriotism in 1789 glorified a different *patrie* from the one Napoleon had been writing about in *Corsican Novella* or *Letters from Corsica,* and made a different set of claims for it. The French were not concerned with national independence, as the Dutch and the Americans had been. The Revolution in France was about confronting the monarchy in the name of national sovereignty; it consisted of the ideas of freedom and democracy, of government of, by, and for the people, of "Liberty! Fraternity! Equality!" and "Vive la Nation!", of political parties and free elections, and the whole apparatus of democratic government.

But once this juggernaut left the station, it raced forward with a speed that bewildered, then stupefied people, not least the revolutionaries themselves. The "absolute" King Louis XVI of spring 1789 first found himself the "constitutional" ruler of summer and fall; then found himself without a crown at all, and eventually, in January 1793, without head to wear it on. From mid-1792 on, France was a republic, but not like the Corsicans had been from 1755 to 1768. This was a bellicose, paranoid regime—with some reason to be both—at war with her neighbors and, worse, with a large fraction of her own citizenry. The guillotine and the Terror replaced earnest admonitions.

It all played havoc in little Corsica even as it provided radically new possibilities and challenges for certain Corsican patriots of French formation and culture.

DIVERGENCES:
CORSICA AND NAPOLEON IN THE REVOLUTION

Napoleon now underwent a process of disillusionment, although he would never have admitted to it. He was not yet a man to see himself critically, still less to admit to succumbing to illusion. Nevertheless this is what happened, and the effect of the events of this period upon him was profound and lifelong. At an age where people may change, he did.

The young officer enthusiastically threw himself into bringing the Revolution to Corsica, for he was convinced that in it lay not only an improved future for himself, but the means of liberating his island from the heavy yoke of royal governance. Late September 1789 found Bonaparte in Ajaccio seeing to the distribution of French tricolor cockades, setting up the sort of "patriot" clubs that were forming all over France, giving speeches, and writing proclamations. But he did not act alone. The Bonapartes, represented by three politically talented and hardworking brothers—Joseph, Napoleon, and eventually Lucien, who was politically active from the time he was fourteen (in 1789)—all proved categorical in their support of the Revolution. The Bonaparte clan of Ajaccio acted as one unit, and, at least in the beginning, it would be unfair to call Napoleon the unquestioned leader. With him occasionally stuck with his regiment on the mainland, Joseph became the family's front man on the island. The brothers advised, corrected, and directed one another as well as their mother. The family was among the first to take advantage of the Revolution's nationalization of Church lands to purchase some excellent plots at scandalously low (insider) prices the moment they came on the market.

In late 1789, Corsica still languished under the tutelage of the royal government, headed by Comte de Barrin, Marbeuf's successor. The old aristocrat watched with a jaundiced eye all that was transpiring in Paris and did his best to keep it off his island. This was a losing battle, but as Barrin commanded the military forces on Corsica and held the formal apparatus of power in his manicured hands, he was able to draw out the contest. In short, Corsica presently descended into the sort of civil war that much of provincial France would experience.

The only issue that mattered to Corsicans was: What about us? Can we use the present situation to gain our liberty? And what does "liberty" mean? Complete independence or a form of autonomy under France? The island was divided on the last matter, but many of its young activists pressed hard from the outset for the French option, notwithstanding that in

Napoleon's case, to judge from *Corsican Novella,* one would have concluded that separation from hated France should have been his only desired goal. However, a year or so had passed since he wrote that novella in the quiet of his tiny Auxonne quarters. Now, immersed in the struggle at hand with the local forces of anti-revolution—a party closely associated with the old aristocracy, a fact that hardly left him indifferent—he found himself caught up in the political process—the fight—itself. The battle was a serious one for the future of the island, but in order to win it, the young radicals needed the National Assembly's unstinting support, and this could hardly be forthcoming via declarations of independence, American style, which ignored France's "revolutionary step forward."

Accordingly, though Napoleon leaped into the suddenly tumescent political life of Corsica and brought with him all his devotion to his *patrie,* he yet took his cues and his political vocabulary and style from France. His enthusiasm for the opening of the Estates-General (May 1789)—an event largely overlooked in Corsica—evoked in Napoleon an unusual paean to liberty. "In an instant everything has changed. From the depths of this nation, an electric spark has exploded. . . . Man! Man! How despicable you are in your slavery, how great when the love of freedom enflames you!" he writes to Paoli, in the famous "I-was-born-when-the-*patrie*-was-perishing" letter of June 12, quoted in Chapter 1. And he signs it, "Napoleon Bonaparte, Officer in the La Fère regiment": one is hard pressed to imagine that here is a man ashamed of his station in the very (French) army that has bloodied itself repressing his homeland.

His peculiar Corsican-French blend of patriotism is evident in a proclamation signed by a host of other pro-Revolution Corsicans who beseeched "*Nos seigneurs* [our Lords] of the National Assembly . . . to deign to concern yourselves with us. . . . Deign to cast an eye now and again on those who were formerly liberty's most zealous defenders." Another petition that shows some signs of being written by Napoleon "reminds" the National Assembly that Corsica wished to become "an integral part of France," adding, "for our security, let us be French forever."[8] Through it all, Napoleon was in touch with a Corsican deputy in the National Assembly—a man with a future on the island by the name of Christophe Saliceti. He, in turn, operated closely with a talented but still comparatively unknown deputy named Robespierre.

The result was that on November 30, 1789, the National Assembly proclaimed "the island of Corsica" an integral part of "the French Empire" subject to the same (future) constitution as the rest of France. Corsica was now as French as Champagne. When, presently, the Revolution reformed the nation's administrative geography, the island became a department, just like the eighty-three others. This development satisfied the Francophiles on the island but left many Corsicans scratching their heads.

The next surprise evoked no ambivalence in the mass of islanders: their beloved Paoli returned from his London exile. The grand old man of Enlightenment statesmen had been no less stunned by fast-moving events than everyone else, but he managed a deft reaction. After a triumphal tour of Paris, where he swore the oath of allegiance to the new French constitution, Paoli returned to Corsica in July 1790. Napoleon and Joseph participated in the Ajaccio reception committee. Paoli was elected president of the Corsican General Council and named commander of the National Guard on the island. The latter was a citizen militia, in existence all over France, which competed with the old Royal Army.

Although his prestige on the island remained unique and his position was strong, Paoli enjoyed nothing like the power situation he had occupied in 1755, when he ruled Corsica alone, with an iron fist in a velvet glove. Times were very different. Now he was subject to the Revolution and, more specifically, to its strongest local advocates. These were not the Bonapartes—who definitely counted but were junior—but men like Christophe Saliceti, Barthélemy Aréna, and others. They were Corsican-born *paolisti*. Saliceti was elected as one of the island's four deputies to the Estates-General, where he swiftly learned the complicated politics of "radical" overbidding that led to advancement (if also anxiety and disunity) in the National Assembly, and he turned his ever-improving situation to his own and his island's advantage, in that order. Saliceti was at first named by Paris to be administrator of the newly created department of Corsica, and early in 1793 he was named by the National Convention (a successor body to the National Assembly) as its effective proconsul in situ on the island. His "sacred" duty and unremitting challenge were to press home the revolutionary agenda in a land considerably more ambivalent about it and culturally underdeveloped than most of mainland France. Specifically, he had to lever the prestige and power of the faraway Paris ruling assemblies into Corsican politics, manipulating the language of the Revolution locally in order to impose Paris's edicts. For the politically dexterous, the role offered irresistible power exempt from supervision, but it was also a difficult and unforgiving role that exposed the player to physical danger as well as the constant threat of sudden dismissal from Paris, followed by disgrace, imprisonment, and (easily enough) execution.

Saliceti had no more loyal and hardworking allies than the Bonapartes of Ajaccio, which was not to say that they (or he) were hostile to Paoli—far from it. In an overt sense, there was no question as to where Bonaparte loyalty lay in any choice between Saliceti and Paoli. For a long time, the choice never got stated, though it had to have been thought about as time went by. Saliceti proudly reminded people he would never permit a shadow of discord to arise between himself and the *Babbù*; they shared the same vision for a free Corsica in a free France. Yet the potential for rivalry and conflict was omnipresent not only in the two men's age difference, but above all in their profoundly different insertions in the ongoing political process that had sucked them all so completely into itself. Paoli was Corsica-based and Corsica-viewing; Saliceti took his cues from Paris.

In these early days, Paoli seemed pleased with events and prepared to march hand in hand with revolutionary France toward rebuilding a more justly administered and taxed, democratic Corsica. Joseph and Napoleon went to see him in the Franciscan monastery he used for his headquarters in Corte. Paoli received them as friends; he had earlier given Joseph a nice souvenir—a playing card that had once served Carlo and him as a secret identification. Yet Paoli remained what he had always been: a philosophically inclined, temperamentally authoritarian but flexible and pragmatic politician who was wedded to his homeland's well-being measured largely by its unity. He was also a religious Catholic and a liberal reader of Montesquieu.

There was much that Napoleon shared with the *Babbù*, beginning with the temperament and including the love for Corsica, not to mention their sharing of Paoli's high esteem for Paoli. But at twenty, Napoleon was not the flexible and pragmatic politician he would become. Here and now, however great his love for Corsica, he had become an *inconditionnel*—an uncompromising devotee—of the Revolution. In a letter to Joseph, he notes that a noble was killed in a duel by one of the leaders of the National Assembly, adding, "That's one fat aristocrat less." That sort of remark put him stylistically with Saliceti, not Paoli, a social conciliator.[9]

Napoleon wanted to remain in Corsica to press home the Revolution. This gave him and his brothers a radical reputation; they were collectively known as "the Gracchi," after the Roman brothers of the second century B.C. who championed the rights of the plebeians vis-à-vis the oligarchical Senate. Such a role put Napoleon into conflict with his military superiors. For an officer of the Crown to foment uprisings in units of the Corsican National Guard against local elements of the Royal Army, as Napoleon often did, was to go far out on a limb where only the political power of the National Assembly could save him from being cashiered, if not tried and imprisoned.

But in return, Napoleon landed well-aimed blows for the Revolution. By 1791, he had become a republican—something he would later deny[10]—with a taste for Machiavelli's brand of civic humanism. That same year, his gift for political infighting led to his first publication, the *Letter to Matteo Buttafoco*, a pamphlet written at the behest of the Patriotic Club of Ajaccio, in which the entire Bonaparte clan was inscribed. The club had it printed and distributed. Buttafoco was a man of Paoli's generation, born into a better Corsican family than the Bonapartes, who, like Napoleon, had studied in France and received a commission in the French army. He had served Paoli as a diplomat, negotiating with the chief French minister, Choiseul, at Versailles over the island's fate. Though the evidence is unclear, it would appear that from this time on Buttafoco had worked for the French more effectively than he worked for Paoli. By 1771, Versailles had made him a count. When the Revolution broke out, the logic of the count's previous choices naturally set him at odds with the egalitarians of the National Assembly.

In the state of affairs prevailing in 1790, Buttafoco made an easy target for demolition. Yet Napoleon's *Letter* is a masterful piece of fast-paced polemic that deploys irony to good effect. It skewers the count by defending him with the sort of cynicism that was common in the late old regime (and a favorite target of "sincere patriots"). Buttafoco, for his part, wrote but never published a response. The latter is an unapologetic statement of sincere attachment to France, pointing out that Corsica's precariousness and her geopolitical importance exclude independence in any case. The island has to be kept out of English hands. But he adds, for good measure, "Liberty is a chimera; the democratic principle rests on virtue and in Corsica, all is vice. The monarchical regime suits us better than republican institutions." Paradoxically, there is nothing here that Bonaparte the First Consul might not have said, if he had even bothered to elaborate on why Corsica should remain French—a policy too obvious to him to need explaining. When, in 1801, he was shown copies of the *Letter to Buttafoco,* he responded brusquely, "That tract has no point, it should be burned."[11]

Napoleon's *Letter* also makes a low bow to Paoli, in whose good graces its author very much wished to be. Napoleon describes the record of the French National Assembly as if its actions were an update of the reforms Paoli had wrought in his 1755 constitution. That is a flattering portrait of this older regime that in fact was more of an authoritarian, "consular" democracy than it was a liberal monarchy like the France of 1789. Even so, Paoli was unimpressed with Napoleon's screed. His letter of April 2, 1791, written in Italian, reached the lieutenant at Auxonne where he had finally been obliged to rejoin his regiment and admonished Bonaparte for engaging in partisan polemics. ("Don't go to such pains to refute the falsehoods of Buttafoco," he tells the recipient querulously.) This admonition contradicted the whole ethos of the Revolution, which demanded fierce contestation of "aristocratic" positions by "patriots" (and vice versa), but then Paoli, the father of his country, had returned to the *patrie* intending to conduct a policy of peace and unity, while Napoleon, Saliceti, et al. were up to their necks in the French-begat process of political radicalization that set them at odds with their fellow Corsicans.

Paoli also took exception to Napoleon's *Letters from Corsica*, which he read at about the same time. Here, too, the author had heaped praise on Paoli, comparing him to Cincinnatus, Cato, and Themistocles, in return for which the "ungrateful" statesman offered no syllable of thanks or encouragement, even declining to assist Napoleon by sending him documents that the lieutenant requested in order to finish his work. Paoli found the work too dramatic and disputatious, not what was called for. "History is not written in youth," he added, it required "maturity and balance."

One wonders if even the "right" response from Paoli would have galvanized Napoleon to complete a work that breaks off its narrative of Corsican history at precisely the point where the French take over. Consistency would have required him to be as hard on them as he had been (in his *Corsican Novella*) on the Genoese, or the monarchical French, and that would have been impolitic now. The Revolution had altered Napoleon's perceptions. As he noted in a letter to the French philosophe Raynal, "henceforward we have the same interests, the same concerns, there is no longer a sea separating us."[12] In sum, whether with his regiment in Auxonne and Valence, in Paris watching breaking events firsthand, or running the length and breadth of Corsica for Saliceti, Napoleon had the French perspective—it was the key to his success and his failure in the battle to bring the Revolution to Corsica. And that, not the formerly sacred issue of insular autonomy or independence, was now *the* issue.

STYLES OF PATRIOTISM:
PAOLI VERSUS THE BONAPARTES

Union with revolutionary France offered Corsicans considerably more than they bargained for. The Revolution fostered conflicts among even its most hardened supporters that never let up. The new bodies governing France—first the Legislative Assembly (1791–92), then the National Convention (1792–95)—pursued their predecessor's nationalist, or Gallican, religious policies. Having expropriated Church land and abolished the monastic orders, the regime now sought to control the practice of religion by turning priests into paid civil servants and obliging them to swear a civic oath of allegiance to the nation. Roughly half the clergy of France, including virtually the entire bank of bishops, found the oath incompatible with their spiritual obedience to Rome. The "non-swearers," as they were called, were harassed and prosecuted, and the country fell into deep divisions over whether or not to support them.

As the situation gradually degenerated into an all-out attack on the Christian religion, the pace of political change also heated up. Louis XVI and his queen, Marie-Antoinette, caught in open collusion with the counter-revolutionaries both inside and outside France, were deposed and a republic was declared (September 1792). At the same time, popular attacks on unarmed prisoners, resulting in the kangaroo trials and executions (massacres) of well over a thousand people horrified Corsica as well as Europe. So did the king's trial for treason and his execution.

Corsica in 1792–93 was a rather minor theater of operations for the French, but of course, not for the Corsicans. While many facets of the Revolution proved controversial here, the sliver that stuck most painfully in the Corsicans' throats was religion. One need not visit Corsica to understand the importance of religion on this island, but it helps. The campaniles towering over the towns, the profusion of tombs, encasing saints and martyrs with names like Santa Restituta, the processions of confraternities of somber young men carrying palanquins supporting wooden reliquaries with saints' parts, give some idea of what the revolutionaries were up against when they sought to bring the Church to heel on this island.

The Corsicans did not accept, if indeed they even grasped, the Revolution's ideological point where religion was concerned. It was not that they were so religious, it's that Catholicism figured powerfully in Corsican patriotic self-image and history. From the islanders' perspective, for example, the Franciscan monks had amply demonstrated their patriotic bona fides, supporting various rebellions and the Paolist experiment of 1755–68. Yet here the French were, abolishing the order simply because its members were religious. This sort of ideological logic defied belief in Corsica, especially among the old guard. Lucciano Buonaparte, Napoleon's uncle, who died in October 1791, had had no use for France, royal or revolutionary, and still less for the anticlericalism the Revolution was now exporting.

Paoli, for his part, was determined to put a good face on things and to remain well inclined toward the French. Whatever deep-seated affection he had developed for England in his twenty years there, his official policy was that of honoring his oath to the French constitution. The problem by early 1793 was that the French constitution of 1790, together with the liberal monarchy it gave rise to, had been relegated to history's dustbin. Louis XVI was gone. (Saliceti had been the only Corsican deputy to vote in favor of "Citizen Capet's" beheading.)

Paoli's oath to the king was therefore a dead letter and his Catholic faith was outraged, the more so as Pope Pius VI's condemnation of the Revolution was eventually known throughout Europe. Yet, still, the *Babbù* recoiled from separating Corsica from "la mère patrie," as he willingly called France. He assured the National Convention that he wished himself and his island "to live and die free and French."

Napoleon, meanwhile, progressed in the opposite direction, becoming ever more a soldier of the Revolution, hoping against hope that doing so would, contrary to appearances, pay out in the form of success for Corsica—and for himself, in Corsica. He sided with the oath-taking clergy against the Catholic loyalists, tried to provoke duels with important aristocrats, and generally was a ringleader of "the friends of France." The phrase "soldier of the Revolution" is not just metaphorical. In March 1792, Napoleon was elected lieutenant colonel (second in command) of an Ajaccio National Guard volunteer battalion. This was a privilege for one so young, but it put him even more in the position of doing the work, and sometimes the dirty work, of the Revolution, including fomenting civil disruption and division. Napoleon found himself suppressing the counterrevolutionary insurrections among his countrymen that arose, for example, among non-oath-taking priests and their supporters. He even faced as adversaries men of his own La Fère regiment stationed in Ajaccio, who took exception to their colleague's attempts to propagandize among their troops. In short, like Saliceti, Napoleon played fast and loose, gambling that his actions would be whitewashed by the National Convention. By and large, this was the case, but there were anxious moments.[13]

In May 1792, Napoleon and Joseph were coldly received by the *Babbù* in Corte. Paoli was furious at them for implicating him in their activities by trying to cover their actions with his good name. Following this interview, Joseph imperatively urged his brother to disappear for a time; Napoleon left for France forthwith and did not return to Corsica until October.

INTERLUDE:
WRITER IN THE MAKING?

Claims that Napoleon's genius extended beyond politics and the military to the kingdom of letters are longstanding and of excellent pedigree—Stendhal and Hugo made them in the nineteenth century, Jacques Bainville and André Malraux in the twentieth. Paul Valéry, the French poet, deplored "what a pity [it is] to see a mind as great as Napoleon's devoted to trivial things such as empires, historic events, the thundering of cannons and of men. . . . How could he have failed to see that what really mattered was something else entirely?"[14]

Napoleon's mature literary output, his superb pithy letters and his stirring declamatory proclamations, is perhaps comparable to Caesar's (or De Gaulle's), while his youthful works, on the other hand—several dozen fragments, novellas, stories, dialogues, and essays all date from 1791 or before—fall into the class of President Eisenhower's paintings and Henry VIII's or Frederick the Great's musical compositions. But even that is rather remarkable when you consider Napoleon was in his late teens and early twenties when he penned all but one of these compositions. The youthfulness shows; the pieces are in indecipherable penmanship, contain execrable spelling, and some pages are decorated with caricatures and drawings in the margins. These writings focus on philosophy-of-life (suicide, love, happiness), history, and politics, and afford us more insight into the writer than do his mature works, with which they present a sharp contrast for self-revelation. In their unabashed idealism, the youthful writings provide a limitless number of quotations on which to hang the mature Napoleon in irony—for example, this line, the coda of a very short story called "The Prophet's Mask": "To what extremes does the need to be famous lead a person?" This is a facile and unfair activity, however; most political leaders were idealists in their youth.

In quality, the youthful compositions range from the utterly prolix, grandiloquent, and derivative (usually of Rousseau)—"effeminate moderns, you languish, nearly all of you, in your soft slavery, these brave heroes [of the past] are above your cowardly souls"—to moments of tenderness and lively imagination. The propagandistic pieces on Corsica, despite their torrents of emotion, reveal the least originality and are based on a highly selective use of secondhand research. Yet the body of work contains what surely must figure as some of the lovelier and more insightful prose written by a teenage artillery officer:

> Ever alone in the midst of men, I return to my lodgings to be by myself and to dream, to give myself over to the ardor [*vivacité*] of my melancholy.

> The ivy embraces the first tree it comes to. There, in a word, is the story of love.

> My soul, alive with the vigorous feelings that characterize it, made me support the cold with indifference; but when my imagination grew cold, then I felt the rigors of the season and I went inside.[15]

The literary showpiece of Napoleon's young manhood was an essay, "The Discourse on Happiness," that he submitted to the Academy of Lyon in 1791 in answer to the question "What are the most important truths and feelings to instill in mankind for its happiness?" The prize was equivalent to a lieutenant's annual salary. In organization and feel, the fifteen thousand words are pure Rousseau—from the glorification of feeling to the glorification of liberty ("When the Stoic Cato spilled his guts so as not to survive the Republic, . . . I feel proud of my species"). The forced belief in human perfectibility is pierced by shafts of familiar Napoleonic pessimism ("boredom, sadness, black melancholy, despair succeed one another in a man's heart and, if this state continues, he will kill himself"), and the general undertone is one of sadness and loneliness. Truth be told, the topic was ill chosen for this young writer.[16]

Although Napoleon was aching to get back to Corsica when he penned the essay, nothing in it bespeaks hatred of France nor desire to break with her. In the paeans to liberty, emotion, and nature, and right down to the crushing coda of lachrymose sentimentality (a dying father spews platitudes to his son), one has the impression that here is a man who wants to achieve fame in the French Republic of Letters, and who imagines the best way to do so is to imitate the leading French philosophers of the day. The last thing he seems to have consulted was his real thoughts or used his real style. Years later, Talleyrand, the First Empire's foreign minister, maliciously unearthed a copy of the "Discourse" and presented it to its author, congratulating him on winning the gold medal—which, of course, Napoleon had not—the jury had rejected his submission for a whole host of reasons, including that it was "badly arranged, disparate, and rambling." The Emperor took a look at a few pages, then flung the essay into the fire.

By August 1792, Napoleon, soon to be deeply implicated in Corsican politics, notes that he "no longer had that small ambition to become an author." With one exception, there will be no more literary efforts. Previously captivated by many of the passions common to his stage of life (love, death, literary fame), Napoleon yet returned, in all of these early writings, to politics. He describes one of his fictional characters thus: "He believed himself to be guided by the tenderest friendship, but another passion had in fact taken hold of him, all the more furiously for being hidden, including to himself."[17] In the story, the passion is a secret amour for his best friend's wife, but the words could suit Napoleon and his passion for politics. The painful sincerity of the early writings surely weighed on their patriot-author, amounting to a romantic-patriotic myth that he could not sustain belief in. The French scholar Jean Tulard notes with his characteristic taste for paradox: "It is only when he ceased writing that Napoleon becomes a writer."[18] Another way to say it is that he became sincere and expert in his writing when he quit trying to impress himself (and his reader) with his sincerity; he found his true voice when he lost his self-consciousness, which was when he submitted his writing to the politics he relished, or as Natalie Tomiche so nicely puts it, "to the nervous rhythm of facts."[19]

NAPOLEON IN FRANCE
(MAY–OCTOBER 1792)

Napoleon's return to France had another purpose than to distance himself from retribution in Corsica. The family felt that he must regain his standing at the La Fère regiment, where his reputation was under a cloud, not least because he had been gone since the previous summer. Fortunately for him, the army had lost most of its officer corps to emigration and desperately needed trained leaders. Lieutenant Bonaparte's long absences were thus overlooked, and he was promoted to captain and given a large sum in back pay. As for his questionable actions in Corsica, Napoleon correctly believed that a political fix would save him. The minister of war, based on reports from the royalist regimental colonel in Ajaccio, said he would readily hale Napoleon before a court martial, but the matter was taken out of his hands and put with the Justice Ministry, where it died.

Napoleon's gratitude took the form of a profound fascination with French political events.[20] But the challenge was more than following the players in a complex drama. The street held dangers for even the spectator in revolutionary Paris. August 10 witnessed the great attack of the mob on the Tuileries. Walking along the rue des Petits-Champs to go watch, Napoleon met "a band of hideous men" who, finding him reasonably well dressed, took him for a noble, as of course, technically, he was. They insisted he cry "Vive la Nation!" to prove his bona fides. "You may well imagine I did so," he said. The experience that struck him most was what he saw on arriving at the palace. Louis XVI's Swiss Guard had been instructed not to fire on the crowd, but it set upon them, killing them by the hundreds. Their corpses littered the gardens while women from "the vilest rabble" committed indecencies and atrocities on them. Once again Napoleon's appearance, the impassive—and very likely, disapproving—expression on his face, aroused hostile and suspicious looks. Official terror—the State's use of violence—was a recourse he understood; violence from the bottom up was another matter.

The experience of this, the most famous *journée* (day) of the Revolution since the fall of the Bastille, marked Napoleon gravely, as it marked many, including some of the Revolution's most fervent supporters. In 1791, when his regiment pledged the oath to the new constitution, the twenty-two-year-old "patriot" had felt a strong democratic impulse. Before then, he noted to Emmanuel Las Cases at St. Helena, "If I had received the order to turn my cannons against the people, I do not doubt that habit, prejudice, education, the name of the king, all would have made me obey it. But the national oath, once taken, put me past these things. Now I knew only the nation. My natural inclinations from then on were in harmony with my duties and fitted in marvelously with the metaphysic of the [National] Assembly."

But after a very full year of intense political action in Corsica and France, Napoleon had become hardened and disillusioned by what he had seen himself and others do. His views on many things were evolving, but especially on that great eighteenth-century ideal, "the people." "When you get right down to it," he said, talking of August 10, "the crowd is hardly worth the great effort one takes to curry its favor." The Parisians, he continued, were essentially the same as the Corsicans in their "pettiness, wickedness, and their disposition to slander and tear down . . ." As for the quality of political leadership in this era, his view was no different: "Those leading [the crowd] are poor examples of men, I have to say." As heartfelt as this may have been, it was mainly the day's received opinion, even among adepts of the Revolution. Napoleon's solution to the problem was his own, however, and had nothing to do with education, social reform, or refinements of the constitution. In a letter of August 10 to Joseph, he noted, "If Louis XVI had climbed up on a horse, victory would have been his."[21] In other words, had Louis assumed the role of the "patriot" king, rather than a petitioner for foreign assistance, he might have saved the monarchy.

The second half of 1792 saw the emergence on the political stage of other Napoleonic siblings. When Louis, age fourteen, penned a proclamation, Napoleon wrote to him, "I read your proclamation, it's worthless. There are too many words and not enough ideas. Chasing after pathos is not how you address people. They have more sense and tact than you think. Your prose will do more harm than good."[22] Napoleon also advised Lucien, age seventeen, to be moderate "in all things." Lucien was the arch-revolutionary in the family and took himself with a censorious seriousness that would have done a Jansenist deacon proud. His letters of the period would be amusing except for the mischief he provoked: he speaks of himself as a "sensitive patriot" and fervid democrat; he is certain he possesses "the courage to commit tyrannicide," and that he will "die with a dagger in my hand." Lucien hero-worshipped Napoleon far less than Louis did. Indeed, from his perspective as ideologue, Napoleon had become a pragmatist. Lucien wrote to Joseph: in a Revolution, it is essential to hew to a line, not "follow the wind" or "suddenly change sides." Napoleon, he felt, was capable of both: "I've long discerned in him a completely self-centered ambition that outstrips his love of the common good. I really believe in a free state, he is a dangerous man."

Lucien's remarks are constantly cited by historians and biographers of Napoleon, but whatever their value in the long run, in the short, they were wrong. What is remarkable is how steadfast, not mercurial, "the dangerous man" proved to be in the final months of the Corsican drama. Late summer found Napoleon eager to return to his family and homeland. Having squared himself with La Fère, he engineered yet another leave, fetched his sister Elisa at her fashionable boarding school, and arrived back in Ajaccio by mid-October. It was a happy homecoming, especially for Letizia: for the first time ever, all the Bonaparte siblings were together in the *casa* on Saint Charles Street.

FORCED DEPARTURE
(1793)

It is curious to see how sincerely Napoleon appears to have believed he could simultaneously pursue the Revolution's policies with zeal yet also maintain his relationship with Paoli. While in France, he had counseled Joseph, despite all that had occurred, to "hold tight to Paoli. He is everything and can do everything." Yet Paoli blocked the oldest Bonaparte's election to the Convention, just as he refused Lucien employment in his entourage. Joseph summed it up: Paoli was "impressed" by Lucien's talents "but he does not want to ally with us. That is the heart of the matter." Paoli even tried to stop Napoleon from returning to his colonelcy in the National Guard, forcing him to threaten to resort to Parisian political pressure. By then, the *Babbù* had long allied with other families—notably, the rival clan of the wonderful name Pozzo di Borgo (town well). The Pozzos, like the Buttafocos, were an old Corsican family of higher standing than the Bonapartes. Charles-André Pozzo di Borgo became Paoli's right hand man in Corsica—and Napoleon's bitter enemy. The logic of his choices would soon lead him into the counterrevolutionary cause, and he would serve a distinguished career in Vienna and St. Petersburg, fighting against the Revolution and Napoleon, standing with Wellington at Waterloo. The Emperor would forgive Paoli for the political separation of 1793, but never Pozzo.

The event that set in motion the final drama was little Corsica's expedition against some islands, the Maddalenas, off the Sardinian coast. The expedition of February 1793, in which Paoli named Bonaparte to head a battalion of Corsican volunteers, was a disaster, but it is not clear from available evidence why. Some historians have Paoli secretly instructing the commander of the expedition to make it fail and to "lose" Napoleon in the process. And indeed, Napoleon, together with an artillery battery, did nearly get left on a beach under attack. Other historians exonerate Paoli and blame poor communication, confusion, and enemy action. The fact is, Paoli, as chief of State, had final responsibility for what happened, and the outcome—whatever the cause—probably pleased him.

Napoleon wrote a complaint to the war minister, asking that the culprits be punished. Although he did not name Paoli, the *Babbù*'s reputation was already at low ebb in the Convention, thanks to Saliceti; the Maddalena expedition finished it off. Saliceti and two other deputies were dispatched to Corsica with full powers to investigate; Saliceti returned to his home island in the role of inflexible ideologue and petty tyrant, finding "counterrevolutionary tendencies" and dispensing rhadamanthine justice, making arbitrary arrests and playing the demagogue.

The impending break between the Bonapartes and Paoli was further speeded by Joseph and Lucien. The older brother was known to be misappropriating and pocketing public funds, probably with Saliceti's complaisance, but to the stern disapproval and disgust of the high-minded Paoli. As for Lucien, he, not Napoleon, was turning out to be the mercurial Bonaparte. In a short year he went from idolizing Paoli to despising and calumniating him. As begetter of mischief, Lucien now emerged without peer, and if he does not give the impression of being the consummate egotist, it is only due to the completeness of his confusion of himself with "the Revolution."

Lucien, thanks to Saliceti's influence, managed to place himself as secretary to a high French diplomat, in which capacity, he traveled to the mainland. There, in the Toulon Jacobin club, six weeks shy of his eighteenth birthday, Lucien Bonaparte gave a rambling two-hour discourse, carried on by cheers from his audience. The words that poured from his mouth, printed up and promulgated around France, were a frontal attack on Paoli. The *Babbù*, whose "caresses" just a year or so before "had made me drunk with pleasure," now heard himself accused of every treachery, including secret collaboration with England. Meanwhile, in Paris, the Convention, thanks to Saliceti's preparation, dismissed Paoli from his positions in Corsica and summoned him to appear before its bar. When he did not, it declared him an outlaw.

A family drama now unfolded within the historical one. Napoleon did not know of Lucien's speech, but he was aware of the onslaught on Paoli being mounted from France. Though Napoleon had assisted in creating it, the reality made him flinch. It was one thing to duel with Paoli in Corsican politics, but quite another to see his father's friend and the family's great hero unjustly accused of heinous political crimes for which he would be guillotined if the Convention got hold of him. Napoleon knew perfectly well that Paoli, even after Louis XVI's death, continued to stand by the French connection.

So Napoleon Bonaparte picked up his pen and dashed off probably the most eloquent defense of Paoli ever written. With scalding phrases and implacable logic, he demonstrates what nonsense it is for the Convention to maintain that "the patriarch of liberty, the precursor of the French Republic" would, at seventy and in poor health, abjure a life of dedication to the cause of democracy and side with the counterrevolution. The coda seems heartfelt: "We [Corsicans] owe him everything, including the happiness of becoming citizens of the French Republic." He then went to Corte to stand by Paoli in the crisis.

What the young Napoleon, caught up in this dramatic final flash of his old Corsican patriotism, does not seem to have grasped was how long past the right hour any of these speculations and declarations were: his own and Paoli's intentions, swallowed up by the maw of the French Revolution, had implacably set them against one another. It was a mistake many made in the French Revolution to overlook the deep and constraining logic of choices and events, but it is surprising in one as canny as Napoleon. Or did Napoleon only become canny after great youthful disappointment and failure? Was his inner Corsican "patriot" still at odds with his outer French one? Or did he dream that Paoli would name him his generalissimo?[23]

Paoli calmly defended himself in an equally eloquent statement sent to the Convention, again asserting his own and his countrymen's commitment to France and the Revolution. None of it made a scintilla of difference. The positions were locked into the polarity of revolution and counterrevolution. Word now hit Corte of Lucien's speech at Toulon. The Corsican custom of the clan required Napoleon, at this point, to kill or disown Lucien or to assume his words and leave Corsica. Napoleon did not hesitate to stand by his blood. Nevertheless, he wrote the French minister of war, whom he trusted, frankly admitting that Lucien's presence in southern France was "dangerous not only for him but for the commonweal," and requesting the minister to have Lucien sent back to Corsica.

Now, finally, after months of tergiversation and hypocrisy, the daggers were openly drawn between Napoleon and Paoli, as between the Revolution and Corsica. Now, the Bonapartes heard their forebear calumniated: in the Paolist government's decree condemning the family to "civil death" (loss of all property and citizen status) allusions were made to Carlo Bonaparte's swift desertion of the Corsican cause and his close relations with Comte de Marbeuf. Ironically, the Bonapartes suffered the same fate as the Buttafocos: disgrace—chased from their homeland for political reasons—and for the same charge: treason on behalf of "the French party." The *casa* on Saint Charles Street was pillaged and perhaps burned; its inhabitants went into hiding and then fled the island.[24] But not before Napoleon, on Saliceti's orders, launched a military attack on Ajaccio's fortress, using available republican (French loyalist) troops. It was as dismal a failure as the Maddalena expedition. The Bonapartes sailed for France, disembarking on June 13 at Golfe-Juan, the site of a famous future Napoleonic landing.

The Convention's paranoia led to the realization of its fears in Corsica. Paoli was driven to do what his enemies had wrongly assumed he wanted to do all along: open Corsica to the English. It was either that or sit tight in Corte, awaiting arrest and the guillotine. The Anglo-Corsican regime of King George III was established in 1794; its monarchical constitution accorded Paoli far less power than he had had under the French. The *Babbù* got along so poorly with the English viceroy that he was forced to retire to London in 1795. The island was retaken by France in 1796. When Napoleon became First Consul, he hoped to coax Paoli out of exile to return and run Corsica for France. This was not to be, although the *Babbù* did reconcile with the Emperor before his death in 1807. (In his will, Paoli—true, to the end, to his Enlightenment principles—left money for the reestablishment of a university at Corte.) Those whom Napoleon sent to govern Corsica were, to a man, *ex-paolisti*. Their task: to make Corsica definitively French. Neither they nor successive French governments have fully succeeded.

Napoleon's rupture with Paoli was something he was ashamed of and spent the rest of his life trying to explain away. The excuse he concocted was that it had to happen and was not his fault (as indeed, in a sense, it was not). The problem, as Napoleon explained it at St. Helena, was that Paoli had been a secret Anglophile and counterrevolutionary all along, while the Bonapartes were loyal to the French Revolution. This, of course, was partly wrong. True, Paoli harbored great affection and admiration for England, as Napoleon never did, but Paoli was not desirous of breaking with France and the Revolution. Napoleon once wrote that the only unforgivable action in history was when a man took up arms, not against his king, but against his *patrie*—that is, when Paoli returned with the British to reclaim Corsica. But the actual situation was more complex than that. The French Revolution may have fed on the idea of *patrie,* but at the same time it exposed the ambivalence of the word and the difficulty of pursuing a coherent patriotic program. *Both* Paoli and Napoleon had long considered Corsica their *patrie.* Revolutionary France came along late in the day and created a situation in which the two men ended up attacking their *patrie:* Napoleon, in alliance with the previously hated French; and Paoli, aligned with the previously beloved English.

Indeed, if anyone evolved in his sense of what *patrie* meant, it was most certainly Napoleon, not Paoli. A line in a self-exonerating report Napoleon wrote in summer 1793 for the French War Ministry demonstrates this. He notes that Saliceti and the other French commissioners who arrived in Corsica "must surely have found a large number of good patriots there."[25] It is a perfectly casual sentence, yet it reflects a tidal shift, for what the author of *Letters from Corsica* now means by "patriot" is no longer Corsican freedom fighter but someone who is, not even just pro-French—*Paoli was that*—but pro-Convention, pro-Jacobin, as well as anti-Paoli. This is the new meaning with which the language and logic of the Revolution have endowed the word, and which Napoleon has accepted as unconsciously as Lucien and Joseph. The sacred idea of *patrie,* in short, has come 180 degrees from the way he deployed it three years before. For Napoleon, Saliceti, et al., *patrie* has ceased having a largely irredentist significance ("independent Corsica for-ever!") and instead has become a nodule element in a complex politics of democratic revolution and imperial aggression.

The gravamen of the report to the War Ministry is to recommend a French military incursion in order to retake Corsica for the Revolution. Militarily, it would be easy, the author claims. Why? Well, because "Paoli finds himself with no general."

BEYOND PATRIOTISM

Recalling young Napoleon's confessed "weakness" that he had "a too sincere awareness of the jaded human heart," we may ask if his youthful enthusiasm has not by now painfully "evaporate[d] under a keen knowledge of men." As he sailed from Calvi with his family on June 11, 1793, we think that here is a man who knows himself and "men" better than he used to—perhaps bet-ter than he wishes to. Napoleon's time of *kairos* is over scarcely before it has begun.

Where does his hasty departure leave him: Corsican or French? True, he always kept the sallow features of one who "has been suckled on olive oil," but that could characterize a Frenchman of the Midi as much as a Corsican. If "absence diminishes small passions and inflates large ones, as the wind extinguishes a candle but whips up a fire," as La Rochefoucauld said, then the cyclone of the Revolution destroyed any residue of Napoleonic passion for Corsica. Many speculate that the indifference to Corsican affairs on the part of the Emperor was a direct result of the artillery captain's defeat and disillusionment. Napoleon told Gaspard Gourgaud one day at St. Helena: "Of all the aspersions spread about me in libels, the one I was most sensitive to was to hear myself called Corsican." True, on other occasions, he said he missed hearing the bells of the Angelus sounded in St. Helena churches, as he had heard as a boy on Corsica. But what if, rather than emphasizing Napoleon's remaining Corsican and/or becoming French, we consider that he was neither? What if, instead, we see him, like Caesar, as the perpetual outsider? Caesar, born into the aristocracy, was an outsider by choice; Napoleon, born into the impecunious provincial gentry, was one by blood. Both ended up *seen* as outsiders. Napoleon, like Caesar, was not a child for long; they both grew up fast because they had to. And we could add, Napoleon was not long possessed of any nationality, either (as, indeed Christian Meier claims that Caesar was not).[26]

Napoleon's actions in Corsica, 1789–93, promised little, and say little, about his future. True, he displayed courage and, at times, audacity, but more often he displayed recklessness and lack of foresight. We see a strange unrealism and poor judgment on the part of a Corsican who should have known a number of things and men better than he did—notably, how the French Revolution was dividing and destroying his beloved homeland, how his closest ally (Saliceti) was a poor specimen of a human being, and how his two brothers were undermining his own aims. These were the failings of youth and idealism; they were not signs of great things to come. Even in strictly military terms, Napoleon's early career here was mixed, at best—more often evidenced by defeat (e.g., the Ajaccio uprisings, the Maddalena expedition) than by success.

The Corsica years have intrinsic importance only in the political apprenticeship they afforded Napoleon. As he left Corsica definitively in 1793, Napoleon was becoming, like Caesar, a citizen of the generic republic—that is, of the *res publica,* or "the public thing," in general, not of some particular (e.g., "patriot") version of it. He was on the journey to becoming an adept of the political process—of simply "the political" (*le politique*), as the French call it. Discussing the power of myth over human minds, the British writer C. S. Lewis distinguishes between truth and reality. "Truth is always about something," he says, "but reality is about what truth is and therefore every myth becomes the father of innumerable truths on the abstract level."[27] The French Revolution, with its hideous tableaux and profound disillusionments, proved to be for Napoleon a ruthlessly effective teacher in disengaging him from notions of political truth, while at the same time holding him fascinated with the myths and realities underlying and generating them. Napoleon's passion for politics was redoubled, as he gained wisdom and insight into how society distributed power, used it, vested and justified it.

By mid-1793, if not sooner, he had lost his political virginity, which was his Corsican patriotism. It did not withstand his insertion in the Revolution and the "transvaluation of values," to use Nietzsche's language, which the Revolution effected on Enlightenment politics. Napoleon came to see "patriotism" in quotations, as the modern might see it—that is, as one form (one mask), among others, of public action. That is not so terribly surprising. "Patriotism" was quintessentially the language of opposition. As a British prime minister later put it: "Every government fails in it, every opposition glows with it."[28] This could not have sat well with the budding Statist in Napoleon. "France [under the old regime] was not a State," he used to say. Once it did become one, with the Revolution, Napoleon gravitated toward the State's point of view, not the opposition's. This could occasion, as we shall see, some rather bizarre political affections and alignments depending on who headed the State. It explains, in any case, why Napoleon so steadfastly saw the French Revolution not as an uprising of the people against the head of State, the king, but as an uprising of the middle class against the nobility. Louis XVI, in this telling, would have led that revolt if he had been smart.

Napoleon's evolution may also be seen in his writing. The more political the topic, the better off he was, the faster and more compelling the pace, the more incisive the images and rapidity of the narrative. That is what makes his political writings of 1793 and after vigorous and centered, with a force that presses the reader forward. They lack the heavy-handed idealism of the earlier pieces, but they are not cynical, either. Here, for example, is a letter written not long after he stopped trying to pen prize-winning essays on philosophical abstractions:

> Europe is divided between sovereigns who command men and sovereigns who command cattle and horses. The first understand the Revolution perfectly, they are terrified of it, and would willingly make financial sacrifices toward contributing to destroy it, but they would never tear the mask off it, for fear it would take fire in their countries. . . . As for the sovereigns who command horses, they do not grasp the constitution; they despise it; they believe that it is a chaos of incoherent ideas that will bring the ruin of the French empire.[29]

Napoleon is now interlacing his Rousseau with shots of Machiavelli and Voltaire. He has a point of view but is anything but maudlin about it, and in all events, he sets it off with his capacity to observe and analyze: "One should not judge men in revolution as in time of peace. Revolution is a state of war. . . . Then it is a matter of watching them and not foaming at the mouth or talking as a man who has taken leave of his senses."[30] He would say on St. Helena: "My great talent, what characterizes me the most, is that in everything I see clearly. . . . I can see, under all its aspects, the heart of the matter." This was not a badly inflated opinion.

Napoleon, as he sailed from Calvi to Golfe-Juan, was roughly the same age as Caesar at the end of the great Sullan civil war. Both men learned the same thing from their experience in war and great civil strife: the lesson that anything goes. As Meier says of the young Caesar, so we may say of the young Napoleon: he was "no longer locked into his environment." He no longer believed his or anyone else's rationales, as his opponents still did.[31] From the true believer's—e.g., Lucien's—point of view, this made Napoleon "a dangerous man," a cynic, a trimmer. Whether he became these things after the experience of years of "world" power is another matter, but in the summer of 1793 he was not these things.

What was he, then? This is where Napoleon diverges from Caesar, if only because the age in which both men lived so differed. Ancient Rome knew politics, of course, but it did not know ideological politics, as the French Revolution was introducing it to the mass of the population. In the Rome of Caesar's time, there was no distinction made between State and society, and certainly members of the latter did not readily contest the fundamental purpose and design, *the nature*, of the former. Rome's people were citizens but not apprentices to "the political," as we use the term—that is, many or most of them were not what today we might call "true believers." But if nobody contested the existence of the Roman *res publica*, virtually everyone had an opinion about (and many had a design for) what should *be* the State in 1790s France.

Napoleon, in the short decade between 1784 and 1793, lived the true belief that was the most characteristic belief of his era: patriotism. Incredibly quickly and thoroughly, he was led by raw experience to "see through" it—to see it, as it were, in quotations. The French have a saying that "one exits ambiguity at one's own risk." Napoleon, after his forced departure from Corsica, embraced ambiguity. It made him neither bad nor good; it made him modern—perhaps the first, certainly the most important, *homo politicus*.

IV

Robespierre on Horseback

[D]espite the torrents—the tsunami, really—of defenses and illustrations, few, if any, minds were made up or changed by words.

—William Doyle[1]

The family of Corsican refugees set themselves up first in the small village of La Valette, near the port of Toulon, then at Marseille. Their position, precarious at best, would have been desperate had Saliceti not watched out for them, getting them the small relief of a government allowance. That, in addition to Napoleon's captain's pay, is what, for a time, they subsisted on. Letizia and the girls took in sewing. Napoleon rejoined his regiment at Nice where it was serving with the Army of Italy. Here, as luck would have it, he ran into the brother of his former commander, Du Teil. Du Teil *frère*, unusually for an aristocrat, had come out for the Revolution, and so was sympathetic to Napoleon. He made him his aide-de-camp and put him to work in the service of the French coastal batteries, set up to fire at passing British ships.

The country to which the Bonapartes fled was, if anything, worse off than the island they had left. The Army of Italy, despite its name, was soon to be caught up in the civil war raging throughout the French Midi (south). Summer 1793 was the nadir in the Republic's fortunes in the battles against its enemies. All the news was bad: the Convention's fiscal policies were proving ineffective against the first inflation in history, while draconian wage-and-price controls did nothing to stop food riots from rending the country's larger cities. The Vendée region in the west burst into open revolt on behalf of the king, and in Paris, a leading radical of the day, Jean-Paul Marat, was stabbed to death in his bath. Finally, the Convention's two leading political factions, the Girondins and the Jacobins, were literally at each other's throats. By the time the Bonapartes disembarked at Golfe-Juan, the Jacobins—also known as "the Mountain," because their deputies occupied the higher rows of seats in the amphitheater where the legislature sat—had purged their enemies, who would soon be sent to the scaffold. The result: much of France, notably the port cities where Girondin support was strong, declared its independence from the Revolution.

This Federalist revolt—so called because its protagonists, many of them Girondins, sought to dismantle central authority in favor of greater regional autonomy—began in Marseille in April, and spread to Bordeaux and elsewhere, while Paris desperately struggled to reassert (and tighten) its authority over the country. Meanwhile, in the foreign war that saw France matched against most of Europe, a top French general (Dumouriez) defected to the enemy, while the great naval port of Toulon, home base of the French Mediterranean fleet, presently turned itself over to the British.

The Jacobins did not need Dumouriez and Toulon to understand that their republic was surrounded by enemies. The "Revolutionary Government" they presently proclaimed was a wartime regime characterized by both extreme centralization and the suspension of the normal rule of law. Everyone who was not a "proven patriot"—a vague concept—was a traitor—a very specific concept. As Napoleon was rejoining his regiment at Nice, the guillotine in Paris was dispatching "traitors" at the rate of two and three dozen a day, giving fresh meaning to Edmund Burke's earlier reproach to the Revolution: "You began ill, because you began by despising everything that belonged to you."

Six weeks after his arrival in France, Captain Bonaparte shared a meal with several local businessmen, during which a lively debate ensued over the rights and wrongs in the civil strife currently rending the Midi. The discussion afforded Napoleon a chance he had been strenuously looking for, to establish himself in the good graces of the Jacobin authorities. He returned to his lodgings and penned "The Supper at Beaucaire"—a dialogue among five people: an officer favorable to the Convention (Napoleon himself) and four civilian businessmen in sympathy with the Federalists. The latter's chief interlocutor is a merchant from Marseille, a city under siege by republican forces. At one point, early on, he says to the officer, "You go so quickly that you astound me." This would become a common complaint among Napoleon's opponents.

Certain new elements stand out in the piece—for example, a degree of realism and an openness to presenting opposing positions, a combination of military and geopolitical argument. What most strikes any reader familiar with Napoleon's previous work, however, is the tone. Gone are the thick emotion, the high dudgeon, the ubiquitous ideology (the "patriotism") of "The Discourse on Happiness"–gone, too, the sarcastic (if effective) irony of *Letter to Matteo Buttafoco*–replaced by a cool, analytic grasp of one who is aligned but far from a wild-eyed *engagé*. The piece is thus different from much Jacobin polemic in this era. True, the author speaks in the accepted language of "the genius of the Republic" and "the genius of the Revolution" rather than the faintly reactionary "France," but he also grants (more than once) that Jacobin leaders have been "sanguinary." Then, too, the merchant is permitted to land some decent punches, as in his argument that the people of Marseille are also "citizens" who fly "the tricolor," not royalists, like the peasants of the Vendée, and that they are justifiably tired of the bloodshed and factionalism caused by Paris. To these arguments, the officer's replies are not crushing so much as cumulatively persuasive; they draw attention not to the speaker and Jacobin doctrine, but to material considerations like the protection of private property. Above all, he is relentless in his military demonstration that Marseille cannot stand against "the entire Republic," and that to try to do so is to play into the hands of the British.

In short, "The Supper at Beaucaire" is an accomplished piece of political polemic, and one is unsurprised to learn the Jacobin leadership ordered it printed and distributed. One feels himself in the hands of a writer fully aware of the "war and revolution" dialectic, how the two feed one another and interact. Thus, a number of military insights turn up in the dialogue which will soon make their appearance in material reality when Napoleon goes to war in a less literary fashion. Already, he grasps the advantages of a war of movement over one of lines and positions, of offense over defense. Indeed, the gravamen of the *militaire*'s case is that the Federalists are fighting in a lost, more than a wrong, cause.

The ideological underpinnings of "The Supper at Beaucaire" are of a subtler strain than the bold stripes of classical Jacobinism: the *militaire* assumes the State's perspective, which, by his definition, is not a political–read, a factional–point of view, but the voice of the common good. Factions, indeed, are precisely what the *militaire* disapproves of and wants to delegitimate. At one point, he implies that it might indeed be the case that the Girondin adversaries were not *really* guilty of conspiracy. Nevertheless, what matters is not some abstract ideal of truth, but the practical fact that "guilty" is how they were adjudged by the government in time of war. Reason-of-State, in short, is what the officer defends, though Napoleon is clever enough to put the crucial points in the mouth, not of the officer, but of one of the four merchants who has been brought around by argument.

The Republic recaptured Marseille on August 25, but two days later Toulon opened itself to the English fleet of Admiral Lord Hood.

RECOGNITION

On September 16, Captain Bonaparte was escorting a slow-moving convoy of powder wagons from Marseille to Nice when he dropped in to pay his respects to Saliceti at Le Beausset. The former Corsican proconsul was now a representative on mission to the Republican army before Toulon, and he had a problem. The besieging force was without an artillery chief, the previous tenant of the job having recently been placed hors de combat by a wound. Legend has it that Bonaparte happened into Saliceti's presence at this lucky juncture and received the appointment, but it is more likely that both of them had since July been angling to get Bonaparte into an important position where he would be working with and for Saliceti.

Toulon, like Marseille, was further proof of Napoleon's argument in "The Supper at Beaucaire" that what began as civil disobedience must inevitably become part of the surrounding war. Toulon's population doubtless wished to be left alone by all belligerents to run itself in freedom—for example, the city was permitting a recrudescence of Catholic religious activity, while throughout Jacobin France the campaign of dechristianization was reaching its paroxysm. The Toulonnais were not, in the main, royalist and they were even less pro-English, but they were under siege, hence without food. The British fleet was promising victuals, on condition that the city admit their ships and recognize Louis XVII, the infant son of Louis XVI. After days of agonized debate, the Toulonnais reluctantly accepted Hood's offer. This was a disaster for the Republic—as bad a defeat as the English victory at Trafalgar in 1805—for the British burned twelve French warships and towed away nine more, without losing one boat. Their fleet now controlled the harbors of Toulon, while a combination of Toulonnais and some Spanish troops occupied entrenched land positions around the port. Arrayed against them was a steadily growing army of Republican troops sent from various points in the Midi.

As Toulon will prove to be Napoleon's emergence on the larger stage of history, it is important to understand what comprised the test here. What was needed first off was not strategic brilliance per se but discernment. Toulon did not require a full-blown siege, as some military and political leaders believed.

A close look at a relief map will show that the strategic key to the port is a hill called the Needle Point (l'Aiguillette), lying on a promontory jutting into the inner bay directly south of the port. In this regard, by the way, Toulon resembled somewhat the port of Ajaccio, dominated by the Aspreto hill—a fact hardly lost on Napoleon. If the Republicans held the Needle, then they could emplace artillery and rain a continuous fire on the English ships in the harbor, forcing them to evacuate it—at which point the city would be stranded. An initial infantry attack on l'Aiguillette was repulsed, after which the British built a fort to protect the point. Napoleon's strategy called for the Republican forces to dig in and launch a long-term artillery barrage of "petit Gibraltar," as the French called the British fortifications, and only after it was seriously weakened, launch another, more determined infantry attack.

What was in order now was a steady buildup of French firepower, notably artillery, followed eventually by a coordinated, sustained, and doubtless costly ground attack. The challenge sounds obvious but the Republic's forces, one must recall, were not in the hands of professionals, most of whom had emigrated. The current commander when Captain Bonaparte arrived, for example, was a former court painter, completely unversed in siege warfare and justifiably worried that a disaster might cost him his head. Command would change several more times before passing to a soldier (Dugommier) who was experienced in military leadership. Keeping attention fastened on l'Aiguillette rather than a generalized attack or siege of the city was not easy. If one keeps in mind that the Republic was fighting on a dozen fronts, transferring artillery to this sector was by no means a foregone conclusion, given that its military commanders were all making requests.

Success at Toulon thus demanded more than analytical and strategic skills; it required adroitness, the capacity systematically to impose oneself amid a profusion of competing plans, requests, voices, and needs; knowing whom to contact among various military and political authorities, locally and in Paris, and how and when to apply pressure. It meant knowing how effectively to oppose indecision, timidity, confusion, and incompetence among individuals of (often) far superior rank and position, without getting oneself sacked or marginalized. It required, above all, perseverance: keeping up the pressure until the people in power did what needed to be done. And, of course, it finally required that when the moment of truth came, one could see to the military execution of the plan with precision, and effectiveness.

As a mere captain (major after October 19) of artillery, Napoleon would not have had a chance of imposing his ideas for taking the Needle Point, let alone being a principal in the taking of it, if he had not had the ear of Saliceti and others. Through Saliceti, Napoleon met other representatives on mission—including Paul Barras and Louis-Stanislas Fréron, men of greater importance in the Convention than Saliceti—and impressed them not simply with his ideological dependability—no small matter in a republic still reeling from Dumouriez's defection—but his technical competence: he just seemed to know what he was talking about. The scores of letters Napoleon wrote and the plans he submitted to authorities in the three months from mid-September to mid-December attest to indefatigable energy and unfailing perspicacity: He imposed his plan, and thereafter, thought of every contingency, dealt with every new development, figured out how to repeat himself in different ways, again and again and again. He could, at one and the same time, scour the terrain for materiel—amassing eleven batteries of nearly one hundred guns on the western shores of the smaller harbor—and navigate (sway, counsel, cajole, and impress) at headquarters. He thought more quickly, rose earlier, went to bed later, and talked more than anybody else.

Napoleon's plan worked: the British fleet duly evacuated the inner harbor when they realized that French artillery commanded the entrance and could prevent ingress or egress. Thereafter, successful assaults were made on the Allied infantry positions. In the final attack on December 17, Napoleon figured as a leading planner and coordinator, but he also took part in the fighting. He had a horse shot out from under him and took a bayonet thrust to the thigh, the only real wound he would ever receive.

In recompense for services rendered—services for which Saliceti, Barras, Fréron, and Dugommier made every effort to take personal credit—Napoleon was promoted to brigadier general on December 22 and later named to head the artillery force of the Army of Italy. He was twenty-four—young for the grade, but not extravagantly so. Davout, Hoche, and Marceau were all twenty-three or twenty-four when they became generals. If anything singled out Napoleon Bonaparte from the other favored young generals, it was not his age but his closer relations with the Jacobins; he was a political general. He took away more than a star from the Toulon chapter. He also met two of his future marshals of the Empire: Andoche Junot, whom he made his aide-de-camp, and Auguste Marmont, a man who would one day spectacularly betray the ruler from whom he accepted so much.

THE DINNER AT ANCONA

There have been good Jacobins. At one time every man of intelligence was bound to be one. I was one myself.

—Napoleon Bonaparte

A little over three years later, in mid-February 1797, after ten months of brilliant campaigning, the general in chief of the Army of Italy is preparing to march with his victorious troops on Rome. At dinner with several officers in the Adriatic town of Ancona, he gives vent for two entire hours to his reflections on France and its government in the revolutionary Year II (1793–94). His fascination with the topic was familiar to close associates but not to tonight's diners, to whom Bonaparte's thoughts presented a "painful surprise."

The focus of these Napoleonic musings was the France of 1793–94, the Revolution's extravagant moment that marked it for literature and posterity. It was the era that saw people addressing one another as "citizen" (including "citizen minister"), wearing red ("Phrygian") bonnets and striped trousers, rather than "aristocratic" knee breeches, or culottes—hence the term "sans-culottes," for the revolutionary people of the era. Political correctness forbade the use of titles from the old regime to the ludicrous point that, speaking of insects, one thought it best to say "president bee," not "queen bee." The crowds of sans-culottes wore heavy wooden clogs, or sabots, that could be wielded destructively (hence "sabotage"). A leading revolutionary boasted, "In twenty years no one in Paris will know how to make a pair of shoes."

The foregoing may strike a modern reader as merely curious or interesting examples of ultra-radicalism, but the Year II had other facets that still today elicit disquiet. The guillotine and the Terror were, of course, first among them, but hardly less so was the frontal attack on religion. Around France, churches were closed, saints' names removed from the streets, clerical dress forbidden in public, and holidays like the "Feast of Brutus" invented to replace Easter or Christmas. Meanwhile, the aptly named *enragés* followed talented demagogues like Roux and Hébert and tried to impose the "Nation's will" on the Convention. When even radical revolutionary leaders like the great Danton were led away to the guillotine, many—perhaps most—people felt that "things have gone too far," "have gotten out of hand."

The effective ruler of France in this improbable era was a former attorney from Arras whose personality dominated the Committee of Public Safety as surely as that group of twelve dominated the National Convention. His

name: Maximilien Robespierre. It was on him that General Bonaparte held
rapturously forth at the dinner in Ancona. His table companions found his
admiration for "this man who was superior to all around him," this creator
of "the only strong government France has had since the start [of the Rev-
olution],"[2] a puzzlement, as have students of Bonaparte's life. After all, the
first Emperor of the French is generally regarded as the last word in pragmatic
governance and the French Revolution's great stifler, while the "Incorruptible" is construed as its most advanced avatar, a Jacobin *illuminé* who put ideology ahead of everything.

The commonest explanations of Napoleon's association with the Jacobin
party are necessity and ambition. Saliceti, we recall, was the only thing standing between the Bonaparte family and destitution, and Napoleon sought further advance, particularly after his military success at Toulon. But if these
motivations were a key part of the package, they do not explain Napoleon's
strange fascination with Robespierre. In the spring of 1794, General Bonaparte had met Augustin Robespierre, Maximilien's brother, a Jacobin representative on mission in the Midi. He became impressed by the Corsican
officer (whom he met through Saliceti), so impressed that he wrote to Maximilien in Paris, "I would add to the list of patriots the name of citizen Buonaparte, general in chief of the artillery, an officer of transcendent merit. He
is . . . a man who resisted Paoli's caresses, and who [as a result] saw his property ravaged by this traitor."[3] "Transcendent merit" was strong language; it was
more than was said about better-known and more successful republican generals, such as Hoche or Masséna.

With Augustin's backing, Napoleon and his views received attention at
the top of the Jacobin regime during the last months of its tenure, though
the exact measure of what his entrée did for him is hard to gauge, for the
Committee of Public Safety was largely caught up in the no-quarter
internecine political conflict raging in Paris, while General Bonaparte's
agenda had to do with military strategy. He never met with the elder Robespierre, and the one job that the latter may actually have offered him—command of the Paris National Guard—Napoleon declined. The embattled
Incorruptible fell six weeks later, and it is unlikely that even Bonaparte could
have saved him. The consequence of trying and failing to do so would have
spelled the guillotine for him, as he well understood, and was doubtless a
key motive for turning down the "opportunity."

What Napoleon did become was a listened-to "spinner of plans" (*faiseur
de plans*) for the northern Italian theater in the regime's foreign policy.
More important, he enjoyed, thanks to his frequent contacts with Augustin
Robespierre, a bird's-eye view of what was transpiring in Paris. Napoleon

reflected closely on the events of the Year II for the rest of his life, and the views he developed about Robespierre, which so shocked his dinner guests at Ancona, are both interesting in themselves, they are historically clever, insightful–and for what they tell us about him.

Essentially, Napoleon construed the Jacobins as a moderate party of government, as conservative managers of his beloved State. Napoleon's Robespierre was not the wild-eyed radical of conventional depiction, but an opponent of terror and factionalism–above all, a supporter of strong central government. Democracy, for *this* Robespierre, was not the "sovereign people" rising up as a mob, parading itself as "the nation"; it was the rule of law and of representative institutions. The Committee of Public Safety he dominated moved boldly to break the street factions, sending several of their leaders to the guillotine. As Napoleon noted, it was during Robespierre's term at the tiller of State that "for the first time since the start of the Revolution, people were sentenced to death as ultra-revolutionaries, rather than for trying to stop the Revolution."[4] Beyond this, Napoleon attributed to Robespierre a vast plan for "regenerating both the century and the country," for endowing France and the world with new institutions and mores. In sum, the Incorruptible was a man without personal ambition who stood for "the triumph of the Revolution," by which Napoleon meant containing, consolidating, and defending, but not expanding it.

A curious codicil to the foregoing was Napoleon's evolution in the matter of religion. We know his earlier view that religion was dangerous for the competition it gave the State. Several years of witnessing the Revolution's hammer blows on Christianity, and the divisive and destructive radicalism that accompanied it, however, led Napoleon to reconsider the value of religious belief in conserving the social order and braking men's impulses. He now saw the utility in Voltaire's tenet: "If God did not exist he would have to be invented." Thus, no minor part of Napoleon's admiration for Robespierre resulted from the latter's attempt to reverse the attack on religion. Robespierre had believed religion to be indispensable to orderly society, so he launched–indeed, he became virtually the high priest of–a State cult of the Supreme Being. This bizarre episode had few admirers–either at the time or subsequently–but Napoleon Bonaparte was one of them.

The opinion that must have most shocked the General's dinner companions at Ancona, however, was their host's take on Robespierre's dramatic fall from power on 9 Thermidor (July 27) 1794.[5] Napoleon saw Robespierre perishing "for having wished to halt the Revolution"; his interlocutors saw a dictator steeped in blood, deservedly mounting the same scaffold to which he had dispatched so many innocent victims. They saw his death as a salvation for France; Napoleon saw it as "a great misfortune."

Thermidor brought death to Robespierre and his closest collaborators, including his brother. It also brought retribution for the Incorruptible's associates, large and (sometimes) small. If Napoleon were an opportunist who had become Jacobin from self-interest, then post-Thermidor would have seen him abjure his faith, as it saw innumerable other Jacobins do. The success of the self-styled Brutuses who conspired against Robespierre—men no less notoriously bloodthirsty than he, by the way—lay in getting most people to think of themselves as moderates and of their foe as crazy. In Thermidor, for the first time, "Jacobin" became a term of opprobrium, as the white terror of well-dressed lynch mobs replaced the red terror of the guillotine. "The Terror," as Isser Woloch notes perceptively, "changed the destiny of France . . . [for it] unleashed a cycle of recrimination, hatred, and endemic local conflict that made future prospects of a democratic polity in France very dim. General Bonaparte represented one possible outcome of that dilemma, or a cure worse than the malady, depending on one's point of view."[6]

Napoleon admitted that the downfall of Robespierre "rather affected me, for I rather liked him." This is a far cry from the bitter disappointment he received at Paoli's hands, but there is a trace of political idealism in his stubbornly expressed appreciation of the Incorruptible—even if it does not equal the wild (and unrealistic) courage of his minute-to-midnight stand by Paoli in early 1793. As First Consul, Napoleon would grant a pension to the Robespierres' sister, Marie, and on St. Helena he said that as Emperor he should have ordered the printing of Robespierre's final speech to the Convention. This regret was a velleity at best, and more probably an instance of disingenuousness, but the fact is, there was something of the Robespierre in Napoleon, and vice versa. One of the cleverest observers of the French scene, Germaine de Staël, saw beneath ideological appearances to observe the State's man (if not the statesman) in Robespierre and in Napoleon. Just after the 18 Brumaire coup d'Etat, she looked at the new First Consul and called him, "Robespierre à cheval."

Napoleon, in sum, was a party-line Jacobin for less time and with less fervor than he had been a conventional *paolisto*. His Jacobinism, if that is the word for it, was a continuation of his gratitude for the Revolution's freeing him from the effects of aristocratic caste prejudice. Remaining outspokenly loyal to his version of Robespierre was a way of not renouncing himself, as many did, despite the disappointments of 1789–93 on Corsica, and of 9 Thermidor in France.

Ten months after Bonaparte's arrest, it was Saliceti's turn to fall afoul of the

Convention, which declared him an outlaw. Napoleon knew exactly where his old collaborator had taken refuge, but he said nothing to the authorities.

THE SPINNER'S PLANS

A young man of about 27 years [sic] who is to be feared as troublesome, of ardent republican spirit, of vast knowledge in things military, of great activity, and great courage . . .

—Description of Napoleon in 1794
by an Austrian minister[7]

We must not forget that the French Republic was at war during all this time. Trying to account for the Terror of 1793–94 by considering only the logic of French domestic history—a tendency that has taken hold in recent years—is like trying to analyze a game of chess from the moves of the white pieces only. War, civil strife, and terror were often fatally entwined. One can put it with cogent succinctness, as does Arno Mayer: "War revolutionizes revolution,"[8] or explicate it brilliantly, as does Paul Schroeder: "The parallel to terror as a revolutionary means of combating internal insecurity was war as the means of combating external insecurity. In both cases, the problems were real and serious, the methods natural and almost inescapable, but self-defeating. Widening the use of terror was intended to produce a genuine, unforced revolutionary consensus within France; expanding French power and influence by war was intended to end encirclement and hostility on the parts of Europe. Both attempted to solve intractable problems by trying harder, by overcoming reality instead of facing it."[9] The Jacobin regime faced as many as six States (Britain, Austria, Prussia, Spain, Holland, and the northern Italian monarchy of Piedmont-Sardinia), as well as numerous internal enemies in the west and south of France. Against all of these foes, it fielded fourteen armies. Sometimes some of them won, sometimes they lost, but either way, the situation was perilous, costly, and provoking of constant anxiety the length and breadth of the country. War is certainly where General Bonaparte's thoughts and concerns lay, more than with Paris politics.

The Republic "nationalized" war, to use the new expression of a leading Jacobin journalist. The new regime's conduct of foreign policy constituted a break with traditional diplomacy: it permitted open parliamentary debate of external relations, often punctuated by intervention from gallery spectators; it published secret diplomatic correspondence and promulgated decrees declaring that "the French people" extended "fraternity and assistance to all peoples seeking to regain liberty" (this was so unrealistic a measure that it was revoked five months later). This nation-talk threatened subversion of the monarchies: "the French people" henceforward declared wars on sovereigns only, not on their "peoples"; they concluded "national" treaties with other "nations," not with their crowned heads or royal governments; France held elections and sought to set up democratic regimes in its conquered territories. Even if it was true that the actual substance of European State relations—e.g., the lands fought over—might have struck Henry IV or Louis XIV as familiar, we cannot conclude thereby that the new ideological element disappeared or became minor in significance. More than any other factor, it is what led the French Republic to demonstrate "an unwillingness to accept the validity of other perceptions and . . . no consistent willingness to compromise with other states to any serious extent."[10] That, in turn, added the dimension of abiding distrust, hatred, and vengeance to European relations that it is critical to recall in order to understand the nature of the war—and the role of generals—from 1792 to 1815.

It is nevertheless true that the First Coalition did not crystallize *only* because its members were appalled by the Revolution or frightened of its potential for subversion. As time went by, what pressed France forward on the road to territorial expansion was not missionary revolutionism but old-fashioned territorial greed, military strategy, and—perhaps above all by the time General Bonaparte appeared on the scene—economic necessity: war had to *pay*, not just for itself, but to support the regime, in subsidies that flowed into a public treasury depleted by inflation and economic distress. The Republic made much of a geopolitical doctrine that asserted the legitimacy of France's expansion to her "natural frontiers": the Rhine, the Alps, the Pyrenees. A close look at regional maps, however, will show that these are not the neat geographical lines or walls they sound like, not to mention that they defied a host of cultural, ethnic, and economic realities.

In effect, successive French regimes convinced themselves that the country's "national security" would not be ensured unless the Republic controlled, via puppet regimes or occupation, a swatch of western German territory up to (and even across) the left bank of the Rhine; much of the present Benelux countries; and, in the southeast, the counties of Nice and Savoy which then belonged to the kingdom of Sardinia. France, in short, wanted hegemony in Western Europe. England, for her part—in addition to control of the seas—wanted a weak France. That, at bottom, was the cause of the longstanding enmity between the two countries.

War also had a compelling new Gallic logic of its own, aside from standard interests. Carried on by the Republic with huge citizen armies raised by *levée en masse,* war was the principal arena in which the revolutionary élan of hundreds of thousands of men expressed itself, now that the era of internal insurrections had passed. These swollen armies won battles for the Revolution, but this in turn mired the Republic ever deeper in a readiness to take the military solution. More than in most eras, France in the years 1792–1815 was a society whose political and economic as well as military elites looked to war.

By the turn of 1794, with Napoleon coming off his brilliant action at Toulon, the war of the First Coalition had been waged on and off for nearly two years on several fronts in the Low Countries, western Germany, the Pyrenees, and on the Franco-Italian Riviera. This last theater was the least active and, in some senses, the least important. This is a critical point to keep in mind, for the unstated motive of every one of Napoleon's writings in this period was a burning desire to get more attention, manpower, materiel, and funds diverted to the Army of Italy so that it could live up to its glorious name. Early 1794 found the two French units in this sector, the Army of Italy and the Army of the Alps, occupying ground they had held for over a year, notwithstanding that their principal enemy, the Sardinians, had little taste for continuing the war. The Sardinians were nearly bankrupt (their king would soon have to pawn the Crown jewels) and paralyzed with suspicion of their far more powerful Austrian allies.

Napoleon fairly throbbed with impatience. Martial glory—and war spoils—had some months earlier started flowing back into the coffers—rarely empty but never full enough—of young French generals everywhere, *except Italy.* In April, Jourdan (aged thirty) had saved the Republic at Fleurus, in Belgium. Pichegru (age thirty-one) had gone from lieutenant to commander of the Army of the North in under two years and was famous throughout France. Marceau, at twenty-four, was performing brilliantly as commander of the Army of the West; Moreau, at twenty-nine, had just been promoted major general for distinguished service, and Desaix, twenty-five, was a major general in the Army of the Rhine. Two notably republican officers—Bernadotte, thirty, and Hoche, twenty-five—were major generals, the latter about to cover himself with glory by hurling back the Anglo-émigré forces at Quiberon. True, Napoleon had attained star rank at a younger age than any of these men except Marceau, but he was junior to them in the hierarchy and in success. Finally, unlike them, he had no command of his own, and no prospects for one, for all was quiet on the southern front. The commander of the Army of Italy was General Dumerbion, an experienced soldier but old and sick. Spring saw his artillery commander, General Bonaparte, pressing him hard, both directly and through his connections with the several representatives-on-mission to the Army of Italy, notably Saliceti and Robespierre *le jeune*. Napoleon would submit studies to them, and they would send them on, under their own names, to the Committee of Public Safety in Paris. These memoranda had to commend themselves to men who daily treaded water through an ocean of documents. Turn of phrase and polemical style mattered little; careful reasoning and, above all, a sense of how to address politicians were what counted. Napoleon's tightly packed sets of connected observations, considerations, and deductions, or conclusions, succeeded brilliantly.

The best of them is the "Note on the Military and Political Position of Our Armies of Piedmont and Spain," a 1,500-word gem that hides extraordinary scope in the flattest of prose. From one step to the next, the author proceeds from the humdrum need for more cavalry harnesses to the primordial issue of "the absolute necessity, in an immense fight like ours, for a revolutionary government and a single central authority." The course Napoleon has set himself amounts to a veritable steeplechase of contradictions. He must first reiterate the myth that the war here, as everywhere, is primarily defensive in nature and then proceed to detail a wholly offensive strategy. Second, he must revive interest in the Italian front at a time when other fronts—e.g., Spain—are bubbling with successful activity. Yet he cannot ignore the fact that France's greatest land-based enemy is *not* the Sardinians but the power lurking *behind* them: Austria. (Britain is bankrolling the Habsburg armies.) The campaign on the Riviera and in northern Italy must therefore be shown to have a direct payoff in debilitating the House of Habsburg. True, such a strategy had once been a classic French line of attack against its inveterate Austrian enemy, but in recent years French strategic thinking focused almost entirely on the high road to Vienna over the Rhine or through Alsace or Switzerland. Nothing better sums up the casuistic genius of Napoleon's "Note," therefore, than the line "Strike Germany, never Spain and Italy," which is followed by details for a campaign in . . . Italy.[11]

So Napoleon reasons that the Army of Italy is best situated to deal the most efficient blows at "our most implacable enemy" (Austria). The French must drive a wedge between the two allies—the Sardinians and the Austrians—and then turn to finishing each off in detail. Once the king of Sardinia has made a separate peace, the Army of Italy will attack the Tyrol, in the Austrian heartland. This is a neat project, which General Bonaparte's "Note" makes seem like one continuous action, each step leading naturally and easily to the next. In fact, of course, it is a breathtaking fantasy. No French general stationed in the southern theater—Dumerbion, Masséna, Scherer, etc.—was proposing plans as bold as these, only designs for localized duels with the Sardinian forces in and around the Riviera or the Ligurian coast.

Signed and delivered to his brother by Augustin Robespierre, the text also offers an adroit mix of the political and the military, the author being of the Clausewitzian persuasion that war is but an extension of politics. The Republic is committed to war and revolution, and the two must drive each other. Napoleon speaks of "gouvernement révolutionnaire" and endorses the "overthrow of the throne [of the House of Savoy]." He is clearly aware that his principal reader harbors the radical dream of revolutionizing all of Italy. To a gimlet-eyed Jacobin like Robespierre, Napoleon might have seemed like a military equivalent of Saint-Just, the Incorruptible's loyal collaborator and ideologue of the committee.

As ill luck would have it, Napoleon's "Note" made it to Robespierre's desk hardly more than a week before 9 Thermidor. With the Incorruptible's fall, the artillery general's ideas fell into the hands of men like Lazare Carnot, the Republic's chief military and geopolitical strategist, who were far less inclined to pursue *la guerre à outrance*. For Carnot, indeed, one of Robespierre's several "crimes" was his wish to pursue such a risky war of aggression into Italy, exposing the Republic to attack or counterattack. The gospel of revolutionary war, as Carnot understood it, dictated that every inch of the national soil must be protected—an idea with which Napoleon's ideas played fast and loose.[12]

The post-Thermidor representatives on mission in the south were still amenable to Bonaparte's bellicose designs. Napoleon's post-Thermidor plans for Italy suggest inflaming the Genoese populace against their oligarchical governors and distributing publicly copies of diplomatic correspondence as a means of forcing the governors to do the French bidding. By and large, however, Bonaparte's post-Robespierrist notes emit less ideological scent—their author, as always, taking the measure of his readers' designs while seeking to advance his own. With the passing of Robespierre from the scene, Carnot's moderation won out, illustrated by the appointment of hesitant, usually older commanding generals to the Army of Italy. From a strictly military point of view, the French undoubtedly lost an opportunity to carry successful military operations into Lombardy, but no one understood better than General Bonaparte that war bent to policy. In any case, by then he had other subjects that demanded his attention.

VENDÉMIAIRE, YEAR IV

The fifteen months between the fall of Robespierre and the creation of the first Directory is a period unofficially known as Thermidor, or the Thermidorian Reaction, for the contrast it made to what preceded it. In crucial ways,

Thermidor offered relief: an end of the emergency regime and the Terror, an end to price controls, the recrudescence of religion and social life. The regime's main task was to write a new constitution, which it did, but the government betrayed a certain ambiguity in its nature and irresolution in its policy. If things changed in style and tone, *institutionally* Thermidor offered more of the same. The National Convention–minus, of course, Robespierre et al.– now transfigured themselves into penitent ex-Jacobins. Thermidor was in part an era of hypocrisy, of revolutionaries deconstructing themselves in order to retain power.

Napoleon had supporters and admirers among certain leading Thermidorians (Barras, Fréron, and others), but he did not go out of his way to establish himself as a new man. This might have gotten him into trouble but for the comparative modesty of his reputation–he was better known in the Midi than in Paris–and the high quality of his work. Still, the new faces on the Committee of Public Safety and the new war minister, Aubry, were wary of Robespierre's people and could not consistently decide how to use the artillery general. In the winter of 1795, Napoleon was pulled from the Riviera-Italian front and put to work designing plans for the invasion of Corsica– a project that ended when it became clear the French could not challenge British naval hegemony. In May, Napoleon was ordered to report for duty in the Army of the West, under the command of Lazare Hoche.

There is an old Latin saying that translates as "the French attack each other like wolves." This may be unfair–to wolves, who seem to get along in packs. Few conflicts in the length and breadth of France's long history more sadly attest to her people's mutual enmity than the war that raged in the Vendée from 1792 to 1795 between the peasant armies (*les Chouans*), often led by priests and royalists, and the blue-coated armies of the Republic. As many died here as in the Terror. Yet it was a Frenchman, Chateaubriand, who made the fascinating observation that "civil war is less unjust and revolting, as well as more natural, than foreign war." There is a deeper and more purgative truth to fratricidal conflict, to killing someone you love for a reason you find compelling, than to killing someone you do not know for territorial gains that matter to you little. For a military commander, civil conflict is particularly risky and dangerous; however, it can pay. Thus, all of Caesar's battlefield laurels won over eight long years of battles in Gaul were not worth the single victory at Pharsala over Pompey's Roman legions. Napoleon well understood both the appalling and the appealing sides of such conflict.

The one good thing that could be said about the Vendée assignment was that it offered Napoleon a brigade of his own, for he yearned to come out from behind a desk. But the deficits piled up. The appointment was in the infantry—a step down in status for an artillery officer—and there was the matter of political danger and personal distaste. General Hoche himself had sought to avoid a job that entailed making war on his compatriots, while other fine officers like Kléber and Kellermann had been sickened by this duty. Hoche, like so many brother officers, had faced arrest on flimsy political charges, on one occasion nearly going to the guillotine. Early in 1795, Hoche had written to the War Ministry complaining of how many of his officers in the Vendée were putting in for reassignment.[13] Lastly—no minor consideration for Bonaparte—the war in the west had effectively ended in April 1795 with the peace of Prévalaye between the rebels and the Republic. This left only mopping up to do. The drawbacks of the Vendée job so proliferated that Marmont called the appointment "a disastrous blow to Bonaparte's career."

Yet Napoleon appears to have stifled his ambivalence and steeled himself to take the job, but he kept putting off the time of his departure to the Vendée. He, Junot, and Marmont lingered longer in Paris and, though impecunious, enjoyed the pleasures that the capital offered in this season of gaiety regained. Napoleon profited from the time to go to the opera, visit the Observatory, and hear lectures by Lalande, the famous astronomer.

Summer of 1795 was a time where, despite Napoleon's letters and other people's memoirs, we cannot say with certainty what was our subject's state of mind or heart. It is possible to take the evidence as it lies: the man seems to be serene, gay, and optimistic. But it is also possible to pore over the same evidence and say that it lies: he is inwardly depressed, dour, restless.

This reader is impressed with the sheer amount of epistolary space that Napoleon accords his brothers—for example, witness the pleasure taken in seventeen-year-old Louis's visit to Paris and Napoleon's chagrin at his departure ("I feel his absence so keenly," he writes Joseph on September 6, "he was of such a great help to me"). He tries to arrange a visit for Jérôme, aged ten. He writes less about Lucien, though he goes out of his way to get this brother released from arrest (Lucien—a.k.a. Brutus Bonaparte—was too Jacobin for the Thermidorians' taste). As for his affection for Joseph, it is the defining sentiment of his emotional life to date. He is constantly assuring him of "mon amitié," telling him to be "worry-free about your future," which he, Napoleon, will ensure. In one letter, his feeling for his older brother is so great, he says that he must break off writing. The letters to Joseph constitute the backbone of Napoleon's correspondence in this period; they are newsy and descriptive, full of chat about parties, women, and the gaiety redefining life in the capital in Thermidor.

In short, one comes away from reading these letters with the sense of a

Napoleon of a certain (perhaps hard-won) self-possession, notwithstanding that he had reason to feel anxious and perturbed: the 1794 gains on the Riviera, for which his plans had been in part responsible, have been lost to an Austro-Sardinian counteroffensive; the woman he loves—or thinks he loves, or claims he loves—has not been answering his letters frequently enough; finally, most seriously, his status in the army remains ambiguous. He is officially due in the Vendée, yet he stays on in Paris thanks to various sick leaves and special permissions. Remarkably, he complains little of any of this (except the woman's unresponsiveness) in the letters.

What he shows instead is a speculative and philosophical side that has led some to question how happy he was. He writes (August 12): "As for me, I'm not especially attached to things. I approach life without grasping for it. I find myself often in the mood one enters on the eve of battle . . . when it would be foolish to be anxious. Everything makes me indifferent to fate or destiny." The author might—surely, he *must*—be anxious about his future, but he strains not to let it affect his brother. "You have no reason to worry about me, whatever happens; I have many good friends who are decent people, whatever their party or opinion" (September 6). "The future is a matter of contempt for the man of courage" (September 8). In public, Napoleon displayed reserve and imperturbability, or, as some would have it, "glacial silences" and an inappropriate unwillingness to laugh uproariously at the theater. Such reactions might simply indicate the malaise of being poor in high society, as well as the absence of a taste for hobnobbing therein. One can do worse than to close with the judgment of one of Napoleon's most perceptive future associates, Charles Maurice de Talleyrand: "His true feelings escape us, for he still finds a way to feign them even when they really exist."

On August 19, Bonaparte was named to head the army's Topographical Bureau, a kind of general planning staff directly attached to the Committee of Public Safety. Something of a coup, the appointment showed he still had some political clout, even in Thermidor. A leading figure of the day, Boissy d'Anglas, recommended him to the new minister of war, Pontécoulant, who met him and described him as "a young man, of pale and yellowish complexion, grave and bent over, looking sickly and frail."[14] Napoleon, put off by the thirty-year-old minister's lack of military knowledge, did not follow up this connection, so the politician had to pursue the young general whom he wished to have work with him. Bonaparte's request for reassignment to the Sultan of Turkey (to help him build up his artillery arm) was, after some vicissitudes, turned down because the petitioner's services were deemed too important for him to be released.

Then, on September 15, something strange occurred: Napoleon's name was inexplicably dropped from the army's active list. We do not know precisely why—whether from bureaucratic mismanagement or the sleepless phobia against Jacobins. The former is the more likely, given that the same day the General received notice he could proceed to Constantinople (permission later revoked). In all events, he was angry enough to resign his commission. This would have been the end of his military career, at least for now, but once again his luck held.

In view of the official repression of Jacobins, the famous flourishing of political life in Thermidor was largely a right-wing affair. By no means were all of the people who reemerged to public life sincere royalists; many were simply propertied bourgeoisie, successful profiteers of the Revolution who had acquired Church or noble lands, who speculated in declining assignats or the arms trade, and who sought to bring an end to "anarchy." Still, historian John Holland Rose's conclusion—"the history of the Revolution proves that those who at first merely opposed the excesses of the Jacobins gradually drifted over to the royalists"—is incontrovertible.[15] The men of Thermidor, being mainly ex-Robespierrists and regicides (i.e., Convention members who had voted for the death of Louis XVI), could only view this renascent Catholic, aristocratic, and quasi-royalist sentiment and activity as a threat to their regime.

They reacted heavy-handedly: the decrees of August 22 and 30 stipulated that two-thirds of the new legislature, for which elections would soon be held, must be made up of former members of the Convention. That law provoked disgust and set off a strong reaction. Ensuing weeks also saw growing agitation in the capital among many of the lower classes for whom the high price of bread created mortal peril. When evidence arose that the Paris National Guard was joining the "moderates" (read: royalists), it became imperative to act. Early in October the men of Thermidor placed their fate in the hands of Paul Barras, a leader of the military forces that had brought down Robespierre. He approached the simmering Paris situation with practicality and shrewdness. As the enemy—at least its organizers and most effective carriers—were right-wingers, he released from prison a number of Jacobins to help him oppose them. He appointed a number of Robespierrist officers to commands, one of whom was Bonaparte, a soldier he knew and respected from Toulon.

Now, Napoleon undoubtedly shared the political right's desire (but then it was also the moderate left's) to see an end to revolutionary anarchy and the gains of 1789 consolidated into a stable system of government presiding over a thriving society. Nevertheless, what was the alternative to fighting alongside Barras, a man he despised for his notorious corruption? It is likely that Napoleon's reasoning at age twenty-six was how he described it when he was fifty: If the Convention lost, what would become of "the great truths of our Revolution?" Defeat of the regime's forces "would seal the shame and slavery of the *patrie*." There is no gainsaying that conclusion, however much the reasoning may also have been intended to justify the self-interest of the reasoner. The anniversary of Vendémiaire[16] was celebrated as an official holiday until the Consulate.

The 13 Vendémiaire was the last time that a Parisian crowd would try to force a government's hand and the first time in the entire history of the Revolution that the regime used the standing army against the people. No one had dared before then. The fighting lasted six and a half hours; hundreds died, but in the end the effective street maneuvers by five thousand to six thousand well-armed, well-led troops of the line defeated four to five times their number of wretchedly organized forces of insurrection. The victory was largely Barras's, but in significant measure Napoleon contributed. Certainly, he was by far the most energetic of Barras's subordinates. In the words of other military men, his decisions and directions were "clear," "laconic," "rapid"; he showed "extraordinary aplomb," was "always sure of himself, a born leader." General Thiébault writes: "From the first, his activity was astonishing: he seemed to be everywhere at once: he surprised people by his laconic, clear, and prompt orders: everybody was struck by the vigor of his arrangements, and passed from admiration to confidence, from confidence to enthusiasm."[17] Napoleon was also the most prescient of Barras's seconds: he ordered a cavalry major named Murat to lead his troop to seize the artillery at Sablons and bring it back to central Paris. Those eight-pounders were carefully arrayed by Bonaparte to control the principal streets leading to the Convention—notably those near the Saint-Roch church, where hundreds of insurrectionaries were mown down like fresh hay by cannon fire. The artillery made the difference. The ill-led attackers made several more assaults, took even heavier losses, then withdrew and went home.

Wisely, the Convention dealt with its foe humanely, by the era's standards; only two Vendémiaire leaders were executed. Napoleon's personal intervention spared Menou (the previous commander of the Republic's troops) from being court-martialed for incompetence. (Menou would join him on the Egyptian campaign three years later.) For his good work, Bonaparte himself was named a divisional general and commander in chief of the Army of the Interior.

The end of this, the most decisive day of his life to date, cannot occur for Napoleon until he has shared it with Joseph, so at two in the morning of 14 Vendémiaire, he pulls a sheet of paper toward him to write, "At last it is all over and my first thought is to give you my news." The day's events follow, written in lapidary turns of phrase. Other letters over the next fortnight apprise Joseph of the profit that will accrue to the family from Napoleon's new position, prestige, and pay (48,000 francs per year): a diplomatic consulship for Joseph, a lucrative government appointment for Lucien, Louis's nomination as his brother's aide-de-camp, Jérôme's admission to a fancy school. There are lesser rewards for more distant family members. It is just the beginning. "The family will want for nothing," he assures Joseph. The tone in these letters is matter-of-fact and innocent; the writer in no way senses he is doing anything wrong: his family has been in dire straits, and he has taken care of his own. He was well aware that he was acting no differently from most of the men who attained political power in this era. The abuse—and with it the traces of bad conscience—would come later.

Whether he was happy or sad, ambitious or stoical, in this era is finally impossible to say conclusively. However, in reading his letters, one cannot fail being struck by an absence of pessimism, let alone of cynicism, in his cheerful and hopeful descriptions of the teeming life of Thermidor. He did not respect the Thermidorians—few did—but he was fascinated by the political process, and even showed the new institutions a certain respect. Aside from a negative remark about "the moral state of the country" (August 12), he is mostly upbeat: "The people of Paris are, in their mass, good" (August 24)—not a usual Napoleonic observation. Furthermore, he says: "[From the new constitution] we expect happiness and tranquility . . ." and then he adds, [it] promises to have a long future in France." The constitution is "the principal object of everyone's hopes" (June 23, August 1 and 12). Then, too—perhaps oddly, for a soldier—he is happy about the peace with Spain and Naples, and in the Vendée: "Peace is so necessary to the Republic"; "peace will be good for commerce" (September 15, 23).

If there are shards of cynicism and pessimism that stick in the reader's throat, it is when he or she reads the thoughts of the middle-aged Napoleon looking back on this period twenty years later: "A dreadful system of reaction afflicted the interior of the Republic. . . . The Revolution had lost its novelty. It had alienated many people by adversely affecting their interests. . . . All parties were tired of the Convention—it was even tired of its own existence," etc. Napoleon's success was going to make a different man of him, but the process was only starting in the era of Toulon and Vendémiaire. He wasn't born Machiavellian, he became it.

BOOK II

Le jour de gloire est arrivé

V

Love and War

CLISSON IN LOVE

The man who feels bumps is right. You have the bump of love.
—Balzac, *The Human Comedy*

I definitely believe that love does more harm than good.
—Napoleon Bonaparte

The political life is an exacting mistress; no wonder that the powerful seldom make famous lovers—even less so when love requires a serious professional sacrifice. Exceptions spring to mind, but they are few: Marc Antony went to war for Cleopatra; Henry VIII made a reformation so that he could marry Anne Boleyn (though we well know that other gods than Eros were bearing down hard on the Tudor). Louis I of Bavaria might have proven to be the exception, except that in the crunch he reluctantly sacrificed *la belle* Montez to her enemies in his government. Is it possible then that Edward Windsor's abdication on behalf of Wallis Simpson is the only instance we have of Jove's sincere bending to Eros among ranking statesmen? Is William Bolitho right to suggest that the "sexual direction . . . is no part of the definition" of great politicians who tend to move "exempt from the quasi-gravitational pull of sex on the trajectory of their lives"? Is he right to claim that "in the Law of Adventure, male adventure, love is no more than gold or fame—all three, glitterings on the horizon, beckoning constellations"?[1]

Bolitho's words do not hold for the young Napoleon Bonaparte; he may offer an exception to the foregoing, for in common with at least two of his brothers (Lucien and Jérôme), he loved to distraction, madly, unreasonably, obsessively.

Our march into this theater of operations is fortunately clarified by the many signposts provided by the volatile and verbose writer in Napoleon—and above all, by the disappointed lover. *L'amour* is a familiar, almost a constant theme of his outpourings, from the oft-cited dialogue with a prostitute in the Palais-Royal, written when he was eighteen, to myriad observations in essays on other topics, and finally to the short novella *Clisson and Eugénie*, where love resumes its role of leitmotiv of his musings. By then, however, our young writer was, as Catherine the Great told Diderot, "writing my wishes not on parchment but on the infinitely more sensitive [*chatouilleuse*] flesh of human beings."

The expanse of Napoleon's thoughts about love is wide. "What is love?" he twice asks himself in a journallike entry when he was twenty-one years old.[2] The answer he gives is hardly a happy one: it speaks of "solitary or isolated men" "pierced by feelings of weakness." Their experience with love is titanic, shattering; having "tasted the sensations, the intoxication of love, they now fear a horrible solitude of heart, an emptiness of feeling." Small wonder that men flee such disequilibrium by throwing themselves into their careers. A few months later, however, a more didactic Napoleon produces a similar take, in the wonderfully revealing *Dialogue on Love*. Two characters—Bonaparte and des Mazis—have what is traditionally billed as a debate, but is in fact a tongue-lashing administered by the Corsican to his lovesick friend. Des Mazis takes it badly—no doubt, in part, because he is barely allowed to get a word in edgewise. He is told that he has changed for the worse since he met Adelaide, that love is "harmful to society" as well as to "the individual happiness of men." Love is a "state of illness, the pursuit of a chimera," and des Mazis is in "servitude," he has broken the social contract. Better that he think about his friends and his duties, about being prepared to leap into action if the *patrie* is attacked.

Des Mazis replies that these platitudes mean nothing to him compared to a kiss from Adelaide. He adds that clearly Bonaparte "has never been in love."

Although the character of Bonaparte—whom it would be a large mistake to collapse into Napoleon *tout court*—sounds more than faintly ridiculous, it cannot be denied that the author has an intuitive grasp of a profound truth: nobody can easily tolerate *two* great passions at the same time—in the event, patriotism and love, what the classical Greeks called *philia* (brotherly love) and *eros* (romantic love). If a man seeks to have both deeply, he will end up in conflict with himself; if he be a man of State, his love will war with politics; if he be a soldier, it will war with war.

Or at least, so it is in the realm of ideas and logic. In the realm of life, Napoleon's first experience with eros showed him to be no des Mazis, while his later experiences only brought him reluctantly back to Bonaparte.

Early in 1794 the newly minted general and his brother Joseph met the family of a wealthy soap merchant named Clary. Both men were drawn to Clary's younger daughter, Désirée, sixteen. Napoleon presently made the specious case to Joseph that the girl's older sister, Julie, in her early twenties, was the better choice for him, as she had a decisive character while he was a waffler. For exactly the reverse set of reasons, Désirée suited him, Napoleon added. The indecisive Joseph acquiesced in this self-serving argument, which in fact turned out to be a happy choice for him: he and Julie married in August and had a good life together, notwithstanding his many mistresses. That left the good-natured, plump, short, comely, and above all, highly impressionable and tenderhearted Désirée for Napoleon. He would have married her forthwith, for "the marriage folly is taking hold of me," as he told Joseph (September 5, 1795). Indeed, this was the marrying season for Bonaparte men. Lucien, wildly in love, had taken as his common-law wife an innkeeper's daughter whom he would later refuse to leave, on Napoleon's orders, for the Infanta of Spain, just as Jérôme would refuse—for a time—to leave his American wife, Elizabeth Patterson, at his brother's bidding.

But Napoleon did not marry Désirée. Her father, though fond of the young general, balked at having two promising but unproven sons-in-law from the same family. Napoleon continued to visit Désirée, whom he called by her middle name, Eugénie (he would often rename the women in his life); however, we do not see him letting go in the way he had lambasted des Mazis for doing. Rather, it was the romantic Désirée who fell into a deepening infatuation with her extraordinary "ami."

Napoleon's attitude toward sexual intimacy, by the way, was anything but taken for granted. The journal entry written after the nineteen-year-old's first experience with sex, via a prostitute, concludes with one of the more extraordinary mixes of coyness and coitus in French letters: "I was far from scrupulous," Napoleon writes to himself, "I exasperated her, and thereby held her attention so she would not leave in haste, by pretending to be supremely honest, the better to prove to her that, in fact, I was not."[3] The young man's insecurity at finding himself in a new and vulnerable situation is common; what is fascinating is the compensation he deploys: the naive fantasy of a complete inner and outer mastery, before and after the fact; the fear of conceding he might have learned anything from a girl who had doubtless heard his sort of story many times.

Soon after (perhaps) knowing Désirée intimately, the lovers were parted:

Napoleon left for Paris and his betrothed accompanied her mother to Genoa. His letters to her indicate that for a time, he fell under eros's thrall. To Joseph he was often impatiently inquiring about Désirée, demanding to know why he wasn't hearing more from her. He refers to her as his fiancée and writes letters to test her: "Tender Eugénie, you are young. Your feelings will weaken . . . [but] don't think that if they do I will accuse you of injustice." In July he tells her, "Oh! Mon amie, I love you even more, if that is possible." Throughout these months, he is constantly "begging you, don't let a day pass without writing to me to assure me you love me." Withal, he is also sending her a stream of Napoleonic directions and advice on everything from dress to politics to protocol, so that, as many commentators suggest, these are not the letters of a man in love. Rather, they represent an attempt in a time of uncertainty, straitened circumstance, and new experience to hang on to various emotional anchors.

For the student of Napoleon, the relationship with Désirée gave rise to something of greater heuristic value than the relationship itself for understanding the man's psychology, and that is the strange short story that Napoleon produced in September 1795. *Clisson and Eugénie,* as it is known, is a nine-page biblically simple, romantic fantasy.[4] Written at the height of his feelings for Désirée (= Eugénie), it is best seen as a transparent expression of his own ideals and hopes about love and about himself in love. And in case the reader may still not get the point that this is autobiography, Bonaparte crossed off "et Eugénie" from the title when he had finished the manuscript.

Clisson, twenty, is a rather humorless man of war who "understood nothing of word play . . . , whose power, sangfroid, courage and moral firmness only increased the number of his enemies . . . , [who] disdained love and despised luck." He meets two sisters, of whom the younger, Eugénie, is sixteen. "Without being ugly, she was no beauty," we are told, "yet goodness, sweetness, lively tenderness abounded in her naturally." To Clisson, she was "the nightingale's song." "One would have said nature gave them the same heart, soul, and feelings." Meeting her, Clisson "for the first time takes stock of his life, his tastes, his state. . . . Like most men, he desired happiness but had achieved only glory."

War now goes out the window, as the two marry, settle down, have children (only sons, of course), and "remain lovers." They stay to themselves and have few acquaintances. Six years of bliss pass when news comes that war has not forgotten the man who forgot it. Clisson has been mobilized. "The folly of mankind" has broken up another happy home. Clisson goes off to fight as commander of the army. He wins victory after victory, "surpassing the hopes of the people and the army." Eugénie writes him daily; years pass; he is grievously wounded and sends his loyal aide-de-camp, Berville, to apprise Eugénie of his plight. Now Berville "is at the dawn of passion" and develops a yen for Eugénie, "all the more imperative for being unrecognized, even by himself." The expected happens; Clisson is betrayed by his friend; letters from his life's love arrive rarely, then not at all. He resolves to die, but first writes to Eugénie to tell her to "live contentedly without thinking of the unhappy Clisson." She must "kiss [my sons] for me; may they not have the ardent soul of their father, lest they be victims of men, of glory, and of love." Clisson then leads a charge and falls "pierced by a thousand blows."

The innocence and earnestness of these idealized portraits are touching to some, cloying to others, but in any case they are common. So is the prose; the author was apparently too desperate to get it down to bother much with style. As it lies on the page, *Clisson and Eugénie* is thus reminiscent of what a romantically minded youthful consumer of Rousseau and Plutarch might have exuded after his first amour. The difference is: he or she would not then proceed to live it out, for what is striking about *Clisson and Eugénie* is its predictive value. Napoleon, we shall see, will stand in the shadow of this fantasy when presently he meets his real Eugénie. Reality, when it happens, will, in a sense, bring him nothing new; his predictions will become his strictures; like the bell for Macbeth, they will invite him to act. It will, in any case, be to Napoleon's self-image as a forgiving cuckold that a certain Captain Hippolyte Charles will one day owe his life, and his paramour will owe the fact that she is not the recipient of a divorce proceeding.

Returning to Mlle Clary, Napoleon was apparently cuckolding her, in spirit if not in fact, in the summer and fall of 1795. But he kept Désirée on the back burner well after the time he had begun frequenting salons where he met a certain widow from Martinique. And when he broke with Désirée in January of 1796, he did so shabbily. Knowing she was underage, he wrote to insist she marry him forthwith. The girl could only refuse but she was heartbroken. When, a few months later, Napoleon briskly informed her of his marriage to Josephine, Désirée wrote him a letter that contains a line as noteworthy for its pathos as for its veracity: "The comparison you must make [between me and your wife] could only be to my disadvantage, your wife being superior in all respects to the poor Eugénie, except not surpassing her in her extreme attachment to you."

A ROSE BY ANY OTHER NAME

In everyone there sleeps
A sense of life lived according to love.
To some it means the difference they could make
By loving others, but across most it sweeps
As all they might have done had they been loved.
That nothing cures.
　　　－Philip Larkin, "Faith Healing" (1964)

On August 15, 1795, Brigadier General Napoleone Buonaparte (as he was *still* calling himself) was twenty-six. To look at him was to see a slender and pale, olive-skinned man. True, he was short, at five feet three,[5] but not dramatically so for the era. The height of the average soldier in mid-eighteenth-century France was five feet five; the Archduke Charles, the best of Austria's generals in this period, stood five feet. Understandably, therefore, contemporaries had not the obsession with the diminutive aspect of Napoleon's person, or with his tendency to fold his right hand into his vest (not an unfamiliar pose in eighteenth-century portraits), that posterity has had. He could be brilliant and talkative; more often he was simply taciturn and reserved, apparently tense. But any real portrait of him—then, as now—was a function of the beholder's (usually strong) opinion.

Those who disliked, or came to dislike, Napoleon—often aristocratic women (de Chastenay, de Rémusat, de Staël, etc.)—emphasized his "dog ears," his shoulder-length uncombed, unpowdered "greasy" hair. They noted the large hat pulled down to the eyes, the swift but uncertain gait, the spidery, dirty gloveless hands; they referred to him as thin, with hollow cheeks and a "ghostly pallor"; others said, simply, "skinny," adding that his reedy legs looked funny in his large, unwaxed, and cheaply made boots—giving him a "Puss 'n Boots" air, to use Josephine's nickname for him. The naysayers also noted a head disproportionately large to the body, with eyes that were dominant and a look that was piercing, frightening, readily expressive of displeasure. The mouth, they said, formed a natural sneer, which fitted a brutal and brusque manner. Finally, they commented, this Corsican spoke accented and Italianate French.

Those who admired, liked, or were impressed by Napoleon—most often men (the banker Ouvrard, the poet Heine, the painters Gros and David, most military officers)—compared his face to the "marble heads of the Greeks and

Romans." They spoke of large almond, almost femininely expressive eyes, framed by wide eyebrows, of a noble aquiline nose, high cheekbones, and a broad forehead. They acknowledged he had a large head for a small man, but said it made him impressive, suggesting great intelligence. The wide and extended upper lip, in this reading, revealed a sensitive mouth. Overall, an imposing face, his admirers said, especially the eyes. Bonaparte may have been no Hoche—open-faced, wavy-haired, pleasant, and pretty like an actor—but they insisted he was striking and handsome in an unconventional way.

In manner, what the critics of Napoleon saw as frightening, the votaries saw as arresting, awe-inspiring; they recalled how people immediately noticed this man when he entered a room. The gauche gait now became a stride—military, brisk, in constant forward motion. Favorable historians would point out how Napoleon's walk would be copied by later military men as diverse as Patton. If his manner was designed, his defenders reply, it was designed to put off people who had nothing to say, who would waste this man's time. The admirers, like the critics, granted that here was a man customarily tense, rarely relaxed; only the former take these facets as expressions of thought, direction, purposefulness.

And so it goes, and will go, as aesthetic taste bows to moral judgment, but rarely so strikingly as in the case of Napoleon Bonaparte, who nearly inevitably strikes people as handsome or ugly, as they find him good or bad.

The Napoleon of mid-1795 was a male acutely aware of the female. Laure Permon, the future wife of General Junot (she would have the title Duchesse d'Abrantès), had it right that when he arrived in Paris that spring, "he was in love with all women." His letters to Joseph often mention female attractiveness and the new role of women in Thermidor and Directory Paris. Unusually, his Corsican misogynism is somewhat contained, the disapproval of what he calls "the empire of women" in social and public affairs, for once was not overwhelming. "Here, alone of all the places on earth," he wrote to Joseph, "[women] appear to hold the reins of government, and the men make fools of themselves over them, think only of them and live only for them."

Désirée's star was presently lost in the brilliance of a much nearer and brighter sun. With the Vendémiaire action, Bonaparte's reputation was established in Paris beyond what it had been in the Midi, thanks to Toulon. Among other benefits, it made him something of a catch in salon society, notably the drawing room of one of the great beauties of her time, Thérésa Tallien, "Our Lady of Thermidor," the wife of one of the perpetrators of Robespierre's fall. Mme Tallien was also the (or a) mistress of Paul Barras, about to become the moving force on the Directory—the panel of five politicians who constituted the chief executive authority of government under the new constitution. Although Napoleon's clothing improved along with his bank account when he made full general, his personality and accent might have proven an obstacle to reception in society if this were Habsburg Vienna or papal Rome, but in the Paris of the late 1790s originality was far more appreciated than condemned. He may not have had the physical appeal of an Hoche, but he offered the impression to some women that he was seething with a passion, which the right woman might tame, or at least taste. He rarely took part in center ring discussions chez Tallien, but when he did speak out, it was with sudden abandon and effectiveness—sometimes with gaiety and vivacity—that stunned and charmed. General Bonaparte, in a word, was a presence, a cynosure, as he had not approached being before then. Men and women alike understood that here was a man both driven and going someplace.

One who noticed was Rose de Beauharnais, née Tascher de la Pagerie, who had come to France in 1779 from Trois Ilets (Martinique). She was six years older than Napoleon and is an easier figure to describe than he, for there was more agreement about her portrait. Minus now the full bloom and chubby cheeks of youth, and with suggestions of lines around the eyes, Rose remained a seductive woman of a whole other level than the dewy-eyed teen Désirée. She had small round eyes, long lashes, and delicate features. Her dark hair fell in wispy curls and gentle waves covering her forehead, making her face seem more delicate than it already was. The mouth, with its slight overbite, gave her a sense of innocence and mystery that was enhanced by her smile. No picture depicts Rose with her mouth open, for the woman knew her own shortcomings, and bad teeth was one of them. She had thus developed a somewhat enigmatic, Mona Lisa smile that did not show them. When Rose was serious (not often), her eyes could be sad and have a faraway look, but sad or gay, her eyes were warm and sympathetic.

Rose was a widow. Eighteen months before, her husband of fourteen years, Viscount Alexandre de Beauharnais, had perished on the scaffold. He had been a general and an important politician of the early Revolution—for a time, even president of the National Assembly—and it is quite possible that had he lived (he was executed by the Robespierrists, mainly for being born a noble, only four days before rescue was at hand), he might well have attained greater things. He and Rose had produced two children—Hortense, twelve, and Eugène, fourteen—but theirs had not been a happy union. Alexandre soon took up with Delphine de Custine, the wife of a general; Rose, for her part, fell for Lazare Hoche, Bonaparte's great rival for up-and-coming republican general. The loyal Rose, however, did join her husband in prison toward the end of his life. After his death, however, the widow soon became merry and began seeing Hoche (though she got angry with him for getting his wife pregnant). At the same time, she developed another "sentimental attachment" with Paul Barras. It was through him that she met the much-talked-about General Bonaparte.

In style, la Beauharnais conveyed both a maternal and a sexual aura; she appealed as a friend as well as a lover, which made her that rare combination: a man's woman and a woman's woman. Her animated expressions were so sweet, her makeup so clever, her gaiety so contagious, and her affection so sincere that she could compete for attention at Mme Tallien's with younger and more conventionally beautiful women. Someone experienced with people, however, might have sensed that beneath the grace and kindness, the negligent poses and nonchalant movements, the exotic languor and natural suppleness was a woman of quiet desperation, possessed of a potential for dependence, a ferocious striving for security, and a frantic need for pleasure.

Napoleon and Rose—Josephine, as he presently dubbed her—met in the early fall of 1795. It is so common to note that they were not equally in love with each other that one can easily overlook how fast their alliance became profound. They began seeing each other regularly on the evening of October 29, and their banns of marriage were announced on February 7: one hundred days. Indeed, their chemistry was so soon strong that it created confusion in their minds as to what precisely each meant to the other. True, Napoleon was unquestionably the more infatuated in the romantic sense, though other considerations counted, too: Josephine's social standing, for example—her "calm and dignified bearing of the society of the old regime," as he later put it—was no matter of indifference to him. De Rémusat has him gloating over his beloved's rank as an "authentic viscountess." If true, that hardly made him unusual, even—perhaps especially—among republican politicians, many of whom had blue-blooded mistresses and wives.

Josephine, for her part, if she was not conventionally in love ("I don't love him; on the other hand, that doesn't mean I want him to go away, either)[6] was sufficiently impressed by the young officer to want to wed him in short order. In an age where marriage had, in any case, less to do with love than with reasoned assessment, one can only but remark on how quickly La Beauharnais elected to harness herself to the Corsican. The combination of the young general's success and prospects (it was soon clear he would be named commander of the Army of Italy), his extraordinary personality and intellect, his genuine affection for her children, and the advice of her friends, notably Barras, all functioned in her decision.

Napoleon, however, fell violently in love, though whether he did so with this particular woman or with his preconceived idea of her and of love, it is difficult to say. Given the power of imagination in his life and the relative sparseness (how could it have been otherwise?) of his acquaintance with Mme de Beauharnais, one is tempted to value highly the role of obsession in any account of their early story. Then, too, no minor factor in precipitating "his first passion felt with all the vigor of his nature" (Marmont) was Napoleon's comparative inexperience in sex. Though he had been sexually active since he was eighteen, regular physical relations with one woman had not fallen within his experience until now. In sum, Napoleon was far more vulnerable than he realized or certainly than he appeared to be; he was inclined toward hopeless infatuation and overestimation of his beloved. His idealism, in short, like Clisson's, was expressible in love as well as politics. His political idealism and romantic passion were a sublimation of an extraordinary drive to eros.

They were married on March 9, 1796; Barras stood up for them. Two days later, the General left to take over his new command, and thereafter their relationship became epistolary. This is fortunate for us, for the record it left, and probably for Josephine as well, given what his presence would have been like in view of these letters. He wrote her daily, sometimes more often—and we do well to keep in mind that he did this at a time when his schedule (which allowed for, at most, five hours of sleep) was that of an army commander on campaign, a diplomat conducting negotiations, and a proconsul governing large areas.

The letters—curiously addressed to "Mme de Beauharnais" until after their author gained fame for his victories in the field, then addressed to "Mme Bonaparte"—fell on their intended in a hot, crashing cascade that must have taken her breath away for the munificence of his gifts and his demands: "By what arts have you captivated my faculties and concentrated in yourself my entire moral existence?"; "If only I could enclose you in my heart, I would put you there in prison"; "my heart has no corner that is not yours; I have no thoughts that aren't of you; all my force, my arms, my spirit are yours; my soul is in your body"; "to live in my Josephine is to live in Elysium." He begs her to be less lovely, less kind and good, so that he may love her less wildly. In short, Clisson is talking.

But it is *not* Eugénie who is answering. Bonaparte's letters often sat unopened while their intended was off at a party exclaiming, "Comme il est drôle, Bonaparte," or because she was disinclined to imbibe yet again the heavy Corsican accent wafting redolently up from the phonetic spelling, the dreadful grammar and worse diction, the violently underlined erotic passages, scratched nearly through the stationery. (The paper carried the head: "l'An

IVe de la République Française Une et Indivisible, Bonaparte, Général en Chef de l'Armée d'Italie.") Napoleon's and Josephine's relationship would gradually evolve, as, over time and most painful experience, they came to know each other, but for now, he was asking her to throw herself into his raging torrent, and she was not remotely interested in doing so. To her, it was not what she had married him for. "All her indolence rebelled against the violence she felt in Bonaparte," writes Evangeline Bruce perceptively.[7]

Nothing is sadder or more tedious than observing Napoleon's self-imposed torments and gyrations, expressed in this first year of letters to Josephine. The lover senses his affection is not returned in the ways he so desperately wants it to be. No one theme is commoner throughout than Napoleon's piteous pleas and dark reproaches at Josephine for not writing him often or ecstatically enough. But it is a truth he is not ready to accept; he will not accomplish the act of moral courage it would take to do what he constantly advises others to do: to align internal and external reality. *He will have this fantasy*: "Never has my destiny resisted my will," he writes her, as if in warning. When Josephine won't play the part of Eugénie, Napoleon reminds her of what she must feel: "You cannot have inspired a love without limits without sharing it yourself"; "You know the pleasure your letters give me, and I am certain that you love writing them, too." Or he puts words in her mouth: "Make sure you tell me that you are convinced you love me beyond what it is possible to imagine."

Recalling "Bonaparte's" high-minded advice to des Mazis (*Dialogue on Love*) about the superior value of service to the State over "enslavement" to a woman, one can only shake his head in wonder at lines penned to Josephine such as "Let those who love glory do so, and those who serve the *patrie* do so, my soul is suffocating in this exile, and when my beloved is suffering and is ill, I cannot coldly do the calculations of [military] victory." Josephine's failure to answer as desired drove Napoleon wild, as did her refusals to come to Italy to be with him (she had been deploying subterfuges, such as that she was ill, or even that she was pregnant). The Directory began to worry that if Josephine persisted in avoiding Italy, the Republic's best general might not actually leave his post and return to Paris. So Paul Barras intervened; Josephine, very much against her will—she was currently having an affair with a young officer named Hippolyte Charles—was shipped off to join her husband across the Alps in July 1796. With incredible nerve—or was it insouciance?—she brought Charles with her.

Man and woman reunited in Italy proved a disaster, as Josephine's tepidity in passion became evident even to this Adam whose famed realism had taken leave where his Eve was concerned. Confronted by reality, Napoleon could no longer delude himself: Josephine was no Désirée in her love for him. The situation climaxed in late November when the General returned to Milan. Believing Josephine to be waiting for him, he charged up the grand staircase of the Serbelloni Palace to find an empty bedroom: Mme Bonaparte was in Genoa, he was informed. She was, by the way, almost certainly traveling with Charles—an as-yet-unplumbed woe for Napoleon, who was one of the few not to know about their affair.

The conqueror of northern Italy nearly swooned with dismay, and fell ill with migraines. He lingered nine days in hopes that "Madame" would return to Milan, meanwhile writing her pathetic letters of rage and disillusionment: "I abandoned all just to be able to hold you . . . the pain you have caused me is incalculable," etc. But the nadir had been reached, the cup drained. In one of his letters, he tells her, "I was wrong to demand of you that you love me as I love you. How can lacework weigh as much as gold?" Thereafter, the dreadful grace that may attend suffering descended on Napoleon, and he began to let go of the worst of his infatuation with his wife. He would continue to love her—indeed, one is tempted to say that he was now free to love *her*, not simply track his obsession—and he would occasionally prove capable of penning her passionate letters, replete with pleas to write back promptly. But the moment of the complete surrender of reason was past, and a sea change is palpable in the tone of his letters to her after late 1796.

What was broken in Milan was what, at the political level, had been broken in Corsica by Paoli's "betrayal": the fantasy of Dionysian abandon and mutuality. Napoleon never loved like this again. The year of living dangerously with eros ended with 1796. Paoli and "early" Josephine had seen the rawest, fullest expression of the man's considerable capacity for altruistic (i.e., "other"-oriented) idealism. Neither person had returned his feelings in full. So, after making a herculean effort to bend reality to his will, the young man did what most sane people would do: he bent himself to reality; he began to moderate his investments in individuals. In the realm of the political, as we saw, this meant starting to lace his Rousseau with shots of Voltaire and Machiavelli. (True, his admiration for Maximilien Robespierre might have developed a full-blown cult, but 9 Thermidor ended that possibility.) In matters of the heart, it meant that the fictional Clisson gave way to the character of Bonaparte. Napoleon's later feelings for Josephine, as his attachment to Marie Walewska, Marie-Louise, et al., amounted to the erotic equivalent of his brief political attraction to Robespierre: significant but controllable.

There would be other major traumas in the relationship between Napoleon and Josephine, but they were hers, not his. In mid-1799, while in Egypt, Napoleon finally found out about (read: stopped ignoring) the

Charles affair. He resolved to divorce her and wrote his brother Joseph to inform him of his decision, adding: "You alone are all that is left to me on earth. Your friendship is so dear to me [that] I think I should become a misanthrope if I lost it or if you betrayed me." (The letter was intercepted by Admiral Nelson and published in the London *Morning Chronicle*.) Despite Josephine's mad love for the young officer, she saw with horror what she stood to lose—rank, fortune, a loving stepfather to her children, and, not least, the treasured friendship of a man she now fully realized was extraordinary. When Bonaparte returned from Egypt in the fall, she played the tragedian's scene before his locked bedroom door, pleading, weeping, begging, and "reasoning" her way back into his "friendship." Napoleon, to many people's disgust, forgave her. The wife of the minister of foreign affairs wrote of her incredulousness at "this man who manifests every form of audacity, every kind of courage, yet tolerates his name being dishonored and dragged in the mud" by his wife, whom he pardons.[8]

The pardon, like the affair itself, recalls the Philip Larkin poem on page 88. In a letter to Josephine, Napoleon, speaking of his all-encompassing love for her, observed: "That, nothing cures." Yet at the end of the day, Napoleon did cure himself of his infatuation and, at the same time, showed a generosity toward his wife that is far from negligible. Despite the bitter disappointment of his heart's primal fantasies, his mature concern for Josephine as a person, his kindly impulses toward her, if they did not "know no bounds," yet won out over rancor and self-centeredness. Napoleon did not let his anger and frustration lead him to do to her what his power might have permitted, including, of course, to have Lieutenant Charles severely punished (if not shot on some pretext) and his career ruined. Pride may be the deadly sin displayed here—or uxoriousness, if one is biblically minded—but not anger or abuse of power.

As with all else in his life, so with his one *grand amour*, Napoleon developed a different take after the fact, and notably at St. Helena. It now became vital to him—in his own mind perhaps, but certainly where the public mind was concerned—to reduce the dimensions of love's victory over his young heart and to swell the dimensions of his own worldly wise disdain. Napoleon, post-infatuation, returns to a version of the Bonaparte character from the *Dialogue on Love*, getting off arch observations to his collaborators on the order of:

"Love doesn't really exist. It is a feeling engendered by social mores. I'm probably the wrong person to judge it, however, for I am too rational."

"One must not get caught up in arguing with women; it is best to listen in silence as they talk irrationally."

"I will in no way have my court an empire of women. That was the mistake that Henry IV and Louis XIV made; my job is far too serious than that of those princes, and the French have become far too serious to forgive their sovereign open ties with official mistresses."

Yet at his more honest, Napoleon was also capable of regretting that he had not given more time to women—even just to talking with them, sitting on a sofa. "I could have learned a lot of things from them; they are a river to whom one must bring water." And the concession, "I really loved Josephine," followed immediately by the pulled punch to salvage pride (or Corsican male vanity), "but I had no respect for her." Then the admission, she would also be for him, "une vraie femme"; then the derisive, "Actually, I married her only because I thought she had a large fortune." And so on. She mattered to him.

We may ask: Would the young Napoleon have actually given it all up for love? Was he in earnest when he wrote to Josephine, "Would that I could pass my every moment with you, having nothing to do but love you"? Even to pose the question strikes us as silly, knowing what we do about this man's subsequent public life. But that may not have been how it felt to him at the time. Napoleon was becoming and learning who he was. The overinvestment in Josephine might have indicated to him what he already suspected: that he had an exceptional capacity for investment in the creatures of his imagination. And if he also perhaps discovered that there were limits to his capacity to make reality conform to his fantasy, he nonetheless plainly saw that he had remarkable force of will.

The more interesting question is what would have happened if Josephine had responded as her lover-husband wished?

The probable answer is: nothing very different from what did happen between them in the long run. There is no winning in the realm of fantasy; there is only, eventually, the death of fantasy due to the "death of a thousand cuts" that reality imposes. Napoleon and Josephine would have presently gotten on with their lives, much as they did. But we—posterity—would be much the poorer, for then we would be absent this priceless, painful portrait of erotic obsession.

THE IMPROVISER OF VICTORY:
THE FIRST ITALIAN CAMPAIGN (1796–1797)

Hannibal charged across the Alps, we outflanked them.
  –Napoleon Bonaparte

The West has exited from the most violent century in its past and is well sick of organized death and destruction. We still resign ourselves to wars for contingent goals, but in war itself, we see nothing redeeming, and little that we readily associate with words like "moral" or "spiritual." We have deconstructed Christopher Columbus and Father Junípero Serra to the point of all but conflating them with Cortés as conquistadores.[9] We assimilate Frederick the Great or Napoleon to Hitler and Stalin. We now respect generals for the punches they pull, the cities they do *not* take, and for the lives they (perhaps) save, including the enemies'. People of the eighteenth century, as in previous periods of the European past, still largely looked at things differently. Certainly, they had no affection for the suffering, destruction, and inconvenience of war, yet they also saw war as a potentially ennobling, not just an aggrandizing enterprise. They saw it as a theater of life where a huge spectacle of human grandeur and greatness—and yes, of course, misery—unfolded. They respected war as well as feared it; above all, they adulated great warriors, particularly when they were conquerors. Even (or especially) the radical left championed a bellicose and imperialist foreign policy; such a stance, indeed, had become a large part of what made them revolutionaries and neo-Jacobins.

If we do not understand all of the foregoing, we shall not see how Napoleon Bonaparte's accomplishments as warrior made him so widely respected and even beloved, not only in France but among many who lived in adversarial countries.[10]

We left Napoleon in the autumn of 1795, commander of the Army of the Interior—a post that filled neither his time nor his aspirations. Interior counted 94,236 men, all stationed in the environs of Paris, making it the third largest of the Republic's standing armies—a comment on the absence of domestic tranquility in France even after the Terror. Although the job was derided by many generals, its task of holding the Revolution's domestic enemies at bay made Interior the most critical force in the Republic. It is likely that Napoleon had agreed to do the Directory's domestic dirty work in this post for a limited time only. Barras did not have a great deal of difficulty imposing the victor of Vendémiaire on his more hesitant colleagues (including Carnot). To clinch the appointment, he stated flatly, "Promote this man or he will promote himself."

"General Vendémiaire," as Bonaparte was now known, remained the republican general par excellence, his political reliability more solid even than Hoche's. Such a reputation required a certain zeal and inventiveness in daily life; Napoleon, for example, construed his marriage to the aristocratic Josephine as "another gauge of my firm resolve to find my happiness only in the Republic," while the bride had worn a tricolor sash over her wedding dress of white muslin. As chief of the Army of the Interior, Napoleon dismantled the politically undependable National Guard and purged many of Aubry's crypto-royalist appointments in the War Ministry. On the other hand, he closed down the left-wing Pantheon Club, the leading society of neo-Jacobin agitators in the capital. His duties included drumming up public displays of patriotism, and his daily reports to the Directory never failed to mention the number of times that "La Marseillaise" was played in Paris theatres. Perhaps the best attestation to his patriotism came from his enemies: the royalist Mallet du Pan, who hated him for his role at Vendémiaire, called him "a Corsican terrorist . . . , a professional scoundrel and the right arm of Barras." Early in the new year, Bonaparte learned that he would be named to Italy.

In 1796 only three States still tilted against the Republic. The Habsburgs of Austria, with small assists from the waffling Savoy king of Piedmont, mounted a land threat, while England ruled the seas and the banks, and generously stoked the collective fund of anti-French animus. However, Spain, Prussia, and several small powers had been defeated and had made separate deals with the Republic. Spain, indeed, was a French ally, as was Holland, which had undergone a revolution of her own and was now styled the Batavian Republic. The former Habsburg land of Belgium constituted five departments of the French Republic.

The grand strategy of France's "organizer of victory," as Carnot had been dubbed in his long season of military success in 1794–95, was simple: General Moreau's Army of the Rhine would push into Swabia, in southwestern Germany, while Jourdan's Army of the Sambre-et-Meuse would attack the territory lying beyond the Belgian-Dutch frontiers, west of the Rhine. The left bank—considered fair game for annexation by adepts of the French theory of natural frontiers—was a congeries of ecclesiastical and secular semi-sovereign cities and "statelets," such as the Rhenish Palatinate, Aix-la-Chapelle, Coblentz, Mainz, Trier, and Cologne. They constituted important parts of the old and very prestigious Holy Roman Empire—that ancient monarchy that had been instituted by Charlemagne and the pope in 800. The Empire's traditional champion had always been noble Austria—the Habsburgs having, centuries before, established a lock on election to the imperial title—but France and, more recently, Prussia were very much challenging Vienna for leadership in Germany.

In Carnot's plan, the Army of Italy would serve the merely diversionary function of attacking Austria's holdings in Italy; especially rich Lombardy, with its thriving capital of Milan. This would oblige Vienna to pull troops out of the German front. If the Army of Italy emerged victorious from its encounters with the Austro-Piedmontese forces, then it would march north to join Moreau and Jourdan for a drive to Vienna. A clear plan, to be sure; however, "in strategy everything is very simple although that does not mean that everything is very easy," as Karl von Clausewitz wrote.[11] We know that the French forces on the Rhine could easily stall or go into reverse, while the Army of Italy had only very recently, thanks to Bonaparte's plans, made any aggressive moves at all. It was arrayed against Allied forces with a paper strength of double its own effectives, confronted by the Alps and Apennines, by the Po and its innumerable tributaries, by impregnable fortresses like Mantua, by a hostile indigenous population, and by neutral states like ducal Modena, Parma, and Tuscany that leaned more toward monarchical Austria than republican France.

Bonaparte's swift and total imposition of himself and his authority on the klatch of skeptical, surly, and far older generals who held the subordinate commands in the Army of Italy is the stuff of legend. Masséna's, Augereau's, or Sérurier's prejudices against the skinny, callow youth—"the political general," "the general of civil war"—endured barely a quarter of an hour under the heat of his intensity and the hammer blows of his informed questions. It is nonsense to imagine the respect of professionals like these could have been taken in by Napoleon's Paris connections or by his touted republicanism. With his generals, Bonaparte was all military: style, language, knowledge. The degree of authority he exercised over them ("this little bugger of a general frightened us," Augereau conceded) was unique in their experience, and they became his men to a degree they were never anyone else's.

The miserable condition of the Army of Italy, whose effective manpower was low, at about 38,000 men, is also the stuff of legend, though it should be said that all armies (and not just the French) were badly off at this time, and complaining constantly. Bonaparte did what he could to improve his men's outfitting; the army's commissioners (purveyors) had probably never seen their lives so plagued by the demands and criticisms stemming from a commander in chief. Nevertheless, weeks into the campaign, the troops were still wearing threadbare uniforms (if uniforms, at all) and had no baggage trains because there was no baggage—a condition that arguably improved their mobility, however. The entry into Milan in mid-May—a "grand event" only in Stendhal's telling, in the opening of *The Charterhouse of Parma* (1839)—amused observers for the "striking contrast between the luxury of the Milanese and the grotesque attire of the [French]."[12] Yet rarely have appearances so stood at odds with reality, for if the Republic's soldiers looked like the dregs of humanity, they fought like Caesar's legions in Gaul. One did not join the armed forces expecting to be well provided for, but because the alternative in the village or the urban gutter was worse.

The wars generally associated with the adjective "Napoleonic" attained a degree of violence previously unknown in Europe, but paradoxically, this first campaign, which established Bonaparte's name, was in some respects typical of the war of maneuver and limited engagement that characterized the old regime. Typical, but speeded up. Under its new commander, the compact French divisions not only floated like butterflies and stung like bees, they also darted among the foothills and plains of northern Italy with the speed and suddenness of hummingbirds. The kingdom of Piedmont and France had been at war since 1792, yet four years of sieges and small engagements had changed nothing decisively. Now, in less than a fortnight, it was all over. On April 11 the allies attacked the French unexpectedly, but their offensive was uncoordinated and the French seized the initiative. Twelve days later, after half a dozen actions, including sort-of battles at Montenotte and Mondovi, the Piedmontese general was asking for terms. Napoleon did nothing drastic strategically or tactically, but under his hand the army and its divisional commanders performed the familiar routines of march and countermarch, attack and fallback, feint and envelopment, so well and so swiftly that they struck with the force of the new. A Piedmontese officer meeting Napoleon for the first time wrote of "the impression one had of this young man was one of a painful admiration; the intellect was dazzled by the superiority of his talents."[13] King Victor Amadeus III—inveterately suspicious of his Austrian allies (and they of him)—deserted the coalition and made peace with the French Republic at Cherasco.

On April 27, Bonaparte wrote the Directory: "Tomorrow I shall march against [the Austrian army under General] Beaulieu. I shall force him to retire behind the Po, which I shall cross immediately after him. I shall take all of Lombardy, and, within the month, I hope to be in the Tyrolean alps, there to meet up with the Army of the Rhine and, with them, carry the war into Bavaria." In the event, the plan unfolded far less seamlessly than these self-confident declaratives suggest; still, this is largely what happened, though final victory required closer to a year than a month: the Austrians were of another mettle from the easily demoralized Piedmontese. Seemingly heedless of defeat in the field, Vienna dispatched general after general, and perhaps 150,000 troops in all, to try to hold on to their emperor's beloved Lombardy. These men fought hard, and sometimes well, and the campaign was anything but the French cakewalk that historians, judging only by the outcome, have made it out to be.

The campaign turned on French efforts to take Mantua, the great Habsburg stronghold of northern Italy. The defenders within the fortress resisted valiantly for long months, while their comrades—army after army of them—sought desperately to relieve them. The Austrian preoccupation with Mantua was like a bull's obsession with the matador's cape. Had they learned more quickly, they would simply have gone after the matador (the French army) and disabled or destroyed him, for his vulnerability was total. As it was, the French suffered tactical defeats and near disasters at Castiglione (August 3) and Caldiero (November 12). A few days later, at Arcola, they deployed a suicidal plan that left them open to annihilation in the swamps of the Adige, but they eked out an unexpected victory.

Autumn 1796 was an especially difficult time for the French. Had the Austrians discerned how extended and undermanned the Republic's army was, they might have attacked with focus and zeal, and ended the campaign. Bonaparte's letters and dispatches at this time are often full of the blackest pessimism. He and his men were tightrope walkers working without a net. No matter how many tricks they performed, one false move could have brought the end. On the other hand, their glory was the greater for the skill and daring shown, and this was an age when glory counted for a great deal, and the military kind represented its highest form.

The greatest Austrian problem was that their numerically superior forces, using the so-called cordon system of defending territory, were strung out over a large area. Napoleon, from his effective placement at the geographical center of the enemy's conjoining forces, struck at his divisional opponents separately, defeating one, then going on to the next. Although he was often forced onto the strategic defensive, he never abandoned the tactical offensive—he was always attacking—thus keeping the Austrians off guard, having to fight at the time and place of their adversary's choosing. The French outflanked and threatened communications lines; they concentrated their force so as to have numerical superiority at crucial junctures; they effected river crossings with only the materials they could scrounge up locally. None of this would have been possible without superb generalship at the divisional level, notably by Masséna ("victory's tot," as Bonaparte dubbed him), or without Napoleon's complete control over his commanders and every element of his army. Then, too, the commander's willingness to take breathtaking risks—exposing his men to crushing counterattacks—counted for something.

At Rivoli (January 13, 1797), the French defeated the final Austrian relief army. Mantua finally surrendered on February 2. Bonaparte had preserved his army, dumbfounded his opponents, and astonished Europe. Yet he had not inflicted the sort of total defeat on the enemy that would become the Emperor Napoleon's hallmark in many of the later set-piece battles. Arcola and Rivoli—the "great" victories of 1796–97, honored by metro stops, monuments, and streets—fended off disaster and eked out small credits, thanks to the slow reactions of older, more conservative Austrian generals. They were close shaves, the successes of scrambling, endurance, and luck, but they were not the snapping in twain of an opponent's force, morale, and resolve. Despite Napoleonic ingenuity and French valor, the Austrian army always evaded their clutches and lived to fight another day. Even when, in March and April, the Army of Italy covered four hundred miles in thirty days and reached the Semmering Pass, within eyeshot of Vienna, the Habsburgs only reluctantly requested an armistice; their army was not destroyed nor their government demoralized, while the French army was at the end of its tether.

"THREE TO ONE": THE "MORAL" ELEMENTS OF VICTORY

Fighting . . . is a trial of moral and physical forces through the medium of the latter.

—Clausewitz, *On War*

Clausewitz is surely right that war is not really a science or an art, though it has aspects of physics, choreography, directing. If war *has* to be compared to another human activity, he continues, then we might think of commerce (the "clash of human interests and activities"). The problem, however, is that commerce, even in the hands of its most unrestrained practitioners, does not entail direct violent and potentially mortal attacks by large numbers of human bodies on each other. War is even more maximal, competitive, elemental, and more unchanging in its basic nature than moneymaking. It is the *ultima ratio regum*—what a king, a government, or a man, may have recourse to in order to stay alive.

Lending itself poorly to similes, war is also too ultimate and multiform an activity to be captured by theory. The successful pursuit of a war requires talent and practice, neither of which ensues from a study of theory or history. Napoleon had certainly read widely on war (notably du Teil, Guibert), but he never maintained that doing so provided him with more than points of reference or a convenient way to describe campaigns after the fact. Napoleon, for all that his own practice of war set records for originality and furnished Clausewitz with the inspiration (and provocation) for his masterpiece, *On War*, did not contribute any new theory of war. *On War* doesn't, either, but it does explain, among other things, why such theory would not be truthful or useful.

If we ask ourselves what Napoleon did better than successive Austrian commanders (Beaulieu, Wuermser, Alvintzi, and Archduke Charles), a trait that stands out was his capacity to sift possibilities on a complex and moving force field. Rapid perception and discrimination, followed by rapid decision making (including mind-changing), followed by rapid direction giving and acute surveillance. We might perhaps compare it to the work under pressure and time constraints of a cryptographer and a stage director or a choreographer. Napoleon thus saw a potential weakness in a line of battle or a geographical anomaly about some terrain quicker than others did. He sifted scenarios faster.

But superior perception, as vital as it is, is the lesser part of the matter at hand. The key element in Bonaparte's military success was the psychological. "The conduct of war," Clausewitz writes, "resembles the working of an intricate machine with tremendous friction." That friction produces tension in every actor on the stage of battle, but in none more than in leaders. A commander must display various kinds of courage, but the greatest is not physical bravery, it is moral courage: *accepting responsibility* for decisions that will doom many, perhaps even a State. Such acceptance arises best in him who feels at home in hell, we might say, so what is transpiring around him—the gigantic and distracting presence of suffering, death, and destruction—becomes to him second nature, a medium readily appropriated. Clausewitz again: "Only if the mind works in this comprehensive fashion can it achieve the freedom it needs to dominate events and not be dominated by them."

Bonaparte throve in war making, such that his knowledge and his personality became disposable to him in the "action in a resistant element" which is combat. His older aristocratic opponents were pros with solid reputations, but war was their métier, not their self-expression and their meaning (nor, we should add, their fortune and their future). While they toiled hard, they were not indefatigable, they were not able to snatch a few hours of sleep, day after day, and still function well. They did not exist on a permanent knife edge of despair and elation, in a state near to nervous exhaustion, even if hidden behind apparent calm. War was an important job for them, but not their titanic personal struggle, the imposition of their very selves.

Paradoxically, one of the results of displaying Napoleonic will was to undermine the will of one's opponents. What nerve the Austrian generals summoned arose from an uncritical and external reliance on the conventions of eighteenth-century warfare. To flout these conventions, even just by speeding up, was therefore to discomfit them and to threaten disarray in their regiments' complex formations and movements, and disarray on a field of battle can turn into rout with the speed of lightning. The Austrian commanders who were force-fed a steady diet of such flouting of convention by Bonaparte were soon bereft of ideas as to how to respond, and they grew discouraged.

At the opposite pole, Napoleon's confidence and courage inspired his own troops to such a degree that their morale, more than their commander's tactics and strategy, was the "secret" of Napoleon's success as a general. This is the more remarkable when one considers that the morale of the Army of Italy had bottomed out before he took over. There had been mutinies over back pay and general conditions; pillaging and violence against civilians were common, as were insubordination and disobedience. The new general's reforms (e.g., his decree that the men would henceforth be paid half their salaries in specie), his firm stand against pillage, his swift and implacable treatment of infractions, especially those committed by the hated and crooked civilian purveyors, counted heavily in the reimposition of discipline and spirit in the Army of Italy.

But more important was Napoleon's hold on the psyches and the psychology of men in uniform. If one may speak of his genius at war, it consisted of this: he took an army materially and spiritually on its uppers, and in a month or less turned it into one of the finest fighting forces of the century, perhaps of all centuries. And the means he used were not primarily material but psychological, what the era would have called "moral" or "spiritual." The General knew not to confuse soldiers' gripes with their actual state of mind, their mood with their obedience, their appearance with their battle-readiness. He knew "that a horse will perish from want much sooner than a man" and that to drive men beyond their apparent endurance could be a source of inspiration, for "the soldier is as proud of overcoming hardship as he is of surmounting danger." Above all, he understood that "of all the passions that inspire man in battle, none . . . is so powerful and so constant as the longing for honor and renown. . . . According to their origins these feelings must surely be reckoned among the noblest in human nature, and in war they are the true breath of life that endows the monstrous body with a soul." The words are Clausewitz's, but Napoleon put the same thing more succinctly: "Moral force rather than numbers decides victory. The moral is to the physical as three is to one."

Bonaparte's relations with his troops were not mediated through a steep hierarchy of social class and conventions, as Austrian army relations were. Then, too, the Republic's men were mainly French, while Austria commanded polyglot armies of Serbs, Czechs, Germans, Hungarians, etc. Napoleon's proclamations to his army shared the glory with the soldiers and projected onto them the author's indefectible confidence in his own destiny: "All of you want to be able to say, when you return to your villages one day, I was in the conquering Army of Italy." Napoleon grasped as few have done that esprit de corps and the glory that flowed from success in battle would, for many, prevail over even their feelings for their families, and that men might come to love him more than they loved their wives or their children. Most of the generals and many of the soldiers of the Army of Italy would be with Bonaparte at his coup d'Etat three years later; indeed, this army stands as perhaps the most fanatically loyal of all of Napoleon's armies. What Plutarch says of Caesar and his legionnaires might be said of Napoleon's mastery of the Army of Italy: "Those who in other expeditions were but ordinary men displayed a courage past defeating or withstanding when they went upon any danger where Caesar's glory was concerned."

Finally, we come to the ideological dimension of this army's effectiveness. Many of the era's shrewdest observers believed that the outcome of the Revolutionary and Napoleonic wars had been all but decided before the fighting began, in the mobilization and spirit of the French Republic's nation in arms doctrine. The dangerous (because subversive) dream of the eighteenth century's military reformers like Guibert had been to forge the ultimate "patriot" army—the fraternal band of citizens, led by a new Cincinnatus, who would crush the professionals sent against them because they fought harder, better, and for enlightened principles. With all of its deficits—from unwieldiness and cost to conscription riots and high casualty rates—the *levée en masse* of the Year II seemed to realize the dream. Those infernal French columns and hordes charging into battle shouting "Vive la Nation!" and "Vive la République!" worked a stunning effect.

Official consciousness-raising among French soldiery had peaked in the Robespierrist period, when the Committee of Public Safety and many army commanders published up to seven and eight newspapers for distribution among the troops. Such propagandizing abated with Thermidor, but the sans-culotte "style of the Year II," as Jean-Paul Bertaud calls it, continued to prevail in certain armies, above all, that of Italy, whose militancy stood out from the rest. Thus, for example, the inhabitants of Salzburg expressed surprise on seeing French soldiers not salute when they encountered their officers, or at hearing them request of the civilian population in the conquered city that it refrain from deferring to the French soldiery.

More than any commander in chief of his era, save Hoche, the young Bonaparte held the high, or idealistic, view of soldiers as patriots and citizens, not just as men at arms. They were carriers of the Revolution, as well as defenders of the homeland, and a critical function of military leadership as he saw it was to foster their politicization. He organized the publication of newspapers, which, if they lionized the commander in chief, also fostered political correctness. Bonaparte assiduously saw to the celebration of the great patriotic holidays of the Revolution–not only Bastille Day (July 14) but also the more controversial anniversary of Louis XVI's execution, which he himself found distasteful. Bonaparte's first order of the day (March 26) spoke of his "satisfaction" with his men's "devotion to the Republic," their "commitment to freedom as much as to discipline." They would find in him, he said, "a brother-in-arms, strong in the confidence of the Government of the Republic, proud of the goodwill of patriots and determined to realize a destiny worthy of the Army of Italy."

That destiny went beyond the traditional role of armies in military defense and conquest, as Europe had known for centuries, to include the forcible spreading of the values, principles, and *institutions* of the French Revolution. Initially a source of puzzlement and derision among the Austrians, such a practice soon spread disconcertment, as the Army of Italy began piling up victories and Napoleon began setting up republics where previously there had been aristocratic or monarchical governments. No appreciation of the military effectiveness of the army and its commander can fail to note this aspect of their offensive.

LODI

"GRANCOSA"

Lodi is a town on the Adda River, about twenty miles southeast of Milan. The name suggests a rich vein, as in mother lode, or a guide, as in lodestar, or even a magnet, as in lodestone. In Napoleonic history, Lodi has been all of this:

a vein of lore, a guiding star for Napoleon (but after the fact), and a magnet for legend. Lodi is many things except what it was purported to be by the command of the Army of Italy: a major military victory.

On May 10, 1796–that is to say, nearly at the beginning of the Italian campaign–the bridge at Lodi was the scene of a minor if hard-fought action between a few thousand French advance guard and a similar number of the Austrian rear guard. The army of which the latter were part was retreating as rapidly as it could, and if the French had simply waited a day, Lodi and its bridge would have been theirs without firing a shot. But Napoleon wanted action. It was not enough that he had, a few days before, executed a magnificent crossing of the Po River, in the teeth of an unsuspecting enemy–a feat that has gone down as a classic in the annals of military history for its speed and precision of execution.

Bonaparte felt he needed a nameable success against the mighty Austrian army, so much more significant in the eyes of Europe than the force of Piedmontese he had just whipped. Taking the Lodi bridge, therefore, became a bloody affair because General Dallemagne's division, on Bonaparte's orders, forced the issue. The Austrians stood firm for a time and had a clear shot on the bridge, so the French operation ended up a sort of daredevil, life-consuming challenge, with most of the key French officers trying their hand at leading a "Vive-la-République!"–shouting column headlong into enemy fire. French dead numbered 350, over twice that of the enemy. In truth, May 10 was, on the whole, a French military disappointment, for General Beaulieu and his Austrian army got away. Four future marshals of the Empire (André Masséna, Louis-Alexandre Berthier, Jean Lannes, and Pierre-François Augereau) risked life and limb that day to prove their bravery. Their commander, for his part, directed the French artillery emplacements firing on the enemy at the far end of the bridge, but though his exposure to fire was slighter, Napoleon won the historical sweepstakes for Lodi.

And he did so because cultivated legend plays a large part in our conception of the past, a truth that few understood better than this general. On the eleventh, Napoleon dined with the bishop of Lodi, who asked him about the fighting on the previous day. "Non fu grancosa [it was no big deal]," the French commander replied, and turned to other topics. Yet that same day, he wrote Carnot: "The battle of Lodi gives the whole of Italy to the Republic." Both statements are true, curiously. True, the second is an overstatement, but not a gross one: the Austrian retreat, although owing little to Lodi, spelled the imminent fall of Milan, as happened four days later, which in turn meant that the large, rich province of Lombardy was now in French hands. Though not "all of Italy," it was perhaps "grancosa."

As for Lodi, many pairs of hands memorialized it in the marble of memory as a true battle, in which Napoleon distinguished himself by his personal bravery under fire: journalists at the brace of newspapers published for the army and for French home consumption, the Republic's political commissioners (including Saliceti) posted to the Army of Italy, and, perhaps mostly, the word of mouth of French soldiers themselves, more ready than anyone else to lionize their general in chief. The future Consul's and Emperor's historians and an enamored French public would ensure the legend's survival. And legends, in turn, sprouted sub-legends, in this instance, the affectionate diminutive of "Little Corporal." The French soldiers were said to have coined it as they lovingly watched Napoleon labor over cannon emplacement and aim at the Lodi bridge, but the name was the creation of flacks and memorialists long after the action.

Bonaparte's own contribution to the myth of Lodi was substantial. At St. Helena he confided to Emmanuel Las Cases that "it was only on the evening after Lodi that I started to believe myself a superior man, and that the ambition came to me of executing the great things which so far had been occupying my thoughts only as a fantastic dream." No one can contradict a man about his own thoughts, but the assertion has struck some observers, including some devoted to him (e.g., Arthur Lévy), as unconvincing. Bonaparte's belief in his own superiority was strong and clear, and it predated Lodi, going back perhaps to Toulon, certainly to Vendémiaire. The Italian campaign would make his name a household word throughout Europe, but Lodi was not the end of that campaign; it was only the end of the beginning. Napoleon had won, to date, three or four modest battles on a secondary front; he had not yet displayed his gifts for diplomacy and statecraft. All of this, as well as some harrowing military moments, lay in the future on this spring night. We would be better off seeing the famous St. Helena statement as a good example of Napoleon's lifelong need to know everything before anyone else, to have foreseen it all. In any event, two Napoleonic statements made immediately after Lodi strike one as more plausible. One took the form of a remark to Marmont, speaking of the Directory: "They haven't seen anything yet. . . . In our time, no one has the slightest conception of what is great. It is up to me to give them an example." And the other was in a letter to the unfaithful Josephine where he wrote: "I shall go berserk if I do not have a letter from you [tomorrow]."

Lodi would see itself upstaged by another myth about another battle at another bridge: Arcola—a larger military action, three tributaries and eighty miles to the east of Lodi (and six months later). Antoine-Jean Gros, David's most gifted pupil, painted *Bonaparte on the Bridge at Arcole* for the 1801 salon and was justly celebrated for it. The work is an oil on canvas depicting an Ossianic if youthful Napoleon, all noble gravitas and reproach, flag in one hand and saber in the other, leading the attack. Deconstructing the twenty-six-year-old Gros's painting is a common academic exercise; he was a court painter, after all, so he made the First Consul strikingly handsome and put him in a mythic setting. (The truth? Bonaparte fell off the bridge into a swampy canal where he would have drowned had he not been rescued, with difficulty, by his frantic aides.) Yet the master painter's acute geometries reveal something profound about Napoleon in this era, about his ability to stir and to hold his contemporaries, something that goes beyond the physical courage and dynamism that are also depicted here. There is a strength in Gros's Napoleon that dispels fear and inspires courage and sacrifice. Using a modern colloquialism, we might say that "the force" was with him. The setting and the trappings are not noticeably military; Bonaparte is now the generic and unquestioned leader, not just a general rallying soldiers.

With *Bonaparte on the Bridge at Arcole,* we are both a long way from the French Revolution—this is a solitary individual, not "the People" or "Liberty"—yet at the same time, close to it, for no court painter at Versailles would have depicted a divine right king in quite so tenuous a posture (whoever Bonaparte is leading *could,* after all, fail to follow), nor would an "absolute" king have felt the need to be so depicted.

VI

Apprenticeship in Statecraft: Italy and Egypt

Who would not want Bonaparte for legislator, captain, father, and for spiritual chief?

—Ugo Foscolo (1778–1827),
Last Letters of Jacopo Ortis

Napoleon put more of his interest and imagination into State-building than into military campaigns or diplomacy. In that sense, he differs from Alexander the Great, who spent nearly all of his thirteen-year reign as king of Macedonia in conquest, and from Caesar, who spent most of his fourteen years of power in military campaigns and provincial governance. All three men were, of course, politically sui generis—indeed, Caesar's life, as we know, gave rise to a common political adjective, "Caesarian." Nevertheless, only Napoleon might be remembered for his political thought per se; only he consciously put so much of his imagination and will into State-building; only he among the three had a real chance to build a State at home.

But he began abroad. For the naysayers, the keepers of the Napoleonic black legend, Italy and Egypt are apprenticeships in opportunism, megalomania, and dictatorship. For the historian and the cultural anthropologist, the two episodes—back-to-back in Bonaparte's life, one lasting nineteen, the other fourteen months—present nothing but contrasts. However, from the biographer's perspective, they both express the impulse to political creation in the order and the style that the French Revolution had brought into being.

The effect that Bonaparte had on Italy and Egypt was both profound and long-range, and ambivalent and immediate; it joined greatness and newness of vision with greed, brutality, and reason of State. As such, he was (and is) both hated and appreciated by the peoples there whom he affected. Yes, Napoleon was an opportunist and a conqueror, and he certainly enjoyed power, but he enjoyed and envisioned more than just power. The choices, in viewing him, are thus not either/or but both/and.

"CISTER" REPUBLICS

If the Italians can now prove themselves worthy of recovering their rights and getting free government, we shall one day see their patrie *gloriously standing among the powers of the earth.*

—Citizen General Bonaparte,
January 1, 1797

May 19, 1796: Milan has been force-fed the Army of Italy's victory parade and a rigorous diet of reparations. Nothing unusual in this; "the right of conquest" is an old concept in history. But now a proclamation issues from French headquarters over the name of the commander in chief, General Bonaparte.[1] Unauthorized by the Directory, it announces "to the *people* of Lombardy" that "liberty" is declared. This is the sort of rhetoric—but is that all it is?—that has characterized the Revolution's first years—the era when "virtue" and "justice" (but not "terror") have to be written in quotations. Now here it is again, this time with the force of conquering bayonets. The statement is troubling, and not just to the men in Vienna who held power in Lombardy. Italian historians later will speak of May 19, 1796, as a defining moment in their national history, the beginning of the movement that blossomed in 1870 with the unification of Italy.

The eighteen months from May 1796 to November 1797 constitute perhaps the most complex period in all of Napoleonic history. Italy at the time was made up of over a dozen States, each with its own changing set of responses to the French presence. Similarly, French policy toward these States was anything but a homogeneous doctrine emanating from Paris; it was a flight of arrows, a spray of vectors, issuing from the conflict among five directors and their general-proconsul in situ as well as with the omnipresent and indefatigable forces of ultrarevolution and counterrevolution tearing apart French society. To lose sight for an instant of French internal politics is to miss the clarifying factor in an otherwise impenetrably dense and charged Italian magnetic field.

The Directory had not seriously conjured with the possibility of a major military victory in Italy. Suddenly, the large and rich province of Lombardy lay at their feet, and the five men holding executive power in Paris proved to be irresolute about what to do with it. They all shared with Bonaparte and his army an unquestioned belief that the fate of the Revolution hung on maintaining French supremacy in a Europe of hostile regimes, but on specifics they disagreed—for example, over the limits of desirable expansion: the moderates holding to the natural frontiers thesis, while their radical colleagues would spread the Revolution (and their own power) everywhere.

As a group, the directors had their eyes fixed on the Rhineland, with its flourishing cities and quality farmland—the shimmering goal for French governments since Louis XIV, if not earlier. Lombardy, in this view, made a good bargaining chip to induce Francis I to condone the Republic's occupation of some or all of the left bank of his Holy Roman Empire. Had the Directory shown the force and will of Robespierre, it would have set the French Italian policy, and French generals would have served their end, but the small committee of five was a poor cousin to the unified twelve who had ruled as the Committee of Public Safety. In the vacuum created by directorial infighting and indecision, a newly victorious general could make room to work.

It was not as much room as he wanted—the Directory was not *that* feckless—nor as much as his high-handed ways and regal style at the Mombello Palace outside Milan, where he had moved, would lead us to think, but it was enough to absorb him in the possibilities at hand after the fall of Lombardy. He was not indifferent to French fortunes in the Rhineland, but the chance to experiment in the governance of millions beckoned him, as it had tempted other generals since Caesar. Indeed, Hoche, as thirsty for glory as Bonaparte, would soon be trying to establish "his" ("Cisrhenan") republic in the Rhineland. But to the youthful author of regimental constitutions and essays on the best means for "inculcating happiness in people," the opportunity in Italy in 1796–97 was .22-karat gold asking to be wrought. Italy—both the "Italia" of the ancient culture that was mother to his family and the imminent "Republic" of his ideological dreams—interested him.[2]

The "Jacobin general" thus turned State founder when Lombard patriots (*giacobini*) pressed him to overthrow their old regime and declare a republic. Initially, Bonaparte and the Directory's commissioner to his army, the inevitable Saliceti, considered republicanizing all of Italy, or as much of it as fell into French hands. Such a grand design was akin, in its unreality, to the tsarist dream of freeing eastern Christianity from Moslem overlordship.[3]

Napoleon settled for sculpting out of Lombardy and nearby lands an entity he dubbed the Cispadane Republic (October 1796). It was soon aggrandized by further French conquests and became the Cisalpine Republic (July 1797). The Directory argued the name should be prefixed by "trans," indicating the far side of the Alps from Paris—that is the Transalpine Republic. But Bonaparte, significantly, took the perspective of Rome, hence "cis," indicating "this," or the near, side of the Alps. It certainly flattered the Italians.

The old city-state of Genoa also reformed itself at Napoleon's direct instigation, and became the Ligurian Republic—a matter of satisfaction to a former Corsican patriot, but opposed by most of the Directory and its commissioner to Genoa. Even the most backward state of the peninsula, the Bourbon kingdom of Naples and Sicily, underwent a revolution, thanks to Napoleon's influence. Indeed, that might have been the most authentic, in the sense of home-grown, revolution to take place in the peninsula during the so-called *Triennio* (the three years from 1796 to 1799). Unfortunately, the Neapolitan experiment was so swiftly and bloodily repressed by Naples's former rulers that it has become more famous to history as a monument of counterrevolution.[4]

Although some of its members in theory favored exporting the Revolution, the Directory, for its part, never approved of these republican experiments. The government in Paris worried that new republics would make their own jobs of ensuring French national interest harder. In at least one case, the Directory puts its foot down: the Piedmontese patriots would not be allowed to overthrow the House of Savoy, for that monarchy was seen as too valuable to France as leverage against Austria.

Bonaparte did not invent the concept of "sister republic," but he experimented with it in Italy (and the following year in Switzerland) beyond what anyone else had done. True, he saw to the adoption of French constitutional models and methods, but the space he made available for Italian flourishes was not small, while the manpower and energy of the *giacobini* were what turned the wheels of these republics. Much of the time, Bonaparte was indeed having to contain the zeal of the local patriots, for whom the date was the Year I of revolution, not (as in France) the Year V. He declared to the Milanese: "You can, you must, be free, but without undergoing the misfortunes that the French people knew." But the situation was paradoxical and delicate: three years after the revolutionary dynamic had been broken in France, it was flourishing in a conquered territory. No French general would have repressed the *giacobini*—they had functioned as pro-French partisans in the war—but Bonaparte gave them more support than another general might have done, even if his rhetoric on their behalf doubtless sounded a little hollow coming from a soldier who had shut down the Pantheon Club in Paris.

Things did not go well. The Italians came to realize "that the presence of any army, even a liberating one, is a calamity" (Stendhal). All Italians, even the patriots, resented French financial exactions, which proved greater than sums extorted from Italy by past conquerors. The Directory, like the Convention before it, staggered under debt and depended for salvation on war reparations. These reparations did not suffice, and the Directory declared partial bankruptcy in September 1797, the only time a French government did so between 1770 and the present day.

Reparations were old news for European powers; what gave things a new twist was the wholesale expropriation of works of art by the French. This was not the "rape of Italy by Bonaparte," of anti-Napoleon legend. He, like other French military leaders in Italy, simply applied a policy decided several years earlier by the Convention.[5] The French revolutionaries had elaborated a self-serving theory that held that, just as Rome had "inherited" Greek culture, the "new Rome" (the French Republic) could "repatriate" art that had been created in the "night of barbarism." In this view, Rubens's true *patrie* was not Antwerp but Paris. Louis XIV, of course, had seized Flemish art without needing a theory to justify it. The policy mocked the Revolution's best principles—the *giacobini* begged the French to turn Italian art over to "the people"[6]—but virtually no French leader of the era seriously questioned or refused to execute it.

So unlimited deference and gratitude were not shown to the "mother Republic" by her "children" in Italy. Then, too, the Cisalpine and Ligurian governments were themselves isolated in the peninsula. Bonaparte and the *giacobini* discovered to their chagrin how little resonance revolution had throughout the Boot. This was not the Batavian Republic, which enjoyed the benefits of a reforming middle class and a long history of insurrection against Austria. The paucity of patriots in Italy was matched only by the stubborn resistance shown to the revolution by the peasantry and most of the nobility. When elections returned anti-republican majorities, Bonaparte executed small coups d'Etat to maintain the *giacobini* in power, but doing so further undermined the Cisalpine Republic's legitimacy in its own people's eyes. Ultimately, the problem came down to the sort of intractable conflict that had wracked Corsica: between Jacobin-universalist principles, on the one hand, and old-fashioned irredentist nationalism ("get the French the hell out!") on the other.

Bonaparte also dissented from the Directory in matters of religion. Paris pressed him hard not only to occupy Rome but to overthrow the papacy, or at least humiliate Pope Pius VI. The General, knowing from Corsica the power of religion to dissolve a body politic into civil war, and aware of the loyalty Italians showed to the Church, did only part of what he was told. He left the pope his office, his dignity, and some of his territory. But he was not afraid to challenge Church opinion on occasion. For example, his divisional general, Vaubois, took his staff to a Livorno synagogue on July 14, 1796, to the indignation of the numerous devout Catholics.

DEATH IN VENICE
(OF A JACOBIN REPUTATION)

O France, that mockest Heaven, adulterous, blind,
And patriot only in pernicious toils!
Are these thy boasts, Champion of human kind?
To mix with Kings in the low lust of sway,
Yell in the hunt and share the murderous prey?
—Samuel Taylor Coleridge,
"France: An Ode"

A peace that follows a decisive contest in the field may be draconian, but the peace ending the first Italian campaign was not crushing, for the Army of Italy had not won an overwhelming victory against Austria. With the armistice made at Leoben in April 1797, Realpolitik increasingly came to dominate Bonaparte's calculations, for he was aware that the final and most important battle of this conflict was to be won over a green felt table, not in an Alpine valley. The war had, of course, been political all along, as Clausewitz observed, but the political dimension was harder to discern in the bloodshed, high drama, and purely military logic of a campaign. After Leoben, the contest reverted to being open politics; diplomacy was war by other means.

The Directory expected to direct negotiations for France. It was prepared to appoint to the task men of brilliance and renown: Benjamin Constant and Emmanuel Sieyès, respectively, among France's premier writers and political theorists. But Bonaparte indicated he would handle things alone, thank you, and the Directory was in no position to challenge a soldier who had given it so much desperately needed money and glory. Nor, frankly, was anyone other than Constant and Sieyès themselves at all sure that they could impose themselves on Bonaparte. The Directory had earlier dispatched

General Henri Clarke to represent its authority with the commander of the Army of Italy, and Napoleon had swept him off his feet. Clarke was heralding Bonaparte as "the new Alexander." (He did, however, grant that the general, like Alexander, could be abrupt and imperious, and that he asked for too much too quickly.)

Diplomacy is more often a marathon than a sprint. The official and unofficial sessions that climaxed with the Treaty of Campo-Formio[7] in October stretched out over weeks. In them, the accent lay on a nimble wit and a sure knowledge of international law and history. It helped to know when to talk softly, when to call a late-night session (i.e., if your opponent was tired or drunk), when to leave the table, and when to show emotion (Napoleon was excellent at feigning anger and indignation). It also helped if you could drive a wedge between a diplomat's viewpoint and his government's, or know when to separate yourself from your own government's position. Sometimes, you needed to save your interlocutor's face, other times to make him look weak or foolish in public opinion. In short, a subjective sort of contest with few rules and even little guidance from experience.

The Austrians sent an A team led by Count Louis Cobenzl, a forty-four-year-old seasoned diplomat of irony and artfulness, long of wind and nimble of wit, a man with a major political future in Austria. Cobenzl counted on his twenty-eight-year-old adversary to be inept and impetuous, to try to bludgeon Austria, thereby winning sympathy for her, while giving France responsibility for a resumption of the campaign. Napoleon, for his part, was not as free as he would have liked to be, for he was aware both of his army's precarious military position and of the Directory's opinion that Austria ought to be dealt with high-handedly. He disagreed with the Directory's view: there could be no diktat forced down the Habsburg throat; Austria had to be bargained with.

Napoleon got off some well-aimed shots. An infuriating matter to the French was the fact that Francis II did not formally recognize either their republic or the Cisalpine. In response, Bonaparte varied from the cavalier ("So what? Does the sun need recognition?") to the menacing ("Beware that Europe does not come to see the Republic of Vienna!"). What impressed Cobenzl in his adversary was his strange concern, seemingly neither in his own nor France's interest, to ensure the security and grandeur of the Cisalpine Republic. "Why do you have more interest in taking care of those little republics than you do in dealing with us?" he asked him once. Cobenzl ought also to have been impressed with Napoleon's canniness in intuiting what really scared the Austrians: their fear, bordering on neurosis, that Prussia would replace Austria as a German, and then as a European, power. The issue under endless discussion was the matter of Austria's compensation for losing Lombardy and for recognizing French claims on the Rhine. These were huge concessions, and adequate redress had to be forthcoming or the war would recommence. Redress was to be Venice—the "republic of the Beavers," as Montesquieu had called it. But Venice was a neutral power, not to mention Europe's oldest government, enjoying a precedence dating to the fifth century. She was thus poisoned fruit both for Vienna, toward whom the doge had tilted in the recent war, and for France, whose revolution renounced conquest and proclaimed the rights of people to dispose of themselves.[8]

Yet if neutral and old, Venice was not completely honorable or innocent, but a corrupt oligarchy that was a shadow of its former glory and "virility" (to use a Napoleonic word). Napoleon had previously dreamed of folding Venice into his beloved Cisalpine Republic; and indeed, progressive groups within the city-state's patrician class did support the French Revolution. However, the populace largely hated the French, and proved it by an Easter uprising in Verona (a Venetian holding) where four hundred French soldiers, including the sick and the wounded, were massacred. The French may have fomented the uprising; the evidence is unclear. Napoleon and the Directory, in any case, agreed that "saving" Venice for republic status was not worth the "forty thousand French lives"—the rhetorically high figure that Bonaparte claimed it would cost. Venice could thus be turned over to Austria. That action made of the Treaty of Campo-Formio another shining instance of the sort of diplomatic skullduggery sheathed in hypocrisy which had, several times earlier in the century, led Russia, Prussia, and Austria to carve up Poland among themselves. The treaty's overt clauses ensured Venetian and German integrity while its secret ones sold them out. As for the fate of the Rhineland, the treaty shifted responsibility from the current diplomats' shoulders onto those of delegates at a "high-level congress" to be held "later" (at Rastatt).

Only one director had the courage to vote against ratification of the treaty; his colleagues and their ministers understood that there was no choice. Sieyès or Constant could not have done better, given France's burning desire for peace, England's implacable enmity, and Prussia's refusal to play into French hands. To call the treaty "Napoleon's peace," thus, is tendentious, notwithstanding that his lonely signature adorns the treaty for France, next to those of four Austrians. Campo-Formio was not what he desired, but it was the best that a negotiator could get, short of a resumption of a war that the Army of Italy was in no position to undertake. It was also, incidentally, atypical of Napoleon's later peace treaties, for it was an ambiguous and indecisive compromise. In a letter to Foreign Minister Talleyrand, Napoleon made it clear he considered Campo-Formio a makeshift until a future war brought definitive peace.

No less a critic of the Consulate and Empire than the historian Michel Vovelle concedes that Campo-Formio might have been a "personal ambition," but in saving Milan at the price of Venice, it was a "noble ambition which in a certain sense played a positive role in the origins of the movement for Italian unity."[9] The same may be said of Napoleon's political record in Italy. It is not as impressive as his military record; and neither one of them is as impressive as Caesar's record in Gaul. Bonaparte's authority, though extensive, was far less absolute than Caesar's, and Napoleon was divided against himself in ways that Caesar, servant of Rome, was not: specifically, Napoleon was divided between the role of Italian republic-founder and that of French proconsul. The former saw Napoleon as aspiring Solon or idealistic young Epaminondas, handing down laws and founding States; the latter saw him as a reluctant, put-upon, and increasingly cynical governor, a Pontius Pilate, if you will. Trying to do both jobs, he did neither to his own satisfaction, and still less to the satisfaction of the unambivalent partisans who daily assailed him with advice.

It is perhaps strange that a man so insistent about his ability to foresee *all* did not draw on his recent experience in Corsica to foresee the impossible political dilemmas and violent social divisions that would face him in Italy. As governor, Bonaparte failed in the most basic requirement of that job: keeping order, fostering unity, galvanizing participation. Notwithstanding the roads built and political infrastructure created, if Napoleon's record stood on his statesmanship in the literal sense, he failed—no doubt, in part, because he succeeded so well in the proconsular role of siphoning off funds, art, and manpower from conquered provinces. That failure is what accounted for his becoming disappointed and disgusted at what he saw as Italian peasant conservatism and official French obtuseness. As time goes by, his evolution toward an increasingly instrumentalist view of Italy will take place, but it will never completely replace the early idealism.

Napoleon at St. Helena looked back on 1796–97 and chose to see only the solar prominence of his role as idealistic young general—"more Italian than Corsican," heroic founder of the "Cister" republics, acclaimed bringer of popular sovereignty to a decadent peninsula, sweeper away of corrupt old regimes that had subverted a natural ethnic entity that should one day be a nation. "I always had the idea of creating an independent and free Italian nation," he would say. He even concocted an ingenious justification for the Realpolitik of handing over Venice to Austria: it was salutary for the Venetians to undergo a test to see if they had a true vocation for freedom and for national unity—an argument along the lines of "prison is good for a man if it doesn't kill him." This is, of course, nonsense, and not even interesting nonsense.

Italians, for their part, including especially the patriots and *giacobini*, proved ferociously critical of Napoleon after the fact. "There is no more horrible thing than Bonaparte's conduct in Italy; he began by announcing war on the tyrants and peace to the peoples, and he ended by making peace with tyrants and submitting the people to slavery." But it is the anger of a disappointed "brother," not that of a national raising his fist at the foreigner, and when we look more closely, we are not surprised to find that the *giacobino* who wrote it, Pietro Custodi,[10] was working for the *Età napoleonica* in its civil administration.

Curiously, Italian national memory has tended toward the St. Helena idealistic view. The fact that two centuries later, Italians celebrated both the *Triennio* and Bonaparte's role in it is a good indication that now, as then, Italians understood there was something more at stake here than repression, reparation, and disillusionment. Ugo Foscolo's *Last Letters of Jacopo Ortis,* (quoted as epigraph at the beginning of the chapter) and his ode to "Bonaparte liberator" were both written in 1799, well after Napoleon had abandoned the Cisalpine Republic for newer sailing, and things were fast going from bad to worse in Italy.

The Italians have never forgotten that Bonaparte was born of their blood and spoke their language natively. Gabriele Rossetti, the father of the English poet, wrote: "In this unique man who was Italy's vanquisher, Italy showed the world what her sons are." A strange way to speak of a hated memory. The inhabitants of the peninsula, whatever their reactions to the French presence, feel they owe part of their Risorgimento and their national unification as a liberal secular regime to the start given by Bonaparte and his like-minded army. Italy has thus always remained Francophile in a way that Germany, which also owed its strong early impulses toward unity to Napoleon, has not. But then Bonaparte, whatever else he did, imposed Italy on France and on the world as surely as he imposed "Italy" on Italians.

FRANCE SEEN FROM THE ARMY OF ITALY

France Seen from the Army of Italy and *The Mail of the Army of Italy* were newspapers of Napoleon's intended for both the army and the French homeland, for Bonaparte in Italy, not a whit less than Caesar in Gaul, kept a sharp eye cocked on events in the capital. Bonaparte's editorial statement in the former journal read: "Our purpose will be to publish the truth on how the army of Italy perceives the situation in France and how it can defend there the cause of its friends against the partisans of tyranny or terror." *France Seen from the Army of Italy* was the less radical of the two papers—it hoped to unite all factions and social strata against the royalists—but both it and the more radical *Mail* were "thoroughly republican."[11]

In these days of elemental political and ideological clashes, nuance yet survived. The Paris police, for instance, deployed a curious dualism between the labels "republican" and "revolutionary": the former indicated "dependable" supporters of the current regime; the latter, "wild-eyed" radicals who wanted a return to the Year II. Had these classifications been applied to the field armies, one would have found that the Army of Italy harbored far more than its fair share of revolutionaries. It would indeed be fair to say that many of the soldiers commanded by Bonaparte, had they been civilians living in Paris, would have flocked to the very Pantheon Club that their general shut down when he headed the Interior Ministry. But in his soldiers and his generals, Bonaparte tolerated—indeed he cultivated—far higher degrees of politicization than he tolerated in civilians.

France Seen from the Army of Italy was, in addition, a disquieting perspective for Bonaparte's soldiers, who took their patriotism straight up. Jullien, one of the editors of *The Mail,* had been secretary to Robespierre; he had been a fellow traveler of Babeuf's (executed for sedition in May 1797), and a friend to Buonarotti, who was deported from Italy for sedition and moved to France. The French soldiers were not pleased by what they saw, or were told was transpiring, in their *patrie.* The gravest threat to the Republic in the Year V (1796–97) was, for them, not "neo-Jacobin" agitation, but the flood of "moderate" and royalist propaganda and elected officials. The legislative elections of the spring had returned an overwhelming conservative majority to both the Council of the Five Hundred and the Council of Elders, despite the regime's unseemly electioneering on its own behalf. The councils proceeded to nominate, in replacement of a retiring director, a new man (Barthélemy) whose political convictions were unorthodox, if not overtly royalist.

Meanwhile the right-wing press tilted openly at the remaining directors; at Bonaparte, whom they accused of treason; and at the war in Italy, which they considered imperialist. Ironically, the royalists, backed financially by the reactionary Austrian government, defended the "rights of peoples"—e.g., Venice. The brouhaha, if it did nothing else, certainly decided the Directory and Bonaparte to back each other more firmly than they might otherwise have done in a policy of expansion. Everyone wanted peace in a general sense, but to demand it at the price of returning to France's old (1789 or even

1792) borders was a policy branded by association with counterrevolution.

How objective was the right's threat to the Republic and the Revolution? It is difficult to say, and would remain so even if we could go back in time and take a look for ourselves. Evaluating such a threat involves making a myriad of judgments about how individuals and groups would have evolved once they were established in centers of power, as the moderates and royalists were bidding to be. The two categories, moderate and royalist, were not the same, even if the Paris police, which had fewer nuances for descrying the right-wing than the left-wing threat, was willing to reduce any and all expression of dissatisfaction with the Revolution to "royalism." On the other hand, there was no dependable way to separate the categories from each other, and the Clichy Club where these activists came together was at pains to make the task more, not less difficult. A formula plastered on a handout read "Long live the good faith Republic!" but when the sheet was folded in a certain way, it read "Long live the King!"[12] General Pichegru, elected to preside over the Council of the Five Hundred, held nominally republican views, yet he was in the pay of the English and, given a chance, would undoubtedly have helped the royalists stage a coup, as he did in 1804.

The Republic's field armies reacted to events in Paris largely according to the views of their commanding generals. In the main, the soldiery's violent messages to the home front (and "front" is precisely the word for how they saw Paris: as a kind of battlefield) were aimed at supporting the Directory by threatening its opponents. Sometimes they ended up frightening them both: "Tremble! From [Italy] to the Seine is but a single step" (Augereau). "Has the road to Paris any more obstacles than that to Vienna?" (Masséna). "We can fly over the mountains separating us from France with the speed of the eagle if that's what's necessary to maintain the constitution" (Napoleon). On the other hand, the Army of the Sambre-et-Meuse, under Moreau, stood out by its silence: no address to Paris. But then Moreau was a friend of Pichegru's, and covertly in touch with the Austrian minister.[13] Overall, two themes stand out in the military addresses to Paris: unremitting war on "aristocrats" and their allies; and the army (not the people) as regenerator of the body social of the Republic.

The directors did what they "knew" their opponents would do if they occupied power: they staged a coup d'Etat. They named Lazare Hoche—the "Bonaparte of the North," as he was known—minister of war, and ordered his army to march on Paris. A gallant soldier and a staunch republican, Hoche was nevertheless reluctantly convinced that a dictator was a temporary necessity to deal definitively with the royalist threat. But if he was a Galahad in his idealism, principles, and naïveté, Hoche was no Lancelot in the joust, and when the legislature rejected his appointment (he was under the age set for ministers by the constitution of 1795) and the Directory backed off from cramming him down their throats, Hoche retired from the field, humiliated.

The directors then looked south, where Bonaparte had been following the situation closely; he had even offered a subvention out of his army's treasury for the underfunded Army of the North. The General hesitated; precipitous action on behalf of the besieged and ridiculed Directory might "tarnish his glory" (especially if the action failed). Instead, he dispatched the stalwart but slow-witted blusterer Augereau. Using Hoche's troops, Augereau reprised the Vendémiaire action of 1795: Paris was invested on the night of September 3–4, 1797 (18 Fructidor Year V) and the legislature purged of its offending members. Two directors were got rid of: Barthélemy and Lazare Carnot, since Thermidor no longer as Jacobin he had once been. From the army's point of view, their action under Augereau represented a return to the Year II, with the soldiery acting as vigilant citizens in place of the people.

Napoleon, it appears, had contacts with Barthélemy, and he surely did with Carnot. The latter is unsurprising, in view of the two men's prior collaboration and Napoleon's skepticism about ideological purges of men of quality. Does Bonaparte's indirect participation in Fructidor therefore make him a cynic, concerned simply to cover all bets? Some say so. A popular historian of the nineteenth century, Henri Martin, wrote that "never was a man less abashed at contradicting himself nor less loyal to his word." There were generals on the scene who fit Martin's bill: Pichegru, for example, progressed from being a protégé of the Committee of Public Safety to working for the Bourbon pretender; or Bernadotte, hardly less a political chameleon, was often paralyzed by prudence and conflicting instincts and ambitions.

But Bonaparte in the Year V was no Pichegru and no Bernadotte, and if we must compare him to another officer, then, curiously, it would be Hoche, the general he is usually contrasted with. Both brilliant young generals, founders of "Cister" republics, the men admired each other, which says something, given their competition. At a patriotic celebration, a subordinate general raised his glass: "To Bonaparte, may he—" he began, but Hoche cut him off: "To Bonaparte, *tout court,* the name says it all!"[14] Hoche died suddenly in September, and his much-mourned passing allowed contemporaries and posterity to see in him "the noblest Roman of them all," rather than a human being in the round, including a prima donna of great vanity.

To read Hoche's letters to the Directory is to believe at moments that one is reading Bonaparte's: the lightning-bolt insights flashed without preparation, the unswerving self-confidence (the same capacity to identify oneself with the nation), the irritated impatience at time lost, the outbursts of pique followed by the insincerely offered resignations meant to put pressure on the recipient; the denunciations of corrupt war commissioners and recriminations at other commanders; the mood swings from black pessimism to sudden accesses of energy and excitement. Hoche had more taste for revenge than Bonaparte did, and less talent for self-mastery. He seethed with rancor at the Directory for setting him up in July; his determination to wreak revenge—he kept a long list of names he intended to purge—seems as consuming in him as the tubercle bacillus that apparently killed him.[15] He died convinced that Fructidor had not gone nearly far enough in establishing tough government in France. Though intelligent and thoughtful, Hoche lacked the Corsican's insularity and cool. If neither man was a Washington (but would French political circumstances and traditions have sustained one?), Hoche was also no Caesar, for his pride and his emotions clouded his judgment, and kept him from imposing his will.

Another trait Hoche lacked was Bonaparte's (or Caesar's) capacity for irony—that is, for holding a critical and distanced sense of the whole, while still being committed to a point of view. The twenty-nine-year-old Hoche, on the eve of his death, was still an *engagé*, reminiscent of the young Napoleon with Paoli. The twenty-nine-year-old Bonaparte simply construed people and events through a thickening filter of realism about what he took to be possible and desirable in a society built and torn apart by the Revolution. Some would say disillusionment, but if so, then it was disillusionment tempered by a genuine respect and passion for the political life in the broadest sense, and to certain principles for organizing the commonweal—principles that, in their era, were progressive.

Italy nevertheless took its toll on Napoleon's attitude about political possibility, although his personal life there, surrounded by his extended family, gave him many happy moments. The court that the young hero created at Mombello swiftly became one of the more brilliant in Europe, drawing to it many of the leading Franco-Italian writers, poets, and scholars of the day. It also increasingly rigidified itself in a rather severe etiquette that no longer permitted the proconsul to receive officers and aides at his table, in haphazard fashion.[16] A look at Bonaparte's letters indicates that what surprised and sickened him was no single event, but rather the process of watching the majority of Italy's population prove indifferent, when not hostile, to their own republic and to the whole project of social progress represented by the French Revolution. He knew the Cisalpine could not be abandoned—had the French left, the *giacobini* would have been massacred—but he understood that its preservation and progress were imperiled "by the prejudice and character,

and by the habit of centuries [in Italy], which one dares not overlook."
Where Bonaparte can perhaps be criticized was his failure to remain in Italy
to work at the task of helping the young republic solve some of its crushing
problems, not least those very French exactions that Bonaparte, if he had had
a mind to, might have modified. He had told a collaborator that he would
not leave Italy "except to go play a role in France," but he did leave Italy, and
not in order to spend much time in France. In his absence from the peninsula, disasters overtook the Cisalpine Republic—indeed all of Italy—which
Bonaparte's presence might well have prevented.

PARIS INTERLUDE

General Bonaparte arrived in Paris on December 5, 1797 dressed in civilian
clothes, thinking political thoughts and complaining to Bourrienne, his
friend from school days, that "If I stay long with nothing to do, I am lost.
They remember nothing [of previous accomplishments] in Paris."[17] He was
avid to take part in the high-stakes game going on in the French capital. In a
fortnight, he met with the leading players from all points of the political spectrum, including two men who had made names for themselves early in the
Revolution. The Abbé (Father) Emmanuel Sieyès had authored *the* pamphlet
that opened the French Revolution: *What Is the Third Estate?*[18] It virtually set
the terms of the ensuing titanic clash between the privileged castes and the
bourgeoisie. For a time in 1789, Sieyès had the impact and wielded the sort
of influence that most political philosophers can only dream about. The
essay propelled its author to a political career in the National Assembly, for
which his prickly but timid personality, and his weak and hoarse voice
would, on their own, never have promised him. But his career, as that of so
many, was cut short by the wild ride of the Revolution itself. A leading moderate, he managed to survive the Terror ("j'ai vécu," he famously put it) by
becoming a "mole," in Robespierre's words.[19] The mole emerged from his
hole in 1795, older and more experienced than most of the political actors on
the scene, and still enjoying his distinguished reputation as a political theorist. Bonaparte and Sieyès met at dinner early in December, and the sparks
did not fly. The philosopher had contempt for the officer, and vice versa. For
the moment, neither was at all convinced he couldn't do without the other.

Bonaparte's new political confidant of this time was Charles Maurice de
Talleyrand-Périgord, the Republic's new foreign minister. A scion of the
highest nobility, Talleyrand had been bishop of Autun under the old
regime, and played no less a role in the early Revolution than Sieyès. Vir-

tually on the eve of throwing off his holy orders to make a career for himself in secular politics, Talleyrand consecrated the Constitutional Church's first four prelates, thus maintaining apostolic succession in the nominally Catholic cult and winning himself eternal damnation in the eyes of Rome. For Talleyrand, too, the Jacobin period proved too hot for his moderation; he went into voluntary exile in England and the United States. He and Bonaparte actually already knew each other quite well, having entered into a rather thoroughgoing political correspondence in the summer of 1797. They now spent time together in Paris, and what emerged was not a friendship—a concept presupposing trust and selflessness—but a quiet entente cordiale, based on mutual interest and respect.[20]

By mid-December, it was clear to anyone who was watching closely that the "victor of Rivoli" had determined to stand back from the immediate political arena. There was no domestic role or initiative he was ready to take on his own. On the contrary, he recognized only too clearly that his reputation as conqueror of Italy, while gigantic, was vulnerable to being frittered away in political factionalism where he had nothing to gain for now—and a great deal to lose. He remained aloof from all parties, and spent his time attending meetings of the National Institute to which he was recently elected.[21]

The problem was to find for the conquering hero of Italy a worthy assignment. The Directory, eager to be rid of him, named Bonaparte (January 10) to the command of the Army of England—theoretically, a *very* grand project, indeed. But after several weeks of troop and installation inspections on the Channel coast the General determined that a successful invasion was out of the question. He so advised the Directory.

There loomed another possibility.

Talleyrand, for some time now, had been proposing to his government a military expedition to Egypt, then a province of Ottoman Turkey—or the Sublime Porte, as it was known. As the foreign minister had intoned grandly in his report of the previous July, "Egypt was a province of the Roman Republic, it must now become a province of the French Republic. The Roman conquest was a period of decadence for this beautiful country, the French conquest will usher in a period of prosperity." Bonaparte, for his part, was also on record advising the Directory that an aggressive Eastern policy was desirable. He had demanded that the Republic should hold on to the port of Ancona at the peace ending the Austrian war: "It will give us great influence on the Ottoman Porte and will make us masters of the Adriatic sea, as we already are, from Marseille and Corsica, of the Mediterranean." On August 16 he refined the advice considerably "in order to truly destroy England, we shall have to take Egypt."[22]

So the Directory bought the idea that an indirect strike at India-via-Egypt was somehow a realistic possibility and a perilous blow to "Perfidious Albion" (England). If there was an element of the fantastical to this line of reasoning, it is crucial to recall that the French had only recently (1763) lost India and her North American empire to the British, and the stain on her honor, as well as the hole in her commerce, was anything but forgotten.

Napoleon Bonaparte's experiences in 1796–97 led him to keep a far distance between himself and the factions—more easily done, no doubt, in the absence of anyone on the current French scene who remotely presented the will, clarity, or force of a Paoli or a Robespierre. The General had strongly advised his subordinate Augereau, when he sent him to Paris at Fructidor, not to ally too closely with even the party of the Directory, on whose behalf he was going to strike a military blow. And even before he experienced the infighting in Paris, Bonaparte reportedly told an Italian collaborator that "for now" he was choosing to "march with the republican party rather than the Bourbon faction," but he would "wait and see" where his self-interest might lead. Napoleon may or may not have said these words, or something like them; it is also quite possible that the reporter (Miot de Melito) intentionally or unintentionally missed an intended irony behind them. Napoleon was unquestionably ambitious, but his ambition was constructed on certain basalt principles of the Revolution, not on a *purely* instrumental view of ideals and principles. A strong distaste for parties and politicians did not make him a cynic, unless De Gaulle or Washington were cynics. The day would come when Napoleon would break with the republican *party*, but when it did come, the break would not carry all before it; a core of republicanism would abide.

A PASSAGE TO INDIA:
EGYPT, 1798–1799, THE MILITARY OPERATION

The most accomplished traveler and best writer could not convey to a European reader what we saw and suffered here.

—General Charles-Antoine Morand[23]

If ever an enterprise were overladen with causes and reasons yet without a guiding plan, the Egyptian campaign was it. The most decisive factors leading to the departure of the three-hundred-boat flotilla from Toulon in the spring of 1798 are the least interesting—the domestic political intrigue in Directory Paris, and the geopolitical considerations of the war with the "sea-girt realm," which could not be invaded from the Channel. But these are only the visible portion of a large, mysterious, and old iceberg. The year 1800 was a time when the best and the brightest and the politically correct looked with fervent approval on what today would be labeled "colonial imperialism." Napoleon Bonaparte's youthful notes speak of Alexander as an enlightened conqueror whose attack on the Persian Empire, which included Egypt, had been self-evidently a good thing, for the rule of the shahs represented the old regime, while the Greeks brought progress.

One is hard pressed to cite a French traveler, trader, thinker, diplomat, or still less a soldier who on principle discountenanced the expedition to Egypt, or believed it anything but manifestly justified by the "superiority" of the West. The Turkish Empire, which nominally ruled here, was regarded as an immoral and declining power, so the French saw an opportunity to revive civilization in an area whence it had sprung. As early as his stay in Ancona (February 1797), Bonaparte had become enamored of the idea of an "Alexandrian" conquest; he had meditated on the idea and, in correspondence with Talleyrand, fleshed it out. By the following winter, once it was clear that an invasion of England was out of the question, Napoleon readily revived "the Oriental dream." Even those critical of his high-handed ways cut him slack for such an adventure.[24]

Supporting the Army of the Orient and its commander in this imperial perspective was a group of some 160 of France's leading scientists, artists, engineers, physicians, and scholars (with a poet and an actor thrown in), whom Bonaparte decided should participate in the expedition for the purpose of advancing human knowledge.[25] Most of them had yearned to be recruited, even though they were uninformed of the destination. The prestige of Bonaparte's name alone rallied them, as did Bonaparte himself, who went out of his way to flatter the easily flattered intellectuals and scientists. In December 1797 the General himself had been elected to France's leading academy of savants, and since then had taken to placing "Member of the Institute" before "General in Chief" among his titles. A significant sum of money was set aside from military expenditure and used for equipping *les savants* with scientific apparatus and a traveling library. Even in the most dire straits of what would be Bonaparte's most arduous campaign until Russia, the scientists were accorded priorities to explore terrain, collect samples, and do experiments. The Institute of Egypt was founded in Cairo in July 1798. Its meetings were the one place Bonaparte tolerated criticism (sometimes excoriations) of himself and his policies. The army, for its part, felt slighted and contemptuously referred to *les savants* as "the General's favorite mistress."[26] The "mistress," in fact, outlived everyone on the expedition, for the work that the savants accomplished in Egypt (and after) virtually founded the science of Egyptology and was perhaps the only unmitigated success of a highly controversial adventure.

En route to Egypt, the French seized the strategic island of Malta from the order of knights that had governed it since the Crusades. The move was a bold but risky venture, for it would antagonize the Russians, whose tsar was Protector of the knights. On July 1, the French tricolor flew for the first time on the continent of Africa, as the Army of the Orient set foot on the beach of Marabout, near Alexandria. It numbered 36,000 men—the size of Alexander's army when he embarked for Persia—and had until now been known as the "left wing of the Army of England," to confuse Britain about its true destination. Talleyrand had assured the Directory that the invasion would be comparatively easy, inexpensive, and quick, requiring six months of execution. As his prediction has taken a large share of historical mockery, recall that it was not altogether unreasonable, given current (mis-)information about the state of Egypt's defenses and its wealth, and given that the British fleet had quit the Mediterranean the year before.

The effective government of Egypt at this time was in the hands of the Mamelukes, an equestrian feudal order of slave origin that had long held power over a disparate population of Moslem Arabs, Coptic Christians, and Sephardic Jews in the name of the Sultan in Constantinople. The Mamelukes flouted Ottoman sovereignty, paid them no taxes, and sought to suck Egypt dry for themselves; few of them even spoke Arabic, the language of the people they governed. The French casus belli for the attack on Egypt—the insults to her nationals resident in Cairo and Alexandria—was far-fetched, but Bonaparte and the Directory had hopes the Sublime Porte—long an ally of monarchical France—would tolerate an armed incursion to deliver a "deserved punishment" to the insolent Mameluke governors of a prize colony.

On a purely military plane, little of great novelty transpired in Egypt, for all that the Army of the Orient under Bonaparte's command racked up several legendary victories. The campaigns here had moments as harrowing and hideous as those in the Russian theater in 1812, but these were not due to the quality of Mameluke (or, later, Turkish) generalship, soldiery, or strategy. Massed infantry arrayed in mobile rectangles deploying modern firepower easily vanquished disorganized sorties of scimitar-waving cavalry. Thus, at the famous Battle of the Pyramids (July 21), the French lost 300 men to the enemy's 2,500. Nine months later, at Mount-Tabor, two undermanned French divisions routed a Turkish army of 30,000; at Aboukir the following July (1799), the now decimated Army of the Orient all but annihilated an Ottoman force many times its size. These victories struck contemporaries as

"Alexandrian" in that they recalled the Macedonian king's crushing defeats of the vast Persian hosts of Darius III. A general of the sterling quality of Jean-Baptiste Kléber, Bonaparte's number two on the expedition—but *not* an unconditional devotee of his commander—blurted out to Napoleon at Mount-Tabor, "General, you are great like the world, and the world is not great enough for you."

On the other hand, military disaster also struck the French—and early on. In Aboukir Bay, near Alexandria, in August 1798, a British fleet under Admiral Horatio Nelson caught up with the French and destroyed the Republic's Mediterranean fleet. The Battle of the Nile ended French naval presence in the Near East and destroyed the Republic's ability to reinforce its army there. Thus began the process of erosion of the French position in Egypt that eventually made a mockery of Talleyrand's predictions and destroyed any hope of long-term success for the Republic there. It was the first, but not the last sign of the importance of sea power, which Bonaparte ignored—to his and France's detriment. Instead, he shrugged off the naval defeat and reminded the army that Alexander the Great had sent his boats home. He told the men, "We are stuck in the obligation of having to do great things. And do them, we shall. Found an empire? We shall found it. Seas that we do not master separate us from the *patrie*, but they do not separate us from Africa or Asia."

The specters that now fell upon the French, however, required more than bombast to exorcise them. Egypt was a society in full economic crisis; it proved to be as far from the classical paradise of the invaders' imaginations as revolutionary France herself was from the Roman Republic she so constantly invoked. To the expedition's stunned disillusionment, the land of the pharaohs turned out to be a filthy backwater of flies, mud huts, disease, howling dogs, and superstition. Alexandria offered nothing worthy of its grand name.

The Army of the Orient was barely coping with this reality when, at the end of 1798, the Porte declared war—unexpectedly, to the French, if to no one else. Early in 1799, Bonaparte marched with 13,000 men north into Syria, anticipating a Turkish invasion from that direction. The army racked up a number of easy victories, but at Jaffa they encountered their worst enemy yet: bubonic plague. The combination of thirst, heat, pestilence, and homesickness drove many French soldiers to despair, some to mutiny, not a few to suicide—some doing so in front of the commander in chief. Then came Bonaparte's first personal military defeat. At Saint-Jean-d'Acre, his siege failed, for the city was provisioned and reinforced by the British, by sea. On May 21, with extreme reluctance, he lifted the siege and marched his men back across the blistering desert to Cairo.

Now is when the situation of the French in Egypt becomes interesting for the student of biography, for what transformed the retreat into Xenophon's "anabasis" instead of a disintegration was one man: Napoleon Bonaparte. It is one thing to be constantly invoking the classical names, it is another to repeat classical greatness. Like Xenophon leading his Spartans out of Persia, Bonaparte met the challenge head-on. With the troops, he could by turns be grandiose—telling them, "Are you forgetting that if I owe you my glory, I made you yours?"—and implacable: scorning their mutterings of mutiny and their officers' "ultimatums" (leading one of their spokesmen, General Mireur, to commit suicide). Yet he could also be stoic and patient. He stood silently while an angry engineer, in despair at losing his friend in combat, violently insulted him in public. Finally, he could be gentle. With the soldiers who were plague victims at Jaffa, Napoleon not only laid hands on them—against the strenuous objections of the doctors ("You must know Bonaparte very poorly to imagine there are easy ways to change his resolutions or intimidate him with dangers," a leading physician, Desgenettes, said)—he also worked with the sick for a time in an effort to show them that the disease was not contagious (as of course, it was) and that he, Bonaparte, had no fear of it. It was important for soldiers, he felt, to show no fear. Later, at a meeting of the Institute of Egypt, he had an angry exchange with Desgenettes over the issue of whether soldiers on campaign should be informed if they had a contagious and often terminal disease. The doctor felt it was right to do so; Bonaparte opposed it. "You'd rather watch an army or a society perish than sacrifice one of your schoolbook principles," he shouted at Desgenettes. He had another set-to with the physicians over whether a lethal dose of opium should be provided to the dying men who could not be evacuated before the advancing Turkish armies. The doctors found the idea repugnant; the General, knowing what the Turks were capable of, was in favor: "I shall always be disposed to do for my soldiers what I would do for my own son." The doses were left.

Bonaparte thus had Caesar's capacity to make morally or spiritually perilous decisions without blinking. The most controversial in this campaign was his decision to execute three thousand Turkish prisoners taken at Jaffa (March 1799). The men had surrendered on a promise of quarter by French officers who had no authority to offer it. Many of these Turks had previously been captured and released on oath not to fight the French again; they had thus broken their word. Arguing military necessity—there was no way the army could have imprisoned or fed such a number, and to release them again was clearly folly—Bonaparte ordered them executed.

In short, Bonaparte's strong proclamation to the army after the Nile defeat—that he intended to persevere—was matched by his unique authority to persuade, beg, cow, and command his men and officers to do the same. The French dug in, and it is fortunate they did so, for the adversities that fell upon them would have beaten most hosts. Napoleon all but willed the army not to disintegrate under the hammer blows of desert, defeat, and disease. General Morand, an intimate of an officer who killed himself after a confrontation with the commander in chief, called Napoleon in Egypt "the greatest general of the century." But his memoir makes it clear that that title did not ensue from the General's being considerate, humanitarian, or just, as some generals were considered. Kléber, for example, was known for being kind to his men, sparing of their blood. Desaix, Bonaparte's other right hand, was called Sultan El-Adel, the Just Sultan, in Upper Egypt, where he ruled. Bonaparte, however, took his enemy's breath away and seized his own troops' imagination, as if it were a redoubt. He was called Sultan El-Kebir, the "ruler of fire."

Here is a description of him given by the young French portrait painter Michel Rigo (1770–1815), who had come with the expedition. The night before the battle of Aboukir, Rigo slept near Bonaparte and was fascinated by his face and his movements. There was, he later told a colleague, "something in [his face] so acute, so thoughtful, so terrible, that it always impressed him, and that this night, when all the rest were buried in sleep, he could not avoid watching him. In a little time he observed Napoleon take the compasses and a chart of Aboukir and the Mediterranean and measure, and then take a ruler and draw lines. He then arose, went to the door of his tent and looked towards the horizon; then returned to his tent and looked at his watch; after a moment he took a knife, and cut the table in all ways like a boy. He then rested his head on his hand, looked again at his watch for some time, went again to the door of his tent, and again returned to his seat. There was something peculiarly awful in the circumstances—the time of night—his generals soundly sleeping—Buonaparte's strong features lighted up by a lamp—the feeling that the Turks were encamped near them, and that before long a dreadful battle would be fought. . . . In a short time Napoleon called them all up, ordered his horse, and asked how long before daybreak."[27]

SULTAN EL-KEBIR—GOVERNING EGYPT

Bonaparte landed on the beach at Marabout armed with no master plan to found a colony, revive mercantilism, or create a sister republic. However, he had long meditated on what he might find here and on how he should react. He was keenly aware that a world-historical event had altered the "Orient," as the eighteenth century called the Near East since Alexander's day: the eruption of Islam. Between the French army and their revered classical forebears fell the shadow of the Crusades. The Army of the Orient was the first European military force to set foot in the Dar-al-Islam (Islam's equivalent of "Christendom") since 1250, when the French king Louis IX had been defeated and taken prisoner near the very beach where his successor disembarked. The centuries of mutual incomprehension and popular indifference that followed Saint Louis's misadventure had led Volney, the top French "Egypt expert" of Bonaparte's time, to warn his readers that neither England nor Turkey blocked a French insertion into Egypt; Islam did.

Bonaparte was already at war with England, and now with the Turks, but he had no wish to make war on Islam. To the contrary, he proclaimed far and wide his good feeling for the religion of Mohammed. "The Roman legions had protected religion," he said, and the French army would do even more than that. The French dated their proclamations in both the Islamic and the Revolutionary (but not the Christian) calendars; they promulgated them in Arabic as well as in French. The Arabic versions often contain more strongly phrased religious language than do the French.[28]

But if Bonaparte's interest in Islam and Egypt was sincere, he did not regard the Franco-Egyptian exchange as one between equals in other realms than religion. In culture, politics, technology, and social organization, he, his army, and the savants arrived eager to teach lessons. The counterpart to the French protection and appreciation of Islam and Egyptian classical history was the newcomers' intention to bring "enlightenment" and "development," to blend "the rights of man" with "the law of the Koran." From Egypt's perspective, the Europeans dropped suddenly onto their scene as an alien, hostile force majeure. Whatever the poor impression Egypt made on the French, the country was not a stagnant backwater, nor a tabula rasa yearning to have gun-toting foreigners force on it their ideas of modernity. Its economy was in depression, true, but it had made significant progress in the eighteenth century, and the country was also undergoing something of a cultural flourishing.

What eluded Napoleon's anticipation was the degree and persistence of Moslem mistrust of the French, coupled with their comparative indifference to Western notions of reform. He also misjudged Islam's presumed malleability at the hands of the State. He saw in Mohammedanism (as it was known) a religion without hierarchy or clergy, as Catholics understood these things, and he therefore assumed it could be controlled by lay authority. In fact, it was the other way around: the State, in the Dar-al-Islam, was itself an expression of religion, and to the degree that any government or political institution was not a figment of religion, it was condemned as foreign. Finally, the Napoleonic view of the Mohammed himself—as the figure from the Voltaire play *Mahomet*, a dramatic popular leader and pragmatic philosopher whose teachings were readily squared with eighteenth-century ideas of *lumière*—was not *quite* how the Moslems saw the Prophet.

For a time, surprisingly, things went well, and not merely due to French power. It was possible to make a case to the peoples of Egypt—"Egyptians" is an anachronism for these disparate social and cultural groups—that the overthrow of the Mameluke was indeed a boon akin to the French overthrow of their old regime, while other French reforms—e.g., public works, creation of hospitals and medical facilities—pleased more people than they offended. Finally, the labors of the French scientists on the expedition were not confined to high culture in the Nile delta, but focused on projects that benefited the entire country (or would have, had they had time to be realized).

This said, the meeting between the cultures failed to produce a real spark. The French—their ways, their language—were so foreign as to seem to be from another planet. They often conducted themselves as arrogant aggressors. Franco-Egyptian interaction thus often evoked the same mutual appreciation that each side had of the other's music: none. The preponderance of Egypt's populace sincerely believed that anything worth knowing was already explicit or clearly implicit in the Koran. More seriously, many Napoleonic measures outraged people. Some regulations were seen as invasions of family life, while military security credited rumors that the French were intending to massacre the Moslems. Decrees on behalf of women, Jews, and Coptic Christians, and the requirement to fly the tricolor from the minarets of mosques, went down almost as badly as the imposition of high taxes to support the French army.

Intent on proving to the world that he could govern Egypt by winning Moslem hearts and minds, Bonaparte tried a bold strategy—the more interesting in that it ran at right angles to the lay policies he championed in France or Italy. Traditionally, the Ottomans and Mamelukes had sought to diminish, so far as possible, the direct role of religious authority in the political sphere. The French therefore would magnify it, accentuating, for example, the importance in Egypt of the distant "chérif" (or head imam) of Mecca, a religious leader of prestige but no power in the Ottoman Empire. More important, having booted out the political caste of the Mamelukes, Bonaparte created a council, the divan, which he stocked with indigenous

Arab social and religious leaders (sheiks and ulemas), as well as with middle class traders who had wealth but no political influence. Mainly a mechanism to facilitate French taxation, the divan yet proved successful in bringing new elites to a position of broad social influence while associating them with a specific kind of change and an authoritarian, though populist, tradition represented by the French. It would be difficult to deny the conclusion of the French historian, F. Charles-Roux, that "never was [Egypt] better governed since the Turkish conquest nor endowed with a coherent and efficacious government, so adapted to its needs, than under the French."[29]

Uniquely, Napoleon governed in part by deploying religious language, Koranic quotations, and Islamic arguments to illustrate or justify his rule. Back in July 1798, when he arrived, Bonaparte had proclaimed his "respect for God [Allah], his Prophet, and the Koran," but that was only the beginning. The decree of December 21, for example, written in elegant Arabic by Al-Mahdi, the most brilliant sheik of his era, orders the ulemas to inform their flocks that only Allah could have given victory to Bonaparte, and "anyone who doubts this is a blind fool." From our vantage point, after two centuries of colonialism and decolonization, this idea seems arrogant and imperialist, as well as naive—almost ludicrous. But in its era, given the French Revolution's missionary and ideological form of politics, it made a kind of sense.

It made more sense, no doubt, when it was backed by the equally unique Napoleonic mind and personality, which quite simply floored much of the population here, whether they approved of the French presence or not. Bonaparte's wooing and the obvious pleasure he took in many aspects of Egyptian life were as hard to resist as his anger. When the divan managed to keep order and peace while Bonaparte was absent in Syria, the commander in chief delivered up parades, festivities, flattery, bribes, and compliments, including the famous one (facetiously intended) in which he noted that the people of Egypt were "showing themselves to be good Frenchmen." For his qualities of mind and his (at times) accessible, jovial personality, and, above all, for his frightening persistence and strength of will, Sultan El-Kebir thus carved out a unique niche of authority, not merely power, for himself in Egypt. Locals rose when he entered a room and remained standing in his presence.

But it was all to no avail. Napoleon as "lover of Islam" came on too strong. He was naive and impatient, too ready to deploy force or corruption. He had an idée fixe of what Egypt should be in his hands, and a limited amount of time to devote to seeing that it did. The French hold on Egypt thus remained what it started out as: force operating behind a façade of hypocrisy, of myriad forms of persuasion and manipulation, and of some genuine sympathy. A contemporary noted that "the empire of [his] flattery was so strong that he

[Napoleon] mastered the feelings of hatred that any Moslem at this time felt for every Frenchman." In the long run, might this have evolved into a securer and deeper foundation?

But there was no long run. The Sultan in Constantinople, as we saw, emboldened by the French naval defeat at the Nile and pressed hard by the British, declared war. That declaration led Bonaparte to switch images. No longer merely liberator of Egypt's underclasses from the Mameluke yoke, he now billed himself as the would-be liberator of "the Arabs" from the distant Turkish overlord. The issue remained religion, however, for in Egypt there existed little or no sense of Arabness in the way that the French understood national identity. Napoleon, as Henry Laurens, puts it, could not get around the fact "that each time he spoke of Arabness, they replied, 'Islam.' "[30] The Sultan's attack on the French came wrapped in religious language, with messianic and prophetic overtones; it was a jihad against "the French people, a nation of inveterate infidels to religion."

Bonaparte gave back in the same currency he got, seeking (again, in Laurens's words) "to conjoin in his person the double personality of Alexander the Great and a new Prophet of Islam." A French proclamation of July 21, 1799, even appeared to share the Moslem prejudice against Christians that they were polytheists—i.e., believing in the Trinity, instead of "the one God [Allah], the Father of Victory, Clement and Merciful." Allah had "ordained that I [Napoleon] should come to Egypt," and Moslems who sided with the British "are damned." But the strategy failed, perhaps because its bad faith was so visible. Revolts occurred, followed by brutal repression, reparations, and then, of course, Moslem mistrust and hatred. For the mass of the populace, the French could not get out from under the burden of being seen as the "Christian enemy," the crusaders returned. In that perspective, the Ottomans and even the Mamelukes were preferable because at least they were not infidels. The French reminder that their Revolution had uprooted Catholicism helped little except to convince some Moslem religious leaders that these foreigners were atheists.

The French understood that they were but a "gentile" drop in a Moslem sea. They increasingly, reluctantly, felt they had no choice but to strike out at religious fanaticism when it attacked them, and to sustain themselves with policies of punishment and reprisal, including the occasional profanation of mosques. Bonaparte himself tried to exercise restraint and clemency (thereby angering his generals), but he could not be everywhere at once, and many atrocities were committed. The French enjoyed worse relations here than they would with any conquered people until Spain a decade later. Even so convinced a Napoleonophile as Vivant Denon worried "that we have simply replaced the Mamelukes." Others of his savant colleagues began to suspect that their presence here was now useful mainly for political purposes: to cover the material disaster that the expedition was becoming.

In July 1799, Bonaparte inflicted a crushing defeat on Turkish and British forces at Aboukir, and on that victorious note, decided to leave Egypt for France, twelve months after he had arrived.

It is said that he grew more disillusioned with humanity while in Egypt. He would later make the oft-cited remark that Rousseau had got human nature wrong when he sang the praises of "natural man." Egypt, he would say, had taught him differently. Egypt indeed taught Napoleon a great deal (as he, Egypt), but to say that it disillusioned him is to imply that he arrived with illusions about human nature, and I rather doubt that he did, after Italy. Napoleon already well knew how men, including popes, statesmen, and international savants, may be dominated by their interests, passions, greed, ambition, and fear. If he needed reminding, Egypt occasioned it, as much among his fellow Frenchmen as in the populace. Vivant Denon's easily piqued vanity, just as easily rectified by Napoleonic flattery, might have been an amusing example. Less amusing was the personal corruption of Bonaparte's old friend Sucy, a war commissioner with the army. Perhaps the commander in chief felt disillusionment about his own inability to enforce "modernity" on indigenous peoples.

As late as the spring of 1799, Napoleon was thinking of staying in Cairo and was mulling over the idea of having his quarters there remodeled. His health was never better than in Egypt; the headaches, colds, and lassitude that had afflicted him in Italy disappeared in Egypt (only to return in Europe). He loved the feel—sights, sounds, and smells—of North Africa, and resonated to its ways. A few years later, he dilated to the young Claire de Rémusat about his sojourn in Egypt. The passage is oft-quoted, for it is expansive and evocative even by Napoleonic standards—for which reasons, it must be cited and read, but perhaps not taken too literally:

> In Egypt I found myself free of the drags of inconvenient civilization. I dreamt all things and I envisioned the means of fulfilling them. I would create a religion! I saw myself mounted on an elephant, marching toward Asia, a turban on my head, in my hand, a new Koran, which I would have composed to my liking. I would have united for my enterprise the experience of two worlds, digging about in the ground of all history, attacking English power in India while renewing in that conquest my relationship with old Europe. The time I passed in Egypt was the most beautiful of my life, for it was the most ideal. But fate decided differently.

In sum, we may concede that Bonaparte left Egypt, as he wrote Kléber, "with the deepest regret," and that "nothing but the interests and honor of my country, a sense of duty, and the extraordinary events taking place at home, could decide me to risk my way amidst hostile fleets to regain Europe." Some historians have taxed him for abandoning his army; and it is true that he left under the cover of night with a small, select party of generals and savants, for he knew his departure would be unpopular with the men. On the other hand, Bonaparte, as commander in chief, held the authority to do as he liked, while the previous May the Directory had sent him specific instructions (which did not reach him) authorizing him to come back to France. The government and Bonaparte had anticipated a six-month campaign, and over a year had passed, and the General was much needed on the home scene. But he was aware that his leaving would be criticized.[31]

Post-Bonaparte, the French had two more long years in Egypt. Under the successor governors, Generals Kléber and Menou, revolts occasionally occurred and were followed by brutal repressions, which in turn were followed by Moslem reprisals. Kléber, a crack soldier, wound up assassinated by a dagger-wielding religious fanatic. Both of Bonaparte's successors persevered in the General's instructions to apply the Napoleonic policy, the gist of which was: nothing matters more than parrying the view that the French are infidels, and the best way to parry it is to continue to use the ulemas as mediators between French administrators and the people.

EGYPT: A BALANCE SHEET

As to [Caesar's] war in Egypt, some say it was at once dangerous and dishonorable, and noways necessary.

—Plutarch

[Napoleon's] colossal foot left an eternal trace in the moving sands of the desert.
—Victor Hugo

Napoleon's lapidary summary of his accomplishment in 1798–99, as he wrote it in *Campaigns in Egypt and Syria,* reads: "He was absent from Europe 16 months and 20 days. In that time, he took Malta, conquered lower and upper Egypt, destroyed two Turkish armies, captured their general, their equipment, their campaign artillery, ravaged Palestine and Galilee, and created the foundations, henceforward solid, of a most magnificent colony. He had brought the sciences and arts back to their cradle." The paragraph contains a mix of true and false. The truest part is his military achievement. As a general, Bonaparte scored several exceptional victories and he met with one sharp defeat (Acre). It is the risk of this line of work that one defeat can sink you. This happened to the French fleet at the Nile, and thereafter—if not ineluctably—to the expedition. But the naval battle per se was not Bonaparte's fault. In themselves, his land victories were, as noted, Alexandrian for their efficacious concentration of force against number. He even improved on Alexander in that the French army never mutinied nor imposed its contrary will on its leader, as did the Macedonian host on its king.

As purveyor of culture, Bonaparte might be said to be responsible for bringing "sciences and arts back to their cradle," although one would add that a military expedition was not theoretically (perhaps, only practically) necessary to do that.[32] As a political intelligence, Bonaparte made one whopping mistake, but it was one that he shared with the entire French political class: he half convinced himself that the Sublime Porte would permit this intrusion without fighting, and that it was itself on the way out of history's little melodrama. It would, in fact, take the cataclysm of World War I, more than a century later, to dislodge the Osmanli sultans from their weak but tenacious grip on the throne of the caliphs. Bonaparte's record as a State-builder also had its Alexandrian colorings—for example, in his brilliant use of outstanding subordinates, such as Kléber and Desaix, or in the extraordinary impact of his own personality on people and on history. Then, too, Bonaparte's religious policy recalled Alexander's project of fusion with the Persians. Napoleon was Alexandrian in his gigantic arrogance and his impatience, though the twenty-nine-year-old French general remained in Egypt four times longer than did the twenty-four-year-old Macedonian king. Overall, Bonaparte's record in Egypt was more mixed (even) than in Italy.

To read Napoleon's fast-paced and vivid *Campaigns in Egypt and Syria* is to see anything but a work of world-weariness or cynicism. It is the writing of an older man who is retrieving a full measure of the excitement and will of another era—who is making contact with what the French call his *imaginaire*: his mental picture and its animating energy. Bonaparte's *imaginaire* of Egypt was, of course, one of control, instantly recognizable to us as colonialist. We could be reading Cromer, Faidherbe, or Lyautey. In the colonialist vein, too, was Napoleon's affection for Roustam, the young Mameluke slave, and for Sultan, the magnificent pure-bred, jet black Arabian, both of whom he took back with him to France.

But that is the point: these famous names from the annals of colonial governorship all came later. Here, as in so much else, Bonaparte came first. To write that he brought merely "traditional answers to eternal problems . . . nothing more than an empirical response to old problems"[33] is thus to judge him anachronistically. Bonaparte's sort of colonial imprint only *became* old in the course of the contemporary era. At the time of the French expedition to Egypt, it was very much *new*—a novelty that set into motion a large historical dialectic that would affect far more than Egypt. France's self-proclaimed "civilizing mission" in the nineteenth century indeed became a transparent façade for a good deal of cold-blooded colonialism, but it first had to happen before the historian can sigh and smirk about it.

Historically speaking, this discontent the French met with meant little or nothing, however. State-builders neither expect nor require popular affection. Bonaparte was only too aware that the sheiks and ulemas he had appointed to the divan did not like him or trust the French. That was not his purpose; what mattered was: Did they permit him to govern through them? Was his government gradually taking hold? And the answer to both questions is "largely, yes," though it had probably less to do with his religious policy, which persuaded few, and more to do with French power and utility. If we ask, did Bonaparte create "solid foundations" of "a most magnificent colony," the answer is "no, not in the short run," and since that was the only "run" there was, then "no," for the record.

But that is not all there is to it.

External factors alone were what drove the French out of Egypt. It comes back to the consequences of the Battle of the Nile, which robbed them of time, to see if their investment would pay off. Had the Republic found the means—and First Consul Bonaparte would surely try—to reinforce and revictual the colony, they would likely have remained, for Kléber and Abdallah Menou were good colonial governors (though Menou was a poor general). For much of 1800–1801, Great Britain was all but resigned to leaving the French there, and was mainly concerned to find adequate compensation for themselves. A British expeditionary force finally, barely, defeated an exhausted and undermanned French army in the summer of 1801. Had Menou held out four more months—that is, until the peace discussions at Amiens got under way—France's position in Egypt would have been a given in the complex set of negotiations, in which the French arrived at the green felt table very much the geopolitical overall winner.

Bonaparte once wondered what "fifty years of prosperity and good government" would have brought to French Egypt.[34] Egypt did turn out to be, as Napoleon thought, a country congenial to "development" and "nationhood," in the European senses of these terms. The French invasion would likely have turned into a forceful but ultimately peaceful colonization, increasingly better adjusted to the religious and cultural landscape. The organ transplant could easily have lived for decades, as was the case for the British colonial occupation of Egypt, from 1882 to 1952.

It is revealing that when the process of modernizing did begin, less than a decade after the French departure, it was led by an authoritarian statesman named Mehemet Ali, who made a fabulous political career boasting of being "born in the same country as Alexander and the same year as Napoleon." He ran the Mamelukes out of Egypt, and he never tired of speaking in Napoleonic accents while invoking the French memory (if not, it is true, inviting in Emperor Napoleon's aid). The legal documents that Ali ordered drafted to justify his taking of power in 1805 were written by the same wise and skeptical old sheik who had written Bonaparte's proclamations, and the language of Al-Mahdi for his new patron is too delicious not to cite: "According to the ancient usages and legislation of Islam, *the people have the right to set up and throw over princes who are oppressive and unjust.*"[35]

Perhaps the surest sign of the continued Franco-Napoleonic presence in Egypt lies in the two-century tradition of arguing over it. The exogenous seeds that Bonaparte planted in the Egyptian garden may have flourished under Mehemet Ali, but they have not been matters of consensus among all Egyptians (the term may now be used). If the Westernizers and developers in Egyptian history (e.g., King Fouad, Colonel Nasser) invoke the French influence, the Islamicists reject it as an alien intervention. The former participated in the bicentennial commemorations of the French expedition; the latter had nothing to do with any of it. In short, the French introduced, or magnified, here the same kinds of ideological clashes that their Revolution posed at home, in Corsica, in Italy, and all over Europe. That was their genius, we might say.

In 1991 a ballet entitled *The Three Nights of the Sphinx* was performed in Cairo. In it, the characters of Napoleon and Mehemet Ali dance before the Sphinx in a long pas de deux, during much of which they are in embrace. But whether it is an embrace of love or a wrestling match is impossible to say.

VII
Power (I):
Taking It (Brumaire)

Stop searching the past for examples that will only slow us down. Nothing in History resembles the end of the eighteenth century; nothing at the end of the eighteenth century resembles this moment.

—Bonaparte, to the Council of Elders,
November 9, 1799

Bonaparte departed Egypt on August 23 and, after a five-day stopover in Corsica (the last visit he would ever make to the island), landed in France on October 9. One month later, to the day, he and a cabal of politicians in office overthrew the Directory and established a Consulate. The next morning, he set to work, and in the space of thirty months, he oversaw the drafting of a new constitution for the Republic, ended the civil war in the provinces, secured more domestic tranquility for France than she had enjoyed in a decade, won the War of the Second Coalition against far larger armies than the First, and forced peace on a reluctant Britain after nine years of continuous Anglo-French warfare. Working with a superb team of associates, he then laid the legal, political, educational, and administrative foundations—the so-called blocks of granite—on which much of the French State stands to this day. Withal, he reconciled with his wife, purchased (with her) a small gem of a chateau named Malmaison, survived a murderous assassination attempt, and invented a tasty chicken in tomato sauce with no cream.

In short, the period from October 1799 to mid 1802 offers a roaring cascade of activity and achievement that can easily submerge writer and reader in a flood of color and narrative, as it can submerge the biography of Napoleon Bonaparte into the larger history of which he is a decisive and unique part. One must try to steer an orderly course, even if it means some time spent at the outset poring over charts and maps. If we grant that there is more to be said about Bonaparte's political evolution than that he was a mako shark who fed on anything that floated by, then the task of clarifying this evolution requires time and some tools.

"POLITICS" AND "THE POLITICAL"

The concept of the [S]tate presupposes the concept of the political.
                    —Carl Schmitt,
                        The Concept of the Political

The French language affords a neat distinction between *la politique* and *le politique*. *La politique* is commonly used and easily defined; it means politics, and is what comes to mind when a newscaster speaks of politicians, campaigns, lobbies, and diplomacy. In France, as in the United States, politics has a bad reputation, although its very *déclassement* is itself a curious political phenomenon at a subtler level. That level is where *le politique* enters the picture. This is "the political" in a larger sense, but the moment you press it for more juice, disagreement arises, for the term has no succinct or uncontested definition. For some thinkers, *le politique* pertains to the nation or *la patrie*—that is, to the beloved community of the whole, the citizenry. The American political theorist Sheldon Wolin, for example, considers "the political [to be] an expression of the idea that a free society composed of diversities can nonetheless enjoy moments of commonality when . . . collective power is used to promote or protect the well-being of the collectivity."[1] The likeminded liberal French historian Pierre Rosanvallon holds *le politique* to be "the place where the multiple lines of men's and women's lives weave themselves together . . . the ground whereon the face of true community is progressively built."[2]

For others, however, *le politique* pertains to the State, not the nation. Carl Schmitt, a conservative German philosopher (1888–1985) lately much cited and discussed despite his service to the Nazi Reich, understood "the political" (*das Politische*) as arising in irremediable group conflict—and more particularly, in the discrimination of one's own group from "foreigners." In this realm of "friend or enemy," where Realpolitik reigns, it is the State, not the community nor the law nor some ideal of justice that is, or ought to be, the monopolist of "the political."[3] Anything less is liberal euphemism and hypocrisy.

In short, the very notion of "the political" is tendentious, as is the act of separating it from "politics,"[4] and how one defines and uses the term is a function of one's own views and goals. But whatever its reference, the concept has cachet, for it refers to something powerful and grand, if vague, and one wants to be seen as dealing in its currency. (By comparison, mere "politics" is debased coin.) *Le politique* transfers attention from the rough-and-tumble of the struggle for gain in the public arena to the larger picture, which is the forms, uses, and distribution of power in a society. As such, it points to a vast range of phenomena—from social organization and economic structure to culture and intellectual production. For example, a thing as seemingly removed from "politics" as religious faith may yet be shown to participate in *le politique,* for the mere presence in a society of organized Christianity has a profound effect on the action of power in that society, regardless of whether or not the Church's practitioners intend this to be the case.

The *le/la* distinction is useful in illuminating Bonaparte's evolution as a political animal, and it does so, moreover, in terms that the man himself would have understood. Bonaparte was passionately interested in "the political" and implicitly understood that it touched on all dimensions of social life. He enjoyed reading political theory, and had even taken his hand at writing it. Writers like Machiavelli gave him food for thought about the use and legitimation of power in the larger sense. And like Machiavelli (or Carl Schmitt), Napoleon tended to believe that "the political"—the use of power and the containment of conflict—pertained to the State. Community forms like *patrie* and nation were, in his view, far more emanations of the State—ideal (and ideological) constructs and projections of official power—than they were the actual coming together of "the people" in mutual affection and support.

But not just *any* State. *L'Etat,* in Bonaparte's view, was not simply an empty vessel to be filled by a "great-souled" leader (Aristotle's phrase) in *any* form he chose, as twentieth-century Germany would see in *der Führer.* The Bonaparte of autumn 1799 was still the son of the Revolution in his certitude that the only legitimate State could be one that styled itself and derived its justification from the *res publica*—the "public thing." What the republic entailed by way of governmental institutions remained a topic of sanguinary debate among the French, and Bonaparte, as we know, had shed the Rousseauism of his youth. Italy and Egypt had strengthened in him the beliefs that men and women are weak and malleable, if not necessarily evil, and that true political leadership therefore was less a matter of correct doctrine or constitution, as he had once believed, than of safeguarding a few basic "interests." Crucial among the latter were national unity, civil equality, security of person and property, and strong, fair, neutral (unpartisan) leadership. The State also fostered glory . . .

Despite his distaste for ideology and his somewhat instrumentalist and sparing invocation of ideals, Napoleon yet adorned all this meat-and-potatoes of "interests" with one sprig of theoretical parsley; and that was "national" or "popular sovereignty," of which the State, of course, was the supreme avatar and guarantor. "[Sovereignty of the people]," he wrote Talleyrand on September 19, 1797, "is the only thing I can see that we have truly defined in the last fifty years." "Defined" is doubtless the wrong choice of words, for "national" and "popular" were among the most flexible and vague words in an already elastic lexicon of French revolutionary discourse. Nonetheless, the formality of democracy, with its sacred talisman of "sovereignty of the people," is what "republic" had come to mean to Bonaparte. This was what the Revolution had ushered in, and there was no turning back from it, however great the acknowledged gap that now yawned between ideal and reality in the turbulent practice of democracy.

All the rest, however—the doctrine of the separation of powers, an independent judiciary, an active legislature, responsible ministries, universal suffrage, a bill of individual rights, a multiple executive, etc.—had become, to Bonaparte's way of thinking, the hobbyhorses of factions, the stuff of *la politique* (politics). Safeguarding the generic republic, in short, was not the same thing as defending the First Republic.[5]

His apprenticeship in Italy and in Egypt thus saw Napoleon confirmed in his belief in a hierarchy of the two "*politiques*": *le* and *la*. From "the political" flowed daily "politics," but the former was ideally the parent of the latter. We might almost say that for Napoleon, "politics" was "the political's" fictional character in a historical saga of which power and the State were to be co-authors. At least it was supposed to be thus. In reality, the problem arose that "politics" kept turning out to be a creation with a life of its own—one that bucked at playing a character to the State's "author," and that indeed turned on the State. "It is politics which leads to catastrophe without there being a real crime," Napoleon once noted, and the confirmation of his judgment came from his experience in Italy, where the Cisalpine *giacobini* had been so distracted by doctrines and factions that they failed to unite effectively behind their French Solon's magisterial views about State- and community-building. Bonaparte had anticipated resistance or subversion from the royalists and the pro-Austrians, but he had been blindsided by his own patriots' infatuation with politics and ideology. They turned out, he felt, to be rigid doctrinaires who laid claim to the wrong heritage of the French Revolution—its indomitable factionalism underlying the cant about patriotism, its taste for vengeance lurking within the calls for social peace, its rigid but constantly shifting and hypocritical devotion to "ideology" and "metaphysics," rather than to the critical (and ironical) sifting of ideas.

This derogation of "politics" was something that Bonaparte shared with most of his countrymen, the great majority of whom, if they did not despise the free play of parties that characterized British parliamentary life, strenuously believed that it was inapplicable to France. The "Anglo-Saxon" approach to power management via decentralized government and active parties of the loyal opposition was considered by Frenchmen of both the *ancien régime* and the Revolution to be an invitation to social dissolution in a free-for-all of market forces and factional or corporatist interest. The British way diffused "the political" into "the social" and "the economic," and it deified partisan politics. Bonaparte was anything but alone among his countrymen in the belief that only a very strong State could guard French society against the centripetal forces of self-interest, religion, doctrine, and party. Only it—buttressed by a formal rationale compiled in a written constitution (Britain had only a customary one)—could sternly serve and preserve the "General Will." In short, be it revolutionary, monarchical, or moderate, the French State must stride resolutely forward in its mission to centralize and administer the nation—and reduce and contain "politics."

Italy and Egypt had taught Bonaparte that he preferred the political life to the military, even if he preferred war to "politics." He returned to France after nearly three years of absence believing that "politics" was only one, *and not the best,* means of serving "the political"—that is, of building State and community. This said, he had brilliantly mastered the techniques, shady or sunny, of the politics of his era—including demagogy, manipulation (his threats to the Directory to resign in order to get his way), dissimulation (e.g., his notoriously padded reports from the front), and the deployment of propaganda. Some indeed would say that the Institute of Egypt was pure public relations, though others call it a serious enterprise undertaken for sincere reasons. Perhaps the great French historian Jules Michelet was right that the best sham is the sincere one.[6]

Passing time led Napoleon to become more aware of what he imagined to be the limitations of "politics." In his visits to France in 1796–98, for example, he had become convinced it was a grave mistake to indulge revolutionary factions in their frontal attack on religion, in the form of "dechristianization" or militant anticlericalism. He was equally unimpressed with the doctrinaire

alternatives to religion that took life as State-fostered patriotic cults, the latest of which, theophilanthropy, struck him as ridiculous. Bonaparte now
agreed with his former mentor, Robespierre, that the people needed religion,
but he believed that the dictator had been wrong to imagine that he or any
other politician could cobble together a meaningful religion out of secular
and natural elements.

So if "politics" as a means of effecting "the political" (the organization of
power) thus had its limits, *what else counted*? Two things: leadership and
action. Italy and Egypt gave Bonaparte a redoubled, experience-tempered
sense of the centrality of the leader—his person and personality, his qualities,
style, temperament, and, most of all, his deeds: the fact of action.

I was going to write the "simple fact of action," but action, if it is efficacious, is not often simple, it only may appear so. Deciding what to do and
when, precisely, to do it requires intelligence. Clausewitz notes that no great
military commander was intellectually less than brilliant. The French of this
(or any) period were not short on smart statesmen and generals (Talleyrand,
Fouché, Constant, and Chaptal were not slackers), yet Bonaparte stood out
for the impression he made on people for his brains. This was no small element in his imposition on his contemporaries. The naturalist Geoffroy de
Saint-Hilaire, who went to Egypt with the French expedition, commented on
the General's extraordinary ability to focus on several things at once. He
recalled a scene, the day before the departure for France, when Napoleon
simultaneously heard out an aide apprising him of provisions packed for the
journey and an ordnance officer describing a problem; took leave of his
clingy mistress (resentful at not being taken along); and debated with Gaspard
Monge, France's leading mathematical physicist, over whether or not Isaac
Newton had already "answered everything." No, Bonaparte maintained,
Newton had not: there remained this big matter of small particles moving at
high speeds over small distances—what we today call particle physics, and
which indeed did have to wait for its latter-day Newtons. Time and again,
"the four-thought Caesar,"[7] as Saint-Hilaire called him on this occasion, was
experienced as remarkable, even intimidating for his intelligence, though one
suspects that contemporaries' reactions were also a function of Bonaparte's
imperiousness, self-confidence, and perhaps above all, youth.

In Italy and Egypt, he sharpened several of the most startling (political,
in the larger sense) traits of his "greatness," as the classical world, and therefore the eighteenth century, understood greatness—qualities of leadership
that are rare because they are so difficult of enduring acquisition: for example, the capacities for isolation, apartness, and self-mastery. They figure in
Aristotle's portrait of the "great-souled" man who is indifferent to opinion.

If Bonaparte did not possess these qualities quite to Caesar's degree, he had them enough to hear himself compared to Caesar.[8] (He confided to Pierre-Louis Roederer, however: "I am often in a most painful agitation, which does not prevent me from appearing very serene to the people I'm with. I just beam for them, like an expectant mother. . . .")

The foregoing qualities rarely bloom alone; they bear other fruit, some more, some less, savory or salubrious. Despite his reserve and his avoidance of close identification with individuals or groups, Bonaparte had an easy way that surprised people who harbored conventional notions of how "greatness" acted. With his family, friends, and troops and officers, Napoleon was usually affectionate, loyal, and generous, even munificent with gifts, as he was tolerant of their peccadillos and failings. In public, he dressed and held himself with "republican" modesty, listening often, speaking occasionally, with cogency and simplicity. His style, in short, clashed with the Directory era's taste for ostentation, affectation, and glib fluency. Bonaparte had a mongoose eye for undulating pretentiousness or snobbery, and a short fuse for the ill-advised who displayed them, though in such cases, if he reacted, he did not nurse grudges. Corsican vindictiveness and a taste for feuds were not his way.[9]

But if Bonaparte, like Caesar, was not particularly vain, he was (also like Caesar) proud—and pride, too, in a leader can become a political quality in the larger sense. The Greeks and the Romans expected that "great-souled men" would sin the sin of hubris. Bonaparte, like Alexander, felt little or no need to acknowledge dependence on people around him or even on the community. He loved France, to be sure, but he avowed, "France needs me more than I need her." He rarely, until the end of his life, pondered his vulnerability to the ubiquitous tremors that stir the human condition: loss, bad fortune, guilt, fragility of meaning, mortality. He felt slight sense of gratitude, and gave us little evidence that he felt he lived in debt to anyone or anything except possibly the Revolution.

What was crystallizing in Bonaparte while he was abroad was the conviction that he was always his own best judge, that other people's opinions of him were incomplete at best and more often mean-spirited. His disinclination to admit mistakes was hardening into a refusal to share credit. His inward detachment, which permitted him to be so acutely sensitive to his own designs and the claims on his own heart, required a corresponding insensitivity to the thoughts and claims of others. Like the Macedonian who had taken Egypt before him, Bonaparte brooked less and less opposition; he always "knew better," "knew" that his motives were purer, "knew" that his grasp of the essential was surer than that of any rival or would-be rival.

Finally, nothing Bonaparte saw in Italy or Egypt altered his view that he had already held in 1791, that if the strong may well be good, the weak are nearly inevitably wicked. This, too, was an attitude with profound political implications when held by a statesman. Napoleon's unblinking look at events and people brought him more and more to the opinion that the weak were guileful, treacherous, and "untransparent," that they burdened themselves and others with an ostentatious baggage of principles and ideals—"freedom," "love of humanity," etc.—which they did not really believe in, but used to their own advantage. To Bonaparte, "the game of politics," if it was to be played well, could not be played pettily: the charlatanism had to be great, but in a sense honest—played with a sense of irony, no doubt, but not with false idealism hiding small ambition and self-interest.

Theoretically, of course, nothing distinguishes Bonaparte's view from similar ones held by dictators of any age, all of whom knew (know) how to "lie big." The differences among them—and they are sharp—may in fact not lie in any inner moral sense or conscience—an atrophied organ in "heroes," of any era, it would seem—but rather in what is permitted them by their contemporaries. Which forms and actions of "great ambition" do the times condone? Which do they discourage? If a society wishes to avert dictatorship, it cannot hope to do so by strangling all potential dictators in their crib; it can only try to create a milieu wherein dictatorship (and the taste for conquest and glory) will not flourish and be widely embraced. The France that had exited the Revolution was not such a place, even if it was also not a place where a despot could set himself entirely outside the law, openly spurning mediating institutions, and governing entirely by exception. Good political order was seen by the turn-of-the-century French to require norms (laws) as well as respect for norms, even if they also acknowledged that emergencies arose. When the latter happened, the sovereign leader must be ready to determine "the exception" and make the "decision," but only in order better to defend the rule of government by norms and institutions.[10] As J. Christopher Herold writes with matchless grace and wisdom: "It may be a costly process for humanity to produce Napoleons, but if humanity should ever cease to produce them it would be a sign that its energies are exhausted. In order to turn its Napoleons to better enterprises than conquest and war, humanity first would have to turn away from war. To prove Napoleon wrong humanity must change."[11]

Heroic temperament (and temper), great intelligence and knowledge, remarkable qualities of personality, and even Nietzschean reservoirs of will, energy, and ambition amounted to a base or plinth, however. They were fulfilled and redeemed only in the act. Great political leadership, as the eighteenth century understood it—and had seen it in a Danton, a Robespierre, or a Frederick the Great, or had mythified about it in classical heroes like Alexander and Caesar—must issue in something strong and dramatic that dazzled the thousands or the millions, and perceptibly changed their lives. Napoleon's contemporaries, who had lived through what was widely considered to be the disgusting and boring era of the late Directory, longed for the sort of bold and distinguished action that they imagined had characterized an earlier time. From a warrior, dazzling deeds were de rigueur.

And the prize reserved for the achiever of great deeds of battle was the greatest prize of all, though it is one that moderns have placed in the museum of human ideas: glory. *La gloire* was as much a Roman notion as—and no less a political one than—the *res publica*. *Gloire* had animated the French monarchy and had flourished in the Revolution; and it remained nearly as strongly tied as ever to military conquest. As Albert Sorel writes, to Napoleon's contemporaries, "It appeared as natural that the Revolution should . . . invade, conquer, pillage, dismember nations and reconstitute states and peoples as it seemed natural to Louis XIV to dispute, split up, and seize the heritage of kings."[12] From this, far more than from drafting legislation or working the corridors, issued glory, and to overlook or downplay glory is to reduce Bonaparte to being just one more crafty Machiavellian, and thus to miss why his contemporaries were, even before the coup d'Etat of November 9, 1799, placing him above everyone else.

Few grasped as well as this general did the role of glory in organizing power—both domestically ("we have drowned the Revolution's earlier shame [the Terror] in floods of glory") and abroad: When Lombardy's provisional government beseeched Bonaparte for laws to ensure their republic-to-be against counterrevolution, he replied, "But don't you find guarantees of your independence in the daily victories of the Army of Italy? Each victory is another line of your constitutional charter. Deeds take the place of a declaration that by itself would be childish."[13] At the end of his life, Bonaparte got off a line—the valediction of his will, hence his last public utterance—which reads thus: "The love of glory is like the bridge that Satan built across Chaos to pass from Hell to Paradise: glory links the past with the future across a bottomless abyss. Nothing to my son, except my name!" *Voilà le politique*, Napoleonic style.

But in autumn 1799, Bonaparte had not yet reached either Paradise or Hell, he was only contemplating the Republic of France from the quarter deck of the frigate *La Muiron*,[14] as it hove into view in the port of Fréjus, on the morning of October 9. The feeling he shared with virtually all his countrymen was that the "strong men" of 1789–94 were long gone, and in many cases much missed, and more needed. It would not take long to see how his victories were playing in France—among which social strata—and how that might permit him to act. He would discover what his combination of ideas, qualities, and glory could do with the republican form—how capacious it could become in the hands of the great-souled man.

"THE NATIONAL MESS":
THE STATE OF FRANCE, 1798–1799

As between those who want to take power and those who are afraid to lose it because they will be hanged, the latter always have more to lose.
                                                                —Mme Germaine de Staël

While Bonaparte was in Egypt, events on the Continent had taken a sorry turn for the French and its sister republics. If anything should convince us that Bonaparte and Italy would have done better by each other had the General remained in Milan for another year, it was what transpired in the peninsula following his departure. The Treaty of Campo-Formio failed after barely seventeen months. The Austrians could not adjust to their losses in Italy nor tolerate continuing French machinations there; the Republic surfeited its greed so much more effectively than the Austrians did theirs. Ultimately neither Habsburg nor Hanover could swallow the swollen France of "the natural frontiers." And yet, typically, it was the Directory, in its Diogenes-like search for a domestic fix via foreign aggrandizement, that resumed hostilities. They could not keep their hands off the pope, whom they despoiled and arrested; they unleashed the *giacobini* in all directions, setting up republics in Rome and Naples that could not survive; and they drained all the pro-French allies of funds and goodwill.

The War of the Second Coalition first saw fortune smile on the Allies, whose ranks were greatly augmented by a Russian army under a first-class field commander named Alexander Suvorov. The French were beaten in Germany, in March 1799, and obliged to evacuate Switzerland before a superior Austro-Russian army. In Italy, the new and old sister republics fell like ninepins, leaving Masséna besieged in Genoa. The French army sent to restore the situation in Italy was smashed at the battle of Novi (August 15), where its commander, Joubert, breathed his last. At the same time, the news hit Paris that an Anglo-Russian expedition had landed in Holland, a French ally, and the Dutch fleet had gone over to the British. Last but never least, the royalist parties and their peasant supporters in southern and western France, having lowered their heads for a year, were encouraged by Allied victories and backed by British support to rise in insurrection. A hardscrabble army of some 10,000 men rallied to the Bourbon fleur-de-lis.

In short, for the French, a "national mess." For the first time since 1793, the Republic faced imminent invasion and subversion by the counterrevolution. Much of the foregoing was known to Napoleon in Egypt, thanks to a clever British naval commander (Sir William Sydney Smith) who had European newspapers passed to his adversary, doubtless in the hope it would persuade him to leave for France. The Republic's domestic state, in most accounts, was hardly less parlous, although it is unlikely Bonaparte got much detailed information about this until he landed. Harmoniously functioning liberal democracy does not usually arise from war, religious and social schism, and lethal political clashes between the legislative and executive constituents of the government. The illegal *pis-aller* that had been the Fructidor coup of 1797 only kept the Directory alive; it did not keep it well or wise. Each subsequent year's legislative elections delivered "unacceptable" results, whether too many "moderates" or too many "anarchists," which in turn resulted in further official illegal measures to "right" the situation. The mortal duels between counterrevolution and revolution were complicated by conflict among the revolutionaries—between the strivers to consolidate and the *zelanti* to go further.

Thus the Directory staggered on; for all of its corruption and infighting, it yet carried the burden of war and domestic conflict without succumbing for four years,[15] making it the longest-lived regime of the tumultuous revolutionary decade. It preserved a republic grown territorially larger than the kingdom of France at any time since Charlemagne, and it began some domestic reforms, notably in finance. What it could not do was dull the razor-sharp shards of French society shredding the common fabric. (In fairness to it, no French regime succeeded at that for the next century.) The Directory's political blows undercut itself, yet it had to deal them.[16]

For the Directory to have succeeded in riding the tiger, the government would have had to be seen as other than hypocritical, nest-feathering parvenus and factional politicians. These lawyers decked out in ostentatious, military-style uniforms designed by David needed to sport more than ostrich plumes; they needed panache. The one principle they stubbornly clung to—an orthodox, if socially conservative, republicanism[17]—inclined them in times of crisis to a policy of no-enemies-to-the-left. This entailed policies that elicited widespread ridicule and fury (e.g., travelers could be refused entry to

Paris for not wearing a tricolor cockade; or a production of a play about the Roman general Hadrian was not permitted to have the central character named emperor, as the historically accurate script required it).

What the Directory badly needed was to break with this factionalism and make a great act of trust in its own people, entailing sacrifice of some of its own policies and style, while showing magnanimity to its sworn enemies. And then it needed to sit tight. But no director had this degree of courage or imagination, moral reputation, political authority, or corporate unity with his colleagues to bring it off. None appears to have been even capable of such a plan, except perhaps Carnot who had been purged as a reactionary in Fructidor. The Republic and the Revolution still inspired myths and allegiance, but the directors were not widely seen as their avatars, rather as frightened, vengeful, arbitrary, intolerant, and weak men. The Revolution had had bloodier moments, but few or none where public spirit and morale were lower. Lafayette, from his exile abroad, spoke of the situation in France as "the national mess" (*le margouillis national*).

And then, as if to remind people that history hangs by a thread, fortune took another turn. During *La Muiron*'s six-week passage to France, when its illustrious passenger was without news, the royalist insurrection in the Midi was bested, Suvorov was beaten in Switzerland, and the Anglo-Russian forces were extruded from Holland. Was a "savior" needed, after all?

THE RETURN OF THE PRODIGY

> *Caesar's experiences . . . may have inclined him to consider the existing order provisional and its institutions superficial, and to judge its leading figures not according to their rank, but according to their nature—wearing institutional robes that on the one hand fitted them too tightly, but on the other, had become too capacious. He could not appreciate the huge burdens imposed on them. He can have had no sympathy with them. His standards required them to be measured not by the yardstick of the possible, but by that of the necessary.*
>
> —Christian Meier[18]

Bonaparte had left home famous; he returned more famous. Yet during his absence, he had slowly ceased to inform people's thoughts and calculations; indeed his royalist enemies put out that he was dead. It is striking, therefore, and must have been gratifying, to see how instantly his fame reignited. Even before he set foot on the Continent, he had become the cynosure of conversation around France that he had been in 1796–97. His victorious progress through the Midi in early October 1799 was only a shade below the overwhelming triumph of his return from Italy. Spirited crowds gathered in the towns; Lyon, the Republic's second city, illuminated her houses and improvised a play in his honor, *The Return of the Hero*. His arrival in Paris on October 16 was followed within a day by the news of Bonaparte's "glorious victory" of Aboukir.[19] Banquets were given, including a huge one by the government at which—and this is a comment on the era's skullduggery—the guest of honor ate only the eggs and pears that Berthier brought in his pockets, because he was concerned about being poisoned. Lucien Bonaparte, a thriving politician, was named president of the Council of the Five Hundred—a gesture of esteem for his brother, which the twenty-four-year-old took as an overdue acknowledgment of his own genius.

Bonaparte thus returned triumphant, and any charge of desertion of his army was an issue raised late in the day by the handful of his political adversaries. His return was that of a Scipio or a Fabius, not Augustus or Hadrian—that is, he was feted as a conquering *republican* soldier, not an imperial potentate or crypto-monarchist. If he was no longer known as the Jacobin general, he was still girded about by a strong republican carapace. Criticisms and doubts about his intentions and designs smoldered on both of the political extremes, but far more among royalists than among the neo-Jacobins. The latter, undergoing a small revival, were ambivalent in their feelings about Bonaparte. By and large, they did not seek to impugn his reputation as a republican officer, not least because his fame peaked among one of their best constituencies. The workers of the faubourgs "sang the triumphs of our armies and the return of our father, our savior, Buonaparte."[20]

The foregoing merits clear statement because there is an irresistible tendency to portray Bonaparte as slinking home in disgrace, frantic to be selected as the general-in-charge of a coup d'Etat in the offing, in order to make himself dictator. This misconceives his situation on arrival, when his star outshone that of any other soldier in Europe, and it probably misconstrues his initial intentions. Bonaparte departed Egypt when he did because the news from home painted a dire picture, and he believed rightly that the Directory had desperate need of him. He hardly admired that body, nor was he prepared to lash himself to their mast. Napoleon was critical of "these lawyers"; he had once asked a close associate, Miot de Melito: "Do you imagine, that it is for the grandeur of . . . a Barras that I have triumphed in Italy?" Still, confidences reported decades later by a hostile politician must be weighed against the *fact* of Bonaparte's support on his return from Egypt for the regime that had stood by him since 1795.

Paul Barras hoped to use Bonaparte to help him make some kind of coup of his own, both men having once agreed that Fructidor had not gone far enough in "consolidating" government (read: in putting Paul Barras more firmly in charge). To this end, Barras was hoping to make Bonaparte a director, even if doing so entailed amending a constitution that required directors to be forty or more years of age. Barras hoped General Vendémiaire would feel grateful for what Bonaparte owed him from the past, but he was also aware that much had changed.[21]

Paris politics at the moment of Bonaparte's reinsertion made tenth-century Byzantium look simple and innocent. Cliques of every coloring–centered in newspapers, clubs, foreign embassies, and secret organizations, not to mention, in most organs of government–muscled one another for advantage. Atop this writhing heap, the Directory clung with uncertain purchase, and never more so than during the early defeats of the War of the Second Coalition. Then, it had kept power at the price of radical measures that starkly recalled the Great Terror of the Year II: renewed measures against priests; laws permitting the holding of members (hostages) of émigré or noble families in custody; measures forcing the wealthy to lend money to the State; a mass military conscription reminiscent of the hugely unpopular *levée en masse*; and, withal, measures that reduced freedom of the press and association. None of this surprised Bonaparte, who was familiar with the tradition that saw French governments fall back on "the Jacobin legacy" when foreign crisis threatened. (He would do the same.) It was just that he no longer believed such policies worked.

Not the least fascinating facet of French factionalism in the latter portion of the revolutionary decade was the revival of Jacobinism after the fall of Robespierre and his Committee of Public Safety. The neo-Jacobins, as the heirs were known, flourished after 1795, despite periodic persecution by the regime, and in June 1799, thanks to the renewed war, they underwent a "hundred days" of influence and power that vaguely recalled the Year II.[22] All of this Napoleon had missed, including, most recently, the virulent anti-radical backlash by the Directory, now that the foreign foe was temporarily at bay.

It would be wrong to see neo-Jacobinism as the extremist counterpart to royalism. Not only was this new left not formally illegal, as royalism was, but it was far from universally loathed among French revolutionary political and intellectual elites. Neo-Jacobinism was widely felt as the conscience and heard as the true voice of the Revolution, and even its staunch adversaries in government dared not damn it in principle, for neo-Jacobinism's proponents (or their predecessors) had "made" the Republic and "saved" the Revolution in the Year II–and in every crisis since then, where royalism reared its head, the government had mobilized the left. Many directors and ministers were men visited by the ghosts of Jacobinism past and neo-Jacobinism present. Opposing them, thus, was not like taking on the royalists; it was like fighting a brother. When the government moved against the left, it hid behind far-fetched excuses such as that the radicals' "extreme patriotism" was somehow or other "a royalist front"—or at least a pretext for a royalist backlash. Here was a testimony to the directors' bad conscience.

This said, the neo-Jacobin movement had sprouted some genuinely disturbing aspects in the eyes of certain social groups and their political representatives. Neo-Jacobinism's new social revolutionary program appealed to working- and lower-middle-class urban strata and amounted to a dialectical advance beyond the politics and ideology of 1789. Drawing on the semi-communist or socialist thought of such men as Gracchus Babeuf, the neo-Jacobin program called for "economic equality" to "round out" civil equality. (Babeuf's faction called itself the Movement of Equals.) This horrified the revolutionary fat cats who supported the Directory. At bottom, the France of this era was a sort of oligarchy characterized and governed by what we might call "revolutionary *arrivisme.*" This new middle class had acquired nationalized lands and made great profits, which it soaked from army supply and in speculation in equities or in monetary trading. Their fortunes indebted them to the Revolution, yet made them desperate to halt it, lest the churning maelstrom engulf what they had made. In short, the *arriviste* ex-Jacobins of government and their wealthy bourgeois supporters were increasingly developing an ideological conflict with the aspiring neo-Jacobins of the clubs. The trench between them had not yet become a chasm of full-blown (proletarian versus bourgeois) class conflict—and indeed the neo-Jacobins were politic enough to know to play down their Babeuvist socialism—yet it was more than a quarrel over the purely political question of "who's on first?" in the government.

In this clash with revived (or neo-)Jacobinism, the Directory had its point man in Emmanuel Sieyès, the familiar and respected figure on the political stage whom Bonaparte had met in late 1796/early 1797, before going to Egypt. A key to Sieyès's principles and his fastidiousness is that when he was first elected to the Directory, he declined the post because he did not approve of the constitution of the Year III, even though he had had considerable influence in drafting it. If he now accepted a place, a few months before Bonaparte's return from Egypt, it was because he intended to change things—to set into place a "conservative system,"[23] to use his phrase. But the constitution required a nine-year process for amendment, and Sieyès was in a hurry. His backers included most of the brightest lights in the cultural firmament—for example, the writer Germaine de Staël and her companion, Benjamin Constant, the philosopher. They also included the so-called Ideologues, the leading political faction at the Institut National—that gentlemen's club of France's best minds, which had dispatched a number of savants to Egypt. All of them shared the eighteenth-century conviction that society's problems were amenable to improvement by a better *document*: in the event, a better and more prevenient constitution, which, in small print, meant the creation of a smaller and stronger executive.

Director Sieyès had struck at the left in another of those small, date-designated coups (this one called Prairial, for June 1799) that virtually defined this regime in the public's eyes. Out went the team of neo-Jacobin directors and ministers who had mainly taken office during the war crisis; in came moderates whom Sieyès felt he could count on to change things, hence we shall call them "revisionists," but because they were anti-radical, we may also call them "moderates."

One notable Jacobin old-timer, however, actually entered the government due to sheer talent, despite his political past and his beliefs. Joseph Fouché (1759–1820), the new minister of police, is a man worth pausing over because he would become one of Bonaparte's longest serving and most skilled associates. Fouché duplicated a few of his patron's qualities, while yet remaining a simulacrum of him. An ex-cleric,[24] like Sieyès and Talleyrand, Fouché did a good deal more than live through the Terror; he served the Convention as one of its most efficient henchmen, pressing the attack on counterrevolution in numerous cities throughout provincial France, where his name was written in the blood of thousands of executed (sometimes massacred) in 1793–94. He then turned against "the tyrant, Maximilien I" (Robespierre), and starred in the plot to overthrow him. That accomplished, Fouché notoriously did *not* convert to Thermidorian moderation but remained an old-time Jacobin. He even associated with Babeuf and the "Equals," avoiding prison or exile only by the quality of his secret police work for Barras. Whenever the Directory faced a royalist threat (often), there was Fouché to help save the day. He did not have Napoleon's education or culture, but he had something like his intellectual candle power—Balzac called him a "singular genius," "the best head I know." Unlike many politicians in this era, Fouché was uncorrupt, led a quiet family life, and had many friends to whom he was loyal and generous.

What is said to stand out is Fouché's expediency. With Talleyrand, he is commonly regarded as one of the great cynics of French history. Yet unlike the former Bishop of Autun, it is not clear that "cynic" is the best word for the ex-Oratorian, though if "wary," "shrewd," and "proactive" are taken to

be synonymous with "cynical," then he was that. Fouché knew how to protect his flanks and to navigate the swirling and changing tides of power, but
he was a man who clung to core beliefs, and, as minister, he laced his competence with charity and a certain acceptance of human nature. He proved
to be "the last recourse against violent antijacobinism, the defender of the
Revolution," in Michel Vovelle's words,[25] and if he turned against the Directory it was because he found it "weak, therefore oppressive." The oft-cited last
line of Fouché's memoirs, "I wanted to win for the Revolution," is not a fan-
ciful figment of his imagination *if* one keeps in mind that he, like Bonaparte,
understood "winning" to include ending the forward pitch of the Revolution
for its own sake. Like his future boss, he believed that consolidation would
require a compromise with the elites of the old regime, which would not
become harmonious reconciliation anytime soon.

Prairial made Sieyès more powerful than any figure since Robespierre, but
that is *not* to say he had the force to be able to rebuild the regime to his
heart's desire. He needed "a sword," although not one likely to be drawn, just
to be on hand in case. The neo-Jacobins, for their part, entrenched in the legislative councils, the army, and in their high-profile clubs around France,
dreamed of a government closer to the image of 1793. But the far left was in
something of a bind. With Sieyès and the moderates moving against the
Directory regime, the neo-Jacobins now let themselves get caught in a tactical
legalist defense of a constitution that was not theirs, which many among
them would also have liked to overthrow. They fought hard against Sieyès et
al., bringing charges against the moderates and vigorously attacking them in
their newspapers. In July they even got Talleyrand kicked out as foreign minister. Both sides had their generals—the Sieyésians looked to Moreau and Joubert; the neo-Jacobins, to Jourdan and Bernadotte. Bonaparte was in Egypt,
but he could have been sought by either side. Most of these officers played
both sides of the fence. Joubert, for instance, though an outspoken army
Jacobin, yet plotted with Sieyès to mount a coup, and, withal, had contacts
with the royalists. It is fair to surmise that virtually any one of the leading generals would have fallen in with a neo-Jacobin or a Sieyès coup—and some of
them, even with a royalist—if it were well brought off.

Once *La Muiron* landed with its distinguished passenger, however, this
poker game among the military top brass ended, and all bets were off. The
sudden return of "le grand absent" precipitated grumbles and whispers
among the epaulettes and the ostrich plumes, but as of Bonaparte's triumphant return to Paris, no one was prepared to stand up to him. Joubert,
even had he not been killed in action in Italy, would not have survived the
disaster of his defeat at Novi with his reputation intact. And even if he had,

would he have been willing to go head-to-head with the commander (Bonaparte) to whom he owed his general's stars? Augereau might have postured and threatened, but it is doubtful that he, either, would have marched against his former boss, let alone done so victoriously. The proud Bernadotte would have been the most willing to oppose Bonaparte, but breathing over his shoulder was his wife, Désirée Clary, and his brother-in-law Joseph Bonaparte, reminding him that this was also a family affair. Finally, there was Moreau, the only general with a remotely (but still not) equal military reputation to Bonaparte's. Moreau, however, understood where things stood—no one could rival the "conqueror of Italy and Egypt"—and in any case, he generally avoided active politics. Sieyès, in fact, had been buttonholing Moreau to join them when news of Bonaparte's return arrived at his office. Moreau turned to Sieyes and remarked, "There's your man."

In sum, although it is fashionable to argue that the "political culture" of the French Revolution looked askance at "cults of personality," the inescapable fact is fin-de-siècle France greeted Napoleon Bonaparte with open arms, seeing in him both the arbiter of internal conflict and the deliverer from military defeat—above all, the bringer of glory. If anyone could smash the Coalition, it was said, it was the Corsican. "Ah, Monsieur Pitt," wrote one newspaper, "what terrible news for you coming at the same time as the Anglo-Russian defeat in Holland! You'd have been better off losing three more battles than having Napoleon Bonaparte back."[26]

Bonaparte took in the new situation. As the foreign crisis was no longer catastrophic, the Directory was disconcerted by his return. In their reflections, the thought must have recurred: "Will he blame us for what has happened?" For Bonaparte, the regime had not only continued to be politically inept, it had lost "his" Cisalpine Republic. The decision to join the action against the directors was thus nothing he can long have paused over. The conviction that he, Bonaparte, was by far the best person to take the Republic in hand came deeply and naturally to him—the more persuasively, as he was being begged by both the political left and the right to do just that.

But the issue of act with whom? was another matter, and remained open for a good week or ten days after his return. Napoleon's exact political inclinations in these pre-Brumaire days are a subject of disagreement. Some have him pondering whether to side with the neo-Jacobins, who represented, after all, his past and were strong in the army. Then, too, some of their leaders courted Bonaparte. Other experts note that the General's current "anti-Jacobinism sat well with Sieyès."[27] It is best if we keep in mind that the pending action was less an ideologically driven matter than a catfight over power among republican factions. And Emmanuel Sieyès was not sitting in the catbird seat—that is, was *not* in a position to select among candidates to be his sword. Bonaparte had imposed himself on one and all simply by returning, and the exact details of the General's latest thoughts about the ever-changing French political game mattered less to the contenders than hitching their bandwagon to Napoleon's matchless *gloire*.

For Bonaparte, it came down to a decision between two men more than among political ideas. There was his old patron and marital advisor, Barras, a politician thoroughly corrupt and debased in the public's eyes (his latest exploit: trying to extort millions out of the royalists in exchange for helping them), yet undeniably enjoying entrée with Bonaparte. And there was Sieyès, whom Napoleon found tedious, stiff-necked, and self-important, notwithstanding that Joseph and Lucien had been courting him in their brother's absence (and in his name). It is a reflection on his preference for old loyalties that Bonaparte invested time and effort into feeling out Barras, whom, at bottom, he probably would have preferred to work with. But Barras had no ready plan and no steady allies, while Sieyès did. Too, Sieyès understood something Barras missed: "Bonaparte is the most civilian [of the generals]." Sieyès made it clearer than Barras did that he appreciated Bonaparte's *political* qualities, not just his military genius, and that he would admit him to a political, not just a military, future in the new regime.

Nevertheless, Bonaparte's and Sieyès's vanity had attained such a tensile strength that neither man would make the first move toward the other; only the tireless intervention of seconds eventually made this "love match." Then, too, Sieyès suspected from the outset that Bonaparte's glory, savvy, and ambition would know no limit. "J'ai vaincu" (I vanquished) beats "J'ai vécu" (I survived) any day, as the theorist well knew.[28] At his first audience with the Sieyès Directory, Napoleon dramatically put his hand to his sword hilt and swore "never to draw my sword except in defense of the Republic and its government." The words would turn out to be duplicitous, but then duplicity was the word of the day. The very men pressing Napoleon to act included directors, ministers, and legislators—that is, men who *were* "the government." Behind them stood the elite of the nation, eager to make a change, though some would soon be having second thoughts. As for "in defense of the Republic," *all* sides in the present scramble justified themselves as acting in defense of "Republic"; it was a nuanced word in the eighteenth-century France, loaded with possibilities.

The project almost didn't happen. On October 30, riding at his brother Joseph's estate, Mortefontaine, Napoleon was thrown fifteen feet from his horse. He lay unconscious, as his horrified relatives waited tensely. After a few hours, he came to. Had he died, "he would have gone down in history as the republican soldier, better even than Hoche, for he had already shown more genius than his emulator in glory."[29]

BRUMAIRE: AN ACTOR'S NIGHTMARE

The modernity of Bonaparte's coup d'Etat stems from the fact that 18-Brumaire is not a simple seizing of power by violence, but a new way of conquering power by relying on an apparent display of parliamentary legality.

—Curzio Malaparte[30]

Nearly a century later, another French political general by the name of Georges Boulanger, a soldier regarded as Napoleonic by many of his supporters and opponents alike, will be pressed by one of his leading backers to stage a coup against the Third Republic, rather than plod tediously on, racking up expensive electoral victories, as he has been doing. The backer points out that Boulanger obviously has France behind him and must therefore do what the country "needs." Boulanger replies with more wisdom than he usually musters: "To make a coup," he says, "one needs to know in advance that he has nine chances out of ten, and even then he hesitates." Might he be thinking of Bonaparte at Brumaire? Perhaps.

Forms were vital, in Bonaparte's time, as in Boulanger's. The French political class did not see their regime as a banana republic, at the mercy of every military cabal in sight. The goal of the drama set to open to the public on 18 Brumaire (Saturday, November 9) was thus the political equivalent of abiding by the classical dramatic unities: in the event, staying within the grounds of legal forms and postures, while convincing the audience that one's enemies were breaking (or about to break) the rules—i.e., that they were outlaws, to use the label of highest horror in the revolutionary lexicon. The revisionists' plan called for precipitating a crisis of government via the sudden resignation of a majority, and perhaps all, of the Directory. This would serve as the pretext to persuade (or constrain) a majority in the legislature to vote the regime out of existence and name a commission to draw up a constitution for a new one.

The immediate rationale for this theater was the necessity of preempting a strike by the so-called drinkers of blood and the proponents of a new Terror, the enemies of peace, order, and property—that is, by the very neo-Jacobins whom Bonaparte had been courting and was courted by, right down to the wire.[31] The larger justification for action, however, was compellingly anchored in public perceptions: the ongoing crisis of legitimacy of the

Directory as a regime. Public disillusionment, and it alone, is what allowed skeptical and savvy people to wink at the brandished "anarchist threat" and swallow the craziness that followed, for it was all but universally conceded in France that something *had* to be done. Most of the Council of Elders and a large part of the Council of the Five Hundred were known to side with the actors; many of the two councils' officers figured in the cast. Two of five directors—Sieyès and his shadow, Roger Ducos—were arch-plotters, and it was assumed (correctly) that a third (Barras) could be bought off quickly. Finally, finding prescient bankers to front the necessary funds for the opening performance of this "play" was not hard to do (they'd see about a second or a third funding). A week before the coup, Bonaparte had asked Pierre-Louis Roederer, a collaborator, if he worried that it would be difficult. He replied famously, if without experience of such things, "It would only be difficult *not* to do it, it is three-quarters done."[32]

Saturday dawned with signs posted around town invoking Bonaparte's "glory" and alleging that the Directory had sought to "exile" him in Egypt. "But his glory, his life, and his national abilities are necessary in France, not abroad." Paradoxically, this glory-talk concluded that "Bonaparte must be in Paris to give us peace," though the paradox of expecting peace from a general is dispelled somewhat when we read a proclamation to the soldiery that spoke of "victory and peace restoring the Republic to the place she held in Europe." The French political class of this era never meant just *any* peace.

The first day, which was more like a morning, unfolded with a precision that would be lacking on the morrow. The Council of Elders, meeting in its usual chamber in the Tuileries (but minus a number of its left-wing deputies who had not been advised of the convocation), exercised their right to reconvene the entire government, deemed to be under threat, to the pre-chosen beautiful chateau of Saint-Cloud, a few miles southwest of the capital.[33] This would make for a tighter, more easily controlled theater of operations—a venue where a popular uprising of the people of Paris could not prove immediately decisive. The Elders also named General Bonaparte to the command of the seven thousand troops in the Paris region. Sieyès and Ducos duly handed in their resignations, as did a while later Barras, bowing to an enormous monetary gift and the threat of exposure of his turpitudes. Barras's departure under escort finished off the Directory as a corporate body, despite the fact that the remaining directors, Louis Gohier and Jean Moulin, both Jacobin sympathizers, refused to tender their resignations.

To the troops drawn up before the Tuileries, the General made the only strong speech of the next two days—more forceful because it seemed improvised, though in fact it was inspired by a discourse given recently in a neo-

Jacobin club in Grenoble! During the harangue Barras's personal secretary arrived to deliver a message to Bonaparte. He must have regretted coming, for the General, catching sight of him half hailed him before the soldiery, and there delivered a public harangue: "What have you done with the France I left you so brilliant? I left you peace, I find war! I left you conquests, I find the enemy at our borders! . . . I left you the millions of Italy, I find misery and extortionate laws! . . . Where are the brave hundred thousand soldiers I left, covered with laurels, my companions in glory? . . ." The rest of Saturday, Sieyès could now devote to horseback riding lessons, which he had commenced some days before, in anticipation of the coup. He understood the appeal of a mounted leader.

Bonaparte sensed that Sunday might not go as easily, for the element of surprise would no longer be with the revisionists. He was not wrong, yet it must be said he resisted Sieyès's suggestion that they order the arrest of forty leaders of the opposition, and he countermanded Fouché's directive to close the gates of Paris. "Why all these precautions?" he asked, "when we march with the nation and with its force alone." What he might have done, however, was prepare himself and his supporters in the two councils with more precise instructions about how to handle a strong parliamentary opposition. The drama of Day Two, unlike its predecessor, unfolded before an audience— and what an audience. Sunday saw *le tout Paris* betake itself to Saint-Cloud to watch something happen. Very important people, handsome carriages, picnic baskets, and umbrellas dotted the landscape in and around the chateau. It might have been Longchamps, given the tension that laced the excitement. Not a few of the watchers had their pockets stuffed with money and a rested team of horses standing by.

What Sieyès and Bonaparte had underestimated was how stubbornly the opposition would dig in. The left, taken by surprise and excluded from yesterday's events, had had twenty-four hours to open its eyes and to see what was coming down. They now saw plainly that General Vendémiare had opted to act, but not with them. Decked out in their dramatic red togas, several score of neo-Jacobin representatives in both houses of the legislature overcame their internal divisions, their surprise, and their remorse, and found in extremis traces of the nobility and courage that had characterized so many of the ancient Roman senators whom they imitated in garb, language, and self-importance.

The opposition in the Five Hundred and, to a lesser extent, the Elders pressed to strong effect the "outrage" of the sudden transfer to Saint-Cloud, the inadequacy of the explanation for it, and the rumored strong-arm tactics brought to bear on some directors to get them to resign. The left in the Five

Hundred was the only body in a position to act, and it was intending to do so. The representatives brandished the threat of Caesarism; they gave "liberty or death" speeches and dramatically swore an oath to the very constitution many of them would have snapped like a dry twig if Bonaparte had but sided with them. In the Elders, where neo-Jacobins were a minority, they yet made noise, insisting to know why this crisis could not simply be resolved by appointing three new directors, and everyone going back to work. Both houses bogged down in argument and catcalls.

Bonaparte and Sieyès were only too well aware that time was not their friend and that they had lost a tempo. Their present force was nothing without impetus, while the opposition's strength, all *in potens,* could materialize with the swiftness of a monsoon. Gohier and Moulin were proving to be men of unexpected courage who, removed from house arrest by General Moreau, could become the backbone of an opposition. They could count on several ministers and top generals like Bernadotte and Jourdan who had backed off only grudgingly and temporarily to watch the results of their colleague's move. The left also controlled the Paris municipal administration, while the populace of the faubourgs, though it had not risen since 1795, was always a horrifying possibility. Finally, there was the enigmatic Fouché. For now, the police chief was betting on and abetting Bonaparte, but he was studying events closely, and could change sides in the rustle of a saber.

Ultimately, what the neo-Jacobins in the councils had was a vague and unspoken entrée to the hearts and consciences of innumerable of their colleagues, including many moderates and even perhaps a few Sieyésian revisionists. If, by their example, they could be brave, and by their words, they could present what was happening as an attack on the Republic and the Revolution, then the attack would be repulsed. Having emphasized earlier the importance of Bonaparte's "self-mastery," we are confronted with a choice instance of his failure in it. Christopher Durang's bizarre and effective play *An Actor's Nightmare* tells the story of an actor trapped on stage, not knowing his lines, with his life at stake if he does not say them correctly. It was hardly less for Bonaparte with both councils on 19 Brumaire.

It is one thing for an officer, in the company of his mates, to toss around in scorn clichés about "a bunch of lawyers"; it is another to step into a hall of convoked legislators, all of them older (most far older), wearing Roman togas, and formally imbued with the status of "representatives of the Nation." Momentarily overwhelmed by this utterly new challenge, Bonaparte lost his patience, and then—most unusually—his way. He had not prepared himself, and he found he could not improvise when he was this nervous and angry. He strode into the Elders and "with a soldier's candor" fired off a bad metaphor: "You are," he warned them, "sitting on a volcano." Then, choosing a peevish tone, he complained that he was "tired of being calumniated as a Caesar or a Cromwell," adding that if he had wanted to head "a military government," he would not be spending these past two days cooling his heels, waiting on the legislators.

"And the Constitution?" someone yelled.

Bonaparte smashed back an answer in prosecutorial style, when there was no grandstand to play to, just representatives whose support he needed and had imagined he had. "The Constitution?" he replied in mock disbelief. "You yourselves have annihilated that. On 18 Fructidor, you violated it; on 22 Floréal, you violated it, and you violated it again on 30 Prairial. It has no further respect from anyone." The Elders insisted he be more specific about the "anarchist plot." He replied vaguely, "If liberty perishes, you will be accountable to the universe, posterity, France, and your families." They pressed him to name the "traitors"; he stammered "Barras and Moulin"—tired news, indeed.

Napoleon sensed he was in trouble. He seemed not to know what to say, and in desperation, took a menacing line: "Don't forget," he barked, "I walk with the god of war and the god of victory!" Such words may have worked wonders on the sheiks in Cairo, but they were a scandalous thing to say to the Republic's elder statesmen. (Napoleon later admitted as much.) Murmurs were heard. Compounding his error, Bonaparte instructed the soldiers at the door, "If anyone of these orators, in the pay of the foreigner, dares to declare your general an outlaw, let a lightning bolt smash him instantly to bits." He walked out, his supporters relieved to see him gone.

The ham fist would next come smashing down on the Five Hundred. Lucien was in the chair when his brother strode in—illegally, for he was armed and unbidden; it was the first overt breaking of the law. Napoleon had composed himself after the Elders, but his jaw was set. At the sight of him, cries went up of "Death to the tyrant!," "Down with the dictator!" and "Outlaw!" The representatives crowded around the General, and one of the larger of them grabbed him by the shoulder and yelled in his face, "Was it for this you won [your victories]?" Bonaparte's officers and several grenadiers came to his rescue, blows were exchanged, and one of the soldiers was slightly hurt. The victor of Rivoli, enveloped in grenadiers, was taken from the hall. In the courtyard, he mounted his horse, then fell off it, to the alarm of his men. Whether he swooned or was pretending to be hurt we cannot say, but he certainly appeared undone; nothing like this had happened to him before. Lucien Bonaparte, having failed to dominate "his" council (which was moving a measure that declared his brother an "outlaw"), now joined the soldiers outside. Here, the allegation was running rampant that one of the Five

Hundred had uncloaked a dagger and wounded one of the guards with a blow aimed at the General. The troops, like everyone else, were only too aware of the Brutus-Caesar precedent, though today few historians credit the knife theory with veracity. The fury of the Five Hundred could be heard in the courtyard, and it, along with the General's ashen look and evident disorientation (he called Sieyès "general"), strongly affected his soldiers.

The nadir of the coup attempt had arrived. Sieyès feared the revisionist cause was lost. A grand pause opened, but no Mirabeau emerged from the Five Hundred, as had happened in the Estates-General of 1789, to solder unity among the frightened representatives and stiffen their backbones as the royal troops entered. No Jacobin general stepped forward to lead the troops in the Saint-Cloud courtyard on behalf of "the Nation's representatives" against the tyrant, Bonaparte. Instead, Lucien Bonaparte rose to the occasion. Not known for keeping his head, he yet understood two things very surely: to permit the Five Hundred to pursue their "outlaw" debate would be disaster, and, on the other hand, the soldiers would not act if they thought they were committing atrocities against the Nation's representatives. So Lucien uncorked an impromptu speech for the history books.

"Citizen soldiers," he said, using the great revolutionary apostrophe, "the president of the Council of the Five Hundred declares to you that the large majority of the council is, at this moment, falling under the terror of a few representatives armed with knives . . . and undoubtedly in the pay of England." He warned the grenadiers that if these representatives were not stopped, they would restore the Terror and chop off "some of the most needed heads of the *patrie*." "In the name of this [French] people which, for so many years now, has been the plaything of these miserable children of the Terror," Lucien "confided to you warriors" the task of delivering the majority of the council from the knives of the minority. Then, turning to his brother, he took a sword and pointed it at Napoleon's heart, and said: "I swear to plunge this into my own brother's chest if ever he threatens the liberty of the French!"

And that was essentially it. While the drums beat the charge, Murat led the troops to clear the makeshift hall where the Five Hundred were meeting. The neo-Jacobins did not resist, but fairly fell over one another to escape the bayonets. Resistance, of course, would have been foolhardy—except politically: a carnage of martyrs would have done wonders for their cause and stained the new order beyond cleansing, in just the way many hundreds of dead stained Bonaparte's nephew's coup d'Etat in 1851. Réal, the number two of the police, who had sided more openly with the revisionists than had his boss, Fouché, called Brumaire a "farce," and he was perhaps better advised to use that word than the "tragedy" of Karl Marx's more famous telling.[34]

The neo-Jacobins, having exited stage right and left (or jumped into the audience), the grenadiers returned to their quarters singing the revolutionary hymn "Ça ira." They surely saw themselves as having saved the Republic. The ex-abbé and the General were now able to return to their fastidious play with form. The revisionist members of both councils were permitted to have dinner, then they were reconvened for an all-night session. Here, in the baroque great hall of Saint-Cloud, softly lit by torch and candle, yet a bit eerie for all that, some 100 (out of 750) legislators affixed their simulacrum of an imprimatur to the dissolution of the old regime and the creation of the new. Bonaparte, Sieyès, and Ducos emerged as interim "consuls" (ubiquitous shade of Rome), and at 4 A.M. on 20 Brumaire, they pledged their oath to the Republic. A commission was established to draft a new constitution.

Popular reaction? Virtually none. The workers and artisans of the faubourgs stayed at home. However, the era's equivalent of the stock market leaped 10 percent as an expression of investor confidence in events. "The great orators who dominate political assemblies by the glitter of their words are generally the most mediocre statesmen," Napoleon would say later, no doubt defensively thinking back to Brumaire. He might have added this story: when someone asked classical Greece's greatest orator what was the most important quality in his art, Demosthenes replied: "Action." And the second quality, he was asked. "Action," he replied. The third? "Action."

As important as Brumaire was at the time, it has proven still more fateful in history. For nearly two centuries, it has stood as the great watershed of a classic view of Napoleonic biography. Pierre Larousse—the French Noah Webster—famously set the terms by offering two separate entries for "Bonaparte" and "Napoleon I" in his *Great Universal Dictionary of the Nineteenth Century* (published in 1862), possibly the most influential work of the French nineteenth and early twentieth centuries. Here is his succinct definition of "Bonaparte (Napoleon)":

republican general, born at Ajaccio (Corsica), 15 August 1769, *dead at Saint-Cloud* [emphasis added], the 18th of Brumaire, the Year VIII.

Today, French historians think differently. Thierry Lentz, for example, demonstrates conclusively that Brumaire, as viewed in the French countryside, was construed as a coup engineered against the right wing, on behalf of the Revolution.[35]

Views change.

VIII
Power (II):
Using It (The Consulate)

It is one thing to face the music, it is another thing to dance to it.
—Saki[1]

THE PASTICHE OF THE YEAR VIII

Bonaparte: A constitution has to be short and ...
Roederer: Clear.
Bonaparte (hearing nothing): Right. It has to be short and obscure.[2]

Few people woke up on the morning of the twentieth and concluded they now lived in a *military* State because a general was in power. The appurtenances of repression—from special tribunals and summary justice to election-tampering and rule by decree—had been quite visible since 1797. And then Bonaparte was a general who wore civilian clothing, literally and metaphorically. As he told a colleague, "If I were to die in the next three or four years, I would leave a will warning the nation to beware of military government, saying it should name a civilian head of State."[3]

The provisional consuls were Bonaparte, Sieyès, and Roger Ducos—the last named an ex-director with the sort of radical past and moderate present that typified politicians since Thermidor.[4] Closely allied with Sieyès, Ducos was astounded enough by Bonaparte to have already evolved. When the consuls met the day after the coup, Ducos proposed that the General, "by right [of conquest]," should chair the Consulate. Bonaparte waived off the proposal and called for a rotating daily presidency—an act of modesty that characterized him at this time. A politician's wife described him then as "modest but domineering," adding that he made a happy contrast to vain and weak directors.[5] People appreciated the fact that the Brumaire "revolution" ushered in no severed heads or imprisonments. Sieyès had given orders to take revenge on the Jacobins, but Bonaparte countermanded these deportations; he refused to get the regime off on that only too familiar foot. The consuls also repealed the law of hostages and the forced loans, and issued a new amnesty law inviting back many of the émigrés (Lafayette, among them). As Jean-Paul Bertaud eloquently sums things up, "The bayonets of the Republic would have become the Republic of bayonets without the intelligence of Bonaparte who grasped that if the army guaranteed his power, it could never subjugate French society."[6]

The provisional government's goal was to produce a constitution for a new regime. Pressed mercilessly by Bonaparte, it did so in record time (under seven weeks). In the meantime it had to govern, and this Bonaparte intended that it do, from the center, not the extremes. The ministers the consuls appointed were mainly Bonaparte's choices, as evidenced by the fact many of them kept their portfolios (or received promotions) in the new regime. Bonaparte's appointments tended to disestablish strict political orthodoxy. Fouché, at Police, would seem to disprove the turn away from revolutionary political correctness, except that he was appointed on competence alone, very much despite his past. The Justice Ministry went to Jean-Jacques Cambacérès, an ex-noble and that rarity, a former *Conventionnel** moderate. Charles Maurice de Talleyrand-Périgord, who received Foreign Affairs early in 1800, was the best example of the blue blood of 1789 who long ago learned to tack with events. "I know he doesn't belong to the Revolution except by his misbehavior," Bonaparte told a dubious Cambacérès, ". . . his self-interest [as a deserter of his status and order as a bishop and noble] answer for him."

The provisional Consulate never saw a great set-to between Sieyès and Bonaparte for predominance. Events unfolded as they had in recent weeks, Sieyès pleading nolo contendere. He had little choice; his supporters, from Cambacérès and Boulay to Roederer and Lebrun, had all gone over to the "enemy" without so much as an adieu. Some accounts even have Sieyès counseling submission to his followers, to avoid further conflict: "Gentlemen, you have a master. Bonaparte wants to do everything, knows how to

*A deputy who served in the National Convention, 1792–95.

do everything, and can do everything." Curiously, in the one department where Sieyès, political philosopher, might have been expected to make a contribution—constitution drafting—to the general surprise, he had no draft ready, as he had indicated he had, while the notions he disseminated amounted to a salmagundi of contradictions that stood in contrast to the clear and forceful lines of his sulfurous pamphlet of 1789, *What Is the Third Estate?*[7]

Although the plotters of Brumaire had convinced the Council of Elders that "the constitution can no longer save the Republic," in Bonaparte's words, the Republic yet needed a new constitution. A hastily cobbled-together draft took effect on Christmas Day 1799, though it was not approved by voters until the following April. The constitution of the Year VIII contains no declaration of rights, just a short preamble that concludes with the defining statement of the regime: "Citizens, the Revolution is fixed to the principles that started it. . . ." Then, the biblical phrase: "It is finished." The document is a prodigious pastiche of Sieyésian paradox and Bonapartist demand, containing self-neutralizing structures of theoretical interest, but mattering very little compared to the personality and will of the man whose statecraft the document was written to sustain and to enhance. At a public reading of the new constitution, a woman was reported asking her neighbor what it all meant. She replied, "It means Bonaparte."[8]

Bonaparte had given a strong hint of his intentions as early as 1797, in a letter (September 19) to Talleyrand, where he frankly notes that the executive (not the legislative) "power of government in all the latitude I would give it, ought to be considered *the true representative of the nation.*" (Emphasis added.) In this, Sieyès agreed with him, for the axiom both men adopted in 1799 was "confidence comes from below, power from on high." Can it thus be any surprise that the legislature elaborated in the constitution added up to two chambers of little account? The Legislative Body had the august right to vote on, but not to initiate or discuss, bills sent it by the executive, while the Tribunate could discuss but not amend a bill. Notwithstanding the classical prestige of its name, the Tribune held none of the interfering powers on behalf of the people of the Tribune cunctators of ancient Rome. These councils were only distantly a result of universal suffrage; a steeply graded, trilevel process ensured that common voters could express mainly confidence.

Rather, "the true representative of the nation" was what Bonaparte intended it to be: the Consulate itself. This executive consisted of three magistrates—a First, Second, and Third Consul, but the last two held merely consultative power. The First Consul received an annual salary of 500,000 francs; his colleagues received 150,000 francs apiece. The First Consul held most administrative and diplomatic, civil and military powers over the Republic. He was assisted by a Council of State, whose membership included many of the best minds in France. Bonaparte had no qualms about riding these men ruthlessly into the small hours of the morning, but they, at least, had the satisfaction of real debates issuing in important decisions, as the legislature did not, to anywhere near the same degree. The measures they presently turned out remain the foundation of the modern French State.

There was one ringer in the mix that betrays an unadulterated Sieyésian mark. A new body, the Senate, took life. Bonaparte, well read in Roman history, wanted no breeding ground of opposition and conspiracy, but as this institution was one that Sieyès clung to, the General admitted it. At its inception, the Senate-Guarantor (*Sénat Conservateur*), to use its correct name, was not a popularly elected legislative body (nor was its American eponym, at that time). The mission of the 60 (later, 80, and eventually, 120) who were appointed lifetime senators was akin to that of the U.S. Supreme Court: to adjudicate the constitutionality of measures taken. But the Senate would soon take on further tasks and become a central part of Bonaparte's regime(s).

The constitution, like that of 1793 and 1795, was presented for "the acceptance of the French people" in a plebiscite (a Roman institution) where it appeared to have garnered 3 million "yes" votes to a few thousand "no's," out of a possible 5.5 million ballots. Given the rates of abstention under the Directory, that appeared to be a formidable victory. However, some years ago, a French scholar uncovered the truth: the minister of the interior, Lucien Bonaparte, cooked the plebiscite results, so that the actual "yeas" were half of the number proclaimed. In other words, only 20 percent of the electorate approved the new regime.[9] Some historians see this as a defeat, but we must recall: contemporaries *had no idea* of Lucien's monkey business. The vote went down with the public (and with posterity, until 1972) as a victory. Then, too, even if we limit ourselves to the corrected numbers,[10] the plebiscite of the year VIII is *still* a success, given the prevailing socioeconomic crisis that was inconducive to voting. For if fewer people cast "yea" ballots than for the Jacobin constitution of 1793, it remains true that hundreds of thousands more voted for the 1799 regime than had voted for the Directory constitution of 1795, or in any intervening election.

And Sieyès? In return for bending to the General's (if perhaps also the general) will, Bonaparte graciously allowed him to name the three new consuls who would replace the provisional ones. It was a formality; the names, beginning with Napoleon's, had been decided: for Second Consul, Cambacérès; for Third, Charles-François Lebrun, a former deputy of the Third

Estate in 1789 and a moderate royalist in the Council of Elders. Lebrun, it was hoped, would placate, perhaps rally, "moderate" opinion. The gesture to Sieyès was essentially an expensive floral arrangeemnt sent to the man's political funeral. There was no question that he would not serve as Second or Third Consul—"You want to be king" and "I don't want to be your aide-de-camp," figure among the statements he allegedly said to Bonaparte. He "received" the Senate as his domain, as well as a real domain—a chateau and lands called Crosnes, worth 480,000 francs (more than Bonaparte and Josephine paid for their estate, Malmaison). Accepting this buyout, after having sold out by helping to draft a constitution that compromised his own views, was a sadly characteristic way for Sieyès to go. There is instructive pathos in this intellectual's swift descent from being a sort of dictator in the summer of 1799 to getting pushed off history's stage by the real thing in the fall.

With a revolution and regime to consolidate and a war to win, Bonaparte was impatient to get on with things in the new Consulate. Roederer had recently reminded him—not that he needed it—that right moments neither come often nor linger. Observe Lafayette in 1790, Roederer had said; the young general was, if anything, *more* popular than Bonaparte was now, "yet he proved unable to found anything."[11] This, Napoleon was absolutely determined, would not happen to him, but it meant he was in a terrible hurry.

The Consulate, once it was established, unfolded amid greater perturbations and raised more opposition than the Brumaire coup had done, but by and large the new regime prevailed—and quite quickly. In truth, it did so more easily than a neo-Jacobin, Directorial, or moderate-royalist regime would have done in its place, thanks to the simplicity of Bonaparte's ideas, the superiority of his preparation and mind, and the occasional use of his mailed (or ham) fist. The consuls continued with the policy of conciliation and moderation—for example, the body of the great seventeenth-century general Turenne was reinterred at the Church of the Invalides, amid great panoply (a very unrevolutionary act).

On the other hand, as a testimony to Bonaparte's belief that to be credibly moderate he must be seen as strong, the government closed down all but ten political newspapers in Paris, on the pretext that the country was at war and public opinion could not afford articles that ran "contrary to the respect due to the social compact, the sovereignty of the people, and the glory of the armies." There was little unusual in his measure; it is unlikely that any party, coming to power at this juncture in France, would have refrained from doing it. From its origins, the press in France had been linked to the State; papers were virtually a tool of the royal ministers in the old regime, though that fact had not insulated them from censorship and restriction.[12] A tight official grip on the press was a policy that French society found largely unobjectionable, for the press did not enjoy the prestige then that it does now; people deemed it partly responsible for the overheated atmosphere of the Revolution, and they knew that republican governments after 1793 had taken action against it.

In general, too, Bonaparte moved more swiftly and effectively than the Directory had done against brigandage (criminal and political) in the west and the Midi, for which many communities were grateful to him, even if it entailed renewed official violence and martial law. The new regime installed some "booted justice,"[13] as Howard Brown calls the recourse to special military tribunals in areas of the west and the south where counterrevolution revived, but there is little doubt that the French as a whole were disposed—and many were *well* disposed—to make a good-faith trial with Bonaparte.

In France, few people minced words; they recognized the new regime as a potential dictatorship, but in the clean, clear, Roman style of a dictatorship of emergency or of public safety, under the strong hand of a consulate, no longer the ineffective, diffuse oppression of the Directory. Joseph Garat, a neo-Jacobin sympathizer and a man with a long past in revolutionary assemblies ("the optimist of the Revolution," some had called him, though others preferred "political eunuch"), overcame his misgivings about the new Consular constitution and made a speech celebrating it. As for Europe, it knew Napoleon Bonaparte far better than it knew the ex-Abbé Sieyès. Some regarded the new First Consul as a great hero; others, as the scourge of God; and a few, like the Queen of Naples and Sicily, as a bit of both. Contemporaries referred to the latest coup d'État with the same word they used for the previous ones: "revolution," but few failed to grasp that there were important novelties this time around: Brumaire was understood to be a move *away from* radicalism, an attempt to fix the Revolution on a plinth of property, order, and grandeur. No less an arch-enemy of Bonaparte's and the Republic's than William Pitt wondered for a time if this might not be the advent of a "moderate" or "American-style" republic in France.

WAR IN ITALY (AGAIN):
THE SECOND ITALIAN CAMPAIGN, 1800

*Fundamental conflicts of interest did not make an Austro-French armed struggle
inevitable; the belief in an inevitable armed struggle created a conflict of interest.*
                                                    —Paul Schroeder[14]

As the body of the first Emperor of the French was being carried to its grave
on St. Helena in 1821, the pall over the coffin was said to be the cape he had
worn at the battle of Marengo. Fitting, if true. Rarely did Napoleon need or
profit more from a victory than the desperate one he pulled out of a hat in
the afternoon of June 14, 1800, on a plain in Lombardy. France was at war,
and the convolutions of a new constitution would not suffice for the survival
of "the god of war." The constitution amounted to so much expensive wire-
walking apparatus purchased by a daredevil, when all that mattered was,
could he walk the line? For General Jourdan had been right: "The people saw
in Bonaparte only a general always victorious, destined to restore the honor
of the arms of the Republic."[15] Consul Bonaparte's first proclamation to the
French after Brumaire spoke of the need to make the Republic once again
"respected abroad and feared by its enemies . . ."[16]

When the Consulate took power, Austria, as usual, was the only enemy
still actively in the lists, the Russian tsar, Paul I, having taken umbrage at his
allies and withdrawn from the Second Coalition, while the British, as usual,
were fighting only at sea. Bonaparte, as expected, made a move for peace in
two unexpected (and unorthodox) personal appeals directly to George III and
to the Holy Roman Emperor, pleading for peace on the basis of a return to
the status quo of Campo-Formio. But why should the Allies accept that?
England remained untouched, while the Austrians still occupied nearly all of
northern Italy—and when it came to territorial avidity, Francis I was a match
for any French director or consul. No, the letters to the crowned heads
(penned on Christmas Day 1799) were in fact aimed at a French public eager
to know that its new government wished for peace, even if it was constrained
to fight. The so-English arrogance of George III's refusal to deign to reply to
Napoleon's appeal ("it is much below my attention," the Hanoverian wrote
in his journal) could only have brought a smile of satisfaction to Bonaparte's
face, for its impertinence infuriated the French.

The First Consul's grand strategy was to attack Austria along an extended
front stretching from the Rhine to the Swiss Alps to the Ligurian coast.

Unfortunately, his subordinates—Moreau, in Germany, and Masséna, near Genoa—were unable to hold up their ends. Moreau would not move with the required dash, while Masséna split his troops and allowed himself to be penned up by the Austrian commander, Melas, in the port of Genoa. So Bonaparte reconceived his strategy, telling Moreau's chief of staff, "What [Moreau] does not dare to do on the Rhine, I shall do over the Alps."

Bonaparte now secretly gathered the Army of the Reserve in the vicinity of Dijon, by the Swiss border. He needed to engage Melas and win a decisive, speedy victory, and could not afford to get caught up in a protracted campaign, as in 1796–97. No longer a fledgling general proving his military capability, he was now a head of State, frantic—his letters amply demonstrate it—to get back to Paris and take up the work of State-building. With stunning daring, Bonaparte forged the Alps over the lofty St. Bernard Pass, early in the year (May), with a fully equipped army of 35,000 men. It was a move so incredible that it had no modern precedent; a startled world was inevitably put in mind of the one ancient soldier who had done it: Hannibal. Debouching into northern Italy in late May—"We have hit the Austrians like a thunderbolt," he wrote to Joseph (May 24), "the enemy was not expecting us and still seems barely able to believe their eyes"—the Army of the Reserve swarmed over the Austrian rear, cutting their communications lines, and regaining in a fortnight most of the territory taken from the Republic in the spring of 1799.

Hard on the heels of such astounding strategy, however, Bonaparte committed a grave tactical blunder: he left himself wide open to an Austrian counter-move. The aged Melas, for once acting the part of his adversary rather than that of a ponderous Austrian general, *attacked*—swiftly and unexpectedly. He crossed the Bormida River at dawn and smote the French on a plain near the village of Marengo. He caught Napoleon with his forces depleted, for he had dispatched Desaix's corps to the south, and was outnumbered nearly two to one. Not until later in the morning did Bonaparte realize the truth and send aides chasing desperately after Desaix, carrying the message, "I had thought to attack Melas. He has attacked me first. For God's sake, come up if you still can."

Awaiting reinforcement, Bonaparte fought his men well in a terrible situation. Yet when Desaix arrived at 3 P.M., the latter concluded, "This battle is completely lost." But glancing at the sun, still high in the sky, he added, "But there is still time to win another battle." Desaix advanced with his corps in brigades, perfectly combining artillery bombardment with infantry assault. The Austrians were taken by surprise but resisted stubbornly. Then one of their artillery wagons exploded with an earth- and morale-shattering bang. At that moment, young General Kellermann, son of the commander who had won the Revolution's first victory over the Austrians (at Valmy, 1792), chose to lead his cavalry regiment in a full charge against the stunned Austrian left flank. As Chandler writes, "It was the moment of truth which converted near-defeat into crushing victory."[17]

But it came at a price: Desaix—his invaluable right hand in Egypt, a man as close to being a friend as Bonaparte had—was dead, shot in the chest while leading a brigade into action. At nearly the same time, fifteen hundred miles to the southeast, the equally gifted Kléber, military governor of Egypt, was assassinated in Cairo by a Moslem fanatic. And so the First Consul had his badly needed success, though truth be told, even if Melas had won at Marengo, the Austrians were still in such a strategically difficult scrape, thanks to Bonaparte's descent from the Alps, that they would have lost the war. Indeed, we should recall that if Moreau and Masséna had been able to follow the First Consul's original strategy, the French victory would have come sooner and been greater. One is nevertheless put in mind of a line from a letter Bonaparte wrote to Talleyrand some years before (October 7, 1797): "It is only a step from victory to disaster. My experience is that, in a crisis, some detail always decides the issue."

Despite his hurry to get back to Paris, the First Consul took the time to try to undo the damage wrought in the peninsula during his two years of absence. Poor Italy had met with hard times in 1798–99, first at French, then at Austrian hands. The strapped Directory annexed Piedmont, broke the Cisalpine and Ligurian Republics with economic vassalization, and permitted French military governors to run amuck. The Cisalpine and Ligurian Republics proved to be travesties of Bonaparte's policies; they imposed official anticlericalism in Rome itself (Pius VI was arrested and died in French captivity) and permitted the *giacobini* to stage revolutions in venues where violent reaction could only ensue—and did. War returned to the Boot in 1799, and, with no Bonaparte in the field, the Austrians enveloped Italy in a savage wave of repression, reaction, and pillage. Most of the distinguished and progressive men in Lombardy were imprisoned. It was enough to make the Italians miss the French (at least, until they returned).[18] The First Consul resurrected the sister republics in Genoa and Milan, but he forbade acts of vengeance or retribution against parties that had cooperated with the Austrians. He gave more territory to the Cisalpine, along with a new constitution, aligned on the current French one. And presently, he also consented to a new name for the Cisalpine, a fateful one: "the Italian Republic."

Egypt, too, lay heavily on Bonaparte's mind in these months. On becoming First Consul, he began conceiving ways of relieving the expeditionary force there in order to hold the colony. He ordered Admiral Ganteaume to sail to Alexandria with reinforcements (including a troupe of actors for the men's diversion), but the plague delayed the fleet's departure, and when it finally did set sail, the British prevented Ganteaume's delivery of men and materiel to the new French colony.

The First Consul returned to his capital in time for the July 14 celebration. He had previously notified Lucien that his return was to be "unannounced," ordering the minister of the interior to hold no victory parades or build no triumphal arches. "I have too high an opinion of myself to attach value to trifles like those. The only triumph I want is public approval." That, he had. And he had something more. He had a powerful new friend in Paul I, perhaps the most rash and mercurial tsar ever to reign over All the Russias. Paul had recently bolted the Second Coalition when he became convinced that England and Austria had not properly deployed or supported his expeditionary forces. After Marengo, he turned another notch: from ferocious hater of the French Revolution and friend to the Bourbon pretender, Paul suddenly emerged as a great admirer of the First Consul, in whom he felt he saw his own strength personified. The autocrat brusquely withdrew his subsidy of the Comte de Provence, Louis XVIII, and ordered him to leave Mitau (in Russian Poland), where he had been living and plotting in comfort. As the British went white with surprise and concern, the autocrat and the dictator discussed by letter projects for Egypt and India.[19]

And finally, the First Consul had something that has proven to be longer-lasting than any of the above: a recipe. On the eve of the battle, Bonaparte's chef, Dunand, had no cream for the sauce for the chicken dish he was preparing for the commander, so he whipped together one out of tomatoes, white wine, and garlic—*et voilà, poulet marengo.*

Marengo was not of itself a sufficient military triumph for France to oblige the Austrians to sue for peace. Notwithstanding the eloquent personal appeal for peace that Bonaparte penned to Francis I from the battlefield, the Habsburg tergiversated. In theory, his alliance with Great Britain prevented Francis from making a separate peace; but as Bonaparte refused to negotiate with Britain and Austria at once—and in any case, Prime Minister Pitt was not ready to throw in the towel—the Austrians had no real choice. They dispatched the faithful Cobenzl to open dilatory negotiations at Lunéville (in Lorraine).

But in December, yet another Austrian general (the Archduke John, brother of the emperor) was crushed by General Moreau, at the battle of Hohenlinden in Germany. With Moreau's troops preparing to march on

Vienna, and with Masséna mopping up Lombardy, Cobenzl dealt in earnest. Austria begged for terms—and of course came off the worse for having waited. As Lunéville was moving to resolution (winter, 1801), the Pitt government fell. His successor, Henry Addington, was a thoroughgoing dove and as close to a Francophile as the British political class produced. First in London, then in the northern French town of Amiens, the diplomats negotiated—Joseph Bonaparte, representing the Republic; Lord Cornwallis, of Yorktown fame, Britain. (The latter's view of the former: "a man of good will rather than a man of great skill.") A bone of contention on which the talks broke off for a time was Egypt—the First Consul insisting on being permitted to reinforce it; the British refusing.

The Treaties of Lunéville (1801) and Amiens (1802) were only the high points of a remarkable set of peace agreements all concluded at this time between France and eight different countries. Together with the Concordat, concluded with Pope Pius VII, these amount to a *summum bonum* that gave Bonaparte almost the same reputation for peacemaker that he had for war. France made some territorial gains, significantly in her colonial holdings, but essentially, she reemerged as she was after Campo-Formio. Yet things were very different from 1797. Campo-Formio had been like the police closing of a floating crap game; the wiser players knew that one day things would start up again. The treaties of 1801–2, however, were envisioned as something closer to a true settlement. France did not simply dominate western Europe, *she was acknowledged to.* Britain, as always, held the seas, and Russia, which had withdrawn from the war after her defeats (1799) in Italy and Switzerland, was vaguely conceded the east.

The Morning Chronicle, an opposition newspaper in Great Britain, harangued the government in early October 1801: "It would have been better for us all if we had accepted peace at the start of 1800 [when the new Consular regime had first offered terms]." The paper reviewed the French victories and gains of 1800, ending: "We now have nothing, France has everything. . . . All we managed to do was spend nearly 400 million pounds and contribute to establishing the Republic on the foundations of eternal and unshakeable glory."[20]

THE BLOCKS OF GRANITE: *LE POLITIQUE*

[The Revolution] destroyed everything; now it is time to rebuild. We have government and its powers but what about the nation? So many grains of sand: scattered, without system, unity or connection. . . . You think the Republic is definitively established? You seriously delude yourselves. We are in a position to do it, but we have not done it, and we shall not have it until we raise up a few great granite blocks on the sands of France.

—Bonaparte to the Council of State,
May 8, 1802

Perhaps the Revolution was not so finished, after all. The "blocks of granite" that the authority-driven government of Brumaire proceeded to raise, in a three-year period following its leader's return from Marengo (July 1800), consisted of deep-seated structures of sociopolitical reconciliation, religion, law, finance, administration, education, and society. It also consisted of an attempt to re-create a French colonial empire with a wider and more modern purpose. In some instances, these policies were new, even shocking ideas; in others, they were reforms that had been mooted for years, but left uncompleted by preceding regimes, for want of time, will, concord, and energy. In one area (colonies), the measures proved to be such a failure that posterity has stopped seeing the policy as foundational (in intention). The handprint of the First Consul is clearly imposed on each; on most, it is the principal mark. Men far older than Bonaparte, far more experienced in government and affairs, were impressed by the "unrivalled sagacity of his opinions relating to every part of the huge system of public administration."[21] The new structures would persevere, resolutely retained by later regimes, which, politically speaking, were as unlike the Consulate and Empire as these latter differed from the old regime. Many of the reforms still stand in the Fifth French Republic, lending plausibility to the First Consul's assertion that he was "only doing what people want, governing them as the majority wants to be governed."

And Bonaparte? A counselor of State one day thought to warn his colleagues of the workload looming over them on a particular matter. It might, he stated solemnly, require "thirty sessions" of the Council. The First and Second Consul (Cambacérès), workaholics of the first order, glanced at each other and smiled. "And so?" Bonaparte said, "what's the problem? It's that many more tasty bones for us to chew on."

Consular action was guided by a number of premises, which eighteenth-century Americans might have called "prejudices," so much did national temperament vary between the two republics on either side of the Atlantic. The French generally inclined to the rather un-Anglo-Saxon notion that the State all but subsumed society; indeed personified in the government, it was not only regulatory but a normative agent, a veritable producer of the social and the guardian of French specificity.[22] In Bonaparte's words, "The government is the center of society like the sun: all the various institutions must orbit it without ever deviating . . . so that all come together in general harmony." General Thiébault once observed that the French people had become "flabby" under the Directory. The First Consul disagreed. "A nation," he said, "is always *what you know how to make it*. [Emphasis added.] . . . For a good government, there is no such thing as a bad people, just as there are no bad soldiers serving under good generals." In short, the burden of success in social organization was seen to rest on the shoulders of its political leadership.

If Bonaparte struck out in all directions, the acts he performed or oversaw, from the small and symbolic to the large and material, were characterized by a high degree of coherence. The First Consul brought to port the Revolution's projects for administrative centralization, such that a leading jurist of the day (Portalis) would purr with satisfaction over "the great nation, composed of many different men having but one sentiment, one thought, marching and conducting themselves as if the whole depended completely on one man."[23]

Thus, Consular coherence was peculiarly French, and the American reader does well to pause a moment over another era and mind-set. The kingdom of France had been a congeries of discrete provincial customs, rights, and institutions, not dissimilar to the American states or the British counties and regions. But where English speakers conjured easily with the paradox of *e pluribus unum,* the French Revolution saw this "society of societies" as no cornucopia but an "immense chaos"[24]—a bulwark of aristocracy and monarchical despotism (notwithstanding that the kings had done their level best to snap provincial independence). The Consulate, following the lines of the Revolution, determined to rationalize the nation.

The cornerstone of the granite blocks was social peace. Everyone within and without France agreed that peace was the goal of goals, but how to have it was a by-now badly splintered bone of contention. Did one wearily strive for healing in further annealing, bonding "the nation" ever more tightly in blind exclusion of nobility, royalty, and Church? That had been the Revolution's way, but its failure—widely alleged even by some of the very men (like

Sieyès) who had once convincingly championed it—was the justification for
Brumaire. Bonaparte, at the outset, made clear he intended to act boldly in
this matter. The day after the coup, he had appeared at a Paris prison to lib-
erate the Directory's political hostages, and thereafter he undertook measures
to heal the wounded polity by easing émigré and anticlerical policy.

Thus far, even a good many Jacobins like Fouché were willing to go along.
The First Consul wanted something stronger, however, and in the spring of
1802 he got passed through the Senate a law that granted full amnesty to any
émigré returning to France before September 23 of that year. The bill was
thus aimed at up to three to four million people, if we include the families
of the 145,000 proscribed. The Consular reconciliation measure, which
included admitting a number of distinguished or talented émigrés to government service, was an act of reparation and pacification that illustrated, as
the French historian Albert Vandal notes, "patriotism and courage." It
made a strong start at the sort of generous policy desperately needed in the
Republic at this time, but which the Directory, despite its *astuce,* had not
proved capable of providing: a policy of largeness of spirit, of imagination,
and heart.

Social reconciliation entailed two large movements by the First Consul.
The other one, raising even more hackles than amnesty, was religion. This
granite block was a mass.

CONCORDAT

*Progress, far from consisting in change, depends on retentiveness. When change
is absolute there remains no being to improve and no direction is set for possible
improvement: and when experience is not retained, as among savages, infancy
is perpetual. Those who cannot remember the past are condemned to repeat it.*
—George Santayana[25]

The word "religion" comes from the Latin *religere,* meaning "to bind
together," yet religion had ever been the cause of France's most fundamental
divisions. "Peace," in the French Republic of 1800, meant delivery from
domestic conflict possibly even more than it meant victory in foreign war.
The end of civil strife, in turn, was inseparable from the question of religion.
Bonaparte returned from Egypt more aware than ever of the impact of the
institutions and beliefs of organized religion on "the political," in the larger
sense, while at the same time he was no less convinced that religion's min-

isters needed to be strictly curbed in their ability to influence day-to-day "politics." After Marengo, few associates got away without hearing a discourse on "the crucial role of religion in society," on the order of "In religion I see not the mystery of the incarnation, but the mystery of the social order." Or again, "When a man dying of hunger observes another who is glutting himself, the only way the dying one will accept it is if an authority exists who can say to him, 'God has willed it so . . . but in eternity, [it] shall be otherwise.'"[26]

The First Consul never considered pressing home a hands-off solution of condoning all cults—Constitutional, Catholic, Protestant, Jewish, and freethinking—side by side. Religion, he believed, was too important to be left to its practitioners; benign neglect might work in a new polity like the United States, but not in France where, for centuries, religious institutions and conflict had virtually defined the national history. Church-State separation had already been much criticized both by supporters of the Revolution, for diminishing the control of "national sovereignty," and by Catholics, for "relegating" religion to the private sphere of people's lives. The policy had not ended social conflict; above all, it had not ended the fierce animus between the two cults, both nominally "catholic" (Roman Catholicism and the Constitutional Church), which did combat for the souls of thirty million Frenchmen.

Still, a republican regime, if it chose to embark on a policy of religious reconciliation, presumably owed loyalty to "its own" church: the Constitutional Church. The CC, though disestablished in 1795, was a Revolution-inspired institution, in some senses the Gallican equivalent of Anglicanism. Since its independence, however, the CC had watched the number of its faithful plummet, not least because many republicans in authority scoffed at or even persecuted it. The CC had not managed to rally a majority of the nation's Catholics, nominal or devout. Empirical evidence of the sort Bonaparte took seriously—e.g., soundings by local authorities—buttressed his impression that the CC's great rival, the Roman Catholic Church, flourished in many areas and was far from dead even in some regions hardest worked by anti-Christianization. The thousands of nonjuring Roman priests who had elected to stay in France to tend their flocks operated under great duress and in semiclandestine conditions, yet in the way that religion has of flourishing during adversity, Catholicism was undergoing a strong revival and enjoyed widespread moral authority.[27] Truth be told, many of the hotheaded anticlericals of the Year II were now asking that their children take first communion. Here was living proof of the failure of the cold and high ideal that had been Christianity's civic replacements, which ended in worse than failure; they ended in ridicule.

Then, too, the papacy as a political institution was potentially useful and, in any case, too dangerous to be left unrecognized. The sale of Church property, the abolition of the old ecclesiastical tax, and the secularization of births, marriages, and deaths all remained under a permanent shadow of contestation, mute or spoken, since 1791. Finally, perhaps most important, the Church was a powerful weapon in the hands of the counterrevolutionaries in the West and their British allies. A deal with Rome permitted Napoleon to disarm the counterrevolution of the greater of its two chief weapons: crown and altar. In sum, to ignore the Church was, in Napoleon's matchless metaphor, like saying "there are men about the house with lighted torches, but leave them alone, and arrest them only if they set it on fire."[28] At the end of the day, the Church of Rome bestrode the path, as immovable and as unbreakable as ever. Bonaparte put out feelers to the Holy See.

The political forces arrayed *against* his attempt to reconcile the French Republic and "the real pope—that Catholic, apostolic, and Roman one, the one who lives in Rome"[29]—were worthy of the First Consul. The entire French political class, as well as the army, stood violently opposed to revealed religion. To them, the Church was the most malignant of the tumors excised by the Revolution. Any accord that permitted priests and popes to regain entry into the lives of the French was a blasphemy against the great idol of "sovereignty of the people." A leading savant and a great champion of the Egyptian expedition, Volney, lit into Bonaparte to his face at a meeting of the Institute.[30] Talleyrand, the ex-bishop, was beside himself, and Fouché, a man who loved his job, got himself fired as police minister for refusing to bend in good grace to this policy.[31]

Looking back on the arduous negotiations that resulted in Roman Catholicism's reestablishment in France, a principal actor in the drama said that the project was the "work of a hero and a saint."[32] This is not a claim posterity has agreed with. The Vatican has not opened the cause for canonization of Pope Pius VII, while Bonaparte's role, here as elsewhere, remains subject to violent criticism and disagreement. Still, there is something to be said for these words. The "hero" enjoyed one big stroke of luck at the outset in that the "saint" whom Providence raised up to deal with him happened to be a Benedictine monk by the name of Luigi Chiaramonti, recently crowned Pope Pius VII. A French bishop would tell the story that Chiaramonti, having examined a copy of the "constitution of the clergy" of 1790, noted matter-of-factly that if he had been a French priest, he would have signed the oath.[33] That story, if true, is astonishing, for though it is far from showing that the new pope *believed* in the Revolution, it does show him to be a moderate inclined to look for the best in new things. The First Consul, for his part, told an underling to treat the pope "as if he had 200,000 soldiers." It is an inapt simile. Pius, for better or worse, was a man of genuine faith and humility, who approached issues from a resolutely spiritual stance. This would work out well in the short run for Bonaparte, and badly in the long run. The pope would turn out to have both far fewer and far more than "200,000 soldiers."

Pius trembled with joy at the unexpected grace that was the possibility of the return of the Church's "Eldest Daughter" (France) to her bosom. He would stand by the gratitude, pride, and admiration he felt for the "son" who occasioned this grace throughout long months of agonizing negotiations, and even across future years, when Napoleon's behavior exhausted the goodwill of many lesser ecclesiastical hearts. On the altar of reconciliation, and in a desire to show the world that the Church was less concerned with wealth, precedence, and power than her enemies claimed her to be, Pius refrained from making a bone of contention out of the issue of the papacy's territorial holdings in Italy, which the French had seized in the recent war.

The hammering out of a concordat required eight grueling months and twenty-one drafts, and took place in secret in Paris, Bonaparte fearing that the news of such discussions would raise a hullabaloo in the government. The Republic's chief negotiator was the Abbé Bernier, a former royalist priest from the Vendée turned devoutly "bonapartist." The Church was represented by its cardinal secretary of State, Hercule Consalvi, a decent and clever prelate (Bonaparte called him "a lion in sheep's clothing"), whom the French treated ruthlessly.[34] The hardest part of the deal for Pius VII, being the man he was, was to remove the entire bank of French old regime bishops: an act of unprecedented papal ingratitude and authority (a *coup d'Eglise*, as it has been called). The old Gallican bishops had stood by the Holy See at the cost of exile and dispossession. Now, these long-suffering servants from some of the noblest families of France were being asked to resign their sees in order to make way for an episcopacy, to be named by the republican dictator. It is just as well that the pope did not know at this point that Bonaparte intended, for the sake of true reconciliation, to name to the new sees a dozen of the unrepentant "Constitutional" bishops of the old CC. And he stoutly refused to force these "schismatics" (from Rome's point of view) to make any public retraction of their prior vows and views.

Pius's pleas were unavailing; later Catholic historians like d'Haussonville have faulted him for not breaking off negotiations at this point and entrusting the Church to the faith of the hundreds of thousands of French Catholics willing to suffer for their religion. Bonaparte, in turn, has been criticized for his hard-ball approach to the negotiations, though it should be said that he was out on a limb here and could not go back to his people with less than draconian conditions for a restored Catholicism. If the pope marched "to the doorstep of hell,"[35] as Pius himself put it, it was because he and Consalvi well understood that the *only* Frenchman of any stature or power who favored resurrecting Roman Catholicism and who was willing to sacrifice the schismatic CC in order to do so was the First Consul. The pope signed the Concordat and even tacitly acceded to the unilaterally declared Organic Articles, the legislation by which the Republic set the Concordat into French law, though the articles would remain a thorn in Pius's flesh.

The proud old *Eglise de France*–the vast, wealthy, and independent First Estate of Europe's first realm (counting, in 1789, 130,000 clergy, arrayed in 135 dioceses, governed by 150 bishops)–thus became the Concordatory church, a reduced corps of civil servants, manning sixty jerry-built, unwieldy dioceses. These 60 bishops and 36,000 priests have been called "prefects in purple" and "mayors in black,"[36] but that is too flattering, for this clergy no longer tended the prestigious registries of births, marriages, and deaths. Most of the monastic orders were gone altogether, and no corps of chaplains was raised for the Republic's armies–probably just as well, given the military's views on religion.

The treaty amounted to a revolution (and a counterrevolution) in the Revolution that no contemporary foresaw, and no one perhaps but a hero and a saint could have brought off: an immense act of uncoerced (O rarity, for the French Revolution) reconciliation, which showed "that the principles of 1789 could be baptized," as Martyn Lyons puts it.[37] When the abundant dust settled, each leader got the fundamentals of what he had wanted: the pontiff saw the public return of Catholicism as the acknowledged "religion of the great majority of the French people"–an event that would have stunned his predecessor, Pius VI, who died in French captivity. He got something else as well–no less real for being unintended and gradual: by his single-handed removal and appointment of two entire national episcopacies, Pius VII laid the foundations of the modern Catholic "monarchy" based on papal infallibility–the Church's unfortunate answer to the challenges of the modern world. Consalvi punned about "the labors of Hercules" that he had performed in his hog-trading with Abbé Bernier, but the credit was mainly the pope's, who time and again swallowed his pride. His successors would be grateful for the power that accrued to their holy office.

And what did Bonaparte get? Well, on Easter Sunday of 1802 he got to hear the bells of Notre-Dame de Paris peal joyfully for the first time in a decade. He got to attend a pontifical high mass at the cathedral (where the defaced statuary was hastily covered over) and to hear a sermon preached by the prelate who had held the pulpit at the coronation of Louis XVI at Reims in 1775. (But the anticlerical General Delmas was not impressed: "A lot of pretty monkish mummery," he sniffed to Bonaparte, "nothing was wanting except the million men who lost their lives pulling down what you are laboring to raise up.")[38] The First Consul could now give skeptics living proof that the Revolution was both *finished and safe*. The Concordat and the Organic Articles amounted, from the regime's perspective, to "putting a mace in the hand of Hercules,"[39] for in one move Bonaparte deprived the royalists of half their appeal while recruiting a formidable ally for dealing with Catholic occupied territories in Belgium, Italy, Holland, and Germany.

Recalling Bonaparte's idle speculation to Mme de Rémusat about "founding a new religion," the Concordat was as close as he ever came to doing it. By ensuring one of the Revolution's deepest impulses—its official agnosticism—the Great Consulate took a decisive step toward political modernity. It had imbibed both the Enlightenment's philosophical critique of religion and the Revolution's sharp laicity—that is, its dissociation of society and revealed religion. Bonaparte firmly rejected the pope's desperate plea that Catholicism be recognized as "the [French] national religion." The First Consul saw Catholicism as a cult, and all cults as equal—accountable not by their truth value but their usefulness. Jean Étienne Marie Portalis, a Catholic jurist who worked hard for the Concordat, put it thus: "The essential point for public order and values is not that people have the same religion, but that each man be attached to his own."[40] This was not how things had ever been in France, and it was certainly not how Pius VII wanted them, but it was how they were now. The Napoleonic regimes would practice a kind of "positivist laicity"[41] that stood in sharp contrast to the indifference and unavowed hostility to religion characteristic of both earlier and later eras of French history. Whether it was good or bad is not a question the historian may pronounce on; it will depend on a reader's view of religion and the State.

ECONOMY, STATE, AND SOCIETY:
BOURGEOIS CONSOLIDATION?

Is it possible to conceive of a science where the scientists are in no agreement as to the principles which form its theoretical structure?

Philippe Steiner[42]

It was not only in ecclesiastical matters but in many other fields that Napoleon sought pragmatic policies that fostered social peace. Doubtless, he was hoping to win plaudits while trying to impose or strengthen his rule; many of the reforms have their own distinctive 'Bonapartist,' perhaps even Corsican, flavor. Yet they would not have survived in the increasingly democratic political culture of modern France if they were mainly responsive to one man's philosophy and goals.

Finance

The politically wise of 1799 well understood that the vexing problems of taxes and credit had set in motion the crisis that brought down the old regime; they were even more aware that State finance during the Revolution and its wars—entailing the issuance of paper money and ill-fated State bonds—had ultimately worsened things. The Directory's plight remained a smoking disaster requiring the immediate attention of the men of Brumaire. There were virtually no funds in the Treasury; public finances were in quasi-desperate straits. Bonaparte had excellent advisors in Gaudin, Barbé-Marbois, later Mollien, Chaptal, and others, while he himself grasped what was needed. The arcana of monetary and fiscal policy must not be permitted to distract us from the fact that underlying the charts and figures lay a clear matter of social psychology: the imperious necessity of creating a mood of confidence among the movers and shakers of a nation's economy, and of reassurance among the broad mass of taxpayers.

And this, Bonaparte instinctively understood, was a political matter. This is important for us to note at the outset: Bonaparte's general approach to matters economic was resolutely political and pragmatic, as one might expect in a head of State, though he did have some interest in the fledgling science of political economy and even cautiously admired the current free-trade theories of the era's towering economic philosopher, Adam Smith (1723–90). However, despite their admiration for Smith, the French, including their economists, well understood that Britain had not won her economic stripes through any literal-minded application of laissez-faire ideals, but via a quite ruthless State-led protectionism and *dirigisme*. The free-trade ideals only came afterwards, when Britain, now in the catbird seat, wished to impose her industry, commerce, and credit on her less developed neighbors. (A German economist of the early nineteenth century would call this strategy "kicking away the ladder.") In France, the debate was not over any imagined "purity" of economic motives and actions—*au contraire*, it was well understood that the economy played a crucial political role in society, and was therefore a fit object for government action—but over how much *dirigisme* was called for. In sum, a great, undefined sympathy for "freedom of commerce" was everyone's "apolitical" ideal in this era, completely honored in the breach.[43]

The mere declaration of the will to move in this area improved the situation. From a statesman's point of view, the question of credit—from the Latin verb *credere,* "to believe (in)"—towered over everything else. The regime ached for the sorts of financial-fiscal structures that would ensure secure, long-term, and sufficient monies for the State. Such structures were familiar in England or Holland but not in the French Republic. For belief of this sort to happen, the money had to be put on a sound basis. Everything turned on a stable currency, yet it was equally true—then, as now—that a regime that monkeyed with the money played with its life. Bonaparte took counsel and moved swiftly. The Germinal franc, named for the month of the Revolutionary calendar in which it was reestablished (April 7, 1803), created a stable single currency. If it endured until 1928, it was because, for the first time, the money was convertible into metal (primarily silver, but also gold).[44] Unfortunately, even the First Consul did not have the courage to force the innumerable competitors to the franc out of the tight grips of the lower classes, so some monetary confusion reigned in France to Waterloo (and beyond), precipitating or supplementing the occasional economic crisis, but not seriously imperiling economic activity.

The tax system also required no innovations per se; it required only the great novelty of returning a dependable yield so that the State could fight its wars in peace, so to speak, and not constantly be having to feed and clothe the armies by desperate ad hoc measures. Bonaparte preserved the Revolution's direct taxes and did not quaver before the unpopularity of restoring several of the hated indirect taxes (e.g., duties) of the old regime. (It might be noted that Britain taxed her citizens twice as much per head as France did, but then Britain had a quarter of France's population.) The resultant system, though undemocratic, was well adapted to economic growth, for it favored high profit margins in the hands of the larger economic actors. It lasted until the First World War, when the graduated income tax finally made its relatively late appearance in France.

Credit institutions had to be built from scratch. The most celebrated—if not the largest (that was the Sinking Fund, a means of reducing the inherited State debt)—was the Bank of France. It took wing in 1800 as a semiprivate affair (the Bonaparte family figuring legion among its share owners), but it capitalized on its grand name and on its State-granted monopoly to print money and to discount private notes and loans (it took only the safest). Like the Germinal franc, the Bank of France was anything but an overnight success; it (along with the Sinking Fund) was for now largely for appearance's sake—to inspire investor and popular confidence. It would require years (long beyond the First Empire) before it played the role in French economic life that the First Consul had intended.[45]

Administration

Despite all talk about the splendor and majesty of the French State, France, as a country, was *under*-administered in the Consulate (and the Empire). Indeed, the number of ministerial bureaucrats fell considerably from the 6,500 men and women who served the Directory.[46] As there were not enough civil servants and administrative structures to carry out State policy effectively, render services (notably, provide security), or bring in the taxes, data, and conscripts deemed to be due from a population rounding onto thirty-seven million (including annexed lands), the Consulate layered on new levels of *fonctionnaires*—notably the prefect (a Roman title) at the head of each department and the subprefect at the head of each of four hundred arrondissements. It was these men's productivity and efficiency, not their number, that was extraordinary and marked the era. For this, Bonaparte—by his personal example of work and his outsized demands on his subordinates— was largely responsible. The prefects, by the way, did not enjoy their ancient forebears' power to govern independently; the Napoleonic prefect was intended to be simply the State's (read: the First Consul's) voice beyond Paris. In addition to prefects and subprefects, Paris took on appointing lower offi- cialdom (including mayors of communes of over five thousand in popula- tion). This represented a full retreat from the policy of electing civil servants and magistrates that had characterized the Revolution.

The prefects were touted as a reform favorable to the interests of the local- ity—a not entirely implausible claim when we consider the turmoil that had been occasioned *en province* by the Revolution's ad hoc representatives on mission (recall Saliceti in Corsica). Yet in its annulment of local political- electoral life, the new system constituted a big change. Few of the ancient intermediate institutions that had complicated the old regime—sovereign courts, provincial assemblies, customs agencies, ecclesiastical bodies, etc.— remained standing between the citizen and Paris. The prefectorial adminis- tration was, as a young historian puts it, "one-dimensional—from the top down" and constituted "a turning point" in its conception of power.[47] The sta- lactites of authority reaching down were few, long, and large; the stalagmites of confidence reaching up were diffuse, numerous, and small.

Legal Code

Bonaparte once conceded that he had "dreamed it would be possible to reduce all of law to simple geometric demonstrations, so that whoever could read and write and put two ideas together would be capable of pronouncing on it." A very *Etatiste* dream, this, for it effectively removes law from politics. The First Consul, in the next sentence, admitted that this was "an absurd ideal," but he did not say that it was not still an ideal.

The block most inseparable from Bonaparte in posterity's eyes was the Civil Code, renamed the Code Napoleon in 1807. The First Consul carefully chose the handful of jurists who compiled it, and pressed them mercilessly until they got the job done. He personally attended nearly half the meetings of the Council of State where the code was discussed, and weighed in frequently with opinions, his heavy-handed manner earning him the title of "the Achilles of the Council." The code is that rarity among great legal pandects in being wieldy and concisely chiseled. Stendhal claimed to have reread it annually for style.

The code seems to spout platitudes on the order of "the family is the building block of society," "the law is applicable to the entire nation," or "the State is the unique source of this law." When considered in their era, however, these are distinctive positions: for example, marriage and family are no longer "alliances" in the aristocratic sense but bricks in the wall of the *patrie*; God and Church are no longer the source of law. Yet the code seemed so natural to the average Frenchman that he regarded it as national.[48] Even the restored Bourbon kings will not dare to relinquish it, though its retention sanctified the juridical overthrow of the world they had fought and died for, for a quarter century. But the code does have its originality, its tilts. While, in general, it exemplifies the Enlightenment's search for a rationalist universalism, it also quietly inters certain individualistic and democratic laws of the Revolution. To combat the facility of divorce or the equality of sons vis-à-vis their fathers, which the Revolution legislated, the code returns to certain old customary rights—for example, the Corsican (= Napoleonic) nod toward the patriarchal family, including a tightening of the rules for divorce and the subordination of women to their husbands and fathers.[49] At bottom, the code affirms the legal moorings of the Revolution's expropriation of the First and Second Estates on behalf of the Third. "Property, equality, and liberty" were Bonaparte's replacement for "liberty, fraternity, equality."

The First Consul cared for the code; he directed that a copy of it be made available to every citizen of the Republic. He cared for it more than for any constitution, and it is not hard to see why: the code *became* the effective constitution of France far more than the pastiche of the Year VIII (or its successors) ever were.[50] It was received by a combat-weary public as the deliverance of French public life from the "politics" of constitution-drafting and *loi*-making by a party-driven legislature. It delivered society instead into the hands of State-named judges who applied "public law (*droit*)" and of prefects who administered it.

Public Instruction

The regime created State-supported high schools, or *lycées,* a word dear to the First Consul, for its classical associations. However, *lycées* were costly, and only forty-five of them were actually created. Scholarships supported 6,400 male students, of whom 2,400 were sons of the military and civil administrators. That left 4,000 for the best of the rest, but almost no poor boys and few enough lower middle class ones ever aced out a son of the *grande bourgeoisie* for a spot at, say, Lycée Charlemagne.

The *lycées* and the few other elite institutions (*les grandes écoles*) of his era were little reminiscent in their goals or methods of the lyceums of Aristotle or Plato. Military in style and mainly technical-scientific in curriculum, these schools were institutions of public instruction, not education, in the Anglo-American understanding. "Instruction" stems from the Latin verb *instruere,* meaning "to construct, to furnish, or to form"; while "education" derives from *educere,* "to draw out." Bonaparte carried out the revolutionary notion of public instruction by creating institutions to "construct" a politically quiescent citizen and "furnish" him with a strongly technical curriculum.

Baubles

Finally, the Legion of Honor (1802) has also come down to us in the fittest of health. Another block that was 100 percent Napoleonic in inspiration and execution, the legion was (and is) unique for rewarding *both* civilian and military excellence. Roman in name (from the *Legio honoratorum conscripta* of antiquity), in symbolism (eagles), and in organization (sixteen "cohorts" around France), the Legion broke with the old regime in being open to everybody,[51] not only nobles, officers, or the wealthy. It nevertheless dismayed many contemporaries who saw in the Legion's prestige and its four grades of hierarchy a rift in the fabric of civic equality. Bonaparte met their objections at a meeting of the Council of State: "I defy you to show me a republic, modern or ancient, that did without distinctions," he said. "You call them 'baubles,' but let me assure you it is with baubles that men are led!" The French, he claimed, had not changed much in ten years of revolution: "They are still the proud and volatile Gauls of yore, and are still motivated by one sentiment: honor. . . ."[52] Duly, the motto of the Legion became "Honor and *Patrie*." Few, then or now, have declined the award (there were 113,271 "legionnaires" in 2001), although the Marquis de Lafayette did.

Colonial Empire: A Failed Policy

The First Consul's colonial policies between 1801 and 1803 reflected his burning desire to undo the humiliating defeat of 1763, when France lost her vast North American and Indian empires to Britain and Spain, and to divert Frenchmen from their obsession with domestic politics by offering them a cause for a great national undertaking. Talleyrand's famous paper of 1797 had dwelt on the need for a "restless nation" to seek "new avenues" in colonial expansion—at the time, Egypt. For Bonaparte, Egypt was but the first step in a direction that the late nineteenth century was to call "social imperialism"— that is, a vision of colonies no longer held for mere mercantile reasons, but as sites of a vast and multifaceted national investment: politically, socially, morally, as well as, of course, economically. This idealistic vision enjoyed an early development in René Chateaubriand's *Atala* (1801), a dewy-eyed and greatly influential novel about former French Canada, dedicated to Bonaparte.

In the immediate, Bonaparte's policies entailed the dispatch of a fleet and an army to suppress native rebellion in French insular possessions in the Caribbean (Saint-Domingue, Guadeloupe), the restoration[53] of slavery in the French colonies after the Convention had abolished it (1794), and military reconnaissance missions to Egypt[54] and India in the guise of trade and scientific voyages. Napoleonic neocolonialism enjoyed strong backing from the powerful colonial lobby and the great majority of the political class, for had it succeeded it would have taken back Egypt from England, tightened the French hold on the trade-rich Lesser Antilles, and given France an extended purchase in (British-held) India. Then, too, the First Consul, in collaboration with the Institute, his great ally in the Egyptian expedition, had drawn up a "great plan" for an expedition to (mainly British-held) Australia.[55]

Success would also have entailed—perhaps uppermost in Napoleon's mind—the exploitation of the Louisiana Territory, which like Egypt, was intended to be developed, administered, and eventually colonized. A newly

French Louisiana, geopolitically and economically oriented to Saint-Domingue and the French Caribbean, was to have been a great jewel in the French colonial crown, even at the cost of war with the United States.[56] Only the premature return of the war with England in 1803 destroyed these hopes and led Bonaparte, most reluctantly, to sell off Louisiana to the United States for $15 million. "I know the value of what I abandon," he told an associate, ". . . I renounce it with the greatest regret."

None of the foregoing, even the return of slavery, sustained the degrees of dissent that other granite blocks (e.g., the Concordat or the Legion of Honor) had to face. Abolitionism did not become a force in Europe or America until the next generation. Protest, when it blazed about colonial policy, blazed over failure, for example, the annihilation of the French expeditionary force of 30,000, led by the First Consul's brother-in-law General Leclerc at the hands of disease and the great Haitian leader, Toussaint L'Ouverture—the "Black Bonaparte" as he called himself.

Whether sincere or self-serving, and undoubtedly both, Bonaparte's colonial vision was marked by the Revolution's messianism.[57] It would turn out to be an expensive venture for the nations inclined to it later on, to the point that future generations would "sincerely" honor themselves and their "sacrifices" with euphemisms such as "taking up the white man's burden" and "*la mission civilisatrice.*" For we should not forget: social imperialism was long seen as a boon for mankind, before it took on a very different set of labels. Napoleonic policy in this domain proved costly, not least in revolutionary principle, and ended in sharp military defeat and diplomatic checkmate after the premature return of the war with England. Yet for its era, his colonialist hope was a bold novelty, which, had it even partly succeeded, would have been heralded as one of the greatest of the granite blocks.

Summarizing Consular reforms commits the writer by what he chooses to accent: consolidation of the Revolution or reaction against it? a gingerly posture toward the future or a new openness to the past? The granite blocks are impossible to sum up in bold strokes. The Legion of Honor "brought partisans of the Revolution together," but it also served its creator's wish to lay up "clusters of interests attached to the regime, who, in return for advantages and honors, were expected to secure the loyalty of the populace by virtue of their influence upon the wage-earning classes."[58]

Even measures as technical as financial reform defy unambiguous conclusions. The Germinal franc and the Bank of France prepared France for a century of economic growth, but at the same time amounted to "a kind of accountant's minute scrupulosity and timorous orthodoxy."[59] They aimed at removing the ulcer of government finance from the realm of political conflict, yet that act was accomplished by fiat, making finance a matter of bureaucracy, not of trust in the private sector or of parliament. It is perhaps scarcely surprising, therefore, that the credits these institutions afforded were inadequate to the policies of the State that held finance in so tight a grip. The Bank of England permitted Britain to finance her wars against Napoleon via borrowing against the future—deficit-financing—while the Napoleonic regimes, traumatized by the Revolution's experience with the assignats, rejected State debt and paper money.

Or the Civil Code, a modern document in its extrusion of religion and privilege from the realm of law, yet contains much that reacts against the democracy limned in the early Revolution. The code is frequently stigmatized by some of the greatest historians for being "bourgeois," and so it was. But in its time and place, it could hardly have been pro–working class, or even, after the Terror, resolutely democratic. "Bourgeois," moreover, is a broad and much-abused word. The bourgeoisie, after all, participated in and profited from the Revolution, yet a bourgeois merchant or industrialist of 1800 would not, professionally speaking, have found the Civil Code particularly congenial or farsighted, for its notion of "property" was based mainly on immobile forms of landed wealth—an "aristocratic" notion, actually.

The granite blocks, then, were the means by which a property-owning society of the eighteenth century, led by an Enlightenment general, strove to make a good exit from the most extravagant political ordeal of modern times—an ordeal that the General and his supporters regarded as greatly admirable and greatly pernicious. They had lived out Dickens in advance of his writing; they had seen the best of times and the worst of times, and their challenge lay in separating the two. They agonized less over what they had seen than they worried about what could happen if the ordeal continued—not only by way of war and invasion, but by way of popular unrest and demands. They felt degrees of social fear. Toward the goal of domestic peace on their own social terms, they made reforms or consolidations, which effectively sacrificed politics to administration.

Yet the men of Brumaire were also stubborn in their grip on the fundamental social gains of the Revolution, and they believed that their willingness to sacrifice in the political sphere was not unlimited.

The leader they had chosen—mainly for his military glory and intellectual brilliance—was a minor noble from a traditional rural (and foreign) society. His social and economic vision was slightly behind that of most of the men he worked with. In the crunch of the short term—and the government was always staggering from one crisis to the next—the General had a tendency to fall back on what he knew best and trusted most—the traditional rural, landholding Catholic society and its imagined harmony—rather than to reach for the newer society of commerce and industry that may have tempted him for the future. None of this proved to be a serious problem.

It was otherwise, however, with the General's temperament and personality, and their intended and unintended political consequences.

THE POLITICS OF DEPOLITICIZATION . . .

Political news daily loses some of the pressing interest we used to feel when, each morning, we learned of some great crime or conflict or read the announcement of a great law that had been conceived, drafted, and adopted in the space of fifteen minutes. . . . Today, the most fervent of every party have adjusted to a new tranquility and seem to have renounced their factions. The time we used to devote to combating errors can now be put to projects of public utility.[60]

—*La Décade Philosophique*

Recall the Terror: Robespierre, though a dictator, is hostage to the popular societies and the political newspapers that he simultaneously mistrusts yet needs, his arms and legs in the wild flight forward that he and the Committee of Public Safety glumly elect. Implacably, with bitter reluctance, the Virtuous One sends his political foes to prison and to the guillotine by the tens of thousands. He suspends elections and governs by decree, and never has a political party or an opposition been less safe (nor more called for). Yet the stock of his enemies does not diminish, and the political fever never flags in a land worked over by representatives-on-mission. Isser Woloch writes aptly of the "grim paradox" that is "the simultaneous expansion and contraction of democratic space."[61] All this politics and so little choice, so little progress; so much talk of "virtue" and *patrie,* not enough patriotism.

The historian H. A. L. Fisher considered one of Bonaparte's best political insights to be this: "You cannot rule a nation unless you adjust your political contrivances to suit the peculiar temperament."[62] Well, the "new tranquility," superbly described in the newspaper citation above, was the First Consul's principal "political contrivance" to rid society of "politics," to remove it from "the dictatorship of the event." Bonaparte knew from his youth and his young adulthood in revolutionary Corsica what it was to be powerless, hence politicized. He had found the experience vertiginous, demoralizing, and career-upending. In his resolve to put the drama of political polarization behind him, he was nothing less than typical of many in the political class of his generation. Politics was or ought to be the preserve of power, of the State—specifically, of the head of State. "[T]he great statesmen you believe to be violent, cruel, and so on," he impatiently lectured guests at Malmaison, "*are merely being political.* [Emphasis added.] They know themselves, they judge themselves better than you can." The result was predictable. In Mme de Rémusat's words, "It was with the magical power of this sacramental phrase, *ma politique,* that he crushed the thought, feelings, and even the impressions [of people] . . .")[63]

In sum, the fervent desire to have done with "all that" motivated Consular reform and its reception. In place of the breathlessness of daily political life in the Revolution, the Brumaire regime offered forms of politics crafted for a post-political society. Politics may be minimally necessary, Bonaparte believed, but it must not be too serious, not deal with ultimates, lest it become too divisive. In this sense, Napoleon shared the liberal and legalist vision. By taste, talent, and temperament, Bonaparte absorbed the color, the power, the politics, and the charisma into himself. He and his doings provided the show—and some show it was—and most of the vast audience turned to watch, in passivity and appreciation. French interest in elections had been steadily declining since 1793. In place of local elections with its factions and newspapers, civil servants now provided efficient "public services." In place of national elections, there were rare plebiscites on single, simple questions. With such structures, and in a polity where 46 percent of the males (and 66 percent of the females) were illiterate, it was felt a safe and clever bet to resurrect universal male suffrage—a way to create the form of "democracy."

What overtook Consular France was government by administration. In the First Consul's words, "When all is organized . . . it is natural that the work of administration should increase and that of legislation diminish."[64] Rule by decree, whether Bonaparte's or a prefect's, invoked law "derived from the administration, enforced by the administration, interpreted by the administration. In theory the doctrine of popular sovereignty is upheld; but the control of the legislature is necessarily diminished."[65] If the word "technocrat" had existed, Bonaparte might have used it to describe what he was looking for in his appointments: men of competence, above all; most had a revolutionary past—few in the political class didn't have one after ten years—but they had been "reconstructed" by events, and some of the ex-Jacobins were outright repentant. A few may have been sympathetic to some form of royalism, but almost none supported the old regime.

It all more or less fell into place after 1802, as Bonaparte wished. That large domain of political action that in Great Britain belonged to the sphere of Parliament or in the United States to Congress fell, in France, to the bureaucracy.[66] The results have been inimitably captured by Balzac in his description of the Empire as a regime: "The nosiest, most meticulous, most scribbling, red-tape mongering, list-making, controlling, verifying, cautious, and finally just the most cleaning-lady of administrations—past, present, or future." A political opposition developed, as we shall see, but it was a small (if prestigious) fraction of the elite. For the broad base of society in most parts of France, the prefect of Seine-Inférieure's report is illustrative: "When a people has made a good and serious delegation of public power, it can do no better than to busy itself with everything else."[67] Adolphe Thiers puts it: "The better minds, tired of political turmoil, happily turned themselves to whatever had to do with industry and commerce."[68]

. . . AND THE "NATIONAL" FIX

You may well imagine I cried "Vive la Nation!"
—Napoleon Bonaparte,
  recounting his run-in with
  a suspicious group of sans-culottes,
  August 10, 1792

Ideology is the imaginary relationship people have with the real conditions of their existence.

—Louis Althusser

Bonaparte scorned theory, but theory was not done with Bonaparte. For all that the First Consul rejected "metaphysics," certain identifying traits of his modus operandi had already struck contemporaries. By the end of 1797, for example, the neologism "Bonapartismo" was circulating in northern Italy; admittedly vague, it pointed to something that was simultaneously a doctrine, party, principle, and temperament—all of it distinguishable from the ambient forms of Jacobinism that also jockeyed for position in progressive circles in Milan, Turin, or Genoa.[69] We shall see later what bonapartism might amount to, but for now let us see how it talked.

A curious and quiet evolution has occurred in Bonaparte's language. His letters and writings of 1793–97 speak in the "correct" tongue of the later Rev-

olution: the point of reference is always "the Republic." To protect and glo-
rify the Republic, the General wins his victories, and is even prepared, or so
he tells Carnot (May 14, 1797), "to sacrifice . . . every idea in my head." Rare
are Napoleonic references to the less politically correct "France."[70] As for the
freighted "nation," Bonaparte, like all republicans, used it as a facile synonym for "Republic," as in this line from the leading Constitutional
bishop, Grégoire, which the pre-Consular Bonaparte might have easily
said: "There is not a 'people' of Menton, nor of any other city in France.
There are citizens of Menton, Nice, Paris, *but there is only one 'people,' that of
the entire Republic, . . . of the entire Nation.*"[71]

Then, in the summer of 1797, a new locution made its appearance in the
Napoleonic repertoire: *La Grande Nation.* The flattering phrase instantly
became common coin in the late Directory,[72] for it neatly took for granted the
territorial expansion of the French Republic to the north and south. "Great,"
or aggrandizing, "Nation" was a new, usefully vague way of saying "natural
frontiers" ("national" and "natural" being virtual synonyms in the eighteenth
century). But it did grander business than that. As Jean-Yves Guiomar astutely
notes, the phrase was "more than a spatial and territorial concept, it was
France putting herself with Greece and Rome at the top of human history, as
the most recent (the last?) great emancipating civilization." The Great Nation,
Bonaparte seemed to imply, "wasn't great because it was quantitatively large; its
growth was simply the normal due and visible testimony of inner greatness."[73]

Despite the revolutionary catechism that admitted no shadow of difference among the three classic nouns, "Republic," "Nation," and "France,"
there yet remained crucial nuances among them, as Bonaparte was aware. By
the time he returned from Egypt, we notice that "France" and "nation" were
becoming preferred usage in his letters, dispatches, and proclamations,
although in official language, he could not avoid "Republic." At a public banquet, he drinks "to the union of all Frenchmen," while his fellow honoree,
General Moreau, toasts "to all the loyal allies of the Republic." The more
savvy among the guests at the affair surely understood the strain of fusion or
conciliation that was present in Bonaparte's version—the readiness to reach
out to moderates with a less charged nominative than "Republic," while
Moreau opted for revolutionary orthodoxy. Around the same time Bonaparte
upbraided the Directory, "What have you done with this France [*not* this
republic] that I left you so brilliant?" True, the immediately post-coup
proclamation "To the French" interchanges "France" and "Republic," but if
we look at the carefully worded declaration (December 28, 1799) "To the
Inhabitants of the departments of the West," we note that it treads lightly on
republic-talk. In a land where counterrevolution simmers, Bonaparte prefers

to write, "Let those who want the *glory of France* separate ourselves from the men who persist in wanting to mislead us."

In a letter to an inhabitant of the occupied territories in Belgium (November 24, 1799), the new consul tells Baron Beyts that he wants him and other local notables "to rally the mass of the people. The simple title of French citizen is worth far more than that of Royalist, Clichien, Jacobin, Feuillant, or any other of the thousand-and-one labels that have sprung up in the past ten years out of a spirit of faction, and which are hurling the *nation* into an abyss from which the time has come at last to rescue it, once and for all." Arrogance lurks in the assumption that patriotism for Belgians cannot possibly mean wanting the French the hell out of their *patrie,* but what is more interesting for our present purpose is that "France" and "nation" are preferred to "Republic," for "Republic" rings too partisan. (Beyts, as it happened, rallied and eventually became prefect of the Loir-et-Cher.)

The Consular regime sang even more loudly the chords of "nation" and "France." Another proclamation "To the French," dated March 8, 1800, entreats citizens to pay taxes and answer the colors: "Frenchmen, you want peace. Your government [*not* the Republic] desires it even more ardently." There follow four references to "France," two to "government," two to "nation"—and none to "Republic."[74] Later, judicial officials drop their old oath "to be faithful to the one and indivisible Republic, founded upon liberty, equality, and the representative system," and instead promise "to remain faithful to the Constitution and to fulfill scrupulously the functions entrusted to them."[75] Bonaparte's message to the Senate (May 20, 1803) informing it of the likelihood of renewed war with England, makes no mention of the Republic, saying, rather, "It is not in [the British] government's power to curb the majesty of *the French people.* [Emphasis added.]"

What does this all mean? The shift from "Republic" to "nation" registers at the level of language the escape from *la* into *le politique* in Consular France. No passionate imbiber of Rousseau, as Bonaparte once was, could fail to understand the French longing for unity.[76] "Nation" was the sacred word of 1789 that vocalized that longing, that re-created on the imaginary level the unity and harmony, which the real conditions of social existence denied to the French. This desire for unity and harmony packed powerful normative and expressive significance into an apparently simple, objective, uncontested pair of nouns, "nation" and *patrie.* They were regarded as sacred, as scoffers were the first to understand. In 1793–94 a person could be arrested if even his child or spouse shouted "To hell with the patriots!"—as did a boy who lost a card game in a cafe. That young man went to the guillotine. So did an exasperated older fellow heard to mutter, "Merde à la nation!" in a crowded street.

Words counted. "Nation," "national," and "patriot" were talismans that signified nonpartisanship in the revolutionary popular imagination. A Jacobin club
billing itself "The Antipoliticals" flourished in Aix-en-Provence during the revolution; its members proclaimed themselves devoted solely to "true patriotism"
and they shunned "la politique."[77] Yet, in the reality of social life—in the turbulent swirl of "le politique"—"nation" and "patriot" were *partisan,* as that
unlucky boy and older fellow both understood, and as Bonaparte himself
understood, if only half consciously. In a famous line, the First Consul
announced, in effect, that *his* party was not a party: "To govern through a party
is sooner or later to make yourself dependent on it. You won't see it happen
to me: I'm *national.*" Paraphrasing Bonaparte's letter to Carnot, cited earlier,
we might say that one of the "ideas" he has proved himself willing to "sacrifice" to "France" is "Republic."[78]

Eighteen hundred was a late era for "nation," however. Nation-talk had, for
an endless decade now, become a notorious vehicle of partisan work. Sieyès
had launched the gambit with *What Is the Third Estate?*: the answer to the title
question being "it is the nation." In four short words he had thus excluded
the most powerful and wealthy castes of the kingdom (the clergy and nobility) from being French. When, ten years later, Bonaparte boasted to Sieyès, "I
have made the Great Nation," Sieyès is said to have countered, "You could
not have done so had we not first made the Nation."[79] A clever enough retort,
but cynical in the measure that it gives the ghost away on what has come, by
both men's admissions, to be a kind of ploy. "Nation," one has the impression, should now be written with quotation marks. Bonaparte summed up
the revolutionary use of "nation" with his usual brutal frankness: "When the
rabble gains the day, it ceases to be rabble. It is then called 'the nation.' If it
does not [gain the day]—why, then some are executed, and they are called rabble, rebels, robbers, and so forth. Thus goes the world." According to Karl
Marx, a relatively influential nineteenth-century Socialist, workers have no
nations. Or we might paraphrase the socialist philosopher Pierre-Joseph
Proudhon (1809–65), "Whoever invokes the nation wants to cheat."[80]

For Bonaparte, as for Sieyès, the term "nation," whatever it started out as
in their hearts, evolved into an abstraction to be manipulated. In the course
of a fascinating—because it was open-ended and candid—conversation in
1803 with the twenty-three-year old Claire de Rémusat, the wife of the
Comte de Rémusat, a nobleman who had rallied to Bonaparte and was soon
to be made Prefect of the Palace, the First Consul noted in passing that he
had "always known," from the first moments of the Revolution, that this
event's "advantages" would never accrue to the actual "people" who
acclaimed it and in whose name its vast works were done.[81] "Nation" was cru-

cial for what it did *not* denote—that is, the king (or "god")—not for the actual population it denoted.

"Nation-talk," as we shall use the term here, in sum, is not just *any* expression of patriotism. Occasional references to "nation" are pandemic among all the actors on the political stage in the modern era; in that sense France may indeed be considered to be what the great historian C. J. H. Hayes called her: "a nation of patriots."[82] However, if we reserve the phrase "nation-talk" to refer to reiterated, intense, and significant use of the concept, "nation," and its crucial derivative, "national," then we shall quickly see that it includes only *some* (and actually rather few) parties and individuals. Although all the players on (and off) the political stage "love France," and repeatedly say they "love France," and even occasionally invoke the "French nation," *not all players do so systematically.* "Nation" and "national" turn out to be hard to invoke systematically, for doing so arouses expectations and awakens possibilities that are difficult for political actors, especially in positions of State power, to live with.

Nation-talk, in sum, is a particular style of politics—the theory of the statesman who affects not to believe in theories or parties. Despite advice to the contrary, Bonaparte refused to create a bonapartist party. Nation-talk became his way of not being seen as partisan or political. He needed to hand over Venice to Austria? He prepared the way by asserting that the Venetians were too corrupt and effeminate to be any longer considered "a nation." The French were certainly a nation in the First Consul's telling, but their nationhood must be "constituted" more firmly. This required "centralizing power and increasing the authority of government." Consider Bonaparte's justification for "public instruction": "So long as the people are not taught from their earliest years whether they ought to be republicans or royalists, Christians or infidels, the State cannot properly be called a *nation.*" From an outsider's viewpoint, "constituting the nation" has meant imposing, in the guise of unity, a most political sort of uniformity. There is even a degree of Orwellian nonsense involved, as in Bonaparte's commissioning Méhul to compose a "Chant national" with the message: "Victory, victory will win peace."

The Marquis de Lafayette, we recall, despaired over the "national mess" *(le margouillis national)* that France had fallen prey to. Bonaparte, we might say, applied the "national" fix. In the last analysis, the quotations around the term are necessary. Bonaparte is a Corsican who has lived through and discarded a sincerely passionate attachment to patriotism. His fundamental take on nations is best expressed in a letter of 1805 to his viceroy (and stepson) in Italy: "The time will come when you will realize that there is little difference between one nation and another."

NAPOLEON AND THE BONAPARTES

With Napoleon, the private man must not be judged by the public one.
—Arthur Lévy[83]

His appearance still depended on the attitude behind the eye of the beholder. Some described him as "moderately stout due to a frequent use of baths," while others thought him "looking very thin and yellow." People did agree that he now wore his hair (thinning on top) short, but his expressions varied, and few were around him enough to get a sense of the whole. His secretaries and valets disagreed whether he was most often calm, grave, or meditative; Bourrienne, for one, thought he was more temperamental than that. All concurred that when he got angry ("and he seemed to be able to control these explosions at will," notes Méneval), his eyes "flashed fire, his nostrils dilated, and he was swollen with the inner storm." In good humor, or when wishing to please or charm, his expression was "sweet and caressing, and his face lit up with a most beautiful smile." The smile, whether a smirk or sincere, was always recalled.

He tended to dress simply, except when he did not—which suited his anti-aristocratic aristocratic style. In the midst of a magnificent reception for Lord Cornwallis at the Tuileries, amid the strutting peacocks of his court, he stood out for the simplicity of his Chasseur's uniform,[84] but also for the brilliance of the Regent diamond, sparkling on his sword hilt. When thoughtful or working, he paced back and forth, his hands held flat behind his back, staring intently at the floor. But when he looked an interlocutor in the eye, he was intimidating. A royalist meeting with him to discuss reconciliation at first took Bonaparte for a domestic. Then, however, "he raised his head. He had grown in stature, and the fire of the look suddenly hurled at me signaled Bonaparte."[85]

The personality was every bit the equal of the look and the role of a great (and a *French*) head of State. It constantly surprised people for its apparent guilelessness. The Prussian ambassador quickly fell under Bonaparte's charm: "He speaks frankly and truthfully. He has a savvy about men and about affairs, and above all, he has a gift for inspiring confidence in people." Marmont believed that the famous Bonaparte charm "which no one could mistake" came from its possessor's simplicity of heart. Bonaparte, he wrote, was "one of the easiest men to touch with true feeling, . . . [he had] a grateful and welcoming heart, I could even say sensitive." Charles James Fox, a leader of the English opposition, had a different reaction to the First Consul when he visited Paris in 1802. What stood out in his mind was the man's "disenchantment," which Fox attributed—in a priori fashion, one senses—to Napoleon's having "lived through a revolution that was begun for humanity but shipwrecked in blood."[86]

If his enemies could still refer to his being foreign (Corsican), Bonaparte himself felt entirely French. At a State dinner given by Talleyrand for the king of Etruria (in northern Italy), the monarch took Napoleon aside and said to him in Italian, "But honestly, you're Italian, you're one of us." The First Consul replied dryly, "Je suis français."

The opening years of the new century saw Bonaparte search for, but never quite find, a home of the true sort that he had had in Ajaccio. It wasn't for want of trying. Returning from Egypt, he moved into Josephine's little house in the rue de Chantereine (the street having been redubbed the rue de la Victoire[87] in his honor). Within weeks, they moved to an exquisite country house, to the west of Paris, which Josephine had copurchased with Napoleon, each contributing half the required amount.[88] Malmaison, despite its name ("mal," because it had once been a hospice for the seriously ill), became a place of connubial and familial happiness for the pair. The Bonapartes being an expansive and inclusive couple, with a large extended family, Malmaison became the lustrous center of many lives in the early Consulate—*young lives*. At thirty-nine (in 1802), Josephine was self-conscious about being "old," but all around her was youth and the celebration of youth. Her children were nineteen and twenty-one, her husband, thirty-three, his siblings and in-laws, his officers, and even some of his advisors were all in their twenties and early thirties. (The oldest of the men Bonaparte worked with regularly in government were only in their forties.) For the rest of his life, Josephine's son, Eugène de Beauharnais, would recall the luminous days of Malmaison—the women (girls, really) dressed in white, as the First Consul preferred; the officers decked our far more gaudily, in their splendid uniforms. Future Marshals Ney, Macdonald, Bessières, and Lannes all met their wives at Malmaison. It might have been a West Point prom except that these were real generals.

Still, Malmaison was a weekend refuge and not grand enough to be the principal residence of the First Consul of the French Republic. Too, it was—and would always be—Josephine's place (she would retire here after the divorce, and die here in 1814). So after Brumaire, Bonaparte took over apartments at the Petit-Luxembourg, on the Left Bank of the Seine. He stayed there but only a couple of months, for the palace was on the miniature side, and was too associated with the Directory. In February 1800, he moved to the former royal palace of the Tuileries, across the river. "Moving into the Tuileries isn't everything," he told Bourrienne. "You have to stay here."

The First Consul resolved to make his "court" the most imposing in Europe, if only to show monarchical Europe that republican France could win at that game, too, however personally tedious Bonaparte found it. The ex-revolutionaries among the men of Brumaire did not complain, at least not loudly. A Swedish aristocrat familiar with the old regime at Versailles remarked upon the "grandiose public splendor, far greater than what you see in our time in most courts," and the Prussian ambassador informed his sovereign that the opulence of the liveries and rigidly enforced etiquette at the Consular Tuileries were "unimaginable" in Berlin.[89]

And yet, and yet: the First Consul continued to use "citizen" in address—a habit or whimsy widely remarked on, if difficult to read.

The palace where Louis XVI endured the final ignominies of his ill-starred reign did not completely satisfy the First Consul, either, although the Tuileries did remain the official residence of the First Consul (and Emperor). Bonaparte wanted something else, more natural and with more of nature.[90] So Bonaparte presently selected the palace where his own stately story had begun: the elegant chateau of Saint-Cloud, a favorite dwelling of Marie-Antoinette's—a fact that pleased him. The classical chateau, with its acres of beautiful parks and neighboring woodlands, sat on a bluff above the Seine, southwest of Paris, a quarter of an hour by carriage from the center of town (far faster than by Citroën limousine in today's traffic). A mere three million francs, spent between 1801 and 1803, did the repairs needed to bring Saint-Cloud up to Consular standards.

There would be other Napoleonic residences, *many* of them—notably Fontainebleau, the Renaissance hunting "lodge" of King Francis I; and Compiègne, after his marriage to Marie-Louise—but none pleased their restless occupant. He once carped, "Why have all the architects who have built residences for sovereigns pulled it off so badly? I've seen no chateau, no palace, that can please me."[91] Perhaps the reason he found no angle of repose in a building had to do with reasons other than the architectural.

With public activities taking up most of his time, Bonaparte held fewer wide-ranging conversations with his associates, though he continued to trust implicitly a handful among them, notably Cambacérès, the Second Consul, whom he entrusted with his most delicate and important political assignments. But he had no friends—a much-commented-upon fact, though true of many great heads of State. Bourrienne might have remained the faithful Achates to his old classmate's Achilles, for he was indispensable in the Consul's daily life, but the old classmate let his cupidity lead him to abuse Bonaparte's favor ("he had the eye of a magpie," Napoleon said of him) and get himself trapped in commercial scandal. The need for Bourrienne's dismissal weighed heavily on the First Consul, embarrassing and saddening him so much that he put it off, until finally, one day in 1802, he blurted out, "Give any papers and keys you have of mine to Méneval, and leave. And never let me see you again."[92]

Would-be friends and close associates were replaced by family in Bonaparte's daily and emotional life. In his devotion to his family, he is commonly said to have remained "very Corsican," but for that to be true, it would need to be shown that extended French, Irish, and American families do not also often prefer each other, take exuberant pleasure in their company, and systematically advance one another's designs. The Bonapartes argued fiercely and famously, and accorded their brother rather less than the grateful docility he wanted, but with one exception, he remained close to them, spending his free time with them, and showering them with wealth and positions.

Joseph, as always, was incomparable for the trust he inspired in and received from Napoleon. He was thirty-four when he negotiated the Treaty of Amiens for France. At Mortefontaine, where he lived in luxury with his wife and two daughters, he received many of the leading intellectual, literary, and political lights of the day. Lucien, still brilliant, still a loose cannon, became interior minister—his reward for his priceless action at Brumaire. In the spring of 1800, he became a widower; it required all of a month for him to recover from his "profound despair" and begin dating again. Louis, full of filial devotion to Napoleon, agreed to become a soldier in spite of himself (he had no fiber or taste for the military). He was a colonel at twenty-one (in 1800). Jérôme, the Benjamin of the pack, was a freshly commissioned officer in the French navy.

The oldest and least comely of the Bonaparte sisters, Elisa, had married at twenty, in 1797, to Felix Bacciochi, a plain-witted, unambitious Corsican who was a captain in the army. Napoleon, displeased with the match, nonetheless resigned himself to promoting Bacciochi. In 1802 the couple were living grandly in Paris, where Elisa kept a salon frequented by the Catholic writer Chateaubriand and a rising political star, Fontanes. Felix would soon be a general and a senator. Napoleon's favorite, Pauline—a beautiful and vivacious woman—fell in love with one of her brother's more gifted officers, Victor Leclerc. They wed in 1797 at Mombello, with the family present. Five years later, Leclerc was dead in Saint-Domingue of yellow fever—fortunate not to have fallen into the hands of the Haitian rebels he was sent to suppress. Napoleon arranged Pauline's second marriage to a scion of one of Rome's grandest houses, the Borgheses, granting them French citizenship so that his beloved "Paulette"—perhaps the sibling who loved him best—could live in Paris. Caroline, the most ambitious of the sisters ("in her," Napoleon would say, "the head of a statesman sits on the shoulders of a pretty woman"), had married Joachim Murat, her brother's most famous general, and a great cavalry commander. He would soon receive the prestige post of military governor of Paris.

But the epicenter of Napoleon's emotional life remained his wife. The climactic crisis between them, on his return from Egypt, had, as we saw, lanced his great obsession. Thereafter, the self-cauterization of that wound (for survival)[93] and Josephine's unexpectedly, but truly, falling in love with her husband led the pair to settle into a happy relationship. Napoleon wrote her one day of the "magnetic fluid" which he imagined flowed between them, as between all "people who love each other." It was a great satisfaction to her that Bonaparte adopted her children. (Eugène, at seventeen, had distinguished himself on the Egyptian expedition, and was a brigadier general at twenty-one, in 1802. Hortense would soon be wed to Louis Bonaparte.) Josephine had known her man all along but now she proved it. Napoleon would say at the end of his life, "Josephine possessed an exact knowledge of the intricacies of my character."

Their life together was far from perfect. Josephine suffered profoundly from psychological and other insecurities, not a few of them (e.g., her sterility) well founded. It was a source of the deepest frustration for her and Napoleon that his family remained stubbornly unwilling to accept or even to be kind to "that woman." Napoleon forced the Bonapartes to accept her, but the tension at being with her in-laws was never far from her consciousness. Then, too, Napoleon occasionally took mistresses—the actress Mlle George, or Eléonore Denuelle de la Plaigne, by whom he had a natural son (the Comte de Léon). He insisted, however, that these women posed no threat to Josephine. "She worries far more than she should that I will fall seriously in love," he told Mme de Rémusat. He asks the rhetorical question, "What is love, anyway?" to which he offers the common romantic answer: "[Love is] a passion which sets all the universe on one side and the solitary loved one on the other." Then he says, "It is certainly not in my nature to surrender to any such overwhelming feeling." The reader of Mme de Rémusat waits to see if the author—an appreciative, yet critical, and always perceptive observer of Bonaparte—will respond to this last bit of banter. But she says nothing. She cannot know of the First Consul's letters to his wife from 1796 to 1799.

Has Napoleon himself forgotten them? Is this a stunning example of clinical repression or a stunning example of disingenuousness? Or is he posturing for the pretty twenty-three-year-old prefect's wife?

BOOK III

Contre nous, de la tyrannie

IX

Power (III): Naming It
(From Citizen Consul to Emperor
of the French)

The most dangerous enemy of the people is the people: the flu-
idity of its character, the mobility of its ideas and affections. It is
this propensity for infatuation that makes a single fault efface
fifty years of virtue in their eyes, and the wrongs of an entire century disappear in the face of a single promise to fix them.

—(Constitutional) Bishop Grégoire

PARALLEL LIVES, PARALLEL PLOTS (1800–1802)

Some chroniclers—the hostile ones—date the start of the First Consul's
"reign," as if his regime were already a monarchy, from his return from
Marengo. This is reasonable if we are gauging the past by what followed, but
it may not be how Bonaparte himself experienced things. He was celebrated
for his victory and given a largely free hand to sculpt the "granite blocks,"
yet he was far from having yet amassed the pure cobalt of power, and the
sole name "Napoleon Bonaparte" should not blind us to the larger context:
the French Republic remained the only State in Europe where power was
formally derived from "the nation." The plebiscite, however notorious its
failings, was not felt to be a necessary sham in the autocracies of Russia,
Prussia, Austria, or Naples. Lucien Bonaparte's machinations in the refer-

endum ratifying Brumaire prove the lengths to which the government was willing to go to get popular legitimacy, "or at least to claim it."[1]

In the early years of power, the First Consul encountered opposition. Like Caesar or Robespierre, he was obsessed by it and perhaps overestimated it, for as it stood, it usually was of slight account. There were, after all, only thirteen newspapers still permitted to publish—only eight in Paris, with a combined readership of 20,000 in a population of 500,000. The opposition, in fact, posed only one major threat to the First Consul: death. Politically speaking, assassination attempts may be (and certainly were in this instance) a sign of the opponents' despair over their inability to deliver a successful challenge to their enemy's power and legitimacy. Indeed, Bonaparte's adversaries accomplished the opposite: they fostered the strengthening of his position.

The opposition's weakness had many faces and many reasons—starting with their foe's political skill and ending with his popularity—but among the rest the chief one was their own disparateness: the opponents were varied and disunited; they often hated or feared one another more than they did Bonaparte. They included disgruntled liberals of the Institute, the salons, and the legislature; Jacobin radicals who had opposed Brumaire; royalists driven to frenzy at the success of a moderate regime sporting monarchical overtones; and, finally, a cabal of rather vain and feckless army generals, some of whom were Jacobin in sympathy, some royalist, and some (the two most important) a bit of both.

The liberals did not seek Bonaparte's death, literal or political, only his acknowledgment that they played a crucial role in public life as the loyal opposition. The constitution had created a legislature whose members were paid handsomely, but their function and value were not commensurate with their salaries, and this disturbed them.[2] They had supported Brumaire and execrated (and feared) a revived Jacobinism; they fairly fell over themselves praising Bonaparte's intellectual brilliance and were not averse to seeing a strong regime emerge. Only gradually did they come to oppose the First Consul on principle, by which point it was far too late.

Bonaparte was willing—indeed, eager—to establish personal relationships with the parliamentary deputies, as he had with the savants at the Institute. Time and again, he suggested, "Instead of declaiming from the rostrum, why don't you come and talk with me privately? We could have family conversations."[3] But legislators with high ideals and high ambitions to make careers as parliamentary paladins envisioned winning for themselves measures of the kind of prestige and countervailing weight that accrued to Parliament or Congress. The First Consul, however, conceived government as the work of administration, by contrast to which the deputies' burdens were light: an annual review of the budget, receiving petitions from "the people," and the pro forma ratification of bills sent over by the executive. Degrees of boredom and underutilization among deputies were almost to be expected and encouraged. Argument and discussion had a role, but in the closed-door sessions of the Council of State—not the public venues of Tribunate and Legislative Body where criticism could become the stuff of newspapers and factions, ambition and interest. That, in Bonaparte's view, was the Anglo-Saxon way, not the French.

The great majority of the tribunes and the legislators agreed with, or at least accepted, the Consular view. A few, however—including some of the brightest lights (e.g., Benjamin Constant)—set out to test the waters. Their critical rhetoric met with fury, shock, and retribution from the First Consul. (Bonaparte had fewer problems with legislators who made criticisms quietly, avoiding resounding speeches.) The legislative opposition dug in over the petty and the principled, and sometimes over both at once: for example, the use of the word "subjects," not "citizens," in an article of a treaty with Russia. The legislators were capable of making a fuss over a minor bill about the archives but saying nothing in protest at the return of colonial slavery or the annexation of the Rhineland. What most irritated the First Consul was the Tribunate's and Legislative Body's refusal to give him the unanimous vote for the Concordat, which he had specifically requested. Too, a noisy minority also opposed the creation of the Legion of Honor, another "reform" they considered counterrevolutionary.

But what the parliamentary liberal opposition signally did *not* do was develop a powerful politics of protest around "republican" values or "national" protest, as previous oppositions had managed to do. *Au contraire,* it was the government that successfully tarred them with the factional brush. (A typical Napoleonic statement: "These are 12 or 15 men who imagine themselves to be an entire party. . . . I shall oppose against my enemies THE FRENCH PEOPLE."[4]) Objectively, the opposition's rare and disjointed forays amounted to little—a handful of rejected bills, all of them accomplished by the government via other means. Those experienced in revolutionary legislatures commented to Bonaparte that he had got off lightly.

The First Consul thought not. He was indignant over criticism and unaccustomed to defeat; these speeches, he felt, made him look ridiculous. His police operatives reported every useless detail of what was said among the deputies and in the elite salons they frequented, and Bonaparte counted it all. As Irene Collins notes, there was "an air of fantasy about most of these rumors, and of comic opera about police attempts to spy on [the legislators]."[5] In another era, public opinion might have backed the deputies, many of whom were skilled and well-meaning men, but this was a time of wide-spread "fatigue of pure reason" (or "cant"), so to speak, and any trace of trou-blemaking in the deputies was read by the public as obstructionism, disloyalty, or self-interest. Bonaparte expressed himself with revealing asper-ity: "Do these phrase-makers and ideologues imagine they can attack me like I was Louis XVI? I won't stand for it. I am a child of the revolution, sprung from the loins of the people, and I won't suffer being insulted like I was a king."

The Consulate faced a greater threat from the far left and the far right. A group of discontented Jacobins struck at Bonaparte with an assassination plot in October 1800, but it was defused by Fouché's police. The First Consul bided his time, waiting for an occasion to have done with the "anarchists." The occasion did not dawdle. On Christmas Eve, a devastating bomb ("an infernal machine") was exploded just after the Consular carriage passed a spot on the rue Nicaise, on its way to a concert. Bonaparte was unharmed but a number of soldiers and bystanders was killed. The First Consul and some of his associates were convinced it was a Jacobin plot; Bonaparte was so furious that he declared himself "ready to constitute myself as a court of justice and have the guilty arraigned before me."[6]

Fouché, however, suspected the infernal machine was a royalist deed, and proved it with extremely skillful police work.[7] By then, however, the First Consul, eager to profit from public indignation, was already hot on the Jacobins' traces. This was so very bonapartist: to kill two birds with one stone. The special tribunals set up to prosecute Consular enemies raised a hue and cry in the legislature, which accused the regime variously of reverting to the Terror or abandoning the Revolution (as if the Terror were not the warp and woof of the Revolution). The deputies' charges highlight a contrast in the deployment of the key nominatives, with "republic" now being placed in opposition to "nation" and "France": "Let the government rally more wholeheartedly than it is doing to *republican* principles, *republican* institutions, to *republican* opinion. . . . Let the reins of government be confined to *repub-lican* hands."[8]

Another Jacobin initiative came from disgruntled army officers. A cabal at Rennes, which perhaps included Bernadotte, hid pamphlets in butter jars containing phrases like "Soldiers, you no longer have a *patrie,* no longer a Republic. It is a vain word. . . . A little Corsican tyrant now dictates his laws to you. . . . Soon a Bourbon will be on the throne or Bonaparte will have made himself emperor."[9] Here, too, the police were five paces ahead of any and all plotters, while Fouché, true to his political roots, did his best to trans-fer the blame onto the royalists.

The wake of the rue Nicaise attack, it was believed, was no moment to protest the means chosen by Bonaparte to repress his assailants; the regime and its supporters convincingly asserted there was greater danger in their enemies' abuse of liberty than in their own use of special authority. Bonaparte sensed the social fear aroused by the Jacobins among the haves. Making "a great example" by deporting 130 "terrorists" would, he said, "attach to me a middle class all too tired of being threatened by mad wolves, ever in wait of the right moment to pounce on their prey." Punishing these "anarchists" was an issue of "guaranteeing the social order," and no protests from the legislature backed by a handful of "metaphysicians"—a reference to the self-named Ideologues at the Institute—was going to stop him from doing so. It was one of the most unjust and abject abuses of power in Napoleon's career. Adolphe Thiers, as famous a defender of the bourgeoisie as French letters or politics has ever produced, judges that Napoleon's deportation of these men without due process was "the only mistake he committed in this time [1800–1802] of perfect conduct."[10]

The First Consul's alacrity in pursuing the revolutionary old guard did not mean that he was remiss about the royalists. His critics accuse Napoleon of favoring the right over the left, and it is true that he was more eager to win the nobility to his colors than to rally the left. He was considerably more flattering to noble *ralliés* than to Jacobin *ralliés*, but then he knew the latter better and took them more for granted. In fairness to Bonaparte, he had a far greater chance of rallying some or most of the 150,000 émigrés than he had in converting a few hundred neo-Jacobin intransigents. Both extremes were family to him: the nobility representing his social origins, for all that they looked down their blue noses at the Corsican *nobliau*; the Jacobins representing the Revolution, hence his ideological (or adopted) family. And both, of course, were, or could be, *frères ennemis*, instilling in him their own variety of special fear and loathing. At the end of the day, he was harsh on the well-known recalcitrants of both sides, and eager to rally their nameless flocks.

The Bourbon pretender was at first so relieved to see an anti-Jacobin regime arise in France that he confused it with an anti-revolutionary one. He wrote Bonaparte after Brumaire to feel him out about a restoration of Louis XVIII. He was badly mistaken, however, about the limitations of the new moderation and the limitlessness of the First Consul's pride. Bonaparte's was not a head to be turned by promises of royal largesse. He replied courteously but succinctly: "Sacrifice your interest and your rest for the happiness of France. History will thank you."[11]

The conspiracies, assassination attempts, and stirring up of civil strife continued, as did the Consulate's sweeping and successful repressions. By the end of 1802, both the counterrevolutionary party and the extreme revolutionary party were decimated and demoralized. Germaine de Staël summed it up acidly: repression "was the one kind of impartial justice from which he never flinched, so that he was only able to make friends out of those to whose hatreds he ministered."[12]

At the height of this febrile climate of joy at the Republic's victories, cut by anxiety at the nation's vulnerability in having its fortune hang on the life of one man, Lucien Bonaparte, with the likely connivance of his brother, floated a brilliant and risky plan to increase the First Consul's power. As minister of the interior, Lucien arranged in November 1800 for the drafting and distribution of a pamphlet under the title of *A Parallel among Caesar, Cromwell, Monck and Bonaparte.*[13] Ostensibly anonymous, it was intended to turn up in an official envelope on the desk of every prefect in the Republic. Whatever might have dismayed them in this essay, its force could not have failed to strike them.

> Individuals appear in certain epochs who found, destroy, and restore empires. Everything bends before their ascendance. Their fortune is something so extraordinary that it carries before it even those who once imagined themselves his rival. Our revolution had given birth to greater events than it managed to give rise to men to contain them. . . . The Revolution seemed pushed by who-knows-what blind force that both created and overturned everything. For ten years, we had sought a strong and knowing hand that could stop it, yet at the same time preserve it. . . . This person has appeared.

The sharp originality of the pamphlet is the parallel between Caesar and Bonaparte—a correspondence that may seem evident to us but was a bold gambit for supporters of the First Consul in 1800. Lucien is willing to risk assuming Caesar's troubling political baggage as the undertaker of the Roman Republic, in order to lay claim to his unique force and glory: "Bonaparte, like Caesar, is one of these dominating characters before whom all obstacles and all wills subside; their inspiration seems so supernatural that, in classical times, one would have considered them as living under the protection of a genie, or a god." No mention is made of Caesar's appointment as consul for life, with the right of naming his heir, but it was not necessary: the author could bank on the intended readers among France's political elites to know the outline of Caesar's life.

On only one question does the *Parallel* adduce a *difference* between Bona-

parte and Caesar. Caesar, the essay states, was "the chief of the demagogues"; he imposed himself by rallying the mob. Bonaparte, on the other
hand, "rallied property-owners and educated men against the mad multitude. . . . Caesar was a usurper and a tribune of the people; Bonaparte is the
legitimate consul." For an 1800 reader, this was a swipe at the opposition in
the Tribunate (who saw themselves as "tribunes of the people") as well as at
the Jacobins of the Year II. Caesar, in sum, was criticized *not* for opening the
path to empire, but for being a kind of Robespierre before the fact. (The
truth was: Bonaparte's achievement lay closer *both* to having rallied the
demos—the democracy—and to having actually based his power on an upper
middle class of independently wealthy [*rentier*] bourgeoisie.) If the *Parallel*
had stopped here, it might not have set off a tempest, but it marches resolutely on. The peroration has just transfigured "Bonaparte, Alexander, and
Caesar" in "the same theater of glory" when it raises a new question:
"What if, all of a sudden, Bonaparte were to be missing to the *patrie*, where
would we find an heir? . . . *The fate of thirty million people hangs on the life of one
man!* Frenchmen, what would you become if all of a suddenly a funereal
voice informed you that this man's life were over?" So *this* is the point: not
apotheosis but anxiety creation.

The remarkably early appearance of the *Parallel* only six weeks shy of the
first anniversary of Brumaire caught the eagle eyes of Fouché, who insisted
to the First Consul that now was no time to distribute such a tract. The police
chief had the support of Josephine; she had a veritable phobia about the matter of heredity—the issue of issues for this now-barren woman. It was well
known in political and family circles that Lucien saw himself, not Joseph, as
the right heir designate in the event that Napoleon gained the Caesarian privilege of naming his successor.[14] Lucien had a furious set-to with Fouché in
front of the First Consul, but the latter stood by his police chief; Lucien was
fired from Interior and sent to Spain as ambassador. The First Consul
declared "my only natural heir is the French people; *they* are my child," and
leaped to dissociate himself from the *Parallel*. Fouché proceeded to have the
pamphlet destroyed,[15] but the hand of Napoleon in its creation is clearly evident.[16] As he told Pierre-Louis Roederer, "The French can be governed only
by me. I am persuaded that no one other than I, were it Louis XVIII or even
Louis XIV, could govern France at this moment. If I perish, it is a tragedy
[*malheur*]."[17]

If the constitution of the Year VIII had provided for the right of executive
dissolution of the legislature in parliamentary fashion, it is all but certain that
Bonaparte's critics in the Tribunate and Legislative Body would have failed

to be reelected. Barring dissolution, the First Consul, it is said, would have done better serenely to ignore them—as he would, perhaps could, not do. But possibly there was a wisdom to his agitation over the opposition. Left ignored, might they not have raised themselves up into the full-blown loyal opposition they wanted to be? If they were of little account, then so was the Consulate's legitimacy still a brittle affair. In any case, Bonaparte became so obsessed with "this Medusa's head" that he imagined glaring at him from parliament, that he prepared to effect an outright purge.

But a purge was the Directory's way—to be avoided, at all costs. The fertile Cambacérès hit on a preferable option. The Senate was the guarantor of the constitution and nominator of legislators; have it publish a decree—a *senatus consultum,* in the high-flown Latin the French Senate sometimes used that would remove the dissenters among those legislators in the upcoming planned legislative renewal of 1802.[18] The men were sacked, and the operation wasn't even technically illegal, for the constitution was silent about exactly how renewal procedures would unfold.

In the spring of 1802, the Treaty of Amiens was signed with Britain, and this temporarily halted the plots being fomented by royalists dependent on English gold and operatives. The right had already lost its Vendée base, thanks to Bonaparte's pacification of the region, not to mention having had the wind taken out of its sails by the return of thousands of *ci-devants* (ex-nobles) who availed themselves of amnesty.[19] A new era dawned for the right, exemplified by the return and rallying of René de Chateaubriand. An admirer of both the First Consul's social conservatism and his dreams of colonial restoration, the young Catholic writer was friendly with Lucien and Elisa Bonaparte. The book he had completed, *Atala*—considered to be a first shimmer in the great rainbow of French Romanticism—contains unstinting praise for the First Consul whom it describes as "one of these men Providence sends as a sign of amends when He is tired of punishing us."

Chateaubriand's larger work in draft, of which *Atala* is a small part, is called *The Genius of Christianity.* Though its literary and theological value is mediocre, its ideological significance is epochal. Dedicated to Bonaparte,[20] *Genius* was published the year of the Concordat and is awash in its glow. The book disproves the notion that émigrés "learned nothing and forgot nothing" in exile, for it shows how a Catholic conservative has been led by the Revolution and its patriotically fueled anticlericalism—Chateaubriand is haunted by the objections and fears of the anti-Christianizing Jacobins—to recast his faith in their terms, not as a ploy but an utterly sincere migration in mentality. The book appears to be an apology for Christianity for its patriotic (not its Truth) value, but it goes beyond that. *Genius* postulates patriotism as a

God-given instinct, the first of any Christian's duties; it effectively subordinates Catholicism to the service of the (French) *patrie*.[21]

Bonaparte approved. *Genius* became one of his ideological arms to be
wielded against the Concordat's opponents.

CONSUL FOR LIFE (1802–1804)

*Wretches, will you hold back your praise because you are afraid that the move-
ment of the great machine might produce on you the same effect as Gulliver's on
the Lilliputians, when by moving his leg he crushed them?*

Napoleon Bonaparte[22]

With the achievement of peace in 1802, France was in harmony with herself
and with Europe for the first time in ten long years. But was she in harmony
with her First Consul? Bonaparte's reputation was legendary now; he reaped
so much credit for Marengo, Amiens, and the granite blocks that even an
opponent could concede: "Except for Washington in America, no chief
magistrate of any republic has ever been so universally popular."[23]

But were credit and the promise of eternal fame enough for him? A
republic can confer infinite measures of recognition and glory on a man, but
are there not limits to the power it can concede to him while yet remaining
a republic? This is the issue of issues with which contemporaries wrestled (as
does posterity) for the second half of the Consulate. Some condemn Bonaparte; others look at the nation that blinded itself by lionizing him. Georges
Lefebvre writes that the aura around Napoleon in 1802 prevented people
from "realizing that he was abusing his power and that he contemplated
objects inimical to their own interests. The French people still saw him as a
hero of the nation at the very moment that he had ceased to be one."[24]

In disowning Lucien's *Parallel*, Napoleon told Roederer, "Heredity isn't
something that can be forced, it happens on its own. It is too absurd to be
legislated as a law."[25] "Absurd" was the Revolution's way of looking at
heredity; "forcing it" was Lucien's way. In 1802 and again two years later,
Napoleon moved deftly to make it "happen on its own." He did it so well
that it almost appears as if the events leading from the initiative to make him
First Consul for Life to his coronation as Emperor of the French were the
sleek unfolding of one predetermined process. Perhaps it was, in his mind.
Many historians believe it was. Yet what keeps this inner logic from having
the same coherence in the world that it did (*if* it did) in his mind will be the

unpredictable matter of external events. In a word, making it "happen on its own" will depend on the unexpected return of war.

For now, however, in the spring of 1802, all was well. It seemed more than appropriate to confer on the great restorer of peace and prosperity a "striking gauge of the nation's recognition." This hint was tactfully conveyed to a sympathetic Tribunate by the faithful Cambacérès, so often (but not always) ready to anticipate, not merely obey, his patron. The problem was that the legislators could not see through Bonaparte's coy disclaimers about "desiring nothing but the right to serve the people"; they did not guess correctly what it was he really sought—the life consulate, with right to name his successor. This was the "gift" that Caesar had received from a grateful Roman Senate, and Bonaparte could ask no less. The French senators—perhaps more, perhaps less *rusé* than their ancient counterparts—chose to take the First Consul's false modesty seriously: they voted him merely another ten-year term in office—until 1820.

Disgusted, Bonaparte called a meeting of the Council of State where Cambacérès engineered a strategy to edge out the Senate. The government, in an extraordinary departure, would put "to the people" the question: "Should Napoleon Bonaparte be made First Consul for life?" A zealous counselor added a second question, "Should he have the right to name his successor?" but Napoleon struck it out as controversial. One thing at a time, he felt; with the life consulship in hand, the issue of succession could be decided. It may be that the decision to hold the plebiscite, *after* the Senate had spoken with its *senatus consultum* offering Bonaparte a reappointment of ten years, was illegal—a *coup d'Etat*.[26] The abashed Senate, for its part, took it as a punishment for its failure to do the First Consul's real bidding. Only a few Councilors of State, such as Théophile Berlier, expressed any misgivings at the Caesarian direction events seemed to be taking, but they did nothing and trusted to their confidence in Bonaparte as a "son of the Revolution."[27]

"The people," of course, overwhelmingly approved Bonaparte's new status. (Recall: the form of voting in a referendum was on public registers; it required considerable courage and conviction to place a *non* vote.) The nominal *oui* vote was 3,653,600, though the figure was inflated and may have been closer to 2.8 million. The *nons* were 8,272. It was the first time in French history that universal manhood suffrage actually chose a head of State. By comparison with 1799,[28] it was still an impressive performance by the era's electoral standards; the rate of participation had definitely risen, even though it came to only slightly more than half the electorate. The regime's berth in popular esteem was more secure than ever, for the vote backed up the First Consul's personal charisma and his halo of military glory with a "democratic election."[29] *Pace* Lucien Bonaparte's *Parallel,* the recourse to the plebiscite was a Caesarian act–democratic, populist, demagogic–not an elitist or aristocratic one. And it had the desired effect: it set a juridical linchpin to Bonaparte's already crushing and unique legitimacy–a legitimacy that effectively swallowed up that of any possible institution or competitor. It certainly drained bodies like the Senate or the two lesser houses of what small capacity or wish they still harbored to raise objections to further developments.

Opponents of the life consulship included Lafayette and Lazare Carnot, a tribune, though both agreed not to crystallize any opposition. Perhaps the most poignant attempt to slow Bonaparte's pace came from Antoine Thibaudeau, a member of the Council of State and a former *Conventionnel.* His private "Note for the First Consul" is a plaintive and candid document that as much as recognizes that nobody will be able to stop Bonaparte, because everyone around the First Consul is tired and afraid–afraid, both of angering and of losing him. Perhaps most of all, they are desirous of pleasing him, in gratitude for what he has accomplished. Thibaudeau is reduced to entreating Bonaparte to limit himself–to want "the real glory," by which he meant, Bonaparte agreeing to be a French George Washington.[30]

A Senate *senatus consultum* (August 1) named "Napoleon Bonaparte" (his first name appearing for the first time in a public document) as Consul for Life. The next day, the First Consul "seized" the Council of State with his project for a new set of "organic laws" that would consolidate his hold on power and further orient the regime as a democratic dictatorship.[31] Another constitution may strike us as superfluous, but that is to forget Bonaparte's mania for form; he wished to be free to do as he liked, but "legally."

The constitution of the Year X (1802) presented a few modifications. The Senate now had the right to dissolve the Tribunate and the Legislative Body, and the government to prorogue them. The former chamber was reduced to fifty members meeting in five separate sections, where they "jabbered" (Bonaparte's word) in secret, not in public. The new president appointed for the Tribunate was Fontanes, the coauthor, with Lucien, of the *Parallel.* The First Consul received few new powers; there was little left to give him. The peace treaties he negotiated no longer required legislative ratification, and he now had the regalian right of pardon. And he received the right to name his successor (one sees why he felt no need to put the question on the referendum). On the other hand, this power completely opened the can of worms that had long sat half opened on the Bonaparte family shelf. Who among his brothers might succeed him? Or would it be the son of a brother? Or would he adopt someone else, like Eugène de Beauharnais? Or get a divorce from his apparently barren wife?

The Council of State now found itself outflanked by a new, much smaller privy council, which advised the First Consul while arguing with him less. The wide-open debates were becoming a thing of the past, as the old council became mainly a venue for technicians and experts. The biggest status enhancement accorded by the new constitution was to the Senate-Guarantor, which, in view of its evolution under Bonaparte's pressure and Cambacérès's direction, should perhaps be redubbed the Senate-Assenter (or even the Senate-Kowtower). Its new powers to interpret and amend the constitution were ratified, and the body acquired the right to suspend trial by jury or impose martial law in specified departments.[32] It would be truer to say, these powers were held by the Senate *for* the government, for they could be exercised only on specific request by the government. The government in turn rewarded its senators. Roughly a third of them were endowed with landed domains (called "senatoriates") whose income amounted to the equivalent of their already outsized salary.

The Senate, in short, stood above all other institutions of the regime, save the Consulship itself. In the eyes of certain legal historians, it was as definitive of the regime as the First Consul himself; its presence made even the life consulate "an imperfect monocracy."[33] If the body was not the full theoretical equivalent of its Roman counterpart—even a Nero or a Caligula had formally held power "In the Name of the Senate and the Roman People" (S.P.Q.R.),* which was not the case in Consular France—the French Senate was yet the only institution of government that was remotely in a position to challenge the Consul, although, for years to come, it would remain Napoleon's compliant backup generator.

The only major change set up by the constitution was a new method of popular election of candidates for the legislature. It replaced the old constitution's lists of notables—that Sieyésian idea that the First Consul had suffered impatiently (he considered it complicated and lifeless). The new "electoral colleges" were Bonaparte's own blend of the *demos* and the *notables*, the local and the national. At their base, the cantonal level, the colleges' members were selected by universal suffrage, while at the top, the department, they were made up of the wealthiest (the highest taxpayers). Membership in them was for life, and the regime did its best to encourage them. Bonaparte obliged many of the leading military and political figures of the day to serve in the departmental colleges; they reinvigorated local life, and with some justification, could be called "the voice of the nation" (in Napoleon's words).[34]

The constitutions of the Years VIII and X, in sum, made the First Consul

---

Senatus populusque romanum.

rather less than the Oriental despot or the Greek tyrant that he was sometimes accused of being. To quote Albert Vandal, they "made Bonaparte the
master of government, but they did not make government the master of
France."[35] It is why the men of Brumaire—men favoring authority but not despotism, and who understood in their marrow that "without power, ideals cannot be realized"—were, with few exceptions, still on board the Consular vessel
after 1802. Not happily, always, and with increasing doubts and premoni-
tions, but on board. It would be some time before some of them grasped the
notion that "with power, ideals rarely survive."[36]

The constitutions conferred powers on the First Consul that were more
extensive than Louis XVI's when he was demoted to constitutional monarch
in 1791, and more extensive than the powers that Rousseau conferred on a
dictator of emergency. But they were still in the straight line of power as conceived by the Revolution. To quote the leading scholar of bonapartism,
Frédéric Bluche, "It was in no sense a question of using authoritarian means
for the sake of authority, but rather of using authority in the service of a conception of public order which, for all that it was meddlesome, was not without explanation given ten years of revolutionary turmoil."[37] If Bonaparte
reigned more supreme than Robespierre, it was for contingent reasons of
charisma and glory that led to his being more widely celebrated and less
often disputed than the Virtuous One; or it was because he knew how to
build a social basis of power that combined *both* the crowd and the bourgeoisie, while Robespierre had governed with only the former. If the First
Consul reigned more supreme than the Directory, it was because he was one
while they were a disunited five.

It is common to comment on the "monarchical" veneer of the Life
Consulate. The government continued to emphasize the national and religious holidays that replaced the revolutionary and republican ones. Chief
among the new ones was August 15, commemorating the Marian feast of the
Assumption and (mainly) Bonaparte's birthday. Too, Napoleon would soon
permit his profile to appear on coins—a sharp break with republican practice.
No living person's profile had appeared on revolutionary coins once Louis
XVI was removed. The First Consul and his illustrious spouse, "la Con-
sulesse," made a tour of Normandy that some compared to a royal progress
of the old regime. General Duroc, although a stalwart republican soldier,
accepted appointment as Governor of the Palace; under him "chamberlains"
and "prefects" enforced a ceremonialism that struggled to appear monarchical. The French minister to Sweden, presenting his credentials at court,
gave a strange little discourse on the monarchical and the consular constitution, concluding that the difference between them was "nominal." It

raised a tempest in a teapot in Paris, such that *La Moniteur,* the government newspaper, had to deny that the ambassador's speech was official policy.[38]

So then was the First Consul for all intents and purposes a king? No, not as the era understood kings. The late Consulate was not an absolute monarchy such as Europe would continue to know until 1914. No clear-eyed Austrian, Russian, or Neapolitan would have confused the French regime's consular style and military panache with the monarchies they lived under. Several classic names of scholarship, including Georges Lefebvre and Pieter Geyl, consider that the First Consul reconciled power and reform in such a way as to become "the last and most illustrious representative" of the enlightened despot tradition—a tradition that included an absolute monarch like Frederick the Great.[39] This is a flattering simile, and one that Napoleon would have considered accurate, but there are great differences between him and the enlightened despots—differences that go beyond the mere fact that as Life Consul, he no longer relied on savants or flattered elite opinion, as he once had, or as Frederick or Catherine had done throughout their reigns.

Napoleon Bonaparte was not now, and never would be, the true equivalent or successor of Louis XIV. Louis had no parliamentary opposition *whatever* to contend with, even a broken one. Louis *could* not be disputed; Bonaparte could be, and was, if with increasing infrequency. Louis did not lose debates in his council, as Napoleon sometimes did—for example, on the crucial issue of whether the émigré nobility should have to accept amnesty (with its admission of guilt), an obligation the First Consul considered humiliating for them.[40] Unlike Louis XIV, the Life Consul could not pass a budget or create new taxes without legislative approval. He could not remove judges or lift judicial due process and place regions under martial law without recourse to a senate. The Consulate's extra-judicial procedures and tribunals, set up in areas afflicted by "brigands," still amounted to a legal regime that the historian Howard G. Brown qualifies as "liberal authoritarian," meaning it was "limited by a liberal legal system. Even under Napoleon, courts required hard evidence before they convicted."[41] In sum, the Life Consul's power is not well described as despotic, enlightened, or royal, as the era understood these terms; these terms had become outdated in France by the democratic revolution that made it possible for Bonaparte to become head of State. His power, both consular and imperial, pointed to something new: a form of democratic authoritarianism.

With the organic *senatus consultum* of August 4, 1802, establishing the new constitution, there was every expectation that the Life Consulate would last—if not a lifetime, then surely a decade. Even if, as many now believe, the seed of the Empire was already germinating in the womb of the Republic, nothing in its nature would have made it bloom as rapidly as it did. The occasion for the changes that surprised everyone, including the First Consul, came from without.

THE WAR OF DIRTY TRICKS

One cannot reign in a land covered with ignominy and glory if one has only ignominy on his side.

–Joseph Fiévée,
royalist turned bonapartist

No one predicted that the Treaty of Amiens would collapse just fourteen months after its signing. Given the fervor that had greeted the peace a year earlier, one is bemused at the widespread complacency on both sides that greeted the war's return.[42] The British war effort, at this time, was mainly maritime and economic, but it had one important land-based component, for which the Addington cabinet earmarked a large budget: covert operations, from spying and internal agitation (e.g., fomenting counterrevolutionary uprisings in provincial France) to propaganda. This new kind of war effort included Britain's blind sponsorship, in collaboration with the Bourbon princes, of terrorist action against the person of the French First Consul. I say blind, because neither His Majesty's Government nor the Bourbon pretender, the Comte de Provence, formally countenanced assassination as a political weapon; yet both parties condoned what was going on.

The British secret service had indeed played a crucial role in the murder of Tsar Paul I (March 1801), when the autocrat had deserted the Second Coalition for Bonaparte.[43] Early in 1804 the British infiltrated into France a handful of royalist agents, notably a great Chouan leader of General Hoche's era, Georges Cadoudal (the name means "blind knight" in Breton). "Georges," as he was known, was a brave man of derring-do and the renown that went with it. Some weeks later the British landed the French general of the Revolution, Jean-Charles Pichegru, the conqueror of Holland in 1794, who had gone over to the enemy a year later. The plan of these men and their confederates was to kidnap Bonaparte as he and his guard traveled to Malmaison; if he resisted, as they knew was likely, then he would be killed: a war fatality, but *not* an assassination (a prized distinction in this set).

This once, British intelligence got outwitted by the French, though it took time for them to get organized, and in the meantime the Anglo-royalists came very near to executing their plans; only the capture of one man and his subsequent revelations saved the life of the First Consul. Elizabeth Sparrow shows the decisive role that Bonaparte himself played in the actual sifting of documents and direction of counterespionage operations.[44] Eventually, the French enjoyed the advantage of the collaboration of Jean-Claude Méhée de La Touche, the principal agent of the Bourbon princes abroad, who began secretly reporting perhaps directly to the First Consul himself. Bonaparte also received fine intelligence from Joseph Fiévée, a London-based royalist who had been struck by the First Consul's superiority.[45] The writer-journalist's remarkable lucidity now went into his secret correspondence with the First Consul, who paid him handsomely and capitalized on his sharp insights and advice.

The dream of the Anglo-royalist operatives within France was to effect a working alliance with the residue of the Jacobin left and all newly disillusioned republicans of Brumaire. This idea worried Bonaparte, ever ready to conflate rival generals, loquacious tribunes, and Institute Ideologues with spies, plotters, and bomb throwers; but looking back, the eclectic union was not likely. France was on firm war footing; juries were suppressed in cases of treason, and death was the reward of anyone convicted of harboring conspirators; notoriously republican and independent generals like Bernadotte and Augereau were distanced from important posts; and the purged and shrunken legislature was tamer than ever, and certainly had not thought to criticize the return to war.

The only soldier left on the scene who has been said to rival the First Consul was Jean-Victor Moreau, the victor of Hohenlinden.[46] The truth would be that he more exasperated Bonaparte than rivaled him. The republican Moreau was widely known to rue his support for Brumaire, criticizing the "despotic" drift in Consular power. Perhaps worse, in Bonaparte's eyes, Moreau seemed to delight in occasionally ridiculing the regime. For example, he dubbed his cook "chevalier de la casserole d'honneur," in mockery of the Legion of Honor, which he himself had refused. In fact, Moreau was a vain man, of no great political talent or even ambition; Napoleon said of him, not without accuracy, that his military reputation was "too heavy for him. There are men who don't know how to carry their glory."[47] If Moreau was dangerous, it was because his reputation made people speak of him; the most minor military plot somehow inevitably ended with soldiers yelling "Vive Moreau!"[48] He was, in short—and this is a comment on Bonaparte's ascendancy—the best that the era managed to cast up as available for visible leadership of a *fronde* (a cabal), so the oppositional parties, including the royalists, acting through Pichegru, reached out to him and aroused his vanity, if not his courage or energy.[49]

The French police were onto Moreau's meetings with Pichegru and Cadoudal, and they arrested him on February 15. The act rather stupefied public opinion and might well have played against the regime, except that further arrests soon after—Pichegru, Cadoudal and his co-conspirators—revealed a wide and perilous web of conspiracy, some of it implicating Moreau. Something else emerged, too: Moreau was merely a stopgap figure in royalist plans—a General Monck, if he wished; a puppet to be discarded if he did not. Once the mortal blow on Bonaparte was struck and the regime had fallen, a grander figure of the House of Bourbon would set foot in France as Lieutenant of the Kingdom, to make ready the way of Louis XVIII.

Who was this prince? A number of possibilities emerged, but the most likely candidate seemed to be the thirty-one-year-old Duc d'Enghien, grandson of the Prince de Condé, cousin of the Comte de Provence. Enghien lived on his British allowance at Ettenheim, just across the German border, in Baden. His ample correspondence—systematically read by the police—indicated he was a zealot who, although admiring Bonaparte in some respects, ached to play a role in his overthrow.[50] It was further reported that Dumouriez, that infamous traitor-general of the early Revolution, was an associate of Enghien's, working in harness with him. The First Consul had been on edge all winter, as new pieces of the puzzle revealed the extensive Anglo-royalist network, aimed at him personally. His reaction to this last report was splenetic: "What! *Now* you tell me the Duc d'Enghien is a few miles from my frontier organizing plots? Am I a dog one shoots in the street, whose killer is to be blessed? They attack me personally! I'll give them war for war!"

The blow he delivered was indeed close to being an act of war: he dispatched French troops to seize Enghien, even though doing so meant breaking the law of nations by crossing an international border without the ruler's consent. The duke was brought back to Paris, on the evening of March 20 and imprisoned at Vincennes.[51] That very night he was hailed before a court-martial, found guilty of treason—though it could not be proven he was in cahoots with Cadoudal—and shot forthwith, his corpse hastily buried in one of the chateau's ditches. Later versions have it that "if only" Enghien's handwritten letter asking to see the First Consul had gotten through to Malmaison, he would have been received and spared. But the most serious studies indicate that the entire course of events, from abduction to execution, was foreseen in the initial decision. The First Consul willed it so.[52]

There can be no question that the deed sounded strident echoes in France and across Europe, stunning the aristocracy and several of the royal or imperial courts, particularly the Russian. The Parisian newspaper *Le Journal des Débats*—got around the censor by publishing a translation of a passage from Silius Italicus's poem, *Punica,* in which a father beseeches his son to desist from his design to assassinate Hannibal. Chateaubriand resigned his sinecure in the Consulate's Rome embassy and returned to the political opposition.[53] Josephine and the "gentle persons" and amnestied nobles in her circle were aghast, but here, at least, Bonaparte made efforts to explain himself, and it is important to note their effects, for the attentions of the "great man" were no minor factor in maintaining his ascendancy over people. Among the most self-searching in his wife's set was Mme de Rémusat, by now a lady-in-waiting. Her words speak for many: "I was not yet at the point where I felt strong enough to win a fight against the attachment I myself felt disposed to have for [the First Consul]. . . . His appeal [after Enghien] had also succeeded with M. de Caulaincourt, who, won back by his attentions, regained little by little his serenity and became at this time one of his most intimate confidants."[54]

The echoes of the Enghien affair have rung down the corridors of two centuries, as historians have joined contemporaries and memoirists in construing the duke's demise as, variously, a crime, a mistake, and a gangland-style execution organized by an angry Corsican bent on winning a vendetta with his social betters. It raises the question: Would there have been a similar outcry over flouted law and the amorality of *raison d'Etat* if it had been the First Consul who was assassinated by Cadoudal? One doubts it.

Enghien's death was all of those things, and something else. As Bonaparte himself pointed out, both at the time and throughout his life, this was a political act, of a sort familiar in the era. At the Congress of Rastatt in 1799 (also in Baden), British operatives planned the massacre of the French plenipotentiaries by the Austrian soldiers.[55] The First Consul's top associates (Cambacérès, Talleyrand, Fouché), although they conveniently changed their minds during the Bourbon restoration, condoned the plan when Bonaparte assembled them at Malmaison for their advice. Some, like Murat, pressed hard for it, arguing that now was no time for clemency or legalisms, which would only be misread by the enemy.

The outburst against Bonaparte in the royal and aristocratic families of Europe would be hard to overestimate. Prince de Condé reviled Bonaparte as "the new Robespierre" and "the booted Jacobin," but the epithets contain an important political truth: with this act, redolent of regicide, the First Consul branded his regime(s) for all time with the mark—the scar—of the Revolution. That the Empire was born in this life-and-death struggle with the political right wing is no minor or merely contingent detail of its inception.[56]

Surely, in the short run, the Consular regime's hammer blow on the Bourbons heartened French republicans, few of whom would have stood for a pardon for Enghien while Moreau sat in prison. Lentz's speculation that even had Bonaparte known that Enghien had no immediate role in the Cadoudal plot, he might *still* have gone ahead with the Ettenheim strike is a view I share.[57] The First Consul did Enghien the "honor" of taking him for what the duke took himself to be: an enemy in war. The day after his execution (March 21), Bonaparte stated grimly, "I have spilled blood and I would spill still more, not in anger but simply because a bloody deed enters into the combinations of my political medicine. I am a statesman. I am the French revolution. I say it again and I stick by it."

The prefect of police noted that popular response to the Enghien affair in Paris (the city had been under a state of siege since February 28) strongly favored the First Consul. His action, people felt, proved that the regime was alert, strong, and ready to act.[58] Thiers, as always, sums it up the best: "People took their Bonaparte, not less glorious, but less pure now. They had taken him with his genius, but they would have taken him without it, they would have taken him any way they could, provided that he was powerful, so desirous were they in the days after the great disorders."[59]

GETTING WORSE:
THE COMING OF THE EMPIRE

How came it, one asks in wonder, that after the short space of fifteen years a world-wide movement depended on a single life, that the infinitudes of 1789 lived on only in the form, and by the pleasure, of the First Consul? Here surely is a political incarnation unparalleled in the whole course of human history.
                                                                —John Holland Rose[60]

[Napoleon] wants the need for his existence to be so direly felt, and as such a great boon, that anybody would recoil at any other possibility. . . . If anybody could say all was so well with the country that if Bonaparte died, things would still be well, then my brother would no longer feel safe.
                                                                —Joseph Bonaparte[61]

Were the two years of the Life Consulate a kind of musical false note, corrigible only when the grand imperial choir sang in tune? In 1812 the

Emperor would tell an associate that the Enghien matter, along with virtually every other event at the time, had all figured in his careful preparations for the reestablishment of a monarchy in France.[62] If this is true, it would be characteristic of the careful planner in Bonaparte, but on the other hand, it would be equally characteristic of him to want to take credit for an omniscience and a political choreography that eluded even him *in medias res*. For contemporaries, 1803–4 brought war and renewed anxiety as much as new opinions about the current regime's inadequacies or the need to transform it. Whatever else concerned him, the First Consul was preoccupied with military affairs—above all, the concentration of an expeditionary at Boulogne, whence it could pounce on England the moment the French fleet secured the Channel even briefly.

All of which is to say that the shocking issue of the return of some form of monarchy to France became discussable, then rationalizable, *under wartime conditions* that included grave personal danger for the head of State. And even then, it was only a kind of monarchy—one of eclectic symbols, strange characteristics, and ideological paradoxes: *a new kind of monarchy,* democratic and representative in origin and legitimacy, Roman in style, liberal in aspiration, dictatorial in substance, occasioned by war but not requiring war, sustained by glory. The Life Consulate came to a man as his reward for accomplishment; the Empire will come to him as a nation's insurance against his disappearance. But what he will do with it will be largely his own choice.

The chronology of events is this: A few days after the execution of Enghien, Bonaparte summoned his co-consuls, Cambacérès and Lebrun, to Malmaison to discuss "the national wish," apparently flowing in from all quarters, that the First Consul accept the hereditary imperium. Bonaparte warned that if the government did not act with dispatch, there was a risk that the army would take matters into its own hands and "proclaim" him "Emperor of the Gauls." The title "imperator," after all, was the rank of supreme military command in ancient Rome, and all present were well aware of the numerous instances when the Praetorian Guard had bypassed the Roman Senate and proclaimed a new emperor. Lebrun, the former monarchist, did not murmur, but Cambacérès, the ex-*Conventionnel,* for once dug in. *Rusé* old operator that he was, he did not buy the idea of outside pressure, and he stoutly maintained that changing the regime to a monarchy was impolitic, and would be seen as a betrayal of the Republic. Two further fears that he did not voice were that the receipt of the crown would remove any restraints on Bonaparte's behavior, and, finally, that in an empire, there would be no place for a Second Consul.[63]

As was his way with associates who agreed to disagree with him in private, Napoleon did not force the issue, but permitted Cambacérès to sit this one out. His point man in the enterprise would instead be Fouché, who for some time seems to have been pressing him to take the crown. ("Fouché," Thiers writes, "agitated like one of those people who have a talent for pushing what walks on its own."[64]) In part, the ex–police chief was simply eager to reingratiate himself with his patron after being cashiered in 1802 for opposing the Concordat and the Life Consulate, but it is also true that the old Jacobin had come to believe that in this time of renewed war and royalist conspiracy the Revolution's best hope was Bonaparte, even (or especially) Bonaparte with a crown. The view is nicely summed up in a government-inspired pamphlet that read, "To better save the *patrie*, Bonaparte must agree to become king of the revolution."

The government communicated the details of Anglo-royalist perfidy to the Senate, which returned a motion to congratulate the First Consul. The problem was coyness: no party wanted to be the one who put the mesmerizing project into clear words. Fouché stepped in; his yoke was easy and his burden was light. This time around, because of the bungles attributed to the legislature during the Life-Consulate project, it took little convincing to organize the politicians. Fouché, a senator, told his colleagues cryptically that he had spoken with the First Consul and now would be an appropriate time to do more than convey grateful salutations. The Senate promptly voted an address to Bonaparte containing the invitation: "Great Man, realize your work by making it immortal, like your glory." Carte blanche, to be sure, but the words "hereditary Emperor" were still not spoken. (Some feinting goes into any romance.) The First Consul replied with a convoluted sentence reminiscent of his journal entry after the meeting with the prostitute when he was eighteen.[65] He stood ready, he said, to do his duty and "adopt all that the experience of centuries and peoples has demonstrated is necessary to guarantee the rights that the Nation has judged necessary to its dignity, liberty, and happiness."

The courtly round might have gone on being sung, except that the Tribunate broke in at this point. Eager to wipe away any remaining stain on its copybook, it debated a proposition to make Napoleon Bonaparte "hereditary Emperor of the French." Now what had been adroit side-stepping became a race to the finish line. The speeches "debating" the motion, the invitation to the First Consul to accept it, and the Senate votes ratifying his acceptance were the incidents of six weeks. On May 16 a *senatus consultum* proclaimed: "The Government of the Republic is confided to an Emperor who shall take the title of Emperor of the French." Two days later Cambacérès—now restored to active duty, in the "beauty part" of Grand Chancellor of the Empire—first addressed Napoleon as "Sire," in a ceremony at Saint-Cloud, where the Senate formally announced the elevation.

Did Napoleon *want* to be emperor? Some were certain he had been ingeniously and remorselessly seeking it all along. Lafayette is said to have ironically observed to the First Consul that the real motive behind the Concordat treaty was "so you can have the priests anoint you one day with the sacred chrism [of the kings]."[66] The supposition is hardly outlandish, considering that Bonaparte was a man with a preternaturally developed imagination. There may even be something fastidious about stating that he could not rest until he had gone as far as there was to go, to the very point where—to put it in the unrefined terms of what psychologists call "primary thinking"—he could lord it over the nose-thumbing aristocrats of Brienne or the Ecole Militaire, until he could himself confer nobility. He told Roederer around this time, "Me, I have no ambition, or, if I do, it is so innate to me that it is part of my very existence, like the blood that runs in my veins or the air that I breathe."[67] And at St. Helena he said: "During the Consulate, my true friends and most enthusiastic champions would ask me, with the best of intentions and for their own guidance: where I was heading? I always answered that I had not the least idea. This astonished and possibly annoyed them, and yet I was telling them the truth."

Both of those statements, of course, could be lies or illusions; but it might also be that the will to ever-greater glory that ran in Napoleon's veins and suffused his air—a will that had little to do with aristocratic goals of service and family honor, even less to do with bourgeois patriotism, and nothing whatever to do with Christian love and humility—was unconscious to him. It was not part of his own self-portrait nor tied to some definite career project that he carried in his mind. It was not Bonaparte's style either to be self-critical or to invoke common rationales and attitudes, and great ambition was a common theme—indeed a leitmotif—of this Ossianic era that lionized Alexander, Caesar, and Frederick. In our day, glory, in the sense of individual immortality, sounds a little wild to our ears, and has become an ambivalent and far less avowable motive. Today political careers are planned virtually before they have begun, with little role being left for the destiny that Bonaparte regarded as all-important. "The older I get," he said early in 1802, ". . . the more I realize that each person must fulfill his own destiny."

Napoleon saw himself as fulfilling, not studying or planning, his destiny. In his mind, he understood what needed to be done in France, and he did it better than anyone else understood or did it, so why should he not go on reaping rewards commensurate with these herculean labors? Destiny, glory, and recognition are all pagan and classical ideas, but they are accurate ways to construe Napoleon Bonaparte. If so, then it means that not only was it beyond Napoleon to aspire to be wise rather than brilliant, self-effacing rather than self-exalting, and master of his passion for *gloire* rather than master of the Empire, but further, that these latter thoughts might never have occurred to him. Napoleonic drive was not the only irresistible force in this process of founding an imperium. Bonaparte was anticipated, perhaps even out-stripped, by his supporters in the political class and even in the nation. The First Consul and his advisors indeed may have been standing atop the political equivalent of a gusher.

What is fascinating in the Tribunate's discussion is the mix of sincerity and bad faith, of honest perception and willed misperception, in the deputies' speeches. They provide a case study in the all-too-human phenomenon that sees words and names become more important than the things they refer to. The speakers are straightforward about conceding so. One of the cleverest passages states frankly: "Nobody here can ignore—we've lived it too long—*the empire of words and the prestige of names.*"[68] In thirty-three orations on "this, the most important question ever submitted to our deliberations" (191), one alone (Carnot's) opposed the proposition. The rest are so nearly fungible that two citations suffice to sketch the whole.

> Never could a wish contrary to our sacred principle of popular sovereignty emerge from this body; the national wish we propose has for its sole object the consolidation of [revolutionary] institutions which alone are capable of guaranteeing the Nation in the exercise of its rights. (201)

> What other glory does not eclipse and efface itself before that of the incomparable Hero who has conquered them all, who has plucked everything out of chaos, and created another universe for us. *Stupete Gentes!* [Be in awe, Peoples!] (83)

It is as if these men have cribbed their orations from Lucien's *Parallel.* The tribunes are drunk on history, explaining to themselves their present reality by construing odd versions of the past, extracting strange truths from it. The French Revolution, which beheaded Louis XVI, now somehow never *really* intended to abolish the monarchy; the 1804 legislature, in voting the Empire, is only fulfilling the true intentions of 1789. (One tribune has it that if Bonaparte had shown up in June 1791, when the royal family sought to flee France, he would have been made king by the National Assembly![69]) France is not "restoring the monarchy," her legislators repeat, she is simply ensuring strong leadership "forever," as if resurrecting heredity somehow put an end to the eternal problems of conflict and change. In this vein, conferring a crown on Bonaparte will preserve liberty and equality. Making him emperor—O vague and thrilling title that reels in Rome and Charlemagne while throwing overboard the old regime—will repel kings. Somehow.

Three themes predominate that are interesting to look at briefly because they establish the unusual, not to say unique political context in which the new emperor existed: clinging to the Republic; acting for the Nation; honoring Bonaparte.

The Republic never shone more lustrously than on the eve of its demise. The tribunes argue that proclaiming the Empire will protect the French Republic. This is preposterous to moderns, but contemporaries could have meant it sincerely. The First French Republic may not have had the prestige (or the longevity) of her ancient Roman sister, yet she had enough to make even the more irresolute among her friends refuse to disavow her abjectly. For the Romans, there had been no alternative to the republican form; it was all that any of them, even Caesar, could conceive of. For the French, the specter of the alternative that was restored Bourbon kingship haunted nearly all of the speeches. Napoleon, like Caesar, *had* to be seen by his partisans as the protector and renewer of the Republic, *not its assassin*. The Empire, the tribunes strain to say, is *only a form of government*. France, even with an emperor, remains the "one and indivisible Republic."

Or does it? We come to the second theme, Nation, which the ancient Romans did not use in the modern sense, and which undercut Republic. One speaker (Leroy) is honest enough to confess, "*Republic* and *religion* are words that have spilt too much blood." The new imperium is justified, he asserts, "by the happiness and the glory of the Nation"; it is "national" (213). A colleague states the "eternal truth" that governments are valuable only as they contribute to the happiness of the Nation. The Empire is indubitably national, he says, with the unmistakable implication that the Republic may not be. "The truly national wish that [we] are going to vote has been for a long time now in the heart and mind of the French people" (144). In sum, Nation was the court of final instance. But it did not stand alone as the *ultima ratio* of the Empire.

Finally, after the abstractions, it feels good to deal with the flesh and blood of the Corsican himself. Napoleon Bonaparte, it cannot be said too often, was these men's "Hero" with a capital *H* (the word arises repeatedly), their new Charlemagne—and indeed, *more* meritorious because Bonaparte was not dependent on someone else's sword, as the great Frank had been on Charles Martel's. Bonaparte, rather, was the greatest military leader since Caesar.

"There is no more worthy title than Emperor *for the glory of Bonaparte* and the dignity of the supreme chief of the French Nation" (206). "Let us then rise to the measure both of the national majesty and the prescience of him who is so far ahead of his time" (163).

A final point: the Tribunate (and later, the Senate) sought to salve its conscience by stipulations that hedged about their offer of the purple with assertions about "the Nation's exercise of its sovereignty, which it will not be stripped of" (201), and that would set up guarantees of liberty and equality. Were they surprised when Bonaparte waived this off without any discussion? Fiévée noted: "An English-type constitution will never be forced upon a ruler commanding three to four hundred thousand men." The legislators shrugged and let it go; they were in for a penny, in for a pound.[70]

Perhaps Bonaparte felt more rapport with the language used in the petitions that poured in from the Republic's armies, the most important of which was that written by General Berthier, the war minister:

> You owe it to France who has chosen you for its chief and regards you as its second founder. You owe it to yourself to assure for your handiwork the same immortality as has your name. . . . Henceforth, French armies will march to victory only under the banners of a Buonaparte [*sic*]. . . . The moment has come when the Nation, proud of its chief, must invest him *with an éclat that will reflect back on itself.* It is time that it confer on him a title more proportionate to his exploits, to the rank he holds in Europe, and to the reach of the French empire. . . .[71]

Gone, any reference to a republic; now, it is all just deserts and glory—both the real glory that "Buonaparte" creates, and the reflected kind, which the Nation basks in. This is a remarkable document.

So very few spoke up against the Empire that Napoleon's valet, Constant Wairy, had it right when he wrote in his memoirs, "If the Emperor usurped the throne, he had more accomplices than all the tyrants of tragedy and melodrama combined, for three-fourths of the French people were in the conspiracy."[72] Some, like Rouget de L'Isle, the composer of "La Marseillaise," and the writer Courier, criticized the act privately to Bonaparte. Others, like Counselor of State Berlier, argued in their institutional venue that the hereditary Empire would place them all in a permanent "false position" vis-à-vis the Revolution.[73]

Lazare Carnot was the only one to speak out publicly (in the Tribunate), going as far as to state that most observers believed Bonaparte had had the imperial goal in mind since the Life Consulate, if not before. Carnot had no truck with massaging the word "republic" into new shapes; it was all quite simple, he said: since Amiens, Bonaparte had had to choose between the republican and the monarchical system, and he chose the latter. He would have done better to recall that the Roman Empire lasted no longer than did the Roman Republic. Carnot, however, made it clear his opposition would not go beyond this speech. "I am always ready," he said, "to sacrifice my dearest affections to the interests of the common *patrie*" (68).

The declaration of the Empire led almost no one to acts beyond speech-acts. Chateaubriand, as we saw, resigned his post. The poet Lemercier gave back his Legion of Honor. A few members of the Institute refused the new imperial oath. Most famously, of course, Ludwig van Beethoven changed the title of a brilliant opus from "The Bonaparte Symphony" to the *Eroica* (a hero). Innumerable republicans harbored doubts, but they forced themselves to swallow the official line: "Have no fear, the man who governs France . . . is himself the child of the Revolution."[74]

A FIRST POLITICAL DEFEAT

And then the newly minted Emperor of the French proved himself famously unable to effect his will in the matter of bringing General Moreau to justice—or to injustice, as some see it. Pichegru committed suicide in prison on April 6,[75] while Cadoudal and a number of his confederates went to the guillotine on June 28.[76] But the victor of Hohenlinden was not easily disposed of. Napoleon's intention had been that the bank of judges whom he chose and instructed ("this is a political, not a judicial, case") would condemn Moreau to death for high treason. The general would then entreat pardon, which His Imperial Majesty would graciously bestow, thus concluding a painful period with an irenic stamp.*

Things did not unfold thus. The case lodged by prosecutors against Moreau was found weak by the judges. The one serious charge, from a mod-

---

*A favorite play of Napoleon's was Corneille's *Cinna* (1640), which tells the story of an associate of Augustus who leads a plot against him. Found out, Cinna decides he is wrong and begs the Emperor's pardon, which he receives. He receives more than that: Augustus offers him their old friendship back. The First Consul told Mme de Rémusat that he had long felt Augustus was inadmissibly sentimental for doing this. However, seeing a fine actor perform the role of the Emperor, Bonaparte realized that Octavius was a lot cleverer than he had recognized. "I understood that his 'Let us be friends then, Cinna,' spoken in that adroit and *rusé* fashion, was anything but puerility; it was, rather, the feint of a tyrant, and I approved the act as calculus where I had disapproved it as sentiment."

ern point of view, was that Moreau had failed to report his meetings with Pichegru and Cadoudal to the authorities, but this struck little resonance with judges who were inclined to the eighteenth-century belief that a soldier of Moreau's high *virtù* would have found such an action dishonorable, shabby.[77] Based on the case logged, the judges determined to acquit the general entirely, and were stayed in their course only when the chairman, in direct touch with the Emperor, made them understand that this finding would force the government to illegal proceedings. So they voted "guilty but excusable," and sentenced Moreau to a derisory two years of prison ("as if he were a handkerchief thief," said Napoleon indignantly).

No less annoying to the Emperor, fickle Paris opinion altogether escaped him on the Moreau question, as it had not with Enghien, except among émi-grés. Much amusement and irony went down at the expense of the new imperial regime—a very Parisian form of entertainment. Napoleon, of course, took it personally. He scribbled an unsigned piece for *La Gazette de France* (September 24, 1804) in which the author (unmistakably Napoleon) heavy-handedly "speculates on the motives" that might have led the Roman emperors Constantine, Diocletian, and Maximian to transfer their seats of government away from the city of Rome. The piece ends on a note of self-righteousness at which it is difficult not to howl with laughter: "Could it be that only the finest spirits cannot stand up against ingratitude?" The new Emperor of the French nevertheless quashed Moreau's prison sentence and exiled him.[78]

A POLITICAL VICTORY

The Emperor had a better time of it with the June plebiscite, held to ratify heredity and imperial succession within the Bonaparte family. This, more than the title "emperor," was the issue that broke with the Revolution's post-1792 principles. In this third Napoleonic plebiscite, "the last act of the sovereign people in France until 1815,"[79] the vote went overwhelmingly in Napoleon's favor: 3,572,329 "yes" to 2,579 "no." The former figure, down by 80,000 (2 to 3 percent) from 1802, was somewhat compensated for by a 70 percent reduction in the "nay" vote, but subtracting for the usual government fraud, we may reduce the "yeas" to below 3 million out of 7.5 million eligible voters—in short, to 40 percent of the electorate. Of the 60 percent who took refuge in abstention, no doubt, many more were opposed than the proportion between "yea" and "nay" indicates, but by the low standards of electoral participation during the Revolution, the "yea" figure was seen as a mild success,[80] and gave muscle to the constantly reiterated claims that the Empire represented the national will. The plebiscite was certainly regarded by Napoleon as more significant than the (nevertheless more legally binding) Senate's organic *senatus consultum* that created the Empire.

Measuring or even defining "public opinion" in this era is difficult to do. The sources that deal more than glancingly with the feelings and thoughts of a widely illiterate population of thirty million people are neither extensive nor trustworthy. Prefect after prefect claimed his region was "enamored" of the idea of making Bonaparte emperor, but we do not know if he was telling the truth or trying to please his superiors (both are possible), or if the consensus at hand was not a slippery, evanescent something that the *fonctionnaire* drummed up for the occasion. So historians speculate about national opinion based on outcomes and the many references to public opinion made in the "high" sources. In this instance, it would appear that there was indeed a persistent and widespread rustle of interest around France to back up the claims being made in the legislature, ministries, army headquarters, prefectures, newspapers, and elsewhere. There seems to have been genuine concern for the "heroic" First Consul's safety and his—and through him, France's—glory, together with anger at the attacks made on him (hence on "the Republic" or "France") by avowed enemies of the country and the Revolution. The matters of empire and heredity evoked some ambivalence, unquestionably, but they existed far less in the public mind than strongly positive feelings for Napoleon Bonaparte, and concern about his safety, happiness, and glory.[81]

Conclusion

In French, the word "empire," in addition to being a noun, is a conjugated intransitive verb form that means "[something] is getting worse." Does this sense also apply here? Were France and its people worse off because Napoleon Bonaparte became the first Emperor of the French? Posterity, judging from hindsight, tends to give a sturdy "yes!" in reply, but contemporaries were more conflicted and ambivalent, while leaning distinctly to "no." If a different question had been posed—"Do you desire the continuation of the Republic or the restoration of a monarchy?"—the French would have voted massively for the Republic. But that was not the question, and nobody figured that it was. The question the people of France were wrestling with, had it been verbalized, would have been a run-on sentence: "Are you grateful enough to Napoleon Bonaparte, and worried enough by the attempts on his life, to give him a fabulous new, albeit strange and unre-publican title, that will raise him to parity with the other crowned heads of Europe, whom we're at war with—or soon to be—while keeping him happy, and increasing our chances of avoiding a civil war if he dies?" Put this way, one can still, of course, find good reason to vote "no"—a few did; but one also has a better understanding of whence came the yeses.

Perhaps we would be better off looking at what contemporaries actually said. The Senate voted the Empire and Napoleon accepted the purple. On May 18, at Saint-Cloud, before the Senate and most of the government, Cambacérès told the First Consul, "The most imposing title we give you today is only a tribute that the *nation pays to its own dignity*. [Emphasis added.] . . . For the glory and the happiness of the Republic, the Senate pro-claims you in this instant Napoleon Emperor of the French." Napoleon replied, "I accept the title that you believe *useful to the Nation's glory*. [Empha-sis added.]" Perhaps it was just as simple as that; they all (or nearly all) spoke the same language for now. If, as William James has said, "Truth *happens* to an idea. It *becomes* true, is *made* true by events [emphasis added]," then the Empire, as of its proclamation, had a good chance of becoming true.

Thierry Lentz, although at times a vigorous critic of the Empire and the Emperor, nonetheless sees fit to prefix "great" to the Consulate (1799–1804). Denominational novelties do not easily catch on among professional his-torians, frugal with honorifics, especially where Napoleon Bonaparte is concerned. If one looks at the long arc of French history over a millennium and a half, one is struck by the ferocity of its internecine conflict and the fre-quency of change. In that regard, one cannot help being somewhat awestruck by the near consensus the First Consul was able to effect for the profound and lasting reforms of 1800–1802. Only one other era (1879–84) in French history stands out for a remotely similar rate and range of change; but even that remarkable half decade in the early Third Republic did not manage to effect a reform package as far-reaching and as comparatively unopposed as the Consulate did with its granite blocks. (The opposition to the Concordat and the Legion of Honor was shallow and short-lived.) Whatever we may think of the impulse that carved these blocks, or of what followed them—for which the reforms themselves are not to blame—the period is unique.

Still, the granite blocks do not stand by themselves, and the story of the Consulate is not over. There is the matter of foreign policy, which is every bit as important, and indeed more world-historical than the domestic reforms. We cannot finally weigh Lentz's suggestion until we have looked at the failure of the peace of Amiens and the return to war (as we shall do in Chapter 10).

STUPETE GENTES!:
THE REPUBLICAN EMPEROR

The republic is the organization that best raises the soul and possesses in the highest degree the seeds of great things. But its greatness devours it sooner or later, for in becoming powerful, it has, of necessity, to found unity of action, which in turn leads to the despotism of a man or an aristocrat.

—Napoleon at St. Helena

How beautiful was the Republic under the Empire!
—A saying in late-nineteenth-century France

The arrival of the Empire, for those contemporaries who saw it immanent in every gulp of air that Bonaparte breathed since the battle of Lodi, must have seemed like a Zeno's paradox. A set of infinitesimal advances that never quite arrived—but now, suddenly *it was here!* And yet so was the Republic, standing wanly in the shadows. True, at the banquet given at Saint-Cloud for the Senate on May 18, the Emperor managed to get through the evening without calling anyone "Citizen," and did not appear to have to strain in the slightest.[82] Was the Empire more of a blow to the Jacobins, much of whose revolutionary baggage it retained, than it was to the royalists, whose style it imitated? Style versus substance is an old quandary for political historians.

Since I started reading academic history, I have been struck by the tendency to conflate the Consulate with the Empire because the two regimes offer so many of the same formal powers to the head of State. "From the Consulate, in all three of its versions—provisional, decennial, and life—would emerge, finally, the Empire, but it was always a question of the same regime."[83] Yet there is a quantum magnitude of difference between calling a political leader "Citizen First Consul" and calling him "His Imperial Majesty, the Emperor," as there is between bobbing one's head and making a full bow from the waist. Napoleon assured a slightly dubious Roederer that "all these titles are part of a system, which is why they are necessary."[84] The new regime indeed presented the full panoply of imperial nomenclature: high dignitaries and potentates; marshals and princes of the blood, pomp and ceremonials, prayers for the Emperor, fancier costumes and uniforms. The power of all of this to capture both the elite and the popular imagination was as important as its power to incline people toward obedience and respect.

The aristocracy, the Church, the army, and the diplomatic corps in Paris did not need it explained to them that the make-believe court of the Consulate was another matter from the imperial court, with its civil and military "maisons" that numbered scores of aides, chamberlains, pages, equerries, *grands officiers,* almoners, chaplains, etc. Cambacérès now became "Arch-Chancellor of the Empire," more than compensating this popinjay for his loss of "Second Consul." Officially, he was to be addressed as "Your Grandeur," but he told his aides it was to be "Your Most Serene Highness" in public (in private they could simply say "My Lord"). As for his duties and importance, Cambacérès remained what he had been all along: "more than a number two, less than a number one."[85] Eighteen generals (four retired and fourteen on active service) became "Marshals of the Empire." It speaks for the absence of smallness of soul in Napoleon that he conferred batons on Augereau, Masséna, Jourdan, and Bernadotte, his "political opposition" in the republican core of the old soldiery.

There is a kind of game of make-believe to all of this strutting and fancifulness, but that does not dispense us from taking it seriously, for it was serious to the players, including those not on Napoleon's side. The Comtesse de Rémusat, deeply—indeed, permanently—marked by Enghien's abduction, was disgusted with herself over the "power, even of persuasion, that sovereigns hold over us! Whatever our sentiments or, to be truthful, our vanity, they are earnestly crowded out [by the new Emperor]."[86] The Bourbons, for their part, did not miss the decisive threat for their tired old royalty in this brassy new imperium. "Usurper" joined the medley of their epithets, along with "foreigner" and "tyrant," they flung at Napoleon.

The Comte de Provence and his family did the French Empire the service—no less important for being unintentional—of seeing, or sensing, that something new was at stake here. They branded the imperial regime "the creature of the Revolution," a kind of oxymoronic label that only added to its capacity to inspire dread and marvel.[87] Truth to tell, there was not a monarch in Europe, including even those allied with France, who did not feel a frisson at the appearance of this, France's "fourth dynasty."[88] The Habsburg head of Europe's first monarchy felt anxious enough over developments to redouble his title; Francis II now became hereditary Emperor of Austria as well as Holy Roman Emperor.

Among the plethora of French imperial titles, that of Prince stood out. There were but two: Joseph and Louis, who were now in line to succeed Napoleon in the event he had no issue. Why not Lucien and Jérôme? The youngest was a naval officer of no great talent or ambition, but obedient to the head of the family—until suddenly he was not. Stationed in the Antilles,

he visited the United States, where he met and fell in love with young Elizabeth Patterson, the daughter of a prosperous Baltimore businessman. With no one's permission but his own, Jérôme asked for her hand, and wed her on Christmas Eve day 1803. Furious, Napoleon summoned his minorage brother home, but the nineteen-year-old resisted for more than a year. During that time the Empire exploded on the scene, and Jérôme missed out on the bonanza. In due course, however, his resolve—defying Lucien's attempts to stiffen it—collapsed, and he agreed to divorce his (now-pregnant) wife and return to sea. He was soon to be a prince, admiral, and finally, as we shall see, king. A tall price for a small soul.

Lucien was of firmer stuff. His rupture with his brother, long in the making, was, at bottom, a function of the younger man's narcissism and his temperamental incapacity to subordinate himself to anyone, even Napoleon. Things came to a head in April 1804, in a violent scene over Lucien's refusal to accept Napoleon's (not unreasonable) compromise on the fraught issue of the imperial succession—specifically: Lucien would enter the succession, but children of his morganatic marriage could not. "Brutus" Bonaparte was not a man for compromise. He departed for Rome, renouncing any further role in Napoleonic affairs until 1814. The incredible squabbling among the siblings, and between them and Josephine, over the succession did permit the Emperor to get off a wonderful line, however: "You would have thought I had finagled them out of their rightful inheritance from our father, the late king!"[89]

As for the Empire's symbolism, it displayed *arriviste* enthusiasm for conventional taste and authority. A fierce zoological debate in the Council of State took place over the cock, eagle, lion, elephant, dove, and bee as to which should be the regime's emblem. The former Third Consul (Lebrun) went so far as to actually suggest it be the fleur-de-lis (the Bourbon lily), as a signal of continuity with the old regime. The counselors opted for the Gallic cock, which Napoleon immediately poleaxed ("it's a barnyard creature!"), so they then agreed on the lion at rest on field azure. Perhaps because the lion (rampant on field gules) snarled on the British royal family's escutcheon, Napoleon finally nullified that choice, too, and had things his way. It would be the Roman eagle, a tiresome choice that France now shared with Prussia, Austria, and Russia.[90] On the other hand, imagination was displayed in the choice of the Emperor's personal symbol—the bee: industrious, collective, and dangerous, and with a rather esoteric cultural heritage in the sixth- and seventh-century Merovingian dynasty.

The shadow of Rome and Rome-like empires, so pervasive in late eighteenth-century France, enveloped the Napoleonic Empire in its fur-

ther choice of other symbols and heritage as well, notably Charlemagne. That this ruler had been king of the Franks, hence German as much as French, mattered little, though his extensive military conquests beyond the Rhine and in Spain and Italy were worthy of note. What really impressed Napoleon about Charles the Great was two things: his founding of a ruling house (the Carolingian) that lasted for two centuries; and his ideological revival of the Roman Empire (the famous *translatio imperii*) in the form of an autocratic Christian monarchy that survived into modern times as the Holy Roman Empire. Any similarity with Napoleon himself and his monarchy was in fact more apparent than convincing, for Charles had been a profoundly Christian warrior and ruler whose principal raison d'être and *raison d'Etat* was protection of the Holy Mother Church. His true heir was the Catholic Habsburg who, for a few years yet, bore the title of Holy Roman Emperor, Francis II.

The new French monarch, on the other hand, was the youngest son of the Revolution, not the eldest son of Catholicism, and if a classical forebear were pertinent, then—as Napoleon himself knew—it was Julius Caesar, a man a thousand times more like himself in mind, personality, and style than the uncouth, long-haired, religious Frank. But—and here is a truth Caesar would have appreciated—the need of the moment was ideological suitability, not hermeneutic truth. Caesar was too much a self-made man and an outsider; he was too controversial, as Napoleon admitted. So the new emperor journeyed to Aix-la-Chapelle, in Belgium (now part of the Empire of the French), to commune with Charles the Great's specter in the city that was his capital. He would not, however, sit on his throne.[91]

Another truth that emerges in the comparison to Caesar rather than to Charlemagne was the persistence in Napoleon's Empire of revolutionary symbols, songs, and language. De Staël had written that "monarchical institutions advanced in the shadow of the Republic," but one could now add, "and some of them lingered in the shadow of the monarchy." The word "Republic" lasted as a denomination for the regime through 1805, when "l'Empire français" formally replaced it. It remained on French coins until 1809. The revolutionary tricolor was kept as the national flag without much debate. "La Marseillaise" never enjoyed Napoleon's favor, as we saw, and had been let go in 1800 (except in certain army units). "Veillons sur l'Empire" (Watch Over the Empire) now replaced it. Despite the title, it was written in 1791 and was, if anything, more radical than Rouget de L'Isle's better-known masterpiece.[92]

The Empire's first government held no surprises, but it did see Fouché returned to his former turf. The "butcher of Lyon"[93] reclaimed the Police

Ministry in return for services rendered in the counterattack on Cadoudal et al. and in the proclamation of the Empire. For those who watched the factional balance sheet (not Napoleon!), Fouché's appointment was offset by that of Portalis, a practicing Catholic, to the newly created post of minister of religion, where he managed the Church and helped his master appoint bishops. Finally, Interior was transferred to Jean-Baptiste de Champagny, France's ambassador to Austria and a former deputy to the Estates-General of 1789. He replaced the distinguished chemist Chaptal—last of the Institute's members to hold a seat in government—who "retired" to the Senate. Both were men of the Revolution who had been troubled by the coming of the Empire, but Champagny acceded more convincingly than Chaptal. Another appointment with a revolutionary past was Hugues-Bernard Maret, a "premature" Jacobin of 1791 who had evolved to moderation by the time of Fructidor (1797). He became the Emperor's domestic chief of staff, with cabinet rank—the civilian equivalent of Berthier in military affairs. Talleyrand stayed on at Foreign Affairs—reluctantly, not for ideological reasons but only because doing so precluded his becoming an "imperial dignitary" (Napoleon declared that political office was incompatible with the exalted position of dignitary). In short, in his choice of ministers, Napoleon, as always, did not like new faces, and he went to considerable lengths, even tolerating skullduggery or treachery, to hang on to familiar ones.

The Emperor's mania for clarity forced the French to assimilate yet a third Napoleonic constitution, that of the Year XII.[94] The Empire itself—in its dazzling size, its unruliness, and its unpredictability—may well have been "the institutionalisation of the Emperor's personality," as Philip Dwyer nicely puts it, but the new constitution was not that, for it populated the regime with certain requirements and restrictions,[95] as well as with institutions that were independent of the imperial office, and that was not a Napoleonic thing to do. The Senate was now swollen with members who sat ex officio, thanks to their status or function; and the Emperor could name new senators as he deemed fit, as Caesar could. But the Senate haunted the background of the State stage every bit as completely as the Emperor dominated the scene (and the audience). Then, too, there was now a High Court, presided over by Arch-Chancellor Cambacérès, composed of the princes, "grand dignitaries," and civil and military "grand officers." It had authority to judge the Emperor's ministers, as well as any act of governmental arbitrary detention or abuse of the freedom of the press. The court never in fact used those powers, *but it held them.* The Legislative Body (*le Corps Législatif*), déclassé as its prestige was, yet had the power to suspend a law, and even, temporarily, the constitution. In sum, the assemblies of the First Empire, in their origin and in theory, were far from paralyzed or vestigial institutions. The Empire was encased in law, it was a statutory, not a traditional or "customary" regime. Napoleon I, unlike Francis II, held office by "the constitutions of the Republic."[96] If his powers and prerogatives "were more absolute than that of the last Bourbons, including Louis XIV,"[97] then they were ad hoc, and for contingent reasons, because Napoleon was Napoleon, and the Senate and the High Court did not care to use their power to challenge him.

But Napoleon also held his Empire "by the grace of God." And in this, the religious theatre, he had something even the Habsburg could not boast of, much as he would have liked to. Napoleon I had an anointment by the Vicar of Christ.

CORONATION

A servile pope has anointed a black demon.
—Nineteenth-century royalist saying

In the classical French tradition, kings underwent a consecration (*sacre*) rather than a coronation. It's not that they did not receive crowns—they did—it's that the Church's anointment, conferred by the archbishop of Reims in his cathedral, was what made French kings special among all other monarchs; they were the "eldest sons of the Church." It thus tells us something that although the first French emperor received the blessing of the highest authority of Christendom on December 2, 1804, he tended to speak of that day as his "coronation."[98] If posterity readily recalls one thing about this man, it is that on that day, standing (not kneeling) at the high altar of the cathedral of Notre-Dame in Paris, he received the crown of emperor of the French from his own hand. Pope Pius VII only watched.

The purpose of Napoleon's coronation, which contemporaries referred to as a *sacre*,[99] was as multifaceted as the ceremony itself was eclectic, but one thing we may assert with certitude is this: the event's significance for the "anointed one" was *not* spiritual, as was the case with many rulers and their *sacres*.[100] There were a dozen reasons Napoleon wanted a coronation—the prestige it would confer in international royalist and Catholic milieux, where the "usurper" desperately needed cachet; the foundation it would give his "dynasty"; the further pacification it might effect among Frenchmen still divided by religion—but its personal religious meaning was not one of them. Napoleon Bonaparte was a self-made man, and he worshipped his creator.

To put the case for the ceremony with forceful simplicity: a papal consecration given in Paris would astound the world and cut the ground out from under the naysayers all over, both in France and without. The papal curia, however, found the idea shocking and presumptuous. Even Holy Roman Emperors (*even* Charlemagne) went to Rome for a papal blessing; the Vicar of Christ did not go to them.[101] But Napoleon played his two strong trump cards: he reminded Rome that he had "saved religion" in France—and in France's large empire; and he noted there had been many Holy Roman Emperors, but there was only one Napoleon. Was he counting on the fact that the pope was captivated by him? He surely was; there is good reason to conclude that Pius VII finally trekked to Paris—against his advisors' objections, and despite the fact that the Church had won no hard gain in its bargaining over this chip—simply because of the profound feelings of affection, fear, and bedazzlement fostered in him by the emperor he was going to consecrate.[102] No other major European sovereign showed up at an event to which all of them were invited and all considered the defining moment of any monarch's life, yet the presence of the leader of Christendom outweighed their collective absence.

Things went less smoothly on the French side. It was an eye opener, and should have been a warning, to Napoleon that his "great idea" elicited more objections than satisfaction among his associates. To them, a *sacre* recalled Reims in 1775, when Louis XVI had been consecrated amidst incense and bells, in an outrageously grandiose and reactionary pageant. If a coronation must take place, they said, hold it on the Champ-de-Mars in Paris, where the crowds could mill, sing, and yell their approval. In short, at least make it a kind of revived Feast of Federation of 1790 (the Revolution's one genuinely successful holiday), "the nation assembled." There, in pithy summary, was precisely how the new emperor did *not* envision his coronation. "I don't see the people of Paris," he replied with asperity "—and still less the people of France—in twenty or thirty thousand fishwives, or other people of that species, invading the champs de Mars. That is just the ignorant and corrupt populace of a large city." The *sacre*, he added, would indeed be "national" and civilian, not military or mystifyingly religious, but it would certainly not be "popular."

The coronation went off largely as Napoleon intended. True, it was not held on the anniversary of the 18 Brumaire, as he had wished—the pope could not make it to Paris in time. Then, too, Pius implacably insisted he would not go through with it unless Napoleon and Josephine agreed to have a religious marriage ceremony, as of course it had not dawned on them to do back in the revolutionary days of 1796. (Cardinal Fesch duly pronounced them man and wife in a small chapel of the Tuileries on the eve of events.) But for the rest, the Emperor got his way. The coronation of 11 Frimaire XIII (December 2, 1804) unfolded remarkably smoothly considering this sort of ceremony was very new in France. There was no eve of prayer preceding the event, no confession, no eucharist, no full-body prostrations before the altar, no "royal touching" of the populace for scrofula, and very little kneeling. Pius VII was there to be seen, not to function. The congregation, as Napoleon intended, reflected "the nation," not the populace of Paris. Present were hundreds of representatives of the provincial bourgeoisie (e.g., presidents of electoral colleges, mayors), of officialdom (prefects, etc.), the army, and the nobility.

The Emperor clearly took his coronation seriously, even if others did not. He "processed" down the central nave of Notre-Dame looking extremely pallid and moved, almost troubled—genuine emotions that clashed with his somewhat comical appearance, dwarfed by his large ermine mantle. He wore the laurel crown of the Roman emperors and the grand collar of the Legion of Honor; he held a globe—the sign of imperial power. The uneven two-part ceremony was held at different ends of the cathedral, to emphasize the disconnectedness of the two facets: the religious (mainly, the benediction by the pope)[103] and the secular, the central moment of which—and of the whole affair, from the government's and the audience's point of view—was the taking of the oath. This was a set of promises that emphasized the restrictions on imperial power and its republican nature: "I swear to maintain the integrity of the territory of the Republic, to respect and enforce respect for the Concordat and freedom of religion, equality of rights, political and civil liberty, the irrevocability of the sale of national lands; not to lift any tax except in virtue of the law; to maintain the institution of the Legion of Honor, and to govern in the sole interest, happiness, and glory of the French people."[104]

The oath is revelatory: if the coronation, in its style, felt as if it were anything but Revolutionary with a capital R, the whole affair was yet so secular in substance that it could not help being seen, near and far, as revolutionary in its historic significance. That is not to say that it satisfied or moved the French, however. The grandiosity and expense of the pageant (in a time of economic downturn) and the bizarre fact of the pope's presence in a city renowned for the guillotine kept the *sacre* questionable in the eyes of most Frenchmen, notwithstanding that Pius VII's humble personality and his accessible, simple manner endeared him to the multitude. There is no evidence of a national outpouring of joy at the coronation. What interest or curiosity it generated was aroused by the personalities of the pope and the

Emperor, not by any deep significance of an event that was widely seen as a gaudy and eclectic show. The Emperor's own almoner (chaplain) called it "veritable child's play."

In short, at the price of satisfying his pride and snubbing the reigning houses of Europe, Napoleon may have offended a large fraction of important French opinion. Truly religious Catholics were not taken in, nor was the Emperor's mastery over them enhanced by this simulacrum of a *sacre*–the less so as within a few years he and the pope were at open odds, anyway. Comments such as that used as the epigraph to this section–"a servile pope has anointed a black demon"–though less clever,[105] were common among Catholics. Finally, Napoleon arguably did not need the further legitimacy, if any, that this syncretism of a ceremony may have conferred on him. Legitimacy, as we shall see in a moment, is a more complex phenomenon than that.

To the senators, perhaps the most moving Napoleonic statement was that communicated to them on coronation eve, when the formal results of the plebiscite were registered. Said the Emperor: "My heart is full with my feelings for the great destinies of this people which, from the army camps of Italy [in 1797], I had already saluted as Great. Since my adolescence, all my thoughts have been invested in them, and, if I may say so, my pleasure and my pain are composed to this day out of the happiness and unhappiness of my people." French historians, including some of the best of them–unlike the senators–see insincerity lurking in these words, for the teenage Napoleon famously hated the French. Readers of this book know how I interpret the young man's feelings. But in a larger sense–and perhaps giving some poetic license to the Emperor's use of the word "adolescence"–Napoleon's "investment" in France's historical destiny, an investment that surely dated from his twenty-first year, if not earlier, was as deep as, *because it was inextricable from,* his investment in his own destiny.

In any case, there is no debate that at the distribution of regimental eagles to the army on December 5, the pageant and the emotions were completely sincere. *L'Empereur* among his officers and troops was a soldier's soldier among soldiers. No less a sign of sincerity: a young medical student–a civilian–rushed out of the crowd toward Napoleon and shouted, "Liberty or death!" He was immediately arrested, questioned, and detained for a time at the Charenton mental hospital.[106]

LEGITIMACY:
THE NEVER-ENDING QUEST

An idea has no greater metaphysical stature than, say, a fork. When your fork proves inadequate to the task of eating soup, it makes little sense to argue about whether there is something inherent in the nature of forks or something inherent in the nature of soup that accounts for the failure. You just reach for a spoon.
                                                            –John Dewey

The hobgoblin of political legitimacy had fascinated and exhausted the French since they destroyed their millennial monarchy in 1793. (It has continued to fascinate and exhaust them to the present day.) The average Frenchman of the beginning of the nineteenth century might have been hard pressed to say what legitimacy was, but he would have recognized it when he saw it. Louis XIV, the Sun King, *had legitimacy,* he would say. Louis derived his sacred office from God's anointment of his family in 987, not from any election by "the nation," and his powers and prerogatives were not mediated through statutes contained in a written constitution. He was an "outside bishop" in the Catholic Church; he had the power to touch for scrofula. He lost major battles and wars, signed ruinous treaties, handed over territories to his enemies, and so completely undermined his personal reputation that in 1715 his corpse was greeted with Bronx cheers as it went to its resting place. But none of this undermined Louis's legitimacy. Louis had not *needed* glory or empire, he only wanted them.

From this traditionalist perspective, *Napoléon Premier* could never win, papal anointment be damned. Crowning himself emperor, he had to stand comparison with the monarchical tradition in the vital area that counted most: bloodline. Here he would always come acropper. Making himself a hereditary sovereign, Napoleon thus made himself heir to the unending neurosis legitimizing his rule and (not the same thing) his "house." He was assisted in this obsession by the crowned heads and aristocracies of Europe who themselves were nothing less than neurotic about disclaiming Napoleonic (and maintaining their own) pretensions.

At home, Napoleon's problem was different, if hardly less anxiety provoking for himself. According to a familiar definition, legitimacy "consists of a tacit and understood accord between Power and its subjects as to certain principles and certain rules that determine its attributes and fix its limits."[107] The "accord" or "pact" between Napoleon and the nation was not the "mystical marriage" that joined the Bourbon king with his subjects. For one, in the latter case, it was the king who was sovereign, whereas in the First Empire, it was—it could only be, in the last analysis—"the people." In "attributes" and "limits," the new emperor's powers were great; they perhaps "resembled more those of the absolutist rulers than those of the constitutional monarch George III,"[108] but resemblance is not identity. Unlike an Eastern despot's power, Napoleon's depended on his genius and charisma, his ability to win military victory, and his ability to hold the Empire.

It yet remained his fervent desire to anchor his power in the deep traditional (or traditionalist) old regime sense, without actually returning to the old regime. But here was the problem par excellence of all governments in the revolutionary (and post-revolutionary) eras. Given Napoleon's aggressive personality, he sought his legitimacy everywhere; he tried doses of every medicine—coronation, plebiscite, republic, democracy, constitution, charisma, dictatorship—regardless of how incommensurate or incompatible the sulfurs were. The coronation had, as its secular center, the oath, which contained a republican bid for legitimation. It also featured the papal benediction, which the Emperor assumed (mistakenly, as it turned out) would be a takeout bid for Catholic-religious legitimation. As for the plebiscite, it was superfluous; the Senate's organic *senatus consultum* juridically sufficed to create the Empire. Moreover, the vote per se held no divine mystery or illusions for Napoleon, who was only too aware of how fickle opinion could be.[109] But the plebiscite did lend a patina of democracy to the rule of a First Consul and Emperor who in fact deeply mistrusted crowds. It made his regimes modern.

Modern and democratic, but not republican, as moderns (especially Anglo-Americans) understand the term. Late-revolutionary France's obsession with "the people" was a true secular religion, but its residual obsession with the "Republic" with a capital *R* was a romance with a word. Thiers makes the shrewd observation about the fate of the Jacobins of the Year II: "What a lesson for the sectarians who had thought, in the first delirium of their pride, that they could make France a republic because history had made her a democracy."[110] Democracy, as Thiers means it, combines the formal principle of popular sovereignty with the practical preoccupation with courting public opinion; it is symbolized by the Consulate's and the Empire's concern for the plebiscite—the exceptional appeal to, and the answer from, the *demos*. Or it is illustrated in Napoleon's title of "Emperor of the French," not Emperor of France.[111] But it is not the American meaning: "liberal, republican institutions." It would require the entire nineteenth century to make the French into republicans, in that sense. Bonaparte

had long since recovered from his small love affair with the (First) Republic—
for him, the regime always smacked too much of *un régime de parti*—yet he
nonetheless dreaded losing the word's cachet; hence the oxymoron of that
bedizened coinage: "Napoléon Bonaparte, empereur de la République
française."

For its part, the constitution of the Year XII might be called a bid for juridical legitimacy, but it was one that misportrayed both the true face of
Napoleonic power by erecting institutions that might have challenged the
Emperor, and the façade of language, by which the regime strove for democratic legitimacy. For not the least paradox of the new constitution is the
absence in it of the word "nation." It is an absence of letter, not spirit; nation-
talk was (and remained) the Napoleonic regime's personal signature, the illustration of the Emperor's striving after democratic legitimacy, his perfecting
of what the Consulate had striven for: the democratic regime in formal and
final, but not material, principles. All was done for the "nation," nothing by
it.[112] Napoleon managed a very modern focusing of the "nation" onto himself as its sole representative. As the political philosopher Marcel Gauchet
puts it, in opposition to the republican principle of impersonal government,
Napoleon "reinvented the monarchical principle at its deepest, yet did so
within the framework of a state of law which seemed to exclude it. It was with
the title of representative of the Nation that Napoleon personified power, and
indeed declared himself *more* 'representative' than those of his predecessors
who had been formally elected."[113] This, then, was the essence of the tradition that the nineteenth century would dub "bonapartism," whose potency
endured well into the twentieth century, not just in France but as far away as
Brazil or Central Africa. Nation-talk was the something new that Bluche
intends when he observes that the regime was neither a military dictatorship
nor a classical monarchy.

Napoleonic legitimacy, in sum, was composed of a Macedonian salad of
traditions and forms, all of them palpably ambiguous, artificial, and opportunist, not to mention mutually exclusive. They amounted, in fact, to "an
alibi of legitimacy," as one scholar puts it.[114] But therein lay the problem: to
be seen to strive *this hard* was itself to undermine legitimacy, an area of life—
religion being another—where perceived pragmatism and effort cannot
work. (Napoleon was an instrumentalist in religion, too.) The salad had only
the small advantage of serviceability; the Emperor could and did move from
one form of legitimation to another, depending on the context and need of
the moment, none of them any more successful than the other.

When we look from the stated to the unstated, we see a contrast between
these formal ways that Napoleon and his supporters claimed and staged legit-

imacy, and his *actual* legitimacy. At St. Helena the Emperor would invariably emphasize that he was his own legitimacy—the "selfness of himself," we might say; his legitimacy inhered in his victories, his brilliance, his glory and reputation, his style, his charisma, and—far from least—his manifest knowledge of (and yes, his perceived love for) the French. This is neither a particularly surprising nor an unusual admission in the modern era; there will be many other political leaders who will seek this kind of individual legitimacy, even if *l'Empereur* remains the first and most remarkable in this self-made genre. This new personalist dimension of politics that the Revolution laid the groundwork for, and Napoleon finessed, cannot be restricted or encompassed by legislation, theory, or even mere consistency.[115]

At the end of the day there is a curious subtle game Napoleon played with himself and the French people where legitimacy was concerned. Consider the following set of commonly cited, plangent observations:

> France understands poorly my position, which is why she so completely misjudges most of my acts. Five or six families share the thrones of Europe and they take it badly that a Corsican has seated himself at their table. I can only maintain myself there by force; I can only get them used to regarding me as their equal by keeping them in thrall; my empire will be destroyed if I cease being fearsome. . . . Thus I cannot afford to let anyone threaten me without striking out at them. Things that would be unimportant for a king of an old house are very serious for me. I shall have to maintain this attitude as long as I live, and if my son is not a great captain [of war]—if he is not able to do what I do—then he will fall off the throne where I have placed him, for it takes a man to consolidate a monarchy. Louis XIV, despite all his victories, would still have lost his throne at the end of his life if he had not inherited it from a long line of kings. Among established sovereigns, a war's only purpose is to dismember a province or take a city; but with me, it is always a question of my very existence as a monarch, of the existence of the whole empire.[116]

This long imperial sigh, regularly exhaled throughout the Empire and at St. Helena, is actually a rather cunning exercise in self-pity. It captures a real historical truth, of course, or it would be useless to its function of evoking a sympathetic response, as it certainly did: "Poor Napoleon! They wouldn't give him the respect he wanted and deserved."

What is less commented upon, however, is the role this sort of reflection has as a rationale for an aggressive child, and *this* it is, more than it is an accurate description of any logic supposedly immanent in the First Empire. The reflection implies that "the French required" wars and empire in order to confer legitimacy on the Emperor, that he was not safely on his throne unless he was mounted in the saddle at the head of the Grande Armée. But that is quite arguably not the case. The First Consul, not to mention the Emperor, had far more legitimacy than he realized. He was the object of great gratitude, admiration, and even affection, and barring cataclysm, his "house," in time, would have been tolerated. The never-ending quest for legitimacy was largely his own rationale for aggressive (and childish) behavior.

X

La Guerre—Encore (et pour toujours)

Where there exist wild men so inimical to humanity as to want perpetual wars of extermination, we must take care not to admit them to our counsel, but rather send them far from family and *patrie* for years on end . . . , or, better, put them amidst the carnage of a battlefield on the day of battle; here, unless all feeling of humanity be extinguished in their hearts, they will surely abjure their atrocious principles.

–Napoleon Bonaparte[1]

THE FAILURE OF THE PEACE

If Bonaparte were an ordinary man, he would not excite our fears and our jealousy, but with a man of such great talents and such genius we cannot rest secure with an ordinary armament. Under the [French] monarchy, it was the nation which gave the tone to the government; but today it is the First Consul who gives activity and movement to his country.

–The Prince of Wales,
January 1, 1803[2]

It is erroneous to believe that a political position founded on economic superiority is "essentially unwarlike."

–Carl Schmitt,
The Concept of the Political

The celebrations that greeted the signing of Amiens—the odes and cantatas, the poems, pamphlets, and paeans to peace in French, English, German, and other languages; the plays depicting Amiens at dinner theatres, vaudeville, and on the legitimate stage—were written and performed with obvious sincerity by the various national publics. Had either side turned out truly to want peace, it could have had it, but if peace was much praised, it was spoken for appearances' sake—so that the speaker would not be blamed for peace's failure. In mid-May 1803, France and England were at war—and with an easy resignation that stood in striking contrast to the enthusiasm for Amiens. Peace was the exception in this age.[3] It is perhaps a comment on the quality of Anglo-French propaganda or the degree of the two countries' gullibility; perhaps just a comment on their familiarity with the old harness of war which they had worn for a hundred years.[4]

After the Treaty of Lunéville (February 1801) between France and Austria, peace between France and England[5] was inevitable for the simple reason that Britain—wealthy, insular, but with a small population—could not readily field an army to fight France on land; she was forced to buy a Continental replacement to do it. The negotiations between England and France, begun with such great optimism in the autumn of 1801, proved so painful and protracted that it left the principals dubious that the peace, finally signed in March 1802, could last. England walked away with little new, but then she had been on the losing side—a point all the more difficult for her to accept in that she herself had not sustained a military defeat. Britain retroceded most of the French and Dutch colonies that she had seized and found herself agreeing to turn over the island of Malta to the Knights who traditionally occupied it. She also had to recognize French presence in the Low Countries and tolerate her gains in Italy. Finally, Britain gained no commercial treaty with France that would open up French markets to British goods—a return to the situation of 1786—as English merchants had fervently desired and expected. In short, writer and parliamentarian Richard Sheridan's description of "a peace which every man ought to be glad of, but no man can be proud of" summed up the island kingdom's reaction to Amiens.

The signatories felt they had gotten breathing space from Amiens. The new prime minister, Henry Addington, Pitt's successor, was not the bumbler of common portrayal; he, no less than Bonaparte, understood that Amiens was likely only a truce, but ideally one that might last a decade or so—as long as most treaties lasted in the war-pocked recent history of Europe—so that he could solve his country's serious financial problems, and only then go back to war with France.[6] The treaty gave Napoleon a new title, "prince of peace," to go with his well-earned "god of war," and the chance to finish proving himself the great legislator at home. But he, too, expected a resumption of hostilities with the "ancient enemy," and he took the opportunity to beef up the navy.

Geopolitically, Amiens ratified a new status in the familiar old balance of power; it recognized the three superpowers—Great Britain, Russia, and France—as tenants of far superior positions to those they had occupied before the wars of the French Revolution. Britain and Russia, in fact—and this is an important point not always noted—gained even more than France did, if you consider the whole of the eighteenth century.[7] This said, there was no denying that the old eighteenth-century disequilibrium that had impaired and insulted France was now more than rectified. France was back, with a vengeance! The map of 1802, in sum, revealed a painfully elaborated coexistence among Russia, Great Britain, and France, in which each country dominated spheres of influence in, respectively, the East, the West, and "the seas" (including colonies). The question for Britain would be: Was the seas enough especially given French desire to compete here, too? Could she, in fact, ignore the Continent, as she in effect obligated herself to do at Amiens?

If Britain thus entered the Amiens era with a bad conscience for having disserved herself, hence on the qui vive for redress, Bonaparte entered it seeing peace as opportunity. What strikes the biographer is how boldly, not to say brazenly, he did not take a breather, but instead pursued—even during the six months of colloquy that resulted in the treaty—policies of expansion beyond what England anticipated. To read his letters in these years is to ponder a ceaseless, implacable river of orders to his diplomats, agents, generals, and allies to take initiatives and execute missions in every direction.[8] Bonaparte proved remorseless at seizing and making opportunities to undertake aggressive expansionism at any price, save war itself, including sowing rebellion, conflict, and international confrontation. Agreements and treaties were not so much obstacles to be furtively rounded as to be triumphantly leaped, while Europe gaped. The First Consul knew he had an opportunity to get away with what he liked for a time, so he maximized his advantage, prepared to fight when the time came, but believing (incorrectly) it would not, anytime soon. His underlying rationale was not so much the narcissistic take, "rules don't apply to me," as the cynical belief, "the other powers play this game, too. I'm just better at it." As with all rationales, it contained a germ of truth.

A partial list of his initiatives dating from the start of negotiations (October 1, 1801) that resulted in Amiens (March 1802) would include:

- the redrawing of the map of Germany, with the French overseeing it;
- annexation of Piedmont, allowed by the peace of Lunéville;

- annexation of the island of Elba;
- Bonaparte becoming president of the Cisalpine (Italian) Republic;
- city-state of Parma turned over to the Italian Republic;
- creation of a French protectorate, the kingdom of Etruria, in Tuscany;
- the Act of Mediation requested by (but also forced on) Switzerland, with Bonaparte being named mediator;
- the detachment of the Valais region of Switzerland as a dependency of France;
- the Leclerc expeditionary force sent to Haiti, intended to go on to Louisiana;[9]
- General Decaen's mission to India, where he was instructed by Bonaparte to "tread lightly, simply, and with dissimulation";
- Colonel Sebastiani's mission to Egypt, supposedly to observe, but in fact to consider the means for retaking the country;
- Holland, theoretically independent, forced to receive a new constitution and to draw closer to France.

What muffles a clear negative judgment on this rather astounding bill of particulars[10] is that some of these measures were requested by leading forces within these countries; other measures were progressive, with (at least initially) liberal or modernizing impacts upon the countries. In Germany, for example, nothing less than a kind of territorial revolution took place under the auspices of French diplomacy, as scores of ecclesiastical and imperial statelets saw themselves replaced by centralized modern, if small, states. Austria was all but pushed out of the ancient Heilige Roemische Reich whose crown her emperor wore, while the French were successfully courting the southern German princes, talking them into alignment with France. Most frustrating from the British point of view, Napoleonic diplomacy was clever enough to accomplish this entire German reform under the formal oversight of the tsar, who was the nominal protector of Germany. Alexander I presently figured out that he had been outwitted, and thereafter he seethed with self-righteous indignation at Napoleon.

Italy was always the *enfant chérie* of Bonaparte. An Italian Jacobin of the era proudly noted, "We in the Italian party were always certain we could pluck a secret cord in his soul, which the French ministers did their best to stifle."[11] Bonaparte called a national "consulta" of the Cisalpine Republic at Lyon in late 1801. The deputies elected the First Consul president of the new "Italian" Republic, an act by which they aimed to flatter themselves as much as the electee. Many Italians, including some of Bonaparte's closest associates (e.g., Melzi, who became vice president), had lost their enthusiasm for the

French connection, thanks to four years of exactions, but they bowed to two realizations—they could not agree on a candidate of their own; and they had no one who remotely possessed Bonaparte's force for holding their republic together while keeping it safe from Austria. For better or worse, he was indispensable to the regime's existence. For the first time in French history, Italy permanently outranked any other theater of operations, even Germany, for concern in Paris.[12]

Bonaparte's election in the Italian Republic[13] shocked the other powers. At Amiens, where negotiations plodded along, Joseph felt the British stiffen over this matter, but they failed to lodge a protest. The eventual treaty said no word about the new Italian states, for Britain did not recognize them. That might serve British pique, but it left Whitehall (the British Foreign Office) ill-placed to protest when France annexed Piedmont (September 1802).[14]

In Switzerland, the British did act, but to no avail. The situation offers a clear instance of what sent the Addington government into conniptions, but what posterity finds harder to judge. Since 1798, the Swiss had tried various forms of government, including a Jacobin unitary republic.[15] None had wrought harmony in this diverse land of Alpine territories. The present failure was the Bonaparte-brokered constitution of Malmaison (1801), which had not kept Federalists, Jacobins, and Oligarchs from one another's throats. Moreover, lacing this already ample intra-Swiss animus in unknown quantities were British agents and British gold, acting on behalf of the Oligarchs (the old regime believers). Their activity included fostering anti-French riots and uprisings.[16] This was enough to make Bonaparte act; he procured a formal "invitation" from the Federalists for the French Republic to intervene. In marched General Ney's corps of thirty thousand men, and presently the Swiss parties were in Paris for a "consultation," in order to devise a final plan of governance—or face annexation to France.

Of course, neither great power, Britain nor France, had any right to be in Switzerland, but this made no difference to anyone, even to many Swiss, who, for their own reasons of self-interest or ideology, wanted them there. For Britain, the Helvetic Republic was an outpost from which to foment trouble in France; for Bonaparte, it was a French preserve—ideologically, since the Revolution had marched in and transformed the country; and geographically, in being a crucial military "march"* against Austria and Italy. To the French, and not just to Bonaparte, the Republic had far greater interest here than did *les Anglais*. The First Consul let loose in self-righteous anger against the British for their Swiss machinations adding the warning that if Addington had dared

*A "march" is a frontier region.

to intervene in an official capacity, then he would have annexed Switzerland outright. He brazenly acknowledged, "My calculations are not based simply upon what the Swiss people would like, but upon what is to the advantage of 40 million Frenchmen."[17]

The Federalist forces that invited the French in were legitimate, strong, and, by comparison to the British-backed Oligarchs, progressive, but they were conservative compared to those Jacobin Swiss who had, under French aegis, founded the Helvetic Republic in 1798. The Act of Mediation that now emerged to found yet another regime, under strict French guidance, permitted the cantons to resume their ancient role in a federal-type (not a Jacobin-unitary) government. The First Consul's reasoning was thus: "Nature herself has made a federalist State for you, and to wish to destroy it is not the act of a wise man." To keep the peace, Bonaparte was named mediator.[18] The constitution, it must be said, satisfied the people for a decade to come. (Switzerland is the only country to still carry the name given it in this era: Helvetic Confederation.) England, of course, rightly viewed the country's virtually umbilical ties to France as perilous. But the Treaty of Amiens had said nothing on the matter, while Lunéville only specified that the Swiss were free to choose their government (as they nominally had done), after which the French would depart (as Ney's corps did). Then, too, the countries to which a French-controlled Switzerland posed the most obvious threats—Prussia and Austria—made no protest; they had other fish to fry with Napoleon. So what could England do?

Would Switzerland have been better off if Addington's interventions on behalf of the Oligarchic party had succeeded and England had replaced France as the Republic's guarantor? That would have entailed erasing even more reforms that the Revolution had introduced into Swiss sociopolitical life. Would the Helvetic Confederation have been better off becoming a center of plots against Napoleon Bonaparte's life and regime, like the British-held isle of Jersey, off the French northern coast? But was it better off as a French launching pad for attacks on the Tyrol or Italy? Reasonable people will continue to answer such questions differently.

Lunéville required the French to evacuate Holland after a general peace was signed, but this did not happen. The French imposed a constitution on the Batavian Republic and left eleven thousand soldiers within its borders "temporarily," but maintained at Dutch expense. The British, though soon regretting it, lived up to their treaty obligation requiring them to restore the Cape (South Africa) to Holland. This they did in early 1803, only to see it fall into French hands, as France began to exercise hegemony in the Batavian Republic. French presence in Holland—as on the left bank of the Rhine, or in Italy and Switzerland—was increasingly felt as an aggression, as French exactions in material, money, and men went from importunate to outrageous, but in Holland, as elsewhere, the puppet regime in office requested French protection and reforms, which, with all the downsides, were preferred to Austrian, Prussian, or English presence or pressure.[19] It is this ambivalence that distinguishes early Napoleonic imperialism from other forms of imperialism.

Then, too, these unexpected territorial gains that were the heart of the contention between France and Britain were accomplished without firing a shot—the result, as one historian puts it, of "Germany's helplessness, Prussia's resignation, Russia's retirement, Austria's defeat and England's exhaustion."[20] Whitehall had itself to blame for the "grievous blunder" of not inserting a clause in the treaty stipulating the independence of Holland and Switzerland.

The same can be said for the disappointing economic consequences of the peace for Britain, whose importance is nearly as great as the political. If peace had proven profitable to English merchants and industrialists, then a great deal of French military-diplomatic aggression might have gone down with the City. Chaptal, Napoleon's minister of the interior, and Lebrun, a former co-consul, indeed favored a treaty with England, if only for the sake of maintaining a real peace. Napoleon, however, was wary, for he felt a treaty risked putting France back in Britain's commercial shadow as, he believed, the treaty of 1786 had done. He leaned toward high tariffs to protect what he intended would be his policy of fostering French industrial growth. So, not without reluctance, the First Consul fired Chaptal, and, despite the fitful attempt to satisfy French commerce, resolutely turned French economic policy toward "patriotic" domestic industrial development.[21]

For the French there was only one true deficit in the treaty, but it was gigantic and personal: the British press's attacks on the First Consul and his family. The quality of the journalists writing this propaganda was high and vicious in the extreme; they demonized Bonaparte ("the Corsican ogre, half-African, half-European, Mediterranean mulatto," "the little monkey of four feet two," "a pastiche of every clown of the Revolution," etc.), maligned Josephine, insinuated that her husband was having sex with her daughter, and recounted endless lies about Napoleon's past.[22] Public opinion had only fairly recently become a major factor in international politics and the press campaign played a large role in envenoming relations. The campaign marched in conjunction with the continued presence in England of several Bourbon princes, together with their active clandestine committees, a dozen dissident French bishops who had refused to acknowledge the Concordat, and leading conspirators, such as Georges Cadoudal. In other words, *the ideological bat-*

tle against the French Revolution continued to be waged in Britain; it did not acknowledge the peace.[23]

The First Consul was so outraged at these attacks that he inserted no fewer than five articles, in his own hand, in *Le Moniteur,* to protest. No source, British or French, doubts that this time his anger was real. The attacks stung his *amour propre,* which in turn all but unhinged him.[24] He, his ministers, and ambassadors repeatedly complained to Addington about his failure to control the press. "Does freedom of the press reach so far," Bonaparte wrote in *Le Moniteur* (August 8, 1802), "as to permit a newspaper to say of a friendly nation, newly reconciled with England, things one would not dare say of a government with whom one was at war?" The British regime could have tried to do more than it did, just as it might have acceded to the French requests to expel the Bourbon princes and the émigrés. Addington did warn the First Consul not to waste his time or further risk his reputation preferring libel charges in a British court against the offending newspapers. It is a sign of how furious Bonaparte was that he did so anyway.[25]

At the turn of 1803, having had to endure the stinging disaster of the Leclerc expedition to Saint-Domingue,[26] Bonaparte was angry, embarrassed, and looking for compensation. He was reluctantly ready to sell Louisiana to the Americans, a sign that he may have been readying for a return to war with Britain. Then, on January 30 he deliberately had inserted in *Le Moniteur* part of Sebastiani's report on Egypt, including the outrageous claim that with six thousand men, it would be possible to retake the former colony. Lucien's memoirs hold that that particular sentence was added by Bonaparte, but the historian Harold Deutsch demonstrates how the First Consul's penciled corrections tended, rather, to mitigate the tone of Sebastiani's words.[27] When the British government protested through its ambassador, Lord Whitworth, the First Consul upbraided him before the diplomatic corps (a political display of temper). Was the publication in *Le Moniteur* intended as a diversion from the rout that the French had suffered in the Antilles? It was certainly a trait of Bonaparte's to try to cover a retreat with a diversion, but it was equally true that Napoleon was obsessed with a "return" of Egypt both to vindicate his personal honor and as a stepping-stone to his "Alexandrian" dream of Eastern empire.[28] Then, too, maybe Sebastiani's piece was also "payment" for the favorable review that the London *Times* (a semi-official newspaper) accorded a book that teemed with libels about Bonaparte's Egyptian campaign.

By early 1803, Britain was so sick of feeling had, that she took a stand; unfortunately that meant formally violating the Treaty of Amiens, as the French had not done. Britain refused to evacuate Malta, an island that had somehow grown in strategic importance in direct measure to Britain's need for a pretext over which to dig in. (Previously she had been amenable to having the Russians take it over.) As Franco-British relations further disintegrated in the spring, His Majesty's government stepped back a bit from some of her previous intractability. Addington offered to turn a blind eye to French "aggression" in Italy and Germany; he even withdrew his insistence that France open herself to British commerce. But on Malta, he stood firm: British troops would stay until French troops evacuated Switzerland.

Unlike the prime minister, the First Consul was surrounded by doves, from his foreign minister to his brothers. While he hardly heeded them, in this instance, he had managed to avoid seeming to be "the autonomous disturber of tranquility,"[29] for all that he had goaded the British lion to pounce sooner than he wanted it to. Addington had earlier warned his cabinet: "We must however take Care, not only to be right, but *very* right."[30] But that was not how things appeared when war broke out. Castlereagh, the future foreign secretary, wrote: "It will be difficult to convince the world that we are not fighting for Malta alone."[31] But it was not just Malta; Addington, in his avid desire for secret intelligence from Paris, had compromised the British embassy in Paris to such a degree that the foreign secretary, Lord Hawkesbury, felt "humiliat[ed] in the eyes of the diplomatic world" for his constant attempts to intervene in French internal affairs.[32] Then, too, the Royal Navy's impatience to begin arresting French merchant ships on the open seas further took the moral edge off the British position, leaving them open to French charges of bellicosity and perfidy.

War thus returned as the result of an unstoppable, if understandable, British slippage into intransigence. As usual, Bonaparte's reflections about it were both on and wide of the mark: "The giddiness that has taken hold of the English government for some months now is not to be believed. They must think we have no arms and no ink." Bonaparte, as it happened, was caught off guard and did not want war *at this point*—it was inopportune for French affairs, from commerce to colonial policy to shipbuilding. Down to the last, the First Consul had figured Addington was bluffing, and he seemed almost surprised when Ambassador Whitworth returned to London. Napoleon indeed went on offering terms to Britain, via Russian mediators, even after war broke out (May 18)—including even allowing the British to keep Malta. But they were no longer in season. Only in declaring war had Britain recognized what she had probably sensed all along: she could not tolerate the way Europe had become and was likely to keep going with Bonaparte at the French helm. Britain would no longer be hemmed in by a misbegotten treaty. War offered her the chance to jump in with both feet where, in peace, she had feared to tread. With ringing aptness one minister cited the famous lines of Cicero in his *Philippics*, "Why then do I *not* want peace? Because it is untrustworthy, because it is dangerous, because it cannot be."

The British fleet retook the islands and commercial outposts in India and elsewhere which had been returned to France at Amiens. The French seized the Brabant (in Holland) and the north German province of Hanover, which belonged to the British royal house. They also occupied the estuaries of the Elbe and Weser, closing all German, Dutch, and, of course, French ports to British trade. Spain, in alliance with France, and even neutral Portugal were prevailed upon to follow suit, though neither country did so securely or sincerely. In June the French had seized the Neapolitan ports. The British deployed their navy to blockade the coasts of their enemies.

Curiously, historians do not remark on the dearth of domestic opposition that the First Consul encountered to his expansionist policies or the return of war. The French people had longed for peace—it is a constant theme in the press and police reports of 1798–1802[33]—yet the policies that outraged the Continental powers and Britain appear to have raised little murmur on the home front. *Au contraire,* the evidence suggests wide popular and elite pride in Napoleon's coups and French aggrandizement. The same was true in Britain: Addington's government took no jabs from the opposition for its firmness on Malta; rather, he was criticized for not being firm enough. The British and the French people had sincerely wanted peace, but not at the price of peace in the world as they found it. War returned to no enthusiasm, just a wan belief on both sides in their own government's righteousness.

For the British, prizing peace above all would have required His Majesty's Government not only to tolerate French geopolitical acquisitions abroad and on the Continent, but to admit strong, renewed French naval, commercial, and industrial competition without themselves being able (thanks to the return of peace and to ongoing high French tariffs) to exert their usual maritime supremacy in the familiar dictatorial fashion. In other words, the British would have had to accept that their longstanding economic superiority, which did indeed amount to military-political power (as per Schmitt), would now be at risk of being gradually lost to the French.[34] This was to ask too much.

For the French, prizing peace above all would have entailed placing it above considerations of national unity of the sort that armed conflict necessitates, beyond a wish for vengeance on the long-hated "national" foe, beyond the love of national grandeur, and—not quite the same thing—of their leader's *gloire* and their own, magnified by his. The propaganda the French read in official statements or in the limited and censored (and self-censoring) press presented a dictator's aims of national and personal aggrandizement in the language of imperatives about national preservation and honor.[35] Then, too, the First Consul's acquisitions for the Republic were not presented to or received by the country as random acts of imperialism. Thanks to the heritage of the Revolution, the government had at hand a ready "missionary" rationale.[36]

Yet when all was said and done, the decisive cause for the rupture of the peace of Amiens lies with Bonaparte, not Addington, Hawkesbury, or Whitworth—and *not* with some war logic inherent in the soul of the French Empire. Without Bonaparte's unique temperament dominating affairs, peace might well have quietly tiptoed forward between the mutually incomprehending rivals for five or ten (more) years. But Napoleon's rashness kept London in a continual state of surprise and outrage, of dispute and controversy; there was not even a temporary pause, from the moment (October 1, 1801) that negotiations for a peace began to the day war returned. The British had stepped into the era of the peace hoping to find redress for a bad treaty, and the French served them up worse—English frustration only increasing with the lack of arousal among other powers.

Talleyrand writes in his memoirs, "Hardly was the Peace of Amiens concluded when moderation began to desert Bonaparte; the peace was not yet completed before he was sowing the seeds of new wars." Paul Schroeder's judgment is thus well founded: "The British went to war simply because they could not stand being further challenged and humiliated by Bonaparte; France went to war because Bonaparte could not stop doing it."[37]

So is it the "Great Consulate," as Lentz avers? If the First Consul's domestic record leads one to concur with Lentz, Bonaparte's foreign policy induces listlessness for summoning the energy to join in this novelty, and the historian's natural conservatism wills out. Bonaparte didn't *have to* drive England to war, but in view of what he did, England *had to* declare it.

FORMING THE THIRD COALITION

Well, Prince, so Genoa and Lucca are now just family estates of the Bonapartes.
—Leo Tolstoy, *War and Peace* (opening line)

The British believed that in the long run their blockade would enforce both the collapse of the French economy and the revolt of the Continental powers against Napoleon's control. And they were right in the long run, but in the spring of 1803, they still had to find an ally, and this was anything but imminent. Whom could they convince to fight? Both the French and the British scurried about making diplomatic initiatives, but France could count up front on an array of satellites and allies: Italy, Spain, and Holland compared favorably with Britain's nearly empty dance card[38] at the start of the long two years of "phony war." It would take a lot of money and effort before Russia, Prussia, and especially Austria would risk getting ground up again in the French war machine; and indeed, gold and persuasion did not suffice— the less so, as Russia and England had as much reason to clash over the Near East as to come together against French aspirations there. But England turned out to have a secret ally in its mission to erect a new coalition.

The First Consul's actions in 1804–5—executing the Enghien affair, of course, but above all making himself Emperor of the French—stunned Europe. William Pitt, back in the saddle at Whitehall (spring 1804), was utterly depressed by the pope's consent to attend the coronation. He sent Alexander I a plan of a treaty for the restoration of the Bourbons—a plan considered so sensitive that only a part of it was presented to Parliament.[39] A year later the promotion of the Italian Republic to a kingdom, with Napoleon as "king of all Italy"[40]—in brazen breach of the Treaty of Lunéville—ended Habsburg hopes in the Boot, as definitively as the Imperial Recess of 1803 had ended them in Germany. For good measure, Napoleon also annexed the Ligurian Republic (Genoa) and handed over two small Italian principalities to his sister and brother-in-law Elisa and Felix Bacciochi[41]—all violations of Lunéville.

In short, Great Britain's "secret ally" in attracting allies was less English credits than French discredit: Napoleon Bonaparte.

Napoleon himself is a focus to keep well in mind in accounting for the crystallization of the Third Coalition, for here, as elsewhere in our story, traditional State policy—the stuff of diplomatic histories of the great powers in their endless rivalries—vies for causal prominence with the personalities, the feelings (above all, the piqued vanity), and the reactionary politics of key individuals. Alexander I, Ferdinand IV of Naples and his queen, Marie-Caroline, and Gustav IV of Sweden all had something of a weakness for the Bourbon Louis XVIII (the Comte de Provence as he was known), but even more, they shared a violent hatred of Bonaparte, redoubled by the Enghien execution and the ensuing declaration of the Empire. True, the tsar could also be fascinated by Napoleon, but never as much as he was jealous and envious of him. The young Romanov's megalomania was of such mettle that, at twenty-four (he succeeded his murdered father, Paul I, in 1801),[42] he yet aspired to replace the French ruler as "organizer" of Europe, only to find himself completely outplayed (for example, in German affairs). He and King Gustav refused to recognize Napoleon as Emperor of the French; they referred to him as "the Head of the French Government" or "Monsieur Napoleon Bonaparte" in official government communications.

Angry feelings led some rulers to outright foolishness. Marie-Caroline, as befitted the sister of Marie-Antoinette, played the double game of maintaining cordial formal relations with France while signing a secret alliance with Britain. Napoleon, of course, was on to her, thanks to his agents; he wrote her one of those frank screeds that only he could send: "Your Majesty has already lost her kingdom twice, would she like to lose it a third time? May you heed this prophecy without impatience: at the first sound of a war that you cause, you and your posterity will have ceased to reign, and your children will wander like mendicants through the different countries of Europe, begging help off their relatives."

With Francis II and Frederick William III, personal and ideological factors weighed less than they did with their brother and sister monarchs, yet even here we dare not make neat distinctions between geopolitics as usual and the particular situation created by "the Corsican usurper" and the Revolution from which he sprang. Francis II's abject humiliations at Napoleon's hands were no minor element in pushing Austria to war again and again. From holder of the most august and perhaps the oldest title in Europe, the Holy Roman Emperor would presently become simply "hereditary emperor of Austria" (as Francis I), with diplomatic precedence ranking him *behind* Napoleon I, whose title of Emperor of the French predated the Habsburg's own by several weeks.[43]

The Prussian king had the least *parti pris* against the French Revolution or Napoleon of any European monarch, perhaps because his revered ancestor Frederick the Great had a fondness (at a distance) for the French Enlightenment. Still, we cannot forget: Frederick William lived with constant pressure from his wife, the fair Queen Louise, a stouthearted patriot and a leading voice of the active anti-French lobby in Berlin. (Louise and Alexander I were having a romantic, if platonic, friendship.) Napoleon at moments courted Frederick William III (at other times he snubbed him); he sent his closest aide, Duroc, to Berlin, and offered the king the neighboring electorate of Hanover in return for an alliance with France, or (later) just for benevolent neutrality in the growing polarization between France and the Austro-Russians. But the Enghien affair—an ideological matter at bottom—disposed Frederick William against accepting presents or alliances from Napoleon, and traditional Prussian State policy of resisting French incursions in Germany did the rest.

Finally, there is the role of the most indefatigable and talented group of napoleonophobes to arise in early-nineteenth-century Europe. Each of these social and political reactionaries was extremely well connected and influential, with complete access to the European courts and the British government; they often communicated using the diplomatic services of these countries. They included the Comte d'Antraigues, a French émigré and the pretender's top operative on the Continent (he worked out of Dresden but had a network of agents, including several very highly placed people in Paris);[44] the Swedish general Gustav Armfelt, Gustav IV's ambassador to Vienna, but soon to enter the service of Alexander I; Charles-André Pozzo di Borgo, Bonaparte's bitter Corsican foe whom we met earlier, variously turning up in Vienna, Rome, and finally St. Petersburg, where, in 1804, he became a close counselor of the tsar;[45] Count Nikita Panin, foreign minister to Paul I and a leading diplomat under Alexander; the great Prussian minister of State Heinrich Stein, eventually, too, to work for the tsar;[46] and last, but first in intellectual influence, the talented Prussian publicist Friedrich von Gentz. Gentz was a counterrevolutionary writer in the style of Edmund Burke and Mallet du Pan ("if there is one man who may be regarded as *the* writer of the counterrevolution, it is he," said Talleyrand),[47] and an indefatigable Francophobe. He left his own king's service for Francis II's, because he found Frederick William too weak-willed vis-à-vis Napoleon. At the court of Francis II, he proved himself an implacable critic of any chancellor or minister who did not make opposition to Napoleon the center of his policies.

This band of zealots, in sum, went far beyond a cabal of mercenary counselors who promoted the interest of the State they happened to serve (while taking subsidies from England and Russia); they were men for whom the drive to bring Napoleon down was their life purpose. French victories would force them to move beyond their enemy's reach, but they grimly stuck to their goal of unseating the "ogre" and putting Louis XVIII in his place. They will constantly return in pursuit of Napoleon—except d'Antraigues, assassinated under mysterious circumstances in 1812—to be present and play critically important roles in 1813–15. Napoleon, on St. Helena, was not wrong when he opined that Pozzo di Borgo had been the single most decisive counsel in convincing Alexander I to take Paris in 1814. And Viscount Castlereagh, the Napoleon-hating foreign secretary of Britain, will be decisive in returning the Bourbons to the French throne. Personal feelings and beliefs counted.

In part, thanks to these men, Louis XVIII and his brother the Comte d'Artois, became ever more heeded in St. Petersburg, Vienna, London, and Naples. The Allied powers—some, more than others—leaned strongly in the direction of putting the Bourbon back on the French throne, in the event of an Allied victory. The British prime minister who eventually succeeded Pitt, the Duke of Portland, was a believer in the Bourbon cause; so were Whitworth and many other British diplomats of the old Pitt-Grenville party. His Majesty's government continued to assign tens of thousands of pounds to promoting royalist activities in France and subsidizing the "Count of Lisle," as Louis XVIII was known in Britain, where he resided after 1807. To all of them, the war on Napoleon was a crusade against "a Jacobin chief who has attained his end, and exercises the unbounded power he has acquired like a successful Jacobin," to cite the redundant words of an abettor of this group, the English diplomat Malmesbury.[48]

Napoleon's donning of the purple changed little in the way he was seen abroad. His becoming emperor did little to reassure the Allied sovereigns in their *public* statements and policies. Talleyrand early on (and easily) brought his master to understand that it was dangerous for French diplomacy to seek to play the revolutionary card. But even if imperial diplomacy largely (not completely) discarded this approach, neither its head of State nor his foreign minister was ever able to make the Empire's opponents change their fundamental view of France or its leader: they were outsiders, including ideologically. One need only look at Louis XVIII's declaration issued at Kalmar, on the same day as Napoleon's coronation (a hard day to attract attention from Kalmar, Sweden, no doubt). The document makes it clear that the "tyrant" and his regime are subversive children of the Revolution. The crowned heads of Europe were all intellectually as aware as the Bourbon pretender that the new emperor's person and policies represented a sharp curbing of the French Revolution, but it didn't matter. Francis, Frederick William, and Alexander had all expressed pleasure, at one point or another, at France's return to the monarchy, yet formally they shared Gentz's judgment on Napoleon's self-coronation in 1804: "It is the French Revolution that is being sanctioned and sanctified." Their inconsistency permitted Napoleon to proffer one of his more interesting insights at St. Helena: "I may have been called 'a modern Attila' and 'a Robespierre on horseback' by the other sovereigns; but if they would search their hearts, they would know better. Had I really been that, I would perhaps be reigning still. But one thing is surely certain: had I been such, they all would long since have ceased to reign."

In the mid-1790s, Constitutional bishop Grégoire sought to justify the French Republic's attacks on the monarchies with a wonderful metaphor: "If my neighbor feeds snakes, I have the right to suffocate them, by fear of becoming a victim." Ten years later it was still true (and would remain true) that her neighbors felt that France harbored snakes. In sum, if there was one legitimacy that Napoleon Bonaparte never had to worry about, it was his revolutionary standing in the eyes of the other monarchs. This man, especially perhaps after he took the crown, galvanized counterrevolution as perhaps nothing had since the execution of Louis XVI.

Nevertheless, it remains curiously true that three years after Amiens lay in ruins, it was *still* not too late for Napoleon to avoid a European war. As would often be true, everything depended on what he would do. The Emperor was as surrounded by doves as the First Consul had been. Many of his counselors were being bribed to speak against war by the British ambassador. It was money wasted. Napoleon did not wish to dress foreign enemies against himself; he just could not act in a way to avoid it. Perhaps even a first-class operator might not have kept Russia from drifting into partnership with England. The two countries shared a mutual greed and cynicism—they bartered whole lands and peoples as they talked alliance; their negotiations ranked with the "finest" traditions of eighteenth-century diplomacy. In the end, Alexander I's piqued vanity had to be further piqued, which happened courtesy of the French emperor when he annexed Genoa (Liguria) to France in mid-1805. Finally, true outrage (and fear) led the tsar to push the restoration of European equilibrium to the top of his real agenda.

Not that the British held any monopoly of virtue in this period of "phony war." Albion's standing took a body blow when the French revealed how extensive was the involvement of Britain's diplomatic corps in spying, assassination plots, and general skullduggery even in neutral capitals. And, as always, what was universally perceived as British high-handedness on the seas, its arrogance vis-à-vis neutrals[49] made for greater appreciation of the French position in the conflict. German-speaking peoples also resented British cynicism in seeking to induce others to fight her battles for her. Napoleon would have had little trouble in prying Austria loose from her disdainful banker ally if only he had tried to do so, as Talleyrand constantly pressed him to do. Francis II asked for so little—*just a role* in Italy and Germany, nothing like hegemony, which the French could keep. Even lavished with Anglo-Russian blandishments, Austria would not have dared fight Napoleon again if she had not felt her entire status as a great power was at stake. The annexation of Genoa to the French Empire (June 1805) was the last straw.

Failing all else, Bonaparte might at the very least have kept Prussia's good will. Notwithstanding Frederick William III's innate fellow feeling and ideological compatibility with Francis II and Alexander I, his fear of Napoleon I would have prevailed. The French government had been able to count on Prussian benevolent neutrality since the Treaty of Basle in 1795. But the combination of Napoleon's disdain for a king he did not respect (the Hohenzollern did give vacillation and indecision a new status) and French adamant refusal to give any guarantee for French withdrawal from Holland or Switzerland (Napoleon wouldn't even discuss Naples) drove Prussia, in the coming crunch, into the shadows of the Coalition.

Did Napoleon feel obliged to adhere to his regimen of expansion and war because he was an outsider, a usurper? Arno Mayer writes: "There is no separating the constructive side of Napoleon's internal reign . . . from his external design and strategy." And he is echoed by Jacques-Olivier Boudon, "The Empire was born of war and survived by war."[50] The problem with both of these judgments is that they have the ring of a rationale, as if something systemic or logical outside the First Consul and then the Emperor were driving him to aggression. Surely, one could argue, *surely* he had enough glory in 1805 to last him a lifetime—or for five or ten years. He was not his weak nephew (Napoleon III) in 1870, and his adversaries were fielding no Bismarck or von Moltke. Late Consular or imperial France was not the Directory, where the government needed to weld together a divided population, and silence a dangerous internal (revolutionary or reactionary) opposition with expansion—with war as distraction, as a source of enforced national unity. In 1803–1805 something at once simpler and more personal was at stake.

What made Napoleon different was his personal Caesar-like restlessness and demonic struggle. He, *of course,* did not share Henry Addington's selflessness (the prime minister was prepared to relinquish the leadership of the government if doing so would suffice to bring back Pitt). Napoleon utterly condemned an attitude like that, and from his perspective he was right to do so, for he was the French Pitt—and more. He outdid the *sacré diables* of earlier in the century. Compared to their parents and grandparents, the present generation of European monarchs were Milquetoasts. Yet even Paul I and Catherine II (the Great) of Russia, Frederick II (the Great) of Prussia, and Joseph II and Leopold II of Austria were not as willful or remorseless in the pursuit of *raison d'Etat* as the Emperor of the French. True, Louis XIV (the Great), of the seventeenth century, was these things, but he ended up a loser by Napoleonic standards. What Napoleon dared, demanded, and did simply put him *hors du jeu* in the rule-bound eighteenth-century diplomatic game among royal thieves.

"Was he not a completely eccentric person, always alone on one side, with the world on the other? This view of the world is what makes his politics."[51] Trust Mme de Rémusat to get it right. The result was that "the world" found it impossible to do business with the man, peace on Bonaparte's terms ended up being more dangerous and humiliating than war. In Albert Sorel's unforgettable words, Napoleon "set out for the Empire as Columbus set out for the New World, imagining that he was encircling the old. Most people were fearing, expecting or blindly seeking the predicted and inevitable Great Man. But [Napoleon] knows him, he is him."[52]

But by Napoleon's own terms—"They succeed who are truly able to know how to master their passions"[53]—he failed. The test of self-mastery that he so often boasted of winning, and was always commending to others, he lost after Amiens—and not by a little. He let his soldier's nature will out over the political man that he also carried within. It had been five years since he sat in the saddle sending regiments into battle; perhaps he missed it. He certainly did not fear it, as virtually every other statesman did.

The wars of the First and even the Second Coalition had erupted out of the clash between the French Revolution and Europe. Though decisive in winning both contests for France, Bonaparte played no role in the origin of the first, and only some role in the second. The Italian campaign of 1797 was fundamentally the Directory's idea and decision, while even Egypt had many fathers besides the general who led the expeditionary force. But this war, the war that opened in 1803 and finally heard the cannons roar in 1805, was Napoleon Bonaparte's war.[54]

THE GREAT CAMPAIGN (1805)

When the French people placed the crown on my head, I confided to you the task of keeping it there in the lofty splendor which is the only value it holds in my eyes.
—Napoleon to the Grande Armée after Austerlitz

History has rendered an interesting question hypothetical, hence nagging: What would have happened if Napoleon and his army had made it across the English Channel ("a mere ditch, to be crossed the moment anyone has the courage to try")? One answer: he might have been sealed off on the British Isles the moment the Royal Navy reassembled in the Channel and scattered or sank Villeneuve's fleet. Not to mention the fact that the Austro-Russian forces would have eventually invaded from the east, and Bernadotte's corps, left behind to fend them off, could not have fought a long-term holding action against far superior numbers. True, London would likely have fallen quickly—military thinking at the time figured it would—but the British, like the Russians in 1812, had no intention of surrendering if the tricolor flew over London bridge. Plans had long been made to move the government to Worcester, or beyond. Meanwhile, how could the French have reinforced their leader and his army, stranded, as they were, in a land *infinitely* more hostile, developed, and populated than Mameluke Egypt? Despite endless French naval maneuvering, the Channel stayed English and Napoleon's prayer stayed unanswered, perhaps the best kind of prayer.[55]

Less speculative is the assertion that Napoleon's hope for a descent on the English coast set back his attack on Austria by several months, allowing the Habsburg and the Romanov to mobilize. It was now late August 1805. With bitter reluctance, with fury at what he took for Admiral Villeneuve's incompetence (the admiral's timorousness at facing superior English seamanship), Napoleon set out to take his second choice to "fight England in Germany," as he put it.[56]

Stopping at the Bank of France to lighten it of the last two million francs in the imperial Treasury, Napoleon embarked on a blitzkrieg against the gathering Austro-Russian forces. It was 1800 revisited: enemy armies massing on the Danube, the French in full domestic disarray, only a great victory can set things right. The Emperor's method of war did not simply thrive on, it required, speed: the troops, as always, were unsupplied, ill equipped—not that it mattered, for transport could not have kept pace with the army. Victory was the usual "question of life or death."

The instrument of victory had undergone a change in name, size, and structure, though in essential ways it was still the Army of Italy. The Army of England now became the Grande Armée, betokening not a force named to a specific theatre of operation but the army of the Empire. Its size—210,000 men—was vastly larger than anything any French general had ever commanded. And "commanded" was the word; what singularized the Grande Armée compared to the forces it faced in this (or the next) campaign was its centralization of command. Though subdivided into seven self-sustaining corps—each a mini-army of all three arms (cavalry, artillery, and infantry), headed by its own field commander—the whole, including even Marshal Masséna's corps dispatched to northern Italy, was controlled by the one mind that composed its strategy.

The army was hardened and plebeian in its makeup; virtually all its officers and half its enlisted men were veterans who had served in the wars of the Revolution or the Marengo campaign.[57] Half the officers (and all the "noncoms") had once shouldered a musket, and so were not socially removed from the men serving under them. The practice of the paid replacement was permitted—a breach in revolutionary equality, but further insurance that the army was an institution of the populace, the poor. Recruits got their training by being poured into the ranks, taken under the wing of older soldiers, and picking up the rest of what they needed to know in battle itself. In sum, they were soldiers of 1789 or their spiritual (or literal) sons, and they saw themselves marching with "the Emperor" against "the kings," including, very much, the Bourbon king (Louis XVIII) who threatened the Revolution. They could expect promotions and rewards if they proved themselves daring and courageous.[58]

The Grande Armée was nothing of a parade-ground show force; these were fighting men whose mission in life was to go all out. As warriors, they retained—and Napoleon somewhat indulged—an independent, often insubordinate spirit, and much of the outlook of the revolutionary tradition. They could expect lavish praise or sharp criticism from their emperor, and some of them got away with saying "tu" to him. Above all, they got Napoleon's complete and enduring attention, as few others did. "I get more enjoyment out of reading these [muster rolls] than a young girl gets out of reading a novel," he told Murat. In battle, the Napoleonic infantry were obedient, brave, and zealous; the brunt of their effect usually came in bayonet charges, to the cry of "Vive l'Empereur!" When these men were deployed with the tactical suppleness of the famous "mixed" order of lines and columns, and coordinated with the cavalry and artillery, as only Napoleon could coordinate them, they mounted continuous attack that confused, exhausted, demoralized, and finally crushed the troops whom they met.

Montesquieu observed that "virtue," meaning "patriotism," was the principle of democracy, while "honor" was the principle of monarchy (and "fear," that of despotism). A debate exists on whether the Grande Armée was motivated more by old-fashioned honor than by the new-fangled revolutionary virtue. A historian has the First Consul constructing "his temple to Honor on the ruins of the temple to Virtue."[59] He has a point: the Emperor famously plied his men with the baubles of honor; he never refrained from arousing their craving for glory—above all, of wearing the Legion of Honor. Robespierre spurned honor as a "childish enthusiasm," but the soldiers of the Empire—especially the induplicable Imperial Guard—*were* the Emperor's children in their own eyes and in his: grumpy, spoiled, brave, and fanatically devoted to their "avenger, protector, and father" who was Napoleon. It is not clear that Napoleonic honor was inferior to virtue as a martial trait, nor that it did not contain large measures of patriotism—patriotism, as we saw, being a word with a notoriously vague referent. The soldiers of 1805 were mostly men for whom the virtue of revolutionary patriotism was anything but an empty memory.[60]

The harder role to play in Napoleonic armies fell to officers who were killed at a fearful rate. The higher they rose in rank, the more prone they were to the states of high anxiety and rivalry that the Emperor liked to keep them in. He rewarded his officers lushly, but in return accepted no excuses, played them (especially the marshals) off against one another shamelessly, or railed at them in towering rages or blistering dressings-down that were never forgotten—except by Napoleon himself, who held no grudges. Most frustrating, perhaps, for the truly gifted among his subordinates: Napoleon never took the time to provide them with a deep intellectual formation in his notions of warfare and grand strategy.

ULM

The art of war is a simple art. There is nothing vague in it, everything is common sense; ideology does not enter in.

—Napoleon Bonaparte

The Allies mounted multiple offensives—40,000 in Hanover, 40,000 in Naples, 140,000 in northern Italy (where they expected Napoleon to show up, as in 1800), and their major effort: 140,000 on the Danube.[61] Napoleon could not fail to dispatch an army corps to northern Italy and Naples, but these forces were too small to do more than maneuver gingerly against superior opponents and play for time, while the Emperor dealt the swift and mortal blow in central Europe against the Allied army. It is customary to write the Austro-Russian army, but in fact, as of late September, when Napoleon crossed the Rhine, the Russian forces were still far to the east of their Austrian allies, lumbering toward them with the speed and agility of a hippopotamus.

The new face in military Vienna, the only important Habsburg commander not to have been beaten by the French, was General Karl von Mack. A talented quartermaster who had effectively and secretly mobilized the men and materiel Austria needed for the war she knew was coming, Mack also felt he knew theory and strategy. He disdained his senior colleagues, most of whom had lost to Napoleon—and he was not afraid to take the initiative. Mack elected the Napoleonic strategy of taking the fight to the enemy. He moved his army of 72,000 dramatically westward until it reached the eastern débouchés of the Black Forest, though doing so required the violation of the neutral electorate of Bavaria. Napoleon, for his part, as late as the opening of the campaign, was busy in his personal diplomacy trying to win over the southern German states to the French side. Mack dug in, in the town of Ulm, prepared to meet and destroy the French as they arrived. Blind optimism never had a more fervent exemplar than this Austrian general, as he stared over Ulm's parapets at the main issues from the forest primeval.

Meanwhile the Grande Armée's "seven torrents"—all within a day's march of one another—swept down from France in record time. Some armies march on their stomachs; this one marched on its legs. "The Emperor has discovered a new way of making war: he makes use of our legs instead of our arms," remarked a foot soldier.[62] In late September the French crossed the Rhine into southern Germany far north of Ulm.

Strategic surprise is difficult to deliver in practice as opposed to theory; tactical surprise on a battlefield is by far the more common. Napoleon had had no grand plan to entrap Mack in Ulm; he simply assumed the Austrian would attack his own extended lines or move south to a more defensible position, where he could be reinforced by the Archduke John. Only when this did not transpire did the Emperor conceive the idea that it might be possible to envelop Mack from the Austrians' rear (i.e., from the east)—much as the First Consul had done to General Melas when he swept across the Alps in 1800. "The Austrians are on the edge of the Black Forest," he wrote to Joseph on September 27. "Please God let them stay there. My only fear is that we'll scare them too much [and they'll flee]."

The noose tightened around Ulm until, on October 21, Mack the hapless surrendered with 27,000 men, not firing a shot, and having made a bit of a fool of himself by proclaiming the day before that he would fight to the last man. His officers and men felt differently. In three weeks of campaigning, with no major engagements, the Austrians had lost an astounding 64,000 men. From a cost-effective point of view, Ulm thus rates as one of the great victories of warfare, and certainly another splendid instance of Napoleonic envelopment (*manoeuvre sur les derrières*). Naturally, its announcement in Paris redressed the public mood and the financial markets.

The effect of Ulm on the Austrians was traumatic. (Mack was courtmartialed and sentenced to twenty years in prison, but paroled by his sovereign.) Talleyrand, ever ready to remove the fight from the battlefield to the negotiating table, sounded them out for a truce, and Francis II might have been willing, but Napoleon was not. Napoleon, in point of fact, might have accepted an Austrian peace initiative if Francis had offered to do a *volte-face* and join the French *against* the Allies, thus permitting the French emperor to turn back to his cherished invasion of England. Francis would not entertain such a notion. Failing it, Napoleon yearned to destroy the Allies; he yearned, as Talleyrand confided to his memoirs, "to date his dispatches from the Schoenbrunn."[63]

Not that Napoleon was averse to diplomacy while he made war—on the contrary. He was quite successful in his efforts during the Ulm campaign to charm the wife of the elector of Hanover (the daughter of George III!) by showing off his knowledge of literature and praising British institutions. The woman, hitherto a leading animator of the anti-French party in northern Germany, now began writing her outraged mother to sing the Emperor's praises. More to the point, Napoleon had the same effect on her husband, the Elector Frederick, who became convinced that salvation for his principality lay in union with France. Cozying up to Hanover, however, offended Prussia, which dreamed of Hanover for herself. Frederick William III was momentarily in the catbird seat, courted madly—indeed nearly coerced—by both sides. He was inclined to the Allied cause but captivated by Napoleon's offer of Hanover; and above all, afraid of fighting the French.

Things suddenly changed when French armies violated the Prussian frontier at Ansbach at the same time as Russian armies arrived at Prussia's eastern frontier, expecting to cross. The complicated situation that arose deserves our attention for what it reveals about the role of monarchical sympathies and ideology in the war. The French penetration was in fact not a true violation, as for example Austria's recent march into Bavaria had been, for the Treaty of Basle, still in force between France and Prussia, had excluded Ansbach in the line of demarcation, meaning its territory could be transgressed with impunity. But Frederick William and his chief minister, Hardenberg, one of the French haters in the Berlin court, chose to take offense at the French violation, and use it as the pretext to do what they had wanted to do all along, that is, join the "legitimate" sovereigns against the "Corsican usurper."[64] Alexander I, though in full campaign, now paid a visit to Frederick William, rendezvousing with him and Queen Louise at Potsdam, where the sovereigns knelt in mystical homage before the tomb of Frederick the Great. They swore fealty to each other and enmity to "le monstre Napoléon." Napoleon could not compete with this. The ensuing secret Convention of Potsdam (November 3) obligated Frederick William to send an army of 180,000 to the Allied relief after December 15.

The convention stiffened Francis II's spine for further battle, as did the news of a distant engagement that had taken place some eight hundred miles to the west, off Cape Trafalgar, near Cadiz, Spain, on the very day Mack surrendered. Here, a Franco-Spanish armada was annihilated by a smaller fleet commanded by Admiral Horatio Nelson: it was an altogether decisive engagement, perhaps the greatest sea battle of the nineteenth century. Napoleon's reaction to the news was momentary agitation followed by a muttered, "I can't be everywhere at once." The English commander, rather

All noble gravitas and reproach.

Bonaparte on the Bridge at Arcole, Antoine-Jean Gros (1771–1835),
© Réunion des Musées Nationaux / Art Resource, NY

The truth: how it happened . . .
Napoleon Crossing the Alps, Paul Delaroche
(1797–1856), © Réunion des Musées
Nationaux / Art Resource, NY

. . . the "truth": what it meant.
Napoleon Crossing the Alps
at Mont Saint Bernard,
Jacques-Louis David
(1748–1825), © Réunion
des Musées Nationaux /
Art Resource, NY

A king who does not *need* to be seen
as a Roman emperor . . .

Louis XIV, Hyacinthe Rigaud (1659–1743),
© Réunion des Musées Nationaux /
Art Resource, NY

. . . versus a French emperor
who is the scourge of kings.

Napoleon in Coronation Robe,
François Gérard (1770–1837),
© Réunion des Musées Nationaux /
Art Resource, NY

"If Leipzig and Waterloo
had left but a skim gain of
a thousand dollars to the
family, she would have
counted it."—William Bolitho,
Twelve Against the Gods (1929)
Madame Mère, François Gérard
© Erich Lessing / Art Resource, NY

Ever right, never victorious,
always there.
Charles-Maurice de Talleyrand,
Ary Scheffer (1795–1858),
© Erich Lessing / Art Resource, NY

The practitioner (and politician)
of virtue.
Pope Pius VII, Jacques-Louis David
© Réunion des Musées Nationaux /
Art Resource, NY

The shifting sands of Alexander's soft,
sentimental, and solipsistic personality
stymied Napoleon's attempt
at seduction.
Czar Alexander I, François Gérard
© Erich Lessing / Art Resource, NY

Truth as propaganda?

Napoleon Visiting the Field of Eylau, Antoine-Jean Gros
© Erich Lessing / Art Resource, NY

Abdication, dejection, abjection.
Napoleon After His Abdication,
Paul Delaroche © Giraudon /
Art Resource, NY

C'est la casquette a papa

Cartoon during the Hundred Days: stealing Papa's crown.
Cliché Bibliothèque nationale de France, Paris

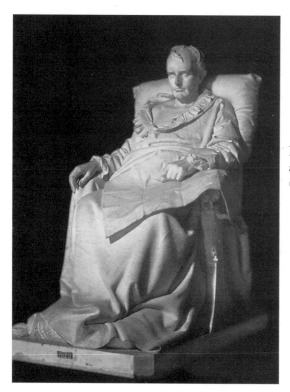

Napoleon on St. Helena:
all gravitas and (self-) reproach.
© Alinari–Scala / Art Resource, NY

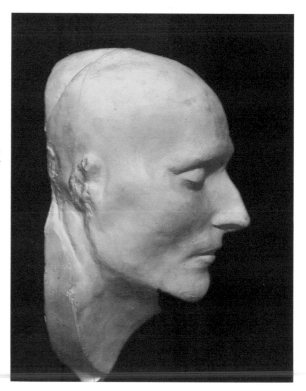

The death mask.
© Giraudon / Art Resource, NY

than attack the superior Allied fleet in the customary line of battle—full front
to full front—transected the Franco-Spanish ships, like crossing a *T,* and
picked off the enemy warships one at a time, due to superior, concentrated
English gunnery. It is hard, in fact, to imagine Napoleon would not have seen
what was coming and at least tried to counter it. Thus, Napoleon was in the
same position he had been in after the naval defeat of Aboukir Bay in Egypt;
and even if he now made himself master of Europe, he was still, in a real
sense, a prisoner there. He would continue a French naval program of shipbuilding, but his mind now turned to strategies of commercial war against the
world's largest commercial power.

For the immediate present, however, the Emperor of the French had more
pressing concerns than geopolitics: the Austrian and Russian armies loomed
ahead of him, on the Danube, while to the north, the Prussian hordes might
descend in the Grande Armée's rear. Frankly, this latter possibility does not
appear to have much exercised Napoleon, for he knew his man in the
Prussian king. Had Frederick William had anything in common with his
"great" predecessor, he would have descended on the French army, in conjunction with the Allies, and made a quick end of it. Instead, the ink was
scarcely dry on the convention before Frederick William became fretful of
what it might entail, and, as he counted the days until December 15, he kept
his communications lines to Napoleon open. The French emperor went right
on waving Hanover in the Prussians' face, while the great French propaganda
and news machine publicized the Ulm victory the length and breadth of
Europe, sowing consternation and hesitation in the Allied and neutral
home fronts, and magnifying the glory and terror of the Grande Armée and
its commander.

AUSTERLITZ

*No battle is decided in a single moment, and to the extent that it can be repre-
sented as such at all, it is only after the event, in a retrospective, teleological construction: the victory mostly gains substance after it has been decided, which is a
paradox.*

—Karl von Clausewitz, *On War*

In war, the French emperor paid more attention to the opposition than he
did in domestic politics, yet in both operations, military and political, we see
the same human identity and character at work: the swiftness of his grasp of

a situation, of the other actors and their potential, the desire to confound and bedazzle them, the certainty that he knew better what was going on, on a confused, complex, and changing field. And if he did not, then it was important after the fact to make it seem as though he had.

Following Mack's capitulation at Ulm, Napoleon ordered his marshals to proceed east at full speed in order to intercept a Russian army that had been racing west, to the succor of poor Mack. The idea was to strike them a death blow before they had sized up the situation. But in the Russian general, Mikhail Illarionovich Kutuzov, the Emperor Napoleon faced a far cannier opponent than in the pompous, purblind Mack. Older-looking than his sixty years, with a marked *faiblesse* for young women and vodka, Kutuzov well understood his foe's desire always to be lunging for the jugular. The necessity in fighting Napoleon, Kutuzov saw, was to slow him down, string out his armies and patience, while keeping one's own troops battleworthy, a constant menace. So Kutuzov retreated, though it meant losing Vienna to the French; he joined up with Austrian and Russian forces near Olmütz, to the northeast.

Vienna was a glittering but empty prize, which, as Talleyrand foresaw, the Corsican *nobliau* in Napoleon could not resist grabbing, though militarily it was of no importance. And indeed, he installed himself in the Schoenbrunn and began issuing proclamations with that provenance. Strategically, however, the French situation was becoming tenuous. In any full-front advance, such as they had been pursuing for eight exhausting weeks, there comes a culminating point whereat the attacker stands to lose the superiority of his drive. To push beyond this point without good chance of an immediate favorable decision in battle is fraught with danger. Clausewitz sums it up with his inimitable pith: "Every attack which does not lead to peace must necessarily end up as a defense."[65] By mid-November, the combined Russo-Austrian forces outnumbered the French considerably, and there was the continuing risk they would be further reinforced from the south by Archdukes John and Charles. And then there was always the Prussian threat, as we have noted. Napoleon needed quick big action, but if the Allies heeded Kutuzov, there would be none—only more skirmishes and maneuvers, while their reinforcements continued to arrive.[66]

Fortunately for the French, Alexander I heeded not Kutuzov, but rather the counsel of a passel of shrill and mindless young popinjays who functioned as his kitchen cabinet. Vacuous and arrogant aristocrats like Prince Dolgorouki noisily assured their master that the French emperor was exposed and could be overpowered. To clinch their argument, they pointed out that even as they spoke, the enemy was abandoning his excellent position along the Pratzen Heights, west of the town of Brünn. Now was the time to attack; Napoleon was on the run; his right flank, in particular, was exposed and getting weaker, as more units there were being withdrawn. "Moreover," added Dolgorouki, "if Your Majesty retreats now, Bonaparte will take us for cowards." "Cowards!" cried the tsar, "better we die!"

Alexander's advisors turned out to be 100 percent right, then 200 percent wrong. The foregoing account is invariably prefaced with the statement that Napoleon intended this great feint, praying that the Allies would fall on his exposed right (southern) flank. The truth is, none of it was foreseen in anything like the lockstep-unfolding of these accounts, all of which, including especially those of the French generals, took their cues from Napoleon's self-aggrandizing rendition in his army bulletins. In point of fact, the battle of Austerlitz[67] is traditionally recounted as the ineluctable movement of a giant turnstile centered on the Pratzen Heights. The Allies began the process, pushing with their left flank against the weakened French right. Here, Napoleon had brought up Davout, his finest corps commander, who arrived in the nick of time, having led his men on an eighty-mile forced march from Vienna. Davout withdrew before the Austro-Russian onslaught, sucking them further in, as they swung slowly around behind the French center. As this process continued, the French left began its push on the northern wing of the turnstile, pressing back the Austro-Russian right and center, which had not bargained on so great a force to contend with, for Napoleon had quietly reinforced his left with Bernadotte's corps, brought up under a heavy cavalry screen, to make its presence invisible to the enemy. Presently, the French were pressing the Allied rear, and the Allies, the French rear—only the Allies were retreating, the French attacking. At the decisive moment, Napoleon hit the Austro-Russian center with his reserve, splitting their army in twain, enabling him to deal with each in detail.

Execution meant everything, for as always, between the cup and the mouth the shadow fell in a thousand unexpected ways. Early on, the Allies spotted a feint, and Kutuzov tried desperately to recall two of his attacking units back to the Pratzen Heights, though they returned too late to be effective. Davout almost collapsed under the vastly superior attack he received and contained (far beyond anything Napoleon foresaw or would have gambled on, if he had). He did not, but it was a near thing. The Allied right might easily have held. Indeed it did, but it wasn't decisive because the Allies were in disarray elsewhere. Finally, the all-important Allied center dug in, despite the concerted French attack. Marshal Soult took the Pratzen early, then lost it to a determined counterattack by the Russian guards. The French gained it back with a charge of the cavalry of the Imperial Guard, under Marshal Bessières. They might have lost it again if Thiébault's brigade had not made a desperate bayonet charge when by all rights they should have retired. Chandler calls this "the single most critical decision of the battle."[68] Even so, the struggle on the Pratzen still had desperate moments; at one point, Napoleon and his staff got caught in the melee of two fleeing French regiments. The French held the heights, however, and by mid-afternoon, Napoleon sent the Imperial Guard, kept in reserve, to smash through the Allied center, splitting their army. From then on, it was a complete rout.[69]

The battle of the Three Emperors, as it is also called, would remain Napoleon's finest triumph, but thanks to perfect intuition, timing, and execution, not a cunning advance plan. Only in the telling, notably by Napoleon (and everyone has followed his version, which accents his foresight), has Austerlitz become a staple of "grand strategy" in the textbooks in military history. "Soldiers, I am content with you," he wrote in opening his proclamation to the army. They got more than kind words; among other rewards, the sons of men killed at Austerlitz were "adopted" by Napoleon. To Josephine, he admitted in a letter, "I am a little weary." It was not, however, the happiest moment of his life; that had been the night before. Visiting the men, he had tripped over a log and fallen down. His aides helped him to his feet, and then the soldiers twisted handfuls of straw into torches and carried them before him as he walked through the camp. The cries of "Vive l'Empereur!" were deafening, carrying to the heights of Pratzen and the Russian camp, where the generals rubbed their hands together and chortled over tomorrow's battle that would see them destroy the French.

Among the prisoners was a Russian artillery officer who spoke good French. He begged his captors to shoot him, preferring death to this shame. The French tried to shush him, saying, "The Emperor will hear you!" Napoleon indeed saw the man and asked him what was wrong. "Sire," he said, "I am not worthy to live, for I have lost my battery." The Emperor replied, "Calm yourself, young man. It is no dishonor to be defeated by *my* army."[70]

Two days later, the Holy Roman Emperor came to the "little corporal's" camp to entreat him for peace. Francis II had no fight left in him; Alexander might have kept on fighting, but even if he had, and even if Frederick William agreed to march two weeks early, it would not have mattered: the Austrians' morale was utterly shattered. The tsar reluctantly retired into Russia, licking his wounds, leaving his allies to come to terms with the French.

FROM *GRANDE NATION* TO *GRAND EMPIRE*

More than ever now, the Emperor . . . departed the luminous and clear realm of
great men who are practical, intelligible, and predictable, to enter instead into
that undefined region, dazzling yet cloudy, where live the heroes made for fable,
not history, who are the object of admiration and preference by stupid people who
put their faith in poetry.

               —Charles de Rémusat[71]

Napoleon was on a roll, so he stayed in role. This had been his war, now it was his peace. "Your Majesty can break the Austrian monarchy or he can raise it up again," Talleyrand adjured him, "but if you break it, it will not be within even Your Majesty's power to put it back together again."[72] Though sore-tempted, "His Majesty" did not dissolve the Habsburg empire. The Treaty of Pressburg fell just short of Carthaginian. Francis II lost four million subjects, a sixth of his empire, in territories torn from him in Italy, central Europe, and eastern Europe. He had to pay a large indemnity to France that broke his government's fiscal back. And perhaps worst of all in an age enamored of titles and precedence, Francis finally lost the greatest crown of them all, the Holy Roman Empire. The thousand-year Reich was at an end.[73] Francis I (as he now was) and his chancellor, Louis Cobenzl, bowed their heads and swallowed the medicine—a supine attitude that drove Friedrich Gentz wild with rage at what he took for appeasement.

Finally, Napoleon got something out of Austria he had long wanted: formal recognition. In the dispatches that Habsburg diplomats and ministers wrote after Austerlitz and Pressburg, "Bonaparte" now became "Napoleon."[74]

The months following Pressburg saw a continuation of Napoleon's phenomenal activity that amazed and exhausted his associates and followers. "What a pity the man wasn't lazy," Talleyrand sighed.[75] The Emperor of the French profited from the victorious end of the campaign to impose considerably more changes on Europe than the mere Treaty of Pressburg. The act of greatest historical import for the future development of a German nation-state was his completion of the remolding of Germany.[76] He created the Confederation of the Rhine (Rheinbund) out of a dozen southern and western German client states of France, including Bavaria and Württemberg, both promoted to kingdoms for their pains in joining the French in the recent campaign.

Another reward for service rendered: Napoleon carved out the Grand

Duchy of Berg for his brother-in-law Joachim Murat. Prussia, in reprisal for her hesitant and deceitful pitch into the wrong camp, had to hand over Cleves and Neuchâtel to France, and Ansbach to Bavaria, and if she was allowed to keep Hanover for the time being, the "gift" came swathed in doubts, for it was known that Napoleon was leaning toward giving the electorate back to England as part of an eventual peace package. Prussia, finally, was permitted to "organize" (dominate) a few remaining states in northern Germany. This recasting of central Europe was vociferously supported by "enlightened" reformists all over Germany, many of whom, truth to tell, urged Napoleon to assume Charlemagne's title, Emperor of the West.[77] Their attitude would change, as they discovered that Napoleonic clientage meant tutelage, but for now the French presence here, as in Switzerland, was still generally associated with progress, in a way that it no longer was seen so widely in the Low Countries and Italy.

Finally, the French emperor turned to the fate of the kingdom of Naples, whose territory he occupied. The army bulletin of December 27, 1805, included the following display of Napoleonic confidence shared with his men: "Shall we pardon [Ferdinand IV and Marie-Caroline] yet a fourth time? Will we trust a court that has no good faith, no honor, no common sense? No! No! The Bourbon dynasty of Naples has ceased to reign. Its existence is incompatible with the tranquility of Europe and the honor of my crown." Napoleon has been accused of seeking "vindictive triumphs," of needing to "defeat and humiliate his opponent,"[78] but in the case of this queen of the *double jeu* and the king of the double-cross, may we not permit him a little glee? The Bourbon dismissal was but an example of rough justice—promised, and delivered. Marie-Caroline at least displayed the courage of candor: "What I'll never be able to console myself for," she told a former minister of hers, "is knowing that I myself have brought misfortune to my family. In a word, I am so very unhappy."[79]

Following Trafalgar and Austerlitz, Great Britain fell back in reluctant relief on her island and her empire, safe from invasion and from boredom, for there was much beyond the continent of Europe to occupy her commerce and her politics. "Roll up that map. It won't be wanted for ten years," William Pitt said. Certainly not wanted by him; he, the "stately column that held up the swaying fortunes of our race"[80] died January 23, 1806. He had long been in failing health, but the coup de grace was the news that Prussia would finally not enter the fray on the Allied side; Hanover was definitively lost for George III. Pitt succumbed murmuring, "My country, oh, my country."[81]

His successors put out peace feelers. The terms England offered were excellent, including recognition of all current French possessions, and the willingness (in a secret article) to extrude the Bourbons from their convenient exiles in Britain. But the French emperor took the British *démarche* in seeking to negotiate as a sign of weakness; he had his own designs, which he knew England would not in the long run tolerate, so any peace for now would be, at best, another Amiens. "Peace is a word devoid of meaning," Napoleon had written to Joseph after Austerlitz. "It is *glorious peace* that we need." The question the older brother refrained from asking was, "what is 'glorious peace' if it brings no peace?"

A dozen other top associates of the French emperor received duchies, or fiefs, carved out of the conquered and annexed regions of Italy. It was the first step toward the creation of a new landed nobility, though not one that enjoyed the formal juridical status of the Second Estate under the old regime. On the other hand, the Statute on the Imperial Family, by which Napoleon took control of the personal and public lives, virtually of the persons, of his own family did faithfully echo ancient royal custom. His notion that the civil status of the Bonaparte princes could not be the same as that of other French people was an assault on the central arch of the revolutionary covenant: civil equality.[82]

The nominations of Joseph and Louis to the thrones of Naples and Holland, respectively, were important matters of the new imperial policy. Napoleon had tried governing the marches of his empire through "vicars" (e.g., Schimmelpenninck in Holland), but he could not control these men completely; they had a disconcerting tendency to care more about their countries than about French policy, and they were not able to preside as well as the Emperor wished over events in their own republics. Each Dutch election, for example, brought turmoil between pro- and anti-French forces. Napoleon's solution was to establish monarchies tributary to Paris. The moment of the brothers was thus at hand. "I can no longer have relatives in obscurity," the Emperor said. "Those who will not rise with me, shall no longer be of my family. I am making a family of kings attached to my federative system." Assured of keeping his succession privileges in France, Joseph was delighted to become Joseph-Napoleon I, while Louis, for his part, had not been consulted. Nor was the French Senate consulted. The act (March 30, 1806) was promulgated on the Emperor's own authority.

Thus, the *Grand Empire* was born. In the wording of the royal appointment to southern Italy is this: the Emperor declared Naples to be a "part of the *Grand Empire*"—as was Holland. Here was a novel conception. Belgium, the Italian annexations, the Valais region of Switzerland, and the Dalmatian gains from the Treaty of Pressburg had all simply been integral parts of a hypertrophic France—of the *Grande Nation,* to use the old phrase of 1798–1800. But

Berg, Naples, and Holland were federated kingdoms, no longer French, yet imperial. There is a nuance between the concepts: "nation," however flexible in Napoleonic hands, referred in the revolutionary sense to "the people" whereas *Grand Empire* referred—it could *only* refer—to "the State." The wheel has turned 180 degrees; Napoleon has, as it were, passed through the nation idea to recover what he has always wanted since his first youthful writings about politics: *l'Etat.*

Time itself turned back as, with nary a bump in public awareness, what would have been 11 Nivose, Year XIII opened instead as January 1, 1806.[83] France's official newspaper of record of parliamentary debates, *Le Journal des Débats* became *Le Journal de l'Empire*; and finally the official rubric bedizening each of the *Journal*'s pages, La République Française, became L'Empire Français.

And so it begins—the odyssey of the Emperor and his Empire, properly so-called. "This comedy of a republic and of equality that we had to play . . . , which annoyed [Napoleon] and fooled nobody save those who wished to be fooled" was over.[84] Some, like Lentz, see the "headlong pitch into a personal and political obsession"[85] occurring well after the Great Consulate, with the battle of Austerlitz. Others, like Paul Schroeder, have seen it present all along, not coming: "All efforts to find some point in Napoleon's career at which he turned wrong or went too far are misguided. His whole character and career were fundamentally wrong; he always went too far."[86] Most lives appear to be of a piece when you search them out—this one perhaps more than most, if only because it has been so much more pondered than most.

Yet it is noteworthy that the proliferation of testimony against the Empire was written after the bright sun of Austerlitz had become the night of 1812–15.[87] At the moment where we are, 1805, Napoleon and his ideas tended, rather, to dazzle most—not all, but most—to sweep Frenchmen and foreigners alike up into an adventure that they considered mythic, sometimes against their better judgment. Contemporaries, whatever their studied thoughts of the French Revolution and Napoleonic imperial policy, were often, like Charles de Rémusat, awed by Napoleon himself, aware that he was a phenomenon such as the world had not seen since Charlemagne or Caesar.

So, we make a mistake to see the Empire, at this point, as largely hated and insupportable. French policy was tough-minded and harshly executed, but the French did not arrive in conquered lands the way Mussolini's army would later march into Ethiopia or Hitler's into Poland. Rather, it arrived trailing the prestige and bringing some of the reforms of the "great" French Revolution—to the profound satisfaction of men of the stature of Hegel, Goethe, Byron, and the young Stendhal. At its worst, the creation of the French *Grand*

Empire was not seen as more terrible or unusual than what the foes of the French would do, or had done, in their place (e.g., the three partitions of Poland by Russia, Austria, and Prussia, or Russo-British discussions to carve up the Ottoman Empire).[88]

True, the Empire represented a sharp recasting of the Revolution, but few saw imperial consolidation as a euphemism for betrayal; on the contrary, most saw it as the salvation of 1789.

It was the Emperor's personality and force of will and, above all, the miraculous string of military successes—his real glory—that were seen as sufficiently extraordinary as to permit titles like "Emperor of the West" to be seriously proposed for him. "The Emperor forged himself a scepter of iron, but the soul of his system was not repression," write Louis de Villefosse and Janine Bouissounouse in their otherwise black portrait of Napoleonic rule. "Napoleon, in the full *éclat* of his triumphs, incarnated more than force. . . . He imposed himself also by his genius . . . , by his superhuman and phenomenal aptitudes."[89] For the time being, then, most people paid the price of Napoleon's "freedom" with more willingness than they later cared to admit.

This was doubly true of the people at the center, the French. "How was it that he could count on the chains that he forged at the expense of the noblest sentiments of the soul?" Mme de Rémusat asked herself. She admitted she did not know the answer; she but knew, "Alas, I can only judge by myself that he managed to do so!"[90] For every Frenchman with the independence of a Lafayette, there were a score whose behavior proved Chateaubriand's point: "Everyday experience proves that the French turn instinctively toward power. . . ."[91]

HOME

When Napoleon had left for the Danube in September 1805, he had received a rather cool send-off from a small crowd in front of the Tuileries. This annoyed him, but it cannot have surprised him, for France was in economic slowdown after two poor harvests and a falloff in exports, and the imperial government was in financial meltdown over the military buildup. We should get used to this: finances were *the* permanent headache for all of the great powers, and could never have been solved without recourse to deficit-financing, which was the English practice, and thus repudiated by the French.

The French solution was ad hoc: the usual minuet danced with private finance. The Treasury minister, Barbé-Marbois, and Napoleon had browbeaten and enticed a group of private bankers to provide the necessary funds;

in return, and acting under the theoretical oversight of the semipublic Bank of France, the financiers were accorded debentures against future tax income and allowed various commercial-financial privileges. As night followed day, the exploitation of these privileges led quickly to speculative schemes (e.g., gambling on the value of the Spanish piaster in light of gold shipments from the Western Hemisphere), which collapsed with the imposition of a strong British blockade and were followed by a scandal in Paris. Rumor ran riot ("X, Y, or Z—even the Emperor—has absconded with the public funds! The banks are dry! The *rente* [the government's rate on bonds] won't hold!"). Before you knew it, people were lining up for blocks outside the Bank of France, bringing their mattresses, and Barbé-Marbois was writing His Majesty desperate messages like "Return, Sire, I beg you, return as fast as you can! Only your presence will make people do their duty instead of secretly following their private interests, thereby troubling order and destroying proper financial operations."[92]

The military triumph on the heights of Pratzen had made possible a political rescue back in Paris. The news of Austerlitz was known in the French capital in mid-December. Napoleon's bulletins were read from the pulpits, in theatres, from government buildings, and on the street. Cannons were fired until everybody was deaf; Te Deums were sung in all of the churches; and enemy flags were distributed to various national and Parisian authorities (who got what was spelled out in Napoleon's missives). The Senate decreed the erection of a triumphal arch (the one that ended up in the Carrousel of the Tuileries), and the statue intended to crown the Vendôme victory column (à la Trajan) would now be one of Napoleon I, not Charles the Great. Republican modesty was out. Prefects, mayors, and bishops made sure that the same scenario was followed in the provinces.

The Emperor returned to Paris on January 26, 1806, and remained there for eight months. Certain collaborators had profited from his absence to express their own "freedom" in the leadership department. Fouché, for example, had apparently taken himself for some kind of prime minister in the opinion of certain of his colleagues.[93] One problem was that there were no permanent mechanisms in place for running the state when the ruler was away.[94] Cambacérès held official responsibility for government, but "Prince" Joseph, the Grand Elector, was formally the second personage of the Empire, and neither man could scheme or maneuver with Fouché's skill. The main point was this: the Emperor never really let go of the reins while he was away. Joseph, Fouché, Cambacérès, and Louis Bonaparte, the military governor of Paris, were expected to (and did) write him virtually daily with their news; and other ministers weighed in often. Napoleon could not be overloaded, but he would snap at a subordinate who hung back. In mid-campaign—in mid-battle—the Emperor was capable of studying and sending reports on a host of distant topics in the capital.

The restoration of confidence—all that was really needed for the financial crisis to begin to resolve itself—was already setting in with the news of the military victories. Once back, Napoleon moved with his usual blunt authority to impose order. For not better overseeing the speculators, Barbé-Marbois was dismissed at Treasury, while the Bank of France saw itself further nationalized. The offending speculators were brought up on charges and forced to hemorrhage large quantities of their ill-got funds. The Danube campaign had paid off: the newly created army exchequer, separate from the imperial Treasury, had a surplus of 65 million francs. The crisis of 1805 would take a year to dissipate, but the point for us is: *it was politically soluble* (as it had been, in a sense, politically precipitated by the weakness and complicity of the government in Napoleon's absence). At bottom, the 1805 crisis was a wartime crisis of confidence, resolved when the war was won and a strong arm took back domestic control.[95]

And Fouché? Well, he nearly got fired; but in the end, he proved to be too valuable.

THE FOURTH COALITION (1806–1807): THE PRUSSIAN AND THE RUSSIAN CAMPAIGNS

If I had experienced pleasure, I might have rested; but the peril was always in front of me, and the day's victory was always forgotten in the preoccupation with the necessity of winning a new victory on the morrow.
                                                            —Napoleon, St. Helena, 1816

Napoleon often complained of the "dictatorship of the event," usually unexpected, often sudden. One sympathizes; the event ruled his life more certainly than he ruled his empire, yet by resorting so readily to war, he further endowed events with an apocalyptic meaning they might not otherwise have had. In early autumn of 1806, the event that surprised him should not have done so. The First Consul would have foreseen better what the Emperor, increasingly blind to any vision but his own, failed to see: Frederick William III was a dog who had been thrashed once too often, and was now ready to bite back. In part, the Prussian had brought it on himself: by going with his own (and more especially his wife's) heart, he had gambled on

Austria and Russia in their recent war with France and come up a loser. Worse, Frederick William's government had tried to dissimulate its stance, especially in the weeks after Austerlitz, which only brought down an ice storm of Napoleonic contempt when he found out the truth. The Hohenzollern next tried groveling–Prussia crept into an alliance with France as of February 15–but this, too, did not save her from humiliation. Napoleon went about establishing French authority in Germany in ways that would confine Prussian influence to just the northeast.

On the other hand, Prussia's choosing "to be a lion only after trying long and hard to remain a jackal"[96] would not have occurred without the covert agency of Queen Louise and the francophobic clique she headed in Berlin, which included key ministers like Hardenberg and Stein, as well as most of Prussia's top generals. Thanks to the queen, an active French royalist agency installed itself in Berlin, whence it influenced the regime and the nobility, and infiltrated France with political tracts for Louis XVIII. Formally–because down to the last, Frederick William could not rid himself of timidity and irresolution–the government proved two-faced: arguing in St. Petersburg that Prussia would take up the French gauntlet and in Paris that Prussia wished only to be a good (read: a better-treated) French ally. The former was the truth,[97] but the latter could have become the case. Prussia, a lesser great power, was having to decide which mentor it would accept geopolitically. Russia was by far the preferred choice, but Napoleon might have imposed himself if he had tried.

He did not. Distracted by his designs and dealings everywhere but with Prussia, Napoleon gave no heed to gathering resentment east of the Elbe. On the eve of war, the French emperor was assuring his foreign minister, "The idea that Prussia would enter the war against me by herself strikes me as too ridiculous to be discussed. . . . If the Prussians lightly go to war, it will be to their ruin."[98] Napoleon was right: the Prussians went to war lightly, in this sense: their famed patriotic revival of 1806 turned out to be shallow, more the effect of the official war party's intrigue and propaganda among the army than a genuine countrywide–still less, a German–nationalism. The bellicose spirit in Berlin that memoirists comment upon was confined to the aristocracy and the officer corps, and consisted mostly of posturing and self-delusions about the glory of Frederick the Great, when Prussia had been "an army with a State attached." The arrogance of the officers of the Noble Guard sharpening their blades on the stone steps of the French embassy was conspicuous but otiose. When war came, only one German state (Saxony) stuck by the German-speaking side; and even the Prussian people betrayed little chagrin at what presently befell their army and its State.

A second way in which Napoleon was right: the Prussian forces did march swiftly "to their ruin." The 1806 campaign is nearly unique in the annals of war among great powers in climaxing so fast—thirty-three days. This, plus the fact that it led to no truce or peace, just the continuation of the War of the Fourth Coalition, marks it for reduced interest in Napoleon's biography. The Grande Armée was still encamped in Germany when the Prussian "surprise" came; Napoleon had been on the brink of ordering it home. The first bulletin of the new campaign indeed blamed the soldiers' inconvenience on the Prussian war party, not the country in general. The Emperor's aim was to attack the Prussians before the Russians (still at war with France) could join forces with their new ally, but the French did not need to rush, for the foe, in full Frederickian confidence, advanced to meet them. Their advance was so helter-skelter, so confused and ill coordinated among its parts (the average Prussian general was over sixty) that the best French intelligence, and Napoleon himself, had no idea where the foe was located. The Emperor formed the army into a huge mobile "square battalion" of 180,000 men as it moved into eastern Germany, prepared to meet an attack from any direction.[99]

They clashed on October 14 in two venues in Thuringia approximately fifteen miles apart. The Emperor, at Jena, believed he had encountered the brunt of the enemy forces when, in fact, it was the Prussian right flank, under Prince von Hohenlohe. The Duke of Brunswick and the mass of the Prussian army were at Auerstaedt, facing Marshal Davout. The two battles (Jena and Auerstaedt) were thus separate and unequal; Napoleon's victory over Hohenlohe, while crushing, was that of a superior force against an inferior. Davout, however, was in the reverse situation: outnumbered more than two to one, he brilliantly bested Brunswick. Marshal Bernadotte had been expected to come to his aid, but he hung back, perhaps because he did not want to serve under a colleague seven years his junior. Napoleon pondered a court-martial for him (which would have issued a death sentence), but in the end he did not even disgrace him. It was not so much that Bernadotte was Désirée's husband and Joseph's brother-in-law as that the Emperor found it hard to punish or cashier, or even confront, those close to him.[100]

This brace of French triumphs destroyed three Prussian armies, took 25,000 prisoners, 200 cannon, and 60 regimental colors. The bulletin declared that "Rossbach has been expunged!"—a reference to the 1757 victory of Frederick the Great over the French. Napoleon entered Potsdam on October 26 and paid homage at Frederick's tomb there—the prie-dieu still warm from when Frederick William, Louise, and Alexander had pledged themselves against him less than a year earlier. The irony cannot have escaped him that if the Prussian army had succumbed, in part due to its slavish imitation of Frederick's (outdated) tactics,[101] he, Napoleon, had been the one who reproduced the nimble and cagey warrior here. The French entered Berlin the following day, and Napoleon did not deny himself the pleasure of ordering that the officers of the Prussian Noble Guard whom he held prisoner be marched down the street where the French embassy stood. Curiously, the crowds expressed no apparent sympathy for them.

True despair overtook the Prussian government only many weeks after Jena, as its remaining forces—numerous and well ensconced in the famous fortresses of East Prussia (Magdeburg, Danzig, etc.)—surrendered one by one, often without a fight, beaten by French bluster and Napoleon's reputation. The colonel at Stettin was not, alas, atypical: having sworn to die at his post, he promptly surrendered without firing a shot. Murat, having captured his counterpart, *Feldmarschall* Blücher, sent the famous dispatch to Napoleon, "Sire, the combat ends for lack of combatants!"[102]

Yet this, Napoleon's greatest campaign *ever*, for swift visitation of total destruction on an enemy's ability to resist, netted him nothing by way of peace, and it was his own fault: he offered the Hohenzollern Carthaginian terms that would have reduced Prussia to second-class power status and financially broken her. There was no way the king could have accepted them when he still had an ally in the field. He and his queen retired to a fortress on their eastern frontier and awaited Alexander's armies. As for the French public, it had not been so much bowled over by the victory this time as possessed of the desire for an end to war in a distant place for unpersuasive reasons. Metternich later wrote that Jena was Napoleon's "apogee." If only he had resisted the urge to destroy Prussia diplomatically, he might have built "a stable, solid, lasting base to the immense edifice that he had managed to raise."[103] It is hard to contest the observation.

Any student of European history knows of the special tie between Poland and France, both in the *ancien régime* and the Revolution.[104] The illustrious kingdom of Poland had disappeared in 1795, as its last remnant was partitioned among Russia, Austria, and Prussia. The Directory had been unable to prevent it. Still, the Polish idea continued to burn brightly, not only among Poles but among progressive forces in Europe generally and among the French in particular. Polish officers fought under Bonaparte in Italy in 1796–97, and won his admiration. And the First Consul, on taking power, had wasted no time in criticizing the Directory for its "cowardly timidity" in acquiescing to Poland's destruction. Now, in late 1806, with the Grande Armée advancing across East Prussia, the Poles, at Napoleon's encouragement, rose up and drove out their Prussian overlords. Polish units soon joined the French army to fight the Prussians and then the Russians.

The French emperor found himself in a bit of a perplexing situation. In all that is murky and debated about Napoleon's famed Polish policy, three things stand out: first, the Emperor was wishing and intending to do something for Poland, regardless of the geopolitical cost vis-à-vis the "central Powers"; second, the Poles must, in return, serve the needs of France and the Grande Armée; and third, anything he did for Poland, short of resurrecting the ancient kingdom as a sister republic—which would have meant war with Austria as well as Prussia and Russia—would not satisfy Polish (or French) patriots, whose point of reference was the early French Revolution. "It comes down to arousing national feeling in Poland without awakening liberal feeling," the Emperor told a diplomat.

Thickening the plot is the curious fact that all of a sudden, in the midst of war, diplomacy, and the close (if absentee) government of his empire, Napoleon Bonaparte, for the first time since "early" Josephine, appears to have fallen in love. The object of these unusual affections was Maria Walewska, a twenty-year-old Polish countess married to a man fifty years her senior. "Marie," as Napoleon called her, was a woman of beauty, modesty, and principle, she is one of few people around the French emperor to hold our interest in her own right, not merely as a reflection of him. Introduced to Napoleon in January 1807 for the crudest of purposes, Walewska was encouraged by her compatriots (including, perhaps, her own husband) to seduce Napoleon "for the Cause." This, she did—indeed, it appears he was rather violent with her in their first sexual encounter—but then something happened: she fell in love with him. He, for his part, did a thing he had not done for a woman since Josephine: he rearranged his whole life so as to be able to spend time with his lady love. The couple's spring idyll (April to June) in the remote castle at Finckenstein was, in its way, a unique and utterly unexpected moment in the life of Napoleon—a period that saw him deploy what one historian of this period of his life calls "a miraculous energy."[105]

It soon became clear to all who knew them that Marie was not a mistress like the others. Her principal biographer titles his work *Napoleon's Polish Wife*, and the Emperor himself was known to refer to her thus.[106] Josephine, waiting in Mainz for word (which never came) to join her husband, heard about the affair despite Napoleon's efforts to keep it from her. She was devastated; this was, after all, a *reversal* of their roles of 1796–98. Napoleon, however, in no ways appears to have enjoyed Venus's payback; he did nothing but reassure her, as best he could by letter, of his abiding love for her. He had great, not petty, failings.

Walewska, like all the Poles whom Napoleon associated with, was a passionate patriot, but her pleas—like theirs—had little impact on French policy.

The thirty-seven-year-old Emperor was far from the patriot of his youth, and he was not, as he put it in a letter to the king of Württemberg, "anxious to play the part of a Polish Don Quioxte," i.e., ready to sacrifice a future relationship with Russia on the altar of "unredeemed Poland." Yet, for all that he complained of and waived off Polish entreaties, the political entity he presently raised up–the Duchy of Warsaw, under Talleyrand's transitional intendancy–proved most disconcerting for monarchical Europe, especially Russia. The duchy would come to play an important part in French foreign policy until the end of the Empire. The oft-made criticism that he used Polish patriotism in order to raise men for his wars, and that he set up a puppet march on Russia's western extreme, is true if mundane; *of course he did*–he was head of the French State, which was at war. The interesting questions we shall treat momentarily are "How far was he willing to go in re-creating Poland?" and "What was the long-range impact on Polish history of the Napoleonic interlude?"

FIGHTING THE RUSSIANS: BATTLE (EYLAU, FRIEDLAND)

The winter battles and maneuvering in Poland and East Prussia were the bloodiest campaign yet, fought under the harshest conditions to date–a foretaste of 1812. In Napoleon's words, "God has created a fifth element: mud." The Grande Armée had had to be reinforced by calling up the conscription class of 1807 ahead of schedule–an emergency act the Senate performed without murmur–while allies and neutrals (Holland, Spain, etc.) had been caged and coerced into raising the number of troops they supplied to the Empire.

A final harbinger of the future: the "God of war" met his first military stalemate–at a town near Koenigsberg called Eylau in February 1807. Eylau attained mythic status among those who fought there, for its savagery and the numbing cold of a February blizzard.[107] Unintended to be a set piece, Eylau evolved from a tangential engagement–turning on the taking, losing, and retaking of a cemetery (no less)–into a pitched battle between the Russian army under Bennigsen and the French under Napoleon. The sides ended up about equal in strength (approximately 70,000 men apiece), but Russian artillery was far stronger. Bennigsen fought his legendary opponent to a standstill. At one point, Napoleon himself would have been killed or taken prisoner had his personal escort not flung themselves into the fray.

Eylau was a fifteen-degree-below-zero hecatomb, with more corpses and wounded (human and animal) littering the field per square yard than in any previous Napoleonic battle. One of the surgeons in chief described the scene as "horrifying butchery . . . all you could see were the cadavers of men and horses. Artillery wagons and vehicles passed over them, cutting them up further, crushing and grinding skulls and members."[108] During the night Bennigsen withdrew; he had arguably bested his opponents during the day, but he and his men could take no more of this. The simple fact of their departure, albeit in fine order, permitted the French to declare a technical knockout, which Napoleon promptly did in his bulletins and instructions to Paris.[109]

Yet Eylau signified to him, now and always, the hell of war. The civilian in the Emperor was a squeamish man; he gave up taking anatomy lessons from Dr. Corvisart because the wax model organs disgusted him. But the soldier was of a different mettle—usually. On the field of Eylau the day after the carnage, Napoleon made every effort to direct his horse around the human bodies, but there were simply too many of them, and finally he gave up and permitted the horse to step where it had to, including occasionally on the dead. "That is when I saw him start to cry," a medic later reported.[110] As he did on other occasions, Napoleon made contact with some of the wounded and gave them sips of brandy, but this time his aides could barely control their nausea at the sight and the stench.

The Emperor's bulletin reporting Eylau very unusually uses words like "massacre" or "horror," and proved so depressing that Cambacérès wrote back to note its dampening effect on the French public. Concerned with popular opinion, Napoleon ordered Vivant Denon to open a competition among painters for a tableau on Eylau.[111] The winner was Antoine Gros, a former student of David, who produced an extraordinary piece that premiered at the Salon of 1808. The Emperor was in attendance, of course, moving along briskly, as if reviewing the Old Guard. But at *Napoleon Visiting the Field of Eylau,* he paused for a time and said nothing. He then distributed awards to other painters and started to leave when, turning dramatically (as he so loved), he walked over to Gros. Removing his own medal of the Legion of Honor, he pinned it onto the artist's coat. (Gros later painted an oil sketch of the moment.)

The Eylau painting is a light-year from a standard triumphalist work, like the dozens that bedizened the galleries of Napoleon's residences. The scene Gros depicts is satanic and hushed, with the figures of Napoleon and his staff relegated almost to supporting roles amidst the carnage and desolation. The Emperor certainly looks "great," but it is a greatness for once drained of glory; his face wears a ghastly pallor, expressing very grim compassion, and there are tears in his eyes. The magnificent golden horse he rides wears a look of horror and revulsion. The viewer's attention is so fixed on the bodies of the dead and wounded in the foreground—notably a Prussian soldier whose face shows, in the terror of Poe, his impending death—that even the Christ-like visage given to Napoleon barely suffices, if it does, to redeem anything. Some critics found the painting in bad taste or went too far in its implied critique. Most agreed that its impact was to "deny spectators the effect of benign or aesthetic contemplation." As propaganda (Gros was never paid by the government), the painting amounts to a risky strategy, for its unblinking look at war's cost. However, Delacroix and Géricault loved it.[112]

Napoleon's smashing victory over the Russians had to wait till spring. On June 14, the anniversary of Marengo, Napoleon caught Bennigsen at Friedland; the Russians let themselves be wedged into the town, with water boundaries on three sides and the French in front. Even so, Napoleon won mainly on a blunder: the Russian could have virtually annihilated Lannes's entire corps, which served as the bait in Napoleon's trap, but had got too far ahead of the Grande Armée to be quickly supported. Lannes's holding action "bears comparison with that of Marshal Davout at Auerstädt," writes Chandler.[113] But if it was a near thing, Friedland was nonetheless a great success, which brought the tsar to the table. The battle, as the Emperor wrote Josephine, "is a worthy sister of Marengo, Austerlitz, and Jena."

FIGHTING WITH THE RUSSIANS: PEACE (TILSIT)

The summit between the Emperor and the tsar—the title means "Caesar" in Russian—was held on a raft in the middle of the Niemen River, near the town of Tilsit, on Russia's western frontier. It was Napoleon who suggested the meeting, which may have misled Alexander as to who was the loser here: he was. "I will have Russia [in alliance]," Napoleon had said at the end of 1805, "if not today, then in a year, in two, or three. Time will erase our [painful] memories, and of all possible alliances, this will be the one that suits me most."[114] There is no mystery in these words; Russia was by far the strongest Continental power after France; she was one of the three superpowers of the era. To befriend her and to turn her against England, as now happened, was to seal Britain's fate, or so it was thought.

True, Alexander himself may also have interested Napoleon; of all the traditional crowned heads in Europe, the Romanov was the only one with any personal qualities remotely worth cultivating. Tilsit was to be considered "a treaty of friendship," not just an alliance, and the two rulers' mutual infatuation has been much asserted. Napoleon noted famously to Josephine, "If Alexander were a woman, I would make him my mistress," while the tsar seemed to be dazzled by "the genius" of the French emperor, whom he attended with the apparent rapture of a student for a beloved teacher. The two rulers were absorbed with each other for the fortnight they were together—often completely by themselves ("you be my secretary and I'll be yours," Napoleon is said to have proposed). Still, it would seem to be Alexander who was the less sincere, for we know from his private letters to his sister how distasteful he found "spending hours on end in *tête-à-têtes*" with "the Corsican."[115] The Tsar-Proteus was keen to affect yet another new role—this one, as a practitioner of Realpolitik—so he steeled himself and embraced the parvenu who could teach him, pretending to be under his spell.

The geopolitical essential of Tilsit was as simple as it was outrageous. When he had proposed a summit to Alexander's envoy, Napoleon had pointed on a map to the Vistula: "Here," he said, "is the boundary between the two Empires." France would dominate west of the river, Russia, east. The Hohenzollern just avoided losing his crown—the French decree removing Frederick William from office was ready in draft—only because Alexander pleaded for his former ally. But the Prussian walked away minus a third of his realm.[116] Several provinces of the kingdom of Prussia were parceled out among Napoleon's loyal German allies, given to Poland, or sculpted into the kingdom of Westphalia, which Napoleon fashioned for Jérôme Bonaparte.

Russia lost no actual territory, even its Polish holdings, but Alexander did have to prove his bona fides. First, he was required to recognize, openly or implicitly, the extended French Empire *and* the Duchy of Warsaw. Next, he must cease supporting Bourbon political machinations and extrude the pretender from where he lived in Russian Poland. As a significant fraction of the tsar's general officers and the Russian foreign service was staffed by French noble émigrés, Alexander fought to retain them, including, above all, the indispensable Pozzo di Borgo. (In the end, Napoleon would have done better to demand their extradition.) Finally, the tsar had to turn on his ally, Britain—not so hard to do: resentment at England ran deep and not just in France.[117] Alexander also needed to demonstrate his usefulness to Napoleon by trying to bring Britain to heel at the peace table (and he could not).

And then, there was the matter of the Duchy of Warsaw—the immortal "Polish Question." In addition to the obvious geopolitical and military importance of a hostile Statelike entity erected on Russia's western frontier, the duchy had sharp ideological edges that sliced painfully into the tsar's deepest attitudes, for the entity that this imperial son of the Revolution raised up was, in some regards, "Poland writ French"—a dependency endowed with French legal codes and a French constitution, albeit overlaid onto Polish aristocratic political traditions.[118] It made little difference to the Russian court that the Polish Jacobins were kept from power; the Duchy of Warsaw, from their perspective, was still Robespierre moved in next door.

In coming days, Napoleon would not fail to bruit about the possibility of one day resurrecting the entire Polish *patrie*—which was the kind of threat or dream he occasionally spoke of for Italy. No one can say for sure whether it was a firm intention or a pragmatic velleity aimed at garnering Polish support in means and men. It could well have been both at different times. The tsar, in any case, did not fail to understand that the Duchy of Warsaw mattered to Napoleon.[119] Napoleon will use the future opportunities of a war won against Austria to increase further the Duchy of Warsaw's limits and its importance. None of this satisfied Poland's (or France's) more zealous patriots, but in a geopolitical context the Russians had every right to believe that he might well one day re-create the formal kingdom of Poland.[120]

In the evening of the Tilsit palavers, one wonders, did Napoleon ponder to himself the tsar's readiness to betray people—for example, Frederick William, to whom he had sworn eternal fealty at Frederick II's tomb; or Britain, his ally. Disgust with its sovereign was certainly the attitude of the Russian court, the imperial family, and much of the Russian government when Alexander returned home from Tilsit. Napoleon's envoy to St. Petersburg, Savary, expended much ink informing his master of the Russian elites' implacable hostility to "Bonaparte" and his peace.[121] It would require a tsar of far greater force of character and clarity of political vision than Alexander I had to sell "the treaty of friendship" to his own realm.

BLOCKADE (I)

It has cost us to return, after so many years of civilization, to the principles that characterized the barbarism of the earlier ages of nations, but we are constrained to deploy against the common enemy the arms he is using on us.
                    —The Berlin Decree (November 21, 1806)

So Britain again stood alone, as one by one, her Continental allies or potential allies got shot away. After Jena and Friedland, there was little of the sham of a peace flurry between her and France. Time and experience had rendered the islanders implacable in their proud imperturbability, and this in turn drove Napoleon wild at "English *morgue*" (haughtiness, disdain), which simply did not, even in extremis, take this buffoon of an "emperor" seriously. Austrians, Prussians, Russians were foes and adversaries, who displayed mixtures of awe, fear, greed, and anger toward the French ruler, but the British, in their icy (and very funny) mockery, were enemies.[123]

It should also be said the British were perceived as adversaries by many on the Continent, for the Royal Navy's manner of enforcement had ever been *sans politesse* (just ask the Americans). The islanders' insufferable sense of their own superiority is nicely illustrated in propaganda that His Majesty's Government disseminated, which readily conceded British ascendancy in commerce, credit, and navy, and cheerfully advised other countries that there was nothing they could do except copy the British example and pull up their own economies and administrations by the bootstraps.[124] Both England and France did their level best to transfer the economic cost of the war onto other countries, but until 1811 or 1812, the French were not perceived as the main "bad guys" in this conflict. "The enemy of the world," as Napoleon called Britain,[127] found itself at war with nearly every power in Europe, at some point or other, between 1799 and 1815.

The two countries took up with alacrity an economic war which, with only occasional respites, they had been carrying on since the early eighteenth century, and in earnest since 1791. This, of course, was an uneven contest, for Britain had attained as much superiority at sea as she had in manufacture, trade, credit, and currency. Britain acted first. As a result of an order in council issued on May 16, 1806 (followed by more such decrees in response to French retaliation), Britain sealed off the French coasts from oceangoing traffic and seized French shipping, the Royal Navy going as far as to arrest private persons and to stop neutral (e.g., American) vessels.

The French, bereft of colonies and trade, and with their navy destroyed at Trafalgar, now retaliated by taking a momentous step. Decrees issued from Berlin (November 1806) and Milan (November 1807) declared the British Isles to be "in a state of blockade,"[125] and transposed onto land the no-holds-barred maritime form of war lately pursued by both belligerents but more flagrantly by England (which had superior means). Land warfare traditionally did not condone or consistently practice the seizure of private persons and property, including those of neutrals, so the French decree—which was, in effect, a rationale for seizing the European coasts—anticipated an outcry; whence the statement of reluctance quoted earlier. Napoleon would continue to portray himself, not as the assaulter on the freedom of peoples, but as "the long-awaited leader of the revolt against England's maritime domination." He periodically reiterated that the current state of affairs would endure only until Britain backed off from these practices and subscribed to a more humane law for sea warfare.[126]

These early Anglo-French decrees establishing the Blockade sounded harsher than the reality they initially created; at this point, they added nothing wildly new to the ancient feud. The mutual prohibition against commercial importation had been the policy in the 1790s, and amounted to a rigorous economic protectionism. However, if the Emperor turned out to mean it when he said, "I intend to conquer the sea by land," then a new form of warfare and imperialism would ensue, as his forces set out to "organize" the *blocus* against England. The Continental System would be the result. In 1806, however, Napoleon had not thought so far ahead; for now, he aimed mainly at depriving Britain of her European export markets. In this scenario, "Perfidious Albion" would drown in her surplus of manufactured goods, while simultaneously going broke from loss of specie, in paying for European (especially French) imports. Economically shut out and shut down, the British government would be driven by the nation's all-powerful merchant-banking class to sue for peace.

Through mid-1808, the French seriously (if never hermetically) enforced their quarantine, with the result that Britain, presently, was sore tested.[127] However, through 1810 there remained great latitude in how the two belligerents enforced the above-named (and new) decrees; hence there remained considerable ambiguity as to what the Blockade actually amounted to—that is, a new weapon of war or a severer version of an old mercantile contest, wherein both sides maneuvered to drain off each other's specie. A critical indicator would be how harshly the two countries would treat neutral trading powers (for now, not so badly).

What neither Napoleon nor the English could foresee—no one did—was how changing circumstance, escalation, and mounting anger would alter both countries' intentions with the Blockade. Even Napoleon did not yet see or feel the "logic" that would involve both countries ever more deeply in Continental affairs than anyone conceived possible or found desirable.[128] But in September 1807, for example, the British bombarded the neutral port of Copenhagen and seized (or destroyed) the Danish fleet because the Danes did not immediately side with England. Napoleon, for his part, then ordered the seizure of German coastal cities, in order to close them to British trade; he demanded that Denmark, which had reluctantly sided with France, close down even its mail service to England. These acts, taken against nominally sovereign powers, were a step down a long slope toward complete control of the Continent, whose consequences would drive the foreign policy of the French Empire to the end.

But to what end? "Napoleon was master in Europe, but he was also prisoner there"[129]

The years 1806 and 1807 were Napoleon's finest hour from the military point of view that counted so in this era. As Adolphe Thiers writes, the victories of the several campaigns of 1805–1807 in Austria, Prussia, and Poland added up to "the longest, the most daring expedition, not through defenseless Persia or India, like the army of Alexander, but through Europe, swarming with soldiers, well disciplined and brave . . . [a feat] unparalleled in the history of the ages."[130]

XI

The Empire—and Its Fissures
(1807–1810)

I love power . . . as a musician loves his violin, for the tones I can
bring forth, for the chords and harmonies.

—Napoleon I, Emperor of the French

IMPERATOR AND IMPERIUM

*To very few men in the world's history has it been granted to dream grandiose
dreams and all but realize them, to use by turns the telescope and the microscope
of political survey, to plan vast combinations of force, and yet to supervise with
infinite care the adjustment of every adjunct.*

—John Holland Rose[1]

France received its emperor back in late July 1807 and bestowed on him the
cognomen "great"—an accolade not awarded since Louis XIV became
Ludovicus Magnus. Huge festivities honored variously his birthday, the
Grande Armée, and *la gloire* in general. The Civil Code saw itself redubbed
with the moniker it has kept: Code Napoleon; while the mega-museum that
Vivant Denon was bringing into being in the Louvre became the Musée
Napoléon. The ironical banter of even the skeptical Parisian bourgeoisie fell
into adulation before *this* degree of world glory; "servitude was acceptable
when thus gold-encrusted."[2]

The human being who bore all these honors was heavier now, as he approached forty. The angular noble Roman that was General Vendémiaire had developed more rounded features, but his movements and moods were still so rapid and changing—"the eyes so alive and penetrating, alternately soft, then severe, terrible, then caressing"—that it made his face impossible of a searching portrayal, even by the best artists (the more so, as Napoleon refused to sit still for a portrait). A film documentary would be needed, but we possess only the film of memory among witnesses who disagree. The Emperor's valet, Constant, felt: "Later on he grew much stouter, but without losing any of the beauty of his features; on the contrary, he was handsomer under the Empire than under the Consulate; his skin had become very white, and his expression animated."[3] Others noted the flaccidity of taut musculature, and the breath of indolence where animation had once been. As the older, cynical Napoleon perhaps lurked in the idealistic, young Bonaparte, so the bronze statue of the Legend was starting to emerge from the physique of the Emperor—in the darkening skin covering the well-chiseled nose, where he sniffed tobacco, in the set chin and the sculptural profile he now preferred to full-face representations.

Although nothing had gone terribly wrong in the ten months he was away, the Emperor yet returned to Paris with both barrels blazing, eager "to be his own prime minister again."[4] En route home, he fired Talleyrand as foreign minister, replacing him with an obedient functionary, Jean-Baptiste de Champagny. The old aristocrat had fallen out of step with his sovereign's unrelenting bellicosity, which he found incomprehensible and self-defeating. He expressed his attitude in a letter to the Emperor after the battle of Friedland, in which he said he earnestly hoped that this would be the "last" victory.[5] The former bishop contained his disappointment—all the easier to do in that he kept his title of Great Chamberlain and received a promotion to Imperial Vice-Elector, putting him just after Cambacérès in official standing.

Despite their emollient greetings, Napoleon's ministers and associates did not succeed in softening up a sovereign who had recently written one of them, "Monsieur le Ministre, peace has been made with the foreigners, now I am going to make war on your offices." The five-, six-, and seven-hour review meetings now recommenced, with ministers and counselors constantly reminded they did not know and had not done nearly enough. Napoleon's rebukes were stinging but impersonal, forgotten the next day. He was simply, as H. A. L. Fisher puts it, "one of those rare men who assume that everything they come across, from a government to a saucepan, is probably constructed on wrong principles and capable of amendment."[6] As Pierre-Louis Roederer put it, "The mediocre came to feel they had talent, and the talented believed themselves mediocre, so much did [Napoleon] enlighten the former and astonish the latter."[7] The Emperor intended to cut as much domestic hay as he could in the sunlight of his military and diplomatic triumphs over the Fourth Coalition.

The Consulate's granite blocks were Napoleon's tribute to the Revolution and its consolidation. The imperial initiatives of post-1805, while more decorative than substantial, were in many cases no less enduring than the earlier reforms. We might construe these initiatives as so many marble or porphyry columns standing upon the granite blocks—sometimes in adornment, other times in defiance. They make the Empire distinctive and impressive, at once different from the Revolution that preceded it, yet nourished by it, variously supportive and destructive of it.

ACQUIRED GLORY: THE COURT, THE NOBILITY, THE LEGION OF HONOR

The marble column that outshone all else for dazzling novelty was the imperial court. The French, Napoleon liked to say, were not a people to want to see their sovereigns "walking in the street." An understatement: the Emperor's personal modesty and simplicity of taste contrasted famously with his policy requiring éclat and magnificence in the nimbus surrounding the sovereign. "Pomp," he had told Comte de Rémusat a few years before, was necessary in order "to throw powder in people's eyes."[8] The splendor of the Napoleonic court was the talk of Europe; no similar corps approached it for panache, power, and pelf. The single Household of the Emperor, with its planetary systems of "grands" (Grand Chamberlain, Grand Equerry, etc.) and "arches" (Arch-Chancellor, Arch-Treasurer, etc.), outnumbered the governments of small powers. If for no other reason than the impetus the court gave to the languishing sector of the French luxury trades (silk, jewels, saddles, embroidery, lace, etc.), some people justified its creation.[9]

This said, it was a strange and mongrel entity that arose in post-revolutionary France and monarchical Europe. It boasted a sovereign who hunted because he felt he ought to but didn't enjoy it, courtiers who (in four-fifths of the cases) could not have been named pages at the Versailles of Louis XIV, an etiquette that was stultifying, amid a syncretism of styles, dress, manners, and backgrounds. In truth, this parvenu court—with its nervy washerwomen become impudent duchesses—offered distinct aspects of the Thénardier clan who run the boardinghouse in Hugo's Les Misérables.

On the other hand, as an engine for furthering meritocracy, its importance

could not be gainsaid. The aristocracy that partly manned these antecham-
bers, for which Napoleon had laid the foundations for in 1806, was brought
into full being early in 1808. The new imperial nobility avoided, first of all,
the very term "nobility," with its strong *ancien régime* accents. *Noblesse*
nowhere mars the official texts, which simply notify the reader that the familiar titles of duke, count, baron, and knight will begin to be awarded in recompense for eminent service and merit. The service and merit were mainly
martial, but also political and administrative, which is to say, to the State—
as personified in the sovereign. Am imperial count put it thus: "One could
not be a favorite with Napoleon, as with any other monarch. One must have
followed him, and been of use to him; for he was not interested in mere
charm. Above all, one must have been more than a witness to his many victories."[10] Newly named titleholders took what only could be called a blan-
ket oath to be "faithful to the Emperor and his dynasty . . . , to raise my
children in these same sentiments of fidelity and obedience, and to march
to the defense of the *Patrie* every time the territory is threatened *or His
Majesty goes to war.*"[11]

In short, the imperial nobility was not the resurrection of a separate social
and legal caste, such as the First and Second Estates of the old regime, but a
grander and more rarefied version of the Legion of Honor. The new nobility, like the corps of Concordatory bishops, was part of the larger Napoleonic
project of social reconstruction based on service. It sought to reconcile old
regime caste elitism with revolutionary patriotism and modern bourgeois
accumulation of wealth.[12] The new nobles were ranking civil and military (or
episcopal) servants. Theoretically, anyone could aspire to a title—and there
were enough famous cases of grocer's or publican's sons become dukes to
keep the prize before many pairs of eyes. In prosaic reality, however, the new
noble titles went to men with a minimum annual landed income (3,000
francs), for Napoleon did not want to re-create an impoverished nobility,
such as the Corsican Buonapartes had been. He aspired to mobilize for the
Empire a well-off stratum of urban and rural bourgeoisie called the "notables," middle-class men of possessions and standing in their local community. Numbering upwards of 100,000 families around France, the notables,
together with the old nobility—among whom Napoleon was making ever-
greater inroads—amounted to a base for his regime.[13]

But if the court and nobility theoretically represented the principle of
equality (equal access), they offered a magnificence fully worthy of the old
regime. This was no minor matter both in attracting people of quality and
in holding the attention of all the rest. Then, too, the Emperor intended
that the new court and nobility would destroy the old Second Estate by

absorbing it, but there wasn't time: in all, the First Empire granted 3,600 titles,[14] comparatively few. The Imperial nobility amounted to a seventh of the former Second Estate. He succeeded with only a relatively few of the *ancien régime* aristocrats—Narbonne, Caulaincourt, Noailles, Ségur, among others—but failed with the great majority of them. Amalgamation was a slow process, and much of the time the Emperor and the military members of the court were absent on campaign. In truth, Napoleon probably never felt wholly at ease with the old aristocracy, for they were capable of making contemptuous comparisons with what once had been. On the other hand, in the end, the prestige of the Empire, if it had lasted, would have proven irresistible to the *ci-devants* (the old nobility).[15]

If the new court and nobility might, in time, have rivaled Versailles for panoply and pelf, it would never have done so for wit and sophistication. But then it was a very different political animal. *La Cour Impériale* was not a city on a hill, set apart from the nation, physically and psychologically rotating around the person of the monarch—his rising, vesting, dining, retiring, going to mass, etc.[16] The Napoleonic nobility served the State, not vice versa, and although many were soldiers, the court was, at bottom, a civilian institution. These were Sunday courtiers, which was, in truth, all that most of them could abide of the excruciating sittings at the Tuileries or Saint-Cloud, with the self-conscious etiquette. In fairness to them, these dukes and counts had jobs to go to during the week; they commanded vast units of men, they ran departments that ran half of Europe. They could not spend their hours refining retorts or discussing the finer points of décor and couture. They went to court out of duty or self-interest, not because it was scintillating. And if they glorified their sovereign, they certainly did not chloroform him. This emperor's outlook was never remotely reduced to peering through the *Oeil-de-Boeuf.*[17]

The Napoleonic policy of fusion of the elites thus went unrealized for want of time, though as clever an observer as Metternich saw it as a "stroke of genius."[18] He might well have; the extraordinary *salade macédoine* that was Napoleon's court—where onetime revolutionaries (virulent haters of the *noblesse*) now addressed one another as "Count," where aristocrats going back to Saint Louis rubbed elbows with swells from Rouen, where sulfurous republicanism smoldered underneath a congealing magma of motley ideas (the future bonapartism), and where imperial titleholders from Germany, Poland, Italy, and Holland spoke French with their French confreres—amounted to a functioning mélange that would have been inconceivable anywhere else.

No less important to the social foundation and political complexion of the Empire was the Legion of Honor, which now came into its own.[19] By 1808 the "mere bauble," as its critics had called it, was a coveted achievement, even among some who affected to disdain it. Its membership numbered 25,000 members in 1812, making it *both* a granite block and a marble column of post-revolutionary French society. The Emperor had a rare affection for this institution; he was indignant when the bishop of Vannes, abducted by royalist brigands, did not refuse to hand over his Legion medal to the kidnappers, though they threatened his life![20] Napoleon alone determined the Legion's beneficiaries, as well as imperial titles, making him a far more powerful monarch for patronage, preferment, and awards than any Bourbon king. The Legion was destined for the new nobility, for many of the notables, and for important scientists, writers, artists, and intellectuals, though in fact, its recipients were mainly soldiers—hardly surprising since France was at war the entire time. Soldiers preferred the Legion to all other awards; there are many stories of their performing prodigies to win it. Still, its unique prestige and novelty inhered in its theoretically being open to all.[21] It also had a political dimension, however—and this had evolved.

The political evolution of the Legion of Honor is revealed in the oath. Although it retained much of its revolutionary language (*Patrie*, liberty, equality, anti-feudalism), by the high Empire, newly minted legionnaires no longer swore to uphold the "Republic," they swore to obey the "Emperor." And in 1811, the year of the birth of Napoleon's son, they swore to be faithful to the dynasty as well as the Sovereign and the State.

WORKS: ARTISTIC AND PUBLIC

When he was still a general, Bonaparte declared, "If I were the master of France, I would make Paris not only the most beautiful city that exists but that ever existed or that ever could exist." Paris would be the new Rome. Not surprisingly, thus, many of the First Empire's marble columns are just that: lintels and columns.[22]

Stand at the Obelisk,[23] at the center of Paris's Place de la Concorde. Looking north, you will see the massive Parthenon-like Church of the Madeleine. East will be the more diminutive Arch of the Carrousel; west, down the Champs-Elysées, there is the great colossus that is the Arc de Triomphe. And looking south, you will see the imposing classical façade of the Palais-Bourbon, the French parliament. Welcome to Napoleonic Paris. And this is only the start. Next comes the Trajan column in the Place Vendôme, the Pantheon, the Stock Exchange, the Rivoli wing of the Louvre, the rue de Rivoli itself, as well as the rues de la Paix and de Castiglione, the *places* de Saint-

Sulpice, Châtelet, and de la Bastille; the bridges of the Arts, of Saint-Louis, Austerlitz, and Jena.[24] Then there is the enormous patrimony in furniture, porcelain, tapestry, medals, glassware, haute couture (including uniforms), and jewelry—all being luxury industries that enjoyed a spurt unprecedented in their history under the First Empire.

Finally, we cannot overlook that temple of high culture open to everyman which is the Louvre, turned into a museum at the First Consul's instigation, and directed by Vivant Denon, under his watchful eye.[25] The Musée Napoléon, as it was called, housed innumerable masterpieces, many commissioned by the Emperor, of the great artists of the day, and many more pilfered by him or by other French generals from all over Europe. One understands why the painter Delacroix would declare, "The life of Napoleon is the event of the century for all the arts."

Some consider the Empire style that soon dominated Europe to be a pituitary monstrosity; others see it as a prodigy, a pastiche of Roman and Egyptian antiquity. (The Pyramid in the Louvre's central courtyard, although contemporary, is rather Napoleonic in size, expense, motif, and motivation.) If you wished to avoid any part of the French capital touched by l'Empereur, you had best stick to the outer arrondissements, which were not part of the city in his day.

Bourrienne notes that the "chief's passion for monuments nearly equaled his passion for war."[26] It would be close to the mark to say that a conquest in the field was not complete until a statue or canvas commemorated it for posterity and "instructed" contemporaries on what it "meant"—much like an army bulletin. Napoleon assaulted the realm of culture frontally, as he rarely did (until later) enemy armies; there was no subtlety about it. The Empire courted and patronized the great architects, painters, sculptors, and artisans of the day, and the day was richer in most of these, especially in painters, than previous centuries: one thinks of the painters David, Gros, Gérard, Girodet, Guérin, Greuze, and Ingres; of the sculptors Canova and Houdon; of the architects Chalgrin and Brogniart; of the furniture craftsman Jacob and the goldsmith Biennais.[27]

But if the French school dominated Europe more than it had even under Louis XIV, Napoleon himself played the role of Maecenas, or patron of the arts, very differently from the Sun King. The motive power of his policy presumed the Revolution: art, not as the preserve of court society, aesthetic philosophy, or a monotonal celebration of the monarch, but art as edifying, regenerative, declamatory, national, and *public*. True, "public" often meant the stated opinion of intellectual or artistic elites, yet the tectonic movement was toward hoi polloi: toward the French, of whom Napoleon was Emperor.

He never ceased tinkering with his complex and evolving policy of representation—of himself, his monarchy, his dynasty, to be sure, but also of the recent national past and the honored dead.[28] Napoleon "recommended" to the Sèvres porcelain manufacturer that it abandon its time-honored motifs of classical nudes or generic landscapes in favor of "historical things that we know." Indeed, to his counselors' grief, the Napoleonic taste barely qualified as an aesthetic at all, rather a yen for facts and resemblance. "What is true is always beautiful," he would say, until Denon finally gave up.

Which is not to say that Napoleon refused to be contradicted—far from it. In this realm, more than any other, he leaned on advisors, and when he did not—when, for example, he insisted on the practical over the magnificent—he was often right, against Denon, Fontaine and Percier (his architects), or David ("first painter to the Emperor").[29] High art was only the smaller part of the First Empire's legacy to the capital. The great royal builders like Louis XIV had had to be pressed into taking measures for Paris (they lived at Versailles, after all); not so, Napoleon. Far from the least difference between the Sun King and the Little Corporal is that "given a choice between bread and circuses . . . [Napoleon] often chose bread."[30] The duller structural needs of the city took precedence over glamorous culture. Strange moments arose, as in 1810 when the Emperor demanded of a commission of experts conferring on a prize in the fine arts that it consider as entrants the Saint-Quentin Canal and the Simplon Pass over the Alps.

The Emperor as city planner was thus responsible for Paris's markets and public cemeteries, for her slaughterhouses, street lamps, and street numbers, for sidewalks, canals, and two miles of embankments (*quais*) along the Seine, for the water supply, the sewer system, the fire department, and—not least—for the Parisian tradition of exhibiting the latest in industry and technology. In sum, a unique accomplishment for fourteen years in power, though much of it is invisible now, or has been destroyed by time. Another decade would have seen these partial realizations united into a full-dress urbanism, with the erection of a new administrative city at the Champ-de-Mars; a palace larger and grander than Versailles, for the King of Rome, atop the Trocadero; and broad north-south (Madeleine-Montmartre) and east-west (Louvre-Bastille) boulevards cutting through medieval neighborhoods.[31]

Finally—and this is another difference between Bonaparte and Bourbon—the wish to build and to (self-)aggrandize was permanently conjoined to the intention to give work to the building and luxury trades, and withal, to keep a weather eye on the State budget. The Emperor was only too aware that the king had ruined France with the extravagance of Versailles, and had lost much of his reputation, in the process. The unbearable tightness of

Napoleon's being thus saw him boast to a minister that he had economized 35,000 francs by suppressing the service of coffee to the staff at Malmaison, allowing them, instead, a supplement of 7.6 francs. This, from a monarch with a civil list of 25 million francs. It is not surprising that he saved roughly half of it, most years.

In sum, Napoleon the builder, Napoleon the art collector, Napoleon the museum creator, and Napoleon the city planner was *not* Napoleon the general, for all that his goal was to win so many cultural and urban Austerlitzes. In the arts and the city, as in war, it was a matter of huge designs and accomplishments, burning impatience, and an unslacked wish for glory. But in the arts and the city, *unlike* in war and diplomacy, far more good than ill was done; the self-interest was enlightened; the profligacy highly controlled; the doer showed a profoundly human tendency to hesitate, back down, accept criticism, refer to opinion, tolerate indecision, change his mind, evolve in his thinking.

To be sure, Napoleon as patron was no aesthete, no detached lover of beauty. Few politicians can afford to be that indulgent in their arts policies, lest they end up as Louis XIV. In any case, Napoleon did not have the temperament, sensibility, or background to be Ludwig II (who broke the Bavarian exchequer). The French emperor's thoughts were always derived from and returned to *le politique,* never straying from the point. As one of the few writers to serve him puts it, Napoleon's tendency to be dominated by an interest or a policy left him "unable to be abstract, he was always concrete."[32] It was not, as some biographers have it, simply a matter of manipulating public opinion; it went beyond that, for in order to "astonish France," as he told Roederer, he "must constantly do." He understood that it also meant serving and regenerating her—and this he did, in the instances under examination here. If the master of the house could not separate his taste for things from his need to self-represent and to self-legitimate, he could also not separate the latter from the wish to do good works.[33]

Was Augustus Caesar so very different, except that he had a year and four decades in which to build his age, while Napoleon I had just fourteen years?

WORKS: LETTERS, EDUCATION, AND LAW

Personally, the Emperor preferred books to paintings. He continued to consume (and that is the only word for it) the printed page at a fearful rate, pushing the pages back with his thumb, a mile a minute, flinging volumes out his carriage window if they didn't please him. He yearned to preside over a literary Augustan age as much as an artistic one, but his luck in this hope ran bad in two ways.[34] First, France as a society had not fielded a team of truly great writers—not philosophes like Rousseau and Voltaire, but literary giants like Racine, Corneille, Molière, and Pascal—since the seventeenth century, the "Century of Gold." The waning decades of the eighteenth constituted a nadir, much deplored and discussed by contemporaries, and only posterity has seen fit to blame Napoleon for it.[35]

On the other hand, however—point two—Napoleon did nothing to help the situation, to the contrary. A tempest raged in his mind between the desire to be *le grand patron des Lettres* and his fierce resentment of criticism, especially any suggestion of ridicule. Unfortunately for France, sensitivity usually beat aspiration. It was not that Napoleon craved, or even tolerated, flattery and adulation in books or the press, but when, for example, a well-known writer of stage reviews (Dupaty) satirized the gaucheries of the new nobility, the Emperor took it personally. Infinitely worse, he took it as an attack on the State, so he responded as sovereign, not just as aggrieved citizen. Dupaty came within an ace of being deported to "the islands."

Then, too, Napoleon could not resist the desire to direct public opinion along lines that he saw fit, so a kind of propagandistic *dirigisme* muscled out what remained of literary liberalism. But even here, his ambivalence was rife. He fully shared the prevailing disgust with the current poverty of French literary invention, yet he was unclear in his mind as to what literature should take up. Novels (a comparatively new species) were definitely out—fiction took too much license. He was drawn to dramatic tragedy in Alexandrian verse, and above all, to history. In these genres, Napoleon was *both* a classicist and a modernist, which is to say, he loved his Caesar and his Corneille—he regretted Corneille wasn't still alive so that he could make him a prince—but he was also fascinated by the idea of current national history, French history, *his* history. Annie Jourdan sums it up nicely in her fine study when she writes: "Between Roman sublime and troubadour pathos, Napoleon was completely at ease. For him, both came together in the present."[36]

So history it would be, history as *tableau vivant*, history as David's vast canvas of the coronation—that is, "corrected"[37] to suit Napoleon's wishes—history to inspire future Napoleone Buonapartes, as they read their Caesar's *Commentaries* and dreamed. Historians, thus, should aspire to write the past from the perspective of the present, with a view to molding future generations. Napoleon limned "the perfect history" as one that was not "susceptible to interpretation," which is to say, one that recounted the story of *le politique* (State-building) while not itself falling into *la politique* (contestation).[38]

As interesting as the foregoing may be as a look at the Napoleonic thought

processes, as a definition of history it fails. The Emperor is extolling the production of propaganda, albeit at a much higher level than was easily available,
given the dearth of talent. Moreover, it is propaganda backed up by the
State's muscle, to prevent competition, to prevent "interpretation." One
can only marvel at his praise of "true facts" knowing, as we do (and he did)
how many slews of "true facts" got regularly censored in French press and
book publishing.

The history that Napoleon had in mind was indeed closer to an anthology of Grande Armée bulletins than to Voltaire's *Century of Louis XV* (which
in fact contains criticism of royal institutions that Napoleon would not have
liked in a book about his Empire). Bulletins were Napoleon's personal
innovation, his own contribution, to the disciplines of history and popular
literature—and by no means minor ones. These products of the imperial pen
are infinitely more captivating than modern propaganda. Aimed (and
received) at all levels of society, foreign as well as French, the bulletins inun-
dated Europe and set off geysers of dismay or admiration. They worked best
on the imagination of soldiers and common people, for they renounced
anything approaching official style in favor of direct simplicity. They are
laconic, dramatic, hypnotic. Each bulletin is personalized, complimenting
this or that general or unit, sometimes individual soldiers; their graceful
accounts of battles are riveting, gilded with statistics and studded with personal asides that share with the reader the Emperor's plans and strategy.
Their narrative is so swift and engaging that they feel like part of the action
whose story they tell, which, of course, in a way they are. In sum, they perfectly illustrate their author's "favorite system, which was to hold people in
what he called 'breathlessness.' "[39] The bulletins drove the counterrevolutionary ideologue Gentz wild with frustration, while they filled his patron,
Count Metternich, with admiration and the desire for emulation.

The Grande Armée bulletins had every possible virtue but one: truth—a
fact well known and accepted by contemporaries, who enjoyed them for the
serial novel they were. History, then as now, is anything but a hard science;
it presents as much of the "mined terrain" of interpretation as fiction does,
but history, then as now, takes truth as a goal, which the Emperor of the
French did not.[40] In the end, Napoleon would have been less frustrated had
he let himself appreciate fiction. Did he not, at St. Helena, after all, claim that
his entire career was one great novel? For sure, novelists have done his person and story no less justice than historians.[41]

Public Instruction: The University[42]

A law of 1806, implemented in 1808, created a body called "The University," which held the monopoly on degree-granting throughout the Empire. The word stuck in the throats of some contemporaries, for *universitas* was a Catholic concept (just as the Sorbonne, since medieval times, had been an ecclesiastical institution). Both the word and the thing had gone the way of the oubliette in the Revolution. What the Republic had dreamed of, rather, was the creation of State-run, secular, free, normative education throughout France, a system of public instruction to mold citizens in French culture and civic (republican) virtue. The Revolution failed in this project, for want of time, focus, and means, but the torch was passed and ready to be relit.

The Emperor, in his founding declaration on "The University," stated the Revolution's ideals in education in his own way:

> I want an educational body whose teaching rises far above the fashions of the day, a body that hews the course when government sleeps, an institution whose elements have become so *national* that one can never lightly resolve to meddle with them. . . . As long as people do not, from their infancy, learn whether they ought to be republicans or monarchists, Catholics or skeptics, the State will never form a nation: it will rest on unsafe, shifting foundations, always exposed to changes and disorders.

The language is purely revolutionary, except–*big* "except"–the goal of the Napoleonic State is to make monarchists and Catholics, not republicans and skeptics. The emerging design of the University–and that is mainly what it was and remained, *a design*–created a huge umbrella corporation (far larger than a modern university), which theoretically gathered into itself virtually every institution of learning in the Empire. The University was given a strictly hierarchical structure, headed by a grand master, supported by a chancellor and council; the Empire was divided into twenty-six academies (districts), each headed by a rector; there were government inspectors, councils, and sundry lower structures. It looked massive on paper; but in reality, for lack of means, public instruction at all but the secondary and higher levels– that is, instruction that concerned anyone but the children of the notables– went on largely as before, with the same personnel.

Why did Napoleon choose the name "University," rather than Ministry of Public Instruction (as it later became)? Here, as in the Civil Code, the Empire stitched together its own pastiche of policies and ideals of earlier regimes, including that of the kings. As the Church had once controlled education, it was now readmitted to that realm, if only because the imperial State could not afford to occupy it completely. Napoleon named as grand master of the University Louis de Fontanes, the moderate royalist who we recall had collaborated with Lucien Bonaparte on the *Parallel* in 1800. Fontanes was a devout Catholic who lobbied for Church schools and episcopal influence. A bishop was appointed chancellor under him, and the reactionary religious philosopher Bonald was placed on the University Council. Second, Catholic "free schools"—autonomous institutions, only nominally in the University (they were run by religious teaching orders)—were permitted to offer competing schools to the State-run *lycées*. Third, religion played a role in some of the content imparted to students—notably the famous (or infamous) imperial catechism, wrung out of resistant bishops by an insistent emperor. It taught "the duties of Christians to Napoleon the First, our emperor [to whom we owe] love, respect, obedience, loyalty, military service, taxes collected for the conservation and defense of the empire and the throne; we also owe fervent prayers for the health and prosperity—spiritual and temporal— of the State."

In light of this, it is little wonder that many historians have concluded that Napoleon ordained a kind of revived clericalization of French education.[43] Yet that finding may be hasty, for in the last analysis, the word "University" may be seen as Catholic window dressing covering a reality that was far more secular than the Church liked. That the University formally enjoined the inculcation of "the precepts of the Catholic religion" in students did not, of itself, make it counterrevolutionary, or for that matter even so very different from revolutionary education projects that called for the aggressive teaching of deism and morality. True, it meant that for a long time the curé and the bishop counted for as much as the prefect and the mayor in setting up and running most of the Empire's schools—*most*, but not *all*, and definitely not the "star" institutions that were intended to replicate the imperial elites.

The Empire's problem—here, as everywhere else—was not to have the means to enflesh its skeletal designs; it was thus obliged to lean on the millennial provider of education (the Church) for a time. In short, we would be better off saying that the University succeeded in eliminating all trace of revolutionary *anti*-Catholicism, but the Empire drifted gradually away from, not toward, any trace of clericalism in its policy of public instruction.[44] Catholic secondary schools began to lose their rating of acceptable, as the Empire went on, while those crown jewels of Napoleonic instruction, the *lycées*, were kept so free of Church influence that the more pious bourgeois families regarded them as irreligious (as well as militaristic).

What the Emperor wanted—though the University failed to achieve it, in its short life span of six or seven years—was to lay the groundwork for national education as the French have *always* liked it: State (not Church, not private) institutions, staffed by State-trained, licensed, and supervised instructors, providing public instruction that saw to the creation of Frenchmen and citizens. Among other ways in which the Empire fell short of the national model that Napoleon's words seem to set out was its reputed neglect of the education of children and women,[45] and its failure to offer free instruction. The outsized defense budgets of the Empire pressed Napoleon to try to make the *lycées* financially self-supporting, and the resulting tuition fees, despite some availability of scholarships, kept them bourgeois institutions in recruitment.

Nevertheless, the fundamental revolutionary/Napoleonic mold was retained by *all* subsequent French regimes until one in particular, the Third Republic, at great cost in both financial and political capital, finally brought into being free, lay, mandatory education in France.[46] It was thought a fine thing a minister of public instruction in Paris could look at his watch and confidently inform a visitor what topic, at that moment, was being broached by instructors to their classes *throughout France*. This was national; this was also Napoleonic.

Law

The Emperor governed a State of law, but he was not fond of the men of the law. He shared Voltaire's conviction that the proud and obstreperous caste of judges and lawyers had undermined the reformist party within the monarchy of the *ancien régime*, and had gone on to foment much of the never-ending turmoil of the Revolution. If further proof were needed of their potential for causing trouble, the role of General Moreau's defense attorneys in mounting a highly visible—and troublesome—case for their client (1804) confirmed Napoleonic prejudices.

Imperial reforms—some of them set out in the new Code of Civil Procedure (1807)—created law schools, certification, and higher standards of professionalism, especially for judges, who were appointed for life. They also permitted the legal professionals to reconstitute themselves into an order—an act that many Napoleonic associates viewed as a reactionary restoration. However, the lawyers remained shorn of the social status and the handsome fees they had once enjoyed, and, above all, they remained deprived of any independent corporate public role. Unlike the past, they were now no longer critical factors in *la politique du jour,* but the Emperor's pawns—like the bishops, teachers, prefects—in *le politique* of State creation.[47]

Criminal law, as revised in a Code of Criminal Procedure (1808) and a Penal Code (1810), had both its progressive and regressive aspects. It persevered in mandating cruel and archaic penalties (branding, cutting off of a parricide's hand before his decapitation, etc.). Yet, it permitted the magistrate leeway in fixing sentences, and—to Napoleon's discomfiture—it maintained the jury system in trials. At the time, even liberal opinion in the First Empire saw nothing too tough in the penalties meted out by the Criminal Code.[48]

GLORY'S PRICE:
CENSORSHIP, POLICE, PROPAGANDA

Bonaparte flies like lightning and strikes like thunder. He is everywhere and sees everything.

—*France As Seen from the Army of Italy* (1797)

We come to a shame on the Empire, which, unlike certain others, need not have been so; the Emperor knew better, wanted different. He was a man of strong impulse and reaction, but he also touted himself a master at self-control, claiming correctly that a true leader had to be this. But he grew less measured as time went on; the narcissism inherent in power got the better of him. The problem, as always, was not imperial annoyance at even veiled criticism, but imperial action. Restrictions on newspapers thus continued to grow during the Empire. Taxes, charges, and confiscations drove up the price of journals, to put them beyond the reach of many readers, and newspapers of vaguely objectionable views were merged with more obedient ones. Papers were arbitrarily suppressed or bought by the government or by its ministers. Yet a social consensus continued to prevail that agreed with two imperial viewpoints: "Everytime there's disagreeable news of the government, it doesn't have to be published," and newspapers ought to propagate the government's views—anything else was politics.[49]

Curiously, however, the prevailing presumption that Napoleon collapsed the journalistic sphere and completely subdued the political role of the press is wrong. The truth is more complex and subtle than we may think,[50] and one of the continuities between the Empire and preceding regimes is that newspapers managed to find ways of expressing political opinion. There were social and technological limitations to censorship; personal rivalries and contradictory agendas flared up among concerned officials and police, who in turn were far from omniscient in their oversight and judgment. Protests still got voiced, as journalists became expert at allusion and circumspection.

Thus, for example, a right-wing paper like *La Gazette nationale de France* could insinuate disapproval of the regime by printing strong criticism of the Enlightenment and the Revolution, while the left-wing *Revue Philosophique* did the reverse. Lavishing praise on 1789–91, it left to its readers to see the obvious distance the Empire had evolved from the Consulate.[51] Other times, journalists slipped in small clues that wars were not going well, or were costly in money and lives.[52] Perhaps the most famous lambasting by inference was Chateaubriand's riff on first-century Rome, published in *La Mercure de France* on July 4, 1807:

> When in the silence of humiliation, no sound is heard but the voice of the informer and the dragging chains of slavery; when all tremble before the tyrant, and it is as dangerous to incur his favor as to deserve his disgrace, the historian appears, entrusted with the vengeance of the nations. In vain does Nero flourish, Tacitus is already born. . . . Soon the author of *The Annals* will unmask all false virtues; the deified tyrant will be revealed as nothing but a mountebank, an incendiary, and a parricide.

The Emperor ordered *La Mercure* suspended for three months.

On the other hand, however, appeals to Napoleon's mercy and vanity could save newspapers that the government was set to shut down—at least until 1811, when the Empire went into crisis and a crackdown was ordered. Thereafter, only four papers were permitted in Paris, one each per department; and all were required to submit their copy to censors before publication. Now the voices of opposition were nearly entirely silenced, though even now there was slippage, as underpaid, inattentive, or bloody-minded censors let pass (for example) that French troops fled before the British in Portugal, or a French general attempted a coup d'Etat in Paris while the Emperor was in Russia.

The period from 1811 to early 1813 was the nadir, the worst suppression of freedom of the press in France until Vichy, but by late 1813–14, things shook loose again, as the regime tottered under the hammer blows of adverse military fortune, and newspapers began to report and comment on events largely as they liked.

Book publishing was another matter, for then, as now, literature was sacrosanct in France. Censorship on this preserve therefore proved a more sensitive issue—beginning, as usual, in the ambivalent mind of the Emperor. The paradox is nicely captured in a famous letter he penned to his stepson, Eugène de Beauharnais, viceroy of Italy: "I want you to suppress completely the censorship of books. That country has a narrow enough mind as it is, without straitening it more." So far, so good; this could be the proconsul of Mombello speaking. But then the Emperor adds: "Of course the publication of any work contrary to the government would be stopped." And there we have it (again): to him, writers would, should naturally use their art, influence, and freedom to support the State, and if they did not, they went against the public weal.

But what was contrary to the government? Was Germaine de Staël necessarily attacking the regime when she wrote,

> . . . the fear [Bonaparte, in 1797] inspired was caused by the singular effect of his personality on almost all who approached him. . . . [H]is character could not be defined by the words we commonly use; he was neither good nor bad, neither gentle nor cruel, in the way that are people of whom we have any knowledge. Such a being, having no fellow, could neither feel nor arouse fellow-feeling; he was more or less than a man.

Was she attacking the government when she wrote, "But the despotism of his character was stronger than his own intelligence"?[53] True, such published words would not have been permitted to circulate freely in most Continental monarchies, and still less in France of the Year II, but Napoleon wished to foster a literary renaissance, or so he said. In his actions, however, he waived off his brother Joseph's advice to manage de Staël, confirming her exile and arbitrarily ordering the suppression of her fiction (*Delphine*) and nonfiction (*On Germany*), though neither work picked up the cudgels against the Empire per se. This was an issue of vanity and pique, not politics. Fouché was right to call his patron "perhaps the most easily offended and most mistrustful man who ever lived."[54] If de Staël were not so already, she certainly became after 1810 a sworn and bitter enemy of the regime. It need not have been so.[55]

Some months after his return from Tilsit, Napoleon called for a full review of literary censorship, for he was uncomfortable with the idea that the police were carrying it out in an arbitrary and heavy-handed fashion. He himself participated in the lively debates in the Council of State, as if it were the Concordat or the Civil Code. He had originally thought that the Institute, as the prestige corps of France's leading writers and scientists, was the natural body for the oversight of book publishing, but its members "descended" too easily into squabbles and polemics—a sign of the Empire's attempt to suppress politics was that politics "returned" in any form it could.

In the end, Napoleon made censorship voluntary—writers would be trusted to submit their manuscripts for official previewing, understanding that if they did not, they ran the risk of having the published book suppressed at their own expense. The number of printers in Paris was reduced to sixty (from 157), the number of theaters to eight, in order to enhance surveillance, and censorship was handed over to a special agency rather than continuing to be confided to the police. The new officials, acting arm in arm with the police, burdened writers and took their toll on the already meager attainments of literature in the Empire. Of the twelve to nineteen works submitted to them each week, one or two were cut. The Emperor would occasionally demand to know "why people of letters 'are doing everything to dishonor the nation,'" when, of course, the truth was that the blame was largely his. Napoleon's bulletins or his pieces in *Le Moniteur* were the only writing entirely safe from interference.

The Napoleonic police and the judiciary structures of repression are regarded as infamous, and rightly so. Gendarmes, agents, and special tribunals dealt in arbitrary arrest, preventive detention, internal exile, and deportation. There were several competing police forces during the Empire, though this multiplicity did not aid their effectiveness any—to the contrary.[56] Withal, however, the worst case of repression remained one that dated back to the earliest Consulate: the deportation of 94 neo-Jacobins out of 130 falsely accused and condemned, after the rue Nicaise bombing, in 1800 (see Chapter 9). Most of the 94 men perished of disease in "the islands." A few years later, but still during the Consulate, the Haitian leader Toussaint L'Ouverture (1743–1803) died in a State prison, in part because the guards would not let him be treated.

During the Empire a few spectacular cases also drew attention, notably that of General Pierre Dupont de l'Etang, who surrendered two corps in Spain in 1808. Napoleon had him thrown in prison and wished to bring him to trial for treason, which would have ended in his execution. Fouché and Cambacérès dissuaded *le patron* from committing blatant infringements of justice, à la d'Enghien, due to imperial pique at this, the regime's first non-naval military disaster. It was not until 1812, in fact, that Dupont was disgraced and sent to prison, but not shot, as Napoleon wanted. (He ended up Louis XVIII's first minister of war, eighteen months later.)

Looking at the forest instead of obsessing over a few well-known trees, one cannot help being struck by how sparse it is. In a nation of 30 million, the number of political prisoners detained in *les prisons d'Etat* by 1814 was

2,500, of whom many were criminal enemies: spies and foreign operatives, Chouans, and brigands.[57] True, another 3,000 to 4,000 political opponents of the regime suffered internal exile—they were forced to leave their homes and dwell in a distant (but French) venue at their own expense and great inconvenience. None of this is to deny the flagrant injustice of the situation, but when one puts it in context of the era, recalling that between 300,000 and 500,000 people had been imprisoned by the Convention (of whom 50,000 were executed), it is surprisingly mild. A similar statistic might surprise those who lightly compare Napoleon with Stalin or Hitler: the budget of one branch of the French secret police in 1811 was 75,000 francs—a derisory sum, only three times the salary of one senator. One former prefect, a man whose memoirs contain their fair share of criticism of the Empire, felt that the Napoleonic police had been unfairly "slandered" in public opinion.[58] Many, like Fouché, retained more than residual traces of their revolutionary commitment, and did what they could to blunt the effect of Napoleon's occasional impulsive orders. Even a police minister like Fouché or Savary did not have the authority to send someone to political prison; only the Emperor could do that.

Then, too, the French Senate had its "commission of individual liberty" that could, and did, investigate cases of judicial injustice. This body was not nearly as busy as it could have been, nor did it ever cross swords with the Emperor, but some prisoners were released due to its activity.[59] Napoleon, for his part, would not relinquish the iniquity of arbitrary arrest, but he also did not cease being disturbed by it. In 1810 he decreed that the cases of political prisoners would be reviewed annually and each prisoner interviewed, lest gross injustices be taking place.

In sum, though the Napoleonic police were perhaps everywhere, the justice given out by the Empire was far less unjust than in the later Revolution. To call the regime a police state is to exaggerate; there was no terror, no kidnapping of political opponents, no torture, no gulag. The Empire, like the Consulate, displayed what we referred to earlier as the "liberal authoritarianism" of a "security state."

Propaganda

The Emperor was a born public relations man, eager to put out his version of everything, with nary a qualm about accuracy, only impatience to get it out faster. "We are not here to discuss public opinion," he told the Council of State, "we are here to control it. Strength is founded on opinion. What is

government? Nothing, if it does not have opinion."[60] Thus, he continued to
fire off pieces for *Le Moniteur,* something few other rulers were tempted or
qualified to do. In them, as in army bulletins, battles were always short and
decisive, the French experienced comparatively few casualties, the enemy
dissolved under hammer blows of the Grande Armée; peace was Napoleon's
goal, always just around the corner, kept at bay by the remorseless bellicosity
of the Empire's foes. Imperial policy (war aims, conscription, morale, diplomacy, etc.) was hardly touched on, but *la politique* of the Emperor's adversaries was stigmatized unmercilessly.

But it goes beyond the printed word. To a degree unique among the
politicians of his era, perhaps *any* era, Napoleon cultivated the garden of his
myths of his State and himself in all sectors. Indeed, if one constructs the
notion of "propaganda" loosely as "the collection of methods utilized by
power with a view to obtain ideological and psychological results,"[61] then the
breadth of Napoleon's motivation and grasp in managing public opinion,
is never-ending—from the printed to the spoken word, from paintings, sculpture, music, and porcelain to parades and feast days, from awards and dec-
orations to uniforms and furniture. If this section strikes the reader as old hat,
it is because the Napoleonic name has for two centuries been synonymous
with propaganda. He is reputed to be the "father of modern propaganda," the
first consciously to replace *politique* with pabulum as an instrument of governance; "It is not what is true that counts, but what people think is true."[62]
Metternich was so impressed with French publicity campaigns that he wrote
his government: "The newspapers alone are worth an army of 300,000 to
Napoleon." He criticized the Allies for regarding publicity as beneath their
dignity, thus ceding the turf to the French.[63]

Well, yes and no. In an age when mass literacy and democratic politics
were young, the demarcation between propaganda and education—particularly "education" defined as "public instruction," in the French sense—is hard
to draw. As many have noted, propaganda is not always or necessarily misleading and evil; one may stage propaganda campaigns for AIDS awareness,
for example. It is perhaps worth recalling that the word has its origins in a
Church mission started by Pope Gregory XV in 1622. Finally, even evil propaganda may attain artistry and brilliance; one thinks of Leni Riefenstahl's film
The Triumph of the Will, for example.

The point is that it may be misleading to call Napoleon a propagandist
and leave it at that, imagining one has said the last word. He was, after all, a
political figure well aware, as he put it, that "it is a large mistake to imagine
that in France you can spread [official] ideas in a clumsy fashion."[64]
Fontanes's and Lucien's *Parallel,* or Ernest d'Hauterive's 300-page remarkable

contrast of French and British foreign relations were Napoleonic propaganda, as was David's immense picture of the coronation or Gros's hardly less vast canvas of Eylau, but then several plays by Pierre Corneille were propaganda for absolute monarchy, while Rousseau's *Social Contract* and Sieyès's *What Is the Third Estate?* were propaganda for the opposition to the monarchy. The four Gospels of the New Testament are propaganda for Christianity. But if these things had an impact, it was not *only* because they were brilliant artifacts of human intelligence, but because they seemed to many people to correspond to truths, even to great truths.

Napoleon, it is said, "cleverly—very cleverly—knew how to pass himself off as a man of Providence. There is the mark of his genius."[65] The unmistakable implication is that his achievement was a victory of propaganda. This is not only wrong, it is also rather an insult to millions of contemporaries, not all of whom were *that* gullible. Many people actually thought him a genius and a man of Providence, independently of the First Consul's or the Emperor's politics of propaganda. Let us consider two grand State-driven mega-events: Robespierre's *sacre* of the Supreme Being (and by strong implication, of himself) in 1794, and Napoleon I's self-coronation. Both were lavish, fastidiously organized ceremonies that could be (and have been) called "cynical." Robespierre's did not work because the populace and the revolutionary elites were not much hooked by fabricated religion (nor, at that point, so widely enamored of his leadership); Napoleon's *sacre* drew criticism but it did work. A study as propaganda, therefore, adds little to our understanding, barring an inquiry into the historical reality behind the representation. Relativism only holds so much water. Consider Bokassa I's coronation in the Central African Empire in 1976; it was *an exact model of Napoleon's sacre* (without pope), but was not a success.

Take the very famous brace of similes, cited earlier—"Bonaparte flies like lightning and strikes like thunder." Propaganda? Of course. But we may ask, what made it potent—that it was clever writing, or that after the first Italian campaign, the words struck people as true? Consider David's portrait of Bonaparte crossing the Alps on a sleek, light gray charger in 1800. "Wrong," some say, "propaganda! He crossed the St. Bernard Pass on a mule, and he was wrapped in furs, without a flowing red cape." Not all people naïvely believe David depicted literal reality; rather they understood that there are literal and metaphorical truths. A painting of Abraham Lincoln breaking the chains of a small African-American boy does not show an actual event either, yet its non-veracity does not detract from its truth.

So while it is true that Napoleon relentlessly, and sometimes cynically, executed a policy of propaganda, he also took interesting risks, and operated often from a base of truth. Recall Gros's painting of the day after Eylau. The Emperor is shown (correctly) mounted on a magnificent steed, wearing a beautiful uniform, and surrounded by adoring figures (some, not all), yet no viewer can mistake Gros's vision of the totality and horror of war, a horror that even an emperor cannot escape. It is remarkable that Napoleon–a leader normally (apparently) comfortable with war–here shared his painter's horrified vision, to the point of rewarding him beyond what he customarily did for a painter.[66] Historians intent on proving that the Emperor never made a disinterested move admit that this painting is not triumphalist and self-aggrandizing in any usual way. It can be called propaganda, but one has not thereby said all there is to say about the complex mesh of Napoleon's feelings, intentions, and policies.[67] The pro-Napoleonic regimes also made use of propaganda, yet enjoyed markedly less success.[68]

Napoleon, it has been said, "brought nothing new to the dazzling myth of the superman–world conqueror–a common enough myth that partook of every day life [in the era]."[69] No, he brought only himself, but that reality was quite enough to suggest myth to contemporaries as fast–or nearly–as Napoleon wished. "To be truly a great man, in whatever field," the Comtesse de Rémusat writes, "you have to have genuinely *made* a part of your glory, thus showing yourself to be above the events that have caused it."[70] Regretfully, she was sure, Napoleon had done that.

NAPOLEON AS ECONOMIC ACTOR

It was in the midst of a political tempest that the principal discoveries were born; and people may well ask one day how a nation at war with Europe, sequestered by the other nations and torn by civil dissension, could yet create industry of the quality that France raised.

–Jean-Antoine Chaptal,
Minister of the Interior (1800–1804)[71]

The Emperor behaved much less despotically in the control of things than he did over persons; his despotism in the economic sphere has been exaggerated.

–Georges Lefebvre[72]

Napoleon did not trust affluence per se–a paradox in one who is commonly accorded the role of "savior" of the middle classes. If in the actual world of

warmly courted provincial notables, wealth trumped heredity, or even natural talent, *in the mind of the Emperor*, it did not. Wealth, he felt, could lead
its possessor to discount faith and patriotism, to misprize the seriousness of
national frontiers and official authority. Mobile wealth, especially, was difficult for the State to keep tabs on; preferable, therefore, were landed fortunes,
for agriculture was "the soul and the first basis of the Empire." For the same
reasons, Napoleon esteemed industry, with its factories and employees,
over banking and commerce, which depended on a handful of individuals
making deals across borders. And, of course, he famously loathed money-
lenders, currency traders, and army contractors, "the plague of the nation,"
as he called them. All of these were common politician prejudices of his day,
which neither stopped Napoleon from encouraging the accumulation of
wealth nor stopped French speculators from playing the markets.

So the Empire undoubtedly reinforced the dependence of economic
activity on the State. Many Napoleonic practices recalled the heavy hand of
previous regimes: the revival of guilds and chambers of commerce, the continuation of grain pricing and labor regulations (prohibitions against unions
and strikes), degrees of State regulation or nationalization of many businesses, from bakeries to minting and tobacco. (On the other hand, the
regime left the gigantic domain of agriculture virtually alone, except for
undertaking a land survey, a *cadastre*.[73]) However, it must also be noted that
these measures satisfied more French businessmen than they displeased, and
to attribute them to the "regimentation [that] was natural to an authoritarian government which prized public order and full employment" is mean-
spirited.[74] Not merely Corsican-born politicians prized public order and full
employment. French merchants were delighted with General Decaen's proposed expedition to India (1803), as they expected it would re-create French
trade there over and against English commerce.

We are familiar with Napoleon's reputation as "restorer of French finance,"
his success at limiting the State debt, at creating the basis for (one day) sound
money, and at laying in place long-lasting fiscal and administrative structures.
As he knew little or nothing about economic issues and language on taking
power, his acquisition of knowledge in these realms was scarcely short of phenomenal. Reading his letters to Count Mollien, his minister of the Treasury,
one is struck by Napoleon's passion for "micro-managing," even in areas like
credit, taxation, or monetary issues, where he had no training. The letters
might almost be those of Mollien to a technical subordinate in his department.[75] Regarding State credit, *l'Empereur* stayed the fiscal realist. He continued to favor indirect taxes, which could be raised without legislative
approval, refused to finance wars by borrowing, and maintained his irrational

fear of inflation and paper money. He kept large reserves ("dead funds," as he called them) on hand, and his rigorous metalism provoked stagnation in some regions, but he clung to his way, haunted by memories of the bankruptcy and ensuing political collapse of the Directory or the old regime. Never forget: this was a man who economized half of his civil list each year.[76] Little wonder that he complained, "My imagination loses its empire in finance."

Such hidebound conservatism, including low rates of State interest paid on loans and procrastination in paying off government debts, was not likely to encourage lenders. Napoleon's philosophy may seem all the more obstinate when we recall that he had at hand the financial example of Britain, whose recourse to deficit financing, paper money, and extensive international banking was financing an industrial revolution a generation ahead of anyone else's, *and* was permitting a country of twelve million people to underwrite a successful war against Europe's most powerful Empire. On the other hand, the French banking sector and the country's financial elites, after their horrific experience in the Revolution, were not ready to lash themselves to the mast of State—to invest massively in the *res publica*—as they had done for the monarchy.[77] This was a fact of life that any French politician had to live with. Laissez-faire liberalism—personified by the respected chemist Chaptal, whom Napoleon appointed minister of the interior in 1800—was formally ascribed to by *all* adepts of the French Revolution. But in the land of Colbert,* one is not surprised to find considerable "fine print" below the signatures. Thus, Chaptal, or even a renowned free-trade champion like Jean-Baptiste Say, not to mention most French politicians and entrepreneurs, simply took for granted measures of State action that would compensate for French uncompetitiveness compared to Britain. When it came to official action, the attitude of French businessmen could still be expressed by this exhortation of a cotton manufacturer in 1786: "Sire, leave us alone but protect us a lot!"[78]

Despite all the wars and the *dirigisme*, much of the economy flourished under Napoleon in France as well as Europe.[79] Having lost the eighteenth-century economic rivalry with England due to inferiority in technology, credit, and commerce that France would surely not have been able to put right, even if the Peace of Amiens had endured a greater time,[80] the Empire at least possessed the advantage of avoiding the deluge (in quantity and quality) of consumer goods flowing out of the British Midlands. A precondition

---

*The great finance minister of Louis XIV famous for his subordination of the economy to State *politique*.

was thus set for a major modulation in the history of French capitalism: the industrial boom of 1800–1810.

As stimulator of industrial development, Napoleon was far from inactive or bereft of imagination. He volubly espoused the eighteenth-century faith in science and technology, and in the spirited role of entrepreneurs—engines of human progress, he believed. (Nor was war bad for many kinds of business, by any means.) He stopped short—and here we see the persistence of underlying free-trade liberal ideas—of fostering a policy of systematic promotion and rigorous regulation, as Colbert had done under Louis XIV. It sufficed for Napoleon to try to create conditions favorable to industry. Under the Empire, due in no small part to guidance, protection, and stimulation from the top, clever French capitalists in metallurgy, textiles (mainly wool and cotton), building and luxury trades, and the chemical industry turned a profit by modernizing their technology and methods, and taking advantage of the protection offered by the Continental System against British competition.

In short, the Emperor Napoleon protected a lot. He also advised, inspired, cajoled, rewarded, gave incentives, lent money, and visited factories and related venues.[81] He pinned Legion of Honor medals on the day's leading industrialists, such as Richard-Lenoir and Oberkampf; while Delessert et al.'s invention of beet sugar (to replace imported cane sugar) went anything but unheralded. At the imperial instigation—and in large measure, to foster economic growth—the State systematically collected information and statistics,[82] handed out subsidies, passed protective tariffs, held international expositions of industry and technology, founded or abetted special museums and schools, wrote a Commercial Code (1808), and founded a Ministry of Manufacture and Commerce (under Chaptal). Then, too, it created (or revived) bodies dedicated to science, commerce, and industry—for example, chambers of commerce, chambers of arts and manufacture, the General Council of Manufacture, and the Society for the Encouragement of National Industry.[83] These semiofficial institutions were not supernumerary players on the economic stage, but occupied key roles in communicating the needs of commerce and industry to government, and vice versa. They would oversee the French industrial revolution for decades after the First Empire. Finally, far from least, the Napoleonic State acted as a client, consuming an enormous quantity of goods and services from luxury items to military materiel. The orders placed by the regime were an expression of His Majesty's ardent concern to stave off unemployment (and its consequences), stimulate prosperity, and/or jump-start an economic engine that was temporarily stalled.

The years 1800 to 1810 were effectively a kind of takeoff of the Industrial

Revolution in France, fundamentally made possible by population growth and greater rural consumption, but also by a host of factors directly related to the imperial government: extensive governmental patronage and, above all, stiff protectionist policies that completely insulated fledgling French industry against "impossible" English competition. The new industrial sector of the Empire may be seen as an inverted triangle stretching from the Upper Normandy to the Rhine, to Alsace-Lorraine, to Milan, and including Paris. Indeed, the capital may be said to have "arrived" when James Rothschild opened a branch of his investment bank here in 1812. By 1810, French industrial production was 50 percent over what it had been in the 1780s, and if it was still nothing like the level of British production (nor growing at its rate), it was yet an accomplishment that should not go unnoted—and suggests a more accurate view than the one that sees Napoleon as "uneconomic." (If the industrial boom did not extend to agriculture, that had little to do with the government, but with the long-term trends. The Revolution had contributed to French peasants' acquiring more land, but their doing so did not noticeably improve farming methods nor raise agricultural productivity.)

Was all this enough to justify Napoleon's "confidence" to Caulaincourt (1812), "It is I who created French industry"? Certainly, he gave the French Industrial Revolution a strong boost, and just as certainly, France would know future regimes that would prove far less congenial to industrial development than the First Empire. Still, the self-congratulation is an overstatement, coming from a political leader who gave priority to agriculture (but then what French head of State would not have, in this era?) and who was not as economically modern as he said he was. For one thing, he sometimes made poor economic choices: the Empire, for example, forbade the common stock company—"the juridical form most appropriate for the concentration of productive capital."[84]

What seriously threatened the Empire economically, and kept it from establishing stable structures (recall that the Bank of France and the Germinal franc did not come into their own until well after 1815), occurred, as we shall see, in the financial sector, despite the ruler's well-known tightfistedness: Napoleonic profligacy in war. By 1812 the military budget will be upsetting the general budget, notwithstanding the constant increases in both direct and indirect taxation (the latter quadrupling since 1806). The proportion of State resources devoted to the army will rise from 60 percent in 1807 to 80 percent in 1813. In 1810 the Emperor created his "special treasury," or *domaine extraordinaire*, which he alone controlled. Into it flowed the hundreds of millions of francs raked off the resources of the satellite States or paid in by countries beaten in war. It funded a large chunk of the cost of the army and the

Emperor's land grants to his nobility and his family. Indeed, these punitive levies accounted for as much as a third of imperial revenues some years, yet despite them, the regime's finances were in disarray by 1813, and grew worse thereafter.

THE CONTINENTAL SYSTEM

[T]he central fact about the Continental System [is]: it was anti-economic from the ground up, in spirit and essence.

—Paul Schroeder[85]

Napoleon's economic contribution to Continental Europe consisted, for better and for worse, of a partly colonialist/partly federative project that attempted to regulate the semisovereign States, while subjugating them to the "French continental market design" or "the uncommon market," as Geoffrey Ellis refers to it.[86] This Continental System—Napoleon much preferred the phrase to *le blocus*—started out narrowly gauged to French interest, and then became more so, as the war went badly for France after 1812. The system thus carried innumerable downsides, including all the moral ones that inevitably attend such imperial projects. Most notoriously, the European ports of the Atlantic and the Mediterranean littorals fell into ruin and never fully recovered. That said, however, these regions were doomed, in any case, as Crouzet notes, and the coup de grace administered by the Blockade was not, in strictly economic terms, necessarily a bad thing. On the contrary, by speeding up the inevitable, the Empire arguably better prepared these regions for a modern economy.

Whatever his long-range hopes or intentions for Europe, Napoleon in the moment sought not the Continent's economic integration but the salvation of one economy: imperial France's. France had suffered the most from the English blockade, including the loss of her colonies and their highly lucrative trade. Her economy was in desperate straits, and any head of State would have defended it. The Emperor's decision to go all out for the development of France along alternative (industrial, not commercial) lines was a thought-out, interesting, and defensible gamble. Keep in mind, too, that "France" now included 130 departments, amounting overall to a truly vast single market and GNP—far beyond Britain or any other great power.[87]

The Continental System also had constructive, not just aggressive and destructive consequences, although from the viewpoint of the old order, it portended disaster. Georges Lefebvre is right to say, "The struggle against France never lost its social character. . . . [T]he *Ancien Régime* aristocracy [knew] that it was doomed for certain if the Continental System was successful." Lefebvre's student, François Crouzet, for his part, considers there are "valid reasons to include the continental system as a precursor" of the European Union though saying so is very much *not* in fashion these days.[88] For one thing, it permitted the implantation of French industry and technology, and it restored France to some of the continental economic dominance that she had lost to Britain. It also bore certain positive consequence for French allies and satellites, both in industrial development and in the bringing down of old barriers. Thus, for example, the Russian textile industry grew from 2,687 factories in 1806 to 3,911 in 1814; a single market was created in the kingdom of Italy[89] and within the inner Empire; everywhere large measures of rationalization and State-driven economic stimulus occurred; new regions (e.g., the Rhine and the Rhône valleys) and new sectors (e.g., textiles) flourished, as trade got rerouted to the French and European hinterland, instead of directed to the coasts and beyond the seas. Finally, perhaps most noticeable, a sense of continental solidarity arose, largely in opposition to Britain, as "Europeans" became conscious for the first time of their economies existing in some sort of whole.[90]

Could the system have become a true economic community? The technological, especially transport, conditions of the era would not have permitted a real Continent-wide integration. Europe remained a juxtaposition of sovereign states, including small ones (albeit many fewer), each with its own tariff barriers—means of raising its rulers' revenues. Above all, time was lacking. But in the brief years the system was seriously applied (1808–12), it did bring about something new: the imposition on most of Europe of a single economic policy. Despite tariff barriers and the difficulties of land travel, the system knitted relations between different regions that had been isolated by the Blockade. Tenacious linkages were established, for example, between northern France and Belgium, Lorraine and the Saar, Switzerland and Alsace. Even a communist historian (Tarlé) writes that despite French misrule, the economic unity of the Continent progressed between 1806 and 1814.

Might the system have evolved to become something closer to an economic union? No one can say for sure, though advisors to Napoleon like Coquebert de Montbret elaborated projects to create a tariff zone over all of French-dominated Europe. The system enjoyed no broad consensus among European elites. There were many interested, as well as many disgusted parties. Might the latter have been brought round, as they saw the success of industrial development in France, where the cotton industry laid the basis for the nineteenth-century industrialization of Europe? Then, too, how would a victorious issue from the war have affected opinion? As Crouzet notes, if Napoleon had returned victorious from Moscow, England's situation would have been desperate.

In sum, the Continental System simultaneously wore many identities and may convincingly be portrayed, depending on the viewer's argument, as a supreme act of aggression against the Continent (Schroeder); a mere pretext (Driault) or a solid reason (Sorel) for French imperialist designs; a defensible kind of Monroe Doctrine of Europe (Schmitt); a traditional French retaliation at British commercial and industrial competition (Tulard); a design for a French industrial takeoff that might have succeeded (Dunan); a classic case of bourgeois economic exploitation (Tarlé); an outgrowth of earlier policies, yet a novelty, both backward-looking and forward-moving (Bergeron).[91]

However, to conclude that the Continental System was *inherently* failure-prone in its economic dimension, due to the sheer fact of the French presence, is unpersuasive; one might as well argue that the British colonial empire was uneconomic because it was maintained (ultimately) by force. One may fault the Emperor for not making up his mind whether the system was finally economic or military, but in each domain it scored successes as well as failures. Early-nineteenth-century capitalism was an irrepressibly dynamic affair that proved profoundly adaptive and resilient, both under British and French hegemony. The latter has indeed been analyzed (by Tarlé and Lefebvre) as a form of capitalist domination unlike, say, twentieth-century communism, which simply overwhelmed and strangled nascent tsarist industrialism.

The Continental System did not fail for economic—or even political—reasons; it was overthrown militarily from outside. Thus, its economic (as its political) fate cannot be known.

THE FEEL OF THE EMPIRE

The gold light, the marble, and the massed battle flags made an image of Napoleonic glory that has always helped me understand the side of Stendhal that is least rational. If brief exposure to the glories of the Empire, a hundred years later, could so dazzle me, I find it easy to pardon the effect upon a lieutenant of dragoons eighteen years old, riding in the midst of the Sixth Light Dragoons, uniforms bottle-green, red west-coat, white breeches, helmet with crest, horsetail, and red cockade.

–A. J. Liebling, on seeing Napoleon's tomb

Only the painters could make [the uniforms] as magnificent as Napoleon wanted them to be.

–Timothy Wilson-Smith[92]

If we could live in the French capital for a fortnight at the end of 1807, how would things have seemed different from a fortnight passed there in the middle or late 1790s? We would find many fewer newspapers, pamphlets, and posters; nearly no illegal assemblies and demonstrations; fewer theaters and printers, no demagogues and few enough speechifyin' politicians. On the other hand, we would see innumerable soldiers, priests, and functionaries; many more active churches, more schools, museums, and *many* more public works. The city would no longer be the decayed wreck it had become in the Revolution, especially the churches and the façades of public buildings. The economic good times after 1806 gave Paris an industrial boom. The Parisian population was surging (from 550,000 in 1810 to 715,000 in 1814), the feel of the city was imperial and cosmopolitan. There would be a sense that Paris, for the first time really, was the center of the civilized world, not just of France–the capital of the greatest empire since Charlemagne, the self-proclaimed rival of ancient Rome, "the envy of the nations." "Empire style," we would know, was the rage in other capitals. There would be *many* foreigners walking around, importantly and admiringly. Had not the greatest writer of the age, Goethe, just met *l'Empereur* at Weimar and talked of Caesar with him? The *gloire* and the pride of Parisians–the sheer arrogance of some–might well strike us as palpable, and the Emperor more talked about and admired than any head of State in Europe since Louis XIV.

Things, in sum, would seem inestimably brighter. David, the great painter, noted, "It seemed to me on my return [from Italy] that I had just had a cataract operation."

Brighter, and also clearer, less complicated and ambiguous. The mood would strike us as infinitely less charged with anxiety and partisan hatreds; less concern, too, about politics, liberty, equality, bread, and foreign invasion, and even (for now) about army recruitment and war casualties. As the "national" had replaced "the political," so the "imperial" was now replacing "national." We would see a few leading lights of the old nobility appearing at salons, and taking positions of importance in the government. Some of their sons were auditors in the newly created and very prestigious Cour des Comptes. We would have less chance of intersecting with a public holiday than if we had visited Paris in 1795, for there were fewer of them, but if we did, the holiday would not be commemorative of the Revolution. The Revolution, indeed, might seem distant to us, though far from gone. Many of the prefects and officers we might see on their way to making reports to a minister would be former Jacobins now stationed in distant departments in southern Italy, central Germany, or Poland. Shrewd observers might even smile to themselves, "The capital, like the Empire itself, had a Jacobin core."[93]

We would sense that Parisians felt the Empire was the accomplishment of the Revolution, of its civilizing mission, that it had brought French reason, methods, and enlightenment to a backward and resistant Europe. The Republic would feel gone—at least until we looked at the change in our pocket and saw the "La République française" inscribed on it. More books would be available to buy, but fewer titles in politics and history. The subjects of the capital might strike us as a far more malleable people than the citizenry of the Revolution had been, a people of greater pride, vanity, and ambition, but also far greater passivity; they would perhaps seem more leadable, if no more inspireable, more "saveable" and responsive, but less active, perhaps possessed of fewer interior faculties of self-doubt and ambivalence.

The regime's slide ever deeper into autocracy occurred in obvious and subtle ways. Following Tilsit, the Tribunate, despite its supine acquiescence with imperial wishes, underwent abolition. It struck the Emperor as a pointless institution, but also a pretentious one in its democratic airs about representing "the sovereign people." Few voices protested the Tribunate's departure from the scene. To show he had nothing personal against the tribunes themselves, Napoleon offered most of them postings to other State structures. The regime was now unicameral, the Corps Législatif taking over both functions of discussing and voting normal legislation. In any case, it mattered less and less, for governmental and administrative regulations, more than voted laws, increasingly did the Empire's business.[94]

What has thus been a Roman-style dictatorship of public safety has now become a democratic variation on hereditary monarchy. The images of Napoleon in imperial habits that adorned official offices offered two representations: a more natural-looking human being, heir of the Republic, à la Caesar, and an idealized, icon-style restorer of the West, like Charlemagne (albeit beardless—that would have been de trop in this neoclassical era). The continuity that made both historical references apropos, however, was this ongoing novelty of nation-talk: the man at the top ever claiming to incarnate the people. A faux pas by the Empress reveals where things stood. Receiving a delegation of legislators in 1808, Josephine—not exactly a political theorist—graciously greeted them as "representatives of the Nation." This, they might responsibly have been called in most constitutional regimes, as the Empire nominally was; in any case, it was not a major mistake. Or was it? A rectification appeared presently in *Le Moniteur*—written by the Emperor himself, on campaign in Spain—denying that Her Majesty could have said such a thing, "knowing so well, as she did," that her illustrious consort, the Emperor of the French, was the first representative of the Nation. *La Nation, c'est Napoleone,* with all the irritating faults of pronunciation and the Italianate neologisms.[95]

The nation indeed knew its place. Any contemporary middle-class Parisian who had survived the Revolution could only have been impressed by (and thankful for) the populace's retirement from the political scene—a voluntary retreat, contrary to a good deal of received opinion. For this burgher and his kind, the loss of the various freedoms (press, assembly, opinion) was dispelled, to a great degree—and for now—by a rebirth in the freedom of security and public order. In the "high" Empire, demonstrations and riots were extremely rare. Conspiracy tended to be (in the words of a historian) "burlesque," a thing of the past. One is reduced to seeking popular dissent in occasional remarks, placards, and rumor. Historian-critics of Napoleon strain to posit a tension between "the nation" and "the Emperor," but the distinction holds little water. The great majority of *le peuple* were fervent fans of *l'Empereur,* in whom they saw a justiciar and a champion, the leader who assured (more or less) bread and jobs.[96]

And who also assured *faste*: show, spectacle. In the same way as it replaced sans-culottes and *Conventionnels* with notables, functionaries, and soldiers, the Empire replaced mass political action with parades, reviews, corteges, vernissages, collections, and above all, uniforms. Marshal Ney, the Duc d'Elchingen, spent 12,000 francs apiece on his dress uniforms. This ostentation may have sniffed of the parvenu to Prince Metternich, but for many people, and not just the lower classes (and not just the French), "the fetishism of tight breeches and swaying plumes and silken jackets, the obsessive display of flags and standards, a stiff breeze blowing everywhere, the tonality of scarlet and gold—is not a romantic version of an uglier reality. It is a real transcription of a mutual willed romance—Napoleon's and French society's."[97]

Yet paradoxically, the reality of the Empire was not *military* rule, such as Frederick the Great's Prussia knew. No more than the Consulate did the Empire depend mainly on raw armed force to hold it all together, nor were soldiers—save the man at the top—generally running the government. The uniform, by the way, identified more than men-at-arms. The State ordained its own choice of livery for everyone from *lycée* students and engineers to legislators and prefects, State counselors, and ministers. Uniforms were a key part of the regime's politics of symbols, of order and grandeur through convention. In a way, Napoleon was the couturier of the French Empire.

Yet underneath the panoply of colors, which David and Gros rendered brighter than they actually were in life, the deeper feel of the Empire was that of a gray hard-working civilian administration. Small wonder that statistics— from the root "State"—got a huge boost at this time. Statistical was the Empire's "political"; to govern was to count. Prefects spent a good part of their time census taking, sending to Paris the kinds of data about the community—the governed—that would obviate *la politique* in favor of scientific *dirigisme,* or so the Emperor hoped. The dominant motifs of the Napoleonic State—and increasingly the values of all levels of its society—were thus not simply hierarchy, authority, and order, but also pragmatism and efficiency. What kept it all from merging into swollen and etiolated bureaucracy was the existence of this one will that received all the information and transmitted all the orders. Napoleon I was the system's singular novelty, who kept bureaucracy and romance in the same sentence. As he himself summed it up in the twilight of his life: "The day France chose unity and concentration of power, which alone could save her, the day France coordinated her beliefs, resources, and energies, thus becoming an immense nation, and entrusted her destinies to the character, decisions, and conscience of the one man on whom she had thrust this accidental dictatorship—from that day *I* was the common cause, *I* was the state."

His Majesty's inimitable presence notwithstanding, politics in the old sense—raw, rife, rampant, and ornery—leaked out all over, and one could never be entirely certain that the old Paolist at the top wasn't a little amused. Napoleon, for example, cannot have failed to hear from Fouché, Fontanes, or Savary that the new professor of philosophy at the Sorbonne, Paul Royer-Collard, was a member of Louis XVIII's "Secret Royal Council" (dissolved by the "king" in 1806), and that his lectures occasionally reflected as much.[98] Or consider the press. Despite the reduced number of journals and the reduced readership (in part because the newspapers were more and more seen as government organs), and despite censorship, roughly a quarter of a million people still read the press—*and had opinions.* The debates over religion or the arts raging between the Institute Ideologues, who still had great prestige, and the men (like the above-named) of the University were never-ending. The literary and artistic prizes that both institutions were periodically called upon to award occasioned huge squabbles, which distracted people, and gave the illusion (but was it just that?) of a certain liberty of opinion. Napoleon was vexed by these squabbles, but he would not end them completely. For one, he needed these men's expertise, lest the imperial prizes (and therefore, the Empire) be seen as ridiculous. So the pent-up politics was allowed to overexpress itself for a time in artistic debate.[99]

Never forget, too, many of these very Napoleonic loyalists (Fouché, Regnault de Saint-Angély, Thibaudeau, etc.) who were administering the new system were "old" men, if not in age (though they were no longer young Turks), then in mentality; they were still, in many cases, the men of the Revolution, which is to say, men with politics in their souls.[100] The reactionary Fiévée, writing about this sort of mentality, noted: "I don't understand why the Revolution, which so lends itself to ridicule, is yet never held ridiculous by anybody. That proves it made a profound impression on people's spirits and that one will forever judge its power by the crimes it has engendered."[101]

Besides parades, administration, and sublimated politics, there was a fourth novel aspect of the Empire even more remarkable to contemporaries than were men in uniform, though this aspect, too, involved men in uniform, in a sense: religion. It would be difficult to overestimate the effect on French society—on the day-to-day lives of people—of the return of the Catholic Church. A full generation had appeared on the scene, acculturated by the Revolution, for whom religion was the great human nemesis. Now these people were being asked to incorporate religion into their lives; doing so cannot have been easy. True, the new state of affairs was nothing like what it had been before 1789; the Church no longer defined sociopolitical existence and, as some would have said, "lorded it over everyone," but Christianity was very definitely back in a big way after the Concordat. Local parishes now sprang into the sorts of multifaceted and absorbing lives that parishes often lead; the "cult," as religious rites were called, was offered daily, but especially on Sunday—once again the Lord's Day, with the departure of the Revolutionary calendar.

Beyond this, priests and bishops, and even monks reappeared in public, no longer in mufti but wearing clericals. There were processions of the Holy Sacrament, Te Deums were sung for many reasons (some complained, for *any* reason), the catechism was taught to the young, and alms and charity were given to the poor (the Church, indeed—and not the government—was the principal venue for welfare). Then, too, Protestants and Jews—or, rather, Protestantism and Judaism—were now accepted public entities. That was a *big* change in this land of the Eldest Daughter of the Church, this sesquimillennial Catholic France. For many people, religion was the novelty par excellence that defined the era—for better or for worse.

THE JANUS FACE OF THE *GRAND EMPIRE*

> *My dear little Marie, you are a reasoner, you are—and such an ugly trait. I have lost a whole quarter-hour trying to explain to you that what seem to you incompatible measures have, in fact, great advantages. Try to understand, the Civil Code has proven itself, and not just in France.*
>
> —Napoleon to Maria Walewska (1809)

Moving from imperial France to the *Grand Empire*, we move to a different system, a different feel, and, in key regards, a different emperor.[102] The formally constituted *Empire Français* accounted for 130 departments by 1812—representing a 64 percent increase over the eighty-three departments of France in 1789. The annexed—the French euphemism was "reunited" (*réunis*)—areas initially lay in Germany, the Low Countries, and northern Italy, duplicating the heart of Charlemagne's (Carolingian) empire, but the spurt of imperial acquisitions after 1809 gave Napoleonic France the rest of the Papal States, including Rome, the Adriatic Coast (called by its old Roman name, Illyria[103]), and further parts of Holland and northern Germany. In all, forty-four million subjects, even if "citizen" was still used.[104]

In addition, the French controlled what was unofficially but commonly referred to as the *Grand Empire* that included forty million subjects. These territories, lying beyond the inner French Empire, were governed either by princes attached to France by piano wire (e.g., the kings of Bavaria, Württemberg, and the Grand Duchy of Warsaw), or by French princes of the "house" of Bonaparte.[105] Elisa and Felix Bacciochi "reigned" as Grand Duke and Duchess of Tuscany, though in 1810 the territory was annexed to France. Joseph-Napoleon I did not stay long on the throne of Naples, but was moved to a far more troublesome Spain in 1808. His replacement was the archi-ambitious

Murats (Joachim-Napoleon I), who governed southern Italy in solipsistic solemnity—"No Bourbons or Habsburgs were so imbued with their royal prerogatives as these princes of an hour"[106]—yet simultaneously deploying elements of populism that, in the end, almost amounted to nationalism. In Holland, similarly, Louis-Napoleon I became "too Dutch" to please his emperor-brother, who deposed him in 1810 and annexed the land outright. Jérôme-Napoleon I, the king of Westphalia, and Eugène de Beauharnais, viceroy (for "King" Napoleon) in northern Italy, did "better," from their mentor's point of view, but the Emperor did not make life easy for them, either.

Thus, a defining characteristic of the *Grand Empire*—aside from its brevity (it endured only two or three years in certain regions)—was its grand shapelessness, whence the difficulty of making hard and fast generalizations about it. The Empire was not a planned or even desired accomplishment but a contingent, ad hoc congeries of conquered lands, satellites, and allies, which turned up over the course of a twelve-year journey. It thus has as many references as it has interpreters, including Napoleon himself, recalling variously the empires of Constantine, Theodosius, Justinian, and Charlemagne—not to forget that of the despotic but highly organized general-emperor Diocletian, to whose "all-pervading imperial eyes" Napoleon, in one of his franker moments, compared his own. But these allusions were mainly rhetorical, for grandeur's sake—"to adorn the untameable urge for action," as Geyl puts it[107]—not analytic or normative concepts. The prosaic truth is that the Empire got built ad hoc by opportunity and necessity and is too "amorphous, variegated and far-flung" to be generalized about as a single entity.[108]

The unforgiving dilemma that confronted *l'Empereur* and his army of kinglets, dukes, governors, and prefects was to square the imperious demands of French policy—notably, of war and fiscal extraction—with Napoleon's idealized, but still real aspirations for "his" Empire. This was a problem that never got solved, only resolved daily in countless ways that pressed Napoleonic government ever further down the path of pragmatism, rapacity, and finally—when resistance ensued—despotism. The imperial letters to the royal siblings and the vice-royal stepson exhorting them to govern "wisely and well" are too often invoked to rationalize a system that, in fact, not theory, was ruthless in ways that Napoleon would never have dared to be in France. A sanctimonious missive to Jérôme, reminiscent of scores of similar ones to other brothers and governors, tells the king of Westphalia:

> . . . only in the confidence and love of the people will your throne stand
> firmly. What is desired, above all, in Germany is that you grant to those who
> do not belong to the nobility but possess talents, an equal claim to offices, and

that all vestiges of serfdom and of barriers between the sovereign and the lowest class of the people shall be completely done away with. The benefits of the *Code Napoléon*, legal procedure in open court, the jury, these are the points by which your monarchy should be distinguished. . . . Your people must enjoy a liberty, an equality, a prosperity, unknown in the rest of Germany.

The mere existence of letters like this one used to strongly influence historians, to the point that a leading scholar of bonapartism early in the twentieth century could write: "It seems easy to forget that the medal [of imperial governance] has a dark as well as a shining face."[109] Times have changed, thanks to the work of European scholars who have studied in situ the effects of Napoleonic rule in the Empire. The pendulum has swung the other way, so today many historians consider these classic Napoleonic communiqués to be the cynical statements of a megalomaniac seeking to portray himself as an idealist.[110] "I only made you king for the sake of my system," Napoleon wrote Murat in a fit of annoyance, which strikes present-day historians as closer to the truth. In fact, in the end, the *Grand Empire* was neither great nor evil, but a mix of both.

The Emperor's general view on policy was classical, which is to say he favored rules of universal application: "Until now you have had nothing but special laws, henceforward you must have general laws. Your people has only local habits, it is necessary that it should take on national habits," he told Italian representatives. "General laws" meant the French model—not that it was French per se, but that it was a product of the Enlightenment and Revolution. "National habits" ensured that the fundamental ethno-cultural traditions of the area would be somewhat respected. The imposed administrative model never included a call for social revolution, but it certainly entailed far-reaching reform. A gruff line of the lowborn, plainspoken Marshal Lefebvre sums up the approach: "We have come to bring you Liberty and Equality," he told the residents of a small Prussian town in 1806, "but don't lose your heads about it."[111]

The kingdom of Westphalia in north-central Germany was to be a showpiece.[112] Napoleon and Jérôme were well aware that this State was the artificial creation of war and geopolitics, yet they both waxed eloquent and earnest over the importance of building a "true nation" here, by which they meant a strong government and loyal subjects. The Code Napoleon, French fiscal structures, and a prefabricated French constitution would supply the past and the traditions that Westphalians were lacking. It is hard to decide which is the more incredible or the more lamentable: Napoleonic arrogance or Napoleonic self-confidence.

It is thus all the more disconcerting to have to report that this hodgepodge of medicines and surgery without anesthesia actually did begin to take: a national sense, as the Bonapartes intended it, began to take root among Westphalia's two million subjects. What seriously inhibited it and led to popular revolt in 1809 was *not the model*—even though it prescribed French as the language of State (!) or committed the "outrage" of pioneering Jewish liberation—but rather the external factors of French greed and need: the forced conscription of many thousands of the kingdom's men into the Grande Armée, the extraction of a large percent of the country's richest resources in endowed estates for the new French nobility, the levying of unexpected taxes to support local French troops, etc. The resources and the goodwill thereby frittered away were critical to State-building, as the dismayed but obedient Jérôme was aware; probably his older brother was, too, but he answered to a different call in Paris.

The *Grand Empire* is Westphalia writ very large. Certain areas of the Low Countries, Italy, Germany, Poland, and Illyria were not forced to swallow the whole package of French reforms—and indeed, in certain regions Napoleon openly favored the old regime arrangements to some degree, if only in order to get his hands on what he needed more quickly. But if no country escaped exploitation, none entirely escaped some reform, either. When war returned in 1809 and Napoleon's needs for soldiers, subsidies, and supplies became more imperious, he felt obliged to bully and threaten his vassal kings and prefects, who in turn bullied the populations under them. As resistance mounted to French exactions, their anointed authorities were punished and repressed (also bribed and played off local elites); and if a prefect or a king hesitated or remonstrated too much, he was stripped of office, as was King Louis-Napoleon I of Holland. Repression surely disillusioned many of the repressers, as well as virtually all of their victims, about French ideals. The Emperor oversaw, virtually micro-managed, everything. The kings, governors, and prefects represented *him*.

A spoils system worthy of ancient warrior kings thus went hand in hand with a thoroughly modern administration.[113] In the "Janus face" of exploitation and subordination versus innovation and progress,[114] the vile visage became the more common and drained off most of the remaining pockets of French welcome, although in many regions a stubborn stratum of pro-French bourgeois opinion and collaboration (whether by self-interest or liberal ideology) clung to the power and influence that the Empire had confided to it. On the other hand, if serious social and cultural resentment smoldered through the *Grand Empire,* it rarely flamed up; full-dress rebellion occurred only under special conditions in Calabria, Spain, and the Tyrol.[115]

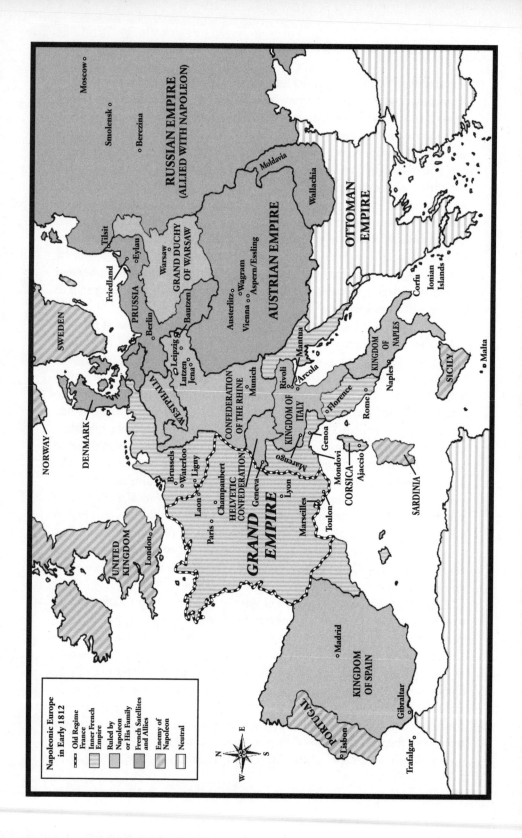

Napoleonic Europe
in Early 1812

- ▨ Old Regime
   France
- ▨ Inner French
   Empire
- ▨ Ruled by
   Napoleon
   or His Family
- ▨ French Satellites
   and Allies
- ▨ Enemy of
   Napoleon
- ☐ Neutral

RUSSIAN EMPIRE
(ALLIED WITH NAPOLEON)

Moscow ○

Smolensk ○

○ Berezina

Moldavia

Wallachia

OTTOMAN
EMPIRE

Corfu ○

Ionian
Islands

○ Malta

SICILY

Tilsit

○ Eylau

Friedland

Warsaw ○
GRAND DUCHY
OF WARSAW

PRUSSIA

Berlin ○

Bautzen ○
Leipzig ○
○ Jena
Lützen ○

WESTPHALIA

SWEDEN

NORWAY

DENMARK

Austerlitz ○
○ Wagram
Vienna ○ ○ Aspern/Essling

AUSTRIAN EMPIRE

Mantua

Munich ○

CONFEDERATION
OF THE RHINE

Rivoli ○
○ Arcola

KINGDOM OF
ITALY

Florence ○

Rome ○

Naples ○

KINGDOM
OF
NAPLES

UNITED
KINGDOM

London ○

Brussels ○
Waterloo ○
○ Ligny
Laon ○
Champaubert
Paris ○
HELVETIC
CONFEDERATION
Geneva ○

GRAND
EMPIRE

Lyon ○

Marengo ○

Genoa ○
Mondovi ○
Ajaccio ○

CORSICA

SARDINIA

Marseilles ○
Toulon ○

Madrid ○

KINGDOM
OF SPAIN

Gibraltar

PORTUGAL

Lisbon ○

Trafalgar ○

N
W ● E
S

True, the French lost nearly all of the goodwill and enthusiasm of their subject populations, but the surprise would be if they had not. Empire-building and modernization rarely proceed on the goodwill and enthusiasm of subject populations, or even (usually) on consensus about empire-building in the home country.

Nor did French loss of goodwill erase all benefits of "French cultural imperialism."[116] This was particularly so in areas (e.g., Belgium, the Rhenish left bank) that had been occupied since the 1790s, but it also held for more distant and recent acquisitions, like Illyria and Dalmatia. The French presence tended to flush out the old regime.[117] As a leading Bavarian jurist warned his king, if the Civil Code were imported from France, it would start a process that would end by dismantling the absolute monarchy. The code was not imported.[118] This is why even in bellicose powers like Prussia, a minority of liberals stubbornly admired the French emperor right down to the end. We may go further, with Michael Broers, who notes that even the downsides, which were military recruitment, fiscal extraction, conscription, and policing, *all* helped lay the foundations for a centralized State—a difficult point to concede if our focus is only the hatefulness of the French occupation.[119] No less a critic than Germaine de Staël recognized ruefully that "the peoples [of Europe] obstinately considered [Napoleon] as the defender of their rights."[120]

So it is a puzzlement, at least by the reckoning of modern notions of rational self-interest; less so, perhaps, if one considers myth and imagination, which Napoleon Bonaparte very much seized hold of among various strata in the "reunited" territories. This is the more apparent if we consider the long-term Napoleonic legacy in the lands of both the inner and outer Empire. It is a legacy which, for particular reasons, in each case, became associated with progressive forces in the histories of nearly all the States and nations that had known the French presence. Reformist and even revolutionary causes in Italy, France, and Germany after 1815 were self-consciously "napoleonic," while the Italian Fascists, Spanish Franquists, and the German Nazis were hostile to that legacy. As for Poland, the fluttering light from the Duchy of Warsaw— shouting to the world that the previous partitions had not been definitive— illuminated all of subsequent Polish history, not only in laws and institutions, but also in the national imagination. The Polish national hymn still sings of Poles living up to "us and Napoleon."[121]

For the biographer, the impalpable question of motive always sits at the center. What did Napoleon intend with his *Grand Empire*? Some argue he had no large intentions for this or anything else. Anatole France writes:

What made him so eminently fit to dominate, was that he lived entirely in the moment, and had no concept of anything but immediate and instant reality. His genius was vast but shallow, his intellect, immense in extent, but common and vulgar, embraced humanity without rising above it. He thought what was thought by every grenadier of his army, but there was an incredible strength behind his thinking.[122]

The words have the ring of truth to them, but surely they apply to more than one empire builder. Alexander or Caesar also had no long-range plans, nor did Charlemagne bring much originality to the table, beyond then-common notions about "restoring the West" and "the Christian empire" (*restoratio imperii*). Immediately before or during an empire's creation, there is little point to inquire, "What are the builder's motives and plans?" He probably has none beyond the moment; the task itself is far too unexpected, thrilling, and large. Historically, "grand ideas" about territorial expansion grow *after the fact*—as evolving rationales and ways to improve organization or to increase the mother country's extraction. Anatole France's cryptic and convenient phrase "an incredible strength behind his [Napoleon's] thinking" is thus question begging. Might not that "incredible strength," once it was free to set itself the task, have conceived some interesting ex post facto ideas and rationales, enough to offer later academics much food for thought and many monographs?

The Emperor wrote to Jérôme (November 15, 1807): "I count more on the effects of the Code Napoleon for the extension and consolidation of your monarchy than on the results of the greatest [military] victories." Does he mean it? Manifestly not, to judge by his immediately subsequent actions, but then not to forget: these actions were very largely taken under duress that was war. Did he simply extend to Europe the (partial) abolition of the feudal regime and civil and religious equality because he strove to ensure French domination? Some plausibly think so.[123] But the question is akin to asking how much he meant the rhetoric of the army bulletins, which so inspired the coming generations of French (and other) poets. Did the words to the soldiers, as Geyl asks, "bubble up from the depth of [his] soul" or were they "the technique of an actor who is master of his craft," or yet again, were they the products "of a calculating turn of mind [that] was directed towards aims that were strictly practical"?[124] There is, of course, room for reasonable men and women to support all these positions as indeed they have for two centuries.

What seems clear is that Napoleon did not distinguish between himself and the Empire. There is something of De Gaulle in this, but "le grand Charles" was ultimately respectful of forms and institutions (notably, the

Republic), as Napoleon was not; the comparison is, therefore, more to Caesar. Caesar did not oppose the Roman Republic, he subsumed it into himself, along with his campaigns, his conquests, and his cohorts; they were instances of the expression, the playing out, of his freedom. Similarly, Napoleon "came in time to see, first France, then the formal Empire, and finally the *Grand Empire,* as extensions of himself, legitimized by the ineluctable force of his destiny."[125] In the light of this overriding identification between Napoleon and this creature, the question just posed of motive thus dissolves into problems of daily contingency (troops, money, materiel, etc.), little more.

But the identification, in turn, revealed a dynamic, a logic, of its own. The power and the glory—above all, the military glory—came to inhabit not just the Emperor's psyche but those of his supporters, of even his subjects, among all of whom grand expectation became and remained the casual unconscious case. The ambivalence that haunted Napoleon himself and his supporters—the Janus face, if we will—started to resolve itself as the myth of all-conquering hero, after Tilsit began to engulf and enslave other myths, like that of revolutionary reformer, but then, as we shall see, the ambivalence will return with still later defeats.[126]

SPAIN

Suppose an accumulation of acts, some making for survival, some for destruction, suppose even that they overlap in time, so that the spectator on the shore of history cannot be sure whether the tide is yet on the turn: still, if he is observant enough, he will record one wave which is the highest of them all, and one which marks the first failure to reach that level.

—J. M. Thompson[127]

In all the rich and fascinating detail of Napoleon's Spanish "ulcer," we should keep one thing firmly in mind. This country, since the middle of the eighteenth century and lasting to the middle of the nineteenth, was caught up in deep, inveterate social conflict that would have flared into serious collective violence regardless of external stimuli. This said, Napoleon's eruption onto the Spanish scene worsened things as surely as his legacy improved them.[128]

Recall that the Bourbon kings of Spain had early declared themselves ideological enemies of the French Revolution, only to come round into alliance with the regime that had executed their cousin Louis XVI. Lost battles and stimulated self-interest will have that effect on governments. But King Charles IV, and his chief minister, Manuel Godoy, did not make for reliable allies for so activist and exigent a leader as Napoleon Bonaparte. A war with Britain meant special dangers for the peninsular kingdom—for example, the loss of the Spanish fleet at Trafalgar; blockaded ports; separation from its vast possessions (and wealth) in the Western Hemisphere. Spain only languidly carried out the high demands of her French alliance, as it only wanly enforced the boycott against British goods. By 1806 Godoy was so eminently sick of marching to the quick-time beat of the French drum that he quietly looked into the possibility of stabbing his nominal ally in the back—that is, by attacking across the Pyrenees, should the Grande Armée come up the loser in Prussia. Well, it did not, and infinitely worse for Godoy, Napoleon discovered while in Berlin documentary proof of Spanish duplicity. Godoy then grovelingly reaffirmed the French alliance (Treaty of Fontainebleau, October 2, 1807), and sought to prove his goodwill by permitting General Junot and a French army to cross Iberia to Portugal, in order to punish that small kingdom, an ally of Britain. Junot occupied Lisbon in December 1807. It was only a matter of time until Napoleon dealt with Spain.

Godoy's treachery of 1806 only confirmed the Emperor in his tenacious contempt for what he considered a "degenerate, reactionary, and superstitious" regime—an attitude he shared with most of his subjects, and indeed even with many of his sworn enemies, the British. What, "enlightened" French leadership asked itself, was one to expect of a land of 10 million people, which employed 58,000 priests and 100,000 monks and friars, virtually all of whom hated the Enlightenment, not to mention the French and their Revolution?[129] In truth, the Godoy government was not priest-ridden or reactionary, but it was composed of men whom self-interest had corrupted. "Proof" of Napoleonic prejudices about Spain emerged presently in the country's fragmentation at the top. The Bourbon monarchy became hopelessly riven by an implacable enmity between Charles IV—a doddering fool who at times fell into insanity (and whose queen was the lover of Godoy)— and a devious Crown Prince, Ferdinand, who schemed against his parents to the point of considering having them poisoned. On March 18, 1808, a mob engineered by Ferdinand's operatives captured Godoy and turned him over to the prince, who clapped him in prison. With that, Charles IV abdicated and his son mounted the throne as Ferdinand VII. Then Charles reneged, however, and both men appealed to Napoleon for support.

One would be hard pressed to overstate Napoleon's contempt for the dramatis personae in this farce, or, honestly, even to quibble with it. Godoy was an intelligent man who had once been an enlightened reformer but had

long since lost himself in intrigue and corruption. Ferdinand had no difficulty turning popular opinion against him—hence, by extension, against
Charles IV, the queen, and the French, their nominal allies. For a time,
Napoleon toyed with the notion of allying with the prince against the
king, and even of marrying off Ferdinand (a widower) to a cousin of
Josephine's, thus pulling Spain into closer dynastic alliance with France. In
that vein, he considered giving Spain a share of Portugal. But the monu-
mental corruption, stupidity, and infidelity of the Spanish Bourbons now
thoroughly disgusted the French emperor, and the idea of lending his name
to Ferdinand disgusted him ("it was opposed to my principles, unworthy of
me").[130] So he leaned instead toward removing the Bourbons altogether; this
monarchy had outlived its day; moreover, its pro-English traditions and
predilections were a permanent threat to the French Empire's back. Better to
install one of his brothers and reform the peninsula. What clinched the matter for Napoleon—to some extent forcing his hand—was the large and unexpected uprising of the people of Madrid (and other cities), on *Dos Mayo* (May
2), protesting the presence of French troops and the removal of the "beloved"
Prince Ferdinand, who had managed to portray himself to the population as
"the longed-for one."

Meeting with the lot of them in Bayonne (France), Napoleon graced the
Bourbons with such a withering blast of insults and threats that they wilted:
the new king (Ferdinand VII) abdicated, while his father (Charles IV) signed
over his own rights to Napoleon. In their place, the Emperor installed a wary
Joseph, Louis having refused the Spanish crown because he was too attached
to his Dutch subjects. Even Vice-Elector Talleyrand overcame his distaste for
the Emperor's aggressive policies and justified this action, on behalf of the
traditions and glory of "the House of France," as he quaintly put it.[131]

To replace the sitting dynasty—the Borbón-Parma, no less—of a major
European country with its own nominal ally was an unprecedented act, the
sort of "revolutionary" initiative that hopelessly compromised what nascent
reputation for moderation the Emperor might have been winning in the eyes
of his fellow monarchs. It was also a serious misjudgment of the Spanish, for
if the government recognized the princes' abdications and Joseph's nomination, the people did not. The *Dos Mayo* should have been a sign to
Napoleon of things to come, but in his mind it was "a simple" matter of acting firmly, as he had done in the French Vendée, a no-less priest-ridden and
"backward" area. The Spanish people would thank him one day, he believed,
their grandchildren would see him as the regenerator of their *patrie*. In the
meantime there was a treasure trove of soldiers, lands, and taxes to be
extracted. In sum, it was not a difficult decision, even if an utterly fateful one.

Murat's troops restored order by the evening of May 2, and *Don José Primero,* an enlightened and sensitive man, made sincere efforts to win over hearts and minds. The constitution imposed by the French at Bayonne was somewhat respectful of local traditions—for example, it did not dispossess the Church or abolish religious orders, although it did overthrow the Inquisition, which was still powerful in Spain. Yet popular opposition grew, and in July 1808 a Spanish force surrounded General Dupont's corps at Baylen, and brought him to surrender. For the first time, a French army was roundly defeated—as it happened, almost without fighting; it was Ulm reversed. Europe was awed, Napoleon was thunderstruck, and the British dispatched more troops to the peninsula. A certain General Arthur Wellesley landed at Mondego Bay in Portugal, and beat Junot at Vimeiro (August 21). The fortunes of the war then seesawed for a time before settling down to an uneasy French "victory." The main councils in Madrid continued to recognize "El Rey José," giving the French the great advantage of the formal support of the Spanish State. Murat was able to subdue much (not all) of Spain, but his 118,000 men could not be everywhere at once in a country of her size. Napoleon himself thus arrived in the peninsula, in October, at the head of 170,000 men, and crushed the Spanish at Burgos and Somosierra. Joseph reentered Madrid, from which he had been dislodged in June, and the British army beat a hasty retreat, evacuated at La Coruña by the Royal Navy (January 1809). The French emperor then hightailed it back to France—literally galloping off on his steed, his staff trailing behind him—where he had other pressing business to attend to.

The sharp Spanish resistance, backed up by English troops, however, had infuriated the Emperor, who now decided to give Spaniards a taste of the Jacobin they were convinced they saw in him. Only a clean sweep of Spain's institutions, he had come to feel, would modernize this country. Over King Joseph's protest, Napoleon imposed a new constitution that dispossessed the Church, abolished monastic orders, and imposed the Code and the Concordat on the country. After the moderate, indeed conservative, reforms that the Emperor had imposed in Westphalia and the Grand Duchy of Warsaw, this was a step back toward the apparently forgotten Revolution. It had the effect of apparently simplifying what was already a complicated social war and a combat against "the foreigners" into a religious crusade against the "Antichrist."

Still, by late 1809, due to superior French military force, the Spanish bloodletting was all but stanched; no one, even the English, considered that Spain would become anything but another Rheinbund, a Napoleonic satellite.

And yet, and yet . . . Resistance survived, often thrived, all over the kingdom—wherever the French soldiery *wasn't*, which was a great many places in
a country vaguely the size of old France. Popular revolts of priest or monk-
led peasants shouting "Dios, rey, y patria" were the backbone of the resistance; but there were also provincial juntas whose liberal bourgeois members
championed reforms even more radical than those imposed by the French.
All these forces, moreover, had complex agendas; the monk-led *guerrilleros*
were also bearers of socioeconomic hatreds at their own land-owning classes
(and against the Church for its tithes), as well as patriots outraged at the
French.[132] The *afrancesados,* as the pro-French forces were called, were, for their
part, far from wild napoleonophiles; they represented a broad gamut of opinion, most simply wishing to restore order and avoid civil war.

As 1809 ended, the French—though they did not realize it—were thus looking at continuous war to reclaim and re-reclaim Spain. Spanish obstinacy, but
mostly Spanish scale, was what defeated them. If Napoleonic France was a
large python capable of swallowing calves, then Spain was a full-grown cow
(Russia would be an elephant). No matter how many hundreds of thousands
of soldiers the Emperor poured into this trough over the next five years
(French losses here were greater than in Russia), or how many tens of thousands of *guerrilleros* they slew, the mass of the Spanish peasantry would not
accede to French domination. "The longed-for one" (Ferdinand VII), held
captive in France, remained the Spaniards' king, in their own eyes, the symbol of their national independence.

It would thus not be Napoleon's famous "realism" that failed him, nor still
less that he had succumbed to (re-)becoming a Jacobin ideologue, even if he
could play that part when it suited him. It is, rather, that Spain surprised
Europe and herself, and the only person she would not have surprised was
a certain young General Napoleone Buonaparte, who warned in 1794 that a
land war in Spain was unwinnable due to the national uprising it might cause.
But he no longer existed, at least for now.

THE WAR OF THE FIFTH COALITION:
1809

All those wars . . . , were they my choice? Were they not rather always in the
nature and force of things, in the battle between the past and the future, in that
permanent coalition of our enemies, which placed us constantly in the obligation
to fight, lest we be beaten?

—Napoleon at St. Helena

Autumn of 1808 saw the French emperor journey to Erfurt, in eastern Germany, there to colloquy, amidst ancient Persian pomp, with his "brother"
monarch, Alexander I. Napoleon the Great sat surrounded by the Tsar of All
the Russias and by his own puppet kings,[133] like some shah amidst his
satraps, recounting anecdotes that began with "When I was a second lieutenant of artillery" (a unique scene in world history). It annoyed him no end
that the tsar conducted himself as his equal, but then, the meeting was at the
French emperor's request: he needed Russian reassurance that when he
marched into Spain with his army—or anywhere else—he could depend on his
ally to support him in the east after he pulled out units of the Grande Armée.

But the degree of enthusiasm and support he hoped for was not forthcoming. Surreptitiously, Talleyrand, who had accompanied his sovereign to
Erfurt, began an elaborate treachery—some would say a "good deed"—of
secretly warning Alexander to resist Napoleon for the common good. Once
back in Paris, the ex-foreign minister would draw close to Metternich, the
Austrian ambassador, telling him that only an "intimate union" between Russia and Austria could "save what remains of Europe's independence."

Vienna, for her part, would have liked nothing better than a diplomatic
revolution that would deliver Russia to her side, for it is a comment on the
abjection of Napoleon's defeated enemies that even the apprehensive Francis I had arrived at the terrible conclusion that only war—the *ultimo ratio regni*—
would recover Austria's lost holdings in Italy and Germany and lost standing
in Europe. So the Habsburg court was a nest of hawks these days, led by the
new empress, Maria Ludovica,[134] and the new chancellor, Johann Philipp von
Stadion, but including the familiar faces of Stein (reluctantly fired by Frederick William III, under pressure from Napoleon), Pozzo di Borgo, Gentz,
Madame de Staël, and a bevy of Habsburg archdukes. The overthrow of the
Spanish Bourbons had hit Vienna almost with the force of the news of Louis
XVI's execution in 1793; it enabled Stadion finally to persuade Francis that

the French emperor would not rest until he had toppled the Habsburg as well: "He wants everything!"

Although grimly prepared to go it alone, Vienna sought allies. She turned up few; many felt called, almost none willing. Prussia secretly promised support but when the time came, proved afraid to deliver. Britain offered up minor subsidies and indicated she would send an expeditionary force to the northern coast of Europe that might drain off French troops. The power that counted most—Russia—was not yet ready to abandon her Tilsit alliance, however reluctantly she had signed (and lived) the treaty. In short, the only real coalition to be mounted in this nominal fifth war of that name was the coalition France created against unhappy Austria; it included the key German States and Italy.[135]

In her desperation and determination, Austria reached for the new and the dangerous. Having enacted far-reaching military reforms—introducing, for example, the French novelties of general (national) conscription and self-sustaining army corps—she enacted another French innovation as well: she boldly stirred the embers of German national spirit. This was an extreme gambit for an imperial, multinational monarchy rooted in divine and dynastic right, not in democracy. Nonetheless, Friedrich Schlegel's "Appeal to the German Nation" was officially diffused to the army and elsewhere, in the hopes that a war between two States might become a patriotic struggle against the French.[136]

Militarily, Austria went all out, putting arms in the hands of more soldiers than ever before in her long history of war—more, indeed, than she would again, until 1866. Her strategy, moreover, was the unusual (for her) one of *l'audace*: attacking and surprising the French simultaneously in three separate, if related, theaters of operation: in Poland, Italy, and, mainly, Germany.[137] Indeed, this would turn out to be her major mistake, doing too much too soon. If Austria had concentrated on the German front alone, she might well have won the campaign, for as usual, Napoleon, for all that he was at ease with war, was not ready for a fight just now—not with Spain smoldering in guerrilla uprisings, England unbending (if bent), and Russia proving to be a dubious ally.

The French emperor had to divide the Grande Armée, much of which was left in Spain; he set up the entity called the Army of Germany, of which he took command in April 1809. His country and soldiery grumbled. The Emperor had boasted to Roederer, "I have had only one passion, one mistress, France. I sleep with her and she has never failed me, she is prodigiously generous with her blood, her treasure. If I needed 500,000 men, she would give them me."[138] The reality, however, was that high conscription rates caused some draft riots in France, despite the fact that only two-fifths of the 250,000 men Napoleon commanded for the upcoming campaign were French, the rest being German, Italian, Dutch, and Polish soldiers. This time, again unusually, the French waited to be attacked, for doing so was the only way to trigger the defensive agreement made with the tsar at Erfurt. Alexander I duly declared war on Austria on May 5, but as he had predator wars of his own raging against Sweden and Turkey, he dispatched only a token corps to cooperate with the French in Poland.

The War of the Fifth Coalition has been called the first modern war because it was characterized by certain organizational and operational innovations that we associate with the latter nineteenth century: symmetrical conscript armies of singularly large size, arranged in organized corps, acting under decentralized commands in separate, if coordinated theaters, maneuvering along very wide fronts. It was a war of magnitude and maneuver more than before, and the decisive factor was attrition more than dramatic one- (or two-)day pitched battles. Success in the 1809 campaign was, to a great extent, the cumulative result of superiority at sequential and continuous tactical actions fought all along the Danube, as well as similar action in Poland and Italy.[139] There were tableau battles, but they were less decisive than the great engagements at Austerlitz, Jena, or Friedland.

Above all, the Austrians fought better because they had to.

In the central campaign, in Germany, Napoleon presently wrested the initiative away from Archduke Charles, outmaneuvering him and driving his army north of the Danube. After a victory at Eckmuehl (April 22), the French occupied Vienna (May 13), the Emperor not resisting the chance to take up residence (again) in the Schoenbrunn.[140] But nine days later the unthinkable happened: at Aspern and Essling, near the capital, "the god of war" suffered a sort of defeat.[141] Napoleonic bulletins blamed the rising Danube for the French withdrawal, but in fact, superior Austrian infantry tactics had repulsed their attacks all day, while the Austrians destroyed the sole bridge that the French had managed to construct across the Danube, and thus imprisoned half the French army on the island of Lobau. If the battle of Eylau had been stalemate and that of Baylen the defeat of a Napoleonic general, Aspern-Essling was the real thing: the personal defeat of Napoleon on the field. To add loss to injury, Napoleon's close comrade in arms and one of his most brilliant field commanders, the gruff old Jacobin Marshal Jean Lannes, died of wounds received in action.[142]

Things swiftly improved. In the Italian theater, Viceroy Eugène de Beauharnais snatched victory trembling from the jaws of defeat and won his stripes as a valuable field commander in his stepfather's eyes. He threw the

Austrians out of Italy, arriving in timely fashion at Napoleon's side for the final battle of the campaign, on the Danube. Wagram (July 5–6) was fought on a larger area and with larger armies than any previous Napoleonic battle. It proved to be a veritable hecatomb: French casualties totaling a stunning 37,568; Austrian, 41,750. Yet even so, Wagram was no Austerlitz or Jena for decisiveness; Archduke Charles's army kept its fight, and only diplomatic considerations led Vienna to sue for peace, for Austria's lack of military success had not persuaded Prussia to enter the war on her side.

Austrian Chancellor Stadion had been wrong in his conjecture that the French ruler was intending to overthrow the Habsburg dynasty in Austria, though *now,* in the wake of his victorious campaign, Napoleon did for a time consider forcing Francis I to abdicate in favor of one of his brothers (perhaps Archduke Charles). The Austrians, on reflection, preferred further loss of territory to the loss of their ruler, so the Corsican emperor obliged them. The Treaty of Schoenbrunn saw Austria lose Salzburg and Inn-Viertel to Bavaria, and cede parts of her western interior and coastal provinces to France. Her Polish holdings (Galicia) got divided up between the Duchy of Warsaw and Russia. Her loss of population included three and a half million of Austria's remaining sixteen million subjects. Overall, the Habsburg empire had lost over a quarter of her territory and her population in four Napoleonic wars. Finally, the Habsburg State was obliged to reduce its army to 150,000 men, declare war on England, and join the French Continental System, and shoulder a crushing war indemnity of 85 million francs. In sum, harsh but not catastrophic terms, not Prussia after Jena.

Austria thus became France's close ally, but it was a caricature of the true partnership Talleyrand had always had in mind. The post-1809 Franco-Austrian relationship was the alliance of a cruel, powerful man on a beaten, broken horse–a horse that accepts any surcease it can get from a master on whom it yearns to take revenge. In that sense, Talleyrand was correct when he wrote in his memoirs: "Each further triumph, including Wagram, was an obstacle on the path to the Emperor's consolidation [of his reign]."[143] Napoleon had missed yet another occasion–perhaps his eleventh or twelfth since taking power–to make a true peace, or at least begin a true peace process.[144]

Thus, Napoleon Bonaparte–the great domestic pacifier of fragmented Directory France–would not make the same effort of sacrifice and self-mastery at the international level, where doing so would have required him to forgo or restrain his need for a "vindictive triumph"[145] on the Spanish rebels, the Habsburgs, the English, and the pope (as we shall see). He would not significantly reduce Prussia's staggering war indemnity, though maintaining it was driving Frederick William to extreme length looking for revenge. He would not make an effort to keep Russia happy by refraining from aggrandizing the Duchy of Warsaw. The Polish puppet State received much of Galicia, and its population now counted five million, instead of three million people—a fact that only increased the likelihood that the tsar's entourage and government would eventually prevail on him to break his alliance with Napoleon. Roumiantsev, the Russian foreign minister, declared that he wished France would choose between the Russian alliance and Poland. France, as it were, did choose: she chose Poland. In the wake of Wagram, however, Russia did not yet dare to budge. As Napoleon confided to Savary: "Let's not kid ourselves; they've all made a rendezvous on my grave, but no one wants to actually be the first to go there."

In short, the hard line all the way across the diplomatic board, as the French sovereign made an "unbridled surrender to his temperament. . . . We may be sure that he understood, for he understood everything, but he looked the other way, and to speak plainly, he was unwilling."[146] What was invisible on the constantly redrawn maps of Europe, as on the obsequious miens of the sovereigns, ambassadors, and lackeys at Erfurt, was the relentlessly rising tide of resentment among Napoleon's enemies and no few of his allies.

Anger at French subjugation and French swaggering now began to fuel strong reactions—and the stronger (and stranger), perhaps, in that they drew on the French revolutionary traditions. At Essling, for example, several Austrian units appear to have actually played the Revolutionary hymn "La Marseillaise," which was no longer common even in the French army. Whether the Austrians did so as an act of provocation or because they believed it was their turn to fight a war of liberation against despotism is impossible to say, but their doing so must surely have given pause to some of the old Jacobins among French soldiers, including perhaps Lannes himself, if he heard it.[147] Then, too, the Alpine region of the Tyrol—ceded by Austria to Bavaria in 1806—erupted into a great peasant revolt in mid-1809, against the Bavarians as well as their French allies. It required six months of brutal repression to put it down, though tough old Marshal Lefebvre proved equal to the task.

Popular bitterness struck Napoleon himself, nearly literally, on October 12, in Vienna. At a military review, an eighteen-year-old youth by the name of Frederick Staps drew near to the imperial person, was arrested and discovered to be carrying a large, sharpened kitchen knife.[148] Staps was interrogated, including by the Emperor himself, who learned that the lad had intended to ask him if he was going to make further war, and if the reply had been "yes" (or if Napoleon had ignored him), then Staps was going to slay him on the spot. The Emperor offered Staps his life if he would admit he was wrong, but the young man declined: "To kill you is no crime, it is a duty." If he lived his life, he added, he would only try again to kill the warmonger whose presence was draining "Germany" of men and materiel.

Napoleon was troubled by the young man's calm and sincerity, by his implacable dedication to tyrannicide. He assigned a top French operative to interrogate Staps, and he followed the case closely. The findings further disconcerted the Emperor, for it presently emerged that Staps had been one of Napoleon's greatest admirers. At Erfurt, the lad had stood among those shouting "Vive l'Empereur!" Furthermore he was a Saxon—a citizen of a kingdom closely allied to France, which had greatly benefited materially from the French wars. But none of this mattered to Staps, any more than did French reforms and French "enlightenment"—all of which he respected. He simply wanted the French out of "Germany," as he called it, and the wars to cease. With his clear answers, his unflinching sangfroid, and his terrible innocence, Frederick Staps might have been Joan of Arc confronting Bishop Cauchon. He might have been Lucien "Brutus" Bonaparte addressing the Jacobin club of Marseille, or another Paolist son of Carlo Buonaparte.

The lad was tried and executed as a spy, not a would-be assassin, for Napoleon did not wish to publicize that he had been the object of an attempt by a "German" patriot. He inquired into how the boy had died: unrepenting was the answer. Staps died relieved that peace had finally come to his beloved homeland; he died shouting "Long live liberty! Long live Germany! Death to the tyrant!" The dead Staps's specter continued to haunt the French emperor—on this, many of Napoleon's collaborators (Rapp, Champagny, etc.) agree. He wrote to instruct Fouché that Staps was to be presented in France as a *fou* (a madman), not as a patriot. Too, Napoleon hurried along the peace of Schoenbrunn, signing the treaty on the very day (October 14) Staps died. And he drew closer to Austria—the design favored by Talleyrand. Beyond this, Napoleon grew more concerned about his own fragility; he would presently decide to divorce Josephine and take an Austrian (= German) princess in wedlock, in order to produce an heir.[149] It was a shame that Lucien Bonaparte was not around for counsel; he, more than anyone else, might have exorcised Staps's ghost from his brother's clouded mind.

If the Staps moment gave Napoleon pause, it does not justify broad generalizations about "irredentist nationalism" in the Mitteleuropa of 1809. The Austrian dissemination of Schlegel's "Appeal" did not work, for the German nationalism it hoped to mobilize did not exist broadly yet. If Fichte and

Jahn, the two nationalist writer-spokesmen living in Prussia, could have read "The Diary of a Napoleonic Foot Soldier," by a certain Jakob Walter or the letters home of Theodor August von Baldinger, they might have put down their pens in dismay.[150] The diarist is a Württemberger in Napoleon's army, and von Baldinger is an officer in the Bavarian army; both are allied with France. Both men are indifferent to the outcome of their respective campaigns (1809 and 1812); one espies no shred of "German" fellow-feeling in them, either toward Austria (in any case, Walter's opponent) or their own, or any other, German State. But then Schlegel, Fichte, and Jahn perhaps understood this, which is why they were writing consciousness-raising propaganda, not descriptions of what was.[151]

On the whole, what widespread resentment existed was not national feeling, but a stew of familiar elements: weariness with French war, taxes, and presence; some social resentment at the local nobility or notability (often allied with the French); wounded Catholic zeal in response to French religious reforms; loyalty to a regnant dynasty.[152] *Pace* Staps, there was mainly just the communitarian zeal of discrete German States (including Saxony), which rushed to Napoleon's (not Austria's) side, drooling over their anticipated gains in the "god of war's" victory. The rulers of the era, including even the Francophobic empress Maria Ludovica, disapproved of peasant uprisings (as, *of course*, of tyrannicide), and felt threatened by "popular nationalism," with its strong democratic overtones. A "friendly" uprising, such as that in the Tyrol (1809), after all, could—and did—turn against the Austrian, as easily as the Bavarian or French, overlords.[153]

At the end of the day, only Napoleon and the "Napoleonides" (his created set of family rulers) courted nation-talk and democratic uprisings with impunity; only they had the savvy and the experience with it. Louis, Jérôme, and Joseph all did so, but the champion was King Joachim I in Naples. Murat had become inebriated with his experiences in governing Poland, where he had been hailed as a national liberator, and in Spain, where he saw firsthand the power of anti-French patriotism. And so, after 1808, Murat boldly identified his and Caroline's government in Naples with the ideal of Italian self-rule, going so far as to promote not just patriots and (anticlerical) Freemasons, but even the Carbonari, a secret sect of revolutionaries who were committed to Italian unity and to self-rule.

THE POPE AND THE EMPEROR

Nemo contra Deum nissi Deus ipse.
(Who can oppose God if not God?)[154]

A unique facet of European history that distinguishes it from other Continental histories is the presence of a third factor in the familiar dialectic between governments and peoples. While in Asia or the Middle East religious institutions are fundamentally elements, not to say creatures, of the State (or they may *be* the State), in the West, a third partner emerges to thicken the mix: the so-called Church Universal, with its leadership in the city of Rome, centered in that extraordinary office that is the Supreme Pontiff, or Pope. Although popes and governors never stopped agreeing about the need for the "two swords" (temporal or secular, and religious) to work in harmony for the benefit of "all souls," the truth was, they often did not, and the long annals of the papacy and secular rulership abound with instances of savage set-tos between kings, emperors, and parliaments on the one hand, and bishops, popes, and sometimes just sincere and stubborn believing laymen like Thomas More, on the other. When a clash did occur, Rome exerted a dramatically different kind of authority from the State's power, but its authority often turned out to be no less effective than force, in the long run, because it exerted influence over the very people whom the State considered its own.

The era of good feeling between Pius VII and Napoleon Bonaparte had been intense—the pope was (and remained) profoundly impressed by this layman's qualities, and grateful to him for restoring religion to the major European theater of Church operations that was France—but short-lived.[155] Already after the coronation, Pius—or at least his College of Cardinals—was smarting over Rome's failure to extract hard gains from Napoleon in return for the priceless value of his benediction at papal hands. The gains desired were both temporal—the return of the central Italian lands called "the Legations" to papal government—and spiritual: the rescinding of the Organic Articles that permitted the French government to exercise nearly complete control over the French (or Gallican, as it was called) Church, independently of papal authority.

The French emperor felt free to ignore plangent papal plaints—because the Concordatory church in France that his regime had set up was as near to being subservient to the temporal sword as any politician could have

wished. Support of the bishops and priests for "the new Cyrus"* was virtually without fissure, extending even to such unorthodox religious institutions
as the feast (on August 15) of "Saint Napoleon"–a largely mythical martyr of
Roman times–and the use of the new imperial catechism (1806), with its all
but cringing deployment of the spiritual authority on behalf of lay power.[156]
As in other countries at war, the Empire's clergy, who enjoyed their renewed
status at the top of the pyramid of etiquette, were patriotic; their homilies and
official letters contained crusader-like accents, urging the populace to accept
conscription for the defense of "the holy cause."

None of this went down well in Rome, which never ratified the new catechism or feast day. Then, too, it need be said, Rome also never admitted the
imperial decrees that granted Protestantism or Judaism equal recognition with
Catholicism. Rome still felt it was acceptable, under certain circumstances,
to have Jewish infants baptized and taken away from their parents–notwithstanding the scandal that doing so created. Catholic resistance to Napoleon
was by no means all over noble issues in words.

But none of this would have created a break between the Church and
France. Something else was needed, and it arrived a few months later, when
Napoleon demanded of the Holy See that it close its ports to British trade–
in effect, that it enter the war on the French side. Wrongly, he imagined that
the pope hoped for an Allied victory over France. But the short and stoop-
shouldered monk-pope, with his bushy head of hair and his large, deep-set
black eyes, would not resign himself to take sides in a temporal conflict. "We
are the Vicar of a God of peace," he wrote to Napoleon, "which means peace
towards all, without distinction."[157]

The imperial position, crystallized by Talleyrand in his instructions to the
French ambassador in Rome, Cardinal Fesch, was that the pope, although
supreme in matters spiritual, was a temporal prince in Italy, and, as such was
"part of the Empire"–that is, of Charlemagne's empire, now the French
Empire.[158] The French strategy was to construct a wide definition of the
notion of the "temporal" at the expense of the "spiritual." The papal position,
on the other hand, held that certain "political" decisions–for example, acts
of war–so directly impacted upon the Holy See's spiritual role and authority as to constitute a clear threat to them, and thus permitted–indeed,
required–a properly religious response. The pope therefore ceased investing
the clerics whom Napoleon named to vacant dioceses in Italy and soon in
France. The Emperor ordered the occupation of the Papal States outside

*The Persian king who permitted the Jews to return to Palestine and rebuild their tem-
ple (538 B.C.).

Rome, and he withdrew his uncle ambassador from the papal court; any cardinal, even dependable old Uncle Fesch, after all, might be tempted to serve
two masters. He replaced him with a professional diplomat, Charles Alquier.
A regicide of the Convention and a seasoned servant of the Crown, Alquier
would surely prove dependable, no? Well, no; the unlikely happened: fewer
than two years on the new job, even Alquier had to be removed because Paris
deemed him too sympathetic to the pontiff. Pope Pius's "fiery counte-
nance, flashing eyes and vigorous words" convinced the French ambassador
that his own government would never be able to prevail in the contest that
was shaping up.[159]

The contest between pope and emperor escalated to a climax. In mid-1809
Napoleon ordered General Miollis to occupy the Eternal City. Pius would
not be intimidated into altering his position; he would not recognize
Napoleon's hegemony nor invest his bishops. Moreover, with the bull
Quum memoranda, Pius excommunicated all who had a share in his expropriation. This went far beyond what many curial cardinals thought prudent,[160]
but the pope himself was directing Church policy (in part because the
French had forced him to revoke his most effective ministers). The bull led
to Pius VII's arrest, at the hands of General Etienne Radet, acting without
official orders but imagining he was fulfilling his sovereign's wishes. (Radet
later wrote: "At the same moment I saw the Pope, I saw myself once more at
my first Communion."[161]) This sort of attitude would prove to be a problem
for Napoleon. The Emperor disapproved of Radet's act when he heard about
it, claiming that it was Cardinal Pacca, the papal secretary of state, whom he
wanted arrested, not the pope, but what was done was done. The Holy Father
was removed to the small city of Savona, in northern Italy, where he took up
comfortable residence in the local bishop's palace. In 1810 an imperial decree
ended the temporal sovereignty of the popes altogether and annexed papal
lands to France. Rome now became the Empire's "second city." (Amsterdam
was its third.)

Historically, none of this was so unusual. Emperors had been excommunicated by popes since the Middle Ages, sometimes with effect, sometimes without, and rulers struck back—usually, with effect. The pope's
predecessor (Pius VI) had died in French captivity just prior to Bonaparte's
taking power. In post-revolutionary Europe, excommunication was not
considered to pack the political wallop it once had—and the less so now, as
Pius had no means of promulgating his bull "to the city and the world." Yet
it was a rash act for the ruler of a Catholic country—the touted "restorer" of
religion—to court spiritual condemnation by the Vicar of Christ; it would be
worse if the ruler were seen as persecuting a reverent old man. The battle

shaping up was one of perception and image, but perception rooted in the reality of persecution and suffering.

Napoleon's strategy was to keep the pope under arrest until he backed down. (The absence of properly invested bishops was increasingly leading to domestic disruption, as much of the corporate religious life of some thirty dioceses ground to a halt.) French propaganda represented Pius as a political ruler fighting for land and advantage, but employing inappropriate (religious) means to do so. In this reading, it was a prosaic contest between two political leaders, not an epic clash between "the two kingdoms" (spiritual and temporal). Pius was no Thomas à Becket or Thomas More, just a clever infighter who wielded the spiritual sword for temporal ends.

On the face of it, the imperial position was far from a caricature, for Pius had indeed issued the bull only after losing his states. The pope, of course, stoutly maintained that these lands assured the Church's spiritual independence, but arguments against that familiar position were rife in the eighteenth century, and the French were by no means regarded as extremist, only as liberal and modern, in their insistence that the papacy did not need temporal holdings in order to do its good works. Nor did it help Pius's credibility that until recently Europe, including no few Roman cardinals, had been impressed by this pope's enthusiasm for Napoleon, rather than by his opposition to him.[162] If the pope were to make his point, he would have to do it differently, not via political, but by spiritual arguments—and in fact not by argument at all, but by suffering.

Napoleon would prove wrong in his casual expectation that the pope's will could be broken by sequestration. *Pio Sette* was a deeply spiritual man whose tenure in the papal office so far was reproachable—nowhere more than in his own remorse-ridden heart—for how *in*sufficiently savvy and political he had been. Pius realized that he had been a victim of his own credulity, that he had nearly given away the store to a ruler whom he mistakenly respected and trusted. Now a prisoner deprived of counselors, means, and even his own clothing, Pius hadn't the luxury of formulating a strategy; he just knew that to give in here was to betray his idea of Church and faith, and that therefore he must stand tall. It helped, in accepting the present circumstances, that he had been a monk who retained his taste for monastic simplicity, discipline, and—not least—penitence.

At Savona, the pope courteously—almost meekly—got on with Napoleon's prefect (Chabrol), expressing thanks for any service or mark of respect accorded him, and betraying no trace of anger or resentment at the ruler who persecuted him. He read the history of Pope Leo the Great, canonized for saving Rome from the "scourge of God" (Attila the Hun), and fretted over his own inadequacy by comparison with the saint. Pius's heart was considerably less serene than his behavior.[163]

As for Napoleon, the goal of his policy toward the Church evolved, as the master became ever more provoked. The Emperor retreated from his conciliatory views of the Concordat era back to the youthful views he had held in the reply to Roustam: religion as the creature of *l'Etat*. Papal institution of bishops no longer sufficed for the Emperor; now, Napoleon would remove the seat of the Church Universal to Paris. Toward this end, in 1810, he had the Holy See's archives and administration, as well as the Sacred College, brought to the French capital.

The Emperor described his goal as "merely" the realization of Louis XIV's "Gallicanism," the policy which held that the French Church must be its own compass in all but purely doctrinal matters. Stating it that way made the policy tolerable—even desirable—to the great majority of the French bishops and clergy who, remarkably, stood by Napoleon in the early years of the clash with Rome—the little they knew about it, for the topic was taboo in the controlled press—just as Louis's bishops had stood with the crown in his day.

But a handful of wise, if reluctant clerics were coming to fear that Napoleon's true goals lay closer to schism, à la Henry VIII—that is, to a reformation of the French Church, to make it completely national. The most prescient grasped that something even larger than that was at stake. Henry Tudor had been satisfied merely to head the Church in England; he did not ask to direct the Church Universal, to reduce the Servant of the Servants of God to being the servant of the English royal State. The true precedent for Napoleon's intentions was the Roman Emperor Constantine, who, in the fourth century, "christianized" pagan Rome, and, in return, dominated the popes and the Church. But what had been possible in the fourth century, in Catholicism's infancy, had long since become unthinkable with the emergence of an independent papacy. Napoleon himself, when he had recourse to the Holy See to unseat France's old regime bishops, had contributed more than anyone to enhancing papal authority. If he now tried to break it, would even the weak-minded among his bishops follow him?

BOOK IV

L'Etendard sanglant est levé

(We raise the bloody standard)

And as the smart ship grew
In stature, grace, and hue
In shadowy silent distance
grew the Iceberg too.
—Thomas Hardy,
"The Convergence
of the Twain"

XII

The Great Unraveling
(1810–1812)

> One need not trivialize life by forcing nature and destiny apart
> and placing one's misfortune apart from one's fortune.
> —Hugo von Hofmannsthal

HIGHWATER: DIVORCE, REMARRIAGE, HEIR

Nothing became Josephine's marriage to Napoleon more than the grace with which she left it. The same might be said of her imperial consort, who had resisted this moment for years. Whatever else the divorce was, whatever political agreement, it was also the sacrifice of a loving, if complicated couple on the altar of *raison d'Etat*. After the simple ceremony in the mayor's office, on the rue d'Antin thirteen years before, then the incredible *faste* of the Notre-Dame coronation, here they now sat side by side in the Tuileries on a sad December day in 1809, reading his and her prepared statements. Josephine had long seen it coming–they all had; she implicitly understood the need for Sire to sire, and thus to remarry. In return for her dignified acceptance of the inevitable, she retained Malmaison, the title of Empress, and an outsized civil list. Their friendship, annealed by this sacrifice, endured to her death.[1]

Some awkwardness naturally arose in this divorce of a "Catholic" couple. Under normal conditions, the Vatican would have complaisantly annulled the marriage, as it had done for a baker's dozen of French monarchs over the centuries (and had done for Jérôme Bonaparte in 1805). But these were not normal times, and the Emperor thought better than to request a favor of his "guest" at Savona. He turned instead to French ecclesiastical authorities, who dutifully dissolved the union.[2] Characteristically, Pius made no issue of it, although a lesser man in his desperate straits would have grasped at the smallest arrows to shoot at his tormentor. Had the pope in any way made an issue of the divorce, the quick and dirty deal that presently ensued with the House of Habsburg would not have been able to occur. (What pained the pontiff more than anything else was the subservience of French Church officials to Napoleon.)

The need for Napoleon I to produce a son and heir of his own loins was longstanding. The passing of years had not raised Joseph, Louis, Jérôme, Murat, or even Eugène in general opinion; their experience in regal and viceregal government had convinced no one, least of all their imperial sponsor, that they were the true heirs of an immortal sire, equal to the task of imposing themselves as the successor of *l'Empereur.* The case for "a womb," as His Majesty gracelessly put it, was plain. Napoleon inquired of the tsar for the hand of one of his sisters. The Romanov, left to his own devices, might have turned over Anna or Catherine to his "ally," notwithstanding that Franco-Russian relations had gone from mediocre to poor since Tilsit, but Alexander reigned over a capital profoundly at odds with its ruler in the matter of the French alliance. So St. Petersburg tergiversated, and presently the Russian imperial family married off the older of the two archduchesses to a kinsman, the Duke of Oldenburg, a prince in northwest Germany. "Disappointed suitor" was a role Napoleon was becoming familiar with in his relationship with this tsar.

Napoleon had "smelled" this outcome early on, and, desirous of countervexing the Russians for their political coyness, he had all along lent an ear to Metternich's proposal for a Habsburg match. The Emperor's counselors leaned toward a Habsburg, as it is likely Napoleon himself did, for he had seen a picture of Maria-Louise and found her attractive. By the end of January 1810, the matter was decided, to the annoyance of the tsar, who had hoped to taste the pleasure of discomfiting Napoleon. On April 2, the formal ceremony took place at Notre-Dame—it would have been fitting if Josephine had given Napoleon away—but the union between Francis I's daughter and the former Jacobin general had already been consummated.

It is difficult to overstate the significance of the marriage to "Louise," (Habsburg women usually had "Maria" as a first name, and so were called by their second name) as Napoleon called his new wife; it stupefied contemporaries as much as the coronation had done six years before. To kidnap and execute one Bourbon (Enghien), overthrow another (Spain), then proceed to marry a Habsburg, is a yarn few storytellers would dare to invent. Not only did the union contain elements of ideological pacification—a "son of the Revolution" marries the grand-niece of Marie-Antoinette, making him the "nephew" of Louis XVI—but it provided France (or seemed to do) with a steadfast ally among the great powers.*

Best or worst, depending on one's point of view, it provided the new dynasty with a successor to its peerless founder, and if this did not thereby lift them beyond all peradventure, it certainly added conspicuously to the elusive legitimacy. June 9, 1811, the baptism of the King of Rome, Napoleon-Charles,[3] was yet another acme of the French Empire and the foundation of "peace," the way Napoleon liked peace: as the triumph of his will—and in preparation for war (against Russia). In memoirs writ long after the collapse of the French Empire, Metternich assures us that already in late 1809, he believed "Napoleon had passed the limits of the possible, and I foresaw that he and his enterprises would not escape sudden ruin." Prescience after the fact is the failing among memoir writers. The truth is, the Habsburg marriage and the King of Rome were almost as much the new Austrian foreign minister's baby as the imperial couple's, and surely instilled in Prince Metternich *at the time* a sense of contributing to foundation, stability, and peace.

From late 1809 to mid-1812, Napoleon was resident in France, mainly Paris. Doubtless, the presence of his new wife, as fresh as a sprig of edelweiss in spring, with whom he got on well (especially in bed), and his child made him loath to leave. They both rejuvenated him. If the State he was constructing may be compared to a work of art—as the great Swiss historian Jakob Burckhardt says all States must be—then the coming of Marie-Louise and Napoleon-Charles finished setting in place an old regime baroque façade on a revolutionary neoclassical structure. The years 1810–11 thus saw the reinforcement of censorship and the reduction in the number of licensed newspapers and the term of the Legislative Body; it saw the removal of the revolutionary trilogy, "liberté, fraternité, egalité," from the frieze of the Hôtel de Ville, and the requirement for domestic workers to carry an employment book. Finally, it saw the annexation of Holland, resulting in a permanent break between Napoleon and Louis (Louis left the imperial scene as completely as Lucien had done[4]). The Emperor's working entourage took on a slightly different coloration now, with younger scions of the "ancient" aristocracy—Pasquier, Molé, Caulaincourt, etc.—rising to positions of power in the wake of a few older "revolutionaries" who quit the scene.[5]

*A noted Cambridge historian writes: "It was rather as if Adolph Hitler had won the Second World War and had then claimed George VI's eldest daughter as his bride. Indeed, as a bachelor, Hitler would have been less encumbered than Napoleon, who first had to divorce Josephine." Timothy Blanning, *Times Literary Supplement*, May 18, 2001, 30.

Legion among the latter was Joseph Fouché, replaced at Police by General Savary. Fouché reputedly possessed the Emperor's own (reported) self-mastery, or "phlegm," to use his word, and he was self-confident to the point of hubris. Fouché stood out from all other Napoleonic collaborators except Talleyrand for being a very independent political entity, with connections across the scale, including even among the "aristos" of the faubourg Saint-Germain. Napoleon felt that he knew Fouché for what he was, and valued him. During the crisis of the English landing in Holland (1809), Fouché had risen to the occasion better than Cambacérès, calling out the National Guard and sending off an army to deal with the enemy. Napoleon rewarded him with the dukedom of Otranto (in Italy). But then, in *echt*-Fouché fashion, he tried to assume *too much* authority (e.g., taking on Interior, at the time vacant). Later, unbeknownst to the sovereign, he extended what the British took to be a French peace feeler. This was enough for a rude dressing down and a dismissal, though as Napoleon had done with Talleyrand, he let Fouché keep his senatoriate and his title, and he gave him a new job (governor of Illyria). With the factotum Savary at Police, life was simpler; the Emperor no longer needed to maintain a spy agency to watch over his police minister, who in turn no longer spied on the Emperor. The Police Ministry, it was said, went from being an institution of State to becoming an institution of the monarch, as liberty saw itself relegated to the private, not the public sphere.

Some descry "megalomania" in Napoleon's post-1809 willingness to accept monuments in his honor that formerly he had waived off, though it might just as plausibly be said that he now believed he had proven himself worthy of marmoreal "petrification." Undeniably, the Austrian marriage aroused his taste for conspicuous consumption, for more and more of the best and the biggest, but as always, Napoleon's pursuit of public works was equally motivated by a desire to place orders and give jobs in economically difficult times. So, megalomania laced with pragmatism and parsimony.[6]

Moreover, as noted, "old regime baroque" was only the façade, not the building itself. Napoleon repeated that *he was the Revolution,* meaning that in him the Revolution retained what was essential, and if liberals quarreled with that pretension, the great majority of the French agreed. In the Champagne region of France, for example, recent research finds that the Empire enjoyed more explicit and tacit support than any regime until the Third Republic, because the regime's muscle made property owners feel safe in their new acquisitions and social acceptance, protected from a return of the old regime and, as important, from the threat represented by the growing number of hungry and unemployed workers in the towns.[7] Similarly, in the northern port cities, ravaged by the economic war between Britain and France, one would expect the commercial bourgeoisie to have turned against Napoleon, but the reverse was true: Rouen merchants stayed loyal and enthusiastic through 1812.[8]

Napoleon exclaimed at the birth of his son, "Now begins the best period of my reign," and if we do not agree, most of his subjects did. It is thus clever but perhaps superficial to say, with H. G. Wells, that Napoleon "could have been father to a new world [but] he preferred to be son-in-law to the old."[9] In the land of the bubbly or the city of Joan of Arc, at least, the Emperor guaranteed the new and the stable, and with the birth of his heir, his regime may even have convinced people that he represented "true peace, universal peace, such as can only be that of France with herself."[10]

But France at peace with herself (more or less) was not France at peace with Europe. If by late 1810, most of Spain was occupied, it was not subdued, and therein lay the problem. A handful of key marshals (who, admittedly, could not agree to work together) and a quarter of a million men could not bring the damn thing to an end, nor keep Joseph effectively and plausibly on the throne.[11] The Emperor should have gone back to Spain after the Austrian campaign, as he said he would do, but he did not. Whether labor or ardor kept him in Paris, he did not leave for Iberia. Instead he sent Masséna with 70,000 men, but "victory's tot" proved unable to dislodge Wellington from Portugal, hence to close down the base of English operations in Iberia.

Clausewitz writes: "In action our physical images and perceptions are more vivid than the impressions we gained beforehand by mature reflection. . . . We therefore run the risk of sacrificing mature reflection to first impressions." But in Spain, Napoleon's problem was the reverse: he remained prisoner to "impressions gained beforehand" about Spain, and did not heed what the past two years should have taught him. A clean victory in Spain in 1810 would have released 300,000 men for other ends, and if that might not have made a decisive difference in the 1812 campaign against "General Winter," as Napoleon put it, it might well have decided the tsar not to go to war in the first place when he did.

Nevertheless, Spain was the exception that proved a seemingly happier rule—Napoleon's rule of his Empire. Madame Mère, a.k.a. Letizia Buonaparte, famous for her sardonic wit, was asked around this time what she made of having one child as king-emperor and most of the rest as crowned heads. "It is fine," she said, "provided it lasts." The French Empire was like a wealthy patient on whom new, brilliant, and apparently successful surgery—including rhinoplasty—has been done. Only time will permit it to work. The great events of 1810–11—the Habsburg marriage and the birth of the King of Rome—seemed to provide that time. The partisans of a Franco-Austrian alliance, starting with Metternich and Talleyrand, had reason to cheer; the Comte de Lille, reason to weep; the British, to gnash their teeth; the pope, to sigh deeply; and Joseph de Maistre, the greatest of the counterrevolutionary theorists, to struggle to discern the apparent good amid all this evil.

> *Bonaparte puts it out that he is the envoy of God.*
> *Nothing is truer. He comes directly from heaven,*
> *like a thunderbolt. . . . He is a great and terrible*
> *instrument in the hands of Providence.*
> —Joseph de Maistre[12]

THE CRISIS OF 1810–1811

Since Tilsit, due in part to a run of good harvests, the Empire had been blessed with overall economic prosperity despite the British blockade. Still, it is a comment on the precariousness of what economic health meant in this era that another cyclical crisis, setting in in late 1810, catapulted everything back into question.[13] The downturn opened with monetary disorders, then moved to the commercial sector, where the collapse of French banks followed hard on those of their Anglo-Rhenish counterparts. It next hit the buoyant French industrial sector, where the problem was speculation, faltering home markets, overproduction, and unemployment.

Finally, and worst, given that agriculture amounted to 75 percent of the French GNP, a spate of sudden storms, heat, and drought decimated the crops of 1811 and 1812. Thereafter, the war returned in earnest, and with it the unexpected military catastrophes of 1812–15. Combined, it finished off any hope of pulling the Empire out of crisis; the depression flowed into the larger end that engulfed the regime at Waterloo, and the military-political disasters lead us to lose sight of the fact that the crisis of 1810–11, per se, would have been surmounted—indeed, things were already on the mend in 1812, and should thus not keep us from registering the overriding prosperity, economic development, and technological progress that took place under the Empire.

Nevertheless, the 1810–11 crisis very sorely tried Napoleonic France and Europe, even in the regions and sectors where things had prospered. The Emperor as economic crisis actor proved to be mainly a reactor. Indeed, it is noteworthy how much the normally hands-on Napoleon heeded his "liberal" advisors like Mollien, and intervened mainly to soothe the effects, not to try to alter the causes, of the problems. Thus, he engaged in extensive public works, placed heavy State orders with certain industries (not just luxury), made loans to a very few others, and distributed "Rumford soup" to the hungry. That said, he did, in Colbertist fashion, award the occasional industrial subsidy from his *domaine extraordinaire*, and he unhesitatingly controlled grain prices, something virtually any French head of State would have done in this situation, though doing so brought down on his head the brickbats of the orthodox free traders.

Mostly, though, Napoleon beefed up police surveillance, for the sporadic riot took place in the larger cities of the Empire, and menacing placards could occasionally be seen on parade.[14] Undoubtedly, the years 1812–15 saw greater resistance to renewed conscription and higher rates of military desertion, and at times it all blended into united bread and peace issues on the part of defiant citizens. Still, considering that 1810–11 was worse than any economic crisis the regime had known until now, one is struck by how little political backlash was unleashed, given the popular habits presumably ingrained by the French Revolution. In the Atlantic port of Caen, six people, including two women and a youth, were executed by firing squad in 1812 for pillaging the grain supply, yet their cause was not interpreted by people as political, and in any case, the affair remained quite local until later. Popular *tristesse* was noted by the police far more often than genuine anti-regime sentiment.

To have struck at long-term problems, Napoleon would have had to relax the Blockade and ease French economic rapacity within Europe, but while he issued the trade licenses (only to French traders) in order to make quick money, he altered nothing else in the Continental System except to tighten the quarantine against the British. In the circumstances of this recalcitrant crisis, it is possible that, recalling that war in 1805–6 had resolved the deflationary crisis in Paris, the Emperor was more ready to jump into the Russian campaign. Financial considerations certainly stiffened his unwillingness to cut Prussian reparations by much.[15]

THE BLOCKADE (II)

Following its auspicious start in 1806–8, the French commercial quarantine of Britain was losing force by 1809–10, as the Isles' industrial and financial

sectors adapted themselves to this harsh form of an old economic battle raging between the island and the largest Continental power. British production now rose over 20 percent of what it had been in 1808. Napoleon had
to decide whether to tighten his *blocus* and turn it into more of a purely military instrument, or continue the longstanding (pre-Napoleonic) policy of
draining off British specie by selling to but not buying from the Isles.

Characteristically, the Emperor sought to do both at once, though he did
not seem to have been particularly aware of any contradiction. We get no
sense from his letters that he *even entertained* the idea—so obvious to a bloodthirsty conqueror—of taking advantage of British crop failures to starve the
Isles into submission. Rather, heaven-sent economic opportunity beckoned:
the British were racked with inflation, their pound sterling was in free fall,
and French wheat farmers were eager to sell. Napoleon thus seized the
chance to make a killing—a metaphorical, not a literal, one. Similarly, the Trianon tariff (1810) permitted the importation of certain British colonial
goods, albeit at staggering duties—the so-called customs terror.[16] Thanks to
specially granted and expensive trading licenses—each one signed by the
Emperor—Napoleon permitted certain French businesses to sell to England.
Britain thus tacitly (re-)became a leading French trade partner as the Emperor
assuaged his country's economic crisis (of 1810–11) and better met his own
needs for war finance. On the one hand, it was "remarkably astute," as Georges
Lefebvre notes, but on the other, it was contradictory, for in the measure that
he permitted Anglo-French commerce, Napoleon reduced the pressure on
England and thus "destroyed his own work," as a contemporary put it.[17]

But not entirely. At the same time as he signed the licenses, Napoleon
tightened the interdiction on Anglo-Continental (neutral) commerce. By
mid-1810, with British banks in disarray, Napoleon decisively reclaimed the
offensive with the Fontainebleau decree, toughening the quarantine, whose
rigid enforcement was proclaimed in French-controlled Europe, and was
demanded of Allied Russia, Prussia, and Austria. Illegal British imports were
burned in port cities' squares, inhabitants looking on ruefully as mountains of
dearly missed sugar, coffee, tea, indigo, or textiles went up in flames before
their longing eyes. Napoleon struck again at neutral shipping, although more
deftly. Having previously (Bayonne and Rambouillet decrees, 1808) come into
conflict with the United States for seizing its commerce with England, the
Emperor this time managed, with no little help from the British themselves,
to so envenom Anglo-American relations that they erupted in war (1812).
Napoleon savored the pleasure of seeing the "great young democracy" the de
facto ally of imperial France in her war to the knife on parliamentary Britain.

The Anglo-American war is a good place to remind ourselves of two facets of this hugely consequential conflict ongoing between England and France. European perceptions of England vis-à-vis France started to change only in 1812–15, as the Anglo-French war took on a desperate finality, and harsh Napoleonic policy made it inescapably clear to neutrals that the French emperor "intended to fight it out to the last European."[18] Now the French policy began to prove harsher on everybody concerned than British maritime and naval superiority. In 1812, Napoleon came close to attaining his objective of dissolving Britain into economic and social chaos. In certain sectors, Britain's dynamic but vulnerable economy was badly mauled; there were riots, insurrections ("Luddism"), and a prime minister (Perceval) was assassinated. Britain compensated by expanding her oceanic trade and her financial dealings with non-European powers.

But France, and more especially the rest of Europe, suffered worse than Britain did from this economic war. For Napoleon and his advisors were missing two things: first, the degree to which the Continent retained its taste for, almost its dependence on, British goods. When push came to shove, many Europeans, including Napoleon's own family, were not willing to forgo coffee, spices, and dyes to suit His Majesty's policies. "Your blockade doesn't block," wrote a Swiss pro-English economist.[19] Legal and illegal trade flourished; the Empire's most respectable bankers, merchants, industrialists, and courtiers were up to their hips in fraud.

More to the point, Napoleon only adequately appreciated or understood the *nature* of Britain's superiority as a financial, commercial, and industrial giant.[20] The French saw British capitalism as a "nightmarish world of Hobbesian antagonists, colliding in pitiless struggles for advancement and mastery at home while engaged in a ruthless drive to embrace the globe in the grip of Protestant values, common law, and the English language."[21] They derided Britain as a nation of shopkeepers devoid of a sense of the public weal and dedicated to self-interest, the scene of a war of everyone on everyone.[22] Napoleon portrayed his system "as the battle of one man against a huge, British-led coalition of the greedy and the treasonous and their accomplices" (i.e., the many Europeans who dealt in contraband).[23]

Yet the British economic system simply worked better than the French did. His Majesty's Government managed a financial miracle that permitted the island to have both guns *and* butter. Britain's public credit and financial organization allowed her to keep her economy going while at the same time rushing "St. George's cavalry" (the name for British subsidies to the Allies) to nearly every scene in time to make the rescue. In sum, Adam Smith's hidden hand both kept the shop open and welded the spirit of the shopkeepers into a functioning unity. Britain will emerge from the wars of 1792–1815 all the stronger for being so shaken, as her economic performance in the nineteenth century will show. The gap between her and France will be all the greater.

By comparison, the credit system of Napoleon's empire, symbolized by the pompous but half-impotent Bank of France, was archaic; the country's conservative finances barely held up under the (admittedly extravagant) strain of war, and only survived thanks to subsidies and forced reparations inflicted on satellite or conquered powers. Even the Empire's vibrant industrial sector was not able to satisfy the Continental markets available to it in the exclusion of British trade. Basically, however, Napoleonic France lived off a conservative agrarian economy whose cautious tenants were as tired of pre-revolutionary competition as they were of revolutionary blows and changes. By the time of the Empire, they were "more intent upon liberty of acquisition than upon liberty for production, seduced by the return of traditional values that would give 'security.' [They were] eager to take a long pause."[24]

But as true as that is in the long retrospective from our day, the fact is, as Crouzet notes, that at the time, it all hung on contingencies impossible to foresee.[25] If Napoleon had returned victor from Moscow, Britain might well have folded, and then we would be making very different generalizations.

THE NAPOLEONIC DREAM:
POLITICAL ECONOMY AS NATIONAL ECONOMICS

Napoleon still regarded the State as its own end, and bourgeois society as a provider of funds, a subordinate forbidden any will of its own.

–Karl Marx[26]

By late 1813, with the war going against France and the end in sight, it became (and has remained) topical to criticize Napoleon *for everything*, including the charge that he was uneconomic. That is inaccurate and unfair. The imperial regime suffers from comparison to a brief period in the late eighteenth century—roughly, the decade of the 1780s—when France experienced something like commercial liberty, which, in turn, led to a wild ride in trade and open competition with England. Whatever may be said of this moment—and certain leading sectors of emerging French capitalism and technology were both able and willing to compete with "les Anglais"—it would yet have been a difficult gambit for the French to have kept on playing, even if war had not gripped the players. The risks and anxiety that laissez-faire entailed were deeply uncongenial to powerful elements in French industry, not to mention the problem of France's lack of coal resources. The proof: even after peace came in 1815, free trade remained the rare exception in French history until the Second Empire. For better or worse, the liberal moment was chopped off at the neck by the Revolution, which derailed the economy. The Empire, thus (to switch metaphors), may be seen as a kind of historical island of rather impressive prosperity and development pressed, from the windward, by the sudden monsoon of the Years I and II, and from the leeward, by the military disaster of post-1812. In itself, the Empire confirmed the doom of many antiquated economic institutions and habits, and heralded the dawn of credit and industrial structures that gave an entirely different economic orientation to France, and stood the country in good stead for the nineteenth century.[27]

It is true that few rulers or historical conjunctures laid a heavier hand on any era's economic life than did Napoleon and his wars on the French and European economies, but then few political leaders in *any* period fail to regard the State as its own end, or to regard the citizenry (particularly bourgeois or noble) as providers of funds. Similarly, few capitalists regard people as other than workers and consumers; and few clergymen regard them as other than souls. If political leaders rarely make attentive or informed economic actors, it is, after all, not their job to do so.

The first Emperor of the French was the head of a State very much in construction, and at war, and given his own background and inclination, and the preferences and limitations of the manufacturers, farmers, merchants, and bankers over whom he reigned, several things are worthy of remark: the Emperor was free of indenture to the era's competing grand economic theories (mercantilism, physiocracy, and laissez-faire) yet knowledgeable about them and cautiously admiring of the newest and most prestigious among them (laissez-faire). Karl Marx, a man of profound views about a great deal, is wrong in this (in the preceding epigraph): the Emperor was willing, within the narrow straits he had to sail, to encourage and allow French entrepreneurs to have wills of their own and as much freedom as many of them actually wanted under the circumstances.

Until 1803, Napoleon might well have tolerated a measure or two of commercial freedom, but with the return of the Anglo-French war and then the destruction of the French fleet at Trafalgar, the Emperor resolutely closed himself and his realms to free trade, and wagered on industrial development. What then emerged was the familiar Napoleon-chameleon or Napoleon-pragmatist, who synthesized elements of all the going economic theories in order to make France a kind of an economic success, *nevertheless*: protector of workers, peasants, and full employment; opponent of class conflict; founder of industry and credit (the franc and the bank); integrator of markets and standards; collector of customs and tariffs; war financier, etc. As military exigency tightened, especially after 1812, Napoleon took things beyond generic French State paternalism to an authoritarian imposition of powerful preconditions on the exercise of *all* economic activity, subordinating it to political objectives and military circumstances. However, at its worst, his was less invasive State war control over the economy than that of the Year II (1793–94). However, if the Consulate and the Empire were mainly wartime regimes, military priorities, though urgent, were *not necessarily structural* nor intended as permanent.

In championing a considerable degree of State authority over, and action in, the economy, Napoleon was to a large extent not being particularly Napoleonic, merely French. His State, as pedagogue, ran and lionized institutions like the Ecole Polytechnique, which turned out engineers who became paid functionaries–technician-avatars of State sovereignty, in the service of the general interest, while at the same time playing crucial roles in the private business sector. Official technocratic know-how (and arrogance) attended economic growth in France, although it did not give rise to the substitution of official norms and structures for private economic decision making. "Technocracy" was (and remains) a feature of the French economic landscape, but we should keep in mind: it was an advance over the old regime where not merely high finance but the law, the army, the Church, and government had each been the property of the nobility. The Empire at least subordinated financial administration to a *State* bureaucracy that recruited from all classes, but it ultimately left economic decision makers to make their own decisions.

We might thus reach for an oxymoron to sum up Napoleon as economic actor: "liberal protectionist."[28] Or, better, we could go with Francis Démier's preference, the "national" school of French political economy–an approach familiar throughout the subsequent century and a half, down to the contemporary era when France became part of the European Union. The French "national" economists included a rather wide variety of thinkers (Hauterive, Chaptal, etc.) who were essentially pragmatists working with the framework of one State (France), to whose economic prosperity they were devoted. They admired Adam Smith and considered themselves reconstructed free traders, but they lived, as they were well aware, in a world where Britain loomed large and needed to be rivaled, and for that, only the State sufficed. "Free" economic society must first install within the controlled "national" environment and then branch out.

What ultimately makes the Napoleonic view (dream, really) of political economy "national," in the way we have understood it in this book, was not, *pace* Démier, the geopolitical cadre of the French nation-State—for Napoleon's vision focused on the entire Continent—but the underlying vision that the Emperor shared with Jean-Baptiste Say and so many other economists of the era: the ideal of an economic development not subject to politics (*la politique*), albeit of course an expression of the political (*le politique*).

The Napoleonic economic bet was not lost, it was cut off, in early stride by military defeat. Those disasters guaranteed the Emperor the historical opposition and criticism of the orthodox free-traders. Yet the dichotomy—Napoleon vs. free trade—emerged only *after* the defeats, in the principal actors' recollections and memoirs.[29] *At the time*, many of the orthodox free-traders served the Consulate and even the Empire, and even later, their complaints were largely political, not economic—e.g., the restoration of Catholicism or the return of the old nobility, the sale of Louisiana, the failure of the regime to rebuild a fleet.[30]

To judge Napoleon's ideas about the economy only by the de facto mercantilism[31] that he was forced to pursue in a highly constricted situation and time period is to narrow unduly our view of the man. Once France herself had developed industrially behind her trade barriers—i.e., the middle of the nineteenth century—then she, too, could "kick the ladder away," and enter into a free-trade agreement with Britain. It is by no means accidental that this treaty (the Cobden-Chevalier Free Trade Agreement) occurred in 1860, during the Second French Empire, and that its imperial sponsor, Napoleon III, would invoke his uncle's views and heritage.

1812 OVERTURE

When Napoleon looked upon Europe—and he scarcely looked away these days—his gaze steadily contracted after 1807. One sees little of the imagination that built the Consular blocks or the imperial columns—even the sort that resulted in the Habsburg marriage. One sees instead a grim, relentless, and predictable severity to toughen the Continental System against England. Based on the accomplishments of the Great Consulate in France, Napoleon was assumed to have "principles" for Europe, beyond the pressing needs of confiscation and conscription. The Empire had at first received important reforms and a kind of integration, but all tuned to the interests of France; there was nothing of solidarity, and no emergent plan of parity and peace. Instead, as time went on, Napoleon became increasingly concerned *only* with confiscation and rule—and with tightening the Continental System.

In short, the French emperor's distaste for politics now embraced the foreign as well as the domestic arena; he looked on other rulers as if they were heads of factions and parties who bridled and schemed against "rightful" government, vexing its plans and troubling the peace of its head, the Emperor of the French. In governing by reaction while offering so little new vision to Europe, Napoleon resembled the other crowned heads whom he despised and towered over intellectually. Like them, he saw governing as all about rivalry, habit, and dynastic tradition. That he was infinitely better at the game of self-aggrandizement than they changed nothing except the scale.

The result of this serving up of coercion or licensed aggression where concert and leadership were wished for led to obstinacy, ingratitude, and unruliness in France's satellites and allies. This was to be expected in Spain or Prussia, perhaps, but Tilsit was to have been that great exception among Napoleonic treaties: a compact of magnanimity, which viewed the loser not as a complete dependent, but as in some senses an equal and ally. Based on later letters to the tsar, one wonders if Napoleon had not almost let himself become a dupe of his own unrequited feelings for Alexander: "Your Majesty has shown a lack of perseverance, of trust, and (if I may say) of sincerity."[32] Despite Tsar Alexander's bad (or weak) faith in his French connection, the years since 1807 might yet have redeemed the bloodletting of Eylau and Friedland. The Pont Alexandre III spanning the Seine at the Esplanade des Invalides might have been named for that tsar's eponymous great-grandfather.[33]

This said, however, let us be clear: the effort required of Napoleon to have stood by the Russian alliance on the shifting sands of Alexander's soft, sentimental, and solipsistic personality, his changeable policies and ministers,[34] and his unmet promises would have been herculean. The one consistency in Franco-Russian relations after 1807 was the unvarying pressure exerted on Alexander by the reactionaries in his midst—men and women who obstinately persisted in viewing the French ruler, against all evidence, as "organized Jacobinism." Compared to them, the reformist French party at court, led by Michael Speransky, never had a chance to pass a new legal code or a fairer law for the Jews, let alone free the serfs. A tsar was an Autocrat, to whose will Russians were said to bend without a murmur, but there was a tradition in the land of the midnight sun of doing in tsars who went too far. Alexander could point to major territorial gains won with the compliance of France: on the Danube and in Finland. Indeed, he could claim to have achieved the dreams of Peter the Great and Catherine the Great.[35] Yet, Speransky, though a personal friend of the tsar, went into exile.

Weighed against these geopolitical successes for Russia were two not inconsiderable counter-interests: first, Napoleon refused to withdraw his hand from the Duchy of Warsaw, and, as we saw, had aggrandized it in the Treaty of Schoenbrunn; second, he demanded that Russia honor her treaty obligations to implement the continental system. The former cost the tsar in his pride and in the "social fear" that convulsed his entourage, who saw Poland (or said they did) as "the source of all the venom"; the latter struck Russian commerce in its pocketbook and ruined her credit and exchange (by having to purchase French manufacture). At the end of 1810 the economy was so badly off that the tsar lifted the quarantine on neutral goods, while slapping a tariff on costly French ones. "[Alexander's] whole attitude has changed," Napoleon complained to an ally, adding that the new Russian commercial policy was "friendly to England and hostile to France; whereas once upon a time, the Tsar was the only person in Russia who backed my alliance against England."[36]

Still, as vexing as the topics of Poland and the continental system were for the tsar, they were yet foreseen in the Treaty of Tilsit, which he had signed and put to self-interested use. Napoleon was within his rights to insist on compliance. But he also did not try to manage Alexander's feelings, but, rather, snubbed him—notably, by annexing (in a French breach of the Treaty of Tilsit) the German duchy of Oldenburg, which the tsar had given to his new brother-in-law—the very prince who "bested" Napoleon by marrying the Romanov sister.[37] In short, Bonaparte and Romanov were being average, not great, in succumbing to the fear that each was getting the better of the other. The tsar's hatred for the Frenchman simply "knew no limits," as a recent Russian historian writes.[38] We now know that the tsar and his generals had been preparing for war from 1810 onwards, and were planning on taking the offensive. Napoleon indeed fired his foreign minister, Champagny, in 1811 largely because he was insufficiently attuned to Russian rearmament and troop movements near Poland.[39] Napoleon claimed Poland as his main cause—it made him seem more national—but he was more bent on beating the British by tightening the continental system into a straitjacket from the loose-fitting corset it had become. To that end, he had (re)occupied Swedish-held Pomerania, on the northern coast of eastern Germany, in early 1812, thus throwing Stockholm into Russian arms, despite the fact that its crown prince was Marshal Bernadotte.[40]

In the last analysis, however, Napoleon had less state interest pressing him to go to war than Alexander did. Russia was only slightly, not egregiously, in breach of the trade quarantine of Britain; the leakage here, as in Spain, was nowhere near worth the price of fixing it. The matter at bottom was the tiresome one of monarchical pride and vanity, of rulers imposing their will on each other: "He's making fun of me. . . . he's grown too big for his britches," wrote Napoleon to Caulaincourt, adding that the tsar had "deserted" him, for England. Neither ruler tried to avoid war but planned for it—the tsar beginning even earlier than Napoleon.[41] The Frenchman had not received the tsar as his equal in the grand disposition of Europe; but then Alexander did not deserve as much, *except for this reason*: it would have been the courageous and wise thing to do.

Finally, Napoleon might have tried to avoid war by replacing Alexander with Francis I as his "great ally." The tsar would not have dared to go to war with France, with a bellicose Habsburg at his mid-section. But "crude bullying and crude seduction"[42] were all the Frenchman ever used in dealing with the Austrian, and this had not changed when his "brother" monarch became his father-in-law. Napoleon could not bring himself to grant the oft-beaten Habsburg parity—another failure to rise to the occasion.

THE FLIGHT FORWARD

When at last, and where, will this Caesar let us be quiet? He carries us from place to place, and uses us as if we were not to be worn out, and had no sense of labor. Even our iron itself is spent by blows, and we ought to have some pity on our bucklers, and breastplates, which have been used so long. Our wounds, if nothing else, should make him see that we are mortal men whom he commands, subject to the same pains and sufferings as other human beings. The very gods themselves cannot force the winter season, or hinder the storms in their time; yet he pushes forward, as if he were not pursuing, but flying from an enemy.

—Plutarch

Napoleon made the decision to fight Russia against the exhortations of many close advisors, including his former ambassador to the tsar, Armand-Augustin de Caulaincourt.[43] In four years in St. Petersburg (1807–11), Caulaincourt had won a personal friendship with Alexander I, and felt he knew him well. At Saint-Cloud he pleaded with Napoleon for seven straight hours, deploying an unheard of candor, to get him to reconsider a war in Russia. Their dispute came down to different takes on Alexander's intentions. Napoleon doubted the tsar would even go to war, once it was clear that Prussia and Austria would march (however reluctantly) with France, but if he did, then the affair would be settled swiftly. Based on the well-known Russian military concentration and strategic aggressiveness at their western frontier, where its armies were fanned out, the Emperor was certain that tsarist strategy, were it actually to come to a fight, would be offensive. The Grande Armée then but needed to match its adversary's combativeness with its own high morale, and it would smash the Russian armies in a brilliant battle or two, in or near Poland. This, after all, is what happened in 1805 and 1807.

Caulaincourt's reply, endlessly reiterated, was that Alexander I would prove more stubborn, and that war with him would require a full-dress invasion—with all that this required and risked. Alexander had assured Caulaincourt that he fully expected to be beaten in the field, adding: "but this will bring no peace." The Spanish resistance had shown him what attrition could do, the tsar added, and he told another French diplomat (Narbonne), "I have space and time on my side. . . . [Napoleon] will have to sign the peace on the Bering Strait."[44]

Napoleon made his own gamble on a comparatively quick war. He turned out to be disastrously wrong but as Clausewitz observes, a judgment based on result alone cannot be passed off as the acme of wisdom. Many a losing bet is a plausible bet in realms martial, as in realms theological, and a miscalculation is not necessarily an absurdity. Given how rapidly Russia threw in the towel in 1805 and 1807, or Austria did in 1809—i.e., at times when a concerted military effort on their part might well have altered the outcome—it was logical to think that Alexander would negotiate after losing face in a large battle in eastern Poland.[45] The Emperor might well have concluded that Caulaincourt's opinion, while sincere, was based on what the tsar wanted the ambassador to believe—and report to his sovereign.

The French crossed the Niemen on June 24, 437,000 strong, and "the second Polish war," as Napoleonic proclamations had it, began.[46] The Grande Armée was more truly imperial in makeup this time out than it had ever been: Belgian, Dutch, German, Italian, Polish, Spanish, and Lithuanian soldiers constituted perhaps 60 percent of the whole. It was reminiscent of the Roman legions that had conquered the known world.[47] Vilna fell without a fight (June 26), and Napoleon built a base of operations there; there was reason to think a rapid victory might be at hand, but then it wasn't. The French initially outnumbered the Russian field forces by a wide margin, so the Russians—despite furious disagreements among its leading generals—withdrew.

Napoleon did not enter the campaign trim and vigorous, "heedless of privation and dismissive of well-being and creature comforts," as General Bonaparte once was. But if he struck some as "fat, sensual, and concerned with his comfort to the point of making it a major preoccupation, indifferent, and easily tired,"[48] it must be said—and notwithstanding that he was often ill or in poor health throughout the war—that he rapidly adapted to campaign form. Then, too, his opponent, General Kutuzov, was far heavier and infinitely more lethargic: merely getting him onto his horse was a half day's work for his aides-de-camp.

To their own, as well as to French surprise and disconcertment, the Russian generals continued to evade battle; they could not agree on a strategy, and their forces were usually outnumbered in most venues. (Alexander had returned to St. Petersburg in disgust and frustration.) Napoleon harangued a captured Russian general (Balachov), "Have you no shame? Since Peter the Great . . . no enemy has pierced this far into your territory. . . . You should fight, if only for regard for your Tsar's honor."[49] At Vitebsk, as at Vilna, the French emperor could only gape in astonishment at the empty spot that a Russian army had just evacuated.

Time and again, Napoleon rethought himself: Wouldn't it be best to hold at Smolensk? Why not winter here, outwait the foe? There was a limit to the humiliation any tsar could bank before his generals and his nobility turned on him. Alexander's newly signed alliance with Sweden and his peace treaty with Turkey would be producing fresh reinforcements in this theater; surely *that* would stiffen the Russian's spine. But of course, this was also an argument for going on: the six-week trek to Smolensk in unrelieved heat punctuated by torrential downpours that glued the Grande Armée in mud had diminished the French by 190,000 men—due to illness, combat, desertion, or assignment to guard communication lines. The Emperor would complain of "General Winter," but in fact "General Summer" mauled his army nearly as badly. They would not long continue to outnumber their foe. Marshal Ney and other top commanders advised the "flight forward," even if Caulaincourt still warned against it.[50]

The Russians, meanwhile, were also having no easy time of it, but were swamped in as much indecision as the French. To resolve his generals' disputes, the tsar now appointed Kutuzov, whom he loathed, as overall commander in chief, but even *he*, though he strongly believed in a "Fabian strategy"* policy (as he had used after Ulm, in 1805), was not politically able to execute it until first he made a stand. With great reluctance, Kutuzov did so, at Borodino (September 7), by which time the Russian army did in fact slightly outnumber the French, by 157,000 to 135,000.[51] Strangely—in part, perhaps, because he was ill with a kidney stone—the "God of War" showed no strategic brilliance in this battle, but relied on head-on assaults, which

---

*So-called after the Roman general Quintus Fabius Cunctator (d. 203 B.C.), known for his delaying tactics.

failed to destroy the foe. Despite stunning losses (44,000 casualties to the French 28,000), Kutuzov made good his retreat.[52]

By now, perhaps a serious defeat might not have mattered; Alexander seems to have come to grasp what was at stake and how best to defend it. The extreme had arrived, and with it, an appropriate strategy: cede ground for time. Napoleon yet stuck to his gamble that he, not Caulaincourt, had the correct assessment of the foe. Moscow fell on September 14, with Napoleon sure that victory was at hand, that "the Russians do not know the effect that the fall of their capital will have on them!"[53] The aristocracy, he "knew," would force Alexander to the bargaining table.

He was wrong; the Russian nobility had long accepted St. Petersburg as the capital of their empire, and they now joined their tsar in the great effort to throw back the foreigner. The burning of "holy" Moscow and its 295 churches was a brilliant move on the Russian part (Count Rostopchin, the Russian governor, had organized hundreds of arsonists), for the tsarist masses blamed the destruction of Muscovy's sacred city on the "godless" French.[54] The war thus took a new turn in Russia: it became, if not a national uprising—that would have terrified the ruling class—then a popular conflict that saw peasants refuse to sell goods at any price to the French. Nobles, too, shared the general sorrow: "I should like Napoleon to be drowned in the tears he has caused to be shed," said a French émigré.[55] Alexander showed a new taste for going to the people; he was, as Henri Troyat nicely puts it, prepared to go from being Emperor of Russia to being Emperor of the Russians, if that was what it took to beat his rival.

Napoleon clung to Moscow as his trump card, waiting for his foe to deal, while around him twenty thousand French horses died for want of fodder or were slaughtered (even by their riders) for food. "A grave suspicion took hold of all of us," writes Ségur, a French officer on the expedition, "had [the Russians] decided that the loss of this man was well worth the loss of their capital?"[56] Desperate to believe the Russians needed peace, Napoleon dispatched envoy after envoy,[57] including one even to the Empress Dowager! Alexander made no reply, writing only to his sister: "I have learned to know him now. Napoleon or I, I or Napoleon. We cannot reign side by side." The hour of leave-taking was at hand—it was, indeed, too late—but even now the Emperor fretted, saying to his advisors, "What a frightful succession of perilous conflicts will begin with my first backward step!" The Grande Armée quit Moscow by the southern gate, a mere 110,000 strong. Disaster now inexorably engulfed the French, as Russia herself and minus-30-degree weather swallowed their prey whole, like a python with a piglet. Given the diminished and demoralized state of French arms, the retreat could, in fact, have been worse: any military force worth its salt would have destroyed them out-right and captured their leader. Kutuzov, however, was leery of Napoleon's reputation, and he held back.

The retreat, curiously, saw Napoleon regain some of the old energy, if not grandeur ("I have played the Emperor long enough! It is time to play the General!" he said at the battle of Krasnoye). At the crossing of the Beresina (November 26–29), he developed a plan of feint and dash–"simple, as of old, but likely to succeed"[58]–which not only saved the army and dealt a smart blow to the foe, but earned him this tribute from two West Point military his-torians: "The *Grande Armée* might be dying on its feet, but neither winter, hunger, rivers, nor overwhelming odds in men and guns could halt it. It trampled them underfoot, and went on. And with it, borne above disaster, marched Napoleon's prestige. . . . 'You should never despair while brave men remain with the colours.' "[59]

Napoleon's great failure in 1812 lay above all in his misconstrual of the tsar. The issue between them might have begun as a game of bluff and chicken, but Alexander grew in defeat and victory more than his adversary grew in victory and defeat. Napoleon would always insist, even at St. Helena, that the war was "merely a political war," but for the tsar and his fol-lowers it became far more than that. "The *Grande Armée*," as a recent British historian writes, "was not bled to death by a thousand cuts, worn down by British-sponsored guerrillas [in Spain] or starved into submission by the Royal Navy; it was totally destroyed at great cost–in Russia in 1812."[60] For this, the Russians paid a ghastly price–roughly 400,000 casualties, all told–a figure that is often overlooked in posterity's fascination with the even greater French losses–around 500,000 men.[61]

Napoleon would remark at St. Helena (not once, but several times), "I should have died at Moscow. Then I would probably have had the reputa-tion of the greatest conqueror of all time. After [Moscow], fortune ceased to smile on me."

THE LEADER AND HIS MEN

Marching and fighting, naked, starved, but merry; don't you suppose we, too, were sick of it? Though we owed him precious little thanks, nevertheless 'twas we whose hearts were true.

—"Flambeau," in *L'Aiglon*,
by Edmond Rostand

The disaster seemed not to diminish the Emperor in his men's affection and respect, at least not to a noteworthy extent. To the consternation of moderns, his standing with his troops remained high, even at the end. Was it that he indulged them in a bonhomie he generally loathed and avoided with everyone else? Was it that he remembered an astonishing number of their names, or the names of their wives and children? Was it that he could force himself to eat military grub in which he found a hair floating, mastering his strong desire to retch because he was with "the men"? To leave things at that would be to trivialize the soldiers' collective intelligence and expectations, which required more than cheap displays of facile affection and concern to impress and fulfill them. Men perishing of exposure did not offer their precious sticks and kindling to their officers "for the Emperor" (whom they well knew suffered from cold weather) because Napoleon took care to court them. Soldiers dying in their tracks did not cry out "Vive l'Empereur!" with their last breath, nor consider themselves lucky to expire within the radius of his sight, because he knew how to mix with them.

It would be presumptuous to state with false assurance why the men loved him, despite his well-known callousness about spending their lives, despite his occasional defeats—never completely concealed in the army bulletins, or despite the deaf ear he turned to his surgeons who pleaded for better care and conditions for the sick, wounded, and dying—thousands of whom were left to their fate in Russia without even a poison pill.[62] The most eloquent testimony is Ségur's simple simile, referring to Napoleon's habit of pitching his tent inside a square of the Imperial Guard: "He camped in the midst of his army, like hope in the human breast."[63]

Napoleon was aware of this aspect of himself. "I win battles with the dreams of my soldiers," he would say. The content of those dreams was myriad, and evolved over time; and the hope had many sources and aspects, including surely the knowledge that their lives were in his hand and that he could well save them in even the most desperate of situations. There was, of course, the familiar glory we spoke of earlier, but far less of that remained as a motive for leader love after the departure from Moscow. Finally, much of Napoleon's effect on his men resided in their incorrigible conviction that this commander was like no other, perhaps since Caesar, and that serving— even dying—under him was their chance to touch world history. This awareness of who he was led them to tolerate much.

The mentality of the Grande Armée in Russia was not the old martial Jacobin spirit anymore, which probably expired with Marshal Lannes at Essling.[64] The revolutionary fervor and "virtue" of the Army of Italy had long given way, as we saw, to more hierarchical sentiments of glory, personal honor, and the cult of the leader—reminiscent of the evolution that took place in the Roman army of the last century B.C., as it evolved from being an instrument of the Republic to being the political instrument of individual commanders, notably the charismatic Caesar. The French regimental eagles (modeled on the Roman ones) were redesigned in the year of the Russian hecatomb; the new tricolors referred to the "Emperor Napoleon, to such-and-such a regiment," and listed the names of the battles in which the regiment had fought. No further mention of "le peuple français," the flags are now the "gift" of the Emperor of the French to *his* regiment, and national patriotism casts no shadow between The Man and his men.[65] It is ironic that a soldier who rose from captain to general, and who thus never lived the experience of "fathering" a regiment—the colonel's role—yet carried a colonel's touch with his men. Napoleon was the apotheosis—and the last example—of the very old tradition of a warrior (and State) chieftain and his men. Alexander, Julius Caesar, Henry V, and Hannibal had such ties with their armies, but not the modern dictators and despots, none of whom was a great soldier as well as head of State.[66]

Perhaps most striking—shocking, almost, when we consider the alleged power of nationalism today—is the tie between the Napoleonic legend and even modern-day Russian soldiers. The devotees of the cult of the French emperor in contemporary Russia among the army or among veterans are numerous, and when they reenact the great battles of 1812, notably that of Borodino, they compete with each other to play *French,* not Russian roles— notwithstanding that the Grande Armée had laid waste their land and butchered their soldiers and their people in the tens of thousands.

The French military mind was not uncritical of "l'Empereur," but it did understand the drag of deeper forces. The poet Alfred de Musset, the son of a Napoleonic functionary in the War Ministry, expressed a more rounded view of it all, when he described his father's generation's feelings:

Never were there so many sleepless nights as in the time of this man; never were there to be seen, leaning on the ramparts of town walls, such a nation of sorrowing mothers; never did such silence envelop those who spoke of death. And yet, never was there so much joy, so much life, so many warlike fanfares, in every heart. Never was there so much pure sunshine, to dry out the stains of so much blood. It was said God made it for this man, and it was called the sun of Austerlitz. But he made them, himself, with his never-silent cannons, which left only clouds of smoke the day after his battle.[67]

HIS MASTER'S VOICE

Retaining a fix on the man as he merges with his creation becomes difficult in this late afternoon of the Empire; the Emperor was consumed by his work, as his private self was consumed by his public persona. He spent few evenings roaming free, in conversation with a single interlocutor. One has the impression that if a Claire de Rémusat had presented herself, he would not have had the inclination to open his breast to her. That is why the following testimony is as valuable as it is unusual.

Napoleon departed the Grande Armée on December 5, soon after it had reached Smorgony, near Lithuania. Some later said he "deserted" the troops, but in fact the commander had stuck by his men for all of the campaign and most of the journey out of Russia. Now the duties of chief of State weighed in, and there was pressing reason to get back to Paris—preferably ahead of the news of the Russian disaster. He made the journey with a tiny retinue, including the very Caulaincourt who had raised strenuous objections to the campaign in the first place. For much of the fortnight trip by berlin—made incognito; it is useful to recall that this was a pre–mass media era, when even a Napoleon went unrecognized by 99 percent of the population—Caulaincourt was the Emperor's sole traveling companion, sharing constant cold and occasional terror (when capture seemed nigh). During that time he was admitted to a degree of intimacy that is all but unique in the imperial years. Caulaincourt listened and talked, but mostly listened—and took copious notes during meal breaks and in the evening. Napoleon's words hark back to the writings of the young artillery lieutenant at Valence and are a harbinger of the ramblings of the exile on St. Helena.[68]

The Emperor's monologues are febrile and discursive, at once therapeutic (he is trying to exorcise demons) and illustrative of the intelligence, force, and fluency we are accustomed to in him. (Even if we recall that the Emperor spoke with an accent—irritating to some, charming to others—and made mistakes in usage, it does not lessen our impression that he is utterly at home in the French language. Indeed one wonders if the mistakes were, or became, intentional.[69]) His humors over the fortnight of the journey varied among three poles, the least frequent of which was dark—that is, reminiscent of the tone I sought to sound at the outset of the book, and which some might call "Corsican": mistrust, anger, pessimism, and anxiety. The other two moods, in greater evidence, stood in contrast: Napoleon could be intimate (congenial, humorous—even playful) and thoughtful (reflective, insightful). He invited Caulaincourt to critical candor, rarely dismissing his words or silencing him. One sees here little trace of the cynicism, petulance, or megalomania that could characterize Napoleon as he got older.

The monologues and conversations are remarkable for the uncanny way that Napoleonic blindness underlies Napoleonic intelligence—an all-too-human condition. The number of specific topics raised is great, but the themes he turned back on again and again, including the joy he took in being a father and his eagerness to see his infant son and his wife again, were fewer: Russia and the present campaign, Spain, England, his hopes for France and the Empire, and the current French political crisis.

What confounds him about the war just past is precisely that Russia has won it, although she lost all the pitched battles, not to mention her "capital." We hear no shred of awareness that France has only won these battles on paper, and that none was decisive, except—at the end of the campaign—in keeping the French army alive. While the Emperor now concedes that he lingered too long in Moscow, he blames his reverses on weather or on Poland's failure to send more troops (as if 70,000 weren't enough). In short, he will not see what war has become since the set-piece battles he studied at the Ecole Militaire or fought at Austerlitz—that is, not some infernal Ping-Pong match of accumulating points, but an inexorable situational outcome. Napoleon frets over Alexander's intentions, deluding himself that the tsar will not move quickly against France or be successful at rallying Austria and Prussia.[70]

Spain—and here is a comment on the finality of the Napoleonic mind when it was made up—does not cloud his consciousness and conscience. If the Emperor discusses it, that is mainly because his companion raises questions. He is satisfied of his reasons for being in Iberia—the morass of the old Bourbon monarchy, the threat and opportunity it represented for France— and if the twists and turns of the Spanish story have proven unpredictable and troublesome (mainly due to Wellington's expedition there), there is no reason to reconsider his policy in Spain. In short, Napoleon's old contempt for the Spaniards carries him along, excusing the inexcusable. His blindness was the political (and moral) failure to grasp that below his shrewd profile and his lists of "excellent reasons" for French presence—his analysis is perhaps the best defense of French-Spanish policy that exists—there is *still* every good reason in the world for the Spanish to want the French the hell out.

If Spain is France's problem, then England is everyone's, in Napoleon's telling, for here is a financial vampire that would drain the world's blood, if he allowed it. Britain holds but a few strategic islands and her colonies; her business acumen does the rest. The "menace" of Britain's position, he insists, "leaps out at you," yet the continent cannot get past its annoyance at not having sugar for its coffee or its "jealousy of France." It infuriates him that Britain's form of dominance is now preferred to France's ("If I left Europe to its own devices, she would throw herself into England's arms"). Caulaincourt tries to get him to see that lately French brutality—e.g., her military reprisals on Hamburg for the city's illegal trade with Britain—has led Europe to see her as solo bully. Napoleon grants only that recent French annexations in northern Germany maybe went too far, but he will not consider that British financial-commercial power, however exploitative and aggressive, is in fact (and not just in perception) more benign and progressive than French military repression since 1810.

The issue of French annexations leads Caulaincourt to press "Sire" on the matter of "universal monarchy," about which rumor has waxed for weeks.[71] Was Napoleon seeking world domination? Caulaincourt asks. The Emperor disavows such intentions ("this business is a dream, and I am wide awake"), though one scarcely sees how he could have done otherwise, given the stark contrast between his current fugitive state and this dream.

Defeat and danger tended to bring out the Jacobin in Napoleon. As he flees the scene of his first true disaster, his mind turns to the progressive, not the self-aggrandizing dream. The flood of stated good intentions that now cascades over Caulaincourt recalls earlier goals and ideals—e.g., the Senate will receive political independence and become a true House of Lords; there will be free public education (the King of Rome will even enroll for a time); industry will be (even) more coddled than it already is; the project for a new navy will get even more attention than it already does; he will visit even more places in his Empire than he already has; and so on. None of this, even the admission—half grudging, half admiring—that it is no wonder his siblings have turned out to identify with the national leanings of their respective realms, lies at wild variance with earlier Napoleonic opinion, mood, or policy, but it has certainly not been in evidence since 1810.[72]

But this liberal turn occurs, as always, within the cadre of a paean to "firm government." Nothing is more forceful in the Caulaincourt dialogues than Napoleon's soliloquy on why American-style democracy "is impossible" in post-revolutionary France, which comes down to this: the constant changes of regime since 1789 have conditioned the French to expect them. "That is an evil only time will cure," he admits, but notes that the evolution is already well in hand. The Empire is winning its bet of rendering France "apolitical"; the French not only do not miss parties, they scarcely remember what they are. Napoleon takes pride in the high "morale" of his government—and it is well here to recall that the thousands of imperial functionaries are nearly as attached to their emperor as the Imperial Guard, for he has made the corps of civil servants uncorrupted, effective, and respected within France. The same affection, he notes expansively, is given him by "the people," whom, for the occasion, he chooses to grace as "the nation." The key here is simple: equality before the law, equality in promotion. ("Voilà mon secret.")

The dissenters to the foregoing live in the posh faubourg Saint-Germain. Napoleon is never at peace with that bastion of old society, but he will, he assures Caulaincourt (himself a scion of the highest *noblesse*), succeed in winning over "their sons, who will prefer what I have to offer them to what their fathers had hope to resurrect [i.e., the kings]. . . . All he needs is ten years of peace, and I will be as blest then as I am hated now."

The dominant theme of these monologues is not dark agitation at the impending geopolitical consequences of the Russian fiasco, nor, still less, agonized guilt at the hundreds of thousands of dead and suffering he has left in his wake, at the no-longer "grand" army, abandoned to its own devices, somewhere east of Vilna. The Emperor's mood is by and large one of energy and almost cheerful defiance ("I never remember seeing him so gay," writes the ambassador) as he contemplates the armies he will mobilize. Caulaincourt, for his part, records his own pride at his leader's resilience in adversity. Napoleon is concerned mainly about what is happening in France. He has long believed that many of his military associates are born conspirators, even though "heroes in battle." "The French," he says, "are always ready to bite your hand," though he adds the rather singular self-observation that "I don't have enough esteem for [most people] to be wicked toward them and exact revenge on them."

The real source of concern is the Emperor's knowledge that six weeks before, an attempted coup d'Etat took place in Paris. And it is in Paris, where he and Caulaincourt are now arriving, on the morning of December 19. "From Malo-Yaroslavetz to Smorgony," Ségur writes, "the master of all Europe had been just the general of a dying, disorganized army: from Smorgony to the Rhine, he was an unrecognized fugitive in a hostile land: but beyond the Rhine he becomes once more the conqueror of Europe, and one last breath of prosperity puffs out his drooping sails."

XIII

The Collapse (1812–1814)

Entendez-vous, dans nos campagnes
Mugir ces féroces soldats?
Ils viennent jusque dans vos bras
Egorger vos fils, vos compagnes.
"La Marseillaise"

MALET

The king is dead, long live the president!

Before dawn on October 23, 1812, a minor general named Claude-François Malet,[1] a man of strong Jacobin leanings and a conspiratorial past, breaks out of the low-security sanitarium where he is being detained. He gathers with several fellow plotters, and then each executes a part of Malet's plan. Armed with false documents that purport to show the Emperor has been killed in Russia and a provisional regime has been set up, the plotters (some of whom actually believe Napoleon dead) suborn five companies of the National Guard and set off on a spree of arresting high officials, most of whom they surprise in their beds. Malet and Company indeed drive the knife through a good deal of butter—arresting, for example, the minister of police (Savary) and the prefect of police for Paris (Pasquier)—before finally hitting steel, in the person of the military governor (Hulin), who takes a bullet in the jaw, and his chief of staff (Doucet), who seizes hold of Malet and rallies loyal troops. By late in the morning, the coup is quashed, and the principals are in prison except a priest who escapes. The men. mostly officers, are speedily tried by court-martial, and twelve are shot on the twenty-ninth.

Napoleon received the news in Russia on November 7, and though it is common to claim that it so rankled and agitated him that he decided to return to France forthwith, the truth is, he stayed with the army for another month.

The coup scenario, curiously, was in fact the same one that had landed Malet in prison in 1808. Among his documents was a false *senatus consultum* that proclaimed a provisional government with General Moreau (still in exile in the United States) as president, and a number of leading political figures, as members, including Carnot, Augereau, and Senators Volney and Garat. These were republicans known to disapprove of the turn things had taken in France since 1804, but they hardly constituted an active and disloyal opposition, and they had no clue that Malet was invoking their names. Other names, too; in the sanitarium, Malet had come into contact with members of the royalist underground—notably, the Knights of the Faith (Chevaliers de la Foi), which boasted a small but loyal network around France, with whom he worked closely. Two key royalists indeed figured in his provisional government, making it an odd mélange of far left and far right.

It is still difficult to know just where to peg the gravity of Malet's conspiracy.[2] Obviously, Fouché is right that it was more than a figment of its leader's imagination. The former police minister adds: if the plot's execution was republican, its underlying principles were royalist. That is a sympathetic ex-Jacobin's way of demeaning a conspiracy that neither he nor Talleyrand (who equally loathed the Chevaliers de la Foi) had anything to do with. On the other hand, a once and future royalist such as Fievée opined that only luck had thwarted Malet, who—were it not for Hulin's courage and Doucet's strength—might well have seized many ministries and the National Guard. And after that, who knew: "The country was susceptible to the contagion of the example."

Well, perhaps. A crowd did roar "Vive l'Empereur!" as Malet passed before the firing squad, though Fievée would doubtless be the first to reply, "Yes," but a crowd could have been found to yell "Vive Malet!" at Napoleon's execution, had the coup succeeded. (Malet replied to an interrogator's query, "All of France and you yourself, Your Honor, [would have joined me] if I had succeeded."[3] The Emperor's point to Caulaincourt that the Revolution had overfamiliarized the French to rapid political change was not only true but stayed true for most of the next two centuries. The Emperor ordered many of the documents connected with the Malet affair to be published—to show the public how unimportant it all had been. Curiously, he also proved thereby that official censorship—and the political illiteracy that resulted—did not always well serve the real interests of his Empire, for a free and active press might well have disclosed something of Malet's plotting, not to mention the incoherence of his Jacobin-royalist plans and confederates.

What outraged Napoleon, and weighed on his heart, was not, in any case, what might have been—he was too fatalistic for that—but *what was not*: a loud and resolute cry from the arrested functionaries declaring, "We already have a regime in the event of the Emperor's death: *the King of Rome*." Napoleon simply could not swallow that "his" prefect of the Seine (Frochot) would placidly have set about serving the new government with nary a sigh. He spluttered indignantly to Caulaincourt: "Frochot, besides what he owed me, had taken an oath to me. Yet thinking me dead, he betrayed his oath, all the while convinced he was an honest man." Two days after returning to Paris, the Emperor shamed a Senate delegation of welcome: " 'The king is dead, long live the king!' That, in a nutshell, gentlemen, is the principal advantage of the monarchy."[4] What is curious from posterity's perspective is how little Malet's success says for the reputation of the police forces of the so-called security State. Napoleon, Cambacérès, and other top officials were quite understandably outraged that Savary, Pasquier, and Desmarest— the heads of the various police forces—would have had no clue what was going on in a nearby sanitarium, where a man serving time for plotting against the State was busily plotting afresh. Then, too, far from having been shot for his machinations of 1808, Malet had received his automatic pro- motion to the next grade of general, while he was in prison!*

Napoleon moved quickly to regularize the succession. A *senatus consultum* named the Empress as regent for her son, not only in the event of the sov- ereign's death but also when Napoleon was off on campaign.† The inexpe- rienced Marie-Louise was only a figurehead; the realm would continue to be run by the same men it had always been run by in the Emperor's absence: Cambacérès, Lebrun, Eugène, Berthier, etc. One name that might surprise us, however, was Talleyrand's. We left the ex–foreign minister in early 1809 about to receive a terrible dressing-down from the Emperor ("You are noth- ing but shit in a silk stocking!"),[5] yet despite excellent reasons for clapping him in irons—e.g., his treachery vis-à-vis Russia and Austria—Napoleon had not been able to bring himself to cast out his favorite bête noire. Instead, he

---

*Parisian wags circulated the following conversation. A man asks another, "Do you know what's happening?" "No," comes the reply. "Well then, you must be in the police," replies the first.

†In violation of the Constitution of the Year XII, still in force.

quietly kept Talleyrand in his councils and even paid off his losses in a business investment.[6] He appreciated the ex-nobleman's entrée in the European
courts, and, then, too, he simply did not like new faces in his midst.

On the eve of quitting Smorgoni for Paris, Napoleon dined with his top
commanders and treated them to a reprise of his favorite lament: "If I had
been born on the throne, if I were a Bourbon, it would have been easy for me
not to make any mistakes!" It was disingenuous, and one bets he knew it. He
surely knew that no ruler or general could have faced a defeat of the Russian
campaign's magnitude without trembling for himself and his heirs. The
past two decades had seen Paul I murdered, Louis XVI executed, and Charles
IV, Ferdinand VII, and Gustav IV deposed; it had seen Frederick William III's
and Francis II's hold on their realms profoundly shaken from within as well
as from without. They had all been princes of ancient ruling families. By contrast, Napoleon was faring quite well, thank you, given that Egypt had been
lost, things were going wretchedly in Spain, and the Russian theater had just
blossomed in disaster. The French had barely murmured at any of this, or at
their loss of freedoms, and not even at the increased taxes and conscription.[7]

True, the Malet matter revealed a dearth of dynastic loyalty. The first
thought of a number of officials, caught with their pants down, was not for
a twenty-one-year-old Austrian-born princess and her infant son: But no one
knew better than Napoleon that a founder cannot simultaneously construct a State and anchor his family in its rule. "I need twenty years" was his
common line, for good reason. So it is unlikely the Emperor nurtured illusions about the newly reformatted regency, or that he was completely surprised by the Malet affair—a hard thing to do to Napoleon. He knew what the
French were ("always ready to bite your hand"), and he understood that the
King of Rome would have to reveal talent and ambition if he were to hang
on to the trapeze his father would one day throw him.

The real goal, on returning from Russia, was not to make law that tried to
foreordain the uncontrollable, but to play well in the present the old game
of "as if," now that the leak of a disaster in Russia had become the news hemorrhage of winter 1812–13. Thus, the receptions, balls, and audiences were
reprised at the Tuileries, the parades took place on the Champ-de-Mars, imperial visits got paid to the Invalides, the theater, the opera, and the Trianon,
masses were attended and long walks taken in Paris. Stags were pursued in the
Bois de Boulogne and at Fontainebleau—sometimes two and three times a
week (although the hunter hated hunting, doing so proved him hale and
"royal"); political nominations were announced.

The Emperor grandly discussed plans with the imperial architect, Fontaine,
for a new palace for the King of Rome, to sit atop the heights of the Chail-

lot, overlooking the Seine; it would be handsomer than the Elysée and larger than the Luxembourg.[8] And withal, stuffy court ritual was punctiliously followed: at dinner, guests were announced by the chamberlains as "Their Excellencies" or "Their Highnesses," visiting royalty as "Their Majesties, the King and Queen of ——," Marie-Louise as "Her Majesty the Empress of the French, Queen of Italy." And finally, while the room waited with baited breath, the Grand Chamberlain announced simply: "L'Empereur!"

Of the many who professed to believe that the Russian campaign was the beginning of the end, most said this decades after. Napoleon himself, in any case, was no Cassandra. Any view of the "late" Emperor (all of forty-three years in age) as slowed by pessimism and lethargy is bound for mockery in the face of the explosion of activity and the "eerie willfulness"[9] with which he rebounded to confront the awe-inspiring panoply of problems before him—domestic and foreign, mainly (it is true) self-caused. Here was not a man to be intimidated unless a sign of intimidation be, as it well may, the setting up of a harder, higher, and harsher façade.

PIUS AND IMPIOUS
(THE POPE AND THE EMPEROR AGAIN)

I know how to win in the battle with myself.
—Pius VII

Cambacérès had noted archly at the coronation (1804), "We should have wished for the Pope's face to bear more of an august imprint."[10] Three long years of house arrest at Savona (1809–12)—often spent without pen and paper, let alone advisors, being spied upon by his doctor (in French pay), being menaced, unsettled, and manipulated by the local prefect and his flunkies, but being completely ignored by their master—brought this pontiff *ad augusta per angusta* (to augustness via anguish), as his personal struggle with isolation, remorse, and deprivation ennobled and strengthened him.

Napoleon, meanwhile, underwent a reverse evolution—from the serene and wise leader who had negotiated the Concordat to an angry spoiled child, shouting at his cardinal-uncle, "I will not be the loser!" as if this were a zero-sum game of virtue with the pope. The Emperor did far more than rant and rave: he ordered petty vexations committed against Pius's person, and constantly lied to or misled him in correspondence; he exiled the Roman cardinals who, in solidarity with their leader, shunned the imperial wedding; he had the respected cleric Abbé d'Astros (a co-author of the Imperial Cate-chism, no less) imprisoned in the fortress at Vincennes because the priest had smuggled the pope's bull of excommunication into Paris; he suppressed the major French teaching and preaching orders, for fear they had become too "ultramontane" (papal) in their outlook; he arrested bishops and forced them to resign their sees because they disagreed with his policy; he suppressed the clergy's newspaper (*Le Journal des Curés*); and withal, he pursued his Con-stantinian dream of controlling the Church. He wrote his foreign minister (January 1810) to say that in the future the popes would not be installed "except after my approval, as they used to be confirmed by the emperors of Constantinople."

None of it budged the pope.

Finally, in 1811, badly needing to solve the spreading problems caused by papal refusal to invest bishops, the Emperor called a national council of French-Italian bishops, including a number of the uninvested candidates. They assembled in Paris, but although nearly all were loyal Gallicans to a fault, they dared not do what Napoleon required of them, which was to over-turn ancient Church practice in the absence of the Bishop of Rome. They did, however, send a secret message to His Majesty to say that they "had the impression they were not free" in their deliberations.[11] Napoleon probably regretted the power he had unwittingly conferred on the papacy when, in 1802, he had demanded of Pius VII that he turn out the entire bank of French (old regime) bishops. Before *that* display of papal power—as now before Pius's example of silent suffering—this national council could only quail and wring its collective hands; its members reluctantly preferred to be called "traitors" to becoming schismatics.

In pressing his bishops too hard, the Emperor finally provoked his docile and sycophantic uncle, Cardinal Fesch, the primate of the French clergy—a man who, until now, had been content to quietly receive (and seek) honors and stipends. Even Fesch had undergone a kind of soul-cleansing. In now frankly warning his spoiled nephew of the risks he ran in so alienating Catholic opinion all over the Empire, Fesch paid the price: he lost his exalted position at court (Grand Chaplain) and had to endure "exile" to his diocese of Lyon.[12] Finally, if further proof were needed that Napoleon was eroding a true pillar of support of his regime, it offered itself in the Malet affair: one of the co-conspirators (Abbé Lafon, a royalist priest) listed among the desiderata enumerated in the false *senatus consultum* that overthrew the Empire this promise: France must be reconciled with the pope, and he must be safely returned to Rome. Had the young Bonaparte envisioned or prom-ised any less in 1799–1802?

The need to batten all hatches and repair all riggings in the wake of the Russian disaster—interpreted by Fesch as God's punishment of his nephew (the cardinal was frankly glad Napoleon had lost!)[13]—led the Emperor to try a different approach. Pius was being quartered at nearby Fontainebleau, Savona having been deemed dangerous due to the proximity of a British fleet off the coast. Napoleon elected to meet with this man whom he had not deigned to write to in three years, nor laid eyes on in seven. His last communiqué concerning the pope—read aloud to Pius by Prefect Chabrol—had informed the Bishop of Rome that he understood less theology than a novice and owed it to posterity to resign his office and make way for a pontiff of greater intellectual ability. (In that vein, the current French police minister, Savary, expressed his "surprise" that the pope spent his time at Fontainebleau sewing or praying, not reading erudite tomes.) Now Napoleon wrote courteously to Pius, expressing "alarm" at Pius's recent illness and "relief" at his recovery. He suggested a meeting.

Thus, on January 18, 1813, with the Empress and their infant son in tow, Napoleon actually descended upon the pope, in his rooms at Fontainebleau, kissing him with effusive false affection. We have no record of the ensuing summit conference between the two of them, though we know it was lively.[14] In subsequent meetings during that week, Napoleon brought with him a number of pro-imperial clerics, who helped him to pressure Pius. The gentle pope was by now an emaciated, pale man who could not sleep or eat properly, who had endured four years of hardship and humiliation, and who was desperate to regain his see, his colleagues, home.

And so, like Joan of Arc, Pius relented—not in *timor mortis,* as crushed the Maid (contemplating the stake), but in a desperate hope to regain his flock and release his brothers who had been imprisoned on his account (notably Cardinal Pacca, his secretary of state). Too, why deny it, Napoleon Tempter *even now* fascinated meek Pius, still seduceable by the dream of working in harness with the "Hero." The pontiff signed a new concordat (the old having been quashed by Napoleon some years before) which conceded all that the Emperor asked, leaving Pius only the chance to go home and to retain some of the Church's states. The battle thus ended in defeat for the Forces Spiritual; the French had been right all along: it was about land and political power.

This "death," as the pope later called it, took place on the twenty-fifth. For three agonizing days, Pius, convulsed by remorse, did battle with "the devil" inside himself; we might say, he discerned and overcame his need to want to please Napoleon at any price. On the twenty-eighth, in an act again reminiscent of Joan at Rouen, he recanted: there would be no new concordat. But of course Napoleon, contrary to their agreement on the twenty-fifth, had already published the "good news," thus extracting his profit from Pius's weakness. The pope now was left to rot at Fontainebleau, until outside events rescued him.

Despite the temporary political fix, Napoleon had been beaten. Pius's trembling and all but involuntary obstinacy had slowly come to show Europe that the "great Emperor," whatever else he was, was a mean-spirited persecutor of a kind old man who happened to be the Vicar of Christ. Cardinal Pacca, from his prison cell in the Fenestrelle, had worried about an "unequal contest" that pitted his frail pope against the gigantic Emperor, yet it was the Emperor who was outgunned. The monk Chiaramonti had won, even if he felt nothing like the cold satisfaction that Wellington would feel. In modern language, the pope redefined the terms of the contest, making a profoundly political set-to into a contest of morality. Again unable to admit a will independent of his own, Napoleon let himself "forget the principle he had raised to a political rule at the start of his reign: that civil peace can only come to pass by religious peace."[15]

Morality aside, Napoleon also made a serious political mistake, in his treatment of "il Papà." He caused insulted Catholics to take refuge with persecuted royalists. The royalists had more figureheads and aristocrat-generals than they knew what to do with, but they had few troops. Now, thanks to Napoleonic outrages on Pius VII, what might have been "the Knights of the King" took life as "the Knights of the Faith," attracting to their white banner far more members among a peasantry, which looked with a rightly jaundiced eye on *ci-devant* owners of nationalized lands than it would otherwise have done.

As for Pius, he will be freed by the Allies in early 1814—freed to go home and pursue, well, politics. He will make a triumphal progress through France, cheered by thousands of former imperial subjects. At Cesena on May 4, 1814, he will elaborate his providentialist interpretation of his recent tribulations and his restoration, stoutly reaffirming papal sovereign rights to the legations and the marches, which the Congress of Vienna will presently award back to him.

Home, at last, to "our beloved Roma"—the Eternal City never seen by "the Immortal Emperor"—Pius VII will set in place for his States a thoroughgoing theocracy, suppressing the Code Napoleon and other French reforms, resurrecting the Jesuit order, reconfining the Jews to their ghetto (and resaddling them with the possibility of baptizing their infants, with impunity) and anathematizing liberal and patriotic societies. It will work out to be the most complete undoing of the French Revolution undertaken anywhere in Europe.[16] Only the great public works begun by the French prefect Tournon, prefiguring a modern city, will remain, awaiting the future liberal and secular hand that will finish them—and forget their (French) origin.

In short, not a bad political haul in return for a profound moral witness.

1813:
THE CRUSADE OF THE SOVEREIGNS

The crisis now approaching was not a matter of wit or eloquence or cabales, it was a matter of State, the most formidable crisis ever witnessed in Europe. And it required not the vain Pompeys and Ciceros whom Mme de Staël never ceased worshipping, but a few of those Sullas and Caesars whom she always abhorred.

—Albert Sorel[17]

On February 12, 1813, as the Emperor rode through the working-class district of Saint-Antoine in Paris, a journeyman from a metal workshop—a certain Solavin—accosted the imperial mount, seized the reins, and cried out to Napoleon: *Tu cours à ta perte* (You are racing to disaster). He repeated himself, then, pale and trembling, ran back into his workshop. The next day he was fired, and vanished from history, his employer left to puzzle over "how such a quiet, well-behaved young man, naturally silent and who never spoke of government matters, could bring himself to such an act of madness."[18]

Solavin, however, was the eloquent exception to a rule that assured the French emperor of, as John Holland Rose puts it (without varnish), "the dumb trustfulness of his forty-three millions of subjects."[19] For the astonishing truth is, notwithstanding the Russian debacle, the French, in overwhelming consensus, responded to their ruler's call for war. Countless municipalities, official bodies, and individuals around the country, knowing the army's need for cavalry mounts, sent to the Emperor their personal mounts (even those used for farmwork). And they sent their sons and husbands, too—by the tens of thousands. After a decade of force-feeding the country conscription via constraint and threat, the imperial government—perhaps to its own surprise—actually succeeded in imposing military service on the national mentality.[20] The new troops, raw and young, were called "the Marie-Louises" (as regent, the Empress signed their call-up papers). It is a fitting name: they were young, naive, and (for the most part) they loved the Emperor.

Napoleon's attitude toward the war was not Solavin's. In an irritated letter to Cambacérès, the Emperor wrote: the minister of police (Savary) should stop "depicting me as some kind of peace-lover; doing so can lead to nothing, and is harmful in the measure that it suggests I am *not* what he claims." Not that the war was Napoleon's to control anymore. The Russian army had crossed the Niemen and was ready to press into eastern Europe. The tsar might have hesitated—one did not lightly *attack* Napoleon, but his leading political advisors at this crucial juncture included three of the most talented activists of the counterrevolutionary clique against Napoleon discussed earlier: Stein and Pozzo di Borgo, who simultaneously advised the new British foreign minister, Castlereagh; and Gentz, who also counseled Francis II. These men supervised the Romanov's ideological self-transformation into "savior of Europe"—a suitably Napoleonic destiny, to appeal to Alexander's vanity. As 1812 had seen his religious conversion, 1813 would see him emerge as the "Christian Caesar," taking the field against Napoleon's Caesar *tout court*. "Dare, Sire, without delay. . . . One must dare!" Pozzo told him, so the tsar, steadied by the presence of a host of émigré French generals holding commands in his army, dared. No one was more impressed than Napoleon himself, who would say on St. Helena, "If I had not been [myself], I should like to have been Alexander." The Emperor's inimitable style was becoming imitable; the chickens were at last coming home to roost.

Some chickens had to be pushed hard. Frederick William III had not his brother tsar's clarity of mutable self-definition or the force of will that went with it. His people's hatred for the French was an emotion he shared, but, as ruler in alliance with France, he did not feel he could indulge it with impunity. But the royal range of choice was fast narrowing. The military philosopher Clausewitz is so intent on demonstrating that politics determines war that he is caught out when the reverse situation is at hand, as in Prussia in 1813: the accumulation of years of lost wars, humiliating treaties, and harsh occupation affected public opinion, which forced the hand of an "absolute" king and affected the way the war would be fought. "Exterminate the French; God at Last Judgment will not ask you why," was the going view in certain sectors of the Prussian population.[21]

The Prussian general staff had long ached to take revenge for Jena. The hope of political-military redress in this northeastern German kingdom was still acute in 1813, sharpened by the French emperor's relentlessly shabby treatment of Prussia, which he "thrust down to the lowest circle of the Napoleonic Inferno."[22] Still, the idea of actually *doing something* seemed a remote and very dangerous possibility to a king as hesitant as Frederick William. Then, in late December 1812, General Yorck, the commander of the small Prussian contingent that had marched with the Grande Armée to Russia, defected with his corps and went over to the Russians. The king was in a tough spot: Did the general's defection point to a profound mutation in Prussian popular consciousness?

May we now speak of a "German nationalist revival" such as Baron vom Stein had in mind when he reassured Tsar Alexander about the broad popular welcome his army would receive when it crossed the Oder?[23] Not all instances of aroused community consciousness may be called "nationalism," lest the term break its historical moorings.[24] Prussian reforms after Jena–e.g., mass conscription, promoting bourgeois (not only noble) officers–entailed measures of raised patriotism, but that was as far as it went. The ruling nobility and regime of Prussia had no desire to precipitate a social upheaval that even remotely threatened to turn into a national crusade, such as France had known in 1789–93.[25] Frederick William hoped to harness the martial energy of inflamed patriotism, but without the political volatility of a doctrine like the "nation-in-arms." The difficulty, in an age that had seen the French Revolution and in a region that been occupied by the French, lay in drawing the line.[26] A *Volkskrieg* (people's war) could easily get out of hand.

He need not have worried. The German nationalist writings of a Fichte and Herder were little read beyond the clubs and secret societies and a handful of Prussian generals and politicians. What they did become–along with the military reforms, the popular hatred of the French, and the memories sparked by the intense military campaigns about to begin–was grist for later myth. In the genuinely nationalist movements of post-1848, the 1813–14 "moment" would see itself redeemed, transfigured into the birth of a united Germany.[27] At that earlier time, however, "German-ness" implied doom for the kings of Bavaria, Saxony, etc.–those very sovereigns Prussia needed to woo away from France–who would lose their sovereignty in a "greater Germany."[28] And if the opposition to Napoleon looked and saw a "German national revival," it was in part wishful thinking and in part the effect of Mme de Staël's passionate polemic *De l'Allemagne* (*On Germany*), which was published in October 1813.

The year 1813–14 is usually depicted as the "rising up of the nations" (notably, the German) *against the French*, when the truth is only France, among the powers, was adept at mature nation-talk, as the post-revolutionary era understood it, and only in France may we speak of a revival where the nation did, to some extent, respond to its sovereign's call and, in turn, make certain national claims on him. This ought not to surprise us, for only France had passed through the furnace of the *nation*'s revolutionary assault on the royal State, and had come out the other side of the ordeal a formed "State-nation," in Philip Bobbitt's neat reversal.[29] But if Napoleon (and Murat) will dare to deploy nation-talk in the war at hand, the "legitimate" sovereigns had good reason to proceed far more gingerly. In sum, Napoleon *did have* legitimacy—of another sort—and it served him in the present crisis.

Napoleon might yet have avoided a diplomatic break with Frederick William, if he had sympathetically received the king's requests for territorial restitutions and for the payment of a large sum owed Prussia as the price of her loyalty in 1812. (This, too, should brake the tendency to envision an uncontrollable Francophobia wild in Prussia.) But after Yorck's deed, it was Napoleon—not the Prussians—who was in no mood to treat honorably with an ally. Truth to tell, he may even have preferred that Prussia join the Coalition, for he intended to annihilate her as a kingdom after his victory. On February 28, Prussia thus completed her diplomatic pirouette, and Frederick William and Alexander concluded the Treaty of Kalisch against the French.

Whither Austria in this winter of diplomatic scrambling? Metternich, now firmly in command of Habsburg policy, had no use whatsoever for a "German revival," whose authors he denounced as "Jacobins," nor even for a continuation and widening of the Franco-Russia war with all its risks for geopolitical and social turmoil. As formal allies of the French—and with the prospect, one fine day, of seeing their own succeed to the French throne—the Habsburg had experienced genuine dismay at the French defeat in Russia. Austrian interest, for a long time now, had lain in survival, hence in peace and balance, in the emergence of some kind of concert that would leave Napoleon the kingpin, yet give him respected partners in Russia, England, and Austria. The only problem was that Napoleon, even if he could possibly envision the first two nations as worthy enemies, persisted in regarding—and treating—the third, Austria, with utter contempt.

The winter of 1813 opened inauspiciously for the timid inspirers of "German" revival. No patriotic volcano erupted to confound Metternich; instead, with his iron grip, Napoleon held on to his empire across the Rhine, declaring inalienable the territories that France had annexed in western and northern Germany (as everywhere else). Hamburg rose up but got slammed back into place, and no other Hanseatic city joined her. France's German allies (Saxony, Bavaria, etc.) held firm, despite grievous losses sustained in 1812—proportionally worse than France's—and despite the new levies imposed by Napoleon. The reasoning of these rulers in the Confederation of the Rhine, of which Napoleon was protector, was all dynastic and geopolitical, not German nationalist; they feared an Allied victory that would disturb or absorb their domains.

They were initially relieved by their decision to stand by Napoleon. In the military contest that opened in Saxony in the spring of 1813, the French Caesar scored some important early victories. At Lützen and Bautzen (May), Napoleon showed he was in no ways sapped by an exhaustion, such as would have inclined him "to yield to entreaties for rest and recuperation."[30] Rather, he sharply beat a pair of top Russian and Prussian generals, Wittgenstein and Blücher, and brought the Allies to the sort of hapless military pass that in another era would have heard them sue for peace.

But a new toughness was now discernible in Russo-Prussian leadership. The tsar heeded Pozzo di Borgo and Stein, and resisted the temptation to withdraw his army to the safety of Poland (which he had taken). Similarly, the patriot Blücher, aided by compatriots at the Prussian court, held Frederick William's feet to the fire. Berlin and St. Petersburg grimly hung on to their union rather than dissolve into the mutual recriminations of yore. An armistice was proposed by the neutral Austrians. Normally Napoleon would have spurned it and driven on to occupy Berlin, but the condition of his army after the costly successes of May was precarious; he needed fresh troops, especially cavalry. Diplomatic chatter allowed him to stall for time.

This failure of the war to end in the spring changed things. Lützen and Bautzen, though Napoleonic successes, ruined any hope of long-range victory for the Emperor, for they reinforced in him the tendency—always near the surface, but most visible in a crisis—to believe he was on a roll. Such an outcome was becoming less likely by the week, and showed a serious misreading of his foes. The Russians and Prussians, for their part, grasped that these opening losses did not matter; the fight would go on until Napoleon was made reasonable. Finally, Austria—war-weary but mortally angry at Napoleon for his contempt—entered the scene as an active mediator, ostensibly neutral, but with a strong tilt toward the Allies.[31]

In the Napoleon-Metternich discussions of late June, which dragged on for hours and contained several Napoleonic moments of selective "ill-breeding," the Emperor proved uncomprehending of the chancellor's goal. More than territorial restitution, Austria wanted a lasting peace based on an active agreement among the powers. It perhaps did not matter that Napoleon failed to understand, for he was not prepared to offer peace in this sense. A "concert" was unacceptable to him, even one that would have allowed France to retain the inner *Grand Empire* (i.e., her "natural" boundaries, plus Italy), for it was too "political," almost parliamentary, involving competing parties and interests, resolving conflict by rules and frequent negotiations, not by the throw of Mars's dice. "My domination will not survive the day I stop being strong and feared," he told Metternich.[32] Napoleon essentially drummed his fingers on the table or went to the theater (he had ordered the

Comédie Française to send a repertory company to Dresden to put on a show, in both senses of that term), as he waited for the means to resume the campaign.

The Sixth anti-Napoleonic Coalition* thus crystallized, as Friedrich Gentz thanked his gods of counterrevolution that the folly of "the Corsican" left Vienna no choice but to join the Russians and Prussians. The British had long been negotiating with Russia for an alliance—the tsar was reticent about granting another country a starring role in this, his greatest perform-ance—but in Foreign Minister Castlereagh, Albion had as brilliant an adept of the arts of harmony and compromise as the Austrians had in Metternich, but without his reputation for dishonesty. Alexander, in any case, had no choice but to share leadership: Russia was broke.[33] British appeal remained in large measure financial—her public credit again stood tall under a burden that would have crushed another power—but the island kingdom also now won its spurs in a more convincing way among men at war: the future Duke of Wellington beat the French decisively at the battle of Vitoria in Spain (June 21), forcing *Don José Primero* to flee his kingdom, and leaving the way open for a return of Ferdinand VII and the full panoply of reaction. Too, it left the way open for a British invasion of France from the west. "Ultimately (I admit) I have myself to blame," the Emperor wrote Savary (July 20). Indeed.

The summer armistice wound down, culminating in the preordained fail-ure of the peace talks at the Congress of Prague. None of the contenders appears to have participated in good faith, but a sort of offer of peace was made to Napoleon based on France's "natural frontiers." He did not respond nearly in time, and that was that.[34] Meanwhile, the generals (including Bonaparte) ached to get back to the fight. Mid-August thus saw the resump-tion of the very sanguinary German campaign—a campaign whose climax was a three-day (October 17–19) hecatomb around Leipzig that was the largest and bloodiest battle to date in European history. Some 180,000 Frenchmen and Germans fought 320,000 Allies, resulting in staggering overall casualties of 100,000 dead and wounded. Leipzig was a resounding victory for the Coalition. After fourteen years of war abroad, Napoleon was obliged to retreat across the Rhine.

At a key moment in the fighting at Leipzig, a portion of the Saxon and Württemberg contingents (perhaps 5,000 men, in all) deserted the French cause for the Allied—the Bavarians having already done so, a few days before. These defections help to explain why the German appellation for the battle is *Die Völkerschlacht*, or the Battle of the Nations. The phrase is mis-

*Or the Seventh, if you count the Russian campaign of 1812, as some writers do.

leading if we imagine that the battle illustrated the sort of ideological fervor on the part of the German soldiers that characterized French troops at the battle of Valmy (1792), when they had rushed to the fray shouting "Vive la Nation!"[35] Leipzig culminated a campaign which, at bottom, was a policy-driven crusade of Europe's sovereigns against Napoleon, and which might have been better called the second (after Austerlitz) battle of the Three Emperors, for it represented the triumph of Metternich's appeal to dynastic self-interest, not Baron vom Stein's appeal to German national spirit.[36]

Would Napoleon, having for the first time to defend the *patrie*, try it?

THE NATIONAL REVIVAL MANQUÉ

I may fall but I will not do so handing France back over to the revolutionaries whom I delivered her from [at Brumaire].

–Napoleon I

The French have an expression so commonly used that it has lost its magic for the striking metaphor it is (except perhaps to foreigners). *Peau de chagrin*, from a Balzac story of that name, means literally "skin of sorrow," and refers to an animal's skin, or hide, that shrinks after it has been scraped, cleaned, and laid out. In ordinary French, the phrase has long come to mean anything that shrinks, not so much naturally as against its will, inexorably losing the vitality and life it would have liked–as the poor animal–to keep. The phrase describes the *Grand Empire* at the end of 1813: the blockade and the continental system had disintegrated in the wake of Napoleon's retreat from Russia (England's trade leaped forward enough to justify the new war loans); nearly all of Germany was lost, and the Confederation of the Rhine would soon be dissolved; the tsar had occupied Poland and would soon make himself king of it; Holland and Spain were in full revolt, and Wellington was on his way across the Pyrenees; the Illyrian provinces were gone; Switzerland had declared its independence from France. Prince Eugène, in the kingdom of Italy, and Count Bacciochi, in Piedmont, were holding out heroically against the Austrians–the heroism and self-sacrifice of the Italian Napoleonic administration here, as in the Rhineland, were greater than most of what we shall find in France[37]–but it was a losing battle. Only Denmark still cleaved to the French alliance, mainly because the Prince Royal of Sweden, Carl Johan (a.k.a. Jean-Baptiste Bernadotte), would not renounce his intention to seize (Danish-held) Norway.

Peau de chagrin may also refer to the shrinking field of Napoleonic faithfuls: two marshals of the Empire (Poniatowski and Bessières) were killed in the German campaign; a similar fate befell the beloved General Duroc, who virtually died in Napoleon's arms, causing him more grief than any death since Lannes's; Napoleon's uniquely efficient chief of staff, Berthier, was ill and hors de combat; his old friend General Junot had gone insane from syphilis and died; the valuable field officer General Reynier was a prisoner; General Rapp was trapped at Danzig, and the best of the marshals, Davout, was holding out (read: no less trapped) in Hamburg. The only good news in obituaries these days was that General Moreau—returned from his American exile at the tsar's invitation, and Alexander's initial favorite to replace Napoleon—has been killed by a loose cannonball (apt) at Dresden in early September. Murat, having fought at Napoleon's side in Germany, was negotiating with Austria in order to ensure his hold on the throne of Naples. He held firm for now—a "wise decision," which Napoleon attributes to Murat's well knowing that "the lion is not dead and one cannot piss freely on him"[38]—but early in 1814 he would jump ship,[39] only to change his mind again thereafter. In mid-January 1814, Denmark fell away. Napoleon was no longer Mediator of the Swiss Confederation and effectively no longer Protector of the Confederation of the Rhine, nor effectively King of Italy (nor his son, King of Rome). He was only Emperor of the French. . . .

But that is a great deal. If the Allies now pause at the Rhine, it is not in pride and wonderment at what they have accomplished since August, but in fear and trembling at what lies ahead. Not only does their crushing numerical superiority not reassure them against this particular lion, but they quail at what the huge French *patrie* is capable of disgorging by way of an enraged nation-in-arms. Recall 1792: arrogant Allied forces had strode confidently across the Rhine, resolved to inflict punishment on France for her sins in executing Louis XVI, and virtually the entire French Revolution rose up to throw them back—and keep right on coming for twenty years. In June Napoleon had warned Metternich that in light of his failure to weld a lasting unity between the old world of the sovereigns and the new one of the French Revolution—something the Emperor had very much hoped to effect with his second marriage—he was now prepared to "bury the old one beneath its own ruins." The Allies are at pains to publish a clever (perhaps because sincere) proclamation: "*We do not make war on France, we only throw off the yoke that your government has wished to impose on our countries. . . . The sole conquest we desire is peace for France.*" They anticipate a long and difficult campaign. So they decide to get on with it and not wait for a spring campaign, as Napoleon so desperately needs them to do.[40]

The France on whose soil the Coalition set foot on December 23 had not seen an invader in a generation (time for a boy to be born and to attain conscription age), yet the country was war-weary to its bones. Unlike *la Nation* of the early Revolution, this France was not now champing at the bit to avenge herself on enemies whose fury she half understood. The Allies would instead find France's "morale broken at the moment when, to save herself, she needed all the patriotic enthusiasm of 1792."[41] Napoleon, on returning from Leipzig, found a France divided. His twin defeats in Russia and Germany had the sudden effect of tearing off the masks of popular belief in his invincibility. The political parties reemerged blaming Napoleon for failing to make a "good peace" after Lützen and Bautzen. (The Emperor ordered Savary to repress the royalists, but instead the police chief made his own bed with them.) Even many imperial ministers and civil servants murmured the peace refrain, knowing that if the Empire fell, their jobs fell with it. Most telling was a new trend among the political elites—perhaps in response to Allied propaganda—who were beginning to separate France from Napoleon, French fault from Napoleonic fault, French ambition from Napoleonic ambition, although for a decade and a half now, no shadow had fallen between the two. The "great Emperor" had become the warmonger; the loss of liberty and the political police were often noted; the glory far less so.

On the other hand, this was still France, the home of Mars. Who knew what she could accomplish when her lands were invaded, and if her "lion" rallied her to do her utmost? She had the population to field an almost endless number of soldiers, and she was known to be capable of virtually bottomless energy, rage, and sacrifice under the right circumstances. France bridled but acceded to new Napoleonic taxes,[42] enacted via decree, in an unusual flouting of legality, which required the confirmation of the Legislative Body. In justice, Napoleon also dug deep into his own vast personal holdings, which he had economized from the civil list—his "pear set aside for when I'm thirsty," as he called it. He also demanded yet another army of conscripts: 120,000 immediately, 180,000 more soon after, while a further 900,000 were to be made ready! If we include the 500,000 Frenchmen who had already marched to the colors in Russia, then it is fair to say that all the armies that marched under a royal banner in the last three centuries of French history did not equal the number called up by the Empire in 1812–14. And yet they would not be enough. What is striking is that sufficient French troops existed. If Napoleon had been able to repatriate his hardened veterans in Spain and Germany (where they were imprisoned in the fortresses they were holding), he would have had another 200,000 quality soldiers—quite enough.

After Leipzig, Savary had written to His Majesty to beseech him to return and lead "a national movement, without which we are lost."[43] The Emperor returned in mid-November and called up the National Guard in the eastern (the most exposed) departments, and dispatched a score or so senators and deputies—commissioners, armed with full powers, reminiscent of the Revolution—around France to bang the patriotic drum and raise men and materiel. Proclamations rained down on "the French," invoking *la patrie,* "France," "honor," "freedom of commerce," "protection of national industry," and hatred of *les Anglais.* The defeat at Leipzig was blamed on the "unexampled defection" of the Saxons and the mistakes committed by subordinates. Readers were reminded of the geographical amputation that would be done to *la patrie*—the loss of the "natural frontiers"—in the event of an Allied victory. Finally, "the country" was coolly admonished to "show itself worthy of a sovereign who acknowledges neither fatigue nor danger when securing the welfare of his subjects and the honor of his Empire is at stake." Let "every Frenchman . . . give fresh proofs of his love of his Emperor, his country, and his honor."

What strikes the reader of all this Napoleonic propaganda production in the fall of 1813 and winter of 1814 is that it sounded the patriotic chord without particularly emphasizing a "national revival"; the language dwelled on France and the French, but rarely invoked *la Nation* and *les nationaux.* This was perhaps not accidental. More than a decade of (ab)use of *nation* at Napoleonic hands had not altogether oxidized the term's original ideological power. In 1814 *nation* retained a good deal of the mobilizing and sacralizing aura it had held throughout the Revolution; and more specifically, it retained a great deal of its primordial association with the frenetic popular movements and moments that had transformed the Revolution and appalled the Europe of courts and sovereigns. It is why, as we saw, the term never rested easily on Habsburg lips, or why—in the memorable words of King Frederick William, *"Nation? Das klingt Jakobinisch"* (That sounds Jacobin).

"Going with the Nation" would have required a willingness to reverse the trends in Napoleon's leadership style. The point is best illustrated in the most noteworthy and unfortunate confrontation of this era. In an effort to effect national union—and to undo the effect of the Allied propaganda effort aimed at separating the ruler from his people—the Emperor unusually convoked the Senate and the Legislative Body. To prove that he had not been at fault in the failure of peace negotiations during the Saxon campaign, he granted select commissions of each body the extraordinary (one-time-only) right to review certain foreign policy documents. The canny old senators, led by Talleyrand, instantly spotted the truth, which was that the Emperor had indeed not responded to Allied proposals in a timely fashion, but they said their usual nothing, their complaisance being the crux of the Empire's political mechanism. The legislators, for their part, failed to discern the truth and were prepared to rally the country behind Napoleon in the teeth of what they took for a warlike coalition seeking to dismember France. Their commission did, however, in the person of its reporter, Joseph Lainé, politely raise a few implicit criticisms of imperial domestic government: the Emperor was "supplicated" to ensure that laws be executed in such a way as "to guarantee the French their rights of liberty, security, property, and give the nation its free exercise of its political rights." Napoleon's counselors saw nothing so untoward or impudent in the report, which, as Thiers notes, rested on the well-accepted Enlightenment principle that national spirit was a product of patriotism tied to justice and liberty: "the soil and the law."[44]

It was otherwise with the Emperor, as Cambacérès and Caulaincourt feared it would be. Acting against the spirited advice of the Council of State, he took the Lainé Report for a hostile and disloyal act in the face of the enemy. If it were allowed to stand, he insisted, it would encourage the legislature to get ideas. He prorogued the body and ordered Savary to embargo the report. These acts created consternation, but it was nothing compared to the sensation that followed a week later at a New Year's Day reception at the Tuileries. His Majesty descended from the throne to upbraid the offending legislators who were present. It is worth quoting for the insight it affords into this man's occasional lack of common sense and failure to be politic, even (perhaps especially) in extremis:

> What do you want, to grab power? And what would you do with it? Who among you could exercise it? . . . And where is your mandate? France knows me, does she know you? She twice chose me as her chief by several million votes, while you were chosen by a few hundred votes in your departments. . . . What is the throne but four pieces of wood and ormolu upholstered in velvet? The throne is a man, and that man is me, with my will, my character, and my renown! It is I, not you, who can save France. . . . I would have heard you out, if you'd come to me privately, your mistake was to wash our dirty linen in public. . . . Monsieur Lainé is a wicked man who is in correspondence with the Bourbons and the British, I have proof. . . . When I throw the enemy back and have concluded peace, then whatever it costs my ambition, as you call it, I shall recall [the Legislative Body], and order publication of your report, and you will be astonished that you could have spoken to me as you did.

The charge against Lainé was, of course, false, but that outrage was lost amid so many others. What is most curious is the misreading this spleen-venting represents of a group of mainly sincere and docile deputies who never in their wildest dreams saw themselves as Dantons challenging the Emperor's Robespierre. Thiers is right to note that publishing the report would not have had nearly the deplorable impact that these subsequent acts and words had. On the contrary, doing so would have given the government a needed ally (the Legislative Body) in its campaign to unite the French around the (false) idea that the Allies, and not Napoleon, were at fault in not wanting peace.

Napoleon went through some of the motions of a national government. He sacrificed Foreign Minister Maret—judged too aggressive—and sought to replace him with Talleyrand, but Talleyrand foresaw doom and chose to make his own way in the coming crisis.[45] Caulaincourt took the portfolio. The Emperor confessed to a private audience of select senators that "I have made too much war . . . I was wrong: my projects were not in proportion to the strength and desires of the French people." These senators then left for the provinces, to rally the nation, but they were an old and conservative group of cronies and included none of Napoleon's well-known critics, which might have added to their credibility. Far more effective would have been a corps of younger, more passionate liberal legislators, but then the Emperor was looking to raise troops and materiel, not sow the social whirlwind—and provincials sensed as much.

Still less, therefore, did the Emperor recall Fouché and a team of ex-Jacobins, so useful in a war crisis, as the Directory and General Bonaparte had understood. The far left was sufficiently frightened of the Allies and of revived royalism that they would have served the hated Emperor, hoping to turn him into a Dictator of Public Safety of the Year II. But if Napoleon now mistrusted the wealthy and the conservative, he could not bring himself to issue carte blanche to the peasants and the workers, with whom his stock still sold high. He could dress-down a foot-dragging marshal, "The *patrie* is in danger, it is threatened. It's time to put on the boots and resolve of 1793," but he did not put on those boots himself. When Sebastiane pressed him to "raise the nation," he replied that that was "chimera. . . . I have already crushed the Revolution."[46]

Which is to say, with his back to the wall, Napoleon did not deliver what he had threatened Metternich with: rebecoming Robespierre on horseback, making himself the First Citizen of the Republic within the Empire. The Emperor of the French only appealed to, he did not go with *la Nation*; he might order the *levée en masse* but only in certain departments (e.g., Alsace, January 4), where, in any case, it went unenforced by the local administration and notables, and Napoleon would not entrust its execution to Jacobins who offered their services. He would not starkly evoke the specter of social conflict between France and Europe, which he might have done, for it had never completely disappeared, even in the years since the Habsburg marriage. Fully accepting the "national" gambit, as the French understood it, would have meant renouncing much of what Napoleon saw himself as building since that marriage, and although he could threaten a Coalition prince with doing so, he could not bring himself to deliver it. It was not what he wanted anymore, even if, objectively speaking, it was what he represented in the eyes of Europe, and even to some Frenchmen. Instead, the imperial-proprietary tone remained the leitmotif of his communiqués, and the National Guard in Paris was armed only in the wealthy, not the poor districts.

The French, thus, did not fully catch fire or rise up en masse—far from it. Peasants shouted, "Long live the Emperor!" but they also shouted, "Down with these taxes!"[47] The Treasury minister observed: "Napoleon would barely assemble enough soldiers to resist the enemy than he . . . would dispense with the smallest regard given to public opinion. . . . [The result was] people said to themselves, 'The Emperor hasn't changed; the lesson of all this misery has been lost.' "[48] In the face of such dejection, even the Empire's remarkable conscription machine failed. Tens of thousands of men evaded the draft (of 300,000 called, 63,000 showed up) or deserted the ranks of the Grande Armée, now a shrunken mockery of its name. Defection proved all the easier as typhus raged in armies already dispirited by hunger, cold, and a dearth of uniforms and equipment.[49] Those provinces not quickly overrun by the enemy were sapped by the royalists and dissident clergy, or by lassitude and sickness. In the eastern departments (politically, the most loyal), Napoleon mobilized the National Guard and set up the free corps, but these remained a dead letter because his marshals assigned to these sectors governed with a heavy and conservative hand.

In the last analysis, Napoleon did not feel he had to radically alter his style, for, in defiance of common sense, he still felt he could win the war with the Coalition—that is, throw them back and force an advantageous peace for France. He had told the senators that he was done with war, and some historians (Thiers) have believed him. Perhaps when he beheld the barely concealed insolence in even the most obsequious courtiers, the lassitude in his marshals, the streams of tears in Marie-Louise's eyes, and the frustration and *tristesse* on the faces of his highest officials—starting with Cambacérès, who was now seeking refuge in religion—perhaps *then* he sincerely believed that he had learned his lesson. Yet one is permitted to wonder. If he had beaten the Coalition, would he have long remained content with a "good" peace? The image that comes to mind is that here was a compulsive gambler who has doubled down twice (in 1812 and in 1813), and has lost big. He solemnly promises that he will stop after one more win, and he asks his backers to stand him again. They do, but with death in their souls.

One who rallied was his older brother. No longer *Don José Primero,* though clinging to the honorific "Roi," Joseph Bonaparte had pouted for a time after returning to France from the disaster of his "national" kingship of Spain. But when Napoleon wrote him to say, "[A]ll Europe is in arms against France, especially against me. . . . What is your intention?" Joseph stood by the throne like the good French prince he was. He was made lieutenant governor of the Empire for his pains, second only to the Regent-Empress.

A fortnight later, the first Emperor of the French "confided" his wife and his son to the keeping of the Paris National Guard, whose leadership had been specially convoked for that purpose. It was a touching but rigorously formal ceremony, nothing of which would have reminded the observer that this was the same great hall of the Tuileries where a mob had forced the late Louis XVI to don the "national" Phrygian bonnet. Later the next night, Napoleon burned many of his private papers, and on the morning of January 25 at 6 A.M., he left for the front. It was only ninety miles away.

THE LION IN WINTER:
THE CHAMPAGNE CAMPAIGN (1814)

War is a conflict that does not determine who is right—but who is left.
                                        —Anonymous

If the canny political and diplomatic infighter in the Emperor has left the scene, the uncanny general remains. Napoleon's owl of Mars flew in this twilight as gracefully as it had flown in the dawn and high noon of his career. The year 1814 has the feel of a drawn-out campaign because it had no mammoth and decisive battles, and because the military and diplomatic states of affairs changed so often, or seemed to. Given the meager French resources in men, materiel, and morale, two months was a considerable length, to which only Napoleon could have drawn things out. Only when we consider that the fate of the Empire and the dynasty hung in the balance does the time frame seem rapid. The French army was outnumbered by Prussian, Russian, and Austrian forces by factors of two, three, and four to one—with the promise of endlessly more Coalition (but not French) reinforcements.

Looking back, one has the fatalistic impression of a man putting up a brave battle against terminal cancer, but that is only posterity's view. To contemporaries, the terminal was not known by anyone, least of all by the victim himself. Napoleon, alone, long kept his faith and his cool, perhaps at the price of his realism. "I have never been seduced by prosperity; adversity will find me beyond the reach of its attacks," he had said before he left Paris, and the record in this ordeal of winter and early spring bore him out far more often than it did not. The Allies, divided and profoundly suspicious of one another, had a hard time teaching themselves that one goal—one alone—must impose on them not merely unity, but endurance and virtually any sacrifice. Once that cup was drained, they could focus on a common strategy, and then the end came soon.

Militarily, this was a sophisticated war of maneuver among seasoned generals and armies; the "Marie-Louises" rose brilliantly to the occasion, not to mention the remainder of the veteran Imperial Guard. But Coalition men also fought nobly and often intelligently, and indeed one has the impression that those fabled, oft-invoked *Patriotes* and *Nationaux* of Valmy (1792) would perhaps not have lasted two hours in the field against any of these 1814 contenders. The campaign took place in a far smaller space than any until now: a vaguely pentagonal area covering 130 miles from west (Paris) to east (Saint-Dizier), and 90 miles from north (Laon) to south (Sens). Since much of the war took place in the Champagne region of France, we might call it the Champagne campaign. As in northern Italy in 1796–97, Napoleon took full advantage of holding the interior lines, planting himself and his small army (usually not more than 30,000 men under his direct command) centrally, then striking out with lightning speed to make surprise attacks on individual Allied armies.

After getting off to a bad start, with a tactical defeat at La Rothière (February 1) which so demoralized the locals that they all but refused to give aid to their comrades in arms, the Emperor pulled himself together, gruffly ordered the government in Paris to "stop with this religious monkey business [having masses said for the fate of French arms], which is scaring everyone to death," and made a miraculous recovery. In the Five Days' Battle (February 10–14) he inflicted triple defeats (at Champaubert, Montmirail, and Vauchamps) on several Prussian generals, including, satisfyingly, Yorck, the turncoat, and *Der Grosser Feldmarschall* himself, Blücher.[50] Then, in an incredible march—forty-seven miles in thirty-six hours!—Napoleon clipped the nails of the Russians at Mormant (February 17), and the very next day, of the Austrian commander in chief, Schwarzenberg, at Montereau. A flurry of negotiations now took place, entailing a flagging in hostilities for a time. When fighting resumed, Napoleon bloodily repulsed the Russian Winzingerode at Craonne (March 7), followed by a costly and indecisive action at Laon (March 9–10). Napoleon retook Reims from the Prussians (March 14), but misread the location of Blücher's main force. In the final phase of the campaign, the Emperor strove to maneuver behind enemy lines, but he misjudged Prince Schwarzenberg, who for once dug in, at Arcis (March 20–21). The French fought him cunningly and valiantly, but the odds were overwhelming, and Napoleon had to retreat to avoid annihilation. Arcis was the last major engagement. Now began a series of rapid, but desperate and futile French marches and countermarches, while the Allies descended on Paris, which fell on the thirty-first. A few days later, Napoleon holed up at Fontainebleau with approximately 60,000 troops.

If the Emperor's generalship in the *Campagne de France* withstands comparison with Hannibal's,[51] the fact remains: his defeats of the Allies were never pulverizing, only demoralizing and humiliating—and most often, more costly in French casualties than Napoleon could afford. Sharp temporary reverses inflicted on this or that Coalition general—even as late as the French recapture of Reims (March 13)—sorely tested Allied nerve and resolve, and *seemed* to throw the whole outcome into the air. The peace congress sitting at Châtillon even offered the French emperor terms in mid-February—terms that Caulaincourt, for one, was burning to accept—but Napoleon's Five-Day triumphs "hardened Pharaoh's heart," so to speak, and he preferred to gamble on complete victory in the field. Given the crushing numbers he faced, the chance of this was as remote as the hope that beseeching letters to his father-in-law might detach Francis I from his allies.

The Coalition may have been frangible, but Napoleon, true to form, kept it monolithic, something William Pitt had said would never happen. He did so, not least, because he insisted on changing the terms he would accept, as his military position improved. This went on into March, exasperating the powers and ultimately resulting in Napoleon's failure to negotiate while he still had anything to negotiate with. Metternich had predicted the previous fall that "Napoleon will not make peace. There is my profession of faith, and I shall never be happier than if I am wrong."[52] In February, just after the victory at Champaubert, the Napoleonic police reported that people were complaining, "If the Emperor is victorious even once, he will no longer want to make peace."[53] The Allies *finally* came to believe this. At Chaumont in early March, they signed a solemn agreement to fight for twenty years, if need be, to have done with this man, for "*so long as he lives, there can be no security,*" said Lord Aberdeen—and then repeated himself.[54]

Many writers maintain that at some point in this ghastly winter the

Emperor relaxed his grip on reality itself and took refuge in illusion, as if his ever-vigorous tendency to recount events as he wished the reader or listener to understand them bled into how he himself saw them. On March 14, after retaking Reims, he swells up to Joseph: "I am the master today every bit as much as I was at Austerlitz." And only a week before the fall of Paris, he assures Caulaincourt that his decree of the *levée en masse* is going to create "a great insurrection" which will turn the tide. As the capital lies invested, on the eve of its surrender to 200,000 Allied troops, he tells Chief of Staff Berthier: "If only I had arrived sooner, all would be saved." The foreign minister concludes: "[T]he Emperor blinded himself to his perils as well as to his resources. . . . He treated counsels of prudence as if they displayed weakness. . . . [H]e thought to escape from the dangers that were crowding him on every side by misrepresenting them to himself."[55]

Yet it is dangerous to decide confidently what Napoleon actually knew or what he was capable of. The Duke of Wellington, having studied this campaign, later said that the French emperor, had he executed his military plan, might well have saved Paris and inflicted a stunning defeat on the Allied host in and around Paris. In fairness to Napoleon, moreover, the terms being offered by the Allies in March, as opposed to those of late 1813 or January 1814 (both variations on "the natural boundaries"), could only be seen by him as an utter humiliation: not merely the reduction of France to her boundaries of 1790, but France's effective exclusion from the subsequent decision-making diplomacy that would dispose of States like Westphalia, Bavaria, Poland, northern Italy, and Saxony, which she herself had created and in whose fate she was deeply bound up. Louis XIV, in the last years of his reign, also fought a disastrous war for imperialist reasons (the French candidacy to the Spanish throne) against a coalition made up of England, Austria, and Prussia. And although the Sun King was militarily on his uppers, he refused the "dishonorable" conditions proposed to him by the coalition, and instead fought it out to the bitter end. Moreover, Louis's "ancient" and "sacred" legitimacy notwithstanding, he also issued a most unusual "letter to our peoples" wherein he justified his action and called for his subjects' support.[56]

So with Napoleon. Prince Schwarzenberg, the Austrian commander, had in 1813 opined that the Emperor must be forced to become, in effect, simply "King of France."[57] If Napoleon, enjoying a strong field position and possessing an army still very much intact, elected to fight on rather than accept that demotion, it was not *simply* because he was crazed with ambition, but because, by his lights, what was being offered was unreasonable and dishonorable, and because he had a shot at doing better.[58]

ABDICATION?

The moment has finally come when Divine Providence seems ready to break the instrument of its wrath.

                                        —Louis XVIII[59]

Two pieces are competing for our attention in these opening weeks of the cruelest month. In Paris, appropriately, we have a vast historical drama, in many acts, with many tableaux, much movement, and a stellar cast (but no single star) being presented before a huge audience—virtually, a world audience, if you consider who was paying attention. Meanwhile, thirty-five miles to the southeast, in Fontainebleau, a small play is being enacted by one man and a handful of supporting players. The man and most of the players will see their production as a Greek tragedy, replete with decisive roles for malign fate and friendly betrayers—and they will have a point. Others, however, will see it as bourgeois drama, if only because the lead player is so self-consciously playing his part. They, too, will have a point.

It is appropriate that a regime that sought to suppress parties and politics should succumb to them, not to military defeat. To Count Pozzo di Borgo went the credit of persuading Tsar Alexander I that the Allies were wasting their time in late March by continuing the duel with Napoleon in the field. Better to outflank him politically, Pozzo argued, by marching to Paris and dealing with his numerous domestic enemies.[60] That he had enemies, the Coalition was well aware, having intercepted dispatches intended for Napoleon written by Marie-Louise and Minister of Police Savary. These made clear not only the low state of Parisian morale but the effervescence of *les partis,* particularly that representing the Bourbon cause. It dawned on the Coalition that the French capital might well follow the recent examples of Bordeaux and Toulouse, which had turned themselves over to Bourbon supporters—albeit not without a "friendly" shove from Wellington and his army. In Pozzo's unforgettable words, "Only touch Paris with your finger and the colossus will be overthrown."

The problem—or opportunity—in Paris was that a political vacuum was about to be opened. In the last week of March, as the Allies' forces approached the anxious city, the debate grew heated within the government about what to do. The Regent might well have heeded the counsel of certain ex-revolutionaries among the Empire's servants, who pressed her to install herself and the King of Rome in the Town Hall and "call out the people." It was estimated that perhaps a hundred thousand might rise up. The clinching argument against this gambit (aside from the fact that there was not nearly sufficient military rifles available in Paris to arm "the people") was two imperial letters introduced by Joseph late in the debate. Napoleon, knowing that his wife was effectively a child, and fearing that she might become the docile instrument of her father and the Coalition, had written some weeks earlier to firmly negate any recourse to keeping the Empress and the King of Rome in the besieged capital.

Neither Joseph nor Cambacérès dared counsel disobedience, though they understood the demoralizing effect the imperial family's departure would have on the capital. On the thirtieth, Marie-Louise and the little king duly left for the Loire (Blois), leaving behind considerable ill will and accusations of desertion. Napoleon, had he been able to be contacted at this point, would probably have ordered them all to remain at their posts and to declare the *levée en masse*—instructing citizens, if necessary, to use their personal (hunting) arms—for he was marching hard for Paris, and was possessed (there is no other word for it) of the notion that he could trap the Allies between his approaching army and the embattled citizens of the capital. If there was a large measure of wishful thinking in this plan, there was also a distinct measure of plausibility, given the mind that had conceived it. Paris gave herself up to the Allies on March 31, after a spirited military action of a single day. As the imperial government had now fled as well, a true political void opened up, about which Napoleon, at Fontainebleau, could do nothing.

Into this void stepped the Prince de Talleyrand with most nimble grace for a man who limped.[61] What cannot fail to strike us is that Talleyrand was alive and available at all—not shot or imprisoned, which is what he would have been had the Emperor been harsh and retaliatory toward the men who opposed or betrayed him. Talleyrand and the House of Bourbon had every reason to loathe each other (he was, after all, the bishop whose episcopal consecrations of four non-juring priests in 1791 had made the Constitutional Church apostolic), but the empire of circumstance was such in Paris this winter as to make these two parties the most satisfied of bedfellows.[62] The Grand Chamberlain insists in his memoirs that he led "no conspiracy against the Emperor," which is true only if one buys his argument that the imperial regime did not exist (as, of course, it did exist, beyond Paris), and that *something* had to stand up to deal with the Coalition.

Another saying of Talleyrand's is more pertinent, however: "I have never abandoned a party before it abandoned itself." After all is said about this man's opportunism and venality, the fact remains that he was most lucid and careful about whom he collaborated with. "His wisdom, moderation, and intellectual vanity," as Jacques Jourquin nicely puts it, "were stronger than his corruption."[63] There was no dearth of reasonable men and women in 1814, including fervent ex-adepts of Napoleon, who believed that their "great Emperor" had "lost himself." The question for Talleyrand was whom to throw his hat to, and here it came down to a process of elimination. The Republic was out of the question, damned by its excesses in the Revolution, and in any case, not remotely sanctionable by the Allied sovereigns. The tsar's early favorite, Bernadotte of Sweden, aroused no sympathy from the public,[64] but the Bourbon cadres had been splendidly effective—far more so than their princes (Louis XVIII or his brother the Comte d'Artois, and Artois's sons) had proven charismatic. They had managed to infiltrate and bring around whole cities and regions (always with English military help, however), giving the impression of a groundswell. The Allies, now, as in 1806, had a secret convention to restore the Bourbons; and the British Prince Regent, Castlereagh, Metternich, and Francis I were all (unlike Talleyrand or Alexander I) personally well disposed to Louis XVIII. However, no one was inclined to cram him down France's throat; all had to be shown that the "third dynasty" was wanted. The Bourbons and their followers understood as much and performed brilliantly. Talleyrand gave them the nod. Where he now demonstrated exceptional skill was in persuading the initially dubious Tsar Alexander that this case was cogent. The principle of legitimacy, in short, was suddenly much in vogue this April in Paris.

Not that the overthrow of the Empire lay within the competency of the royalists. The imprint of Napoleon on France was still so bold as to make it inconceivable to most French men and women that their country could exist without him. Thibaudeau wrote that nearly all Frenchmen still believed the fourth dynasty to be "unshakeable," and the return of the *patrie* to its "ancient" frontiers and its former royal house to be "unthinkable."[65] The royalists, thus, could not have deposed the Empire unless the Coalition were willing to impose (and maintain) them by force, which was out of the question.

However, the servants of the Empire, gathered in the one institution that rivaled the Emperor for authority, could wield the axe on their own roots— if they had the stomach to: the imperial Senate, of which, conveniently, Prince Talleyrand was vice president. There is no need to reach for complex political psychology ("in adulating him, the Senators had always hated him in their hearts")[66] to explain the senators' deposition of the ruler who had made every one of their careers. The empire of circumstance again exerted its irresistible pull, including the consideration that Napoleon had committed "crimes" that betrayed France's "liberty" in numerous ways, among them, "illegal" taxes, conscriptions, and wars. The Senate did without joy what needed to be done (though nothing in the constitution of the year XII gave them the right to depose the Emperor), well aware in their grave and sad hearts of the obvious Napoleonic reproach: "You backed me each step of the way without one murmur. If I am the despot and madman they say I am, consider that you sanctioned my every move and accepted my every gift." To which, the equally obvious, equally crushing rejoinder: "There you sit, in Fontainebleau, pigheaded as ever, with a military solution that no one but you believes in, and, in any case, the Allies have voted they won't deal with you. The people of Paris are abandoned and someone has to tote this load." Did the senators believe as much in what they did now as they had believed in their fulsome speeches of a decade earlier—so far away and long ago—when they had proclaimed the Empire?

In the next few days, the Senate voted the creation of a provisional government presided over by Talleyrand[67] and the formal deposition of the Empire, and they published a proclamation to the army, which did not go over well with the men in uniform at Fontainebleau: "[I]f a man who isn't even French could so weaken the honor of our armies, [then] . . . you are no longer soldiers of Napoleon." The Napoleonic army—the men who had by general agreement suffered the most at the Emperor's hands—were also they who remained the most fiercely loyal to him, *always.*

Napoleon did what he could to influence events that were transpiring where he was not. In this, he received signal service from his emissary, Caulaincourt, who won universal respect for his valiant, if fruitless efforts to cut through the web of intrigue being spun by the provisional government and the royalists. The foreign minister held two trump cards: the tsar's longstanding personal affection for him, and that ruler's new desire, having won his longed-for victory over *le grand Napoléon*, to show himself magnanimous. Posterity can thank the Romanov for keeping the Prussians from acting out their *Rachsucht* (revenge lust), which would likely have led to the blowing up of the Jena and Austerlitz bridges and the Arc de Triomphe.[68] Alexander also exhibited great tact, not to say flattery, in his handling of French sensibilities as a defeated power. In sum, his victory "performance," which is what this was, achieved its goal: it was superior to Napoleon's in similar circumstances.

Caulaincourt now sifted some sand into the provisional government's and the royalists' well-functioning machine. It might have been different had Castlereagh and Francis I been present, but as they stayed in Dijon until the tenth, Alexander had Paris to himself, with little input from Frederick William III, his close but utterly subordinate ally. In his fickleness, the tsar let his imagination be swayed by Caulaincourt's passionate plea on behalf of "saving" Marie-Louise as regent for her "hapless" son, Napoleon II. Pozzo di Borgo, who all along had been supplying his patron with a stream of misinformation about the Bourbons' alleged high standing in the country, now bent himself double reminding the tsar that hesitation, after agreements had been made and institutions set in place, could spell civil war. One of his arguments deserves citation for its cogency: "The French people do not know how to wait nor stay calm in uncertainty. It is important not to give them any pretext to have doubts about their future, unless you want to expose yourself to the greatest problems."[69] His words might yet not have taken but for an act of what the tsar took to be Providence.

ABJECTION

There are days, sad days! when one's duty is obscure and the most honest hearts are perplexed.

—Adolphe Thiers[70]

Meanwhile, in Fontainebleau, the French emperor burned to return this conflict to the field of battle whence it was snatched with such legerdemain ten days before. He had over 60,000 troops and the eventual promise of many more—Suchet's and Soult's veterans from Spain; Augereau's corps in Lyon; Eugène's army from Italy; and who knew, perhaps, at some point, Davout's corps from Hamburg.[71] So he reasoned, on the basis of the information and mostly the hopes that he had. (In fact, none of these units lay within striking distance of Paris, or was likely to be, anytime soon.) To fall on the unsuspecting Prussians at Essonne, while simultaneously detonating a rising in Paris remained his great plan—harebrained in any hands but these, but still unlikely to work, even in his. If Napoleon was thus aching to fight it out in and around the capital—"all the splendors of Paris, were they to succumb in a single day" were well worth the victory[72]—his marshals: Macdonald, Oudinot, Lefebvre, Ney were not. On April 4 they pressed him hard in a painful and extraordinary (indeed, a unique) confrontation, until he gave them a vaguely worded abdication on behalf of his son, and sent them off to Paris to aid Caulaincourt in negotiating with the Allies. The tsar, he knew, was partial to Napoleonic marshals. In fact the Emperor was not thinking so much of actually departing the scene as he was thinking of his attack, and how it would, in one fell swoop, change everything: "Just a few hours, my dear Caulaincourt, and all will change. What satisfaction, what glory there will be!"

Now, in a trice, things did change, but not for the better, as Napoleon understood it. In the epigraph to this section, Thiers comments on the radical divergence in the view of what was "true" between those, like the marshals, who saw Paris and its citizens day to day and those, like Napoleon, who remained *extra muros,* metaphorically as well as literally. Of the twenty-six imperial marshals, he who enjoyed the oldest association with *l'Empereur* was Auguste-Frédéric de Marmont—Napoleon's companion at Toulon, as we recall, an eighteen-year-old sublieutenant who so impressed his artillery commander that he kept him at his side ever after. The two companions, with Junot, had shared poverty and unemployment, pounding the Paris pavement together in 1795. Marmont had been Napoleon's aide-de-camp in Italy and Egypt and he was one of the bravest and most loyal of a marshalate known for its courage and devotion, and if his name is not included in the group of ranking officers who leaned heavily on Napoleon until he offered up his abdication, it is because Marmont did not in fact do so. He was, in his Emperor's eyes, the stalwart.

So of course it was this hand that held the knife. Prince Schwarzenberg had been systematically feeling out the marshals with letters and messengers, for it was well known that as a body they were unsympathetic to continuing the war, which they feared would decline into a civil conflict, and that some of them had other issues with their ruler. Only Marmont proved soft—not just on the patriotic issue of what was "best for France," but also on the political opportunity of being able to play a key role in restoring the Bourbons, whence great rewards would accrue to him. On the night of April 4–5, Marmont's divisional generals marched the VI Corps over to the Allied lines—to the shock and fury of the French soldiery, when it realized what had been done to it.[73] The news reached the tsar just as he was vacillating before Caulaincourt's and Pozzo di Borgo's impassioned arguments. Marmont's defection was, His Majesty felt, the voice of Providence, assuring him that Napoleon's cause was not completely supported even in the army. To the immense relief of the nervous provisional government and of his anguished chief political counselor, he now decided against any continuation for the fourth dynasty.

The attempt to justify Marmont's action by appeal to his concern to end a hopeless military contest must answer to the consideration that Marmont was *already aware* both of Napoleon's abdication and of the other marshals' unwillingness to continue the war. Second, the content of Marmont's exchange of letters with Schwarzenberg points to a *political* defection—that is, he saw himself playing the Monck to the Bourbon's Charles II. Finally, after VI Corps' transfer and the soldiery's newfound fury, Marmont had the opportunity to try to turn things around, but he did not take it; rather, he "humbly" accepted the thanks of the provisional government. Thiers's judgment that the marshal willingly played in the army the role that Talleyrand played in the political arena thus seems sound.[74] Marmont holds another record among the leading soldiers of French (not just Napoleonic) history: no Paris street or metro stop bears his name.

Many who opposed Napoleon tooth and nail, like Lazare Carnot, rallied to him in the defense of France. Viceroy Eugène was begged by his father-in-law, the king of Bavaria, to join the Coalition, but he heeded his wife's reproach: "I do not want my children to have a traitor for a father." Even Madame de Staël took Benjamin Constant to task for attacking Napoleon in print at this kind of time: "Is this the moment to be speaking ill of another Frenchman, when the flames of Moscow are threatening Paris?" And speaking of Moscow, is it not inconsistent to admire the Russians for abandoning—and firing—their "ancient" capital, and in the next breath, criticize Napoleon for his vehemence in wanting to fight for his capital?[75] Paris, in the Emperor's telling, was worth a mess.

The marshal's defection and the tsar's decision brought about the unconditional abdication, for which so much blood had been shed.[76] Events in Fontainebleau were now definitively eclipsed by events in Paris, where, among other novelties, the toppling of *l'Empereur*'s statue atop the Vendôme Column by a band of royalists made momentary news. (Napoleon's comment was what one might anticipate: he rued the day he ever allowed Vivant Denon to "put the damn thing up there.") As the momentousness of the abdication and the awareness of what was being said about him penetrated Napoleon's consciousness—a consciousness freed from its burden of focus on his plan of attack on the Allies—he passed through moods and humors from reflective and resigned to sad, despairing, grave. Caulaincourt found him stoic ("As I saw him in his days of glory and prosperity, so did he appear to me in the day of his distress"), inclined to plaintive meditations on the order of "They [the Coalition sovereigns] are treating me as if they were Jacobins, which is not how I treated them. I might have deposed the Emperor Francis and King Frederick William, as I could have let loose the Russian peasants against Tsar Alexander, but I didn't do it."[77]

Occasionally a solar prominence of a plan will flare up from the surface of the dying star—"[I shall] take back my abdication . . . and retire [with my army] to the Loire and await Soult['s corps, etc.]"—but immediately it is followed by resignation and languor ("I don't have the strength"). In his changes of mind, the Emperor is reminiscent of his recent prisoner in this sad purlieu–Pope Pius VII. E. E. Y. Hales writes: "[W]hereas Pius had suffered the bitter self-reproach of a man who feels he has betrayed the cause of truth, Napoleon suffered the remorse of the gambler who has lost all. And where Pius never ceased to blame himself, and only himself, and did penance for his fault, Napoleon never blamed himself."[78] This is harsh. Constant, Napoleon's valet, however, noticed his patron's "extreme agitation" ("he had torn at his leg with his nails until the blood flowed, without realizing what he had done") and heard his "stifled sighs." Napoleon was acutely aware that "My name, my face, and my sword frighten people. . . . This France, which I so wished to make great, I have left so small!" though it is true that his telltale tendency to blame others was never far away ("Ah, if only these imbeciles had not deserted me, in four hours I could have resurrected [France's] grandeur").

In recent weeks, Napoleon had been more contemptuous than usual of death. At one engagement, he reassured his soldiers, who were anxious at his standing in the line of enemy fire, "Heavens, my friends, fear nothing. The ball that will kill me has not yet been cast." At another battle a few weeks later, he guided his horse directly over an unexploded cannonball, which then went off, killing the horse and throwing the Emperor to the ground, though not harming him further. Now, on the evening of April 12–13, he swallowed a sachet of poison that he had carried around his neck since the Spanish campaign (where, given the rancor and retaliations on both sides, it would not have been advisable to fall prisoner). But either the dosage or the poison was too weak, and it only made Napoleon ill. His valet and later Caulaincourt sat by him and received an outpouring of self-pity that certainly illustrates Hale's judgment at times: "I have not been understood! . . . [T]hey will regret me when I am no more! Marmont dealt me the finishing stroke! The wretch! I loved him! Berthier has ruined me! My old friends, my old companions-in-arms [have ruined me]."

What the first Emperor of the French might have reflected on instead was the nature and limits of his appeal to "his" people. It might have struck him that out of the millions who had cheered him wildly, so very few elected to stand up and speak out on behalf of the Empire for which they had been so wildly enthusiastic when it shone. How could all this awe and admiration, this exuberance and joy that he inspired so suddenly reveal themselves as shallow in their anchorage in people's hearts—at least, in those of the *classe politique* (of notables and nobles), who were all that mattered at the moment?[79]

A person may react to another's obvious superiority with humility, love, and emulation, or, contrastingly, he or she may react with envy and resentment. Much will depend on how the superiority is manifest, how it conducts itself. The Napoleonic quest for *gloire* turned out to be the political equivalent of its author's narcissism, of a style that relied, to gain ends that were often laudable, on bedazzlement and intimidation, on manipulation by self-interest, pride, contempt, and fear. They were thus not a policy and style made for times of trouble and testing, of defeat—but then few political styles are. The political arena in general inspires little of that loyalty under threat and in defeat, which war, religion, and love so often inspire. Few tears are ever shed for a deposed political leader and his regime—and never fewer than in the long history of France.

Instead, resentment, envy, and gimlet-eyed faultfinding now kicked in with a vengeance. They were undoubtedly merited, even necessary, but it would have been infinitely better all around if they had come with measures of self-critical regard on the part of the freshly minted naysayers, who after all had allowed the whole thing to function so well for so long. No minister, no general, no legislator, no State counselor raised his voice and noted with a trace of irony, "But we were in this, too!" The "crimes" imputed to Napoleon for suppressed liberties, raised taxes, and endless conscription were well-known complaints; no revelation came forward about genocide, personal corruption or vice. What weighed now, and weighed heavily, in the balance—perhaps nowhere more than the balance in the Emperor's own mind—was the crime of military defeat.

Among the few who stood by him were some of the important women in his life. Josephine was at Malmaison, but she and Napoleon had never lost their friendship, which divorce, if anything, reinforced, as evidenced in their letters and his occasional visits after 1810. The Emperor's new wife, "Louise," was also a source of consolation, though she was not permitted to visit him. Their incessant letters mercifully soaked up some of his time at Fontainebleau. Finally, the steadfast "Marie" (Walewska) did come to visit him, but on the day she arrived (April 15), Napoleon was so distraught and distrait that he forgot she was there, and never asked her to be shown in. He wrote her a note of apology which ended: "Do not be unhappy. Think of me with pleasure and never doubt me," and he still possessed the ring that she had had made for him years earlier, on the inside band of which was inscribed "When you cease to love me, do not forgot that I love you."

Five days later, on the twentieth, the Emperor left Fontainebleau for his exile. In a very moving ceremony, he bade farewell to "the grumblers" (*les grognards*), as he affectionately called the Imperial Guard, the heroes of his triumphs. The regimental flag that he kissed may still be seen in the Museum of the French Army, in the Turenne room.

XIV

Nation-Talk:
The Liberal Empire

Aux armes, citoyens!
—"La Marseillaise"

"VESUVIUS NEXT DOOR TO NAPLES":
NAPOLEON ON ELBA (MAY 1814–MARCH 1815)

Springtime will bring us Napoleon, along with swallows and violets.
Fouché[1]

The terms of the Treaty of Fontainebleau allotted Napoleon his imperial title, a modest allowance of two million francs a year—payable by the French government—and sovereignty over the tiny (ninety-four-square-mile), mu-shaped isle of Elba, a mere nine miles off the Tuscan coast. The young captain of artillery would have been ecstatic at receiving unimpaired control of an island society in the Mediterranean—an islet with a long past, much disputed by imperial powers, which eventually fell into Tuscan hands, before being delivered over to the sovereignty of this democratic emperor with his Enlightenment vision of political modernity. Napoleon might have had Corsica instead, but he did not instruct Caulaincourt to press Alexander for it.[2] Perhaps it was too late in the day for him to want to become Paoli, though something of an Elban Paoli he in fact did become.[3]

Revealingly, the competition was fierce among thousands of *grognards* at

Fontainebleau to see who would accompany *l'Empereur* into exile, but only three Napoleonic collaborators (Cambronne, Drouot, and Bertrand) elected to go, and none was truly an important figure. Famously, Marie-Louise and the King of Rome were not permitted to go, though Napoleon kept their rooms available in his residence in Porto Ferraio. The tsar had pressed for them to join their husband and father, and just as predictably, the Emperor Francis had nixed the idea. For a time, "Louise" kept hoping (and promising) to visit, but then, and after meeting Count Neipperg, she lost interest.[4] Letizia Bonaparte, on the other hand, although she had spent the Empire living in Rome, believed it her duty to stand by her son in his time of trial, so she came to Elba; so did Napoleon's favorite sister, "Paulette," the Borghese *principessa,* who soon became the "star" of Elban high society. Joseph, Louis, and Jérôme were in Switzerland; Lucien, in Rome; all but Louis might have visited their brother in the fullness of time. Josephine had taken ill suddenly, and passed away (May 29), leaving yet another emptiness in Napoleon's heart.* Finally, the "Polish wife" (Maria Walewska) made a rapid visit to the island with their son.[5]

By and large, however, Napoleon, having not simply been at the center of the world but having *been* that center, was suddenly deprived of the power and people—*the action*—that he thrived on and that had become second nature to him. Gamely, he attacked the governance of the little island with the same zest for large projects and small details that characterized his government of *le Grand Empire.* He devised all manner of ideas and set into motion all sorts of schemes for irrigation, cultivation, construction, exploitation, beautification, and, of course, enlargement. Iron mining was made more profitable (but also social services were made available to the workers), streets were paved, and a pretty fountain with shooting water was built, but typically, most of the plans never even got started for want of time and resources. Not that it mattered, for his reputation with the twelve thousand Elbans, who evolved (virtually overnight) from mistrust and dislike of the new sovereign to "undying affection" for him when they realized the huge rise in profits, activity, and excitement, and the eternal fame his presence would assure them.[6]

We can only speculate about Napoleon's inner state of mind in the sec-

---

*His exile weighed heavily on Josephine: "Ah! Sire, that I cannot fly to you to give you the assurance that exile can only frighten vulgar minds, and that, far from diminishing a sincere attachment, Misfortune lends to it a renewed force." Mme de Staël, visiting Josephine at Malmaison, had had the effrontery to ask her if she still loved Napoleon. Without a word, the Empress left the room.

ond two-thirds of 1814 on Elba, for he did not share it with anyone who wrote it down, nor expatiate about it himself on paper (something he had not done for many years now). It certainly seems that April was the saddest month of his life to date. The perceived betrayals and the abdication were bad enough, but the journey to the coast from Fontainebleau (April 21–27) had been a veritable nightmare. The popular fury (usually royalist-inspired) vented on him grew to become so threatening that at one point Napoleon was obliged to put on an Austrian uniform to avoid recognition. He was, and remained, deeply shaken, or as Thibaudeau puts it, "Struck by lightning, he carried the scar."[7] As always, the reports of observers of Napoleon turn on the prior attitude of the writer—with exceptions: for example, an English naval officer, Captain Ussher, who met him in this period, succumbed to his charm and intellectual brilliance. Others, like Britain's unofficial representative on Elba, Colonel Neil Campbell, simply regarded "Bonaparte [as] a man of ordinary talents who has had a great deal of luck." Marshal Marmont, hardly a fair-minded source, noted (in memoirs written decades later) that the Napoleon of the later years was increasingly "indifferent," "whimsical," "disdainful," "dismissive," "blasé," and "quite passive."[8] People who dealt with him on Elba speak of a return of Napoleon's usual level of energy, activity, and cheerfulness, punctuated by short bouts of lethargy, bath-taking, brooding, and occasional sharp pains in his right side near the liver. To sum up, his life on the island generally seemed "tolerable and peaceful," as Fernand Beaucour nicely puts it.[9] Napoleon himself, looking back on this eleven-month interlude, put it differently to Las Cases: "When you are on a small island, once you have set in motion the machinery of civilization, there is nothing left to do but perish from the boredom . . ."

The rest of this oft-cited quotation is, of course, the famous: "—or to get away from it by some heroic venture." Truth be told, however, the threats pushing Napoleon to leave Elba were every bit the match of his natural inclination to flee. From our perspective, it seems unbelievably naive of men as savvy as the governors of the Sixth Coalition to imagine that they could simply be rid of a phenomenon like Napoleon by confining him to an island in the Tuscan archipelago. There, he was, "like Vesuvius next door to Naples," in Fouché's unforgettable phrase.

From virtually the first moment, most of the Allies, including very much the freshly re-royalized French government, began to regret, to fret about, to renege on, and to plan to alter the terms of the Treaty of Fontainebleau. In Vienna, where they were gathered at a congress to revive and recast the *ancien régime* so successfully that it would survive another century to 1914—and where the interests of Bourbon France were zealously promoted by the new and old minister of foreign affairs, Maurice de Talleyrand—consideration was being given to devising ways to remove the two remaining threats to reactionary Europe: Joachim Murat's increasingly "national" monarchy in Naples, and Napoleon's strange reign on Elba. The name of St. Helena had even arisen in connection with finding a more reliable "final destination" for the Emperor of the French.

The worst of it, from Napoleon's point of view, was not that he was being spied on from Corsica, Livorno, and in his own midst, but that Louis XVIII was not handing over the stipulated two million francs, despite forceful reminders by the tsar that honor required France to do so. Napoleon's exchequer (the 1,863,000 francs with which he had left France)[10] would be exhausted by the end of 1817. More to the point, the unpaid subsidy was an indicator of a more deeply menacing possibility: that he could be the object of other, more sinister projects, not excluding assassination.[11] Nothing in the treaty stipulated that Napoleon must stay on Elba. He was constantly beset by Italian patriots who exhorted him to join Murat and lead a national uprising in the nearby Boot. Napoleon, from his own experiences in governing large parts of Italy, considered the idea futile, and he disdained all such proposals.

But the news from France, and his experience with the French, led him to other conclusions.

THE KINGDOM OF THE WEATHER VANE:
RESTORATION FRANCE

*[A]nd thus France, widow of Caesar, suddenly felt
the pain of all her wounds. She swooned and fell into a
deep sleep, so that her old king, thinking her dead,
wrapped her in a white shroud.*
—Alfred de Musset,
Confessions of a Child of the Century

What is the importance of style in politics? The answer: nearly all, at least in the short run, which is what usually matters. Royalism plodded back to aquilar* France like a swaying baggage mule, following the Coalition army; it would presently sneak out, like a jackal in the night; but in between these

*The *aquila* was the Roman legionary eagle, which Napoleon adopted for his Empire.

times—for the eleven months that Napoleon reigned on Elba—the House of Bourbon acted with a fair degree of wisdom, rather like a pig, which, it is said, is the most intelligent of animals. However, the first Restoration, like the pig, ran afoul of contemporary Frenchmen, as it has run afoul of posterity, for style. It did not help that the gouty *Porc Royal* who now besat the throne weighed 310 pounds, and whose manifest contrast with his predecessor could not have been greater. Alfred de Musset also wrote: "One man only had life in Europe then, and the rest of the world simply tried to fill its lungs with the air he breathed." Not even royalists jostled for a place to breathe Louis XVIII's air.[12]

The penultimate Bourbon king of France proved himself liberal and con-ciliatory in important ways—lifting the censorship, establishing a bicameral legislature with real powers, retaining much of the Napoleonic civil service and administrative structures—but he was reactionary in form: he refused the title that the provisional government offered him, "King of the French," for the traditional "Roi de France et de Navarre." He proved implacable about numbering himself "the eighteenth" and dating 1814 as the "nineteenth year of our reign," as though he had acceded to the crown at the death of the dauphin in 1795. The émigré nobility came back in force, smothering the throne, led by the arch-reactionary Comte d'Artois, brother to the king. Artois and the conspicuously royalist aristocracy ("the Ultras") set a tone of contained fury and expressed disdain; they controlled the court and high society. The venal flocked to the new patronage; in popular eyes, the Legion of Honor had been replaced by the Order of the Weather Vane—a book that became a bestseller in 1815.[13]

The priests were also back. The Empire had welcomed the Church but kept it in its place; in the Restoration, the Church's place was central and indiscreet. The man in the street could once again be charged with a capi-tal offense for desecrating the sacrament. The tricolor cockade was out; the white, notably the white of the lovely fleur-de-lis ("the white shroud" Mus-set wrote about) was de rigueur. Thrones have turned on less, and not just among the allegedly "volatile" French. The American reader might consider this hypothesis: the American colonies have lost the War of Indepen-dence, and George III has reextended his reign over them—only more intelligently the second time around. He concedes the Bill of Rights and much of the Constitution, while retaining most of the members of the Continental Congress and their civil service. Only the founding fathers are gone but not hanged, not even charged. Benedict Arnold, however, is the new governor general, residing in the capital, renamed Georgetown; the national hymn is, of course, "God Save the King" again, and a large memo-

STEVEN ENGLUND

rial is to be built in the Georgetown Mall to the memory of . . . Captain André.

The Treaty of Paris that Louis's foreign minister, Talleyrand, signed reduced French borders drastically from what they had been. The Charter that Louis swore to uphold took France on giant strides toward a constitutional monarchy, and if it rested on an ambiguity at its center—as to the precise limits of the two sovereignties: "national" and "divine right"—then so had the imperial monarchy rested on the same one.[14] As Macaulay remarks (with un-Whiggish concision): Louis XVIII "would not have been a despot if he could, and could not have been a despot if he would."[15] Yet the superficial fact that the king signed the treaty (he had no choice whatever; any government would have done so) and "conceded" the Charter—as though his authority were absolute and divine, like that of "Our esteemed Ancestors," not "national," like Napoleon's—counted against him with the French, more than the charter's liberal content weighed in his favor. And so, the "unity and forgetfulness" which Louis claimed he wanted for France were not to be had, as the well-meaning king stumbled from one gaffe to the next.[16]

The mysterious, powerful, and invisible force called "public opinion"—never seduced by the Bourbons, to begin with—soon shifted badly against them, as workaday Frenchmen, particularly in the army (half of whose ranks had been retired at half pay), convinced themselves that "the Nation" had been snubbed—no, "wronged," no, "oppressed!"—by the new regime. It helped not at all that the government's paid pamphleteers, like Chateaubriand, heaped vilification on Napoleon, for *l'Empereur,* by the curious osmosis of public reception, became *l'Empire,* became thirty million Frenchmen. And thus although Louis owed his throne to the Revolution as much as Napoleon did (both had needed Louis XVI's death to accede), the traditional notion of legitimacy presently became much less legitimate in the nation's eyes than the "democratic" claims of the "usurper." As Thibaudeau memorably puts it: "He who is daily vilified as usurper, despot, tyrant, Nero, Attila . . . pulled himself up by his own genius. He emerged from our ranks, we gave him our own votes, and if he oppressed our liberties, that is between him and us. He was not imposed by the foreigner. *He is obviously national.*"[17]

So it came to pass that Louis the Longed-For, as the Knights of the Faith had so reverently referred to the Comte de Provence in the long years of his rambling exile, became, by the autumn of 1814, Louis the Undesirable. One recalls Emmanuel Sieyès's great remark that "the so-called historical verities [about a nation's political preferences] have no more foundation in reality than the so-called verities of religion."[18]

None of which meant that a revolution was at hand. For that, the action of a single man was needed.

NATION-TALK ABANDONED

We know that nation-talk is not simply a fervent instance of country-love, but is, rather, a particular—demanding and strenuous—form of "apolitical" politics. Frederick William III discovered the difficulties when he encountered his Prussian "patriots" after 1806, and so did the Emperor Napoleon himself in 1813–14. Something happened to nation-talk in France after Napoleon's abdication. The Bourbon Restoration, in the apparent weakness of its unprepossessing head of State, and in the traditionalist trappings of his monarchy, saw nation-talk swiftly regain the position it had long occupied in the eighteenth century, as the language (the "discursive repertoire," to use the technical phrase) of the political opposition. Nation-talk's primary loci of usage, we might say, moved from the Tuileries and the government ministries back to the clubs, cafes, barracks, and newspapers, as *la politique* reinvaded the public space and political parties sought to compete with and differentiate themselves from one another.

Was this all *simply* a matter of words? In one sense, yes, it was, but of course the words required systematic action in order to become plausible, and in this regard, it is interesting to note what happened when four of the greatest political actors of the era—all inveterate *nationaux*: Carnot, Fouché, Constant, and de Staël—each earnestly pressed Louis XVIII to adapt himself and his monarchy to the new idiom.[19] It was not simply a matter of being patriotic—the royal government made its share of *patrie*-inspired statements—but of being *national,* as Napoleon had been *national* (although more so in the early years than in the later). Constant and Carnot pressed the king "to rally to the nation," by which they meant nothing ethnocultural: the king, after all, was French, spoke French, and lived like a French aristocrat. Nor did they mean substantive political reform, for the royal charter offered what was, for the era, liberal constitutional government. They meant, as everyone in France intuitively understood, *a style of governance* using the *language* of nation-talk, with its constant references to: sovereignty of the nation/people, flouted national independence, reduced national borders, abused national pride, the glorious nation-in-arms, and the "sacred" cause of national *revanche* for the Treaty of Paris.[20]

Louis's stammering attempt at nation-talk came at a quarter to midnight—Napoleon was approaching Auxerre, to be embraced by Ney—and can only strike us as pathetic. He put on his Legion of Honor medal for the first time, and he addressed the united chambers of the parliament. In the speech, which he himself had written and which he gave from memory, "national" appears precisely once,[21] submerged in a sea of "my realm," "the State," "my *patrie*," "my people," "good Frenchmen," and "the constitutional Charter that I have given you." Meanwhile, his supporters had long been castigating Napoleon as a "foreigner" (the "Corsican ogre,"),[22] which was a *national* way of doing political business, but a poor reply to the charge that the Bourbons were puppets of the foreigner (the Coalition). Ultimately, it was not merely a case of too little, too late, it was a case of not being able to serve two masters: the fundamental references and symbols of the restored Bourbon monarchy were dynastic, religious, and royal, not *national*. It is harder to be *national* than it is to be French or to love France.

THE EAGLE HAS LANDED

I had as yet no notion that life every now and then becomes literature—not for long, of course, but long enough to be what we best remember, and often enough so that what we eventually come to mean by life are those moments when life, instead of going sideways, backwards, forwards, or nowhere at all, lines out straight, tense, and inevitable, with a complication, climax, and given some luck, a purgation, as if life had been made and not happened.

–Norman MacLean,
A River Runs Through It

If Napoleon had decided on Elba to become the (sort of) writer that he will become on St. Helena, he might have written a novel called "The Flight of the Eagle." But instead he chose to "write" his novel on the world, not on paper, and thus to live up to what he had said at the outset of the Consulate: "The novel of the Revolution is over; it is time to make it history." The episode we now treat is unquestionably novelistic—a full-dress romance—perhaps the most fantastic episode in a fantastic career.

As we are not privy to Napoleon's inner thoughts on Elba, we can only speculate on the moment (surely in the winter of 1814–15) and reasoning that led to his decision to attempt a return to France. Perhaps the clincher was receiving news that a plot was afoot to replace Louis XVIII with his cousin, the more liberal Duc d'Orléans (as would indeed happen in 1830). The truth was, Napoleon on Elba, as one historian puts it, "was like a tiger which has

been put into a cage with the door badly latched; then he has been threatened, harassed, and deprived of food."[24] So like Hernán Cortés setting out to
conquer Mexico with a few hundred men, Napoleon set sail for France, landing at the Golfe-Juan, near Cannes, on the first day of the month named for
the God of War. He had twelve hundred soldiers with him—essentially an
honor guard, not a fighting force.

Despite assurances from his spies and his reading of the press that the
Empire and its sovereign had regained popularity in France in inverse proportion to the appeal of the restored Bourbons, Napoleon cannot have had
the remotest idea how he would be received if he landed on the coast at the
head of a band of armed men like some pirate or adventurer. No one could
have known, which is what makes this escapade such a bold, even outrageous
gesture, akin in probability of success to a young maid's leading a royal army
to raise the siege of a city in 1428. In view of the triumphal end of the affair—
"His Imperial Majesty the Emperor and King Enters the Tuileries" (*Le
Moniteur,* March 20)—it is essential to keep in mind that right down to the
end, events might have gone very differently.

For Napoleon's landing did not have the instantaneous, electric effect on
people of revealing either a Medusa's head or the Holy Grail. Rather, what
occurred was a gradual, increasingly rapid spreading of the word, which had
a polarizing effect on the populations that received it. The "real" country—
French workers and artisans in the towns, and, above all, the peasants in the
countryside (the latter accounting for 80 percent of the population)—was
exhilarated and awed by the news. The "legal" country (the 70,000 or so who
had the income to be allowed to vote)—the notables, the nobility, the
administration—was shocked and dismayed, and inclined toward the king.
From the Riviera to Paris, Louis XVIII could count on the keepers of the
loaves and fishes, including the former Napoleonic administration and the
marshalate, which had largely gone over, after the Emperor's abdication. And,
of course, he could count on the government and the legislature.

Napoleon, however, it presently emerged, could count on a group even
more important than the vast rural population—he could rally the soldiery.
The troops were led to him, over their officers' protests, by the peasants, and
by their own disgust with the regime and their revived feelings of loyalty to
*l'Empereur.** At Laffrey, near Grenoble, an incredibly dramatic event occurred
on March 7: Napoleon stepped before several battalions that had been dispatched to arrest him; he opened his famous great coat and said, "Soldiers

*A droll poster placarded in Paris had Napoleon saying to Louis XVIII, "My good
Brother, it's useless to keep sending me soldiers. I have enough already."

of the 5th Line, recognize me! If there is one among you who would kill his general, his Emperor, he may: here I stand." And so it went: at Vizille, Grenoble, Lyon, Auxerre, the men in the ranks sent to stop him came over to him. In Auxerre, Marshal Ney defected to the man whom he had boasted to King Louis he would "bring back in an iron cage," and received a somewhat cool welcome (for having pressured Napoleon into abdication the year before).

This vast social heating up is not surprising in view of the Empire's popularity with the rustics, but it is remarkable when we consider the imperial regime's cosseting of the notables, and its strong post-1810 tilt toward the nobility and the dynastic-monarchical style. At bottom, the French peasants had not suffered under the Empire (conscription aside), as many in the commercial and bourgeoisie had. Moreover, the rurals had recently had a holy terror struck in their hearts by what they feared (incorrectly) was going to become a Bourbon-led return of the feudal order. Too, in Paris and other large cities, the workers suffered from the renewed economic crisis (high unemployment, becalmed production), due to the renewal of trade with England. In sum, a fairly straightforward class conflict, almost a social war, may be superimposed on the well-known political dichotomy between the royal (Bourbon) and the imperial (Napoleonic) monarchies, with the latter, strangely—in view of its latter-day development—representing the Revolution in spades.[24] The Emperor was now the man betrayed, the Revolution undone.

The next important novelty—again in stark contrast to the conservative façade of the late Empire—is that throughout the Midi, Napoleon rallied "the people" and "the Nation" with the slogans and language of the Revolution— and to some extent made good on it when he got to Paris. Now at last we shall see something closer to the national revival that did not come off in 1814. But then, Napoleon had had a choice; now he did not. The popular uprising of March 1815 was almost more than he wished, and he was occasionally obliged to repudiate "disorder," "anarchy," and "revolution." Politically, the Golfe-Juan landing achieved the rapprochement between the former Jacobin-republicans and the party that was already becoming identified as bonapartist.[25] Here is a good example of where passions and emotions swamped doctrine and even reason itself, as the republicans rallied to the Empire that had persecuted them.

By the nineteenth, Louis XVIII was beaten, but until then it had been a near thing, and even now some of the king's top lieutenants were convinced that if the Bourbon would only stand firm in Paris (as he had melodramatically sworn to do a few days before), he could yet win, for even Napoleon would not have the courage to mount an attack on the capital. But Louis decided against it; blue blood ran in his veins, not red, and Paris, on his telling, was *not* worth a mess. In the wee hours of the twentieth, he "folded his tent like the Arabs, and as silently stole away."[26] That evening Ozymandias arrived, to considerably more fanfare; it was the fourth birthday of the King of Rome. Chateaubriand, though a devout royalist and a minister of the king, could not stop himself from proffering a salute to "Bonaparte," whom he compared to Christ, saying to the old Louis, paralyzed with gout, "Arise and carry your bed away." A hundred days will elapse before the return of the king, but the crucial and decisive period has been the last twenty.[27]

On St. Helena, Napoleon was asked the happiest time of his life: "the march from Cannes to Paris," he replied.[28]

THE HUNDRED DAYS (MARCH 20–JUNE 29)

"Why didn't you re-establish the Republic or the Consulate on your return from Elba?"
"Because the Empire was more popular than the Republic."
                              —Napoleon Bonaparte, St. Helena[29]

Events turn out to make more traitors than opinions do.
                              —Chateaubriand[30]

Tacitus wrote that the "desire for glory is the last thing even the wise are able to give up." Napoleon, on landing at Golfe-Juan, claimed to have given it up.[31] His statements at this time and in the coming weeks made a clean break with his recent past: "I have just lived a year on Elba, and there, as if from the tomb, I could hear the voice of posterity. I know now what has to be avoided, I know now what has to be valued: peace and liberty."[32] His entire political justification now rested on the assertion that "The Bourbons have no legal right to the throne because it wasn't given them by the Nation," while he, Napoleon, with the plebiscites, enjoyed extensive proof of the Nation's mandate. He was, in a word, "national," while Louis XVIII, having been put into power by the Coalition, was the puppet of the "party of the foreigner."

But it was not just a matter of words. The weeks that followed the Emperor's return to his apartments in the Tuileries saw the regime radically alter itself under his hand. And not his alone: Napoleon had important collaborators—old and new. The many familiar faces (Maret, Cambacérès,

Caulaincourt, Fouché, etc.)[33] surprise us for being there at all, even under pressure, given that the political class never really lowered its guard to their former ruler in the Hundred Days. Virtually all of them, however, found the courage to make it clear that their service depended on Napoleon's governing more liberally. The cabinet was no longer young. The average age was now fifty-three; only Davout, forty-four, and Caulaincourt, forty-one, were younger than Napoleon. Fouché, who had opposed Napoleon's return, accepted the Police Ministry, but with no faith in his master's ability to retain the throne. He stayed on the qui vive, looking for opportunities to make his nest in a successor regime.[34] Two new collaborators stunned contemporaries by their acceptance of appointment from a ruler whom they had consistently condemned: Lazare Carnot—as a tribune, he had refused to vote the Empire (1804)—and Benjamin Constant, who, as recently as March 19, was announcing to one and all: "I shall not be a miserable turncoat and throw myself from one power to the next, covering infamy with sophistry, stammering common excuses to cover up a shameful life."[35]

Constant received the crucial charge of drafting blueprints for the "Liberal Empire," which he proceeded to do with very un-Siéyesian dispatch. The result is one of the most curious and contradictory moments in the long history of French constitutionalism: the preamble of the document offers a kind of auto-critique of The Way We Were, while the title—"The Additional Act to the Constitutions of the Empire"—made it out to be simply an appendix to the foundational documents of the Years VIII, X, and XII, on which the First Empire legally rested (but which no one except specialists invoked anymore). But this title was mainly a fig leaf to cover the Emperor's new nudity, for the powers stripped from him by Constant went far to making over imperial France into a constitutional monarchy, possessed of a bicameral legislature with real authority, and with political functionaries legally accountable for their acts. Censorship went by the boards; liberty was confirmed. Setting aside personality and circumstance, Napoleon's powers were technically *fewer* than Louis XVIII's in 1814, even though, nominally (and in contradiction), the regime's former constitutions were still in force.

The *Acte Additionnel* simply and presumptuously reconfirmed the reforms of the Restoration contained in the letter of the charter. That is what is so extraordinary. But of course, Constant's document respires a completely different air, and mandates numerous stylistic changes at odds with Louis XVIII's "legitimacy" (polemically summarized by Napoleon as "the principle that the nation was made for the throne, not the throne for the nation"). Thus, the tricolor was reinstated, the Legion of Honor returned to its prestige, the old regime nobility (resurrected by Louis) broken—indeed, the very concept of *ancien régime* found itself "banned" in the name of the French Nation, whose sovereignty it had flouted. Napoleon demanded a few conservative novelties or holdovers ("You can't push me too far down a road that isn't mine!" he spat at Constant at one point)—such as a hereditary House of Peers and the elitist structure of the old electoral colleges,[36] yet at bottom the French Empire, the perfect model of an authoritarian—many said, despotic—regime, with the pontifical blessing, gave itself far more than a cosmetic face-lift. Whether despite or because of his famed realism, Napoleon was founding institutions of power apart from himself. The legislatures would have a life of their own, made up of 629 deputies who were rather more left wing than their center-right counterparts in the chambers of the Empire had been after Tilsit.

SUB SPECIE AETERNITATIS . . .

The foregoing events in French domestic life are so fascinating that one forgets they were not taking place in a vacuum. Contemporaries, however, were only too aware that they acted *sub specie aeternitatis*—in the shadow of judgment. French public opinion hoped against hope that after all the Allied reverences toward respecting French public opinion, the foreign powers might respect French public opinion—that is, might bring themselves to swallow Napoleon's return and conversion, decked out, as they were, in national language. Such hope never had a prayer; the Liberal Empire came to life under a death sentence that was never lifted or even reprieved, just implacably carried out. It made no difference that Napoleon "solemnly" accepted the Treaty of Paris that had reduced his former Empire to its early revolutionary boundaries, nor that he pleaded the sincerity of his newfound love of peace and liberty. The Allies were not about to forget the innumerable times they had been beaten, diminished, exploited, and (perhaps worst of all) charmed by Napoleon; they declared him "an outlaw" who must, and would, be brought down. Friedrich Gentz's proclamation (May 12) dealt summarily with the argument about French sovereignty: "The wish of the French people, no matter how completely stated, will not have any effect or power."[37] The Seventh Coalition thus, in a sense, existed before the *Acte Additionnel* was even writ. In the Allied view, the plebiscite to approve the *Acte* (June) was simply the French citizenry's illegal reelection of a leader who had been impeached, convicted, and incarcerated. In enveloping him in the coils of her "sacred" sovereignty, France had made herself a criminal's moll.

There is, therefore, little story to tell in the geopolitical theater, though

Napoleon strove to make it seem as if he was making headway in negotiating with the Coalition. The failure of Napoleonic diplomacy to stanch the flow of Allied war preparations—or even make contact with individual sovereigns, let alone divide them, by beguiling the father-in-law (Francis I)—was total.[38] If our piece finally becomes true tragedy—the antithesis of the oft-alleged comedy of rerun history ("a dog returning to its vomit" is Wordsworth's lovely phrase for the Hundred Days)—it is because individual will no longer counted, because the unities of time and place were quite closely respected: the whole piece unfolded on a small stage (even Waterloo will be one of Napoleon's most compact battles) in a short amount of time. And finally, it is tragedy because *so much* individual and collective suffering, death, punishment, and vengeance attend the outcome.

The shadow of judgment raised its domestic avatar in the poison of *attentisme* (wait-and-see) among the notability and the political class, who rallied because they had no choice: Napoleon could (and occasionally did) threaten them with unleashing a social revolution if they did not support him. But their support was a hedged bet. Thus, a police bulletin tells us that the official holders of the tobacco distributorships (a government monopoly) have effaced the word "royal" from their product but are waiting before they print "imperial." Or Fouché notes to a former colleague: "Napoleon will be obliged to leave for the army before the end of the month. Once he is gone, we will be master of the terrain. I want him to win a battle or two, but he will lose the third, and then our turn will start."[39] Only Napoleon could afford to show no doubts in this period, though on St. Helena he confessed that he had been racked by his awareness of the defeatism of the political class around him. He went off to war knowing that only a Marengo or an Austerlitz would suffice to allow him to reimpose his control over the parties on the home front.[40]

But if the shadow of judgment sowed division, intrigue, and bad faith among the notables and the politicals, it was quite other in its impact on the Nation, to whose invokers and carriers, we now return.

THE JACOBIN SPECTER

Does Bonaparte break the surface again in Napoleon or is it simply Napoleon disguising himself in Bonaparte, in order to remain Napoleon?
—Dominique de Villepin[41]

In the face of an Allied expeditionary force of the potential magnitude of the army Napoleon took to Russia, the French left wing faithfully nourished their timeworn illusion that they could conjure away the foreign danger with the counterspecter of the nation-in-arms. This was to forget—so easy to do when one is focused on domestic politics—that the Coalition had "been there, done that" in 1814, when it waved aside the *levée en masse* in France's eastern departments. On the other hand, this was not to take into account the novelty of the ruler-in-arms at the head of the Nation: "Napoleon, not as Emperor, but as the avenging arm of revolutionary France." In this per-fervid view, the French people would make itself one with the French army, and *la Patrie* would become an armed camp.

The most vehement for Napoleon included many former Girondins,* now in their fifties and sixties. One of them, Bertrand L'Hodiesnière, had spoken out against Bonaparte at 19 Brumaire, and been thrown out of the meeting of the Council of the Five Hundred by the General's grenadiers. He and his fellows systematically opposed the Consulate and the Empire, and were never seduced by the Napoleonic genius or style. But as a group, they were so profoundly anti-Bourbon that they overlooked everything, including the virtual certainty of a new war for France, and rallied to the Emperor as an act of solidarity with the Revolution.[42] The other revolutionaries (old and young, original and "neo") who felt this way were numerous, organized, and in touch with several leading lights of the regime (Fouché, Carnot, Maret, and many imperial prefects). They also had the ear of Lucien Bonaparte, who finally made peace with his brother and returned to Paris (May 9). Consistency was never Lucien's strong suit, so the fact that he was now a papal prince (of Canino) did not stop "Brutus" from pressing his imperial brother to seek out the Republic that always lurked within the Napoleonic idea of Empire.

The troops backing up Lucien et al. included a socially heterogeneous (but

---

*The Girondins were rather bellicose republican revolutionaries, and a leading faction in the "Mountain" of the Legislative Assembly and the Convention. They eventually (1793–94) lost out to the Jacobin party, and their leaders went to the guillotine.

largely lower-class) patriotic movement calling itself "the federated" [*les fédérés*]—so named for their incessant calls for unity, which, of course, had the effect of splintering and fractionalizing the body social even more than it already was.[43] Ostensibly these outraged "citizens" (a name they preferred to "Frenchmen") asked only for "their" Emperor's blessing and his permission to bear arms, though they proved so boisterous in their "requests" that they drove the ruler to leave the Tuileries for the more secluded Elysée palace.[44] In truth, however, the tens of thousands of "federated" around France were a dark menace, akin, in potential for violence and uncontrollability, to the *armées révolutionnaires* of 1793. They saw themselves as "the nation betrayed," and were all too ready to believe it was their own government (if not Napoleon) who did the betraying; they were the eternal principle of opposition, and they saw in "their" Emperor a party leader, a dictator of Public Safety, but not the sovereign, which was themselves.[45]

Napoleon dealt with the *fédérés* by deception: he pretended to sponsor them, allowed them to organize into battalions so that they could rival the "bourgeois" National Guard, and he promised to arm them. He replied in kind to their cries of "Long live the Nation!" and "Long live Liberty!" but at the end of the day, he armed only a few "federated," for he had no wish to sire a rebirth of the Terror, nor (still less) to permit himself to become a Louis XVI in the mob's hands. Still, the mere fact that the movement existed and called itself "the Emperor's" was a sign that Napoleon was no longer in complete control of the political "thing," which, since late 1814, was becoming known as "bonapartism."[46]

THE NATION-TALKER:
NAPOLEON CHAMELEON

[If King Louis had been serious about being "national,"] he would have styled himself "Louis I" and dated his reign in its first year. . . . He would have made a pact with the nation. But for that, he would have needed [my] courage, greatness, and energy.

—Napoleon

The inevitable plebiscite held to confirm the *Acte* took place during May— that is, long after the effects of the *beau geste* of the return from Elba were replaced by profound apprehensiveness in the face of inevitable war. The results were published on June 1. The referendum had not been expected to be a great success, and in this, it did not disappoint: only 1,554,112 men voted *oui*; 5,743, *non*; nearly four-fifths of the electorate abstained. The east and Burgundy turned out heavily, but everywhere else the voters stayed away in droves.[47] In part, the abstentions reflected political divisions, but surely in larger measure, they illustrated France's awareness of how little political sense the imperial restoration made. The key point for the regime, however, was that it was a nominal success: "la Nation" could be said—and endlessly *was said*—to have "spoken." The "appeal to the people" (*appel au peuple*) was the plinth on which Napoleonic power rested, never more so than now. In the currency of legitimacy such as Napoleon Bonaparte had reminted it since 1799, even so paltry a showing amounted to wealth in the France of the spring of 1815, compared to the poverty of "divine right."

If the looming war was seen by one and all as a scourge, it yet had its usefulness in rallying a divided country behind Napoleon, while allowing him to impose himself on his political allies and his numerous domestic opponents. French internal conflicts were so great and so apparent in this period that the Duke of Wellington could express hope to a countryman that "even without the aid of the Allies, [Napoleon's] power will not be of long duration."[48] The Emperor never faced a greater challenge. The great French behemoth had to be prodded into life, to be crash-mobilized. Lassitude, *attentisme*, fear, and civil division had to be exorcised, and the country's military defense had to be seen to. Armies, funds, and spirits had to be raised, but though France's resources in money, blood, and spirit were bottomless, the nation *felt* broke, depressed, and exsanguinated once the enthusiasm of the "Eagle's" return had worn off. It is customary to emphasize Napoleon's dejection, defeatism, hesitation, fatigue, and sporadic bouts of torpor in the Hundred Days (looking back, he himself would confess to as much), yet in truth he rose with his customary efficacy to the magnitude of the challenge, unstayed by awareness of the pitifulness of any chance of success. The achievement of the Emperor and his government in the spring of 1815 was, once again, prodigious.

The instrument of Napoleon's political strategy was the very "national crusade" that he had deployed too little and too late in the spring of 1814. The strength of nation-talk is that while it appears to be a call to unity, it also—and very efficiently—designates domestic (as well as, of course, foreign) enemies. The hallowed revolutionary call of "la patrie en danger" now went forth, beseeching "all Frenchmen to rally to prevent civil war and repulse the foreigner," setting aside other than "national" loyalties or considerations: no politics, no parties, no opinions, simply "us" against "them," where "them" included not merely the Allies but French royalists, unrallied Jacobins, and refractory priests. Though he had accepted the Treaty of Paris, Napoleon now played on the revanchist theme of France's unjust treatment at "German" and British hands.[49] The great hymn of the Revolution, "La Marseillaise," previously discouraged, returned open diapason; the "patriotic offerings" of the Revolution were reinstated to help war financing (albeit with only a tenth of the success of the previous year); the corps of prefects was purged, and "extraordinary commissioners" were sent to the provinces to raise patriotism and oversee the repression of enemies. A newspaper, *Le Journal Général de France,* edited by Carnot himself (minister of the interior), blended appeals to patriotism and private property, and, of course, the popular *fédérés* were allowed, and sometimes encouraged, to organize. It is a comment on the times and the Napoleonic tilt to the populace that the latter responded far better than the middle-class National Guard, of whom only one in three showed up.

Yet constant official evocation of "the republic within the Empire" did not suffice to make it so, and sovereignty of "the People" or "the Nation" was a largely notional affair (Napoleon still formally reigned "by the grace of God" as well).[50] A bizarre climacteric of the national crusade arrived on June 1 in the vast assembly on Paris's Champ-de-Mai, where Citizen-monarch was to meet with Sovereign People, in the form of thirty thousand of their delegates from the electoral colleges around France.[51] (One year earlier, in the same venue, a supposedly unified France, under the serene gaze of the Allied high command, had greeted Louis XVIII.) In the event, things worked out rather differently, for instead of thirty thousand delegates, only five hundred were actually convoked, while the rest of the cheering throngs of tens of thousands was made up of . . . soldiers (but only six, out of twenty-two living marshals). These delegates had anticipated that the *Acte Additionnel* and "national sovereignty" would be, as billed, the point of the day, but the Champ-de-Mai instead turned out to be an army- and Emperor-centered affair. The chief delegate heralded "the new contract between the Nation and Your Majesty," but the main point of his regime-expurgated speech was to fulminate against the Coalition for not letting "France be France" and acclaim the ruler she wished.

Napoleon, for his part, announced he owed "everything to the people," and then added a sentence that stuns, even now, for its disingenuousness: "If I did not realize that it was the Nation which the Allies are aiming to bring low, not me alone, then I would gladly give myself up to them." He ended the day in a swirling sea of cheering soldiers, on whom he conferred Legions of Honor and regimental eagles, as they swore to perish, if need be, "in defense of the nation." It is unlikely that even one among them heard that phrase as other than "to die for the Emperor." The forced gaiety of the proceedings, amid the encircling gloom, the absence of outsiders or foreigners, and (perhaps above all) the Emperor's strange decision to deck himself out in full coronation regalia, rather than his usual simple Chasseur uniform, remind one of the final ball in Poe's "Masque of the Red Death." It was with relief that Napoleon left Paris on June 12 to lead the army. Though gone from the capital, however, he could not put domestic French politics out of his mind. At a time when he should have concentrated only on military divisions, he was deeply distracted by political ones.

So we ask ourselves: *Was Napoleon being sincere* when he insisted in March, "I return to collaborate with the nation's representatives in the formation of a family pact that will conserve forever the liberty and rights of the French; I henceforth put my ambition and glory in making the happiness of this grand people from whom I hold everything"? Some, beginning with the man himself, on St. Helena, passionately felt so[52]; others did not, while still others did not care, for many who disliked Napoleon supported him "pour la France." Many among the Emperor's former loyalists stayed away (most of the marshalate), but many among his former enemies returned. Mme de Staël, for example, declared that "Liberty is finished if Bonaparte wins, national independence is finished if he loses," but when Napoleon said the French State would pay her money she felt it owed her, then she rallied. Others like Lafayette did not rally for love or money. And one, Pozzo di Borgo, was appealed to and never even replied.

Nearly the same gamut may be seen among historians: some believe in his sincerity; many do not. Bluche believes Napoleon believed it himself, but he calls him "the man of successively sincere positions," and in any case ever the "ideophobe," allergic to systems and doctrines. If Napoleon's underlying conception of political power "surely had not changed," writes Bluche, at least he now "cultivated equivocation." On the other hand, Dominique de Villepin, the present French foreign minister, entitles his eloquent study of the Hundred Days, "the spirit of sacrifice," which he believes sums up Napoleon's attitude and actions.

Many figures from the past have undergone sharp political evolutions from conservative to liberal. In French history alone, Adolphe Thiers, Jean Jaurès, and François Mitterrand come to mind.[53] With them, however, the change was cumulative and comparatively slow. For something like an epiphany of eleven months, we must look outside France, to a Malcolm X, a Thomas à Becket, or a Saul of Tarsus. In terms of liberalizing his regime's political institutions, social bases of support, and his own governing style and language, Napoleon certainly meant business. Many contemporaries agreed with Benjamin Constant when he stoutly maintained that whatever Napoleon did in the future—assuming he had one—his concessions of the structures and recognition of the principles of the Liberal Empire remained "a great point obtained." Constant gets off a fascinating *aperçu* into what he takes to be the Emperor's true attitude in conceding the *Acte*: "He did not try to fool me about his views nor the state of affairs. He did not represent himself as corrected by the lessons of adversity. He did not even give himself the merit of seeming to want to go back to the regime of liberty. He just coldly examined his own interest; and, with an impartiality close to indifference, he considered what was possible and what was preferable."[54] Of course one cannot forget that it was very much in Monsieur Constant's interest to believe and to report these things.

Not to forget, this was the selfsame Emperor who had written to his older brother only the past year (March 1814): "If the people once see us doing what they like, instead of what is good for them, they will obviously imagine that they are the sovereign, and will have a very poor opinion of those who govern them." On the other hand, in fairness to Napoleon, a great deal had transpired in France in a compacted amount of time, which profoundly shook many psyches. The invasion of 1814, the fall of the Empire, the return of the pre-revolutionary dynasty, the drastic shrinking of French borders—*all* came together to create a widespread political mentality of despair and resentment (and revanchism) that indelibly marked this and the next generation, and powerfully affected the nation's history.[55]

H. A. L. Fisher is probably right that "if the wish of France could have been translated into words, men would have prayed for a continuation of the Empire without the restless egotism of Napoleon,"[56] but France did not have her wish, she had Napoleon's—and she granted it, albeit reluctantly. She persisted in "being France," on seeing the Allied outlawing of Napoleon as an unacceptable violation of her sacred sovereignty and independence. The strangeness of the whole resulting venture is equaled only by its desperation and remorselessness. It is Romeo and Juliet without the romance and youth, preferring death to giving in to mature reasoning. The shock is not that so large a minority of the French people hung back—and for them we shall let the esteemed historian Bertier de Sauvigny speak: Napoleon's return, he writes, "was one of the greatest crimes a leader could perpetrate against a nation"[57]—it is that the great majority stepped forward.

In his unequaled history of the Consulate and Empire, Thiers has his countrymen serving as an illustration to the world of political zeal, which may lead to "great misfortune as well as great glory for a nation."[58] One might note, as we pass to the Waterloo campaign, that "great misfortune" is not the opposite of *grande gloire. Bien au contraire.*

WATERLOO: *VAE VICTIS**

If I draw this account with a paint brush not a pen, it is because in this matter, the most sadly poetic part—the drama—seems to me to have decidedly greater import than the tactical part: the latter is cruelly complete, the former is not. At the distance I now am from the death of glory and of the French patrie, I can better recall the expression on the corpse's face than the architectural lines of the tomb.

—General de Brack[59]

The art of recounting [a battle] lies in deleting what is unimportant and stems the forward march. One ill narrates a battle . . . unless he simply tells what the fate of the day rested on.

—Napoleon

By early June, the first brace of Allied armies—the English and the Prussian— were pressing into the Low Countries and had arrived in Belgium.[60] In the fullness of time, their attack would be augmented by Austrian and Russian armies. There would be no end to the Allied mobilization until the outlaw was brought down. A sliver of French hope may have resided in the signs of reborn pro-French feeling among "the peoples" (Poles, Saxons, Rhineland Germans, Belgians, and northern Italians), who, in under a year, had learned there were things they hated more than the French occupation. King Joachim I raised the standard of "national revolution" against Austria in the Italian peninsula,[61] and declared for Napoleon. With allies like him, however, the French emperor wondered who needed enemies, and the turncoat brother-in-law was not invited to take his accustomed place at the head of the Grande Armée's cavalry in the coming Belgian campaign.

The French commander had few choices: he could await the coming attack, or he could strike out as fast as possible, hoping to beat his enemies in detail. Merely to state the alternatives is to know which course Napoleon

*"Woe to the Vanquished!" A common saying in early-nineteenth-century France, especially in connection with this battle.

elected. Leaving Paris to join his army at the Belgian border on June 12, Napoleon moved his corps so swiftly as to surprise Marshal Blücher at Ligny, where he dealt the Prussians a sharp blow, on the sixteenth. If Drouet d'Erlon's corps of 20,000 men, which Napoleon had detached to keep a weather eye on the English, had returned to the field as fast as the Emperor wished them to, Blücher would have been completely routed, not simply thrown back, and would have been unable to come to his ally's assistance two days later. Napoleon now compounded his mistake: he overestimated Prussian losses in men and morale at Ligny, and assumed they would retire eastward (toward home), rather than westward, to aid the English. The latter, having been dealt a blow by Ney at Quatre-Bras, retired to Mont Saint-Jean, on the road to Brussels (about fifteen miles away). Detaching Marshal Grouchy and his corps of 30,000 to locate and occupy the Prussians, Napoleon met the English on the slopes before a village called Waterloo.

The French army, at 74,000 men, was one of the better ones that Napoleon had commanded. The spirit of the soldiery was ebullient, though their officers were glum and distracted (a ranking general, Bourmont, had defected to the Allies with his staff, on the fifteenth). Wellington disposed of a less politically and militarily dependable force of 68,000, constituted of Hanoverian Germans, Dutch-Belgians, and English guards. The Iron Duke wore his famous cocked hat (*bicorne*), from fore to aft (*en colonne,* as it was called); Napoleon wore his, side to side (*en bataille*). In every other way as well, the two commanders illustrated the classic contrast between cold, dry, canny English aristocrat, and romantic French individualist. The steely-eyed stared relentlessly at the field before him, waiting; the eagle eye flashed in the morning sun, locked on its prey.[62]

Understanding that today was a matter of win or die, the French opened the attack in late morning with a heavy assault led by Jérôme Bonaparte on a fortified chateau (Hougoumont), on the British right flank. Though the French fought with bravery and self-sacrifice, they failed to dislodge the foe, or even require Wellington to deplete his center of men in order to reinforce his right. Thus, when the general French infantry attack (led by Drouet d'Erlon) was launched on the British center, situated around a farm called La Haie Sainte, it, too, proved unable to take and hold the farm despite breathtaking *cran* on the part of the French. Their failure, in turn, necessitated yet another all-out assault, this time by Ney's cavalry, attacking a bit farther down the English line to the east. But despite reeling and faltering, and the occasional rout of an individual unit, the Allied line held; the British infantry squares beat off the French cavalry.

By now it was late afternoon, and Napoleon was very concerned about the Prussians, large segments of whose forces had been poised all day on the French flank, waiting to attack until they were sure the English would hold. Now they arrived and began to attack in larger numbers. Grouchy, in short, had not found Blücher. Worse, though the French marshal could hear the sounds of battle in the distance, he had not thought to rejoin his Emperor, but only to follow his orders to the letter ("find and occupy the Prussians"). Desperate to break the enemy before the enemy broke him, Napoleon now sent Ney the cavalry reserves, but their heroism was also of no avail: they, too, smashed futilely against those awful English squares. At one point late in the afternoon, the French did manage to occupy La Haie Sainte, but by now their commander was running out of troops. In desperation, Napoleon dispatched the few battalions of the Imperial Guard, which he had held back. At 7 P.M. they ascended the slopes of Mont Saint-Jean, east of Hougoumont. Near the summit, they were surprised by massed English infantry fire from the front and right, and to everyone's astonishment, the vastly outnumbered guard battalion recoiled in disorder. The great Napoleonic bumblebees, in the fullness of their glory, thus fell to earth and curled up, without delivering their sting.

The truth is, Napoleon had fought a good, not a great battle, and given the quality and the enthusiasm of his men, he might well have beaten a lesser foe, as he had beaten Blücher two days before. For example, General Pelet's reconquest of Plancenoit with only two battalions stabilized the battle for the French for two hours. Marengo, we recall, had been a very near thing. But the British infantry withstood the best Napoleon had to throw at them, and, with the arrival of the various Prussian units, it was all over—*whether or not Grouchy had returned.*[63] The later recollections of French soldiers—officers and men, cavalry and infantry—attest amply to the disconcerting effect of British sangfroid and steady fire confronting French *fougue* (ardor). The latter broke, with the exception of a battalion or two of the Imperial Guard, which heroically fought to the very last. Napoleon should have perhaps bowed before British imperturbability and conserved his army for another fight, not keep flinging men into the breach. General Kellermann, present on the field, critiqued Napoleonic strategy when he wrote years later: "At no moment in the day could we have reasonably flattered ourselves that we could win. However, with prudence, we might have avoided catastrophe. Usual English caution would have given us that chance [by not following up if we withdrew]. But prudence was not the distinguishing quality of the French commander in chief. As long as there was a battalion to move, a chip to play, you may have no doubt that he moved it and played it."[64] Napoleon's soldiers gave him their best, and their courage was magnificent.*

Waterloo invariably appears high on the lists of the ten or fifteen "most momentous battles in world history," but in fact, the battle of Leipzig in 1813 had been a larger, longer, deadlier, and more historically decisive affair, for it not only dealt Napoleon his first outright defeat in the field, but, more important, it also saw the crystallization of a coalition that would not rest until it bagged its prey. The latter consideration is why even if Napoleon had won at Waterloo—and probably even if he had won again in the battle following Waterloo—it would not have mattered. Waterloo's import lies in its legend of "la guerre nationale" and the political culture of defeat to which it gave rise for the next two centuries of French history.

The evening and night of the eighteenth were a nightmare for the Emperor, as he tried in vain to rally his demoralized army. Arriving at Quatre-Bras at 1 A.M., he rested. Marshal Soult's aide-de-camp studied Napoleon in the firelight: "on his dejected face, of a waxen pallor, there was no animation, only tears."[65]

ABJECTION (II), ABDICATION (II)

The art of the retreat is harder for the Frenchman than for [others]. A lost battle saps his strength and courage, weakens his confidence in his chiefs and pushes him to insubordination.

—Napoleon[66]

Fury took the place of strength, which was wanting.
—Michelet[67]

The French cult of Waterloo was founded by Napoleon himself. The bulletin, written a day or two after the battle, describes the affair as "so glorious, yet

---

*A French soldier wrote to his parents nine days after the battle, with a courage and an eloquence that move this reader profoundly: "I had the misfortune of being wounded on the 18th [at Waterloo], by a ball that broke my leg. As I could not be seen to until five days later, I was obliged to ride ten leagues on horseback. Then, when I did go into hospital, gangrene had already set into the leg . . . Now all my body is swollen, and they tell me it will not be possible to do an amputation. I thus send you my farewell and thank you warmly for all that you have done for me."

so fatal for French arms." This is fair enough, but thereafter, and for the rest of his life, the Emperor could not let go of it. On returning to Paris, he endlessly importuned poor Caulaincourt, belaboring the events and decisions of June 18–how could so much courage and so many brilliant attacks have resulted in panic and rout? But for so little, he might have, *should have*, exited victorious. Defeat was the doing of "malefactors" and "traitors." Etc. Only one possibility eluded him in all of his fancies: the thought that Wellington and the English simply beat him and the French, fair and square.

The defeat notwithstanding, however, Napoleon had no intention of giving up. This was Fontainebleau, spring 1814, revived. The only question in His Majesty's mind on the morning of June 19 was from where he would prepare for the next fight. For a day or so, he remained with the army on the Franco-Belgian border, furiously issuing orders to Joseph in Paris. His regent-brother was directed to call up a further 100,000 men, and mobilize the *fédérés* and the National Guard, while simultaneously declaring the *levée en masse* in the eastern departments. Further, the Emperor was to be granted emergency dictatorial powers for the duration.

But a peculiar thing happened: "Paris" unexpectedly showed it had a mind of its own. In light of the defeat, Napoleon lost the little remaining authority he had over most of the 629 delegates of the legislature. Angrily, the ruler returned to the capital, though Caulaincourt and Joseph opposed the idea: "The army is your strength and your security, stay with it." Arriving at the Elysée at dawn on the twenty-first, Napoleon was in high dudgeon. There might well be another 18 Brumaire, he told General Bertrand–or even worse; he added grimly: "Once I have to bloody my hands, I'll go in up to my elbows." The tension, anxiety, and intrigue rife in Paris were unlike anything seen since the Terror of summer in the Year II.

But the Emperor did not bloody his hands. Although he passionately and cogently argued to put "an end to discussion and disputation," he yet agreed to dance the complex political minuet of "discussion and disputation," dispatching Caulaincourt and Lucien Bonaparte to argue his case before the parliament. The legislators' spokesmen were Lafayette and Fouché; though technically the latter was a minister of the Crown, he was playing his usual triple game, with the representatives, the Emperor, and the absent Louis XVIII in Ghent (Belgium). The positions were antithetical: Napoleon was supremely convinced, as only he could be, that the military means were at hand to fashion a victory. He had a small point in that three times as many men-at-arms were available now than had been in 1814, when Napoleon had also argued strenuously for pressing the war. Had the chambers granted what the ruler now asked of them, Napoleon might well have stymied or stopped Wellington or Blücher for a time. Several of the leading voices of the day, including no less than Emmanuel Sieyès—hardly a Napoleonic regular—agreed with Carnot and Constant that the present was no time to be divided, but to rally behind the ruler.

On the other hand, the legislators had a crushing reply: "Enough is enough; we have stuck with you through Waterloo. The Allies will just keep coming; nobody, even you, can stop them until they have brought you down. But in the meantime, perhaps much good can come of making a show of good faith to the Coalition, by forcing you out."[68] Feeling at once strong and terrified, the deputies voted two extraordinary measures: they declared their sessions permanent—that is, they would not permit themselves to be dissolved; indeed, any attempt to do so would be designated "a crime of high treason." And they freely convoked imperial ministers of State to report to them. Both of these acts were unconstitutional—more so, technically, than had been General Bonaparte's actions of 18–19 Brumaire, where as we recall the legal formalities had been observed. In the new constitution, the Emperor held the right to dissolve the legislature; moreover, "his" ministers were responsible to him, not the parliament. Napoleon was not wrong in supposing that if he had acceded to these measures he would have become Louis XVI before the all-powerful National Constituent Assembly. This was the legislature's version of acting "nationally," and it proved effective.

It was only the beginning. The Chamber of Representatives also conveyed to the Emperor the formal request for his abdication.

Napoleon's first response to all of this was about what we might imagine it to be—"I'll never abdicate to that bunch of Jacobin hotheads, that liberal rabble [*canaille*]!" He threatened the parliament with the use of his Guard, or with a social revolution led by the *fédérés* and the National Guard (though this largely bourgeois institution would probably have obeyed parliament ahead of the Emperor). He ranted and raved about "governing with the guillotine *against* the middle class and the nobility," and declared he had been "wrong ever to concern myself with giving a Constitution or forming Chambers." "Do you hear those cries?" he yelled at a hostile Davout, pointing to the largely lower-class crowds cheering for *l'Empereur* outside the Elysée. "If I wanted to put myself at the head of those good people, who have the instinct of the *patrie*'s true needs, then I would soon be done with those men who have no courage against me except when I am without defense." This was not the march from Golfe-Juan, when there had been at least a hope of a vast countrywide union around "the people's Emperor." This was threat of class war.

But just as unsurprisingly, Napoleon was not a man to provoke a civil war, though he was not above threatening it. He acceded to the deputies' demand and abdicated—for two reasons: he could not shake his stubborn belief that the Chamber, for all its political factionalism and intrigue, yet represented "the Nation"; and he was, by all accounts, overcome "with exhaustion and lassitude," as Constant observed. At St. Helena he will endlessly circle back on "what ought I to have done, in late June?" He will reproach himself (or seem to) "for having abandoned my soldiers, the *fédérés,* and my supporters," just as he will say he sorely wished that he had had Fouché and Lafayette "shot or exiled." Pasquier, the former Napoleonic police prefect for Paris who bolted in 1814 and never returned, claims that the Napoleon of post-Waterloo does "not even know himself what direction he is heading. He appeals to the support of the revolutionaries, yet fears them above all others. . . . He is out of his depth entirely."[69] One is dubious. Much of this Napoleonic rhetoric, now and at St. Helena, was posturing—for himself, too. *Au fond,* the Emperor of the French could never have brought himself to accept becoming "king of the rebel mob [*le roi de la jacquerie*]," as he put it. He was no booted Robespierre.

Following the abdication, early in the afternoon of the twenty-second, Fouché took over a provisional government of five members. Napoleon stayed on at the Elysée, consumed with second-guessing and soliloquy-giving before Carnot, Constant, and Caulaincourt. The one concession he absolutely held out for, and received, was the proclamation of his son as Napoleon II. (The King of Rome "reigned" for less than two weeks, but it was enough to establish dynastic succession, so that one day, when Louis Bonaparte's son acceded to the throne [1851], it would be as Napoleon III.) Napoleon had to be pressed to leave Paris; he left for Malmaison on the twenty-fifth, to be the guest of his former daughter-in-law, Queen Hortense. Here, where it all began, he received and bade farewell to two ex-mistresses, Maria Walewska and Eléonore Denuelle de la Plaigne, and their sons by him. With the British and, more especially, the Prussians closing in, it became imperative for Napoleon to depart even these premises. His closest advisors besought him to go to the United States, and he decided to do so. Joseph, Lucien, and Jérôme were even saying they would accompany him there. It was Carnot's idea that from America, "you can continue to make your enemies tremble. If France falls back under the Bourbon yoke, your presence in a free country will sustain national opinion here."[70]

With the enemy at hand, Napoleon was yet unable to tear himself away from Malmaison. The last family member he saw here was his mother, but the last place he visited there was the bedroom where Josephine had died. Here, alone and dressed (most rarely) in civilian clothes, he penetrated late in the afternoon of the twenty-ninth. In the courtyard below, Bertrand,

Becker, and Savary stalked to and fro, impatient to flee with him, in the four-seater calèche that was drawn up.[71] Napoleon could not, even now, simply go quietly. In a burst of "insight" he summoned General Becker to his side and ordered him to go to Fouché. Tell the head of the new government, Napoleon ordered Becker, "that I offer to lead the French army into battle against the Prussians, and, after I force them and the British to come to terms, I shall depart for the new world." Becker did as he was bade. The former police minister found this idea "cockamamie" and told Becker so. That general returned to Malmaison to find the Emperor decked out in his uniform, ready to be "off to the wars." On seeing his aide's mournful look, he went upstairs and put his civvies back on, then left forthwith.

For the next fortnight, Napoleon peregrinated about western maritime France, ending up in the Charentais port of Rochefort and the île d'Aix, waiting for French ships to take him to America. They waited in vain. The imperial entourage had not bargained on the level of animus against the fugitive who had willfully and knowingly brought down so much pain on everyone's head in the Hundred Days. The Duke of Wellington would not issue safe-conduct passes for Napoleon's voyage, while His Britannic Majesty's government privately hoped, in Lord Liverpool's words, "that the King of France would hang or shoot Bonaparte, as the best termination of the business." The Prussians, for their part, longed to do just that. Indeed, only King Louis XVIII's vow to betake himself personally to the Pont de Jéna sufficed to get Blücher to renounce his firm intention to blow it sky high.

Indeed a "time of the pig" was about to engulf France, such as she would not suffer again until 1871 or June 1940. The second Bourbon restoration made only the vaguest of vague bows toward the ideal of sociopolitical conciliation; the so-called White Terror was, rather, the order of the day, and was *far* more brutal than any domestic repression practiced by the Empire.[72] Two ranking Napoleonic officers, Brune and Ramel, were assassinated at this time, while Marshal Ney and General de La Bédoyère both faced firing squads (as did Murat in Italy); and Maret, Cambacérès, Boulay, Carnot, Masséna, and a host of other Napoleonic officials—including even Fouché—were banished. But then the restored dynasty of "Louis deux-times-new [*neuf*]"[73] had some justification for anger. As the price exacted of the country for the Liberal Empire and its "national" crusade, France, by the second Treaty of Paris, wound up reduced to her 1789 (not merely her 1790) borders, and saw herself socked with a staggering (700 million franc) indemnity—and the pleasure of an army of occupation until it was paid off.

It being impossible for Napoleon to escape—the Royal Navy blocked the western littoral—the ex-Emperor surrendered himself on July 15 to Captain

Maitland of the HMS *Bellerophon,** a warship that had given yeoman service at Trafalgar. Napoleon anticipated, and certainly hoped, that he would be taken to England, but the Allies would not hear of any venue so near at hand. Rather, on August 7, he was transferred to the HMS *Northumberland* for a long sea journey to the South Atlantic. Even Napoleon's opponents, beginning with the English naval officers on board these ships, readily conceded his uncomplaining forbearance as he went from deception to disappointment in his unavailing negotiations for desirable refuge. Ten weeks later to the day, on October 16, 1815, he disembarked at Jamestown, on the British island of St. Helena.

In his note to the English Prince Regent asking for sanctuary in Britain, Napoleon had compared himself to the great Athenian statesman and general Themistocles begging asylum of his former adversaries, the Persians, whom he had thrashed years earlier at Salamis (480 B.C.).[74] The comparison, of course, was inapt, for the first Emperor of the French had never beaten the British in battle—*au contraire*. He might, however, have appropriated for himself the words that Themistocles is reported by Plutarch to have said to his fellow Athenians: "In truth, I know not how to tune a lyre nor play on the psaltery, but give me a small or obscure village, and I shall give it renown and greatness."[75]

*In Greek mythology, Bellerophon was a son of Poseidon, god of the sea. A stupendous warrior, Bellerophon committed the sin of hubris by becoming too taken with his own prowess. Recognizing no limits, he attempted to take over the throne of Zeus himself, for which defiance, the master of the gods sent him to hell, where he died abandoned and alone.

XV

Shadows:
"The Liberal Empire"

Institutions are the shadows of great men.
–Ralph Waldo Emerson

THE NEW "SAINT"

You don't visit Longwood; Longwood visits you.
–Jean-Paul Kauffmann[1]

Napoleon became a resident of St. Helena–a "Saint," as they call themselves–on October 17, 1815.[2] He would never leave the island, and would die
here on May 5, 1821, and be interred locally. Not until 1840 would his body
be brought back "to the banks of the Seine, to repose among the French
nation I have loved so well." So complete and far-flung an exile had little
precedent among major heads of State,[3] brought down in their prime, and the
required adjustment for an intelligence, will, and energy as titanic as
Napoleon's was not easy–and indeed was never fully made. Longwood–the
name of the residence that he was assigned–had previously been a collection
of huts connected into cattle-sheds. It was cheaply reoutfitted for the new tenant; a British soldier would write to his mother shortly after Napoleon's death
that he was "shocked by the wretched state" the house was in.[4]

The Frenchman adapted poorly to the new climate and boredom. The
tropical temperatures, the constant wind and rain, had an enervating effect

on his frame of mind and, very probably, on his health—as indeed they did on the nerves of his confreres and of the Allied commissioners who also resided on "the rock."[5] Napoleon fitfully undertook projects—he kept sheep, planted trees, gardened, etc. He even tried to learn English, albeit unsuccessfully (recalling Mme de Rémusat's judgment that "The Emperor never liked to surrender to anything, even to grammar").[6] Little wonder that he would periodically take to his rooms for days on end in a black depression.

No one among the Emperor's ranking *fidèles* and family elected or was permitted to accompany him to St. Helena. The imperial entourage on the island thus consisted of four Frenchmen, of whom none had figured signally under the Empire. All were officers, two accompanied by their wives, and one by his teenage son. Among Generals Bertrand and Gourgaud, and the Comtes de Montholon and de Las Cases, the level of intellect and conversation was mediocre (though Las Cases had a significant literary culture). Two of the four stayed to the end; two left the island years before their patron's demise—Las Cases in late 1816, ostensibly because he ran afoul of the British authorities (but he was happy to go); and Gourgaud in 1818, invited to leave by Napoleon because he acted toward the Emperor like a jealous lover and could not get along with Montholon.[7]

A fifth presence was Dr. Barry O'Meara, the Irish naval physician assigned to attend the Emperor; he was transferred out in 1818 by the British authority because his loyalties had become Napoleon's, not the Royal Navy's. Despite the confidences that the Emperor vouchsafed this pentarchy—as well as his maître d'hôtel, Cipriani, a Corsican Bonaparte family retainer who died suddenly in 1818—there was nothing approaching the intimacy that a Joseph, a Lannes, or a Duroc had enjoyed with the Emperor. But then these new men had been warned: "You perhaps thought in coming here you'd become my comrade?" the Emperor told one of them early on. "I am not a comrade with anybody. . . . I must be the center." Thus it had ever been since an affectionate Corsican boy and a vulnerable lover of 1795–96 had grown into the emotionally walled-off general, consul, and emperor, and thus it would remain: "The Emperor is what he is," wrote Bertrand, "and we cannot change his character. It is because of that character that he has no friends, that he has so many enemies, and indeed that we are at St. Helena."

Napoleon presently fashioned himself a *raison de vivre* on the island: to bear witness to himself, in the hope that it would shape how men saw him, both now and, more important, in the future. His first, most consistent and continuous effort in this regard was his ongoing set-to with the British authority on the island. Our Frenchman was fortunate indeed in having as his local nemesis Hudson Lowe (1769–1844). No less than Napoleon did the small-minded Sir Hudson live in a prison—in his case, "the clean, well-lit prison of one idea"[8]—reducing his ward to the status of "General Bonaparte." Many were the contemporaries who said or would have said that such annoyances were small punishment for this man's crimes, but it was also true, as a later prime minister pointed out, that Britain denied Napoleon a title that His Majesty's government had de facto recognized in its dealings with the French in 1806 and again in 1813–14. More to the point, it was almost a calculated affront to the French nation, which had twice "chosen" this man as its sovereign.[9]

Had he tolerated such address, Napoleon would have spared himself and his men endless woe, and have partaken of the social "high life" on St. Helena, notably invitations to the governor's residence, at Plantation House. But doing that he would have lost the opportunity that he was ever vigilant to seize: "Martyrdom," he told Las Cases, "will despoil me of my tyrant's reputation"; "misfortune alone has been lacking to my fame"; "[I will gain] a crown of thorns." Surely, it is not unthinkable that *l'Empereur* had watched Pius VII's witness against himself, and had learned something from it. Las Cases again: "The Emperor took up the attitude of dignity oppressed by force, and wrapped himself in a moral cloak."

His lofty witness occasioned its imperial exponent a few moments of high exaltation—"my body belongs to the wicked, but my soul is independent. I am prouder here at St. Helena than if I were seated on my throne, making kings and distributing crowns"[10]—but by and large, it trapped him in a curious paradox: at precisely the time that the creation of his great literary witness—his "memoirs" (see the next section)—strained his every sinew to create the myth of "the liberal and the republican Emperor," his day-to-day life in exile required Napoleon to stage a show. In the rinsing heat of tropical St. Helena, he and his entourage daily performed their opera buffa, entitled "Napoleon I, Emperor of the French, King of Italy," replete with full court dress, regalia, swords, and unrelenting protocol—all for an audience of one (Hudson Lowe), who was not present. Sometimes history repeated *is* farce.

But in summoning up the courage to be, before those more dire existential nemeses guilt, meaninglessness, and death, Napoleon turned primarily to another activity.

MEMOIRS

Au claire de la lune,
Mon ami, Pierrot,
Prête-moi ta plume
Pour écrire un mot.
—A familiar
French song

"Misfortune has its silver lining: it leads you into the truth," Napoleon said at this time. It is far from the case that the volumes we customarily refer to as the Emperor's memoirs are true, but it seems no less likely that the man behind them was often struggling to find truth as he understood it. A word about what we are dealing with here: early on, the Emperor took a stab at producing his own story, and after a few illegible pages—writing being the demanding thing that it is—he gave up. Thereafter, he relied on his four *fidèles* not only to transcribe his dictated words but also to take down casual conversations about the past, which, of course, occurred constantly between him and them. They did their duties to the letter. Often Montholon, Las Cases, Bertrand, and Gourgaud would beg off early of an evening—especially ones containing interesting sets of imperial reflections—in order to get back to their rooms and get it all down. Any journalist or diarist understands that need. The four men are often referred to as Napoleon's "evangelists," which is too flattering to all concerned, especially since at least two of the four, not to mention the Mentor himself, were well aware that a financial fortune lay in their pens.

The first result of all this dictation, transcription, editing, and rewriting was a compendious multi-volume work of roughly a million and a half words, which swiftly became one of the great bestsellers of the nineteenth century, Emmanuel Las Cases's *Memorial of Saint Helena* (1823). As J. Christopher Herold puts it, "And the flesh was made word."[11] It was followed, in 1847, by Montholon's two-volume *Accounts of the Captivity of the Emperor Napoleon at Saint Helena*. To lose oneself even briefly in these, as in Gourgaud's and Bertrand's multi-volume later collections of Napoleon's wandering ruminations—each dated with the day Napoleon gave it[12]—is to realize they do not constitute simply a longer version of an army bulletin. The man responsible for them is one who has recovered, if not his youthful idealism (although there are moments when it seems as if he has), then something of his youthful conscience, and taste for reading, reflection, and writing.

Which is to say, these volumes are not meaningfully described as "a propaganda production," even if they contain strong views and theses. They strike one, rather, as repetitious, painful, and probably futile attempts at self-exorcism and guilt management. Marcel Dunan calls the *Memorial* "a masterpiece of strange and controlled enthusiasm,"[13] but in truth, the control is not nearly as evident as the strangeness—or the inconsistency. It is common to say that Napoleon asserts everything and its opposite in these endless pages, which is only too true, for taken as a whole, the four "gospels" amount to several *million* words spoken over five years. Thus, for example, he may observe to Las Cases: "If I had died on the throne, in clouds of all-powerfulness, I should remain a problem for many people, but today, thanks to my misfortune, every passing hour strips me of my tyrant's skin." A few years later, he tells Montholon: "It would have been better for my glory if I had died at Moscow."

Las Cases's book contains a few outright lies, such as an invented letter to Murat exonerating Napoleon for the war in Spain—but by and large, Napoleon and his "evangelists" proceed by massaging events into whatever slant the Emperor wishes, at that moment, to give, understanding that he will return to the same topic months or years later, and perhaps give it a different one. The cumulative effect is to give one the impression (correct, I believe) that he or she is seeing something of the "real" man in these memoirs more fully than at any time since the artillery lieutenant's youthful writings or the ride with Caulaincourt (1812). Napoleon certainly has his obsessions in these insular years: Marie-Louise, Waterloo, the Russian campaign, the Spanish imbroglio, the fate of the King of Rome (whom he feared would never know his father),[14] etc. He gets off brilliant portraits—unjust to some (Murat), indulgent of others (Robespierre), fairly ferocious about others (Talleyrand and Fouché).[15] He speaks kindly of Pius VII, whom he regrets he treated shabbily.[16]

Generally, however, Napoleon is not afflicted by his memories of people per se; they are not bad, they are weak. He is not Lear on the heath, thundering against his daughters; he is not filled with resentment and the desire for vengeance, which Nietzsche compared to "poisonous tarantulas" in the soul. Rather, the general tone underlying these detailed discussions of every phase of the Empire is a dark one: "When I focus my thoughts on the mistakes I have made, and who it was [i.e., myself] who brought the allies back into France, I feel overwhelmed with remorse,"[17] though it does not lead him to full confessions about narcissism and the corruptions of holding great power. Napoleon is obsessed with how he should have done things, how he really was, and what he really intended.

AUX ARMES, CITOYENS!
—"La Marseillaise"

The Napoleon that Napoleon fashions in the memoirs—both convincingly and unconvincingly (perhaps to himself as well)—is the Napoleon of 1789 and the Napoleon of "1789," as the nineteenth century was coming to understand it—that is, the era of liberal national movements in Poland, Spain, Italy, and Germany. The former reveals the exiled Emperor's recovery of a civic-heroic discourse of "citizen" and "republic," of his "Jacobin" conscience, in opposition to the Restoration monarchy. The latter discourse is the "export" version of nation-talk—of "people's rights" vis-à-vis the State now repackaged as "the rights of peoples" to become nations. In the *Memorial*, Napoleon sees himself as the conscious abettor of "nations and nationalities" in Italy, Germany, Poland, and Spain (Spain not being a nation until it had established popular sovereignty and imposed State control of the Church).

Napoleon's apparent recovery of his Jacobin conscience is an accent we have not heard in him this systematically since well before the first Italian campaign. On St. Helena the references and values of the artillery lieutenant, of the disciple of the Abbé Raynal (if not of Rousseau) and the member of the Institute, the friend of the Enlightenment, all recur in defense and illustration of the Liberal Empire of 1815. It carries with it an implicit repudiation of the high Empire, 1808–13. We hear such mystifications as "the Empire was merely the regularization of the republican principle" and "[T]he imperial government was a kind of republic . . . [because I was] called to be head of government by the voice of the Nation." It is striking how confident he now is after years of anxiety (apparent or real?) about his legitimacy: "There was never a king who was more a sovereign of the people than I was. Without the least talent, it still would have been easier to reign in France [as I did] than it was for Louis and the most gifted Bourbons."[18] Napoleon grants that he may have been wrong to have created a nobility and a court, "because it weakened the principle of equality." He was largely regretful of censorship and political prisons.

In the memoirs, the domestic and the foreign, the national and the international fuse in the imperial mind: "Were I to return [to France]," he tells Las Cases, "I should refound my empire on the Jacobins. Jacobinism is the volcano, which threatens all social order. Its eruption could easily be re-produced in Prussia . . . [and with] all the power of Prussia at my disposal, I could use it as a club to smash Russia and Austria." The prophet, in short, stays armed. The booted Robespierre is never too far away at St. Helena. The man's taste for power abides, but is now envisioned as power thrust upon him by circumstance (as war was), and exercised via a range of ideas and doctrines.

Speaking about the historical Robespierre was a frequent rumination for Napoleon Bound. He was at pains to assert (to O'Meara, as it happens) that it was not right to judge lightly "a character who belongs to the domain of history. Despite what is commonly said against them, they are singular, and do not have despicable characters. Few men have left the mark that they have." In short, great men should not be judged by ordinary rules of morality: The hero as bringer of progress deserves latitude, to act by self-understanding and his own notion of freedom. Only if he acts egregiously should he be condemned.[19]

SICKNESS UNTO DEATH

He gave up to God the most powerful breath of life that ever animated human clay.
                                                    —Chateaubriand

On St. Helena, Napoleon took a greater interest in religious faith than he had previously shown; this is unsurprising in a man who is suffering and ill. It was not unusual for him to read the Bible, sometimes aloud, to the "court." No surprise, either, in his professed admiration for Saint Paul, in whose forceful and successful leadership of the nascent Christian movement the Emperor doubtless saw a kindred spirit. Finally, he talked about ultimate questions of God, life after death, judgment, etc. Sometimes one has the impression that he perhaps believed in more than the deism that he always professed (he was *never* an atheist, a stance he always scornfully disapproved). For example, he tells Montholon, "Belief comes with study and meditation on the marvels of Creation." He respected religion, particularly Islam, but toward the end of his life, he may have come to find more in his native Christianity than he had previously found. He speculated to Las Cases, "Perhaps I'll come to believe again, even blindly [as he did until he attained the age of reason, around thirteen]. May God will it! I certainly wouldn't resist it; indeed, I ask for nothing more. I think it must be a great happiness." At the end of the day, however, he did not really receive the grace of faith, and he confessed to General Bertrand that he doubted there was "anything after death," adding the rather eighteenth- (not twentieth-) century observation, "I am lucky not to believe, for I don't have chimerical fears about hell."[20]

Considering the ruthless treatment Napoleon accorded his body—how little sleep and exercise he gave it, how fast he ingested his food, how fat and sedentary he became—that body gave him yeoman service for almost fifty years. But in 1818 he began having liver and stomach problems, and thereafter his health declined, precipitously so late in 1820, when he took to his bed. He expired at 5:49 P.M. on Saturday, May 5, 1821, attended by two priests sent him at his request by Pope Pius VII.[21] "I die in the Roman Catholic Church into which I was born" reads the imperial will. The death mask made by his physician, Dr. Antommarchi (O'Meara's replacement) shows a sober serenity and an almost youthful beauty.

According to the autopsy performed by Dr. Antommarchi, and more or less subscribed to by other physicians present, Napoleon died from a collection of vaguely related maladies: hepatitis, giving way to stomach cancer, then to an ulcerated stomach lining and a diffusion of the stomach cancer. Modern doctors, reading the death reports, also find strong evidence of arsenic toxicity, and some of tuberculosis. Death itself, they now find, may have had an iatrogenic trigger, or at least been hastened, in the large dose of orgeat-(almond)-flavored calomel (a laxative) administered by one of the British attendings.

As is well known, a new theory has flourished for over three decades, which sees the Emperor intentionally poisoned by one of his entourage, most probably the Comte de Montholon, acting in league with the Comte d'Artois, brother of Louis XVIII.[22] Its only hard evidence—but it is significant—is the high dosage of arsenic found on thirty tested hair samples, presumably (albeit not provably) from Napoleon's scalp. The first thing to be said is that this theory, which has imposed itself sufficiently for the 1999 supplement of the *Dictionnaire Napoléon* to contain a lengthy entry on it,[23] has more anecdotal than truly historical significance, given that after the congress of Aix-la-Chapelle (1818), there was no chance that Napoleon would be moved to a more proximate exile, nor, given the impermeability of the British naval guard at St. Helena, that he would be sprung. In other words, except for his memoirs, which were nearly completed by then, he, as a living person, had no further role on the world-historical stage.

Second, the poisoning proponents have undertaken no archival research to support their case against Montholon,[24] which reposes only on the tested hair samples and (albeit ingenious) conjecture. The one professional historian to have studied the case, Jacques Macé, started out a proponent of the poisoning thesis, but after several years of research for his biography of Montholon, he became dubious. Several serious problems attend the theory: first, the hair samples owned by Betsy Balcombe, given her by the Emperor just after his arrival on "the rock"—that is, *before* he would have ingested the arsenic-laced wine—contain the same high levels of poison as hairs from much later in his St. Helena stay; second, Montholon did not have regular access to Napoleon's wine; third, key signs of arsenic poisoning (notably dark rings around the fingernails) were absent on the corpse; fourth, Montholon, on returning to France in 1821, had execrable relations with the Restoration regime, and appears to have received no money from them. He joined the bonapartist opposition to the government, and lived long enough to see Louis-Napoleon crowned Emperor of the French, and to be rewarded by him.

Notwithstanding, the current generation of hair-splitting poison theorists (as a species, they date back to like-minded surmisers in the Restoration) has succeeded in raising doubt, even if the latest clinical judgment by forensic medicine is that the natural pathology noted in the autopsy, one way or another (we cannot be sure of the exact onset and chronology of the diseases affecting Napoleon), sufficed amply to kill Napoleon. Occam's razor, therefore, would logically slice off any recourse to the poisoning thesis.[25] Logic, however, does not always obtain in human history, whereas the overdetermination of effects by many causes usually does. The high toxicity levels in Napoleon's hair samples raise unanswered questions. Unfortunately, they shall likely remain unresolved by further forensic investigation since the French government has less warrant to open Napoleon's tomb than the American government does to open John Kennedy's.[26]

THE NAPOLEONIC TRADITION(S)

I am constantly struck by the popularity of this terrible personage among the nations of Europe. Everywhere peasants, young and old, will tell you a thousand stories about him and, seeming to forget the evil he did them, will focus on marvels he performed. The magic of glory is very great!

—Adolphe Thiers[27]

I am destined to be the polemicists' green pastures, but I am hardly afraid of becoming their victim. In chomping down on me, they will bite into granite."

Napoleon at St. Helena

In France, Napoleon the defeated exile quickly rebecame an object of sympathy and inspiration, to the disconcertment of historians who impose modern liberal notions of "rational" and "reasonable" on European history.

Even a royalist officer like Lieutenant Colonel Baudus, who considered that the Emperor's death on the battlefield would have been a "boon" for the nation, now regarded his status as a prisoner of Britain as a mark of shame for France.[28] Late in 1815, many more enthusiastic bonapartists roamed Paris's streets and filled her cafes than could be seen in the Hundred Days, let alone after Waterloo. We may attribute this rapid evolution to the tight-fistedness of the second Bourbon restoration, which again snubbed "the national" for the "legitimate," and to the perceived authenticity of the former Emperor's "witness" on his lonely island,[29] but at bottom it frankly defies clear explanation and remains a kind of mystery. François Guizot, that other great historian-statesman (besides Thiers) of nineteenth-century France, summed up the legacy of Napoleon, whom he did not like, with famous economy: "It is no small matter to be, as one man, the incarnation of the nation's glory, a guarantor of revolution, and a principal of authority."[30] Most astonishing of all, Pozzo di Borgo, one of the most remorseless opponents of the Emperor, described the man he contributed so singularly to bringing down as "this phenomenon, the likes of whom we shall not see again; a moral and political universe unto himself. . . . Still not understood . . . , he is destined to remain a mystery, a sublime, gigantic shadow."[31]

Internationally, too, Napoleon's name swiftly claimed association with liberalism and national independence—incredibly, if one considers only the Empire's legacy of tyranny and does not give due measure to the power of myth around a charismatic personality. Napoleon's enemies, as always, advanced his cause mightily with their clumsiness and reaction. "After me, the revolution, or rather the ideas that made it, will resume their course," Napoleon had said. "It will be like a book in which you take out the place mark and recommence reading at the page you left off."[32] Thus, in Spain, for example, during the Hundred Days, liberal elements in the Cortes made contact with Joseph Bonaparte to inquire about French support for a "national" movement against Ferdinand VII. The revolution duly took place, and duly failed, but its martyrdom redounded to Napoleon's benefit.[33]

Relentlessly, too, in Poland, Italy, Sardinia, the Rhineland, and even in Prussia, England, and the Papal States, the Napoleonic name was invoked by progressives, liberals, republicans, and even socialists and revolutionaries.[34] Few did so in ignorance—they understood that the French Empire had had dark sides—but with deliberation, opposing a present reality of reaction that they could not control, via references to a past that could be modeled and selectively invoked. Adam Mickiewicz's epic poem, *Pan Tadeusz,* written in exile in 1834, is a classic monument to his fellow Poles' belief that a political messiah similar to Napoleon will come from the West, to give them free-

STEVEN ENGLUND

dom (from Russia) and justice.[35] And in Russia, the poet Alexander Pushkin, having stigmatized Napoleon as "the universal scourge," now asked, "Where are you, favorite son of fortune and war?"[36] In the United States, where the cult reached a level of popular acceptance second only to France, Thomas Jefferson, no friend of the French Empire's, succumbed to seeing Napoleon on St. Helena in a different and more sympathetic light. The same thing happened with progressive British writers: in their support for the Chartist movement and their struggle with its opponents, they came to construe "l'Empereur" differently.

In mid-nineteenth-century France, the Napoleonic cult (not to be confused with the bonapartist doctrine or political party) exerted a tidal pull on artists and writers, who succumbed not always willingly, and not always uncritically. Victor Hugo evolved from stern disapproval of the Empire and its Corsican adventurer to cautious admirer of the "great Frenchman," while the poet (and future foreign minister) Alphonse de Lamartine, a man who *never* approved of Napoleon, yet wrought verse that celebrated the Empire's glory and accomplishments. The popular writer Béranger–"the national poet," as he was known–also disliked the Empire and its founder, but by 1828, his vast audience had obliged him to evolve, so he celebrated Napoleon's armies and the common soldier in his poems.[37] In the public sector, politicians as eminent as Thiers, and journalists as influential as Armand Carrel (editor of *Le National*), all the way down to the nameless revolutionaries (republican and socialist) who died on the barricades in the myriad insurrections and revolutions that punctuated 1820–48, *all* deployed and profited from the Napoleonic myth, however critical they could also be of the man who engendered it.

As for bonapartism, the *Memorial of St. Helena* became its Koran; the Liberal Empire, its Camelot; the myth of the Napoleonic soldier-laborer emerged as the fountain and protector of "patriotism," the mid-century's stock in trade.[38] Bonapartism's political culmination was the election of Louis-Napoleon Bonaparte (son of Louis and Hortense) to the presidency of the Second French Republic in 1848. He presented himself as a "national," as "the people's choice" (or "wish"), and he won a perfectly legal and triumphant election. But he followed that three years later with a brutal coup d'Etat, which established the Second Empire at the price of hundreds of killed and wounded, and thousands of imprisoned or exiled. The regime's subsequent descent into authoritarianism (and finally liberalism)–ratified, of course, by plebiscites–and its bellicose foreign policy culminated in the disaster of the Prussian War of 1870–71, when France lost Alsace-Lorraine. The bonapartist tradition was dealt a devastating blow from which the formal political movement never recovered.

But it was not a mortal blow to Napoleon's myth—far from it. The definitive establishment of the Republic in France went curiously unaccompanied by the disappearance even of bonapartism, which remained a presence on the political scene into the early twentieth century, or of the literary and popular cult of Napoleon, which flourished on the very revanchism that "Napoleon the Little" had occasioned in losing two provinces.[39] The successors of Béranger—Erckmann and Chatrian, a brace of republican despisers of the French imperial tradition—turned out a bestseller (*The Story of a Conscript of 1813*) that celebrates the patriotic spirit of the First Empire's penultimate campaign. Republicans now became adept—and have remained so—at distinguishing between "Bonaparte" (admirable, progressive) and "Napoleon" (tyrannical, anti-revolutionary). For example, the current French foreign minister can ask the sort of post-modern question (cited in the epigraph on page 433) that no one but a French reader can remotely conjure with: "Does Bonaparte break the surface again in Napoleon or is it simply Napoleon disguising himself in Bonaparte, in order to become Napoleon again?"[40]

One would like to write, "The Great War (1914–18) brought the final disenchantment of the romance of war in France"—and certainly the Marne and Verdun dealt the cult of war a resounding blow—yet to do so would be to forget that Abel Gance produced his masterpiece of romantic napoleonia (*Napoléon*) in 1927, and promoted the film with this unforgettable statement: "Napoleon is the abridgement of the world. . . . [He is] a paroxysm of his epoch, which in turn is a paroxysm of all of Time. And the cinema, for me, is a paroxysm of life."[41] It might surprise some readers to learn that the new or radical right wing in France—the twentieth century's neo-royalist Action Française, the interwar authoritarian leagues, Vichy, Poujade, Le Pen, etc.— by and large have *not* invoked Napoleon. Still less, have communism and fascism as doctrines fed off him—indeed Italian and German fascists were hostile to him. (This has not stopped scholars—notably British—from conflating Napoleon with Hitler and Stalin, inaccurate, anachronistic, and simply unfair as such comparisons are.)[42]

However, the French Gaullist tradition, although thoroughly republican, has proven more equivocal. "Le grand Charles" himself exhibited the classic republican ambivalence: on the one hand, he wrote in *France and Her Army* (1938), Napoleon "left France crushed, invaded, drained of blood and courage, smaller than when he took her . . . , and still [123 years later], feeling the weight of Europe's mistrust." On the other hand, "Must we count as nothing the unbelievable prestige with which he surrounded our armies, . . . the renown of power which the *patrie* still enjoys?"[43] To be sure, Gaullism, despite superficial resemblances and frequent comparisons, is *not* synonymous with bonapartism, but is, rather, a form of civic republicanism, as American democracy represents another. However, the republican tradition in France, though it long ago (in the 1840s) repudiated the Napoleonic tradition, yet retains a far profounder trace of that imprint than it cares to concede.

THE ROAD NOT TAKEN

"It would have been better for the peace of France if this man [Jean-Jacques Rousseau] had never lived . . . , for he prepared the French Revolution."
"I should have thought, Citizen Consul, that it was not for you to complain about the Revolution."
"Well the future will tell if it would not have been better if neither I nor Rousseau had lived."

—Conversation between Bonaparte and Stanislas de Giradin before the tomb of Rousseau, 1801

Napoleon is the path that France historically did not take, but might have done, as Robert Tombs persuasively argues.[44] It is the "other Blue"—meaning the revolutionary–tradition besides republicanism. ("White" was the Bourbon monarchy, and "red" is post-1917 socialism and communism.) The Republic and the Empire, the Empire and the Republic. The twain are certainly not indisseverable, and if they are not as congruent as Napoleon himself occasionally had it, they are also not the radical antinomies that official French republican doctrine has stoutly insisted since roughly the mid–nineteenth century.

The aspect of the Napoleonic tradition that first strikes the modern reader is its multi-facetedness. It is a "compleat" set of political facets: it has its republican (consular) "moment" and also its imperial; it is monarchical but also democratic; it is synonymous with Caesarism, yet the Liberal Empire of 1815 and Napoleon III's Liberal Empire of 1867–70 were parliamentary and, well, liberal. It restored the Church, yet it enthroned the secular State, while later-nineteenth-century proponents of bonapartism were outright anticlericals (and some were even a variety of socialist). It stood for censorship, yet it had a strong intellectual and cultural bent (one cannot forget that it founded Egyptology).

Its very proteanism and emphasis on style make it modern—and so very French—as does its (or at least its founder's) capacity for ironical self-regard. And its style is far more important than its formal doctrines, is second only to the unique charisma and memory of the founder, to which it is inextricably wed. What the tradition shares with the genie of Gaullist republicanism is both obvious and subtle. Obvious in the Consular reforms (like the Civil Code), which are still in force; obvious, too, in the centralization, the State *dirigisme*, the monarchical manner attached to the presidency, the accent on the head of State's ties with "the nation." Less often noted is the State's interest in directing culture toward the greater glory of France. But deepest of all is the ongoing republican mistrust of politics as freely competing private and factional interests. Parties exist in modern France, of course, and are tolerated, as do and are the loyal opposition and regular change in government, but they came late in the day to the Hexagon, and are not entirely at home there. At bottom, the Republic and the Empire seek to sublimate differences and unite interests in the "nation"—the great underlying myth of a polity united only in words.

The French, Napoleon lamented to Constant just after his second abdication, "abandoned me with the same facility that they received me [a hundred days before]." On St. Helena, he complained about the French being "weather vanes" (*girouettes*) in their political faithfulness, though he deemed it "an innocent vice." His appraisal could not have been more wrong, at least where he was concerned. The French, including many in the political class and the upper bourgeoisie, fought a futile fight very valiantly for their *Empereur* in 1815—as indeed they had already done in 1812–14 when a true *girouette* would have changed direction, and some did. At the end of the historical day, looking back over two centuries, the historian might be forgiven for concluding that to condemn Napoleon is to condemn the French. The first restoration discovered this to be true, to its chagrin; the young Victor Hugo observed it, and so have many writers since him—Thiers and Edgar Quinet implicitly, André Suarès and Elie Faure explicitly.

That is not to say that Napoleon cannot be criticized, and even condemned—he certainly has been, including by no few Frenchmen.[45] The "black" legend continues alive and well to the present day—both within France, and without. But it is to say that Napoleon and the nation, the latter word writ both with and without quotations, remain joined at the hip. Indeed one has a hard time naming another modern political leader who is more identified with an entire people, both in his lifetime and especially afterwards, than Napoleon. Virtually the entire literary and much of the artistic-cultural establishment (but not, curiously, the scholarly-academic world) of modern France has devoted seas of ink, acres of canvas and no few tons of marble to conjuring with this man.

Recalling André Suarès's quotation at the end of "Frisson," we should yet have to acknowledge that it is a strange kind of "trembling" we confront in modern France toward Napoleon. On the one hand, the Corsican-born Emperor's adopted countrymen cannot shut up about him. The cascade of nonfiction, fiction, fine art, clubs, private institutes, reenacted battles, souvenirs, places of memory devoted to Napoleon is never-ending; the tree is evergreen. On the other hand, from the viewpoint of the Republic—i.e., the State—*Napoléon Ier, empereur des Français* does not exist. No official commemoration, no monument, no street, no metro stop, no *place* name, no subsidized review, no research center, no professor's chair exists to betoken the State's awareness of the Emperor, though the names of innumerable kings bedizen the street plaques.[46] A metro stop even recalls Robespierre, a revolutionary leader who sent infinitely more of his adversaries to the guillotine or to prison than Napoleon ever did. The French capital fairly breathes Napoleon, and to a great extent displays his handiwork, but as Emperor, he is the love that dares not speak its name. The tomb at Les Invalides was built under the Second Empire, and its use for the Republic is mainly as a tourist attraction—and to reassure the government that *l'Empereur* is truly dead (if he is).

This is understandable, for the French State in many of its deepest foundations and mind-sets is the tossed-off creation of Citizen Bonaparte, during an amazing, brief stint as First Consul at the start of the nineteenth century. Unlike Caesar and Alexander, whom Napoleon rivaled as a conqueror, he was also an Augustus—a State-builder—rather more than they were, and that makes him unique in history. Although the Republic honors many of the kings and saints of the long French past, it would thus be an act of lèse majesté for the Republic to honor its rival—like asking an impertinent Tom Sawyer to acknowledge Mark Twain; or better, like asking Dostoyevsky's Grand Inquisitor *not* to be terrified of Jesus. The French State is both too proud and too weak to do this, so instead, individual statesmen, such as the current foreign minister, write rhapsodic histories of *l'Empereur*, strangely subtitled "the spirit of sacrifice."[47] Napoleon, in short, is the French Republic's "irreducible problem," as one of its most gifted, and strongly republican, historians, Maurice Agulhon, acknowledged.

The French relationship with Napoleon thus remains complex and multifaceted, and in key *official* regards, unacknowledged and unspoken—an extraordinary situation when you consider that the Emperor has been, at one and the same time, "the incarnation of the nation's glory, a guarantor of revolution, and a principal of authority"—in the unforgettable dictum of

Guizot, cited previously. French regimes have never known quite how to integrate *l'Empereur* into their official takes on French history, and the twentieth-century republics have been no exception.[48] They have remained ambivalent and timid about Napoleon—keenly (perhaps *too* keenly) aware that many foreigners agree with the great Dutch historian Pieter Geyl when he wrote that France has long been "a most willing tool in the hands of Napoleon, and after his death, a credulous dupe of the legend."[49] Even were it this simple, which it is not—the French, as Geyl also well knew, have always mounted a very intelligent opposition to, and critique of, Napoleon and his legend—the way to remedy, or exorcise, the situation is not to ignore it.

Yet this is what the Fifth Republic does. Official commemorations, while acknowledging many specific First Empire topics (e.g., recently, a stamp was issued honoring two hundred years of the Legion of Honor), elide Napoleon as emperor.

More seriously, for the purpose of seeking a thorough understanding or even mounting a penetrating critique of Napoleon, this negligent attitude of the Republic carries over into research on the First Empire and its founder. Thus, although the French government subsidizes a vast amount of academic research into the most esoteric corners of French royal history, it declines to fund a useful and unobjectionable review of Napoleonic studies that is head-quartered at the Sorbonne. And when, some years back, a private entrepreneur left a large sum in his will to be devoted to building and maintaining a Napoleonic research center, library, and publication program, the Republic fretted that the money might be diverted to propaganda, or even go to fund a coup d'Etat.[50] Only in the recent past have Napoleonic studies gained any serious purchase in government-run French universities and scholarship centers—and even now, it is a very circumscribed enterprise when you compare it to the formidable brainpower and funds dedicated to the study of the Revolution, or medieval, early-modern, and contemporary history. Consider the most formidable *opus magnum* of French historical letters to have appeared since World War II—*Les Lieux de Mémoire* (*Places of Memory*).[51] Its six compendious volumes contain millions of words, arranged in long essays, penned by the great names of French scholarship, there is nothing on Napoleon himself, and nearly nothing on his legend or doctrines.[52] Yet, paradoxically, popular books about the Emperor, by French writers and politicians going back to Stendhal and Thiers, continue to pour off the presses, and have long proven staples of the French book market.

The main reason for this situation, I would submit, is the subtle but real threat that Napoleonic style and ideas, *by the very strength of their unconscious appeal to the French*, pose to the Republic. Suffice it to say that writers and public figures as different as Dominique de Villepin, France's current foreign minister and a leading member of the Gaullist party, and Maurice Agulhon, a resolute socialist and one of France's greatest social historians, have sought to rethink—and get other French people to rethink—the "irreducible problem" for the Republic of France's greatest conqueror.[53]

NAPOLEON AS TWENTIETH-CENTURY DICTATOR: THE TOTALITARIAN TEMPTATION[54]

"History is not ethics, and the sole tasks of understanding and portraying [Napoleon] demand quite enough of us." The words of a leading First Empire specialist of an earlier era still apply.[55] I find it facile to damn Napoleon as an all-purpose "tyrant," but that is what recent books fall over themselves to do. Their authors prefer that this man had "a humble and a contrite heart"; they see him as the direct precursor of the totalitarian dictators and racist-genocidal atrocities of the century just passed.[56] It has gotten so that a writer—*this* writer, at any rate—feels the need to reassure his reader, "No, neither you nor I would probably *like* Napoleon if we sat down to dinner with him"; and "No, this book would not be, and was not intended to be, well received at Malmaison, the Tuileries, or on St. Helena."

The political theorist Mark Lilla observes that we are obsessed with the Nazi-fascist model, and that instead of seeing Hitlers and Stalins at every turn, we would do well to recover the ancient nuances and gradations among "tyrants."[57] For example, the word "dictator," in its Roman and subsequent French connotation, was a morally ambiguous term, containing the possibility for good as well as evil. It was a term that contemporaries applied to Bonaparte. Cicero was driven to borrow the Greek term *teras* to describe Caesar, his adversary: "a wonderful, frightening, monstrous and inscrutable phenomenon of a higher order."[58]

I have drawn occasional comparisons of Napoleon with Caesar, as with Alexander the Great or Hernán Cortés. If we knew remotely as much about these three men as we do about Napoleon, we would no doubt stigmatize them, too, as trailblazers for Hitler. We surely have more reason to discern the rudiments of modern "political" racism in sixteenth-century Catholic-Spanish attitudes toward the "pagan" Aztec Indians than we do in the imperialist "bureaucratizing" lust of Napoleon.[59] Caesar, Alexander, and Cortés readily imitated previous conquerors, as did Napoleon (e.g., in his Egyptian campaign 1799–1801), yet the French occupation entailed far less carnage, devastation, and pillage—and many more immediate and intended improvements—than did the conquests of the ancient or early-modern worlds, not to mention the conquerors and conquests of our own times.

Two centuries on, learned colloquia and discussion still take place throughout Europe and the Near East over the good and the bad, the beautiful and the ugly, in Napoleonic occupation of various regions, yet no Pole or Dutchman debates the boons and banes of the Nazi occupation, nor do Ethiopians look back on Mussolini as the sort of (admittedly, ambiguous) "blessing" that many present-day Egyptians see in Napoleon. Again, no serious thinker, to my knowledge, argues that Stalin fulfilled the October Revolution of 1917, that Hitler continued the German Revolution of 1918, or that Mussolini was the heir of Garibaldi and Cavour. Rather, it is generally believed that these leaders betrayed these causes. On the other hand, lively debate continues, and will carry on, over a question set in an exam of my youth: "Was Napoleon Bonaparte the heir or the heresiarch* of the French Revolution? Discuss."

Thus, Jean Tulard's ironically intended equation "Napoleon = Lenin without electricity" has provoked its own backlash. Two important recent works display the effects of events and discussion on scholarship: Martyn Lyons's *Napoleon Bonaparte and the Legacy of the French Revolution* (1994) and Arno J. Mayer's *The Furies: Violence and Terror in the French and Russian Revolutions* (2000).[60] In sum, if it is mandatory to reconceive the first Emperor of the French in terms of the experience of the living, I do not believe that he withstands useful comparison with Hitler or Stalin, which is why this book has not pursued that tack. The fact that Napoleon halted the headlong course of the Revolution, or turned some of it against other parts of it, does not, ipso facto, make him a counterrevolutionary. In our own day, we have seen an entity far larger than any empire undergo a reaction against its own recent "revolution." The "restoration" in the Roman Catholic Church brought off by John Paul II, a man with a force of will and mind not far short of Napoleonic, turns on his thesis that his measures represent a "consolidation" of the reforms of the Second Vatican Council. While this is a sharply debated proposition, few dispute either the pope's sincere attachment to the council or the council's perduring role as the plinth of modern Catholicism.

Then, too, there is a major matter of magnitude. In Italy in 1930, for example, twenty-thousand police operations—arrests, seizures of arms and pamphlets, closures—occurred per week, aimed at opponents of Mussolini's regime.[61] While we do not have precise data on the daily activity of the Napoleonic police, we know that at the height of the empire (1810–12),

---

*A leader of a heresy, the chief of a heretical sect.

they did not carry out anything remotely approaching this level of repression. There was simply not sufficient State bureaucracy nor an "official" party to undertake such action, even assuming the will for it existed at the top, which it did not. And that twenty-thousand figure is only for fascist *Italy*. We search the annals of the First Empire in vain for crushing acts of pure evil, on the order of the Gulag, the Final Solution, the Night of the Long Knives,[62] or the "assassination" of the Russian peasantry. The "security" or "authority" State is one thing; the "police State" or "total" State, quite another.[63]

But it is the problem of the anachronism of comparing Napoleon to Hitler or Stalin that is finally the most insuperable. *L'Empereur* was indeed a "thoroughly modern major general," so to speak—in the way he staged a "legal" (or parliamentary) coup d'Etat,[64] in the way he organized State power and established his charisma in a desacralized world; above all, in the way he founded a regime based on the appearance of popular consent. But his modernity, as we post-moderns tend to forget when we think of Napoleon, was of the *nineteenth*-, not the twentieth-century variety, and the leaders he might be properly considered the precursor of—or who invoked or admired him (as Hitler, Mussolini, and Stalin did *not*)—carried names like Cavour, Mehmet Ali, Bismarck, and Napoleon III.

Napoleon, thus, may ultimately be seen as a liberal, in this sense: he sought, via a regime of laws and institutions, to elude profound political conflict. Unlike Hitler or Stalin, Napoleonic nation-talk was not irrationalist (anti-intellectual) or group-ethnic—it did not draw its sources from "us" against "them"—but rather from the Roman-universalist perspective: "us" absorbing (acculturating, modernizing) "them." The first Emperor of the French thus sought to escape, not to bask in, the "primacy of the political," in Carl Schmitt's phrase for the Nazi era. Where, if anywhere, we may discern something of the late-modern (twentieth century) about the Late Empire lies in the rising degrees of animosity that Napoleon unintentionally sparked off among his opponents—i.e., the counterrevolutionaries both within and without France, the States endlessly thrashed by the French, and the societies (nations) increasingly mulched by French taxmen and army recruiters. These were the entities that discovered and embraced their modern political identity via the experience of being Napoleon's *enemy*.[65]

In his personal morality, Napoleon was nowhere nearly as corrupt or as strange as the Prince Regent (future George IV) of England, Charles IV of Spain, or, for that matter, his own brother, King Jérôme (Bonaparte) of Westphalia. He differed from most rulers and high aristocrats of his era only in being rather more blue-nosed, as when he scolded his wife, Empress Marie-Louise, for receiving visitors from her bed, when she was ill: "This is

improper in a woman under forty," he wrote. In his relentless application of
raison d'Etat for geopolitical expansion, Napoleon did not differ qualitatively
from his brother sovereigns of the era; he differed in the success rate he
enjoyed, thanks to his political and military skills, and the power and motivation of the French nation. It was not until 1813 that Britain and the Continental great powers began truly to assimilate the "lessons" of compromise
and alliance, and to moderate their own deep-seated expansionist impulses.
And even at the Congress of Vienna, it was a near thing whether geopolitical and personal greed, and national rivalry and vanity, would not set the
former Allies back at one another's throats.

The comparison of Napoleon to a Renaissance prince (or to a *condottiere*)
is a product of the Emperor's mono-mindedness in the pursuit of policy, but
mostly of his personal traits: his wit, his intellectual "style" and brilliance, his
ability to dissimulate, his abrupt and judgmental manner with people.
These have also been called "antique" qualities, what Nietzsche called "the
ancient world's face of granite."

Fortunately, one does not have to *be* a Nietzschean in order to discern in
the subject of this biography a remarkable instance of the "will-to-power."
This philosopher's proximity in time (born 1844) to Napoleon, his oft-
quoted admiration for the man ("The Revolution made Napoleon possible.
That is its justification."), make Nietzsche a more suitable modern invocation
for Napoleon than the totalitarian dictators, who had little use for Napoleon.
Nietzsche's philosophical view on "objective" moral judgments—i.e., that
they are but the disguised expression of a subjective will-to-power—is a
viewpoint one could imagine Napoleon adopting, albeit not publicly. In the
Emperor's refusal to accept equals or depend on anyone emotionally or politically, and his identification of French national interest with his own will, he
gave rise to what we consider "Nietzschean" myths about himself—as god or
devil, as Prometheus, in a world with an "empty" sky ("God is dead").[66] If
these myths still abide about Napoleon, and they do, it is because, in Lord
Roseberry's words, "Mankind will always delight to scrutinize something that
indefinitely raises its conception of its own powers and possibilities."[67]

Introduction (Misplaced)

This Author, This Book

I conclude my work with the year 1815, because everything which came after that belongs to ordinary history.

—Prince Metternich

The ordinary historian hesitates before the extraordinary moment, and would flee it altogether if he did not have a rendezvous with it since he was a boy. I look through the yellowed pages of "The History of Napoleon the First," which I started when I was at Le Conte Junior High School, in Los Angeles. They leave off, breathless, around page 6, with the author impatient to tuck into the battle of Austerlitz. Jean Tulard, the preeminent French authority on the First Empire, observes that people generally come to Napoleon via one of two paths: art and lead soldiers. Mine was the lead soldiers.

Being true to the boy has been the hobgoblin of my thoughts throughout the writing of this book, although I suspect his adolescent feelings included "sentiment[s] of the most spurious kind, a need for servility and wonder, a craving to be intoxicated by an impression of greatness and to fantasize about it," as the great Swiss art historian Jacob Burckhardt summed up the reasons for Caesar's enduring fame. Yet I have not produced a piece that the boy in me would have drooled over: the present book has only a few set-piece battle tableaux, and is without long disquisitions on strategy and tactics. In fact, it stresses that strategy tended to be imposed after, not before, the fact, making it an exercise in public relations, more than in military planning, per se. My book concurs with current thinking that mammoth pitched battles, including some of my boyhood's most beloved set-tos, were less decisive than the cumulative effects of large campaigns over large areas, in which Napoleon had less direct control.

A word is in order about war in the larger sense, however: War was a by-product of Napoleon's arts of peace. "The Empire was born of war and survived by war," writes Jacques-Olivier Boudon, one of the best of the younger generation of French historians of the First Empire.[1] In the eighteenth century, once the French began to lose, the romance of war came in for serious challenge. The greatest of the early *philosophes,* Montesquieu, had harsh words for the "archaic" wars of Louis XIV (1638–1715), which, "without reason, without usefulness, ravaged the earth to display the virtue and excellence of war."[2] Montesquieu felt the Sun King's disasters had interred the possibility of "heroism," in the classical sense. Then, of course, there's Voltaire's splendid satire *Candide*, which mocks "imperialist" wars, as we would call them.

And yet, and yet. Even Montesquieu had his weakness for the "sublime" Romans, who fascinated him as they repelled him, while Voltaire, in his histories, makes it clear that he had a yen for conquering (not losing) warrior-heroes. The fact is, the late eighteenth century was still an age when triumph on the field of battle was the nec plus ultra of glory, and may well be the single greatest factor in accounting for Napoleon's "greatness" in contemporaries' eyes, for the unprecedented dominion he achieved over imaginations and opinion, as well as territory. His was still a world where a "good death," where even military defeat, if sufficiently grand and courageous, brought some *gloire*.[3] In short, the book at hand is about a world where the famous classical sentence "Ave, Caesar, morituri te salutant" was understood.[4]

War's conduct and purpose evolved in response to the huge political and ideological changes wrought in 1789–1815. War became quantitatively more costly and qualitatively more criticized. Yet the nineteenth century still cherished its Bismarcks, its "Chinese" Gordons, its Skobelevs, and its Light Brigades. One has only to flip through a few paragraphs of Alfred de Vigny's *Servitude and Grandeur of Arms* (1834) to breathe in a redolent whiff of grapeshot and gunpowder, and know what they meant to Napoleon and his troops. "A disordered love for the glory of [the profession of] arms took hold of me," writes the poet at the start of this immensely popular bestseller.

It is unquestionably a good thing that this mind-set lies behind us as a species, but its disappearance is less helpful when we would understand Napoleon. Thus, we leap to stigmatize the Emperor for his so-Corsican love of war and for his reputed insensitivity. "One night in Paris will replenish the ranks," he said, appallingly, after a battle particularly costly in human lives. On closer view, however, we find that in fact that observation was not of Napoleonic coinage, but had been spoken on the eve of battle by Condé, a great French general of the late seventeenth century. Moreover, it was not thought particularly brutish by contemporaries, but had entered the currency of general military "wisdom" on human prolificity.[5] Only 1914–18, with the horrifying hecatomb of soldiers, and 1939–45, with the slaughter of millions of civilians, truly changed mentalities.

Or did it? Recently, I heard a well-known banker who, as a young man, had served in the French Foreign Legion admit, "I love war even when it is not necessary. There is nothing like it; it is not a metaphor for anything. It is a unique test of oneself. I love the danger, the glory, the self-knowledge in the face of death, the self-assertion, the camaraderie. And to be honest, [I love] the uniforms, display, show, and the order-giving." This confession—spoken sheepishly, but with increasing boldness, after an evening of candor, cognac, and conviviality—would have been applauded by a French or Russian officer of the era depicted in *War and Peace,* and would have been found eminently acceptable by much of the draft-age population, and even by many in their families.[6]

After hearing this effusion, I sat a bit melancholic, awash in a tide of conflicting judgments and emotions including, along with the obvious distaste and perturbation, a certain admiration and nostalgia, as though I had just watched a "You Are There" program about the legion's defense of Sidi-bel-Abbès or the last British cavalry charge at Omdurman . . .

In brief, from my adolescent self's perspective, the book at hand is *Hamlet with* the prince, but *without* much of the duel. For this, I apologize to the boy, and to any reader who, wanting what the boy wanted, decided nonetheless to stick with me, as I hope (and think) the boy would have done. Such trust has been rewarded, I trust.

For better or for worse, this is a *political* life, not a military, or an intimate life of its subject. For what it is worth, Napoleon would have approved such an approach, if certainly not most of my interpretations or conclusions. Moreover, this is analytic nearly as much as it is narrative history—which is to say, the author tends to "explain a lot," without a plethora of familiar anecdotes. Here, too, for what it is worth, our subject also made his points that way, in his very effective army bulletins. "The art of telling," observed Napoleon, "lies in suppressing the useless, which impedes the flow." The bulletins, of course, also display "the art of telling lies," and that is not my intention here.

The paradox of his relentlessly political life is that Napoleon successfully "ended" politics—at least in the turbulent, partisan, daily sense that the French had practiced it during a decade of revolution. As First Consul, then as Emperor, he pulled and sucked *la politique* into himself; he, and nothing or no one else, became party, parliament, and politician. The language that was Napoleon's principal means of doing so turned on two pregnant French terms—"nation" and "national," this latter often giving yeoman service as a noun, not just an adjective, as is the case in English. French "nation-talk," as

I call it,[7] carries many more connotations and ramifications than their, by comparison, innocuous English counterparts of the same spelling.

This is a book that takes ideas seriously, in the belief that to fail to do so would be to end up supporting ideas and theories that one knows nothing of, and might not have intended to support, if he had but thought about it. Specifically, in our case, ignoring Napoleonic ideas would run the risk of implicitly favoring "the doctrines which have been elaborated to the detriment of democratic ideas and pragmatic politics."[8]

Finally, it is a book wherein a single personality plays a decisive role on the world-historical stage, as none had so single-handedly done since Caesar or perhaps Charlemagne. A writer may have been educated in, and come to have absorbed, the belief that "forces" usually count for more than individuals in determining historical developments, yet still conclude that Napoleon I was "of another order" in his impact on society and posterity. Napoleon's contemporaries—including by no means just Frenchmen (for example, Hegel, Goethe, Beethoven, and Heine), and including adversaries, like Pozzo di Borgo or Chateaubriand—also believed this man was unique in his power to impose his will on society. Unique, too, in the multifacetedness of his talents and personality, not to mention in the near infinity of ways in which he was reacted to and interpreted by contemporaries and posterity. As a fine Oxford historian of the early twentieth century put it: in Napoleon's unfathomability "lies much of the charm of Napoleonic studies. He is at once the Achilles, the Mercury, and the Proteus of the modern world."[9]

Which is not to say Napoleon was not debtor to "great events," and in ways that even he was not completely aware of. I was going to subtitle this life "The Empire of Circumstance," so great was the power of the French Revolution in determining Napoleon's rise and his enduring attainments. As Abel Gance, the great filmmaker, once noted, "Napoleon was a being whose arms were not large enough to embrace a thing greater than he: the Revolution." The Revolution framed his consciousness and his conscience, leading him to regret many actions both at the time he performed them and for long after. The Revolution determined his ideas decisively, in no way more than in intention to suppress the effects of France's explosive "discovery of politics" of the late eighteenth century. Try as he would to "fix" (read: stifle) the Revolution in France, he remained its legatee more than he became its parricide at the beginning of his career, at the end, and during most crises, but *not* in the middle (1807–13).

Nothing brought this home to me more than a line—a confession, really—in the introduction to a work on Napoleon's maritime colonialism. The author, Yves Benot, is clearly a bona fide left-winger, an uncompromising critic of Napoleon's policies. Yet he feels compelled to share with his (mainly French) readers, "I would not hesitate to say that I can easily imagine myself yelling 'Long live the Emperor' on his return from Elba, or again on the steps of the Elysée Palace, on 21 June 1815, against the return of the Bourbons. And even, I can imagine crying 'Long live the Emperor' at the return of his body, 15 December 1840."[10]

For a number of years, in my thirties, at the advice of a friend who is one of our leading historical novelists, I had thought to treat Napoleon in a work of fiction. It would, he said, allow for treatment of motive and "soul" in ways that "straight" history cannot do. Emil Ludwig produced such a novelized work in 1925, as did Anthony Burgess in 1974, and they are wonderful reads. If I have not elected this path, it is not only because the challenge of fiction is terrifying; it is because, on reflection, I conclude that it is not possible to write *originally* (I do not say "brilliantly," as Ludwig and Burgess surely do) about Napoleon in, and to, our day, *unless* one takes into account the vast scholarship devoted to him and his empire. True, taking it into account might still lead one to essay a fictional treatment—the best recent novels about Napoleon (Simon Leys's *The Death of Napoleon,* Patrick Rambaud's *The Battle,* Odette Dossios-Pralat's *Napoléon Remembers*) take scholarship seriously; indeed, they dress themselves up as "histories"—but our age prefers its myths in scientific form. To quote Napoleon again: "We have finished the novel of the Revolution, it is time to begin on the history."

Yet a life of Napoleon Bonaparte is an unnerving undertaking, and if ever Borges's warning to the biographer—"Every man is two men, and the truest one is always the other"—were well-taken, now is the time. The mystery, at bottom, was known from the outset: in Stendhal's words, "How could a young man naturally possessed of such lively feelings for humanity, in the years to come, have acquired the soul of a conqueror?" In brief, how does Goethe's young Werther become Hegel's young "world soul—riding out of the city on reconnaissance"?[11] That progression or regression has been grappled with ever since. There is, of course no Answer, only answers, only selections and interpretations of well-known historical evidence. At the end of the day, there was something unique in Napoleon's, as in Caesar's, "ability to develop his personality and live life to the full in a world of his own making."[12] In both cases, the leader for a time controlled the narcissism that came with absolute power, but in the end it escaped him.

A recent French writer, Jean-Paul Kauffmann, who eschews special pleading, or even much sympathy for Napoleon on St. Helena, speaks for all of us who have ever put pen to paper in the hope of reducing Napoleon to explanation: "Those who write on [him] have at least one thing in common: at some time or other, they are all paralyzed by their subject—dumbfounded, terrified."[13] What I, and the boy in me, have hoped to do in this biography is to convey to the reader our "tremble" before Napoleon—in fear and dis-approval, but also in admiration and, at bottom, perhaps even in fear of our own longing for him. The longing comes in part from the multi-facetedness of this political Proteus, from the endless, intoxicating possibility in Napoleon, which is ever beckoning political man.

Notes

As space is at a premium in this book, I shall not cite the sources for most of the innumerable quotes from Napoleon that I use, nearly all of which are extremely familiar from the many biographies and histories of this period. For those quotations that are in any way unusual, I do provide a source. Most quotations come from either the semi-official, but woefully incomplete, thirty-two volume *Correspondance de Napoléon Ier publiée par ordre de l'Empereur Napoléon III* (1858–69)–the Fondation Napoléon is currently compiling a far more complete one–or from Emmanuel Las Cases's *Le Mémorial de Sainte-Hélène* (1823). This latter source, along with Henri-Gratien Bertrand's *Cahiers de Sainte-Hélène* (published in 1949–59), Gaspard Gourgaud's *Journal de Sainte-Hélène, 1815–1818* (1947 ed.), and Charles-Tristan de Montholon's *Récits de la captivité de l'Empereur Napoléon à Sainte-Hélène* (1847), amount to a kind of *Iliad* and *Odyssey* of latter-day dictation by Napoleon to his four "gospelers."

Chapter I: Napoleone di Buonaparte

1. The most recent biography is Antoine-Marie Graziani, *Pascal Paoli: Père de la patrie corse* (2002).
2. Dorothy Carrington, an English scholar who lived much of her life in Corsica, wrote: "If he was a despot, it was only in his personality and his hold on his people." *Napoleon and His Parents: On the Threshold of History* (1990), 7. This book is one of a handful of genuine contributions to Napoleon's biography made since well before World War I. See also Dorothy Carrington, *Portrait de Charles Bonaparte d'après ses écrits de jeunesse et ses mémoires* (2002). Finally, see T. E. Hall, "The Development of Enlightenment Interest in Eighteenth-Century Corsica," *Studies in Voltaire and the Eighteenth-Century,* 44 (1968), 165–85.
3. Cited in Carrington, *Napoleon and His Parents,* 7.
4. Graziani, *Pascal Paoli,* 23.
5. Emmanuel Las Cases, *Mémorial de Sainte-Hélène* (1803), August 16–21, 1815.
6. "Buonaparte" was a common enough appellation in northern Italy and Corsica. "Napoleone" was less so, but not unheard of. The surname probably dates from the thirteenth century, when it signified the "good party" in the great Guelph versus Ghibelline conflict that defined that era. "Buonaparte," in short, was a partisan name, a political act, on behalf of the secular party of the Holy Roman Emperor (the Ghibellines), which opposed the religious party of the popes (the Guelphs). See Thierry Lentz, *Idées reçues, Napoléon* (2001), 5.
7. Letizia had a daughter who died at birth, and her next pregnancy ended the same way. Joseph was the first child to live.
8. Ibid., 64–70, 96–97, 102–8, 125–27. Jean Defranceschi *La Jeunesse de Napoléon* (2001) (88–89) argues against the likelihood.
9. Carrington, *Napoleon and His Parents,* 36.
10. Frédéric Masson and Guido Biagi, *Napoléon inconnu: Papiers inédits* (1895), 1: 28.
11. Stendhal contrasts it with the dreariness and pettiness of conversation at analogous homes in France. *A Life of Napoleon* (1956), 8–9.

12. Carrington adds, in the kind of "throwaway" insight that makes hers a great book: Josephine was to possess all of the traits that Letizia deplored, making la Beauharnais his "masterstroke against the adored mother." *Napoleon and His Parents,* 91–92.

13. Orthographic aside: it was Carlo, not Napoleon, who "frankicized" the spelling of the family name, dropping the *u* at the time (1777) that he was granted French patents of nobility. Arthur Lévy, *Napoléon intime* (1893), 7.

Chapter II: The Making of the Patriot

1. M.C.H., *Some Account of the Early Years of the Military School of Brienne* (1797) and *Traits caractéristiques de la jeunesse de Bonaparte* (1803).

2. Cited in J. M. Thompson, ed., *Napoleon's Letters* (1934), 1–3.

3. It is curious how these letters play on different historians' stages. To me, they show intelligence and maturity—granted, the slightly faux maturity of a boy trying to be (because he believes he must be) a man, as well as selflessness and love of family. However, to so deft a reader as Dorothy Carrington, they reveal their author's "calculating objectivity" and "cold scrutiny." They are "pompous in style" and suffused by "a voice that assessed people and situations with an implacable assurance, dispassionate, penetrating and pragmatic." Carrington agrees the letters reveal "lucidity, authority, and [a] sense of responsibility," yet she also hears in them the "voice . . . of Napoleon, general, First Consul and Emperor, the voice that emanates from his innumerable letters, edicts and proclamations, and finally from his will at St. Helena" (*Napoleon and His Parents: On the Threshold of History* [1990], 169, 174). Carrington is right about a great deal, yet are we not better off trying to see Napoleon's letters as they lay in 1784, not viewed through the forty-plus volumes of his collected works? A human being is not an acorn; the mature man is not *completely* present in the seed.

4. It stands there today, largely empty and rather the worse for wear, yet still proudly looking down the Champ-de-Mars.

5. Christian Meier, *Caesar* (1982), 84.

6. Napoleon would one day commute the death sentence of a classmate at the ERM despite the fact that the man (Armand de Polignac, a scion of the highest aristocracy) had played an active role in a plot against the regime. Frédéric Masson and Guido Biagi, *Napoléon inconnu: Papiers inédits* (1895), 1: 95.

7. Carrington, *Napoleon and His Parents,* 190.

8. Arthur Lévy, *Napoléon intime* (1893), 16.

9. Masson and Biagi, *Napoléon inconnu,* 1: 78. In 1802, having fallen on hard times, the general wrote to Napoleon, requesting repayment. He was then, like thousands of other nobles, an émigré, living abroad, banned from France. The First Consul informed him not only that he was welcome to return to his native country but also that he would receive a salary and a pension totaling 24,000 francs annually.

10. See David A. Bell. *The Cult of the Nation in France* (2001) and Edmond Dziembowski, *Un nouveau patriotisme français, 1750–1770* (1998).

11. A late-nineteenth-century historian, Frédéric Masson, handed down a considered judgment that has much influenced subsequent writers on the question of Napoleon's feelings about France. The young man, Masson said, was in the same position as a young man from the Lorraine born the year after the German annexation of the province (1871) accepting a scholarship at a State military academy in Berlin (*Napoléon inconnu,* 1: 70). A nice simile, which undoubtedly came from the depths of Masson's *revanchard* heart, but it won't do. Lorraine had long been an integral part of metropolitan France when it was suddenly turned into an imperial Reichsland. An entirely Frenchified population was obliged, virtually overnight, to

begin the process of integral Germanification: linguistic, cultural, political. By contrast, the Corsica of 1768 remained what it had been in 1668 or 1558, or for that matter, in 1868 or 1968: Corsican. It simply changed overlord. A few decades later in the eighteenth century, it would become British, then go back to being French. All of these changes affected the island only slightly. This was one reason Carlo Buonaparte made the transition so soon after Paoli's flight, and why he did *not* hate the French—and he, after seeing the battle of Ponte Nuovo, had better reason to hate them than did his son.

12. See Benoît Defouconpret, *Les preuves de noblesse au XVIIIe siècle* (1999), which shows the identity crisis set off in the newer nobility by the continuous raising of the bar of pedigree for military promotion.

13. Harold T. Parker, "The Formation of Napoleon's Personality: An Exploratory Essay," *French Historical Studies* (1971–72), 21. See also Philip Dwyer, "From Corsican Nationalist to French Revolutionary: Problems of Identity in the Writings of the Young Napoleon, 1785–1793," *French History*, 16, 2 (2002), 132–52.

14. Not including his attempts at literary fiction, which we'll talk about in a later chapter.

15. "Réfutation de Roustan," in Masson and Biagi, *Napoléon inconnu*, 1: 155.

16. *Oeuvres littéraires et militaires*, (hereafter *OLEM*), 2: 102–3.

17. Masson and Biagi, *Napoléon inconnu*, 1: 53.

18. "Réfutation de Roustan," in ibid., 1: 155.

19. *OLEM*, 2: 87. The unrelieved pathos offers one bloody deed after another, often self-inflicted: for example, a fifteenth-century "patriot" believes his wife guilty of abetting the Genoese, although she appears to have acted in good faith. Telling her that "between crime and opprobrium, there is no middle ground but death," he strangles her before the children. The benumbed reader can only shake his head at the cruel tale of the "slavery" inflicted on a poor people (the Corsican population shrank from 400,000 to 120,000 over the last two centuries before Napoleon's time), their "lamentations" under their various yokes, and the futility of their martyrs' self-sacrifice.

20. Masson and Biagi, *Napoléon inconnu*, 1: 184.

21. "Ah!" Joseph would exclaim in his memoirs, "Napoleon the glorious emperor of the French would never give me anything dearer to me than that time I spent alone with him in 1786. Those days, over again, are what I hope to find in heaven one day." Joseph Bonaparte, *Mémoires et correspondance politique et militaire du roi Joseph* (1853–55), 1: 186.

22. Cited in Masson and Biagi, *Napoléon inconnu*, 1: 199.

CHAPTER III: THE UNMAKING OF THE PATRIOT

1. Stendhal, *A Life of Napoleon* (1956), 12–13.

2. Among traditional left-wing defenses of the Revolution, see Georges Lefebvre, *The French Revolution* and *Napoleon* (1969) or A. Soboul, *The French Revolution, 1787–1799* (1975). For a neoconservative, anti-revolutionary view, see François Furet and D. Richet, *La Révolution française* (1965) and Simon Schama, *Citizens* (1989). For up-to-date middle of the road, see D.M.G. Sutherland, *France, 1789–1815: Revolution and Counter-Revolution* (1985) and William Doyle, *The Oxford History of the French Revolution* (1989).

3. See Arno J. Mayer's remarkable comparison of the French and Russian Revolutions: *The Furies: Violence and Terror in the French and Russian Revolutions* (2000).

4. Cited in Mayer, *The Furies*, 4.

5. Michel Vovelle, *La découverte de la politique* (1993).

6. Cited in Mayer, *The Furies*, 84.

7. I would like to thank the Foundation Napoléon for showing me the autograph correspondence between Napoleon and Joseph, which will be published after 2005.

8. Letter of October 31, 1789, cited in Frédéric Masson and Guido Biagi, *Napoléon inconnu: Papiers inédits* (1895), 1: 92–93, 99–100.

9. Masson and Biagi, *Napoléon inconnu* 2: 123. This is shown even more clearly by Napoleon's adept application to his regiment requesting further leave time. He got the District of Ajaccio to give him a testimonial as one "animated by the purest patriotism," while noting, ominously, "he is not afraid of being exposed to any sacrifices caused him by the resentment of the vile lovers and partisans of the aristocracy." Such a statement, dispatched to the aristocratic leadership of the La Fère regiment, had one purpose: to intimidate them into doing what was asked. They did.

10. See *Général de Caulaincourt, duc de Vicence, avec l'Empereur, de Moscou à Fontainebleau*, ed. by C. Melchior-Bonnet (1968), 288–89.

11. Cited in Charles Napoleon, *Bonaparte et Paoli: Aux origines de la question corse* (2001), 184.

12. Cited in Masson and Biagi, *Napoléon inconnu* 2: 128.

13. *OLEM*, 2: 250–52, 255. He became expert at a style of argument that was the hallmark of French patriots throughout the entire Revolution (and indeed the nineteenth century), and which might be summed up as bringing the whole to bear on any single part. An example is worth examination. In Easter 1792, Napoleon was a leader of a National Guard action in Ajaccio that resulted from a popular disruption against the local oath-taking clergy. Clarity about the episode is lacking, but it appears the guard acted in an aggressively partisan and illegal way. Things ended up with one of their officers dead and half the town in an uproar. Paoli blamed Napoleon, who appealed to the Legislative Assembly in Paris. His long justification contains assertions along these lines: a group of "loyal patriots" (read: Napoleon and his battalion) was set upon in a surprise attack by "brigands, conspirators, and agitators" (read: much of the population of Ajaccio). "The entire nation [read: the Revolution in France] was outraged" by this event. Acknowledging that some of the guard's actions were of dubious legality, Napoleon argued that "the first law [of politics] is the salvation of the *patrie*," and he added that the guard would answer the charge of illegality with "I swear I have saved the Republic!" The statement, from start to last, is an ideologically framed appeal for a political intervention to fix a local matter that could and should have been handled by appropriate local authorities.

14. *Mauvaises pensées et autres*, cited by Simon Leys, *The Death of Napoleon* (1998), 1. The Italian writer Leonardo Sciascia wrote an imaginary piece some years ago entitled "Napoleone scrittore" in which he fancies the Frenchman in an alternate career as writer, only to conclude that, no, Napoleon *had* to have lived the life he did, lest men like Balzac, Stendhal, and Hugo not have become writers, for want of stimulus. Academics have turned out learned studies on Napoleon as writer, some of them quite round the bend. A French scholar, for example, believes the young Napoleon's "aspiration for grandeur and moral beauty took him beyond Rousseau" (Natalie Tomiche, *Napoléon écrivain* [1952], 102). The best and most recent is a highly personal but brilliantly written study by a Cambridge literature professor, Andy Martin: *Napoleon the Novelist* (2001).

15. *OLEM*, 1: 45, 61; 2: 125.

16. Andy Martin remarks, aptly, that "The Discourse on Happiness" is better named "Discourse on Unhappiness." *Napoleon the Novelist*, 24.

17. *Clisson et Eugénie*.

18. *OLEM*, 1: 19.

19. Natalie Tomiche, *Napoléon écrivain*, 125.

20. Admittedly, one would have had to be a cloistered monk (of which none were left

in France) to remain detached witnessing the frenetic kaleidoscope of summer and fall 1792. Even as acute an observer as Napoleon admitted to Joseph, "it is hard to keep track" of the parties, persons, and programs in contest with one another." He added, "I don't know how it is going to turn out, but it is certainly taking a revolutionary turn." Letter of June 14, cited in Masson and Biagi, *Napoléon inconnu*, 2: 389.
21. Cited in ibid., 2: 396–97.
22. In early 1792, when the War of the First Coalition was going badly for the Revolution, Napoleon had speculated that France might be forced to evacuate Corsica, so that Paoli could take over the island. Would he have appointed Napoleon, his general in chief, given his feelings about the Bonapartes? Even if he had, could either of them have refrained from getting entrapped in the French Revolution? No other politician did. Would things then have turned out differently between them or for Corsica? Looking back, it is remarkable that as sharp an observer of society as Napoleon overlooked the divergence between Paris and Corsica over religion. However Gallican his own view of State control over the Church, as a Corsican, Napoleon must have been aware of how unfeasible the policy of radical anticlericalism would be on this essentially Italian island, yet he chose to ignore it. Paoli understood it, and did not.
23. As seems to have been the case. *Correspondance*, 2: #1111.
24. A consequence of the English occupation of Corsica is that a British officer, born the same year as Napoleon, was quartered in the Casa Bonaparte. His name was Hudson Lowe, and he would have a much later appointment with Napoleon on St. Helena. William Smith, *European Dynasties: The Bonapartes* (2004), 12. Masson and Biagi, *Napoléon inconnu*, 2: 467.
25. Masson and Biagi, *Napoléon inconnu*, 2: 467.
26. Andy Martin surmises that Napoleon only became French because he was forced to be, much as the orphan Jean Genet "chose" the life of a thief, because that was what he was accused of being. If Napoleon was French, he writes, "it was (as the existentialists would say) in the mode of not-being" (*Napoleon the Novelist*, 58–59). Chateaubriand recalls that Napoleon continued to sign his name "Buonaparte" until he was thirty-three—that is, until 1802 (*Mémoires d'outre tombe*, 674).
27. See A. N. Wilson, *C. S. Lewis* (1991), 219.
28. Lord Rosebery; cited in John H. Grainger, *Patriotisms: Britain, 1800–1939* (1986), 141.
29. Cited in Tomiche, *Napoléon écrivain*, 138.
30. Bertrand, *Cahiers de Sainte-Hélène*, 2, January 1819.
31. Christian Meier, *Caesar* (1982), 95, 97, 100, 201.

CHAPTER IV: ROBESPIERRE ON HORSEBACK

1. *The Oxford History of the French Revolution* (1989), 133.
2. Cited in Antoine Casanova, *Napoléon et la pensée de son temps* (2000), 139. Casanova's study of Napoleon's thoughts about Robespierre is pathbreaking.
3. Cited in J. M. Thompson, *Napoleon Bonaparte* (1988 ed.), 37.
4. Emmanuel Las Cases, *Le Mémorial de Sainte-Hélène* (1803), June 12, 1816.
5. The French Revolutionary calendar had twelve months, arranged in three decades of ten days, with one day of rest per decade. The months' names are seasonally derived (Thermidor is thus a summer month).
6. Isser Woloch, *The New Regime* (1994), 431–32.
7. Cited in Martin Boycott-Brown, *The Road to Rivoli: Napoleon's First Campaign* (2001), 94.

8. "... much of the revolutionary violence and terror, by virtue of being fear-inspired, vengeance-driven, and "religiously" sanctioned, was singularly fierce and merciless." Arno J. Mayer, *The Furies: Violence and Terror in the French and Russian Revolutions* (2000), 535, xvi.

9. Paul W. Schroeder, *The Transformation of European Politics, 1763–1848* (1994), 157. See also Theda Skorpol and Meyer Kestenbaum, "Mars Unshackled: The French Revolution in World-Historical Perspective," in F. Fehér, *The French Revolution and the Birth of Modernity* (1988), 13–29.

10. J. Black, *From Louis XIV to Napoleon: The Fate of a Great Power* (1999), 168.

11. The "Note" tries to convince Paris that further advances in Spain will be a costly mistake, for they risk precipitating a popular uprising that will prove infinitely harder to defeat than the tired old Spanish army has been. Here was foresight that would later be held against Emperor Napoleon.

12. Napoleon's plans were in fact responsible for a few impressive local victories on the Riviera-Ligurian front (e.g., the taking of Oneglia). In the context of the meager achievements of 1793, these quickstep advances into enemy territory were remarkable, and contemporaries understood Napoleon's strategic planning had been critical. His commander praised "the talents of the General of Artillery to whom I owe the clever arrangements that have procured our success." The most impressive testimonial was that from the Austrian diplomat, cited in the epigraph.

13. "I don't see that there is any less glory to be had here than in fighting against the Austrians," Hoche told the minister, insisting that the latter remind all soldiers that "the *patrie* is as much there [in the west] as it is elsewhere." Letter of 13 pluviôse, l'an III (February 1, 1795), in E. Charavay, *Lazare Hoche* (1893), 10.

14. Comte de Pontécoulant, *Souvenirs*, 1: 365.

15. John Holland Rose, *The Life of Napoleon I* (1901), 69.

16. "Vendémiaire," a fall month in the Revolutionary calendar, is named for "vendage," or the grape harvest.

17. Cited in Rose, *The Life of Napoleon*, 71.

CHAPTER V: LOVE AND WAR

1. William Bolitho, *Twelve Against the Gods* (1929), 128.

2. "Impressions de voyage," February 8, 1791; *OLEM*, 125–26.

3. "J'étais bien loin de devenir scrupuleux; je l'avais agacée pour qu'elle ne se sauvât point quand elle serait pressée par le raisonnement que je lui préparais en contre-faisant une honnêté que je voulais lui prouver ne pas avoir." *OLEM*, 1: 63. This makes one recall Talleyrand's quotation from the previous chapter about Napoleon's faking true feelings. My thanks to Janet Thorpe for her help with the English translation.

4. I am grateful to the Foundation Napoléon in Paris for making available to me new pages of the novel that have recently been unearthed.

5. I have seen a multitude of assertions as to Napoleon's exact height, running from five two to five four.

6. All quotations from Josephine and Napoleon come from Jean Savary, *Napoleon et Joséphine* (1900).

7. Evangeline Bruce, *Napoleon and Josephine* (1995), 157.

8. Cited in André Castelot, *Napoléon et les femmes*, 121. See also Bernard Chevallier and Christophe Pincemaille, *L'Impératrice Joséphine* (1996 edition).

9. Although, in point of fact, even Cortés's story is nothing like the tried and convicted case of a gold-seeking and bloodthirsty conqueror brutalizing Mexico. See, for example, Christian Duverger's remarkable and revisionist *Cortés* (2001).

10. See the essay in Paul Viallaneix, ed., *La Bataille, l'armée, la gloire 1745–1871,* 2 vols. (1985), which examines the birth of antiwar sentiment in this era, as well (e.g., vol. 1: 93–101). For a comparison with Prussia, see Karen Hagemann, *"Mannlicher Muth und Teutscher Ehre," Nation, Militär und Geschlecht zur Zeit der Antinapoleonischern Kriege Preussens* (2002).

11. Clausewitz, *On War* (1976 ed.), 121. This Prussian officer (1780–1831) was the era's—perhaps posterity's—greatest philosopher of war.

12. In fact, the reception in Milan was tepid. See Alain Pillepich, *Milan, Capitale napoléonienne* (2000).

13. C. A. Costa de Beauregard, *Un homme d'autrefois* (1879), 332.

CHAPTER VI: APPRENTICESHIP IN STATECRAFT: ITALY AND EGYPT

1. In March, Napoleon has ceased signing himself "Napoleone Buonaparte" in favor of the French version of his name. Murder and vandalism as part of conquest were not peculiar to Napoleonic armies. For these phenomena in the armies of Generals Washington and Greene, and the British Hessian regulars, see Allan Kulikoff, "Revolutionary Violence amid the Origins of American Democracy," *The Journal of the Historical Society* II, 2 (Spring 2002), 229–60.

2. For the state of the question: Did Bonaparte sacrifice the Rhine for Italy in 1796–97, see the article of the same title by Roger Dufraisse in *Revue du Souvenir Napoléonien,* 416 (1997), 5–20.

3. The simile is Albert Sorel's in *Bonaparte et Hoche en 1797* (1896).

4. Naples's fate, as the historian Michel Vovelle notes with characteristic finesse, was what might have happened to France in mid-1792 if the Austrian army had won at Valmy and occupied the Republic. *Les Républiques-soeurs sous le regard de la Grande Nation, 1795–1803* (2000), 189–224.

5. See the fine work on this by Edouard Pommier, *L'Art de la liberté: Doctrines et débats de la Révolution Français* (1991).

6. And indeed, what arose in opposition to French so-called universalism was a cultural policy that viewed art as a nation's patrimony, to be conserved in museums for all to see.

7. In fact a history-honored French misspelling of Campo-Formido. My thanks to Thierry Lentz for pointing this out.

8. The most recent (and very anti-Napoleon) study is Amable de Fournoux, *Napoléon et Venise, 1796–1814* (2002).

9. Michel Vovelle, *Les Républiques-soeurs,* 184. Many French politicians and historians have yelped—somewhat sanctimoniously—at the "delivery" of Venice to Austria, wringing their hands over the "scandal" of the Republic's becoming a "merchant of peoples." Sieyès criticized the treaty for being "not a peace but an appeal to a new war," while Adolphe Thiers sighs about how much grander it would have been had the doge's domain been folded into the Cisalpine Republic, rather than be exchanged for the his recognition. Stendhal, an admirer of Napoleon's, saw this treaty article as a betrayal: "With the occupation of Venice, the poetic and perfectly noble part of Napoleon's life finishes."

10. Vittorio Criscuolo, *Il giacobino Pietro Custodi* (1987), 494–95.

11. Alphonse Aulard, "Bonaparte républicain," *Etudes et Leçons sur la Révolution française* (1893-1908), 89.

12. "Vive la République de Bonne Foi!" folded properly, thus became "Vive le Roi!"

13. Political friction between Bernadotte's and Masséna's divisions was so great that small pitched battles were fought between them, with dozens of men killed or wounded on both sides!

14. Cited in Sorel, *Bonaparte et Hoche*, 319.

15. It is still not clear exactly how Hoche died; some have held for poisoning by his enemies or suicide in his own despair and frustration.

16. Ferdinand Boyer, *Le Monde des arts en Italie et la France de la Révolution et de l'Empire* (1969).

17. *Mémoires de Bourrienne sur Napoleon (1899–1905)*, 2: 32. The classic study of this short period in Napoleon's life is Albert Espitalier, *Vers Brumaire: Bonaparte à Paris, 5 décembre 1797 à 4 mai 1798* (1914).

18. Sieyès answered the title question by saying that the Third Estate (the non-noble, non-clerical classes) was "the nation," and as for the nobility, it was "a false people that has no useful organs and cannot take root on its own. It necessarily attaches itself to the real nation, like these vegetable tumors that can only live by ingesting the sap of healthy plants, which it soon tires and dries up."

19. It was also said of Sieyès, "if there were a curtain in the room, he would be the one behind it." Albert Vandal, *L'Avènement de Bonaparte* (1903), 78.

20. The most interesting take on Talleyrand in recent years are the pages devoted to him in Robert Calasso's *The Ruin of Kasch* (1995). See also Philip Dwyer, *Talleyrand* (2000).

21. The name, since early in the Revolution, of the French Academy, which brought together leading writers, scientists, scholars—and politicians who could be considered serious men of letters or science. Bonaparte was one of the very youngest members.

22. For the current scholarly state of the question, see Thierry Lentz, "Pourquoi l'Egypte?" *Revue du Souvenir Napoléonien*, 418 (1999).

23. *Lettres intimes du général Morand* (1930), 291.

24. Fontanes, a future minister, put it: "Your conduct hardly conforms to a severe morality, but heroism has its license, and Voltaire would be the first to tell you that you fill the boots of illustrious brigands like Alexander and Charlemagne. . . . The theatre of Italy is already too small for the grandeur of your views."

25. See Henry Laurens, *Les Origines intellectuelles de l'expedition d'Egypte: l'orientalisme islamisant en France (1698–1798)* (1997).

26. And this was to say a lot, considering that the troops were aware of Napoleon's affair with Pauline Fourès, the beautiful blond wife of an officer serving in the Army of the Orient. She was called "Bonaparte's Cleopatra."

27. The colleague whom Rigo told this to was Benjamin Robert Haydon, whose *Autobiography* recounts it. Cited in J. M. Thompson, *Napoleon Bonaparte* (1988 ed.), 131.

28. One of Bonaparte's top generals, Jacques Menou, took a Moslem bride and converted to Islam, becoming known as Abdallah Menou, and though the army ridiculed him behind his back, they used the cachet his act provided with the locals. On St. Helena, Napoleon would go so far as to say that he had seriously negotiated to have himself and his army *follow Menou's example,* though the delicate matters of circumcision and alcohol prohibition were problematic. Contemporary Arab and French records do not speak of any project of mass conversion, but it could well be the case that Bonaparte had conceived such an idea while he was in Egypt, or even before.

29. F. Charles-Roux, *Bonaparte gouverneur d'Egypte* (1936), 210. The author shows how much power Bonaparte gave back to local Egyptian authorities.

30. Henry Laurens, introduction to Bonaparte's *Campagnes d'Egypte et de Syrie* (1998 ed.), 18.

31. En route home, he told one of the savants, "Suppose I reach France in one piece and . . . I beat the foreign enemies. I will receive only thanks and benedictions from our countrymen. But if the English take me prisoner [on the open sea] . . . I will be seen in France as a vulgar deserter, a general who abandoned his army without author-

izatilization." Cited in Yves Laissus, *L'Egypte: Une aventure savante, 1798–1801* (Paris, 1998), 275.

32. An admired Egyptian scholar of French history has this eloquent judgment of the famous *Description of Egypt*—the vast, twenty-four-volume work published by the French savants after their return, which is considered to be the foundation of modern Egyptology: "Sacred it is," writes Laïla Enan, "if only in the price it cost." Laïla Enan, in *L'Expédition de Bonaparte vue d'Egypte* (2001), 20.

33. François Furet and Denis Richet, *La Révolution française* (1973), 241–42.

34. The mathematician Monge, the leader of the savants on the expedition, wrote to his wife: "When this country has been built, planted, and tapped for fifty years by the French, it will be a terrestrial paradise."

35. Mustapha Al-Ahnaf, "Cheikh Al-Mahdi (1737–1815)," in *L'Expédition de Bonaparte vue d'Egypte,* 134.

CHAPTER VII: POWER (I): TAKING IT (BRUMAIRE)

1. Sheldon Wolin, "Fugitive Democracy," in *Democracy and Difference: Contesting the Boundaries of the Political,* ed. Seyla Benhabib (1996), 31.

2. Pierre Rosanvallon, *Pour une histoire conceptuelle du politique* (2003), 14–20, which is Rosanvallon's inaugural lecture as Professor of the Modern and Contemporary History of the Political at the Collège de France.

3. Carl Schmitt, *The Concept of the Political,* trans. George Schwab (1976; originally pubished 1927). Schmitt went on to become a legal-political counselor to the Third Reich, but he did not please the SS, and in 1936 he was forced to retire from his active political role in German legal-academic life. For a view that falls between the French liberal and German conservative vision of "the political," see Julien Freund (1921–93) *Qu'est-ce que la politique?* (1967).

4. "The impossibility of dissociating *le* and *la politique* has given rise to a certain disappointment in modern regimes. It is never a simple matter to separate the noble from the vulgar; petty, selfish calculations from great ambition; true and trenchant language from the tricks of seduction and manipulation." Rosanvallon, *Pour une histoire,* 42.

5. According to Baron Agathon-Jean Fain, Napoleon's secretary (1806–15), as early as 1795, Bonaparte had doubts about the First Republic as it existed, for he felt, as did many, that its reputation had been dealt a mortal blow by the Terror. Thereafter "only dupes and doctrinaires" continued to believe in that government, and Napoleon did not consider himself to be either. This said, Fain added, the General certainly did not renounce *the idea of the Republic. Mémoires du Baron Fain* (1908), 310–11.

6. A caveat: Napoleon, as he grew older, took great delight in recounting his supposedly frequent use of political trickery. But it would be a mistake to take his late-in-the-day statements, meant to impress us with the speaker's worldly and cynical wisdom and his transcendence of worldly concerns, as necessarily reflective of a true revulsion with politics on the part of the young Napoleon, or as proving a complete absence of genuine political sincerity in him. Bonaparte in fact valued "politics" and delighted in it, as far as it went.

7. *César aux quatre paroles* (perhaps "forethought" would be a better translation). Cited in Yves Laissus, *L'Egypte: Une aventure savante, 1798–1801* (1998), 275.

8. A geologist (Dolomieu) on the Egyptian expedition noted, "I never saw someone so much master of himself. I don't believe anyone could guess what he was thinking if he didn't want them to." Cited in Laissus, p. 50.

9. Dorothy Carrington writes, "Napoleon simply grew out of certain Corsican values as of constricting clothes." *Napoleon and His Parents* (1990), 89.

10. Carl Schmitt compared a sovereign ruler's determining an "exception" and making a "decision" to Jesus' infrequent use of miracles—i.e., they were meant to confirm the Gospel. *Political Theology* (1929), 12.

11. J. Christopher Herold, *The Mind of Napoleon* (1955), xxxix.

12. Albert Sorel, *Bonaparte et Hoche en 1797* (1896), 134.

13. Letter of April 12 1797.

14. The frigate was named for an aide-de-camp of Bonaparte's killed in Italy.

15. In fact, five, if you consider that most of its leading politicians had emerged at Thermidor (July 1794).

16. To propose, as some have, that all that was needed was for the Directory to show less paranoia and more goodwill is a feckless suggestion. To have invited the royalist-moderate majority to participate in government would likely have been to sign one's own death warrant, figuratively and perhaps literally. Few, in any age, are the actors on the public stage who will take such risks *pro bono publico*. Historians disagree strenuously over the long-range promise or potential of the Directory, but it is hard to disagree that the regime strangled progress toward a party system. A nineteenth-century writer, mainly (it is true) sympathetic to Bonaparte, noted that one may reproach the General for not founding liberty, but one cannot blame him for overthrowing it in the first place. Albert Vandal, *L'Avènement de Bonaparte* (1903), 23.

17. The men of Thermidor, it has been said, were republican moderates but *not* moderately republican.

18. Christian Meier, *Caesar* (1982), 132.

19. Over the Turks.: July 27. So slowly did news travel then. This Aboukir should not be confused with the naval battle of the Nile at Aboukir the previous year which the French had lost.

20. See Nicole Gotteri, "L'esprit public à Paris avant le coup d'Etat," in Jacques-Olivier Boudon, ed., *Brumaire: La prise de pouvoir du Bonaparte* (2001), 23.

21. Ibid., 3. Albert Sorel is right that "the Directory began to fear everything in this young man whom until then it had been obliged to hope everything," but the words speak more aptly to the directors' guilt over what had become of the Republic in Bonaparte's absence than to actual designs on his part.

22. This movement received its first real portrait from an American historian at Columbia University, Isser Woloch, *Jacobin Legacy: The Democratic Movement under the Directory* (1970). More recently, see Bernard Gainot, *1799, un nouveau jacobinisme? La démocratie représentative, une alternative à brumaire* (2001).

23. The term "conservative" had not yet accumulated its strongly right-wing or reactionary overtones. It was understood to mean "conserving of [i.e., the best aspects of the Revolution]."

24. I use the term broadly, for Fouché was a postulant with the Oratorians and left before taking his final vows.

25. Michel Vovelle, Introduction to Fouché's *Mémoires* (1992), 38.

26. Cited in Alphonse Aulard, *Histoire politique de la Révolution française* (1901), 759. Pitt the Younger became prime minister at twenty-four (!) in 1783.

27. Isser Woloch, *Napoleon and His Collaborators* (2001), 16. For another view, see Jacques-Olivier Boudon, *Histoire du Consulat et de l'Empire* (2000), 35–37, and Thierry Lentz, *Le 18-Brumaire* (1997), 233–41.

28. The comparison is John Holland Rose's, *The Life of Napoleon* (1901), 1: 221.

29. Alphonse Aulard, "Bonaparte républicain," *Etudes et Leçons sur la Révolution française* (1893-1908), 91.

30. Nom de plume of Kurt-Erich Suckert, *Technique du coup d'Etat* (1931), 121–22.

31. Historians disagree about how likely a neo-Jacobin "action" was. Liberal scholars find the "allegation entirely mendacious but not absurd" (Woloch, *Jacobin Legacy*,

17); moderates think the "dangers were nevertheless real" (Lentz, *Le 18-Brumaire,* 265). Jean Tulard, for his part, believes that Bonaparte's coup "saved the Republic. Without Bonaparte, the Jacobins would have seized power, and by a return of the Terror they would have brought not only French opinion but an allied and determined Europe down on their heads." In Jacques-Olivier Boudon, *Brumaire,* 175. See also Malcolm Crook, *Napoleon Comes to Power: Democracy and Dictatorship in Revolutionary France, 1795–1804* (1998).

32. *Mémoires sur la Révolution, le Consulat et l'Empire* (ed. by Aubry), 105.
33. The chateau did not survive the War of 1870–71 and the Commune.
34. In *The Eighteenth Brumaire of Louis-Napoleon Bonaparte* (1852), Marx called the coup of 1799 a "tragedy," whereas history repeated itself in 1851 as "farce." In fact, it was Louis-Napoleon's coup (December 2, 1851) that spilt much blood, and would be better billed as a tragedy.
35. Lentz, *Le 18-Brumaire,* 442 passim.

CHAPTER VIII: POWER (II): USING IT (THE CONSULATE)

1. Nom de plume of Hector Hugh Munro (1870–1916), British writer and humorist, killed in France in World War I.
2. Pierre-Louis Roederer, *Oeuvres du Comte Roederer (1853–59),* 3: 428.
3. Ibid., 3: 353.
4. (1747–1816). Ducos, a jurist, served in the Convention, voted the death of the king, and functioned as a representative-on-mission.
5. Christine Reinhard, *Une femme de diplomate. Lettres de Mme Reinhard à sa mère 1798–1815* (1900). The First Consul also disclaimed having his profile on coins at this time.
6. Jean-Paul Bertaud, "Le 18-Brumaire," in *La Revue du Souvenir Napoléonien,* 414 (September–October 1997), 28.
7. Sieyès had lived through much, and he strove *both* to be true to his old wishes to limit the power of government and his new idea to insulate government from the murderous buffetings from below that had rendered authority and consistency impossible. Too, he faced the psychological problem of the writer whose first book is a huge success that promises a sensational career, and everyone awaits his second with bated breath. The best recent biography is Jean-Denis Bredin, *Sieyès, la Clé de la Révolution française* (1988).
8. Alphonse Aulard, *Paris sous le Consulat* (1903-1904), 1: 55. The anecdote was intended to reflect badly on the General and was originally reported in the royalist-leaning *Gazette de France.*
9. The abstention rate was so high that in Marseille, a city of 100,000, only 1,200 voted. Claude Langlois, "Le Plébiscite de l'an VIII ou le coup d'Etat du 18 Pluviôse an VIII," *Annales historiques de la Révolution française* (1972), 43–65, 231–46, 396–415; "Napoléon Bonaparte plébiscité?" in *L'Election du chef d'Etat en France* (1988), 81–93.
10. And in fact, Bernard Gainot provides evidence that Lucien's falsification was not as universal as once believed. See "Réflexions sur le plébiscite de l'an VIII à partir de l'exemple de la Saône-et-Loire," in *Mélanges Jean Bart,* ed. J.-J. Clère (Dijon, 2001). See also Jeff Horn, "The Bonapartist State in the Aube," *French Historical Studies* 25, 2: 238–40.
11. Pierre-Louis Roederer, *Oeuvres du Comte Roederer,* 3: 336.
12. Jack Censer, *The French Press in the Age of the Enlightenment* (1994); Jack Censer and Jeremy D. Popkin, eds., *Press and Politics in Pre-Revolutionary France* (1987); André Cabanis, *La presse sous le Consulat et l'Empire, 1799–1814* (1975); Joseph Klaits, *Printed Propaganda under Louis XIV: Absolute Monarchy and Public Opinion* (1976).

13. "From Organic Society to Security State," *Journal of Modern History* 69: 685.
14. Paul Schroeder, *The Transformation of European Politics, 1763–1848* (1994), 191.
15. Cited in Albert Vandal, *L'Avènement de Bonaparte* (1903), 237.
16. Bonaparte commissioned a march from Rouget de L'Isle, the composer of "La Marseillaise." The new song contained the line "from victory will we obtain peace."
17. Cited in David Chandler, *The Campaigns of Napoleon: The Mind and Methods of History's Greatest Soldier* (1966), 296.
18. I am grateful to the French expert on northern Italy in this period, Alain Pillepich, for this insight.
19. See Roderick McGrew, *Paul I of Russia* (1992), 260–80.
20. Cited in Edouard Driault, *La politique extérieure du Premier Consul* (1910), 201.
21. Jean-Antoine Chaptal, *Mes souvenirs sur Napoléon* (1893), 100.
22. See Pierre Rosanvallon, *L'Etat en France: 1789 à nos jours* (1990), 95–110 passim.
23. Marceau Long, *Portalis: L'esprit de justice* (1997), 48.
24. Portalis. Cited in ibid., 45.
25. George Santayana, "Reason in Common Sense," in *The Life of Reason* (1905), 1: 33.
26. Most interestingly of all, perhaps, "By becoming Catholic, I ended the war in the Vendée. By becoming Moslem, I established myself in Egypt. By becoming an ultramontane, I won over the Italians. If I was governing a people of Jews, I would rebuild the temple of Solomon." Roederer, *Oeuvres*, 3: 223.
27. Alfred Boulay de la Meurthe, *Histoire de la négociation du Concordat de 1801* (1920), 17. For the Roman Catholic revival, see Olwen Hufton, "The Reconstruction of a Church, 1796–1801," in Gwynne Lewis and Colin Lucas, eds., *Beyond the Terror* (1983), 26.
28. Cited in Henry Walsh, *The Concordat of 1801* (1933), 37.
29. Napoleon's words. Cited in Louis de Villefosse and Janine Bouissounouse, *L'Opposition à Napoléon* (1969), 174.
30. To Bonaparte's protest that the return of the Church was what the French wanted, the savant replied, "And if France asked you to bring the Bourbons back, would you do that, too?" Cited in Lentz, *Le Grand Consulat*, 317.
31. Evidence in the British archives shows Fouché was in touch with the conspirators against Bonaparte. A high-level French police operative, Dossonville (himself playing both sides), wrote the First Consul to accuse Fouché. Soon after came Fouché's dismissal. Elizabeth Sparrow, *Secret Service: British Agents in France, 1792–1815* (1999), 261.
32. Cited in Jean Laspougeas, in Jean Tulard, *Dictionnaire Napoléon* (1987), 456.
33. Cited in Alyssa Sepinwall, "Regenerating France, Regenerating the World: The Abbé Grégoire and the French Revolution" (Ph.D. dissertation, Stanford University, 1998), 257.
34. Consalvi had constantly to operate under a Damoclean sword of threats to break off proceedings, of tactical news leaks, of chicanery. (Bernier at one point tried to fob off on him the wrong draft for signature.) There was also much Consular rudeness and bullying. "I don't need the pope," Bonaparte would say. "If Henry VIII, who did not have a twentieth part of my power, could change the religion of his country, the more can I. And keep in mind, in changing it in France, I'll change it throughout all of Europe."
35. Hercule Consalvi, *Mémoires du Cardinal Consalvi* (1864–66), 1: 343.
36. Jean Godel, "L'église selon Napoléon," *Revue d'histoire moderne et contemporaine* 17 (1970): 841.
37. Martyn Lyons, *Napoleon Bonaparte and the Legacy of the French Revolution* (1994), 93.
38. Cited in Pieter Geyl, *Napoleon, For and Against* (1949), 35.
39. Edgar Quinet, *La Révolution* (1865), 2: 525. Quinet, a violent critic, argues that

Bonaparte would have been truer to the Revolution if he had driven home the Directory's policy of separation of Church and State.

40. Cited in Long, *Portalis*, 66.

41. The phrase is Paul Ricoeur's, cited in ibid., 80.

42. "Quels principes pour l'économie politique?" *Economies et Sociétés*, 22–23, (Jan 2, 1995): 211.

43. See Ha-Joon Chang, *Kicking Away the Ladder: Development Strategy in Historical Perspective* (2002); Georges Lacour-Gayet, "Les idées financières de Napoléon," *Revue de Paris*, June 1, 1938, 562–93; Emile James, "Napoléon et la pensée économique de son temps," *Revue de l'Institut Napoléon*, 1966, 113–23; Francis Démier, *Nation, marché et développement dans la France de la Restauration* (1991), 155–65; Jean-Pierre Hirsch, *Les deux rêves du commerce* (1991); F. Fourquet, *Richesse et puissance* (1988).

44. The franc—the word itself refers to the freedom of the ancient Franks—was a metrically defined monetary unit that had been created by the Convention in 1795 to replace the livre and the louis (the latter a discount currency) of the old regime. Interestingly, when convertibility of the franc was finally rescinded during World War I, inflation and monetary disaster followed.

45. See Louis Bergeron, *Banquiers, négociants et manufacturiers parisiens du Directoire à l'Empire* (1978).

46. C. H. Church, *Revolution and Red Tape: The French Ministerial Bureaucracy, 1770–1850* (1981).

47. Jeff Horn, "Building the New Regime," *French Historial Studies* 25, 2: 248. See also Jacques-Olivier Boudon, *Histoire du Consulat et de l'Empire* (2000), 77.

48. That is, indeed, still the case. A leading French scholar unintentionally bears this out when he writes that the code's "originality lies in that it has no originality." G. Pariset, *Le Consulat et l'Empire* (1911), 166.

49. The slight refocus on custom was a Bonaparte-inspired "homeopathic synthesis, one of the First Consul's secrets for moderating the French Revolution with a pinch of *ancien régime*." François Furet, *Revolutionary France, 1770–1880* (1995), 232.

50. See Jean Carbonnier, "Le Code Civil," in Pierre Nora, ed., *Les Lieux de mémoire la Nation*, 2 (1986), 297.

51. But the first woman (Rosa Bonheur, the painter) was not awarded the Legion until 1865, when the Empress Eugénie, wife of Napoleon III (Napoleon Bonaparte's nephew), accorded it to her.

52. A French historian, Louis Bergeron, writes: "It might more accurately be called vanity." *France Under Napoleon* (1981), 62.

53. It became Haiti in 1804, on winning its independence. The Consulate regarded it as the "maintenance" of slavery, since its formal abolition had not actually been fully realized. It would be as if President Thomas Jefferson had gotten an abolition bill through Congress, but then his successor (Madison or Monroe) couldn't make good on it, and so reluctantly permitted its rescinding.

54. A letter (July 10, 1801) from a British spy reported to his operatives: "Egypt . . . is the only object which interests his [Bonaparte's] personal ambition and excites his revenge." Cited in John Holland Rose, *The Life of Napoleon* (1901), 1: 356.

55. Ibid., 1: 379. Rose notes: "The full text of the plan has never been published: probably it was suppressed or destroyed; and the sole public record relating to it is contained in the official account of the expedition published at the French Imperial Press in 1807."

56. See Sylvain Pagé, the Abbé Garnier, *Bonaparte et la Louisiane* (1992); Pierre Salinger, *La France et le Nouveau-Monde* (1976).

57. Raphael Lahlou, "Le rêve américain et caraïbe de Bonaparte," *Revue du Souvenir Napoléonien*, 440: 9.

58. Georges Lefebvre, *The French Revolution and Napoleon* (1969), 150.
59. Ibid., 42.
60. *La Décade Philosophique,* April 30, 1801.
61. Isser Woloch, *The New Regime* (1994), 91.
62. H. A. L. Fisher. *Bonapartism* (1908), 77.
63. Cited in Claire-Elisabeth de Rémusat, *Mémoires, 1802–1808* (1879–80), 1: 335–36, 325. Emphasis added.
64. Cited in Frédéric Bluche, *Le bonapartisme* (1980), 70.
65. Fisher, *Bonapartism,* 26.
66. See ibid., 25–26.
67. Cited in Bluche, *Le bonapartisme,* 110.
68. Thiers, *Histoire du Consulat et de l'Empire,* 2: 357.
69. Bluche, *Le bonapartisme,* 12, 21.
70. And when "France" arises, it is because he needs a synonym to avoid repeating himself—e.g., his letter to the Directory (April 17, 1797) where, in re Venice, he notes a "kind of alliance of interests exists between Francis II and the Republic." Then, restating the idea a moment later, he speaks of "links between France and the emperor."
71. Emphasis added. Cited in Sepinwall, "Regenerating France, Regenerating the World," 169.
72. Some historians believe Bonaparte was the first to use it. Henry Laurens, *L'expédition d'Egypte* (1997), 28.
73. Jean-Yves Guiomar, "Histoire et significations de 'la Grande Nation,' " in J. Bernet et al., eds., *Du Directoire au Consulat,* 1: 323. See also Guiomar, "La Grande Nation, est-ce encore la nation?" in H. Leuwers et al., eds., *Du Directoire au Consulat,* vol. 2; and Jacques Godechot, *La Grande Nation* (1985); Colin Jones, *The Great Nation: France from Louis XV to Napoleon 1715–1799* (2002), 568–80.
74. *Correspondance,* March 8, 1800. The proclamation "To Young Frenchmen" speaks of "glory" and "nation's glory," not "Republic" (April 21, 1800).
75. Howard Brown ("From Organic Society," 687) makes this point.
76. What the Revolution and Rousseau shared was "the combination of a passionate longing for unity and a rigorous experience of division"—that is, "the Revolution's greatest fidelity to Rousseau." James Swenson, *On Jean-Jacques Rousseau Considered as One of the First Authors of the Revolution* (2000). See also Jean Starobinski, "Rousseau and Revolution," *The New York Review of Books,* April 25, 2002, 59. See also David Bell, *The Cult of the Nation in France* (2001).
77. Paolo Viola, "Napoléon, chef de la révolution patriotique," in Jean-Clément Martin, ed., *Napoléon et l'Empire* (2002), 41.
78. Even French historians may fall for "national" as if it actually were apolitical. A leading scholar of his generation, Georges Pariset wrote thus about the Civil Code: "The Civil Code's originality is not to have one. It is not a creation but a coordination; it is eclectic and nonpartisan. That is what makes it profoundly national" (*Le Consulat et l'Empire* [1911], 166). Now the Civil Code, as we saw, was many things, including very much eclectic, but to say it was nonpartisan is to fall into the rhetoric of the writers of the code and to forget that they had opponents who did not see their propositions as either "natural" or "national." Professor Pariset was a good republican scholar who was anything but a friend of Napoleon Bonaparte's, yet in this description of the code we see the triumph of the First Consul's particular style of politics.
79. Cited in Emil Ludwig, *Napoleon* (1926), 147. Evolutions and transformations may occur within an ideology. As Guiomar brilliantly points out, "*Grande nation* is itself a further sublimation of 'nation,' with all that that [Freudian] term implies by way

of the passage from one level to another more purified level, just as the original meaning of the term 'nation' at the start of the Revolution began to disappear. One meaning is replaced by another more useful one, which erases it, denudes it of all creative value while yet seeming in form to render it the greatest homage." "La Grande Nation," 2: 22.

80. Proudhon had said, "Whoever invokes humanity cheats." Cited in Carl Schmitt, *The Political,* 54.

81. Mme de Rémusat, *Mémoires,* 1: 270–73.

82. Carlton J. H. Hayes, *France: A Nation of Patriots* (1927). Eugen Weber, of course, shows how long it took (i.e., until 1914) to turn most of the *Peasants into Frenchmen* (1976).

83. Arthur Lévy, *Napoléon intime* (1893), 157.

84. After contemplating it for a long time, he decided that his new Consular Guard uniform looked wonderful, but not as wonderful as his old artillery lieutenant's uniform. Roederer, 3: 337

85. Quotes from Benjamin Constant and Bonaparte's valets, Constant Wairy and Claude Méneval. See the extremely useful compilation *Napoleon: An Intimate Account of the Years of Supremacy, 1800–1814,* ed. Proctor Patterson Jones (1992), 45, 52, 53. See also Hyde de Neuville, *Mémoires* (1888), 2: 269.

86. For his part, Napoleon smiled at what he saw as the Englishman's naïveté–odd, he felt, in a statesman. Thiers, *Histoire du Consulat et de l'Empire,* 3: 313.

87. The Restoration returned the street to its old name, but Adolphe Thiers, a key minister under Louis-Philippe, restored "Victoire" (1833).

88. According to the copy of Napoleon's handwritten letter to his brother, Joseph, 27 Prairial IV (15 June 1797), available at the *Archives Nationales* (400 AP 10), Napoleon contributed 30,000 pounds (*livres*) to Josephine's identical amount. He tells Joseph that this amounts to three-quarters of his share of the sum realized in the liquidation of the family's Corsican estate. It is curious that there is no mention of any sums realized from the Italian Campaign.

89. Germaine de Staël captures another aspect of the "royal" tone in her description of a typical Napoleonic arrival one afternoon: "His valets opened the carriage door and hurled down the ladder with a violence which seemed to say that even objects were insolent when they delayed for an instant the progress of their master." *Ten Years of Exile* (unfinished in 1817, when the author died, at fifty-one).

90. It appears that he contemplated Versailles itself for a time, but the Revolution had left the great symbol of monarchy a barren shambles. Then, too, it was *Versailles,* and any occupant, even this one, could not hope to do more than bask in the reflected glory of the Sun King who built it.

91. Musée municipal de Saint-Cloud, *Du Coup d'Etat de Brumaire à la fin de l'Empire: Napoléon Bonaparte à Saint-Cloud* (1999–2000), 145.

92. Bourrienne received another appointment, but the greed went with him, and he foundered again in corruption and scandal.

93. An Order of the Day that Napoleon wrote for the army, on May 12, 1802, dealt with a grenadier who had killed himself over love. Wrote the First Consul: "A soldier must know how to vanquish the pain and melancholy of his passions; he must know that there is as much courage in suffering with constancy the pain of the soul, as there is in standing firm under artillery shot. To give way to emotional sorrow without resisting, to kill oneself in order to get away from it, is to flee the field of battle before you have lost."

Chapter IX: Power (III): Naming It
(From Citizen Consul to Emperor of the French)

1. Jeff Horn, "The Bonapartist State in the Aube," *French Historical Studies* 25, 2: 237.
2. Senators made 25,000 francs per annum; tribunes, 15,000f; legislators, 10,000f. A high-level civil servant in the War Ministry received 15,000f; an ordinary *fonctionnaire* received 1,800 to 3,600f and an office boy received 800 to 1,000f. In society at large, by contrast, a worker was paid from 470 to 1,565f annually while his wife got 10 to 24f per month, but was only hired seasonally. And never forget: the First Consul received 500,000f.
3. Cited in Irene Collins, *Napoleon and His Parliaments* (1979), 41.
4. Cited in Louis de Villefosse and Janine Bouissounouse, *L'opposition à Napoléon* (1969), 169. Capital letters in original.
5. Collins, *Napoleon and His Parliaments*, 38. Collins concludes (46) that Bonaparte "had some ground for saying that most of the criticism in the Tribunate was destructive."
6. "This was precisely the sort of summary illegality that the Jacobins favored during the Terror." Adolphe Thiers, *Histoire du Consulat et de l'Empire*, 2: 318–19.
7. His men's only lead was the head of the horse pulling the cart that carried the bomb, but they managed to trace it back to the seller and got a description of the buyers.
8. The charge is that of Marie-Joseph Chénier, brother of the composer, executed in the Terror. Cited in Villefosse and Bouissounouse, *L'opposition à Napoléon*, 161. Emphasis added.
9. Ibid., 225–26; also Thierry Lentz, *Le Grand Consulat*, 348.
10. Thiers, 3: 559. See also Isser Woloch, *Napoleon and His Collaborators*, 242.
11. He matched the Comte de Provence's "magnanimity" by offering to "contribute with pleasure to the ease [*douceur*] and tranquility of your retirement" (if Provence stopped his war against the Republic).
12. Mme de Staël, *Dix Années*, 36.
13. The actual author was Louis de Fontanes, working under Lucien's supervision. Fontanes was a moderate (royalist-constitutionalist) exiled in the Fructidor coup, who rallied to Bonaparte after 18 Brumaire, and made a name for himself as an adulator of the First Consul. Soon to be president of the Legislative Body, he will become grand master of the Napoleonic University.
14. This was the self-same Lucien who, two months earlier, in the ceremony at the Invalides, had cried out to the assembled throng, "Happy the generation that has seen the Revolution that began a monarchy end in republic"!
15. Pierre-Louis Roederer, *Oeuvres*, 3: 346; also *Mémoires secrets sur la vie privée, politique et littéraire de Lucien Buonaparte* (1818), 73.
16. Lucien claimed that the pamphlet *had been approved by the First Consul*. Bourrienne and Roederer also believed this to be so—even that Bonaparte had amended it (Roederer, 3: 350). The truth would seem to be that the *Parallel* was conceived by both brothers; it was to have been a first testing (or roiling) of the waters, with the younger taking responsibility in case something went wrong, as it did. Such players, high stakes. The best recent consideration of which memoirist claimed what is in Thierry Lentz, "Vers le pouvoir héréditaire," *Revue du Souvenir Napoléonien* 431 (October/November 2000): 2–6.
17. Roederer, *Oeuvres*, 3: 332. Nor does anyone seem to have mentioned that heredity had not been a viable solution in Caesar's time either: a decade of civil war was required for his chosen heir (Octavian) to impose his rule over his rivals.
18. Typically, Bonaparte later gave pensions to a few of the dissenters (e.g., Chénier) who were now without incomes.

19. Talleyrand, however, was wise in predicting that "not all whom the Revolution has pardoned will pardon the Revolution." Many of the amnestied pardoned nothing but posed as arrogant victims—to such a degree that Bonaparte regretted he had not added a guilt clause to the amnesty law. By way of comparison, "American communities after our revolution remained implacably hostile to former Loyalists, even as they allowed some to return from exile. But few Loyalists, especially the wealthiest, regained their property. With little reason to stay, at least 60,000 Loyalists left the country permanently—about 2.5 percent of the whole American population and proportionally *five times greater* than the number of émigrés who fled during the French Revolution." Allan Kulikoff, "Revolutionary Violence and the Origins of American Democracy," in *The Journal of the Historical Society*, II, 2 (Spring 2002), 252–53.

20. In its second edition, which appeared four days before the Notre-Dame mass celebrating the Concordat.

21. The classic study of this aspect of Chateaubriand's book is Henry Walsh, *The Corcordat of 1801: A Study of the Problem of Nationalism in the Relations of Church and State* (1933), 62–75. See also Jacques-Olivier Boudon, *Napoléon et les cultes* (2002).

22. Cited in Mme de Rémusat, *Mémoires,* 1: 335–36.

23. Mathieu de Molé, *Sa vie, ses mémoires* (1922), 4: 216.

24. Georges Lefebvre, *Napoleon from 18 Brumaire to Tilsit (1799–1807)* (1969), 159.I, 159.

25. Roederer, 3: 350.

26. At least in the opinion of Claude Goyard, a historian of law, writing in Jean Tulard's *Dictionnaire Napoléon* (1987), 500.

27. See Philippe Sagnac, "Du Consulat à l'avènement de l'Empire," *Revue des Etudes napoléoniennes* (1925), 133–54; 190–211; also Woloch, *Napoleon and His Collaborators,* 92–94. However, Jacques-Olivier Boudon maintains that the "yes" figures were significantly inflated, while Woloch does not.

28. In 1799 the apparent "yes" vote was 3 million, though in reality, as we recall, it was 1.5 million. Then, too, in the present plebiscite, the minister of the interior (Chaptal) had reluctantly, and unbeknownst to Bonaparte, directed the prefects to "campaign" for the First Consul. A surprise among the yeses was the vote of the respected British philosopher of utilitarianism Jeremy Bentham (who had been named a French citizen in 1792). J. M. Thompson, *Napoleon Bonaparte* (1988 ed.), 190.

29. But a pamphlet, *The True Sense of the National Vote on the Life-Consulate,* by Camille Jordan, a moderate royalist, argues that the French voters were far from giving the First Consul carte blanche to do anything he liked.

30. Thibaudeau's "Note" is discussed in Sagnac, "Du Consulat à l'avènement de l'Empire," 143–45.

31. The government had already (since 1801) begun suppressing the epigraph "liberty, equality, and fraternity" from its official acts.

32. "The arbitrary now enters the Constitution," writes Boudon, *Histoire du Consulat et de l'Empire* (2000), 127. The latest work on the Senate is Vida Azimi, *Les premiers sénateurs français 1800–1814* (2000).

33. "An imperfect monocracy, tempered by the Senate and the existence of a constitutional-juridical control of the legality of governmental and administrative acts," writes C. Goyard, in Tulard, *Dictionnaire,* 497.

34. Borrowing James Madison's ideas, we could say that the electoral colleges contributed to democracy in France without contributing to the Republic or to representative government, as Sieyès understood it. See Pasquale Pasquino, *Sieyès, et L'invention de la constitution en France* (1998), 125.

35. Albert Vandal, *L'Avènement de Bonaparte,* 570.

36. This maxim of Fidel Castro serves as the epigraph to Martyn Lyons's *Napoleon Bonaparte and the Legacy of the French Revolution* (1994).

37. Frédéric Bluche, *Le bonapartisme* (1980), 42, 61–62.
38. Thierry Lentz, *Le Grand Consulat,* 337.
39. Pieter Geyl, *Napoleon, For and Against* (1949), 425.
40. Or on the no less critical issue of whether blood or soil (*jus sanguine* or *jus sli*) determined French citizenship. Bonaparte chose soil (it made it easier to draft a man), but the Council of State opted for blood (for a host of reasons dealing with private property and its transmission), and blood it was. See Thierry Lentz, "Qu-est-ce qu'un français selon Napoléon?" *Revue du Souvenir napoléonien* 439 (January/February 2002).
41. Howard C. Brown, "From Organic Society to Security State," *Journal of Modern History* 69: 685; see also Philip G. Dwyer, ed., *Napoleon and Europe* (2001), 7.
42. The details of the collapse of the peace and the return of the war will be discussed in the next chapter.
43. The definitive work is Elizabeth Sparrow's *Secret Service: British Agents in France, 1792–1815* (1999). See ch. 13, "Assassination of Paul I."
44. Ibid., 279.
45. Fiévée dated "a new era" from 18 Brumaire. "States in revolution are not saved by constitutions but by men," he wrote. Bonaparte was his man. Fiévée pulled away from the royalist cause as he foresaw "there was now every reason to adjourn Bourbon hopes for a long time to come." He added, "and indeed to extinguish them forever if only Bonaparte had known how to practice on himself a bit of the ascendancy he so easily held over others." See Jean Tulard, *Joseph Fiévée* (1997).
46. See P. Savinel, *Moreau, le rival républicain de Bonaparte* (1986).
47. De Rémusat, *Mémoires,* 1: 299.
48. In early 1803, it appears Bernadotte sounded out Moreau on leading a movement of generals against Bonaparte, and was turned down. Moreau's name had earlier been put forward as a successor to the First Consul when rumor had it that Bonaparte was killed at Marengo. Villefosse and Bouissounouse, *L'opposition à Napoléon,* 227
49. "[Political] parties have a marvelous instinct for feeling out the weaknesses of eminent men. They in turn flatter and offend them until they find the way into their hearts, and then they introduce poison." Adolphe Thiers, *Histoire du Consulat et de l'Empire,* 3: 327–28.
50. Jean-Paul Bertaud thinks it likely that Enghien's father, who had once commanded the Comte de Lille's secret services, had a pretty clear notion that something deadly was being planned against Bonaparte's life, and that his son might play a brilliant role. *Le Duc d'Enghien* (2001), 335–37, 436.
51. He came alone. Dumouriez was nowhere to be found in Ettenheim; the police spy had made a mistake.
52. In addition to Bertaud, see Lentz, *Le Grand Consulat,* 547–48; and Jean Tulard and Régine Pernoud, *Jeanne d'Arc, Napoléon: Le paradoxe du biographe* (1997), 95.
53. While he showed courage, it is also true that he had been chafing at the low-level job given him and was generally frustrated at not being lionized by the regime. Jean-Pierre Clément, "Chateaubriand et Napoléon," *Revue du Souvenir Napoléonien* 421 (1998–99). The following year, Belloc, the prefect of the Cher Department, was dismissed for expressing his regrets over the assassination of the duke. Jean Vidalenc, "L'opposition sous le Consulat et l'Empire," *Annales historiques de la Révolution française* 194 (October–December 1968): 478.
54. De Rémusat, *Memoires,* 1: 365. "I suffered much, but I felt myself little by little won over by his adroit behavior to me, and, like Burrhus [in Racine's tragedy *Britannicus*], I heard myself crying, 'Would to God this were the last of his crimes!' " 1: 341.
55. The British tried to stop it at the last minute but could not control the anti-French zeal they had whipped up. Elizabeth Sparrow, "The Swiss and Swabian Agen-

cies, 1795–1801," *The Historical Journal*, 1992, 861–84. In modern times we might consider the reason of State that led the U.S. government to plot the overthrow of Salvador Allende in Chile (1973); the Israelis to kidnap Adolf Eichmann in Argentina (1960) and bring him back to Jerusalem for trial and execution; or the American landing at the Bay of Pigs (1961) or the island of Grenada (1983).

56. "I remain convinced that everything done in this era was done, not for the satisfaction of strong feelings or blind vengeance, but simply due to an entirely machiavellian politics." Mme de Rémusat, *Mémoires*, 1: 291–92.

57. Lentz, *Le Grand Consulat*, 542.

58. Alphonse Aulard, *Paris sous le Consulat* (1903-1904), 4: 732.

59. Thiers, *Histoire du Consulat et de l'Empire*, 5: 55.

60. John Holland Rose, *The Life of Napoleon I* (1901), 1: 24.

61. Miot de Melito, *Mémoires* (1858), 2: 46.

62. Armand de Caulaincourt, *Mémoires du général de Caulaincourt*, 3: 12.

63. The two recent biographies of Cambacérès are by Laurence Chatel de Brancion, *Cambacérès* (1999) and Pierre-François Pinaud, *Cambacérès* (1996).

64. Thiers, 5: 141.

65. "I was far from scrupulous, I exasperated her, and thereby held her attention so she would not leave in haste, by pretending to be supremely honest, the better to prove to her that, in fact, I was not."

66. To which, Napoleon is supposed to have replied, "We'll see, we'll see." Georges Seippel, *Les deux Frances* (1905), 136.

67. Roederer, *Oeuvres* 3: 495.

68. Emphasis added. The discourses have been usefully collected by the Napoleon Foundation in *La proclamation de l'Empire* (2001). Page numbers following citations refer to this work.

69. Isser Woloch makes the convincing point that the recent insistence of historians on seeing the extreme radicalism of 1793–94 to be "already written in the logic" of 1789 should be counterbalanced by contemporaries' willingness to see a very different "logic" in the offing. "[T]he reliance of tribune after tribune on the original intent in 1789 as a rationale for a return to monarchy in 1804 ought to give pause. It suggests that in the National Assembly's initial formulation of revolutionary ideology— the only one that mattered by now [in 1804]—hereditary monarchy stood as one cornerstone for stability in the new regime and should not be dismissed as mere window-dressing." *Napoleon and His Collaborators*, 259 n., 33.

70. One can only speculate on what the human object of all this adulation thought of the double-speak of the legislators. To the extent that they struck him as genuine and disinterested, perhaps Napoleon was moved by their passionate avowals; but as they also seem to be straining, he doubtless smiled at their lack of irony and remove. Would he have agreed with Thiers when the historian rendered this harsh judgment? It merits quoting:

> One would think that the self-disavowal implicit in proclaiming the monarchy after having taken so many oaths to the one and indivisible Republic would have taught these orators a lesson, or at least slowed the pace of their affirmations about the future. But there is no lesson that can prevent the bark of mediocre men from being stripped away by this kind of torrent; they let themselves be washed away—the more completely as they thought of the honors and fortune that lay in store for them. (5: 89.)

71. Woloch discovered the petition (*Napoleon and His Collaborators*, 112), but I have made my own translation from the source, Archives Nationales, BB 2: 850A: *Adresse présentée au Premier Consul*, 22 floréal XII. Emphasis added.

72. Cited in Proctor Patterson Jones, ed., *Napoleon: The Years of Supremacy, 1800–1815*, 100. This is a most useful anthology of the memoirs of Constant (the name "Wairy" was not used) and Méneval, Napoleon's secretary.

73. Antoine-Claire Thibaudeau, *Mémoires sur le consulat* (1913), 460–62.

74. The words are those of a Napoleonic functionary, Regnaud de Saint-Jean d'Angély, cited in ibid. Berlier wrote, "Finally, at bottom the man [Napoleon] was a child of the Revolution, who could not forget his origin. . . . There was plenty of plausible grounds for hope." Woloch, *Napoleon and His Collaborators*, 103

75. Thierry Lentz argues persuasively that it was more in Moreau's or the royalists' interests than in Bonaparte's to have Pichegru killed. *Le Grand Consulat*, 553–54. Elizabeth Sparrow, on the other hand, stoutly holds for Consular responsibility. *Secret Service*, 293. The most dispassionate and longest analysis is F. Barbey, *La Mort de Pichegru* (1909), who holds for suicide.

76. "Georges" is said to have gotten off a brilliant parting shot: "We managed to do more than we thought we would; we came to Paris wanting to make a king, and we have made an emperor."

77. Evidence from the British archives shows Moreau was indeed game for the plot, that he had become a kind of royalist, but that he nevertheless insisted on holding full executive power for a time in France. A British spy reported him as saying, "Unless Monarchy be established in the form of Louis XVIII, he will have no part in the transaction." Sparrow, *Secret Service*, 258, 289.

78. Moreau moved to the United States until 1813, when he returned to Europe and joined the military staff of the mystical and counterrevolutionary Tsar Alexander I– a strange choice for a man who has been called "the rival republican" to Bonaparte. See Savinel, *Moreau*.

79. Woloch, *Napoleon and His Collaborators*, 118.

80. Malcolm Crook, *Elections in the French Revolution: An Apprenticeship in Democracy 1789–1799* (1996).

81. Natalie Petiteau, "Les Français face à l'ordre impérial," in *Terminée la Révolution* (IVe européan Colloque de Calais).

82. On the other hand, Constant, Napoleon's valet, stumbled over "Sire," "Your Majesty," and "Citizen First Consul" for days to come. De Rémusat, *Mémoires*, 1: 371.

83. Claude Goyard, article on "Constitutions," in Tulard, *Dictionnaire*, 494. Claude Goyard is a professor of the history of law and administration who teaches at the University of Paris-II.

84. Roederer, *Oeuvres* 3: 512. On St. Helena, he told Las Cases that he had never wanted people to feel free to "tap me on the shoulder." Under the Empire, such license became even more out of the question than ever before.

85. Pinaud, *Cambacérès*, 130.

86. De Rémusat, *Mémoires*, 1: 341.

87. Evelyne Lever, *Louis XVIII* (1988), 280 passim.

88. First was the Merovingian kings, then the Carolingians (including Charlemagne), and third, the Capetians.

89. *Mémoires de la Reine Hortense*, 1: 166. Louis Bonaparte would not permit his son, Napoleon-Charles, born of his unhappy union with Hortense de Beauharnais, to be adopted by Napoleon and Josephine, because, he felt, it would effectively reduce his own chance of succeeding.

90. See Alain Boureau, *L'Aigle: chronique politique d'un emblème* (1985), for a discussion of the eagle as an imperial symbol.

91. See Robert Morrissey, *L'empereur à la barbe fleurie: Charlemagne dans la mythologie et l'histoire de France* (1997); Jean Favier, *Charlemagne* (1999).

92. The word "Empire" was a common synonym of "realm" or "State" in the eighteenth century. The hymn itself sings of rights being maintained and of tyrants trembling and expiating; the main stanza ends with a rousing "Rather death than slavery!" See Jean Tulard, *Napoléon et Rouget de L'Isle* (2000), 92.
93. Fouché's title during the Terror, when he represented the Republic in Lyon.
94. The expression "constitutions of the Empire" and "constitutions of the Republic" were used interchangeably. Goyard, in Tulard, *Dictionnaire*, 502.
95. For example, projects leading to a *senatus consultum* or peace treaties, alliance treaties, and the exercise of the pardon had first to be passed by the Privy Council, which had to contain two ministers, two senators, two State counselors, two dignitaries, and two grand officers of the Legion of Honor. Frédéric Bluche, *Le bonapartisme*, 41.
96. Theoretically, Napoleon's spending was limited by a civil list—the Emperor's budget being 25 million francs; that of his brothers, one million apiece. As Lentz notes, this was different from the old regime, where spending was entirely at the king's discretion. *Le Grand Consulat*, 570.
97. Ibid., 572.
98. See the *Thirtieth Bulletin to the Army*, for example, where the Emperor refers to his "couronnement."
99. For example, David titled his vast and famous canvas *Josephine's Sacre*, even though it is Napoleon who is crowning (not consecrating) her. French historians *still* refer to it as a *sacre*—e.g., Tulard, *Le Sacre* de Napoléon (1993) and José Cabanis, *Le Sacre de Napoléon* (1970). Frédéric Masson, however, covers his bets with *Le Sacre et le couronnement de Napoléon* (1908; see 1978 ed.). For David's painting, and his willingness to bend truth to suit Napoleon, see Bernard Berthod, "David n'était pas en enfant de choeur, ou les incohérences liturgiques du sacre de Napoléon Ier peint par David," in *Revue de l'Institut Napoléon*, 181 (2000-II), 9–20.
100. Take the consecration and coronation of a Habsburg ruler: "The Emperor walked through the streets of the city as a sign of humility. The procession included the Cardinal-Archbishop, who carried the Host under a canopy, immediately behind the Emperor, bare-headed and carrying a lighted candle. Rudolf, in the eyes of his successors, was the first model of Habsburg piety. At his coronation, the new King of the Romans had no scepter, the symbol of temporal power, so he took a crucifix from the High Altar and declared, 'Here is the sign that has redeemed us and the whole world; let this be our scepter.'" Andrew Wheatcroft, *The Habsburgs: Embodying Empire* (1995), 30–31. If anything could be said to the opposite of Napoleon's coronation, this would be it.
101. The last time a pope had come to France was in 816, when Stephen IV crowned Louis the Pious at Reims.
102. "The Emperor Napoleon exercised on the Holy Father a kind of fascination and bedazzlement that all the public and private calamities that ensued could not stop. It was a mixture of admiration and fear, of paternal tenderness and gratitude." Consalvi, *Memoirs*, cited in Cabanis, *Le Sacre de Napoléon*, 171.
103. Pius VII received as a gift from the Emperor a magnificent tiara—the catch being that the great jewel adorning it had been seized from his predecessor, Pius VI, in the Bonaparte-enforced Treaty of Tolentino (1797). What goes around comes around. A Frenchman of Jacobin tendencies said only, "Dame Guillotine deplored the absence of a tiara from her basket" (i.e., the Revolution never managed to behead a pope). Thierry Lentz, *Nouvelle histoire du Premier Empire* (2002), 310.
104. The souvenir medallions given out at the coronation had, on one side, Napoleon in Roman-imperial profile, with the inscription "Napoléon Empereur." On the reverse the same profile but with the inscription "Le Sénat et Le Peuple." Two com-

ments: Napoleon must share center stage with an institution and a concept, and there is no reference to God.

105. In French, the sentence "le pape serf a sacré un noir demon" is an anagram on "Napoleon, empereur des Français." Jean Tulard, *L'Anti-Napoléon* (1965), 15.

106. Jean Tulard, *Napoléon, une journée particulière* (1998), 91, n. 34. The student was an adherent of General Moreau's cause.

107. Guglielmo Ferrero, a distinguished Italian historian of the early and mid-twentieth century. Cited in Bluche, *Le bonapartisme*, 27.

108. Philip G. Dwyer, "Napoleon and the Drive for Glory: Reflections in the Making of French Foreign Policy," in Dwyer, ed., *Napoleon and Europe*, 127.

109. *Des circonstances actuelles*, 157; cited in Marcel Gauchet, *La Révolution des pouvoirs: La souveraineté, le peuple et la représentation, 1789–1799* (1995), 203. "I shall respect the judgments of the public when they are legitimate, but when they are capricious, one must know how to despise them" was a characteristic question-begging judgment of Napoleon's. (He would have agreed more with Madame de Staël, who noted crisply, "In France, we only allow events to vote.") Cited in Edouard Driault, *Napoléon: Pensées pour l'action* (1943), 31.

110. Thiers, *Histoire du Consulat et de l'Empire*, 5: 54.

111. Louis XVI was required by the Constitution of 1791 to assume the title "King of the French."

112. Charles Durand, "Le pouvoir napoléonien et ses légitimités," *Annales de la faculté de droit et de science politique d'Aix-Marseille* (1972), 12. See also Jacques Godechot, who speaks of the Napoleonic "democratic monocracy." *La Contrerévolution, doctrine et action* (1961), 146.

113. Gauchet, *La Révolution des pouvoirs*, 214. Emphasis added.

114. Pierre Beltrame, "L'utilisation de l'idée de légitimité dans la vie politique française depuis le XVIe siècle," in *Mélanges Audinet* (1968), 251–87. Christopher Prendergast offers this interesting reflection: "No legitimation ideology can resist rational scrutiny for very long. . . . In this very general sense, there is nothing unique in the 'problem' of legitimacy that confronted the Napoleonic regime. It is always a problem. What is distinctive about this regime is the sheer visibility of the problem, despite—or rather in part because of—the assiduous efforts of the propaganda and censorship apperatuses to keep it at bay." *Napoleon and History Painting: Antoine-Jean Gros's* La Bataille d'Eylau (1997), 23.

115. Christian Meier writes about an earlier republican leader (Caesar) who drew the "outlines of a new and potentially monarchic reality" on the republican firmament of Rome: "The horizon of possibilities simply widened to exceed anything that might have been contained within the traditional pattern of expectations, fulfillment of expectations, and expectations of expectations." *Caesar*, 95.

116. Jean-Antoine Chaptal, *Mes souvenirs sur Napoléon*, cited in Octave Aubry, *Les pages immortelles de Napoléon* (1941), 87–88.

Chapter X: *La Guerre—Encore (et pour toujours)*

1. Diatribe against William Pitt in *Le Moniteur,* February 2, 1802.

2. Cited in Harold Deutsch, *The Genesis of Napoleonic Imperialism* (1938), 126.

3. Thomas Hobbes, *Leviathan* (1651). "However much we may prefer to see war as a departure from and distortion of true human nature, the anthropological and historical evidence offer little comfort." Elizabeth Fox-Genovese, "Editor's Introduction," *The Journal of the Historical Society* 2, 2 (Spring 2002): v.

4. The respected French historian François Crouzet describes the conflict as "the Second Hundred Years' War." "The Second Hundred Years' War," *French History* 10 (1997): 432–50. For a more objective take on the Franco-British conflict, by a Ger-

man contemporary, see Johan Friedrich Reichardt, *Un hiver à Paris sous le Consulat (1802–3)* (2003), introduction and notes by T. Lentz.

5. The French of this era—indeed of almost any era—tend far more often than not to refer to "England" and "the English" than to the more correct "Great Britain" (or "Britain") or "the British."

6. Charles-John Fedorak, *Henry Addington, Prime Minister, 1801–1804: Peace, War, and Parliamentary Politics* (2002), 88–111. Also David Johnson, "Amiens, 1802: The Phony Peace," *History Today* 52, 9 (September 9, 2002): 20–26.

7. England's gains in India, for example, were vast.

8. For examples, see letters #5442–5448; 5749 in vol. 7 of the *Correspondance.*

9. Only the return of war with Great Britain finished off a bonapartist grand design on the U.S. mainland. Yves Bénot, *La démence coloniale sous Napoléon* (1992), 331. See also Sylvain Pagé, *Napoléon et la Louisiane* (2003).

10. The rupture between France and Britain is not a topic like Nazi aggression of the 1930s where a scholarly consensus has settled in. Rather, it remains, like the revolutionary Terror or the American war in Vietnam, a topic where reasonable men and women make cases that evoke intense debate from other reasonable people. A classic statement of the French case is André Fugier, *Histoire des Relations Internationales, Volume IV. La Révolution française et l'Empire napoleonien* (1954), 177–85; Roger Dufraisse and Michel Kerautret, *La France napoléonienne: Aspects extérieurs, 1799–1815* (1999), 76–82. The British case is best seen in Paul W. Schroeder, *Transformation of European Politics*, 231–44. A plague on both their houses, but leaning toward France, is Georges Lefebvre, *The French Revolution and Napoleon*, 164–79. A recent overview of Napoleonic foreign policy is Philip G. Dwyer, "Napoleon and the Drive for Glory: Reflections on the Making of French Foreign Policy," in Dwyer, ed., *Napoleon and Europe*, 118–35.

11. Albert Pingaud, *Bonaparte: Président de la République italienne* (1914), 1: 262; see also Alain Pillepich's magisterial *Milan: capitale napoléonienne, 1800–1814* (2001); André Fugier, *Napoléon et l'Italie* (1947).

12. Talleyrand indeed felt that Napoleon's tilt to Italy is what unhinged the imperial system. Michel Poniatowski, *Talleyrand et Bonaparte: Le Consulat*, 18–25.

13. The change of the regime's name from Cisalpine Republic was intended to rally Italians and strike fear into Austrian hearts. It did so less than we may think, however, for only a tiny minority of Italians at this time looked beyond the horizon of their city-state toward a united peninsula. Adolphe Thiers, *Histoire du Consulat et de l'Empire* (3: 388) describes Italy as "a ship without a compass, blown by all winds." Not until after 1820 did the Risorgimento press the case of Italian nationalism and project its own nationalist sentiments backwards in time.

14. On the other hand, in view of Prussia's and Austria's recognizing these transactions, there was little England—a far less interested party—could have said that would have counted.

15. See the two essays in the section entitled "La Suisse Helvétique" in Michel Vovelle, *Les Républiques-soeurs sous le regard de la Grande Nation, 1795–1803* (2000), 269–315.

16. Elizabeth Sparrow, *Secret Service: British Agents in France, 1792–1815* (1999), 263.

17. September 23, 1802, #6339. Translation by J. M. Thompson, *Napoleon's Letters* (1934), 75–76. See also [Bonaparte], in *Le Moniteur,* 7 Brumaire XI (October 29, 1802).

18. He didn't take the title formally until 1806. Latter-day Jacobin historians like Georges Lefebvre see the Act of Mediation as reactionary in that it abolished the centralized Helvetic Republic which the French Revolution had built. On the other hand, the Federalists were not operating in a vacuum; they had the truly counterrevolutionary oligarchs to deal with. *The French Revolution and Napoleon*, 1: 172–75.

The same point of view is that of A. Palluel-Guillard, in Jean Tulard, *Dictionnaire Napoléon*, 1609.

19. *Nota bene*: Dutch memories of Austrian rule in the Netherlands were worse. Then, too, the Dutch had fought three bloody wars with the British in the seventeenth century.

20. H. Stegemann, *Der Kampf um den Rhein* (1924), 464. Harold Deutsch writes, "Neither the letter nor the spirit of any of the treaties ... had been violated, least of all the Treaty of Amiens." *Genesis of Napoleonic Imperialism*, 93.

21. Napoleon would say at St. Helena, "The cause of the rupture of the peace was not Malta but the treaty of commerce ... that I did not want." See also Chaptal, *Mes souvenirs sur Napoléon* (1893), 250–51. French and English scholars find a rare point of agreement on the importance of the economic disappointment as a factor in rupturing the peace. See Eric Hobsawn, *The Age of Revolution* (1988), 100–110; Lefebvre, *The French Revolution and Napoleon*, 1: 165–79; Fugier, *La Révolution française*, 140–56.

22. See, e.g., *The Morning Post*, February 1, 1803; Jean Tulard, *Joseph Fiévée* (1985), 135–38; Simon Burrows, "The Struggle for European Opinion in the Napoleonic Wars: British Francophone Propaganda," *French History* 11, 1 (1997): 29–53.

23. "As long as émigré intrigues were allowed to go on without interference, libels spread, and the Bourbons permitted to flaunt their orders, the situation could hardly be characterized as more than an armistice." Deutsch, *Genesis of Napoleonic Imperialism*, 124. See also T. Ebbinghaus, *Napoleon, England und die Presse, 1800–1803* (1914); Robert Holtman, *Napoleonic Propaganda* (1950); Simon Burrows, *French Exile Journalism and European Politics, 1792–1814* (2000).

24. Even Lord Whitworth, the British ambassador to Paris and no friend of Bonaparte's, admitted, "This is no longer the liberty but the anarchy of the press." Cited in Deutsch, *Genesis of Napoleonic Imperialism*, 115. Bonaparte's articles are dated August 8, October 29, November 5, 1802; May 23, 1803; March 8, 1804. They are unsigned but it is clear they are Bonaparte's.

25. The result indeed worsened a bad situation: the French government won a Pyrrhic judgment against the worst émigré libeler, Peltier. He was found guilty and sentenced to a fine, but then reimbursed by a public subscription that also gained him great notoriety. Alphonse Aulard, *Paris sous le Consulat* (1903-1904), 3: 732.

26. C. L. R. James, *The Black Jacobins: Toussaint L'Ouverture and the San Domingo Revolution* (1964).

27. Lucien's claim in Theodore Jung, *Lucien Bonaparte et ses mémoires* (1882), 2: 165; Deutsch, *Genesis of Napoleonic Imperialism*, 117–18.

28. The British government warned its admirals to expect a French move in the Near East. John Holland Rose, *Life of Napoleon I* (1901), 1: 434.

29. Pieter Geyl, *Napoleon, For and Against* (1949), 406.

30. Cited in Charles Fedorak, *Henry Addington* (2002), 118.

31. Cited in Deutsch, *Genesis of Napoleonic Imperialism*, 146. For widespread anti-British feeling in Europe, see Arnold David Harvey, "The Continental Images of Britain," in Frank A. Kafker and James M. Laux, eds., *Napoleon and His Times: Selected Interpretations* (1989), 92–103.

32. Sparrow, *Secret Service*, 267, 295.

33. Aulard, *Paris sous le Consulat*, 216–20; for a slightly different viewpoint see N. Petiteau, "Les Français face à l'ordre imperial," in *Terminée la Révolution* (IVe Colloque européen de Calais), 101–12.

34. An eloquent and forceful statement of the French position (and illusions) was produced by Alexander de Hauterive, a ranking functionary in the French Foreign Affairs Ministry. *On the State of France at the End of the Year VIII* (1801), written on Napoleon's and Talleyrand's direct orders, offers a brilliant scenario by which

France will obtain—via peace and without having to engage in Britain's risky deficit-financing and exorbitant taxes—the commercial, colonial, industrial, and maritime supremacy that has long escaped her, and which, with her superior population, army, principles, and State, France deserves.

35. H. D. Schmidt, "The Idea and Slogan of Perfidious Albion," *Journal of the History of Ideas* 14 (1953): 604–13. For a critical analysis of the "imperative of self-preservation" as a pretext for aggrandizement, see Peter Minowitz's essay on Adam Smith, in Mark Blitz and W. Kristol, eds., *Educating the Prince: Essays in Honor of Harvey Mansfield* (2000).

36. Stuart Woolf, "French Civilization & Ethnicity in the Napoleonic Empire," *Past & Present* 124 (August 1989): 96–120.

37. Talleyrand, *Mémoires*, 1: 289. Schroeder, *Transformation of European Politics*, 243. Schroeder also writes (225): "The problem, as always, lay in Bonaparte's character: his inability to see a jugular without going for it, to forgo short-run opportunities for long-range goods."

38. The kingdom of Naples, which had an English prime minister, was Britain's one sure ally, but Sweden, under the reactionary Gustav IV, was so anti-French that he was, of necessity, well disposed to a British alliance.

39. Charles K. Webster, *British Diplomacy, 1813–1815* (1921), appendix 1.

40. "Rex totius Italiae" was the title Charlemagne had taken when he put on the iron crown of the Lombards. Napoleon offered the crown to Joseph, who declined it because he did not want to lose his place in the French succession.

41. Tolstoy's opening line, cited earlier, is loaded. Piombino was Elisa's "estate," while Lucca went to her husband. Genoa became a province of the French Empire.

42. When Alexander too volubly reproached Napoleon for executing Enghien, Napoleon "reminded" him of his own filial acquiescence in the assassination of Paul I, by the party that was angered at that tsar's evolution away from the English alliance toward a *rapprochement* with Napoleon. "If the assassins of Your Majesty's father were residing near the Russian frontier, would Your Majesty not act?" Alexander was livid; the truth can sting.

43. The Austrians fought over the issue of imperial precedence to the bitter end in their negotiations with France. It was for them an absolutely vital issue. The best treatment of the Francis-Napoleon relationship remains that of the Austrian scholar Auguste Fournier, *Napoleon the First* (1891–92).

44. Jacques Godechot, *Le Comte d'Antraigues: Un espion dans l'Europe des émigrés* (1986); Léonce Pingaud, *Un agent secret sous la Révolution et l'Empire: Le Comte d'Antraigues* (1894); Le Comte Remacle, *Bonaparte et les Bourbons: Relations secrètes des agents de Louis XVIII à Paris, sous le Consulat (1802–1803)* (1899).

45. A contemporary and friend of Pozzo's, Roger de Damas, wrote of him: "[Pozzo di Borgo] never conceived how, from two young men of the same age, same class, and same city, Fate could choose Bonaparte to be emperor instead of him. And he never pardoned Fate." *Mémoires* (1912, 1914), 2: 88–89. See also P. L. Albertini and J. Marinetti, *Pozzo di Borgo contre Napoléon* (1966).

46. C. de Grunwald, *Stein: L'ennemi de Napoléon* (1936).

47. Jean Tulard, *Dictionnaire Napoléon* (1987), 794.

48. Cited in Deutsch, *Genesis of Napoleonic Imperialism*, 143.

49. In fact, Britain was in the frustrating position of dealing with small powers whose neutrality was purely fictitious; they were French satellites.

50. Arno J. Mayer, *The Furies: Violence and Terror in the French and Russian Revolutions* (2000), 570. Jacques-Olivier Boudon, *Histoire du Consulat et de l'Empire* (2000), 265.

51. Mme de Rémusat, *Mémoires*, 1: 335.

52. Albert Sorel, *L'Europe et la Révolution française* (1908), 5: 179.

53. J. Christopher Herold, *The Mind of Napoleon* (1955), 161–62.

54. A recent general take on the geopolitical significance of all the Napoleonic wars is Charles J. Esdaile, *The Wars of Napoleon* (1996).

55. Frédéric Masson, "Napoléon et l'Angleterre. Napoléon contre la marine anglaise (1797–1805)," *Revue du Souvenir Napoléonien* 400 (March/April 1995); Rose, *Life of Napoleon I*, 1: 487–504; Fernand Beaucour, *Quand Napoléon régnait à Pont-de-Briques* (1978), and "Le Camp de Boulogne ou la grande illusion de Napoléon," in *Les Cahiers du Vieux Boulogne* 49 (2001); P. A. Lloyd, *The French Are Coming!: The Invasion Scare, 1803–5* (1991).

56. For an interesting take on Napoleon's supposed dictation in advance of the coming Danube campaign, see Fernand Beaucour, "La 'dictée' à Daru par Napoléon du plan de la campagne d'Austerlitz eut-elle lieu?" *Bulletin de l'Institut Napoléon* 185 (2002-II), 19–30.

57. The classic studies include Alain Pigeard, *Dictionnaire de la Grande Armée* (2002); John R. Elting, *Swords Around the Throne: Napoleon's Grande Armée* (1988); David Chandler, *The Campaigns of Napoleon: The Mind and Method of History's Greatest Soldier* (1966). For the style of Napoleonic military leadership and his relations with his men, see Henry Lachouque, *Napoléon et la Garde Impériale* (1950), translated into English by Anne K. Brown, *The Anatomy of Glory: Napoleon and His Guard* (1962).

58. "In a society where hierarchy was tending to solidify everywhere else, it was the army which offered the greatest opportunity to merit, and it exerted, consequently, a passionate attraction on ambitious young men." Georges Lefebvre, *Napoleon, from Brumaire to Tilsit*, 1: 219.

59. John A. Lynn, "Toward an Army of Honor: The Moral Evolution of the French Army, 1789–1815," *French Historical Studies* 16, 1 (Spring 1989): 152.

60. Professor Lynn disparages "honor" as being a euphemism for "social control," but John R. Elting, the author of the best study in English on the Grande Armée, makes the point that "what the Jacobins meant by 'virtue' wasn't very different from Napoleon's 'honor.'" See Owen Connelly, "A Critique of John Lynn," *French Historical Studies* 16, 1 (Spring 1989): 174.

61. The classic text in any language is, of course, Chandler's *The Campaigns of Napoleon*, but see his updated essays in *On the Napoleonic Wars* (1994). For detailed maps of all the campaigns, see Vincent J. Esposito and John R. Elting, *A Military History and Atlas of the Napoleonic Wars* (1999). The most recent French synthesis is the articles of Jacques Garnier in Tulard, *Dictionnaire*. See also the provocative *Blundering to Glory: Napoleon's Military Campaigns* (1987), by Owen Connelly. For Napoleonic (and Allied) strategy and tactics, see also Rory Muir, *Tactics and the Experience of Battle in the Age of Napoleon* (1998); Gunther Rothenberg, *The Art of Warfare in the Age of Napoleon* (1980).

62. Cited in Chandler, *On the Napoleonic Wars*, 118.

63. The Schoenbrunn was the palace of the Habsburg emperors, on the outskirts of Vienna. *Mémoires de Talleyrand*, 1: 297.

64. "Never perhaps in history has an incident similar in character to the violation of Ansbach changed a critical situation so completely." Deutsch, *Genesis of Napoleonic Imperialism*, 367.

65. Clausewitz, *On War*, 698.

66. It is telling at this point for us to note a stroke that Napoleon-emperor did not deal, but Bonaparte-general might well have. Urged by some advisors to appeal to Hungarian leaders to declare their country's independence from Austria, and even to call for a social revolution, such as, in certain senses, he had done in northern Italy in 1797, Napoleon refused to make Hungary into a "sister republic," as Lombardy had become. The social conservative in him weighed more heavily than the general in extremis.

67. The best account in English of the battle of Austerlitz is Christopher Duffy, *Austerlitz, 1805* (1977); but for absorbing writing, see Alistair Horne, *How Far from Austerlitz? Napoleon 1805–1815* (1996), 133–89. Jacques Garnier, to whom I owe great thanks for his counsel on this section is preparing a revisionist and definitive account and analysis of the battle, which Fayard will publish in 2004.

68. Chandler, *On the Napoleonic Wars*, 123–24.

69. A very familiar myth, first proclaimed in the Grande Armée's *Thirtieth Bulletin*, and repeated in many histories and biographies, is that the Russian left flank retreated across some frozen lakes near Aujest Markt. Seeing this, Napoleon ordered French artillery to fire on the ice, resulting in the perishing of 20,000 Allied troops. This did not happen: the water was too shallow; probably fewer than a hundred drowned.

70. Lachouque, *Anatomy of Glory*, 65.

71. The son of the Comte and Comtesse de Rémusat, he was born in 1797 and died in 1875. *Mémoires de ma vie*, 62.

72. P. Bertrand, *Lettres inédites de Talleyrand à Napoléon* (1889), #138, 209.

73. This was the First "German" Reich; the Second was the Empire of the German kaisers (1871–1918); the Third was Hitler's, which did not last the thousand years that its founder said it would. See John G. Gagliardo, *Reich and Nation: The Holy Roman Empire as Idea and Reality, 1763–1806* (1980).

74. Deutsch, *Genesis of Napoleonic Imperialism*, 418.

75. Emile Dard, *Napoléon et Talleyrand* (1935), 66.

76. W. Venohr, *Napoleon in Deutschland: Zwischen Imperialismus und Nationalismus, 1800–1813* (1998); Brendan Simms, *The Struggle for Mastery in Germany, 1779–1850* (1998); Marcel Dunan, *Napoléon et l'Allemagne: Le système continental et les débuts du royaume de Bavière, 1806–1810* (1942); Roger Dufraisse, "L'opposition anti-napoléonienne en Allemagne, 1805–9," in *L'Allemagne à l'époque napoléonienne* (1992).

77. Auguste Fournier, *Napoleon the First*, 2: 22.

78. Dwyer, "Napoleon and the Drive for Glory," 132.

79. Cited in Thierry Lentz, *Nouvelle histoire*, 209.

80. Rose, *Life of Napoleon I*, 2: 55.

81. John M. Ehrman, *The Younger Pitt* (1997), 3: 161.

82. Cambacérès strained to justify it before the Senate arguing that "the honors given princes are done especially in the interest of the people"–that is, to give people examples of submission to the *patrie* (read: the Emperor). *Le Moniteur,* April 1, 1806.

83. Officially the return of the Gregorian calendar was done for scientific reasons, as the Revolutionary calendar had become astronomically incorrect. But the Abbé Sieyès, in his comfortable exile on his estates, may have recalled what he had said in 1793 when arguing against any attempt to alter the calendar: the Christian calendar and ways represented "a mass too frightening to move." Matthew Shaw, "Reactions to the French Republican Calendar," *French History* 15, 1 (March 2001): 25.

84. Mme de Rémusat, *Mémoires*, 1: 292.

85. Lentz, *Nouvelle histoire*, 205.

86. Schroeder, *Transformation of European Politics*, 284.

87. For example, the quotation of Charles de Rémusat at the beginning of this section was written after 1858.

88. After all, the logic of most geopolitical strategies is, as Lentz points out, "both right and wrong, depending on one's viewpoint." Lentz, *Nouvelle histoire*, 264.

89. Louis de Villefosse and Janine Bouissounouse, *L'opposition à Napoléon* (1969), 266.

90. Mme de Rémusat, *Mémoires*, 1: 345.

91. Chateaubriand, *Mémoires d'outre tombe*, ch. 24. And Stendhal: "Never has anything more true been said about the French people" than Napoleon's judgment,

'They are indifferent to liberty. They neither understand it nor like it. Vanity is their ruling passion and political equality, which enables them to feel that any position is open to them, is the only political right they care about.'" *A Life of Napoleon* (1956), 42. The Austrian historian Auguste Fournier puts it thus: "The French people as a nation were far too proud, too vain, not to lay claim to a man who gave commands to monarchs, who made and unmade kings, and through whom the name of France had been exalted beyond any point ever reached under her former rulers." Fournier, *Napoleon the First*, 326.

92. Louis Bergeron's treatment of this has become classic: *Banquiers, négoicants et manufacturiers* (1978), 145–50; and *France Under Napoleon* (1981), but see also Jean Bouvier, "A propos de la crise dite de 1805," *Revue d'histoire moderne et contemporaine* 17 (1970): 506–13; Lefebvre, *The French Revolution and Napoleon*, 1: 232–40.

93. An English spy has Fouché as a possible accomplice in any plot the British and royalists might undertake—provided that it succeeded. Whether this was true or only the report of a gullible agent, the fact is, Fouché did have a strong network among royalists, Jacobins, and businessmen. Sparrow, *Secret Service*, 303, 321; Louis Madelin, *Fouché*, 2: 20–25.

94. Jean Tulard, "Le fonctionnement des institutions impériales en l'absence de Napoléon d'après les lettres inédites de Cambacérès," *Revue des travaux de l'Académie des sciences morales et politiques* (1973), 231–46.

95. These men, save one, all made fairly swift comebacks, and there is some reason that Napoleon himself and other high dignitaries profited from the scandal. The crisis of 1805 was essentially a deflationary one of credit, circulation, and hoarding of specie—which is to say, a crisis of the old regime sort: intense but limited, involving the State (Treasury department) and the wild speculation of a few dozen Parisian entrepreneurs, but having no impact on the vast French agricultural sector. J. Bouvier, "A propos de la crise," 511–13.

96. Schroeder, *Transformation of European Politics*, 303.

97. Frederick William sent the Duke of Brunswick to St. Petersburg to assure Alexander I personally that Prussia would never pick up arms against Russia, as the French were pressing Frederick William to do.

98. The Hohenzollern ultimatum, by the way, adduced as one of its bill of particulars the turpitude of the Enghien abduction, although at the time it occurred, Prussia had hardly demurred. The war party at the Prussian court had its ear tuned to the Russian view. Deutsch writes: "There is no question but that Napoleon was honestly offended and that he never forgave Prussia for what he regarded as a stab in the back." *Genesis of Napoleonic Imperialism*, 396.

99. In addition to the works on military history cited earlier, there is, for this campaign, Henri Houssaye, *Jéna et la campagne de 1806* (1912); Clausewitz, *Notes sur la Prusse dans sa grande catastrophe de 1806* (1903). Clausewitz, though himself a Prussian officer, is unrelentingly severe on his own side's leadership.

100. "Bernadotte has no soul. You have to have a soul," Napoleon said to General Bertrand on St. Helena (January 10, 1821).

101. Clausewitz execrates what he calls "the stupidity of 'methodism.'" *On War*, 91.

102. The British writer Alastair Horne notes: "For speed [the French 1806 campaign] would beat even Hitler's mechanized triumph in 1940 when he overthrew France in six weeks." *How Far from Austerlitz?*, 212. Hohenlohe surrendered 100,000 men because he believed (or affected to believe) that Murat, with his one corps, had more than that!

103. Metternich, *Memoirs* (1881), 1: 54.

104. See Marcel Handelsman, *Napoléon et la Pologne, 1806–1807* (1909); Norman Davies, *God's Playground: A History of Poland* (1981).

105. Handelsman, *Napoléon et la Pologne, 1806–1807,* 69.
106. Comte d'Ornano, *Marie Walewska: L'épouse polonaise de Napoléon* (1947).
107. See the unforgettable "Lisette at Eylau," by Baron de Marbot, in Ernest Hemingway, ed., *Men at War* (1949).
108. *Journal des campagnes du baron Percy* (1904), 15.
109. He directed Fouché to spread the news of a victory in an "unofficial manner," which is revealing of what the Emperor knew to be the low probability that anyone believed official reports.
110. Cited in Christopher Prendergast, *Napoleon and History Painting: Antoine-Jean Gros's La Bataille d'Eylau* (1997), 185.
111. Unusually, Denon encouraged artists to (to some extent) acknowledge the fact that Eylau was a disaster. He gave the artists some latitude to choose how they would depict the scene whose general human and topographical outline was communicated to them. Prendergast writes, "he recognized that painting cannot simply be the handmaiden of propaganda." *Napoleon and History Painting,* 142. See also David O'Brien, "Propaganda and the Republic of Arts in Gros' 'Napoleon Visiting the Battlefield of Eylau,'" *French Historical Studies,* 26, 2 (Spring 2003), 281–314.
112. Géricault, on his sickbed, asked his student Montford to paint a copy of Gros's work to look at through the course of his illness. Prendergast, *Napoleon and History Painting,* 171.
113. Chandler, *Napoleon's Campaigns,* 584.
114. Napoleon to Haugwitz, December 26, 1805. The best recent discussion of Tilsit is G. Casaglia, *Le partage du monde: Napoléon et Alexandre à Tilsit* (1998), but, of course, see the invaluable Schroeder, *Transformation of European Politics,* 320–32.
115. P. Rain, *Un tsar idéologue: Alexandre Ier (1777–1825)* (1913), 1: 14.
116. A French Imperial Guard drum major instructed his drummers, when Frederick William hove into view, "Don't beat so loud, he's only a king." Cited in ibid.
117. See Arnold David Harvey, "Continental Images of Britain," in Frank A. Kafker and James M. Laux, eds., *Napoleon and His Times: Selected Interpretations* (1989), 92–103.
118. This came as a relief to the Polish nobility, who lived in terror of a Polish version of the Year II. Much of the Polish clergy saw the French, anachronistically, as "dechristianizers." Napoleon had wanted the republican hero Kosciuszko to join the duchy's government, but Kosciuszko was suspicious of French intentions to vassalize Poland, and he refused. For the long-term impact of the Napoleonic legend on the Poles, see Andrzej Nieuwazny, *My z Napoleonem* [We and Napoleon] (2002, corrected edition). My thanks to my friend Katarzyna Anna Wrzos for her help with this source.
119. The French emperor had thought to name his brother Jérôme to Poland's throne, but then decided in favor of the French ally King Frederick Augustus of Saxony.
120. Paul Schroeder considers Alexander's acceptance of the Grand Duchy of Warsaw to be "the most remarkable thing about Tilsit" (*Transformation of European Politics,* 322). I agree.
121. Savary, himself a strong anti-Jacobin, was nonetheless seen as a "revolutionary general," to whom nobody would rent a townhouse until the tsar intervened. The Empress Dowager, a power in her own right in St. Petersburg, was surrounded by French émigrés and was a regular consumer of British anti-Napoleonic propaganda, freely on sale in the "better" bookstores—even after Tilsit, for a time. See the *Mémoires du duc de Rovigo, pour servir à l'histoire de l'Empereur Napoléon* (1828), vol. 3; also Thierry Lentz, *Savary: Le séide de Napoléon* (2001), 163–69.
122. In an era when the Continent still hesitated to publish violent ad hominem caricatures of Napoleon, an English newspaper depicted John Bull playing a bass violin in the form of Bonaparte, with a sword for a bow. The caption: "Britons strike home." Britons did strike home. Continental caricatures of Napoleon were, in their

mass, a product of a later (post-1812) era, but the British newspapers were unbridled–
and very funny–in their mockery of "Little Boney in a strong fit" (James Gillray, May
24 1803) a decade earlier. See *"Die Kehrseite der Medaille," Napoleon-Karikaturen aus
Deutschland, Frankreich und England,* ed. E. Eggs and H. Fischer (Hanover, 1985), 90.
For widespread anti-British feeling in Europe, see Harvey, "The Continental Images
of Britain," 92–103.

123. Friedrich Gentz, *Von dem politischen Zustande von Europa vor und nach der französischen
Revolution* (1801).
124. Perceptions are still partly a question of nationality. A Cambridge historian prefers
to refer to England at the time as "the fight[er] for the defense of European liberties against French hegemony." Brendan Simms, "Britain and Napoleon," in Philip
G. Dwyer, ed., *Napoleon and Europe* (2001), 194.
125. "Blockade" (*blocus*) is curious usage, given the becalmed state of the French navy,
but words are a part of war, and "blockade" was intended to be frightening. In truth,
of course, it was the British who blockaded the Continent.
126. E. Chevalley, "Le blocus continental," doctoral dissertation, Sorbonne (1914),
166–75. "Land und Meer–Napoleon gegen England," in Roman Schnur, *Revolution
und Welbürgerkrieg: Studien zur Ouvertüre nach 1789* (1983), 52. For an unblinking
look at British eighteenth-century maritime practice, see Nial Ferguson, *Empire:
How Britain Made the Modern World* (2003).
127. Paul Schroeder believes England's stance in 1807–1808 surpasses 1940 as "Britain's
finest hour." *The Transformation of European Politics,* 326. He also writes, "The
Napoleonic Wars put a proportionately greater burden on Britain in terms of lives
and resources than World War One would do," 486.
128. François Crouzet, *L'Economie britannique et le blocus continental, 1806–1813* (1958),
1:203. See also the excellent and very long essay by Roger Dufraisse on "le Blocus
continental," in Jean Tulard's *Dictionnaire,* 219–39.
129. Bertrand de Jouvenel, *Napoléon et l'économie dirigée: le blocus continental* (1942), 191.
130. Thiers, 7: 362.

CHAPTER XI: THE EMPIRE AND ITS FISSURES (1807–1810)

1. John Holland Rose, *The Life of Napoleon I* (1901), 1: 177.
2. Mme de Rémusat, *Mémoires,* 1: 378; the remark is that of her grandson Paul de
Rémusat in the footnote.
3. Cited in Proctor Jones, *Napoleon: An Intimate Account of the Years of Supremacy
1800–1824* (1992), 148.
4. Count Mollien, *Mémoire d'un ministre du Trésor public (1789–1815)* (1898), 2: 138.
5. Emile Dard, *Napoléon et Talleyrand* (1935), 145.
6. H. A. L. Fisher, *Bonapartism* (1908), 75.
7. Pierre-Louis Roederer, *Oeuvres,* 3: 382. Most of this handful of collaborators were
still men of the Revolution, but things would soon start to evolve, as former
nobles returned. Isser Woloch, *Napoleon and His Collaborators* (2001), 183.
8. Mme de Rémusat, *Mémoires,* 1: 407. For the court, see Charles-Otto Zieseniss,
Napoléon et la Cour impériale (1980); Jean Tulard, "La Cour de Napoléon Ier," in *Hof,
Kultur und Politik im 19 Jahrhundert* (1985); Philip Mansel, *The Eagle in Splendour:
Napoleon I and His Court* (1987). See also *Etiquette du Palais Impérial,* which was written by the Emperor's Grand Master of Ceremonies, the Comte de Ségur, for
instruction to new courtiers.
9. Then there was the Empress's Household, the princes', and the adjunct courts in the
Bonaparte-ruled kingdoms–not to overlook the fact that *l'Empereur* had imperial
residences and entourages in seventeen venues, from Amsterdam to Rome.

10. Philippe-Paul de Ségur, *Napoleon's Russian Campaign* (1959), 145.
11. Emphasis added. Titleholders with the means to do so could transmit their title to a son by setting up a hereditary estate (a *majorat*). Natalie Petiteau, *Elites et mobilités: La noblesse d'Empire au XIXè siècle, 1808–1914* (1997); Jean Tulard, *Napoléon et la noblesse d'Empire* (1979).
12. Rafe Blaufarb writes: "Neither restoring monarchical institutions, nor maintaining republican ones, Napoleonic social policy offered new approaches to old problems that had been brought to light by a powerful current of *ancien régime* reformism." "The *Ancien Régime* Origins of Napoleonic Social Reconstruction," *French History* 14, 4 (2000): 423.
13. This enlarged, stable social order, wedded to advancement through merit and service to the State—that is, to acquired, not inherited, glory—was what the more ambitious bourgeoisie and the provincial nobility of 1789 had been prepared to fight for. It is common to refer to these 100,000 notables as the true "granite blocks" of the Empire. See Louis Bergeron and Guy Chaussinand-Nogaret, *Les "Masses de granit": Cent milles notables du Premier Empire* (1979).
14. Usage of the old titles thus remained forbidden under the Empire, while the Emperor strove to rally the great names of Versailles to his court by granting them his titles. The totals: 58 percent going to the bourgeoisie, 20 percent to the popular classes, 22.5 percent to the old nobility.
15. For a different view, see Geoffrey Ellis, *The Napoleonic Empire* (1991), 76–77.
16. See Norbert Elias's analysis of the royal court at Versailles. *The Court Society* (1969).
17. The name of the famous oval window (the Bull's Eye) at Versailles through which the king spied on his courtiers. Marcel Proust offers an unforgettable comparison of the functionality of the Napoleonic court with the "powerlessness and exaggerated affability of the royalist nobility" at Versailles. *Le Côté de Guermantes,* 1: 180.
18. Metternich, *Memoirs* (1881), 1: 295.
19. Jean Daniel, *La Légion d'honneur* (1957). See also the essays in *La Phalère (Revue Européenne d'Histoire des Ordres et Décorations)* 1 (2000), "Napoléon et la Légion d'honneur"; John Lynn, "Toward an Army of Honor," *French Historical Society* 16, 1 (Spring 1989).
20. "The bishop, like any man, should have known how to die rather than commit an infamy," the Emperor wrote to Fouché. It turned out the good bishop had not surrendered his decoration or his episcopal ring. Claude Langlois, "Complots, propagandas et repression policière en Bretagne sous l'Empire (1806–1807)."
21. Legionnaires had a legal right to the rank of knight, but when large numbers began requesting it, the de facto requirement arose of a minimum income (discussed earlier). Napoleon was not happy with this blemish on his ideal, however, and he presented annuities to many legionnaires so that they could make the threshold. And the rest of the legionnaires had the right to call themselves "knight by right of the Legion of Honor." In any case, the statute of 1808 making legionnaires eligible to be knights was never formally rescinded.
22. Sometimes precisely that: in 1807 a cluster of magnificent ancient Roman and Egyptian porphyry columns arrived in Paris—part of a purchase from the Borghese collection in Rome. Annie Jourdan, *Napoléon, héros, imperator, mécène* (1998), 285.
23. The Obelisk was originally a Napoleonic idea, but artists and stonesmiths assured him it was not possible to build one of the huge dimensions he had in mind, out of one piece of rock, as he required. The current Obelisk was a gift to France from the Egyptian government in 1829.
24. They were not all completed in the First Empire. See Georges Poisson, *Napoléon Ier et Paris* (2002 ed.).
25. Dominique Poulot, *Musée, nation, patrimoine, 1789–1815* (1997).

26. Bourrienne, 4: 39 and 53.
27. Not to mention the celebrated composers Méhul and Cherubini. Timothy Wilson-Smith, *Napoleon and His Artists* (1996); Christopher Prendergast, *Napoleon and History Painting: Antoine-Jean Gros's* La Bataille d'Eylau (1997).
28. The Marshals' Room at the Tuileries palace well illustrates the honored dead: it celebrates the Napoleonic companions in arms. Other monuments around the city commemorated Generals Desaix and Kléber, while the Pantheon's central frieze proclaims its raison d'être: "Aux grands hommes, la Patrie reconnaissante."
29. Fontaine won on the matter of exhibiting new machines in the Louvre, however, just as he successfully trounced Napoleon's idea that the Invalides church and veterans' hospital was the right place to showcase the treasures he had brought back from Italy. They went to the Louvre or the Tuileries.
30. Wilson-Smith, *Napoleon and His Artists,* 120.
31. These plans were in fact realized by another Bonaparte and his prefect Baron Haussmann, in the Second Empire (1851–70), but most of the original ideas were the uncle's.
32. Antoine-Vincent Arnault, *Souvenirs d'un sexagénaire* (1833), 4: 7–12.
33. Pierre-François Fontaine, the official architect of the Tuileries, writes in his diary: "Napoleon, during his fourteen years' residence, carried out in the Tuileries much less for his own interest and convenience than for the general harmony, beauty and magnificence of the building he thought of as the sanctuary of the monarchy." *Journal,* 1: 410.
34. For this section, besides Annie Jourdan's book, see Michael Polowetzky, *A Bond Never Broken: The Relations Between Napoleon and the Authors of France* (1993); J. K. Burton, *Napoleon and Clio: Historical Writing, Teaching and Thinking During the First Empire* (1979).
35. Even Napoleon's opponents attributed the dearth to historical change. "Genius burns itself out successively in each country, and is only reborn after certain intervals." Germaine de Staël, *De l'Allemagne* (1810), 417.
36. Jourdan, *Napoléon, héros, imperator, mécène,* 185.
37. The painter followed the Emperor's directions to put Madame Mère in the painting, even though she had boycotted the ceremony, in sympathy with the uninvited Lucien. David put in a series of other details, too, at Napoleon's direction. See Bernard Berthod, "David n'était pas un enfant de choeur," *Revue de l'Institut Napoléon,* 181 (2000).
38. He told the interior minister: "When this work . . . has appeared, no one will have the will and the patience to do another version, especially when, far from being encouraged to do so by the police, he will be discouraged by it." He claimed that Voltaire's *Century of Louis XV* was what he had in mind. Mme de Rémusat, *Mémoires,* 1: 266.
39. Mme de Rémusat, *Mémoires,* 1: 266.
40. One senses he understood this in his heart, for while he toyed with the idea of naming an official historian (and a poet laureate), he rejected it. Such myrmidons, he sighed, wrote satires or panegyrics, but either way, their employer ended up looking foolish. He did ponder the creation of a special school for history and geography, and given time and means, it might have been realized.
41. And in the best of instances, such as Emil Ludwig's *Napoleon* (1926), it is difficult to distinguish the genres.
42. Isser Woloch, *The New Regime: Transformations of the French Civic Order, 1789–1820s* (1994), chs. 6, 7; M. Gontard, *L'enseignement primare en France de la Révolution à la loi Guizot, 1789–1833* (1959); R. R. Palmer, *The Improvement of Humanity: Education and the French Revolution* (1985).

43. Alphonse Aulard, *Napoléon Ier et le monopole universitaire: origines et functionnement de l'Université* (1911); Robert Holtman, *The Napoleonic Revolution* (1967), ch. 7; Georges Lefebvre, *Napoleon, From Tilsit to Waterloo* (1969), 2: 191–92. Woloch is more even-handed but sees the Empire's alliance with the Church as fundamental to its education policy. *The New Regime* (1994), 212–16.

44. Woloch concludes: "In the ironic ways of history, this definitive defeat of the [revolutionary] secularizers was probably a necessary step if public instruction was to go forward." *The New Regime*, 235.

45. Recent research, however, shows that Napoleonic policy made more headway than it is credited for in these areas, and it may be premature to conclude that Napoleonic education policy was "not very bold in its ensemble due to the Emperor's prejudice against the masses" (Frédéric Bluche, *Le bonapartisme*, 64). See René Greveet, "L'Enseignement primaire sous le Premier Empire: une nouvelle donne?" and Rebecca Rogers, "L'Education des filles à l'époque napoléonienne," in Jacques-Olivier Boudon, ed., *La Création des lycées et la politique scolaire de Napoléon*, Actes du Colloque du 15–16 Nov 2002 (2003).

46. The Third Republic added a whiff of anticlericalism to national education, which, at bottom, turned out to be no more profound an element of policy than was supposed Napoleonic clericalism. At the end of the day, the Third Republic, like the First Republic, championed a deistic morality. See Antoine Prost, *L'Enseignement en France, 1800–1967* (1968).

47. A.-J. Arnaud, *Les Juristes face à la société du XIXè siècle à nos jours* (1975), 10–11.

48. The Empire's Commercial Code was published in 1807; the Rural Code–like the huge project of a national land survey (the *cadastre*)–was not completed before Waterloo. See Bluche, *Le bonapartisme*, 58.

49. André Cabanis, *La presse sous le Consulat et l'Empire, 1799–1814* (1975) and Holtman, *Napoleonic Revolution*, ch. 8. "In a nation as gifted as the French for jumping to the conclusion, lively imagination, and susceptibility to registering strong impressions, any indefinite freedom of the press . . . could produce no good and much harm," Napoleon told the Council of State (April 11, 1809).

50. This view is cogently argued by Dennis A. Trinkle, "The Napoleonic Press: The Public Sphere and Oppositionary Journalism" (Ph.D. dissertation, University of Cincinnati, 1993).

51. A sharp set-to took place between the conservative *Mercure* and *La Revue Philosophique* over the Jews. The reactionary Catholic philosopher Bonald, writing in the former paper, called for the conversion or expulsion of these "vile" and "usurious" people, while the writer in the *Revue* defended the imperial policy of integration of the Jews into the nation. *La Mercure de France* and *La Décade Philosophique*, February 8, 1806.

52. *Le Journal de l'Empire* (January 29, 1806) printed the text of a British parliamentary debate that discussed the defeat of the Franco-Spanish fleet at Trafalgar. Trinkle writes: "On nearly all issues of political concern, editors and journalists found means to express and sustain information and commentary contrary to official Napoleonic directives–even on Napoleon's personal power base and public depictions of him." "The Napoleonic Press," 107.

53. Mme de Staël, *Considérations de la Révolution française* (1818), 2: 196–97. These words were not written until 1815, so it is inconceivable that they reflected only the author's impressions of 1797. At St. Helena, Napoleon would say that he found her portrait "true." (Bertrand, *Cahiers*, 328).

54. Joseph Fouché, *Mémoires*, 221.

55. Yet Napoleon was equally capable of taking up the cause of Chateaubriand's *Genius of Christianity* (in a later edition), championing it for one of the Empire's rich

literary prizes, which he had created to the end of stimulating better writing. The Institute, set up to judge the prizes, opposed a work that the Ideologues considered reactionary, and they stuck by their opposition, no doubt reminding their brother member (Napoleon) that Chateaubriand, since Enghien's execution, was no friend of the imperial regime. Napoleon lost; the prize was not given.

56. Fouché had Napoleon himself watched, but the Emperor, using another police network answerable directly to him, did the same with Fouché. See Michael Sibalis, "The Napoleonic Police State," in Philip G. Dwyer, ed., *Napoleon and Europe* (2001), 79–93; Peter de Polnay, *Napoleon's Police* (1970); Jean Tulard, *Fouché* (1998); Thierry Lentz, *Savary* (1993); for daily police reports, see the standards works of Ernest d'Hauterive (1908–22) and Nicole Gotteri (1997).

57. Then, too, conditions in the Empire's seven political prisons were not arduous.

58. If they were "arbitrary, then that was in the nature [of police]," and in any case, they were "far less arbitrary" than the police in other monarchies. They were not cruel, the former prefect said, nor lacking in principles. "For my part, I can guarantee that, in all the ministerial correspondence, I never saw anything that could offend the conscience of an honest man." Antoine-Claire Thibaudeau, *Mémoires sur la Consulat 1799 à 1804* (1827), 355–56.

59. Overall, it doubtless, as Isser Woloch puts it, "offered a ray of hope to individuals plunged into the frustration or despair of prolonged preventive detention." Woloch, *Napoleon and His Collaborators*, 204.

60. Alfred Marquset, ed., *Napoléon sténographié au Conseil d'Etat, 1804–1805* (1913), 35.

61. Jacques Ellul, *Histoire de la propagande* (1967), 3.

62. The classic study from this perspective is Robert Holtman, *Napoleonic Propaganda* (1950), updated by his *Napoleonic Revolution*, ch. 8. French historians, for once, tend to follow suit: e.g., François Monnier, "Propagande," in Tulard's *Dictionnaire*. A subtler take that yet does not offer a different conclusion is Jourdan, *Napoléon, héros, imperator, mécène*; and David O'Brien, "Propaganda and the Republic of the Arts in Gros's *Eyla*," *French Historical Studies*, 26, 2 (Spring 2003) 281–314. See Périvier, *Napoléon Journaliste* for Napoleon's *Moniteur* pieces. For examples of Napoleon's intentions to dominate opinion, see *Correspondance* 10: 467; 18: 71–72; and 21: 242. See all his letters of September 4, 1809, in E. Picard and L. Tuetey, eds., *Correspondance inédite de Napoléon Ier conservée aux Archives de la Guerre*, 5 vols. (1912–1925), 3: 220.

63. *Memoirs of Prince Metternich* (trans. by A. Napier, 1880–81), 2: 225–26.

64. He was lecturing Savary in 1813.

65. Monnier, in Tulard, *Dictionnaire*, 1407.

66. "The painting expressed a concern that emanated organically from the public sphere in opposition to official policy—the cost of unending war . . . [T]he painting's critique of war belonged to a larger propaganda program that preserved the form and protocols of an open public sphere only in order to manipulate opinion." David O'Brien, "Propaganda as Art," 312.

67. For another difficult-to-unravel example, see the Emperor's letter to Portalis on the death of a bishop whom he liked and esteemed. Claude Langlois admits the letter, intended for political utilization, is a "monument of propaganda, all the more clever because it employs real sentiments in its praise of [the bishop]." "Complots, propagandas et répression policière en Bretagne (1806–7)," *Annales de Bretagne* 78 (1971): 416.

68. See Todd Porterfield, *The Allure of Empire in the Service of French Imperialism, 1786–1836* (1998); David O'Brien, "Propaganda as Art," 313.

69. Bluche, *Le bonapartisme*, 72.

70. Mme de Rémusat, *Mémoires*, 1: 334.

71. Cited in Louis Bergeron, "Présentation," to *Chaptal: De L'Industrie française* (1995), 36.

72. Georges Lefebvre, *Napoleon: From Tilsit to Waterloo* (1969), 179.

73. Napoleon, typically, maintained that the *cadastre* was more important than any mere political constitution of the Empire, for once it was finished, it would guarantee property and taxation. He would make the same claim for the legal codes.

74. Lefebvre, *Napoleon: From Tilsit to Waterloo*, 175.

75. If anything, Napoleon was almost *too* facile at number crunching. Complained the minister: "The Emperor imagined he was creating new resources by realigning and recalculating 'the numbers'; he believed he could maneuver figures around pages and in budgets the way he could maneuver battalions . . . [and] it required considerable patience to dispel his illusions, ever-reborn, and of which he was so proud." Cited in "Note Liminaire" (to *Napoléon Ier: Lettres au Comte Mollien*) by Bernard Gille, xvi.

76. One might call Napoleon "his mother's (or his father's) son" in this regard. As William Bolitho writes—unforgettably—of Letizia Bonaparte, "If Leipzig and Waterloo had left but a slim gain of a thousand dollars to the family, she would have counted it." *Twelve Against the Gods* (1929), 207. On the other hand, Napoleon lost most of this savings to crooked underlings in 1814.

77. Louis Bergeron, *Banquiers, négociants et manufacturiers*, 304. "Every time the question of public credit comes up in this country, the first reaction is fear," wrote Fiévée. (Cited in *Napoléon Ier: Lettres au Comte Mollien*, xx.)

78. Cited in Philippe Minard, "Etat et économie en France après la Révolution: quel libéralisme?", in M. Biard, ed., *Terminée la Révolution* (2002), 208–11. Minard speaks of a combination of verbal laissez-faire and actual interventionism.

79. For this section, see *Napoléon Ier: Lettres au Comte Mollien* (1959 ed.), ix; Robert Lacour-Gayet, "Les idées financières de Napoléon," *Revue de Paris,* June 1, 1938, 562–93; Emile James, "Napoléon et la pensée économique de son temps," *Revue de l'Institut Napoléon,* 1966, 113–23; Geoffrey Ellis, "War and the French Economy (1792–1815)," in E. Aerts and François Crouzet, eds., *Economic Effects of the French Revolutionary and Napoleonic Wars* (1990); Crouzet, "Avant-propos," to the issue of *Souvenir Napoléonien* entitled "Napoléon et l'industrie" (January 1971); Louis Bergeron, "L'Etat et l'intervention dans la vie économique (1789–1815)," *Etudes Napoléoniennes* 23–25 (1990), 293–99; Bergeron, "Les Milieux d'affaires, la guerre et la paix (1792–1815)," in Aerts and Crouzet; Philippe Minard, "Etat et économie en France"; Michel Peronnet, ed., *Chaptal* (1988), especially the essays by Poujol, Maurin, Gavignaud, and Georgelin; and André Conquet, *Napoléon et les Chambres de Commerce* (1978); Richard Whatmore, *Republicanism and the French Revolution: An Intellectual History of Jean-Baptiste Say's Political Economy* (2000); Ha-Joon Chang, *Kicking Away the Ladder: Development Strategy in Historical Perspective* (2002); Francis Démier, *Nation, marché et développement dans la France de la Restauration* (1991), 155–65; Jean-Pierre Hirsch, *Les deux rêves du commerce* (1991); F. Fourquet, *Richesse et puissance* (1989).

80. A French commercial agent scouting markets in North America wrote his firm (1804) that American consumers regularly complained of the price and quality of French consumer goods, which were simply not competitive with British ones. L. Bergeron, "Problèmes économiques de la Farance napoléonienne," *Reve du histoire moderne et contemporaine*(1970), 479.

81. A typical example: In the midst of the explosion of the Spanish war onto the French political scene, Napoleon yet profited from his trip to Bayonne (to see Ferdinand VII and Charles IV) by visiting the port city of Nantes, currently sore-afflicted by the Blockade. The Emperor conceived a number of projects for

Nantes's rehabilitation (e.g., deepening the harbor), though typically the time and funds for few, if any, were available before the fall of the Empire. See Louis Villat, "Napoléon à Nantes," *Revue des Etudes Napoléoniennes* 2 (1912), 335–65.

82. Jean-Claude Perrot and Stuart Woolf, *State and Statistics in France, 1789–1815* (1984).

83. The last was founded by Chaptal and joined by Napoleon, Cambacérès, Murat, and the leading economic actors of the Empire. Serge Chassagne, "Une institution originale de la France post-révolutionnaire et impériale: la Société d'Encouragement de l'Industrie Nationale," *Annales, Historie-Economie-Société* 2 (1989): 147–65.

84. Napoleon, however, was merely echoing the Convention and the Directory. Louis Bergeron, "L'Etat et l'intervention dans la vie économique (1789–1815)," 295. Moreover, French capitalists were not equal to all challenges. The iron manufacturers, for example, never managed to appropriate the Huntsman process (for casting steel in a crucible), although its superiority was well known (English steel manufacturing had long been using it). The result: French steel stayed uncompetitive with British–a fact displeasing to the Emperor, who held his industrialists responsible for their failure.

85. Schroeder, *The Transformation of European Politics*, 390–91.

86. Geoffrey Ellis, *Napoleon's Continental Blockade, The Case of Alsace* (1981).

87. Patrick Verley, "Quelques remarques sur l'économie française à l'époque impériale," in Natalie Petiteau, ed., *Voies nouvelles pour l'histoire du Premier Empire* (2003).

88. ". . . and the Emperor's downfall was celebrated as a personal triumph. The Holy Alliance was turned into a kind of insurance against the middle classes and the peasants." Lefebvre, *Napoleon: From Tilsit to Waterloo* (1969), 270. François Crouzet, "Le Système continental, antécédent de la Communauté?" in European University Institute, Florence, Colloquium Papers (1992), 2; Bertrand de Jouvenel, *Napoléon et l'économie dirigée: le blocus continental* (1942). A very different opinion on the roots of European integration is offered in H. Mikkel, *Europe as an Idea and an Identity* (1998), which largely ignores the First Empire.

89. But Italy also took its blows from the system. See Pasquale Villani, "Quelques aspects de la vie économique italienne à l'époque napoléonienne," *Annales historiques de la Révolution française* (October-December 1977), 587–617; Stuart Woolf, "L'impacte de l'occupation française sur l'économie italienne (1796–1815)," *Revue économique* 40, 6 (1989): 1097–1117.

90. Roger Dufraisse, "L'intégration hégémoniale de l'Europe sous Napoléon Ier," *Revue de l'Institut Napoléon* 142 (1984): 11–41.

91. See Paul Schroeder, *The Transformation of European Politics*, ch. 8.

92. *Napoleon and His Artists*

93. Michael Broers, in Dwyer, *Napoleon and Europe*, 193.

94. Charles Durand, "Les Rapports entre la loi et le règlement gouvernemental, de l'an IV à 1814," *Travaux et Mémoires de la faculté de Droit et de Science Politique d'Aix-Marseille* 26 (1977); Jean Tulard, *Napoléon: Le mythe du sauveur* (1977), 307.

95. Napoleon's spoken French added confusing sibilances at the end of the first-person future, or incorrect *ts* at the end of the third-person future. Miot de Melito, *Mémoires*, 2: 248–52. His neologisms tended to be Italian words made into French.

96. For negative opinion in the Empire, see Richard Cobb, *The Police and the People: French Popular Protest, 1789–1820* (1970); Jean Vidalenc, "L'opposition sous le Consulat et l'Empire," *Annales historiques de la Révolution française*, 40 (1968): 472–88; Natalie Petiteau, "Les Français face à l'ordre imperial," in *Terminée la Révolution* (IVe Colloque européen de Calais); Michael David Sibalis, "The Police and the People in Napoleonic Paris: Working-Class Opposition to the Napoleonic Regime, 1800–1814," unpublished paper.

Fouché wrote to Napoleon: "One would deceive oneself if one believed that the mass of the population was not indifferent to all political ideas. . . . The Emperor is everything for the mass of the nation" (September 20–21, 1807). Michael Sibalis, who shares Lefebvre's viewpoint, notes dryly of Fouché's toadying bulletin: "If this was true, it certainly marked a change from only a few years before." Sibalis adduces what evidence he can for working-class opposition to the Empire and concludes: "The evidence is by no means unambiguous, but there are sufficient indications to point to a considerable dissatisfaction with and opposition to the Napoleonic regime among the working class of Paris. But the reader should not be misled. The information presented in this paper has been culled with just such an aim; it is therefore weighted against the regime. That is to say, it ignores all statements which tell us how much Napoleon was beloved of his subjects." Unpublished paper, 2–3. R. Monnier, *Le Faubourg Saint-Antoine, 1789–1815* (1981), 245.

97. Adam Gopnik, *The New Yorker*, November 24, 1997, 82.
98. Vidalenc, "L'opposition sous le Consulat et l'Empire," 479. Yet Royer-Collard also evinced a stubborn loyalty to the Emperor, deciding to support him during the Hundred Days in 1815.
99. Jourdan, *Napoléon, héros, imperator, mécène*, 295.
100. "Far from shunting aside those former revolutionaries, [Napoleon] put them to use in ways that satisfied their most emphatic needs: political security, material self-interest, social status, and (not to be underestimated) the opportunity for high-level public service." Woloch, *Napoleon and His Collaborators*, 156.
101. Cited in Jean Tulard, *Fiévée* (1985), 235.
102. For this section, the central works are: Owen Connelly, *Napoleon's Satellite Kingdoms* (1965); Jean Tulard, *Le Grand Empire* (1982); Stuart Woolf, *Napoleon's Integration of Europe* (1991); Michael Broers, *Europe Under Napoleon, 1799–1815* (1996); Geoffrey Ellis, *The Napoleonic Empire*; chapters by Ellis, Dwyer, Esdaile, Broers, Grab, and Rowe, in Dwyer, *Napoleon and Europe*; Jean-Clément Martin, ed., *Napoléon et l'Europe* (2002); Thierry Lentz, *Nouvelle histoire du Premier Empire*, vol. 1, *Napoléon et la conquête de l'Europe, 1804–1810* (2002). These authors do not always agree: in particular, Ellis (in his contribution to Dwyer's collection) has offered a devastating critique of the theses of S. Woolf, who has replied in "Napoleon and Europe Revisited," *Modern and Contemporary France* 8, 4 (2000), 469–78.
103. Chosen, in part, because to name the region after a people living there (Croatia, Slovenia, etc.) would be to take sides in the Balkans' "nationalist" squabbles, which the French were too "imperial" and careful to do.
104. From the rights of peoples to decide for themselves, the Revolution passed to a system of outright annexation, which was a betrayal of principle. Napoleon's annexations, beginning with Piedmont in 1802, were but a return to the old regime. Gaston Zeller, *Aspects de la politique française sous l'Ancien régime* (1964); "La monarchie d'ancien régime et les frontières naturelles," *Revue d'Histoire Moderne* (1933), 305–33.
105. The British historian David Chandler (*Campaigns of Napoleon* [1966], 450) describes the nepotism as "typical[ly] Corsican," but why not "typically Habsburg" or "typically Bourbon." Any powerful dynasty appointed its members to as many thrones as it could; Napoleon simply had more to give out.
106. Lord Roseberry, *Napoleon: The Last Phase* (1900), 133.
107. Pieter Geyl, *Napoleon, For and Against* (1949), 323.
108. Charles J. Esdaile, "The Napoleonic Period: Some Thoughts on Recent Historiography," *European History Quarterly* 23 (1993), 422; S. Woolf, "Napoleon and Europe Revisited," 476.
109. Fisher, *Bonapartism* (1908), 70.

110. E. Fehrenbach, *Der Kampf um die Einführung des Code Napoleon in den Rheinbund-staaten* (1973); J. M. Diefendorf, *Businessmen and Politics in the Rhineland, 1789–1834* (1980); H. Berding, *Napoleonische Herrschafts- und Gesellschaftspolitik im Königreich Westfalen, 1807–1813* (1973); F. J. Bundy, *The Administration of the Illyrian Provinces of the French Empire, 1809–1813* (1988); Simon Schama, *Patriots and Liberators: Revolution in the Netherlands, 1780–1813* (1977); F. G. Eyck, *Loyal Rebels: Andreas Hofer and the Tyrolean Uprising of 1809* (1986); Michael Broers, *Napoleonic Imperialism and the Savoyard Monarchy* (1997); M. Senkowska-Gluck, "Les majorats français dans le duché de Varsovie, 1807–1813," *Annales historiques de la Révolution française* 36 (1964): 373–86.

111. Cited in Chandler, *Campaigns of Napoleon*, 561.

112. Jacques-Olivier Boudon, "L'Expropriation du modèle français dans l'Allemagne napoléonienne: l'exemple de la Westphalie," in Martin, *Napoléon et l'Europe*.

113. Geoffrey Ellis, *Napoleon* (1997), 112. Still less was the *Grand Empire* the harmonious "integration of Europe" that Napoleon, on St. Helena, claimed he had dreamed of. Tulard, *Le Grand Empire*, 189; Natalie Petiteau, "Débats historiographiques autour de la politique européenne de Napoléon," in Martin, *Napoléon et l'Europe*; Stuart Woolf, "The Construction of a European World-View in the Revolutionary-Napoleonic Years," *Past and Present* 137 (November 1992); *Le Moniteur Universel*, August 17, 1807 .

114. Alexander Grab, "State, Society and Tax Policy in Napoleonic Europe," in Dwyer, *Napoleon and Europe*, 186.

115. Charles J. Esdaile, "Popular Resistance to the Napoleonic Empire," in ibid., 141–42. See also Carl Schmitt, *Theorie des Partisanen. Zwischenbemerkung zum Begriff das Politischen* (1975 ed.).

116. Stuart Woolf, "French Civilization and Ethnicity in the Napoleonic Empire," *Past and Present* 124 (August 1989).

117. "In some respects, Napoleon was an evil necessity, the foreign-political and social equivalent of an enema," writes Philip Dwyer in an effective metaphor. Introduction, in Dwyer, *Napoleon and Europe*, 20.

118. Paul-L. Weinacht, "Les Etats de la Confédération du Rhin face au Code Napoléon," in Martin, *Napoléon et l'Europe*, 100. Fehrenbach (*Der Kampf*) concludes that overall the code was a failure in the German Confederation, which is *not* to say that no Napoleonic reforms occurred in Germany beyond the left bank.

119. Napoleonic gendarmes "brought order, stability, and higher standards of public service to societies which had often tolerated violence and crime as endemic." "[T]hose at the helm of the regime never lost sight of the need for impartiality, or that the real goal of these policies was to end vendetta and the political divisions of the war period, not just to restore order for its own sake. . . . Local communities all over western Europe learned to loathe them for many reasons, but also came to see that, in face of real danger, these same gendarmerie soldiers could be counted on to defend them, from bandits, thieves, or wolves. Most important point, however, was the simple fact that they were there." Michael Broers, "Policing the Empire," in Dwyer, *Napoleon and Europe*, 164, 168.

120. Mme de Staël, *Considérations sur la Révolution française*, 425.

121. Stuart Woolf, "Napoléon et l'Italie," in Martin, *Napoléon et l'Europe*, 123. The anti-Franquists in Spain tended to see Napoleonic Spain in the light of a liberal revolution. Lluís Rouray Aulinas, "Napoléon et l'historiographie espagnole," in Martin, *Napoléon et l'Europe*. 142–43. M. Skenowska-Gluck, "Duché de Varsovie," in Tulard, *Dictionnaire*, 1347; Andrei Nieuwazny, "The Polish Kingdom (1815–1830): Continuity or Change?", in David Laven and Lucie Riall, eds., *Napoleon's Legacy* (2001).

122. Anatole France, *La Révolte des anges* (1914), 249.
123. Bluche, *Le bonapartisme*, 82.
124. Geyl, *Napoleon, For and Against*, 389.
125. Thus, Geoffrey Ellis, who adds: "He evidently believed that he was the personification, the individual summation, of all those domains, rather than the servant of a higher French civilization, the mere instrument of its dissemination across Europe." "The Nature of Napoleonic Imperialism," in Dwyer, *Napoleon and Europe*, 113.
126. Philip Dwyer, in ibid.; Luigi Mascilli Migliorini, *Il Mito dell'eroe* (1984) and *Napoleone* (2002).
127. J. M. Thompson, *Napoleon Bonaparte*, 183.
128. "It is therefore likely that there would have been serious disorders even had Napoleon never been born." Esdaile, "Popular Resistance," in Dwyer, *Napoleon and Europe*, 137. See J. R. Aymes, *La Guerre d'indépendance espagnole, 1808–1814* (1973); G. Lovett, *Napoleon and the Birth of Modern Spain*, 2 vols. (1965); David Gates, *The Spanish Ulcer: A History of the Peninsular War* (1986); Esdaile, *The Wars of Napoleon* (1995); R. Hocquellet, "La nation espagnole face à Napoléon: résistance et collaboration," in Martin, *Napoléon et l'Europe*; F. Lafage, *L'Espagne de la contre-révolution: développement et déclin. XVIIIe–XXe siècles* (1993); J. L. Tone, *The Fatal Knot: The Guerrilla War in Navarre and the Defeat of Napoleon in Spain* (1994).
129. Nearly half (28,000) of the priests held no parish functions whatever, but simply lived off the Spanish Church's immense landholdings. Jacques-Olivier Boudon, *Napoléon et les cultes* (2002), 246.
130. See Napoleon's long and very interesting if rambling disquisition on Spain, given to Caulaincourt, in 1812. Caulaincourt, *Avec l'Empereur de Moscou à Fontainebleau* (1968 ed.), 248.
131. Talleyrand would claim years later (in his *Memoirs*) he had opposed the Spanish venture, but at the time he did not. His reference to "the House of France" refers to Louis XIV, who had deeply engaged the French kingdom in Spanish affairs by setting up his family on the vacant Spanish throne.
132. They viewed "the nation" not in modern nationalist or nationality terms, but as a traditional "community of common destiny." See Pierre Vilar, *La Catalogne dans l'Espagne moderne: recherches sur les fondements économiques des structures nationales* (1962), vol. 1. The British generals well understood that the forces they backed in Spain bore many grudges against fellow Spaniards, not just against the French.
133. "Crowned prefect" is Paul Schroeder's name for the kings of Bavaria, Holland, Westphalia, etc. *The Transformation of European Politics*, 337.
134. Francis I's first two wives had died. Maria Ludovica was a member of the branch of the Habsburg family that had recently been replaced as rulers of Tuscany by Napoleon's sister Pauline.
135. Nominally, the fifth coalition against France contained Austria, Britain, and the Spanish insurgents. The French alliance included, besides enlarged France, Bavaria, Saxony, Württemberg, Westphalia, the kingdom of Italy, etc.
136. Charles J. Esdaile, *The Wars of Napoleon* (1995); Marcel Dunan, *Napoléon et l'Allemagne: Le système continental et les débuts du royaume de Bavière, 1806–1810* (1942); J. Sévilla, *Le Chouan du Tyrol: Andreas Hofer contre Napoléon* (1991); W. Langsam, *The Napoleonic Wars and German Nationalism in Austria* (1930).
137. Besides Chandler and Connelly, see for this campaign Robert M. Epstein, *Napoleon's Last Victory and the Emergence of Modern War* (1994); G. E. Rothenberg, *Napoleon's Great Adversaries: The Archduke Charles and the Austrian Army, 1792–1814* (1982); J. R. Arnold, *Napoleon Conquers Austria: The 1809 Campaign for Vienna* (1995); and Patrick Rambaud, *The Battle* (1997), a fictionalized account of the battle of Aspern-Essling that won the Prix Goncourt.

138. Roederer, *Oeuvres,* 3: 537.

139. See Epstein, *Napoleon's Last Victory,* 59, 69 passim.

140. Maria Walewska was brought to live near the Schoenbrunn. She bore him a son, Alexandre, in 1810 (he already had a natural child, the Comte de Léon, by the actress Eléonore Denuelle). Count Walewski would later play a major role in the Second Empire (1852–70). Maria moved to Paris and later to Elba, to be near the man of whom she wrote: "All my thoughts, all my inspiration, come from him and return to him; he is all my happiness, my future, my life." Constant, Napoleon's valet, records this. See Proctor Patterson Jones, ed., *Napoleon: An Intimate Account of the Years of Supremacy, 1800–1814* (1992), 214. Walewska's Polish husband died in 1815.

141. In strict accounting, Essling was a technical victory for the French in that Archduke Charles was the first to depart the larger field of battle. On the other hand, the French ended the day with half their army imprisoned until a bridge could be rebuilt.

142. Some historians report Lannes's dying words to the Emperor (whom he called "tu") as a diatribe against war, specifically further Napoleonic wars, but the anecdote is apocryphal, added under the Restoration to an authentic manuscript by Cadet de Gassicourt (1812). Lentz, *La Nouvelle Empire,* 470.

143. Talleyrand, *Mémoires* (1989 ed.), 2: 6.

144. Baron Bignon, a Napoleonic diplomat who later wrote an unfinished eleven-volume *Histoire de France depuis le 18 Brumaire jusqu'à la Paix de Tilsit* (1829–41), counted ten occasions before Tilsit that Napoleon might have made a lasting peace but didn't. See Petiteau, "Débats historiographiques," in Martin, *Napoléon et l'Europe,* 24.

145. Philip Dwyer, "Napoleon and the Drive for Glory," in Dwyer, *Napoleon and Europe,* 132.

146. Gabriel Hanotaux, cited in Geyl, *Napoleon, For and Against,* 412.

147. See the moving description by Patrick Rambaud, *The Battle,* 169. Rambaud wrote his account of the battle because Balzac, who intended to write a book about Essling, never got around to it.

148. For this story, see Gchot, "Un régicide allemand, Frédéric Staps," *Revue des Etudes napoléoniennes,* 1922; and Jean Tulard, *Napoléon: Une journée particulière, 12 octobre 1809* (1994).

149. As Tulard puts it, Staps's knife went to Josephine's, not to Napoleon's, heart. *Le Grand Empire,* 140.

150. Edited and introduced by Marc Raeff (1991). For von Baldinger, see Annedore Haberl, "La Destinée d'un officier bavarois au temps de Napoléon," *Revue de l'Institut Napoléonien* 184, 1 and 2 (2002): 45–83, 33–69.

151. For the Prussian revival, see Constantin de Grunwald, *Stein, l'ennemi de Napoléon* (1936); Brendan Simms, *The Impact of Napoleon: Prussian High Politics, Foreign Policy and the Crisis of the Executive, 1797–1806* (1997); Peter Paret, *Yorck and the Era of Prussian Reform, 1807–1815* (1966).

152. Napoleon appealed for a national insurrection in Hungary in 1809 (as he did not earlier), but it in fact did not succeed; the Magyar nobility stuck by its old (albeit ambivalent) tie to the Habsburgs. The Hungarian nation was an aristocratically generated idea and entity; it would require most of the nineteenth century for nation to become a popular, democratic idea. D. Kosary, *Napoléon et la Hongrie* (1977). Nor did the long-promised English invasion—a helter-skelter amphibious operation that deposited 44,000 British troops on the Dutch coast in later July 1809 (i.e, too late to help the Austrians)—foment a people's revolt in the Low Countries. French authorities, notably Fouché, reacted swiftly, their efforts aided by an outbreak of disease among the British troops. In December the Royal Navy ferried away what remained of the British expeditionary force marooned at Walcheren.

153. Michael Broers points out in "Popular Resistance to the Napoleonic Empire," in Dwyer, *Napoleon and Europe,* 156. As Hew Strachan observes, the *ancien régime* "preferred to adopt the trappings of the Nation-in-Arms rather than its essence." "The Nation-in-Arms," in Geoffrey Best, ed., *The Permanent Revolution: The French Revolution and Its Legacy, 1789–1989* (1989), 63.

154. A saying of Frederick II (Hohenstaufen) in his confrontation with Pope Innocent IV in the thirteenth century. E. Kantorowicz, *Frederick II* (1931).

155. For pope and Emperor, see Boudon, *Napoléon et les cultes* (2002); Ph. Boutry, "Pio VII," *Enciclopedia dei Papi* (2000) 3: 509–29; Jean Leflon, "Pie VII, face à Napoléon," *Revue de l'Institut Napoléon* 131 (1975): 3–19; Bernardine Melchior-Bonnet, *Napoléon et le pape* (1958); Robin Anderson, *Pope Pius VII* (2000); E. E. Y. Hales, *The Emperor and the Pope: The Story of Napoleon and Pius VII* (1961); André Latreille, *Napoléon et le Saint-Siège, 1801–1808: L'ambassade du Cardinal Fesch à Rome* (1936) and *L'Eglise catholique et la Révolution française,* vol. 2, 1800–1815 (1970); d'Haussonville, *L'Eglise romaine et le Premier Empire, 1800–1814* (1868–1869); G. de Grandmaison, *Napoléon et les cardinaux noirs, 1810–1814* (1895); Henri Welschinger, *Le Pape et l'Empereur, 1804–1815* (1905).

156. One bishop of renowned integrity, Grégoire, a former Constitutional bishop, contrasted the imperial catechism with "a national one" (*Essai historique,* 227)–the sort of distinction Napoleon strongly objected to.

157. Cited in Hales, *The Emperor and the Pope,* 84.

158. As Napoleon had stated it earlier, "Your Holiness may be sovereign of Rome, but I am its emperor." Pius VII pointed out that Charlemagne had merely confirmed the pope in his sovereignty over Rome and surrounding areas, and had given him further lands. The Holy Roman Emperor, however, had made no claim to temporal authority over the pope. Welschinger, *Le Pape et l'Emperor,* 56.

159. Alquier, it seems, too forcefully reminded Paris that nothing would overcome the obstinacy of a man (Pius) who sincerely believed the Church profited from misfortune and testing. "You do not know this man," he wrote Talleyrand. H. Perrin de Boussac, *Un témoin de la Révolution et de l'Empire: Charles Jean-Marie Alquier, 1752–1826* (1983). I should like to thank the present day descendant of Alquier, Admiral Philippe Alquier, for permission to view his ancestor's letters and other documents.

160. The French chargé d'affaires, Lefebvre, surmised that left to their own devices, most of the Sacred College would have voted to join the French confederation.

161. Radet (1762–1825) would spend much of his subsequent life trying to justify his action. See the *Mémoires du général Radet* (1892).

162. A clever Italian saying had it that "Pius VI, in order to save the faith, lost the Holy See, while Pius VII, in order to save the Holy See, lost the faith."

163. "If you knew what a life of anguish I lead, day and night–the constant grief–you would better understand what at times makes a tempest in my heart," he told an Austrian representative who was permitted to see him. He told the prefect Chabrol: "Don't be taken in by my apparent serenity." Cited in Leflon, "Pie VII, face à Napoléon," 14.

CHAPTER XII: THE GREAT UNRAVELING (1810–1812)

1. Bernard Chevallier and Christophe Pincemaille, *L'Impératrice Joséphine* (1988).

2. Cardinal Fesch, who had married Napoleon and Josephine, the night before the coronation, protested the religious orthodoxy of the ceremony he performed, but just the lack of witnesses was irregular. Jean Leflon asks: Did Napoleon, at the time (1804), wish the ceremony unwitnessed, against the day he would need to dissolve it? "Pie VII, face à Napoléon," 131.

3. The title was similar to that once given to the sons of Holy Roman Emperors: "King of the Romans." Alan Palmer, *Napoleon & Marie Louise: The Emperor's Second Wife* (2001); Frédéric Masson, *L'Impératrice Marie-Louise, 1809–1815* (1902).

4. And went to the same place, Rome, where Letizia also lived. Louis tried his hand at writing novels, and proved himself no master.

5. For the effect on the former revolutionaries, see Isser Woloch, *Napoleon and His Collaborators* (2001), 168. See also Louis Madelin, *La Crise de l'Empire, 1810–1811* (1945).

6. Annie Jourdan sees Napoleon as torn between his desire to go down in history as a Maecenas and his desire to impress the world with pomp and luxury, in accordance with the image of himself as Emperor and sovereign. *Napoléon, héros, imperator, mécène* (1998), 184.

7. The Emperor succeeded "because he and his collaborators listened to what most segments of the local elite wanted and provided it, . . . within the context of a centralized state" that proclaimed the "principles of 1789" and abided by juridical norms and constitutional procedures. Jeff Horn, "Building the New Regime: Founding the Bonapartist State in the Department of the Aube," *French Historical Studies* 25, 2 (2002): 262–63. Thierry Lentz goes so far as to say that imperial practice, even after 1810, was a sign of the final death throes of absolutism. *Nouvelle histoire,* 520.

8. G. Daly, "Merchants and Maritime Commerce in Napoleonic Normandy," *French History* 15, 1 (2001): 26–50.

9. H. G. Wells, *The Outline of History* (1920).

10. The words are those of Cardinal Boisgelin de Cucé, bishop of Tours. Cited in B. Ardura et al., *Le Concordat entre Pie VII et Bonaparte* (2001), 108.

11. Not that they tried: *Don José Primero* and his civil administration had no formal control or informal influence over the marshals, who answered to Napoleon and scorned Joseph's liberal aspirations to "incarnate the Spanish nation." The Emperor, for his part, did not stand by his brother while the war was going on, nor yet allow him to abdicate.

12. Cited in Thierry Lentz, *Nouvelle histoire,* 522.

13. For the crisis, see Odette Viennet, *Napoléon et l'industrie française. La crise de 1810–1811* (1947); P. Coftier et P. Dartiguenave, *Révolte à Caen, 1812* (1999); Fernand Braudel and Ernest Labrousse, *Histoire économique et sociale de la France,* vol. 3, *1789–1880* (1993). See the excellent summary of First Empire economic historiography in Natalie Petiteau, *Napoléon, de la mythologie à l'histoire* (1999), 331–56. I am grateful to Thierry Lentz for permitting me to read the pages he devotes to recounting and analyzing this crisis ("L'ébranlement de l'économie") in his forthcoming volume 2 of his *Nouvelle Histoire du Premier Empire.*

14. One rather threatening one, of May 1811, read "We have been to get the Baker and the Baker's wife [i.e., Louis XVI and Marie-Antoinette], now we shall get the Butcher [Napoleon]." Cited in Michael Sibalis, unpublished paper, 36.

15. C. Lesage, *Napoléon Ier, créancier de la Prusse (1807–1814)* (1924), 209 passim. The Emperor forgave—though not without a groan or three—the unpaid balance of the Austrian war debt to France, when he married Marie-Louise.

16. For a good summary, see Geoffrey Ellis, *The Napoleonic Empire* (1991), 104–5.

17. Cited in Roger Dufraisse, "Le Blocus continental," in Jean Tulard, *Dictionnaire,* 233. Georges Lefebvre: *Napoleon: From Tilsit to Waterloo* (1969), 130.

18. Paul Schroeder, *The Transformation of European Politics,* 310.

19. Francis d'Ivernois, *Effets du blocus continental sur le commerce, les finances, le credit et la prosperité des iles britanniques* (1809), 2. See also François Crouzet, "Wars, Blockade, and Economic Change in Europe, 1792–1815," *Journal of Economic History* 24 (1967), 567–88.

20. See the remarkably searching and honest study by François Crouzet, *De la supériorité de l'Angleterre sur la France? L'économique et l'imaginaire, XVIIe-XXe siècle* (1999).

21. Tony Judt, "The French Difference," *New York Review of Books*, April 12, 2001, 19. Niall Ferguson writes persuasively of the unique combination of profit motive, religious evangelicalism, and colonial emigration to account for Britain's unrivaled success in empire-building. *Empire: How Britain Made the Modern World* (2003).

22. Even as fair-minded an observer as Chaptal described Britain as a country "identified with, all but incorporated into, commerce." *De l'Industrie française* (1993 ed.), 211.

23. What is most curious is how similar Napoleonic criticisms of the British political economy of his time were to current (twenty-first century) French criticisms of the American trade deficits, debt-financed policies, and economic "imperialism."

24. "And so the dominant classes of our country showed themselves ready for a lasting unfaithfulness to the very philosophy of progress that had opened the way to their success." Louis Bergeron, *France Under Napoleon* (1981), 204.

25. Crouzet holds that if Napoleon had won in Russia, he could have maintained sufficient pressure on Britain that she would probably have left the war. *L'Economie britannique et le blocus continental, 1806–13* (1958), 2:804. Frank Darvall, *Popular Disturbances and Public Order in Regency England* (1934), 306–12, demonstrates that if a revolutionary movement were going to arise in Great Britain in this era, the year 1812 would have given it its most likely chances of success than at any other time in modern British history.

26. Karl Marx, *The Holy Family* (1975 ed.), 145.

27. Louis Bergeron, "Problèmes economiques de la France napoléonienne," *Revue d'histoire moderne et contemporaine* (1970), 504–5.

28. The phrase is Jean-Louis Billoret's, cited in Francis Démier, *Nation, marché et développement dans la France de la Restauration* (1991), 159.

29. Napoleon on St. Helena will repackage himself as a free trader.

30. Jean-Baptiste Say, France's leading free-trade economist of the era, supported the Consular regime and served it in the Tribunate. Admired by Napoleon, Say was "invited" to add a defense of the regime to his classic *Treatise on Political Economy* (1803), this work being one that Napoleon largely approved of. Say declined, and by 1804 he had broken with Napoleon, *but not over economic issues*. A careful read of Richard Whatmore's *Republicanism and the French Revolution, An Intellectual History of Jean-Baptiste Say's Political Economy* (2000) reveals that the two men shared a number of fundamental views.

31. Mercantilism is the politico-economic philosophy that holds that a State should try to attain self-sufficiency at the financial expense of other States; it is a State-oriented notion of "the economic." It preceded and stood in contrast to the doctrine of free trade, which held that the welfare of all is best served by the welfare of each (entrepreneur), and that each economic agent is the best judge of his own interests and maker of his own decisions.

32. In his accusatory letter of July 1, 1812 (#18878), he reminds the tsar that he (Alexander) had promised "to act as my second in my duel with England." Napoleon notes that he had tolerated menacing language from Alexander that better characterized "the sort of language the Empress Catherine might have used to the last kings of Poland."

33. Napoleon had wanted to build a single-span bridge in iron where the Pont Alexandre III (a single-span bridge) currently sits, but his engineers said it was not possible in the current state of their science.

34. "Alexander's diplomacy remained in many respects amateurish, always fluctuating with the various personal influences to which he was open. The notion which attracted him most was that of succeeding Napoleon as Continental dictator."

G. J. Renier, *Great Britain and the Establishment of the Kingdom of the Netherlands (1813–1816)* (1930), 36. See also P. K. Grimsted, *The Foreign Ministers of Alexander I: Political Attitudes and the Conduct of Foreign Policy, 1801–1825* (1969). The classic study remains Albert Vandal, *Napoléon et Alexandre Ier,* 3 vols. (1891–96). ·

35. Roger Dufraisse and M. Kerautret, *La France napoléonienne: Aspects extérieurs* (1999), 148. As war approached in 1812, Alexander settled his conflict with Turkey at any cost, retroceding Moldavia and Wallachia but keeping Bessarabia.

36. Russia agreed to join the economic war against England, but not to ruin herself or become an economic vassal of France. By 1810 Alexander realized that Britain was suffering less commercially than her adversaries.

37. Napoleon also had a State interest: Oldenburg's northern coastline was open to trade with Britain, and "needed" to be closed off. It is also true that the duke was offered compensation elsewhere.

38. Oleg Sokolov (professor at the University of St. Petersburg), "La Campagne de Russie/V," *Napoléon Ier,* July/August 2001, 47.

39. Champagny also advised strongly against an invasion of Russia. Napoleon replaced him with Maret, Napoleon's political chief of staff and a man without diplomatic experience or talent—but even more pliable than Champagny. For Russian preparations, see *La Guerre nationale de 1812* (Publication du Comité scientifique du grand état-major russe, c. 1900). Napoleon, too, had been thinking about war, however, and in 1810 had requested extensive maps and documentation about Russia from his War Ministry.

40. Bernadotte had assumed the Swedish succession with no enthusiasm or help from Napoleon, and the two men continued to dislike and mistrust each other. Too, Sweden was traditionally counterrevolutionary; moreover, her trade was being ruined by adherence to the continental system. Nevertheless, she would probably have sided with the French—until, that is, Napoleon's occupation of Pomerania drove her to the other side.

41. I am taking Sokolov's view, but for a contrast—albeit not nearly as anchored in military sources—see Schroeder.

42. The phrase is Schroeder's, *Transformation of European Politics,* 314.

43. For the campaign, see (besides David Chandler) E. Cazalas, *La Guerre nationale de 1812,* 7 vols. (1904–11); Otto von Pivka, *Armies of 1812* (1977); Nigel Nicolson, *Napoleon: 1812* (1985); Curtis Cate, *The War of the Two Emperors: The Duel Between Napoleon and Alexander, Russia, 1812* (1985); and Oleg Sokolov, "La Campagne de Russie," in six installments of *Napoléon Ier,* January–June 2001. A classic contemporary telling is Philippe-Paul de Ségur, *Napoleon's Russian Campaign* (1958 ed.). An excellent short summary is Jacques Garnier, "Campagne de Russie," in Jean Tulard, *Dictionnaire.*

44. Henri Troyat, *Alexander of Russia* (1982), 140.

45. It has been maintained that if anyone had advised Louis XIV to invade Russia, he would have found the idea "silly" (Orville T. Murphy, "Napoleon's International Politics: How Much Did He Owe to the Past?" *Journal of Military History* 54 (1990): 167; Philip Dwyer, "Napoleon and the Drive for Glory," in Dwyer, *Napoleon and Europe,* 132. This is only true, given two factors: Louis's far-from-limitless martial accomplishments and abilities, and, above all, given that France and Russia did not quarrel at the time. If the Sun King had won his every campaign, and if he and Peter the Great had clashed, then the notion of a French attack on the realm of the Muscovites could *easily* have been bruited at Versailles.

46. Technically speaking, this was the war of the sixth coalition (Russia, Sweden, and England vs. France, etc.), though it is universally referred to as just "the Russian campaign."

47. The main force, directly under Napoleon, was mostly French in nationality; the two wings were mostly Italian, German, and Polish. Small Austrian and Prussian forces also marched with the French. The French, by the way, marched in British-made coats—another instance of the Continental System bowing to need, but only Napoleon's.

48. Marshal Auguste de Marmont, *Mémoires de 1792 à 1841* (1856–57), 5: 122. Marmont continues: "If his brain was precisely what it had always been—the vastest, deepest, and most productive that ever was—there was yet no more willpower or resolution, and there was an instability that resembled weakness."

49. Another Russian general, Bagration, wrote General Ermolov, "I am ashamed to wear my uniform." Sokolov, "La Campagne de Russie/II," 43.

50. "He was always asking me what I thought of the Russian movements," writes Caulaincourt. "He wanted to get me to say that they would stand and give battle, as he wished. He was like a man who needs consolation. But believing the opposite—that the Russians would continue to retire—I told him so frankly."

51. The French refer to the battle of the Moscowa (river), while the Russians refer to it as the battle of Borodino.

52. Robert Epstein writes: "What Napoleon did not realize, and would never grasp, was that as opposing armies modernized, the likelihood of winning a decisive battle diminished. . . . None of the major battles [since Wagram] resulted in decisive victory. Which isn't to say, as is often said, Napoleon's capacities as a commander were in decline, or that his troops weren't first rate (that would come)." *Napoleon's Last Victory and the Emergence of Modern Warfare* (1994), 176–77, 117.

53. De Ségur, *Napoleon's Russian Campaign*, 103. In fact, however, a number of leading Russian generals felt that Kutuzov made a grave error not to fight another full-dress battle before Moscow's walls.

54. Here, too, Napoleon miscalculated, for he had always believed Russia's peasants to be "superstitious barbarians, of simple ideas," and that "a terrible blow to the great and sainted Moscow" would "deliver up to me these blind, uneducated masses." Whether because he was confident of victory or from fear of losing a "class war" on eastern Europe that even *he* would not be able to "use," Napoleon refrained from calling on the Russian peasants to rise up against their masters, nor did he abolish serfdom in Russia. See Jean Tulard, *Napoléon, la nation, le pouvoir, la légende*, 128–38; Sokolov, "La Campagne de Russie/V."

55. The Comtesse de Gouffier-Choiseul. Cited in Troyat, *Alexander of Russia*, 159.

56. De Ségur, *Napoleon's Russian Campaign*, 109.

57. The outraged Caulaincourt refused the assignment, so Napoleon sent another diplomat, Narbonne.

58. Owen Connelly, *Blundering to Glory* (1987), 177.

59. Colonels John Elting and Vincent Esposito, in Alastair Horne, *How Far from Austerlitz? Napoleon, 1805–1815* (1996), 323. The last line is a quote from Napoleon.

60. Brendan Simms, "Britain and Napoleon," in Dwyer, *Napoleon and Europe*, 200.

61. Both figures include the reinforcements that arrived in the theatre of operations. The men died of illness, hunger, heat, cold, fatigue, and wounds. Sokolov, "La Campagne de Russie/VI." In truth, there is no consensus among scholars as to the casualty count of this campaign. Some set Russian (and French) casualties much lower. See the discussion in Alexander Martin, "The Russian Empire and the Napoleonic Wars," in Dwyer, *Napoleon and Europe*, 316 n. 22.

62. Percy, an army medic, wrote: "[I]t would seem as if the sick and wounded cease to be human beings when they can no longer be soldiers." Cited in A. Forrest, "The Military Culture of Napoleonic France," in Dwyer, *Napoleon and Europe*, 55.

63. De Ségur, *Napoleon's Russian Campaign*, 243. A soldier wrote to his uncle in an ear-

lier Napoleonic campaign: "I don't think I have ever been as cold as I was that day, and I do not know how the Emperor could put up with it; the soldiers were scarcely able to handle their weapons; but it seemed that his presence warmed us up." Cited in Forrest, "Military Culture of Napoleonic France," 49.

64. "Lannes loved me like a mistress," Napoleon noted, ". . . but he wanted to influence me and he had the character of a political sectarian [*frondeur*]." Caulaincourt, *Avec l'Empereur, de Moscou à Fontainebleau* (1968 ed.), 311.

65. John Lynn, "Toward an Army of Honor," *French Historical Studies* 16, 1 (1989): 165–66.

66. Hannibal was not in fact head of the Carthaginian State when he led the army; that came later. As for Frederick the Great, a great dilettante, he did not have a close relationship with his men. In the modern era, Robert E. Lee, Trotsky, and Eisenhower were only commanders in chief, not heads of State, when they led armies.

67. *La confession d'un enfant du siècle,* cited in Michael Broers, *Europe Under Napoleon* (1996), 1–2.

68. Caulaincourt, *Avec l'Empereur.* Also Jacques Jourquin, "La chevauchée fantastique," *Historia,* January 1984.

69. My thanks to Jacques Garnier for this thought.

70. Finally, he deludes himself entirely about the repose and restoration he believes his army will find when, presently, it regains Vilna, in Lithuania. Thanks to recent archeological digs, we are now more aware than before of the human catastrophe that awaited the residue of the Grande Armée in a frozen Vilna, which offered vastly insufficient food, medicine, clothing, shelter–or goodwill. Tens of thousands in the French army would meet death where they sought salvation. *New York Times,* September 14, 2002.

71. A contemporary–albeit not a trustworthy witness–claims in memoirs writ long after 1812 to have seen in the imperial baggage at the time the elements for a coronation, to be held at Moscow, in which Napoleon would have been crowned Emperor of the East as well. The witness was a French émigré general in service to the tsar, Andrault de Langeron, who claimed that the pope was to have participated in the coronation, and Napoleon's first act as Universal Monarch would have been to reunite Orthodox and Catholic Christianity. A French scholar, André Ratchinski, credits Langeron (*Napoléon et Alexandre I* [2002]), as does Dwyer, *Napoleon and Europe,* 131. Jean Tulard notes, in his preface to Ratchinski, that the "documents are insufficient, notably there are no specific orders of Napoleon to prove Mr. Ratchinski's assertion."

72. Napoleon also concedes that he has treated the "napoleonide" rulers as scarcely more than crowned proconsuls. Caulaincourt, for his part, wishes "all of Europe" could see this side of the Emperor. "All of Europe" doubtless would have preferred the removal of the French gendarme or customs agent.

Chapter XIII: The Collapse (1812–1814)

1. 1754–1812. See Bernardine Melchior-Bonnet, *La conspiration de Général Malet* (1963); G. Artom, *23 Octobre 1812: Napoléon est mort en Russie* (1969); Louis de Villefosse and Janine Bouissounouse, *L'Opposition à Napoléon* (1969), 301–11; Jacques-Olivier Boudon, *Histoire du Consulat et de l'Empire* (2000), 366–75; Thierry Lentz, *Savary* (2001), 309–26.

2. The archival records of the Malet affair are relatively sparse, in sharp contrast to the abundant data we luxuriate in about most aspects of Napoleonic history. Many documents disappeared under the Restoration (1815–30), when the principals in the affair or their heirs and successors removed them from the archives of the Min-

istry of Police. Elizabeth Sparrow, *Secret Service: British Agents in France, 1792–1815* (1999), 353–55, 392–94.

3. His co-conspirator, General Lahorie, compared their coup to the coup of 18 Brumaire.

4. Napoleon insisted to Caulaincourt. "What could [they] have hoped for from a Malet that they have not received from me?" He added: "How blind men are, even to their true interest!" The loyal Caulaincourt did not suggest that this apothegm could apply to His Majesty as well. Napoleon fired Frochot.

5. Talleyrand's sotto voce reply: "What a shame that such a great man is so ill-bred." It was said of Talleyrand that he could be kicked in the ass a dozen times without his face's betraying it to anyone looking at him." Duff Cooper, *Talleyrand* (1932), 86, 187.

6. To the tune of 1.4 million francs. Napoleon purchased a mansion from Talleyrand for considerably more than it was worth. Méneval, in Proctor Patterson Jones, ed., *Napoleon: An Intimate Account of the Years of Supremacy, 1800–1814* (1992), 326.

7. See Paul Schroeder, *The Transformation of European Politics,* 467–68.

8. He discussed his own retirement palace—a Sans-Souci that was to be "comfortable, for a convalescent, or for a man as age approaches." Constant, in Proctor Jones, *Napoleon,* 384–85.

9. Isser Woloch, *Napoleon and His Collaborators* (2001), 214.

10. Cambacérès, *Mémoires inédites,* 2: 17.

11. Henri Welschinger, *Le Pape et l'Empereur, 1804–1815* (1905), 220.

12. Fesch wrote: "You say you like it when people tell you what they are really thinking, and you say you will not take offense when they do. . . . [Then, know that] there is forming within me a conviction that I cannot refuse." Cited in Welschinger, *le Pape et l'Emperor,* 259.

13. Fesch wrote Madame Mère: "I foresee he will be brought down and utterly defeated. All who touch the Holy Ark, the Supreme Pontiff, suffer the same fate. My nephew is lost, but the Church is saved; for if the Emperor had returned in triumph from Moscow, who knows to what further lengths he would have gone?" (R. Anderson, *Pope Pius VII,* 137). Extraordinary confession from a churchman who, more than any other, has built the Napoleonic Church.

14. It is not true, however, as is sometimes reported, that Napoleon shook Pius by his soutane, or that the pope later called the Emperor an "actor" disparagingly.

15. Jacques-Olivier Boudon, *Napoléon et les cultes* (2002), 332.

16. See the article on Pio VII in *Enciclopedia dei Papi,* vol. 3 (2000).

17. Albert Sorel, *Les écrivains français* (1890), 33.

18. Michael Sibalis, unpublished paper, 30

19. John Holland Rose, *The Life of Napoleon I* (1901), 2: 267.

20. As Isser Woloch writes, the response to the draft of 1812–13 was "unprecedented . . . , clearly more than a temporary response to *force majeure* . . . It should be viewed as a structural mutation—not in attitude, for conscription remained unpopular, but in behavior. An instinctive and by now traditional resistance to conscription was giving way to a grudging compliance." *The New Regime* (1994), 418.

21. The later political philosopher whose analysis of this period of "German" history may be preferable to Clausewitz is Carl Schmitt. His *Theorie der Partisanen: Zwischenbemerkung zur Begriff der Politischen* (1975 ed.) focuses on the "friend/enemy" distinction as the root of "the political," a theme developed in Schmitt's later books.

22. Rose, *Life of Napoleon I,* 2: 237.

23. For this later Prussian revival, see Karen Hagemann, *"Mannlicher Muth und Teutscher Ehre": Nation, Militär und Geschlecht zur Zeit der Antinapoleonischer Kriege Preussens* (2002); W. Simon, *The Failure of the Prussian Reform Movement, 1807–1819* (1971); and

Matthew Levinger, *Enlightened Nationalism: The Transformation of Prussian Political Culture, 1806–1848* (2000); Schroeder, *Transformation of European Politics*, 450–59.

24. The term is used so loosely today that we commonly refer to Islamic nationalism, though it is, at best, a metaphor, if not a misnomer, to speak of a religion as a nation. Similarly, we speak of "Babylonian nationalism," though it is clear that ancient Middle Eastern empires were nothing like nations, as we understand them.

25. When the reformer-general Gneisenau placed before his king a plan for a "rising of the Prussian people," Frederick William returned it with the comment "very nice— as poetry." Such a "rising" lay closer to what the king was fighting *against,* not for. Philip Bobbitt, *The Shield of Achilles: War, Peace, and the Course of History* (2002).

26. Levinger, *Enlightened Nationalism*, 241.

27. The process is not dissimilar to the action of later generations of fourth- and fifth-century Christian apostles claiming that Jesus and the disciples had intentionally founded a papal Church and orthodoxy.

28. Not to mention the threat "Germany" posed to the Habsburg emperor, whose central realm (Austria) was German. Brendan Simms speaks of the "primacy of foreign policy" for these middle-rank German states, whose sovereigns faced annihilation by being subsumed into "Germany." *The Struggle for Mastery in Germany,* 1779–1850 (1998), 130–46.

29. Bobbitt reverses the usual phrase to emphasize the degree to which the State conscientiously employs nation-talk to define itself and enforce its now greatly enhanced authority. In England, too, we may speak of a national rebirth in this period. See Linda Colley, *Britons: Forging the Nation, 1707–1837* (1992). "Nationalism," however, is a term of late-nineteenth-century coinage, and best describes political phenomena that were corruptions and caricatures of the original national events of a century earlier.

30. Clausewitz, *On War,* 671.

31. By the secret Treaty of Reichenbach (June 27), Austria associated herself with Prussia and Russia.

32. Schroeder, *Transformation of European Politics,* 485–500. Metternich, in his memoirs, claims he "knew all along" that Napoleon would reject reasonable terms, and that therefore Austria would join the Allies. It is more likely, as Schroeder notes, that at the time Metternich didn't know himself what was going to happen, and was steering through the fog like everyone else.

33. Also her fleet was in British hands, where the Russians had placed it, to avoid losing it to the French.

34. The French public, however, was kept in the dark, to conclude that the Allied peace offer was made in bad faith.

35. Digby Smith (a.k.a. Otto von Pivka) shows that the desertion of the Saxons had to do with their assessment of the likelihood of a French defeat, their treatment at French hands, and their king's ambivalence about the French alliance, more than with German national consciousness. *1813, Leipzig: Napoleon and the Battle of the Nations* (2001), 226–36.

36. The kings of Bavaria, Saxony, and Württemberg joined the Coalition for sound geopolitical motives—they figured Napoleon was a losing bet, and Austria was promising them they could keep their kingdoms—not primarily patriotic ones, flattering as it was to imply so afterwards. These rulers might have been able to foment a national uprising, but they were mortally afraid to try to do so.

37. Italy was the reverse of France. Here the popular classes hated the Napoleonic regime, and the middle class served and respected it. In France, the peasants and workers were loyal, and the coddled nobility were quick to defect. "The revolutionary-Napoleonic state had put down firmer foundations "abroad" than in much

of south and western France. . . . [Truly] Napoleonic Europe was not always synonymous with France." Michael Broers, *Europe Under Napoleon, 1799–1815* (1996), 251, 257.

38. January 26, 1814. Napoleon goes on: "You gave in to the weakness of your nature. You are a good soldier on the field of battle, but off it, you are without vigor and without character! Profit from this act of treason that I attribute only to fear to serve me more usefully. I count on you, on your repentance and your promises."

39. Murat's actions were mainly motivated by his ambition to conserve his throne, but the words he chose for his proclamation have resonance: "I have no further illusions. The Emperor wants war. I would be betraying the interests of my former *patrie,* my own State, and [the rest of Italy] if I did not immediately separate my arms from his. . . . Soldiers! There are but two banners in Europe. On one you may read: religion, morality, justice, moderation, law, peace, and welfare; on the other: artifice, violence, persecution, war, and mourning in every family. Choose."

40. For 1814, see Pierre Miquel, *La campagne de France de Napoléon* (1991); David Hamilton-Williams, *The Fall of Napoleon: The Final Betrayal* (1994); François Rude, "Le reveil du patriotisme révolutionnaire dans la région Rhône-Alpes," *Cahiers d'Histoire* (1971), 433–55; Félix Ponteil, *La chute de Napoléon Ier, et la crise française de 1814–15* (1943); F. Benaerts, *Les commissaries extraordinaires de Napoléon Ier en 1815* (1915); Henry Houssaye, *1814* (1888).

41. Adolphe Thiers, *L'Histoire du Consulat et de l'Empire,* 17: 21.

42. Napoleon nationalized village property, then turned around and sold it to the wealthy, thus denuding thousands of local communities of their precious communal property. See Isser Woloch, *Napoleon and His Collaborators,* 216.

43. Savary, *Mémoires,* 6: 202.

44. Thiers, *Histoire du Consulat et de l'Empire,* xvii, 171.

45. "I am not acquainted with your affairs," he told the Emperor, who only a week before had covered him in invective reminiscent of 1809. The ex-minister was well aware of His Majesty's need for his Grand Chamberlain.

46. Pierre-Joseph Proudhon, *Napoléon Ier* (1898), 46.

47. See Baron Fain's description of this year in his *Manuscrit de l'an 1814* (1823).

48. Count Mollien, *Mémoire d'un ministre du Trésor public (1789–1815)* (1898), 3: 116.

49. Some of Napoleon's letters in this winter might have been written from the Russian campaign. "The army is dying of hunger," Napoleon wrote to the quartermaster-commissioner, February 8, 1814, #21214.

50. According to a leading current French military historian, Montmirail was "a great victory, the best of the campaign." It highlights the difference in clarity and speed of judgment between Blücher, no slouch—who thought he was dealing only with the French flank guard, when in truth it was Napoleon's army—and the French Emperor, who, also initially confused, immediately saw the opportunity in the confusion of his opponent. Jacques Garnier, "La campagne de France (II)," *Napoléon Ier* 19 (March/April 2003), 45–46.

51. "Napoleon displayed during these last ten days a fertility of resource, a power to drive back the tide of events, that have dazzled posterity, as they dismayed his foes. We may seek in vain for a parallel, save perhaps in the careers of Hannibal and Frederick. . . . But their star had never set so low as that of Napoleon's after La Rothière, and never did it rush to the zenith with a splendor like that which blinded the trained hosts of Blücher and Schwarzenberg. . . . [T]here is something that defies analysis in Napoleon's sudden transformation of his beaten dispirited band into a triumphant array before which four times their numbers sought refuge in retreat. . . . Where analysis fails, there genius begins." Rose, *Life of Napoleon,* 2: 397–98.

52. Metternich to Caulaincourt, in the latter's *Mémoires,* 1: 214.

53. Prosecutor's report, February 12, 1814; cited in Michael Sibalis, unpublished paper, 32.
54. Aberdeen was British emissary to Vienna. Cited in Rose, *Life of Napoleon I,* 374.
55. Caulincourt, *Mémoires,* 3: 40; 2: 11, 15–17.
56. The historian Frédéric Bluche compares the king's letter to De Gaulle's famous "appeal of 18 June" made from London in 1940. *Louis XIV* (1986), 797–800.
57. "When he no longer makes war for the army, he will make peace for the French, and then he will become King of France." Schwarzenberg (April 15, 1813), cited in Rose, *Life of Napoleon I,* 2: 368.
58. Some historians disagree. Thus, Charles Esdaile: "If the Emperor fought on, he did not do so because France, the principles of the Revolution, or even his own dynasty, were in danger. On the contrary, he fought on because he could not accept the limitations that the powers were now determined to place on his influence. Far from France betraying Napoleon, then, it was rather Napoleon who betrayed France." *The Wars of Napoleon* (1995), 284. For Napoleon to have betrayed France, he would have had to be in conscious bad faith with her, as he was not, in this campaign.
59. January 1, 1814, Hartwell House, England.
60. Thiers writes of Pozzo: "It takes a rare kind of arrogance to be jealous of a genius like Napoleon" (*Histoire du Consulat et de l'Empire,* 17: 114). At St. Helena, Napoleon credited Pozzo with convincing the tsar to march directly on Paris, hence to change the fate of the campaign and the world.
61. Talleyrand even had the personal satisfaction of knowing that he had counseled Joseph and Cambacérès soundly, if disingenuously, in urging that they and the Empress should stand and fight.
62. The Comte d'Artois (brother of Louis XVIII), however, did have to be regularly reminded not to call Talleyrand "Milord, the Bishop of Autun."
63. "Talleyrand," in *Napoléon Ier* 2 (May/June 2000), 53.
64. Talleyrand observed concerning Bernadotte: "Why choose a soldier when you have just discarded the greatest of them all?" See Alan Palmer, *Bernadotte: Napoleon's Marshal, Sweden's King* (1991).
65. The first dynasty to rule France was the Merovingian, then came the Carolingian, and finally, in 986, the house of Hugues Capet, the Capetians—of whom the Bourbons were descendants. Thibaudeau was a former *Conventionnel,* he served Napoleon valuably in the Council of State before being named prefect of the department of the Bouches-du-Rhône (which includes Marseille). A loyal servant of the Empire, he was also a strong supporter of the Revolution, and perhaps for that reason, Napoleon wanted him out of Paris after the Habsburg marriage. *Mémoires* (1913), 375.
66. Thiers, *Histoire du Consulat et de l'Empire,* 17: 646.
67. But just to show that this wasn't all merely business and that a degree of animus was alive and well in senatorial hearts, the senators and the provisional government appointed General Dupont, languishing in a Napoleonic prison, as minister of war. Curiously, too, as Tulard notes, the Paris Municipal Council, acting on its own, in no concert with Talleyrand or the Senate, had already voted a proclamation disavowing their oaths to Napoleon and welcoming the Bourbons. *Les vingt jours: Louis XVII ou Napoléon?* (2001), 22–23.
68. See Gneisenau's intentions, quoted in Gerhard Ritter, *Staatskunst und Kriegshandwerk* (1954), 110–11.
69. Cited in Ponteil, *La chute de Napoléon,* 86.
70. Thiers, *Histoire du Consulat et de l'Empire,* 17: 697.
71. Leaving 125,000 troops in the German fortresses—an act of vanity and a refusal to

admit the *Grand Empire* was gone—was Napoleon's largest military mistake of the entire campaign.

72. The words are Thiers's, who agrees with this line of reasoning. *Histoire du Consulat et de l'Empire,* 17: 692.

73. The particulars of the defection are worthy of a thriller and a comedy of errors combined, for Marmont changed his mind at the last minute, but his generals—notably General Souham—fearing that Napoleon was onto them, marched to the enemy side. Marmont then had a chance to disown their act, but he did not—on the contrary. For a spirited attempted defense of his forebear, see Gérard Souham, *Le Général Souham* (1990).

74. Thiers, *Histoire du Consulat et de l'Empire,* 17: 717. See also R. Christophe, *Le Maréchal Marmont* (1986); P. Saint-Marc, *Le Maréchal Marmont* (1957).

75. Thiers, *Histoire du Consulat et de l'Empire,* 17: 692.

76. François Piétri forcefully reminds us of Napoleon's respect for legal niceties. "A true dictator," he notes, would, in 1813, have arrested Lainé et al., but Napoleon chose the legal recourse of proroguing the Legislative Body. Now, when the Empire fell, it did so, not due to riots and civil war, but because "the victor of Austerlitz" bowed before the questionably legal vote of a rump in the Senate. *Napoléon et le Parlement* (1955). For a sharp critique of this view, see Charles Durand, *L'exercice de la fonction législative de 1800 à 1814* (1955).

77. "Ah, Caulaincourt, Caulaincourt, men! Men! . . . My marshals would be embarrassed to follow Marmont's conduct, for they speak of him only with indignation but they are just angry that he got the jump on them on the path to good fortune. . . . They would like to acquire the same titles and favors with the Bourbons, without dishonoring themselves, as he did. . . . I had treated him as my child. . . . And I have to say, I counted on him. He is the only man perhaps whom I never suspected of desertion: but vanity, weakness, ambition lost him. The wretched man doesn't know what awaits him; his name will be branded [for always]." Cited in Thiers, *Histoire du Consulat et de l'Empire,* 17: 751.

78. E. E. Y. Hales, *The Emperor and the Pope* (1961), 162.

79. Surely the harshest, most effective attack was Chateaubriand's pamphlet of April 4, in which he deployed to devastating effect General Bonaparte's rude interrogation of the Directory: "What have you done with this France that was so brilliant? What have you done, not with a hundred thousand but five million Frenchmen whom we all know, our parents, our friends, our brothers? . . . Our colonies? Our commerce? . . . You wanted to reign by the sword of Attila and the maxims of Nero." *De Buonaparte, des Bourbons, et de la nécessité de se rallier à nos princes légitimes pour le bonheur de la France et de celui de l'Europe* (1814).

CHAPTER XIV: NATION-TALK: THE LIBERAL EMPIRE

1. To Beugnot, the minister of police. Cited in Louis Madelin, *Fouché,* 2: 321.

2. Corsica was a French possession, and it would have been unseemly for Napoleon to have chosen Corsica, even if he had wanted it, which there is no sign that he did.

3. See Guy Godlewski, *Trois cents jours d'exil: Napoléon à l'île d'Elbe* (1961); Norman MacKenzie, *The Escape from Elba: The Fall and Flight of Napoleon, 1814–1815* (1982); and Fernand Beaucour, "L'île d'Elbe," in Jean Tulard, *Dictionnaire,* 649–52. For this chapter, the classic works are Thomas Babington Macaulay, *Napoleon and the Restoration of the Bourbons* (1977 ed.); Adolphe Thiers, *Histoire du Consulat et de l'Empire,* vols. 19–20; Albert Sorel, *L'Europe et la Révolution française,* vol. 8 (1908); Henry Houssaye, *1814–1815,* vols 3–4 (1898–1905).

4. Metternich assigned her the rather dashing count, who was instructed to all but

seduce the "Archduchess," as Marie-Louise was now called. This is indeed what happened, presently.

5. She stayed only two nights, for Napoleon was worried that spies would inform Marie-Louise of the mistress's visit. Walewska's son by Napoleon, Alexander, would become minister of foreign affairs under Napoleon III.

6. Pons de l'Hérault, the director of the iron mine on Elba, is arch-illustrative of Elban views and their evolution: a firm republican, he was a stern critic of the Emperor's, as he had been a great admirer of General Bonaparte's, but once exposed to "the Emperor," he required hardly a day to regain his admiration—and proved it by following Napoleon back to France, where he was named a prefect.

7. *Mémoires de A. C. Thibaudeau (1799–1815)* (1913), 4: 301.

8. Marmont, *Mémoires de 1792 à 1841* (1856–57), 9: 211.

9. Fernand Beaucour, "Napoléon à l'île d'Elbe," *Napoléon Ier* (January/Frebruary 2001), 10.

10. Far less than Marie-Louise and many of the imperial court possessed. Louis XVIII would presently return to exile, in Belgium, with four million.

11. Mme de Staël even warned the Emperor of plots on his life. Henri Houssaye, *1814*, sifts the evidence for Talleyrand's conspiring to have Napoleon killed, concluding that it cannot be conclusively demonstrated but is quite possible.

12. See Pierre Rosanvallon, *La Monarchie impossible: Les Chartes de 1814 et de 1830* (1994); Stéphane Rials, *Révolution et contre-révolution au XIXe siècle* (1987); Guillaume de Bertier de Sauvigny, *La Restauration* (1990); E. de Waresquiel and Benoît Yvert, *Histoire de la Restauration* (1996).

13. *The Dictionary of Weather Vanes* [*Girouettes*] attributed *girouettes* to various people. Talleyrand saw himself awarded twelve; Fouché thirteen.

14. Rosanvallon's excellent *La Monarchie impossible* discusses this point. Essentially the Bourbon monarchy established itself, intentionally or not, as a neutral center, which did not please its subjects. The French, especially after the Empire, like to know who's on first.

15. The great Whig historian continues: "Napoleon, raised to the thone of France, would have both the inclination and the means." Macaulay, *Napoleon and the Restoration of the Bourbons* (1977 ed.), 91–92.

16. For example, the king, justifying budget reductions that reduced the size of the army, told a group of officers: "Peace has come, we don't need brave men anymore." Lafayette, *Mémoires, correspondance et manuscripts* (1837–38), 5: 86.

17. Thibaudeau, *Mémoires*, 3: 310. Emphasis added. This was not merely a French phenomenon. In 1815 the Genoese petitioned the Congress of Vienna (in vain) to be allowed to return to French rule.

18. Cited in Sorel, *L'Europe et la Révolution française*, 14: 295.

19. Carnot initially called on "Patriots" and "Nationaux" to rally to the king ("Guerre aux pamphlets, ou appel à la postérité") and he wrote a *Mémoire adressé au Roi en Juillet 1814* in which he tells Louis: "What is it that made Napoleon's tyranny bearable for so long? It is the fact that he excited national pride. With what devotion did even those who tested him the most serve him! It was despair alone that finally caused one to abandon his eagles."

20. Some political bodies were selective or self-censoring in how they expressed themselves to the king, especially if they wanted favors. Thus, in April 1814 the Paris Municipal Council, a corps full of nation-talkers in most times, addressed the Comte de Lille/Provence, whom they were inviting to be king, a fawning missive in which no mention is made of "the Nation," only of "our France," "your French," "all the French," "our king," and "his *patrie*." (*Le Moniteur*, March 8).

21. He refers to "this truly national war" against Napoleon.

22. Chateaubriand: "Bonaparte has nothing of a Frenchman [in him]." *De Buonaparte et des Bourbons.*

23. Georges Blond, *Les Cent-Jours: Napoléon seul contre tous* (1983). Cited in Dominique de Villepin, *Les Cent-Jours, ou l'esprit de sacrifice* (2001), 104 n. 3. For this section, see Annie Duprat, "Une guerre des images: Louis XVIII, Napoléon et la France en 1815," *Revue d'histoire moderne et contemporaine* 47, 3 (July–September 2000); 487–504; Jean Tulard, *Les vingt jours (1er–20 mars 1815): Louis XVIII ou Napoléon?* (2001).

24. It is curious, as Michael Sibalis points out, that the workers had not demonstrated on Napoleon's behalf in the spring of 1814, when he was forced to abdicate. On the contrary, the prevailing sentiment in the faubourgs had then been one of relief. Something obviously changed in the interim. Unpublished article, 32.

25. The rapprochement occurred despite the fact that talks among the leaders had broken down in the days preceding Napoleon's return. "Somehow the old revolutionary tradition was far from dead, but had only gone underground. How it got transmitted across the twenty years since Babeuf cannot be answered," Sibalis writes (unpublished article). Contemporaries, by the way, did not capitalize the party name, "bonapartist."

26. Henry Wadsworth Longfellow, "The Day Is Done." The line correctly reads: "Shall fold their tents, like the Arabs, / And as silently steal away."

27. The point is made in Tulard's excellent *Les vingt jours.*

28. On one of several occasions that Napoleon told one of his St. Helena "evangelists" that he wished he had died at Moscow, one of them (Las Cases) pointed out: "But then you would not have lived the extraordinary episode of the return from Elba." "Well, maybe there's something to that," replied the Emperor. "All right then, let's say I should have died at Waterloo." *Mémorial,* November 4, 1816.

29. *Mémoires pour servir à l'histoire,* by Napoleon on St. Helena, cited by Pierre Larousse, *Napoléon* (2002 ed., preface by Maurice Agulhon).

30. "When a government is not solidly established, men for whom conscience does not count, depending on their greater or lesser energy of character, become a quarter, a half, or three-quarters conspirator. They await the decision of fortune; events turn out to make more traitors than opinions do." Chateaubriand, *Mémoires d'outre-tombe,* part 3, book 5, 11.

31. For this section, see Benjamin Constant, *Mémoires sur les Cent-Jours* (1829); L. Radiguet, *L'Acte additionnel aux constitutions de l'Empire du 22 avril 1815* (1911); E. Le Gallo, *Les Cent-Jours: Essai sur l'histoire intérieure de la France depuis le retour de l'île d'Elbe jusqu'à la nouvelle de Waterloo* (1924); Frédéric Bluche, *Le Plébiscite des Cent-Jours* (1974); Alan Schom, *One Hundred Days: Napoleon's Road to Waterloo* (1992); Villepin, *Les Cent-Jours* (2001).

32. "I had conceived magnificent dreams for France. In the days after Marengo, Austerlitz, Jena, Friedland, these dreams were forgivable. I hardly need tell you now that I have renounced them. . . . It is not only peace that France wants, it is also liberty. . . . I have loved unlimited power, and I needed it when I sought to reconstitute France [after the Revolution] and found an immense empire. That is all gone now. . . . I shall be content with a constitutional king's authority. . . . It will be enough for my son to have the power of a king of England! . . . My interest is to live tranquilly and to use the rest of my life to repair the evil that twenty years of war, capped by an invasion, have done to France." Cited in Thiers, *Histoire du Consulat et de l'Empire,* 19: 298, 312, 344.

33. A number of Napoleon's favorite henchmen (e.g., Savary, Montalivet) were too associated with the repressive and authoritarian policies and practices of the old Empire, and so were sacrificed.

34. Fouché had arranged to be chased by the king's police so as to appear more appetizing to Napoleon. As for Talleyrand, he, for once, as Jean Tulard notes, remained loyal and incorruptible. Napoleon did his best to lure him away from Louis XVIII, but Talleyrand stayed on in Vienna, serving the king. *Les vingt jours*, 235–36.

35. *Les Débats*. Constant had compared Napoleon to Genghis Khan and Attila in his pamphlet *The Spirit of Conquest and Usurpation*. His volte-face has gotten Constant into trouble with some historians: e.g., "Again, the character of Benjamin Constant was inferior to his thought" (Louis de Villefosse and Janine Bouissounouse, *L'opposition à Napoléon* [1969], 324). Dominique de Villepin dubs him "Benjamin the Inconstant" (*Les Cent-Jours*, 271), while Napoleon told Bertrand at St. Helena (January 27, 1821) that Constant had, over the years, always wished to work for the Emperor: "I was the one who didn't give it a thought." Marcel Gauchet, however, argues that Constant's "jump from the republican to the monarchical principle occurs within the continuity [of his support of liberalism] so that we could almost call it a natural transition" (*La Révolution des pouvoirs* [1995], 251).

36. Napoleon also had the right of dissolution of the chambers, with a sixth-month delay before elections, in which he could govern by decree. He insisted that the Preamble read that the head of State (himself) "has been replying to the wish of the French nation continuously, since 1799," as though the Restoration hadn't happened. This was, of course, his reply to Louis's placement of himself "in the nineteenth year of Our reign."

37. The British opposition newspaper, *The Morning Chronicle*, however, had a different view: "The Bourbons lost their throne by their own faults. It would be a monstrous thing to make war on a nation in order to try to impose a government it doesn't want!" Cited by Villepin, *Les Cent-Jours*, 400.

38. "The truth of the matter is," Napoleon informed Davout frankly, "there is nothing to any of that. I in fact stand alone against all of Europe. That is my situation. Are you, too, going to abandon me?"

39. Etienne-Denis Pasquier, *Histoire de mon temps: Mémoires du Chancelier Pasquier* (1893–95), 3: 195. Pasquier was in disgrace at this time for having rallied too soon to Louis XVIII.

40. Napoleon's architect, Fontaine, wrote in his journal around this time: "It was impossible for us to rediscover the illusions of the [old] dream. We stayed persuaded that it would all be over soon, yet we knew we must execute the orders we were given." Pierre-François Fontaine, *Journal, 1799–1853*, 2 vols. (1987), 1: 401.

41. Villepin, *Les Cent-Jours*, 244.

42. Jacqueline Chaumié, "Les Girondins et les Cent-Jours," *Annales historiques de la Révolution française* 43, 205 (July–September 1971): 355.

43. Though founded in the west of France, where they arose to combat reborn royalism, the *fédérés* were strongest in Paris and in the eastern departments, which had reeled under the blows of the 1814 invasion. Though mainly lower class, they contained a smattering of all social strata. The authoritative work is R. S. Alexander, *Bonapartism and Revolutionary Tradition in France: The Fédérés of 1815* (1991).

44. Currently the residence of presidents of the French Republic.

45. In their aggressiveness, missionary zeal, and corporateness, the "federated" recalled the civic spirit and unity of the Greeks and Romans more than they did modern liberal individualism. They violently opposed the moderate Liberals like Benjamin Constant, in whose Additional Act they saw an attempt to preempt and contain them.

46. Frédéric Bluche speaks of Napoleon's failure to remain absolute master of his doctrine as "the true revolution of 1815." *Le bonapartisme*, 121.

47. The classic analysis is Bluche's *Le plébiscite des Cent-Jours*. In another work, he con-

cludes that "However you calculate the results, the bonapartists were an electoral minority [touching, at most, one Frenchman in three]." *Le bonapartisme,* 109.

48. Cited in Andrew Roberts, *Napoleon and Wellington* (2002), 145.

49. "Woe to those who would treat us like another Genoa or Geneva, imposing laws on us unacceptable to the Nation" (April 9, *Correspondance,* #21779). An air sung to the tune of "La Marseillaise" included the line "must we bend our humiliated brow beneath the German rod?"

50. Bluche's term is "metaphysical sovereignty" (119), while Stéphane Rials (*Révolution et contre-révolution au XIXe siècle,* 33) sees it as a mystification of the fact that real sovereignty lay in Napoleon's hands. Rials, who is himself a Legitimist, grants that the French passively accepted Napoleon's disparate mix of legitimacies (charismatic, democratic, etc.). He contrasts it with the "clearcut royal sovereignty of the Charter."

51. Don't forget, either, the franchise (not counting the plebiscite) in restored Napoleonic France, which admitted voters to cast ballots for deputies to the legislature, was limited to 70,000 men—fewer than the Bourbon Restoration admitted, and it was not a nominally national regime!

52. "The kings and their peoples were wrong to fear me," he told Las Cases. "I returned a new man, but they couldn't believe it. They couldn't imagine that a man would have a soul strong enough to change his character or simply bend himself before the force of circumstance. I am not a man of half-measures. I would have been the monarch of the Constitution and of peace."

53. Adolphe Thiers (1797–1877), whose history of the Consulate and the Empire we have often cited, made his political career as a Realpolitik minister in the July Monarchy (1830–48) and chief executive of the conservative Third Republic (1871–73), only to end it in alliance with the republican opposition (1873–77). Jean Jaurès (1859–1914) started out as a conservative republican deputy from the Tarn (1885–89), then converted to socialism in the early nineties and went on to become the "father" of French parliamentary socialism.

54. Constant, *Mémoire sur les Cent-Jours* (1961 ed.).

55. Louis Madelin, *Deux relèvements français: 1815–18 et 1871–78* (1951). See also Jean-Marc Largeaud, *Waterloo: La Culture de la défaite* (2004).

56. H. A. L. Fisher, *Bonapartism* (1908), 101.

57. Bertier de Sauvigny, *La Restauration* (1965), 361.

58. Thiers, *Histoire du Consulat et l'Empire,* 5: 59.

59. Cited in Largeaud, *Waterloo.*

60. The classic rendering of the battle is Henry Houssaye, *Waterloo* (1899), and the classic literary rendering is the chapter on Waterloo in Hugo's *Les Misérables.* For more modern descriptions and analyses, see David Howarth, *Waterloo: The Day of Battle* (1968); Henry Lachouque, *Waterloo* (1972); John Keegan, *The Face of Battle* (1976); Andrew Roberts, *Napoleon and Wellington* (2001); Largeaud, *Waterloo* (2004). The best short account is Jacques Garnier, "Waterloo," in Jean Tulard, *Dictionnaire,*1741–43.

61. Murat was the only sovereign who thought Napoleon might win the coming war. His attack on Rome and his wild proclamation "to the Italians!" would have finished off any trace of hope for Napoleon to be taken seriously by the Allies—if one had existed. Murat's "national" campaign was a caricature of nation-talk, so obviously deployed for the ends of intrigue and ambition as it was and evoking no popular response. But it took root as a historical root for the later national Risorgimento. See A. Valente, *Gioacchino Murat e l'Italia meridionale* (1941) and Jean Tulard, *Murat* (1999).

62. For the best thumbnail contrast between the two men, see Georges Lefebvre, *Napoleon: From Tilsit to Waterloo,* 2: 95. Andrew Roberts's (above-noted) comparison is more elaborate but less telling.

63. "Napoleon's successes (Lodi, Ulm, Marengo, and Jena) had all been won through the use of the famous *manoeuvre sur les derrières,* whereas his failures (Eylau, Aspern, Borodino, and Waterloo) had all been the fruit of blind front assaults." Charles J. Esdaile, *The Wars of Napoleon* (1995), 296.

64. Cited in Largeaud, *Waterloo,* 210.

65. Cited in Villepin, *Les Cent-Jours,* 449.

66. Said to Chaptal. *Mes souvenirs sur Napoléon* (1893), 211.

67. Cited in Arno J. Mayer, *The Furies: Violence and Terror in the French and Russian Revolutions* (2000), 36.

68. Lafayette, in the Chamber: "The nation has followed him loyally across the sands of Egypt and the wastes of Russia, across fifty fields of battle; it has shared his defeats as well as his victories. And indeed it is for thus having followed him faithfully that today we count the cost in the blood of three million Frenchmen!"

69. *Histoire de mon temps: Mémoires du Chancelier Pasquier* (1893–94), 3: 177.

70. Cited in Villepin, *Les Cent-Jours,* 492. He will say on St. Helena that he had thought to stay only two or three months in the States before making another "return" to France.

71. He had spoken endlessly of Josephine to Hortense over the past few days, including this lament: "Poor Josephine, I cannot get used to living here without her. I always expect to see her emerging from a path gathering one of those flowers, which she so loved. . . . She was the most graceful woman I have ever known."

72. Six thousand people faced political condemnations. Hundreds were assassinated or murdered by armed royalists. Arno J. Mayer has a powerful discussion of the "beast brought out in both man and soldier" in the France of this era. *Furies,* 578. The future father-in-law of Victor Hugo noted that from this period of the second Restoration came that "wonderful" French tradition of investigating and classifying people primarily according to their political affiliation, no matter what the purpose of the inquiry. Tulard, *Les vingt jours,* 261.

73. Parisian songsters and wags dubbed Louis XVIII, "Louis-two-times-neuf" ("neuf" means both "nine" and "new"). Thierry Lentz, *Napoléon* (2001), 45.

74. Themistocles had been proscribed by his fellow Athenians and took refuge with Artaxerxes, the son of the Persian king whom he had beaten in the great naval battle. Themistocles was a symbol of Athenian democracy, as well as a great general, and he had been beaten by a corrupt oligarchy.

75. Arthur Lévy closes his *Napoléon intime* ([1893], 650) with this story from Plutarch.

Chapter XV: Shadows

1. *The Black Room at Longwood: Napoleon's Exile on St. Helena* (1997, English ed.), 281.

2. For this section, see Lord Roseberry, *Napoleon: The Last Phase* (1900); Paul Ganière, *Napoléon à Sainte-Hélène,* 3 vols. (1957–62); Gilbert Martineau, *Napoléon se rend aux Anglais* (1969); Julia Blackburn, *The Emperor's Last Island: A Journey to St. Helena* (1992); Jean-Paul Kauffmann, *The Black Room at Longwood;* Jacques Jourquin, "Sainte-Hélène, choisie par raison d'Etat," *Napoléon Ier,* 11 (November/December 2001); Jean Tulard, ed., *Napoléon à Sainte-Hélène* (1981).

3. After Napoleon, a few key heads of State went into far less distant and severe exile, which they determined for themselves: Napoleon III, Kaiser Wilhelm II, Alfonso XIII, Juan Perón, among others.

4. Blackburn, *Emperor's Last Island,* 220.

5. "Longwood melancholy gently seeps drop by drop . . . this endless flow of water; it's Longwood's only song," writes Kauffmann, *Black Room at Longwood,* 175.

6. Mme de Rémusat, *Mémoires,* 2: 312.

7. The British nicknamed General Bertrand "Shrug," because he didn't take sides in the feud between Montholon and Gourgaud. Napoleon took Montholon's wife as an occasional mistress, probably with her husband's permission—this was standard practice for monarchs—but he made no headway, in that department, with Fannie Bertrand, not for want of trying.

8. The phrase is, of course, G. K. Chesterton's.

9. Sir Walter Scott, no fan of Napoleon's, wrote: "There could be no reason why Britain, when there was nothing to be got out of him [Napoleon] in exchange, should deny her prisoner a title which she had been perfectly ready to acknowledge when there was something to be gained." The only thing that the several Allied commissioners stationed on St. Helena to observe Napoleon could agree upon, other than the high cost of life on St. Helena and the noxious effects of the weather, was the unsuitability of Lowe to his appointed task. Roseberry, *Napoleon*, 80, 148.

10. Bertrand 1: 17 (August 17, 1816), 107.

11. J. Christopher Herold, *The Mind of Napoleon* (1955), xxxvii.

12. Gourgaud's two-volume *Sainte-Hélène: Journal inédit de 1815 à 1818* did not appear until 1899, long after his death (1852); and Bertrand's *Cahiers de Sainte-Hélène* was not discovered until the mid-twentieth century! Gourgaud is the only one who reports about the very last years on the island, while Bertrand's tale is the most personal in relating Napoleon's daily habits and ways (1949–59, 3 vols.). A useful anthology of selections from all four is Jean Tulard, *Napoléon à Sainte-Hélène* (1981). The most interesting study of the language and thought of the St. Helena memoirs is available in the last third of Antoine Casanova's *Napoléon et la pensée de son temps* (2001).

13. Marcel Dunan, in the introduction to his scholarly edition of the *Mémorial* (1947).

14. For his birthday, Napoleon's aides present him with a bouquet of flowers, supposedly from the King of Rome. "Bah!" he replies. "The King of Rome thinks no more about me than he does about you."

15. "Fouché was the Talleyrand of the clubs, and Talleyrand was the Fouché of the salons."

16. "He is an old man full of tolerance and light. Fatal circumstances embroiled us. I regret it deeply." Montholon, 2: 527.

17. Montholon, May 18, 1818. One day Napoleon reproached Gourgaud for moping and being downcast: "You think you have problems, you? And me? What sorrows I have! How many things to reproach myself with!"

18. Barry Edward O'Meara, *Napoleon in Exile, or the Echo of St. Helena* (1822), February 17, 1817.

19. "He, had he himself asked the question [was he a good man?], would at once have discriminated between the public and the private man. He would have said that private morality hadn't to do with statecraft, and that statecraft, if it had a morality at all, had one of its own. His own morals, he would have said, and indeed thought, were extremely creditable to so altogether exceptional a being." Lord Roseberry, *Napoleon*, 247–48. "[People like Napoleon and Joan of Arc] obey a plan, a superior scheme of things. They 'act under God's orders,' they 'were born for this,' as Joan of Arc expressed it. Their course has been *set* for them, they *follow* their star. . . . [They are] extraordinary natures." Gabriel Hanotaux, "Du Consulat à l'Empire," *Revue des Deux Mondes* (1925) 26: 81–82.

20. Cited by Jacques-Olivier Boudon, *Napoléon et les cultes* (2002), 43. The best recent discussion of Napoleon's religious beliefs (or lack thereof) on St. Helena is Antoine Casanova, "Matérialismes, expériences historiques et traits originaux des élaborations philosophiques de Napoléon Bonaparte," in Natalie Petiteau, ed., *Voies nouvelles pour l'histoire du Premier Empire* (2003), 253–82.

21. The pope also directed his secretary of state (Consalvi) to remonstrate with the British government about moving Napoleon to an exile less "mortally injurious to his health," where "the poor exile [will not be] dying by inches." The pope notes: "The pious and courageous initiative of 1801 has made Us long forget and pardon the wrongs that followed. Savona and Fontainebleau were only mistakes due to temper, or the frenzies of human ambition. The concordat was a healing act, Christian and heroic. . . . Nothing would give Us greater joy than to have contributed to the lessening of Napoleon's hardships." E. E. Y. Hales, *The Emperor and the Pope* (1961), 168.

22. Ben Weider and David Hapgood, *The Murder of Napoleon* (1982), based on published theories of Dr. Sten Forshufvud, a Swedish dentist and toxicologist. A French proponent of the thesis is René Maury, *L'Assassin de Napoléon ou le mystère de Sainte-Hélène* (1994); Maury and F. de Candé-Montholon, *L'énigme Napoléon résolue* (2000). The most recent review of all the evidence and debate is Barbara Krajewska, "Examen des causes de la mort de Napoléon," *Revue du Souvenir Napoléonien* 431 (October/November 2000) and Dr. J.-F. Lemaire et al., *Autour de "l'empoisonnement" de Napoléon* (2002). The most recent sifting by a historian is Jacques Macé, in his biography of Montholon, *L'Honneur retrouvé du général Montholon* (2000).

23. Written by Jacques Macé.

24. Though, for example, the extensive Hudson Lowe archives are available in the British Museum, and could possibly provide evidence of a conspiracy on Napoleon's life. Napoleon's upkeep and surveillance on St. Helena was extremely expensive, after all.

25. Dr. Pascal Kintz, president of the French Society of Analytical Toxicology: "My feeling is that the general state of the Emperor could justify his death [i.e., without recourse to arsenic]." Lemaire, *Autour,* 72.

26. A point made by Thierry Lentz, who also notes the strong ideological bias in Weider's books and articles: e.g., Weider denies that Napoleon's memoirs on St. Helena were written with any intention of serving his own legend! (*Was Napoleon Poisoned?* [1999], 9), in Lemaire, *Autour,* 83 n. Lentz, by the way, is the author of the best book in French on the Kennedy assassination: *Kennedy: Enquêtes sur l'assassinat d'un président* (1995).

27. Adolphe Thiers to Mme Dosne, August 5, 1856, in *Correspondance* (1904), 503.

28. Cited in Jean-Marc Largeaud, *Waterloo: La culture de la défaite* (2004), 256.

29. Among innumerable works on the Napoleonic/bonapartist legacy, see Ph. Gonnard, *Les origines de la légende napoléonienne* (1906); Albert Guérard, *Reflections on the Napoleonic Legend* (1924); J. Lucas-Dubreton, *Le culte de Napoléon* (1960); Pieter Geyl, *Napoleon, For and Against* (1949); Jean Tulard, *L'Anti-Napoléon, la légende noire de l'Empereur* (1965), *Le Mythe de Napoléon* (1971), *Le Temps des passions. Espérances, tragédies et mythes sous la Révolution et l'Empire* (1996); Frédéric Bluche, *Le bonapartisme* (1980); Keith Wren, "Victor Hugo and the Napoleonic Myth," *European Studies Review* 10 (1980): 429–58; Luigi Mascilli Migliorini, *Le Mythe du héros: France et Italie après la chute de Napoléon* (2002; orig. published, 1984); Philip Thody, *French Caesarism* (1989); Michael Paul Driskel, *As Befits a Legend: Building a Tomb for Napoleon, 1840–1861* (1993); Barbara Ann Day-Hickman, *Napoleonic Art: Nationalism and the Spirit of Rebellion in France (1815–1848)* (1999); D. Laven and L. Riall, eds., *Napoleon's Legacy* (2000); J. Benoit et al., *Napoléon au Chat Noir: L'épopée vue par Caran d'Ache* (2000); Thierry Lentz, *Napoléon* (2001); R. S. Alexander, *Napoleon* (2001); Gérard Gengembre, *Napoléon, l'Empereur immortel* (2002).

30. Cited in René Rémond, *Les Droites en France,* 4th ed. (1982), 107.

31. Cited in Alan Schom, *One Hundred Days* (1992), 320. Chateaubriand wrote: "The weight of the chains which he imposed on France was forgotten in their splendor." *De Buonaparte et des Bourbons.*

32. Napoleon to Molé, cited in Casanova, *Napoléon*, 133.

33. The Napoleonic-inspired constitution of Cadiz was reproclaimed, but in 1823 a French royalist army (100,000 "sons of Saint Louis") marched in, with the Allies' permission, and restored the reactionary monarch. Things had come full circle, but Louis XVIII's action in Spain reconfirmed the myth of Napoleonic liberalism. "Ultimately the fate of constitutional monarchy and liberalism in Spain was tied to the fate of Napoleon. . . . [I]t is hardly surprising that following Bonaparte's defeat and the withdrawal of the French armies the restoration in Spain should have become considerably more far-reaching than in France." Mayer, *Furies*, 578.

34. In some of these countries, including Papal Italy, Napoleonic reforms were retained, even as the man himself was reviled.

35. Jean Tulard points out that *Napolon*, the Polish form of "Napoleon" means "Apollo," the sun, in its capacity to exterminate and to enlighten. "Ne" or "Nai," in turn, means "truly," so it becomes "Truly Apollo." *L'Anti-Napoléon*, 24.

36. Cited in Alexander, *Napoleon*, 134.

37. And even so, Béranger, like many who wrote romantically about *l'Empereur*, remained an anticlerical republican, with no interest in bonapartism as a political alternative. Jean Touchard, *La Gloire de Béranger* (1966).

38. See Gérard de Puymege, *Chauvin, le soldat-laboureur* (1993).

39. A leading pro-Napoleonic historian Louis Madelin even wrote a celebrated comparison of the two revanchist eras: *Deux relèvements français, 1815–1818, 1871–1878*. Though the book was published in 1951, Madelin wrote it during the German occupation and Vichy—yet another time of French revanchism and the cult of defeat when the memory of the Emperor served to lift hopes.

40. Dominique de Villepin, *Les Cent-Jours, ou l'esprit de sacrifice* (2001), 244.

41. Cited in Gérard Gengembre, *Napoléon, l'Empereur immortel* (2002), 189. No less romantic is the classic biography *Napoleon* by Emil Ludwig (1925).

42. For example, Desmond Seward, *Napoleon and Hitler* (1989), but in this vein see also Roger Caratini (a Frenchman), *Napoléon* (2002).

43. On a private note, De Gaulle told his son, Philippe, "The French are still not consoled over Waterloo because despite everything, they very nearly won the battle." Philippe de Gaulle, *Mémoires accessoires* (1997).

44. Robert Tombs, *France, 1814–1914* (1996), and "Was There a French Sonderweg?" in *European Identities/Identités Européennes* (1994). Thus the French historian Fernand Rude sees the resistance of 1814, which prepared the way for Napoleon's return from Elba, as a precursor of the "national insurrection" of the French resistance against the Nazis, 1940–44. Thus do myths beget and sustain each other. "Le réveil du patriotisme révolutionnaire dans la région du Rhône-Alpes en 1814", in *Cahiers d'histoire* 16 (1971). Similarly, a contemporary French communist scholar, as virulent a critic of Napoleon as scholarship begets, yet writes: "Let me be clear, however . . . I will not hesitate to say that I can easily imagine myself yelling "Vive l'Empereur!" on Napoleon's return from Elba, or again on the steps of the Elysée Palace, on 21 June 1815, against the return of the Bourbons. And I can even imagine crying "Vive l'Empereur!" at the return of his body, 15 December 1840." Yves Benot, *La démence coloniale* (1991), 11.

45. Most recently, see Marcel Normand, *Il faut fusiller Napoléon* [We have to shoot Napoleon] (2003).

46. The "rue Bonaparte," in the 6th arrondissement is clearly intended to honor the pre-imperial general, not the First Emperor of the French. Yet there are many streets and *places* named for innumerable kings (Philippe Auguste, Charlemagne, Louis XIV, etc.).

47. In Dominique de Villepin's words, "The Empire, it's the Emperor, the charisma of

one man, the genius of a warrior, the ephemeral legitimacy, but in no case the principles and institutions of a regime." *Les Cent-Jours, ou l'esprit de sacrifice* (2002) ends
with a parallel drawn between the destinies of Napoleon and De Gaulle. Jean-Marc
Largeaud notes how clearly, if how unconsciously, Villepin thus fits himself into the
French "political culture of defeat" (i.e., of nostalgia and "rebirth") in the contemporary era, which sees the French nation-State dissolve its formerly clear outlines
into Europe. *La Culture de la défaite* (2003).

48. An excellent discussion of the whole question of official versions of the French past
is available in Robert Gildea, *The Past in French History* (1994).
49. Geyl, *Napoleon, For and Against,* 375.
50. Jean Tulard, *Le temps des passions: Espérances, tragédies et mythes sous la Révolution et l'Empire* (1996), 152–55.
51. Much of which has been translated into English—from Columbia and Harvard Uni-
versity Presses.
52. The notable exception being Jean Tulard's fine essay on the return of Napoleon's
body to France in 1840.
53. As Maurice Agulhon puts it, "It is past high time to write the magic word [*nation*]
apropos of Napoleon," while Villepin—who, revealingly, draws on no English
studies for his beautifully penned, almost elegiac, study of the Hundred Days
(March to June, 1815), compares Napoleon to (who else?) De Gaulle, emphasizing
the two men's mutual dignity in defeat, their "spirit of sacrifice" to French national
interest. See Agulhon's preface to Pierre Larousse, *Napoléon* (2002). For Villepin's
views, see *Les Cent-Jours, ou l'esprit de sacrifice* (2001). For his part, Pierre Nora, the editor of *Les Lieux de Mémoire,* writes "What [Napoleon] managed to 'marry' was, rather,
the prose of the Revolution with the lost poetry of the royalty. It is in this sense that
Napoleon belongs to the Revolution, as De Gaulle does to the Republic." Unpublished paper, "Notes provisoires sur Napoleon et la Révolution: Les Lieux de la
mêlée."
54. "Totalitarian" is a loaded (i.e., a politically engendered) term that conflated Communist with Nazi and Fascist politics. I use it for convenience, but urge the reader
to see the excellent critique of the concept in Arno J. Mayer, *The Dynamics of Counterrevolution in Europe, 1870–1956.*
55. Edouard Driault, *Napoléon en Italie* (1906), 667.
56. A few recent historians see Mussolini, Hitler, and Stalin as following in the French
emperor's path, virtually lock- (if not goose-) step. The quote is from Paul Johnson,
Napoleon, 187. For a systematic comparison, there is Desmond Seward, *Napoleon and
Hitler* (1988), but Johnson, Schom, Alistair Horne (*How Far from Austerlitz?
Napoleon, 1805–1815* (1996), among others, draw the comparison.
57. "The New Age of Tyranny," *The New York Review of Books,* 24 October 2002, 28–29.
58. The definition is Christian Meier's paraphrasing of Cicero. *Caesar,* 313. Whence the
term, *teratology*—the study or science of monstrosities or abnormal formations in animals or plants.
59. Cortés's "battles would lose their heroic aura, and the conquistadors would appear
more like abattoir workers." A. B. Bosworth, "A Tale of Two Empires: Hernán
Cortés and Alexander the Great," in A. B. Bosworth and E. J. Baynham, eds,
Alexander the Great in Fact and Fiction (2000), 38. See also Christian Duvergier,
Cortés (2000).
60. Mayer's book set off a lively scholarly debate (by no means just over his views on
Napoleon). See, notably, the review articles on Mayer's *Furies* in *The Journal of Modern History,* 73, 4 (December 2001).
61. Renzo de Felice, *Mussolini, il duce: Gli anni del consenso, 1926–1936* (1974), 83.
62. In 1934, when Hitler ordered the murders of his counterrevolutionary allies, the

Brown Shirts, who had become a liability to him. Or *Kristallnacht* (November 9–10, 1938), when the Nazi thugs were permitted to attack Jewish homes and businesses.

63. Military losses in war, morally speaking, are far from synonymous with the slaughter of the innocents or the repression of political enemies. We, of course, discuss each Napoleonic campaign as it arises, but suffice it to say here, not all armed conflict during the Empire was simply "Napoleon's fault, case closed." Then, too, there remains a problem of order of magnitude. Over two million men, French and foreign, were inducted into the Grande Armée, 1803–14. Of those, it has been estimated that 900,000 died in battle or as a result of wounds, or who went missing (Jacques Houdaille, "Pertes de l'armée de terre sous le premier Empire, d'après les registres matricules," *Population* 27 [1972]: 27–50). Assuming that Allied losses were roughly equivalent, the number of overall military dead, 1803 to 1814—1.8 million—is still proportionally far below the 25 million soldiers killed on both sides in all wars involving Hitler and Stalin. The civilian dead, of course, were incomparably more in World War II than in the Napoleonic wars.

64. See the useful (and amusing) summary of Curzio Malaparte (alias for Kurt Erich Suckert), *Technique du coup d'Etat* (1931)

65. In other words, it is the *counter*-imperial, rather than in the imperial, historical experience per se, that we come upon the relevance of the "friend-enemy distinction" as the source of "the political," so dear to the heart of its theoretician-coiner, Carl Schmitt, the twentieth-century German philosopher-jurist. Schmitt, we should not forget, originated many of his most profound insights about political man in studying the "German" partisans who rose up against Napoleon.

66. The German writer Goethe never fell for Napoleon as strongly as his contemporary Hegel did, yet when he heard the news of Napoleon's death, he imagined a dialogue between God and the Devil, where the former challenges the latter thus: "If you have the courage to lay a hand on this mortal, then you may haul him through your hellish portal."

67. *Napoleon: The Last Phase* (1900), 226. Curiously, it was Napoleon's exploitation of myth and superstition (his reestablishment of official Catholicism), and his own apparent succumbing to belief in his "star" or "destiny," that put Nietzsche off. On the German philosopher's view, Napoleon, to be consistent with (read: worthy of) himself, should not have attributed his successes to anything other than his talent and will. It was a failure in Napoleon's capacity for self-understanding that thus brought his ruin.

Introduction (Misplaced)

1. Jacques-Olivier Boudon, *Histoire du Consulat et de l'Empire* (2000), 265.

2. Montesquieu, *Mes pensées*, 137.575. I am grateful to Elena Russo for this citation.

3. See *La Culture de la défaite* (2003), the remarkable study by Jean-Marc Largeaud of France's romance with "the culture of defeat." *Waterloo: La culture de la défaite* (2004).

4. "Hail, Caesar, those who are about to die salute you." Alfred de Vigny uses this famous gladiatorial sentence as the epigraph of his book *Military Grandeur and Servitude*. Robert Kaplan's *Warrior Politics: Why Leadership Requires a Pagan Ethos* (2002) provides some post-modern insight into this ancient war ethos, but his goal is less historical understanding than championing a neoconservative political agenda, so his work's value to our endeavor is limited.

5. Marcel Reinhard, "Discussion," *Revue d'histoire moderne et contemporaine*, 17 (July-September 1970): 467.

6. Consider Nietzsche's judgment: "We owe it to Napoleon (and not by any means to the French Revolution, which aimed at the 'brotherhood' of nations and a blooming universal exchange of hearts) that we now confront a succession of a few warlike centuries that have no parallel in history; in short, that we have entered *the classical age of war*, of scientific and at the same time popular war on the largest scale (in weapons, talents, and discipline). All coming centuries will look back on it with envy and awe for its perfection." *The Gay Science*, ed. Walter Kaufmann (1974), section 362. See an interesting recent German study, Karen Hagemann, *"Männlicher Muth und Teutsche Ehre": Nation, Militär und Geschlecht zur Zeit der Antinapoleonischen Kriege Preussens* (2002).

7. See my forthcoming work *The Political Sense of the Idea of "the Nation" in French History*.

8. Frédéric Bluche, *Le bonapartisme* (1980), 10. In Adam Gopnik's superb summary: "Napoleon's legacy is not a reminder of the power of pure action. It has become instead one more demonstration of the power of *words and abstract symbolism to create a reality of their own*. . . . It seems to fill a deep human need for display, order, glamour that no other system of modern honor has yet quite managed to do." *The New Yorker*, Nov. 24, 1997, 84. Emphasis added.

9. John Holland Rose, *The Life of Napoleon I* (1901), 1: 505–506.

10. Yves Benot, *La démence coloniale sous Napoléon* (1991), 11.

11. "I saw the Emperor—this world soul—riding out of the city on reconnaissance. It is indeed a wonderful sensation to see such an individual, who, concentrated here at a single point, astride a horse, reaches out over the world and masters it . . . this extraordinary man, whom it is impossible not to admire." Written in 1806, from Jena. *Briefe von und an Hegel*, ed. Johannes Hoffmeister (1969), 1: 74; *Hegel: The Letters*, trans. Clark Butler and Christine Seiler (1984), 114

12. Christian Meier, *Caesar* (1982), 302.

13. Jean-Paul Kauffmann, *The Black Room at Longwood: Napoleon's Exile on Saint Helena* (1997), 209. This sensitive, first-person exploration has justifiably become a classic.

Bibliographical Comments

I gave a dinner in Paris in the autumn of 2002 at which several experts of the French First Empire were present, including one of the bright lights among younger English-language historians and his counterpart in the new generation of French authors (in scholarly historical circles, anything under fifty is "young"). We got into a discussion about, well, Napoleon—specifically, about the primacy of his role in precipitating war. Within a short time, a pleasant, if animated, conversation had declined into a frankly uncomfortable set-to, with the "Anglo-Saxon," as the French refer to all writers in English, insisting that every last war of the Empire, including even that of the Second Coalition (1798–1802), was the personal responsibility (read: fault) of *l'Empereur*, while the Frenchman stoutly defended the proposition that the coalition powers were also guilty of greed and rivalry, not to mention ugly counterrevolutionary intentions. And so it went, with no quarter given, until the clock struck twelve, and people got up to go home.

What hit me hard—indeed, I cannot stop marveling at it—is how two hundred years of writing, in which the two debaters were deeply steeped, had almost no effect on the passions, or even the arguments, unleashed. For all intents and purposes, the date of the dinner party might as well have been autumn 1802, as an Englishman and a Frenchman debated responsibility for the impending failure of the Treaty of Amiens. One's underlying attitude toward Napoleon is an emotional and cultural affair, not readily amenable to rational shaping. Another historian told me once that if all the works on the battle of Waterloo, a topic on which he happens to be expert, were translated into a neutral tongue—say, Italian, for the person in question is Corsican—he could tell whether a given work was authored by a Frenchman or an "Anglo-Saxon," based on the tone of the first few sentences. Although I did not test his claim, it sounded about right. Napoleon is where the river runs deepest and widest between historians writing in English and those writing in French.

Such a state of affairs makes for a delicate position for an American living in Paris, not blessed with the ability to discern human "souls" and historical realities, as clearly as did the interlocutors at my dinner table. To quote Jean Genet, "My faith is never complete and my opinion is never undivided." It thus struck me that both sides seem to be inmates of "the clean, well-lit prison of one idea," as G. K. Chesterton put it: the revilers failing to grasp the power of the man's uniqueness, and the good he also did; perhaps above all, failing to explain his hold on contemporaries, who were not simply dupes. The hero-worshippers, on the other hand, understate the blood and the mud, as well as the consequences of the Napoleonic myth for human gullibility.

Neither side will be entirely satisfied with the interpretations in this book whose underlying tone might be summed up as admiration bordering on amazement, sharply punctuated with increasingly strong disapproval, often suffused with sadness. This is an attitude I owe to my adolescent self whose interest in Napoleon made me the butt of teases and jokes in my left-wing family. It is indubitably closer to the French view(s) of Napoleon than to those of recent generations of my "Anglo-Saxon" countrymen. The latter's unrelenting repulsion and remorseless wish to cut Napoleon down to size are missing from this book.

On the other hand, I readily agree with Eucrates, when he tells the Roman conqueror

Sylla in the dialogue by Montesquieu, "My Lord, it is surely a blessing that Heaven spared humanity a large number of men such as you. Born for mediocrity, we are overwhelmed by the sublime spirits. For a man to rise so far above the rest of humanity, the cost to the rest is too great." As Montesquieu understood, when such men do appear, which is rarely, *understanding* them is more than a matter of reviling them. In the case of the first Emperor of the French, it is also a matter of understanding why so many of his contemporaries and of our contemporaries—by no means, just Frenchmen—"trembled," and were "afraid of their own longing." This is a more ticklish undertaking.

We are desperate for important new primary material on Napoleon. The horror is that, in certain ways, the most complete and best-written life of this man remains the twenty-volume history of the Consulate and the Empire produced by the statesman, Adolphe Thiers in the middle of the nineteenth century. Since then, comparatively little by way of startlingly new and important evidence for a biography of the Emperor has been unearthed, while little of what is known to exist has remained unsifted. Frédéric Masson unearthed Napoleon's youthful writings early in the twentieth century, while the significant Bertrand and Caulaincourt memoirs turned up a few decades later, as did, more recently, the music for Napoleon's coronation mass. This naturally leads anyone undertaking a book like mine to hope that he, too, like the archeologist Howard Carter, will stumble onto a Tutankhamen's tomb of riches. The chances of that happening are slim, however, and it is clear from the foregoing that I did not so stumble. I did not even (I hope!) fall for a wonderful hoax, such as the one that took in André Malraux, the noted writer and De Gaulle's minister of culture, some years ago.[1] Apart from several unpublished letters of Napoleon's, a more complete version of his unfinished novel (*Clisson et Eugénie*) shown me by Peter Hicks of the Foundation Napoléon, and the private papers of one of his leading diplomats, I have not laid eyes on anything new. The Hudson Lowe papers in the British Museum still await historians, but for the biographer they are unlikely to offer much, except, *perhaps*, on the question of how Napoleon died. A rigorously systematic excavation of the scores of volumes of the semi-official French government record, the *Moniteur Universel*, would flesh out the political history of the First Empire, but would probably not offer startling evidence to the biographer.

A principal source for any biography of Napoleon is, of course, the memoirs of his era. New ones continue to appear all the time, as documents are discovered and editorial courage rises to the challenge of publishing them.[2] Hundreds of Napoleon's contemporaries felt the need, often financial, to recount and comment upon aspects of the Emperor's life. I have made occasional use of memoirs, but a word of caution: the vast majority were written *long* after the events they witnessed, hence in full knowledge of the disastrous outcome—whence each memoirist's tendency to see Napoleon in a variety of shadows, often having to do with the writer's current politics or life circumstances.[3] The memoirs tend to gainsay imperial charisma and to see through imperial beneficence, usually resolving Napoleon's ambiguities for the worse, writing large their (originally slight or nonexistent) differences with the Emperor, and generally striking a tone that is "superior" to what they showed in His Majesty's presence. In sum, they tend to explain the failures, not the successes. Most large political careers finish in some failure or other; this is "the nature of politics and human affairs," as Enoch Powell put it—and knew at first hand. Napoleon's fall was as cataclysmic as his nature was phenomenal, and neither his contemporaries nor posterity is readily able to put his end out of mind. In trying to explain Napoleon's rise and his hold on people and power, a constant awareness of his titanic conclusion is not always enlightening. A distinct effort must be made to see the man, year by year, as he was. So I have used memoirs critically and sparingly.

Napoleon Bonaparte is not a man on whom it will be possible to do a definitive life; indeed, no biography of him before J. M. Thompson's 1952 classic is still widely read. Each generation wants its own takes on the force of nature that was the first Emperor of the French. Which leads me to what I believe is crucial for producing a new and interesting biography of Napoleon—aside, that is, from the writer's insertion in the current changing complex of emotions, conflicts, and questions that society always brings to understanding and interrogating history: this is the scholarship laid up in the past three or four decades on Napoleon and the First French Empire. The titles referred to in the backnotes of this book represent a truly fine and useful collection of books and articles that reflect the best methods and insights of international scholarship: from annotated editions of documents, memoirs, and letters to monographs and larger studies on every aspect of the First Empire and its founder, to a handful of important general works—for example, Thierry Lentz's three-volume history-in-progress of the First Empire. There are hundreds of roses blooming, if only one cared to take the time to sniff them.

Thanks to painstaking and reflective works by the likes of Antoine Casanova, Annie Jourdan, and Frédéric Bluche, we now have an inestimably surer grip than did Thiers on Napoleon's evolving ideas, his rationalizations, his propaganda, his odd tastes (e.g., for Robespierre); on the interplay of social and his personal psychology with surrounding intellectual history. Thanks to Jean-Marc Largeaud, we have a nuanced sense of the "culture of defeat" that began with the battle of Waterloo and has subtly but surely influenced French history ever since. For example, it suffuses Foreign Minister Dominique de Villepin's wonderful book on the Hundred Days without the author's realizing it. Andy Martin's quirky take on Napoleon's youthful writing is infuriating but thought-provoking and instructive, as are Christopher Prendergast's and David O'Brien's study of a single painting by Baron Gros on the aftermath of the battle of Eylau—a painting I shall never look at the same way again. With simplicity of prose and a total command of the sources, Jacques Garnier has quietly reshaped our understanding of the Napoleonic campaigns (and Owen Connelly keeps us mindful of the blunders). Jacques Macé, Jean-Paul Kauffmann, and Julia Blackburn have deepened our feel of Napoleon's experiences on St. Helena, right down to the smells, while Dorothy Carrington's study of Napoleon's childhood and family in Corsica is a perfect gem, as is her posthumously published biography of Charles Bonaparte. With an infinity of patience and expertise, François Crouzet has taken the full measure of the economic face of the war between England and France.

Keep going. Jacques-Olivier Boudon has strengthened our grip on Napoleonic religious and educational policy, as Louis Bergeron has done on the Empire's social and economic life. A large host of international historians—Stuart Woolf, Geoffrey Ellis, Michael Broers, Philip Dwyer, Elisabeth Fehrenbach, Helmut Berding, etc.—have greatly extended and completely revised our understanding of the *Grand Empire*, especially (but not only) its downsides for subject populations. In a more positive light, Thierry Lentz's study of the Consulate (1799–1804) bids fair to have that regime renamed "The Great Consulate" for its unique contribution to French and world history. David Bell has expertly palpated French nationalism in the eighteenth century and early Napoleonic period. The significance of Napoleon's legacy for France and Europe has never been better understood than now, thanks to insightful new works by Isser Woloch, Jean-Claude Martin, David Laven and Lucy Riall, Martyn Lyons, R. S. Alexander, Gerhard Bauer, Andrei Nieuwazny, Luigi Mascilli Migliorini, and others. Innumerable members of the huge Napoleonic cast of characters (e.g., Murat, Fouché, Talleyrand, Cambacérès.) have been the subjects of serious biographies that flesh out broadly our understanding of Napoleon's use of, and interaction with, his collaborators.[4]

Finally, two authors stand out from the rest, as is clear from my notes. Paul Schroeder of the University of Illinois has produced a compendious masterpiece on foreign relations, 1763–1848, which can only have a profound influence on anyone who makes the effort to plumb its insights and carefully wrought analyses, regardless of whether he agrees with many of the author's positions. One is (I am) far the wiser for having read and mentally argued with him. Second, Jean Tulard of the Sorbonne is responsible nearly single-handedly for the establishment of Napoleonic studies as a serious academic enterprise in France, where—astonishingly—it had not been the case before him (for reasons discussed in Chapter 15). This man's indefatigability and productivity are terrifying. He has written books or essays on virtually every topic mentioned above, and several others as well, right down to a study of the interaction of Napoleon with the composer of "La Marseillaise," Rouget de L'Isle. He writes that between the "black" and the "golden" views of Napoleon, "I do not pick a party. I am content simply to state and to register."[5] But, in fact, Tulard is very critical and skeptical, if fair, in his approach toward Napoleon, and like many historians, he admits that the Empire interests him much more than the Emperor who created and ran it.

Etcetera, etcetera, etcetera, and plenty more etcetera where that came from: you get the picture. The foregoing and other unnamed works are what make a biography of Napoleon in and for our time an intellectually exciting and profitable prospect. To ignore this scholarship—or simply to peruse some of it—is to doom one's project, in my opinion. Even a writer of Anthony Burgess's literary octane, who princely ignored scholarship, preferring simply to butt heads with *l'Empereur* (*Napoleon Symphony*, 1974) based on a command of the narrative, condemned himself to producing a brilliant and colorful repetition of familiar romantic views about Napoleon.

Of late, as befits an era of bicentenary reflection, we have suddenly enjoyed a spate of "lives" of Napoleon: five, since 1997.[6] "The more the merrier" is one's first reaction, but in reading them, one becomes aware of the reduced profitability of works by authors who are quicker to pass judgment on Napoleon than to understand him and his era—an era that is emphatically *not ours*.

For a life of Napoleon Bonaparte is an unnerving undertaking, and the problem in recent decades has lain in getting serious biographers to take a serious shot at a life of this man. In 2001, one of the foremost younger scholars in America shook his fist at "the oversized figure of Napoleon [who] has intimidated and repulsed [us] for too long."[7] Would-be biographers confront a great problem beyond the superabundance of sources—far too much for one person to read, let alone master—and that is the infamous ungraspability of the subject. The reader will have judged for himself by now whether the present author has succeeded.

NOTES

1. Malraux fell for Lullin de Châteauvieux's nineteenth-century fake, "Manuscrit venu de Sainte-Hélène d'une manière inconnue," and alerted the publishing house Gallimard that he had a great "find" for them to publish. See Jean Tulard, *Le temps des passions: Espérances, tragédies et mythes sous la Révolution et l'Empire* (1996), 148.
2. For example, Johann-Friedrich Reichardt's *Un hiver à Paris sous le Consulat (1802–1803)*, published in 2003, with notes and introduction by Thierry Lentz.
3. For a sharp critique of the problem of Napoleonic memoirs, see Stuart Woolf, "Napoleon and Europe Revisited," *Modern & Contemporary France* 8, 4 (2000), 469–78; and also his criticisms of Luigi Mascilli Migliorini's *Napoleone* (2001) in a forthcoming edition of *French History*.
4. Isser Woloch's recent *Napoleon and His Collaborators* (1999) is crucial in pulling much of this together.
5. Tulard, *Le temps des passions*, 181. He writes, "You need to have a gambler's spirit to take on the Grand Empire, and we would propose as the dictum of the historian who would do so a line of [Jean] Cocteau, slightly rephrased: 'In order to put on this show, let us pretend to find mysteries in it.'" 186.
6. Vincent Cronin, *Napoleon Bonaparte* (1971); Alan Schom, *Napoleon Bonaparte*

(1997); Frank McLynn, *Napoleon, A Biography* (2002); Robert Asprey, *The Rise and Fall of Napoleon Bonaparte*, 2 vols. (2000, 2001); Paul Johnson, *Napoleon* (2002). Luigi Mascilli Migliorini's *Napoleone* (2001), in Italian, is a masterful work, especially on the Napoleonic political legacy. Finally, Isser Woloch's *Napoleon and His Collaborators: The Making of a Dictatorship* (2001) is not a biography *strictu sensu*, but is an excellent study that cannot go unmentioned. The four-volume French biography *Napoleon* (1997), by Max Gallo, was the basis for a four-part television movie on Napoleon, with Christian Clavier in the lead role. Unquestionably, the finest biography to date is Jean Tulard, *Napoléon, le mythe du sauveur* (1978), published in English in a wretched translation, in 1985: *Napoleon: The Myth of the Saviour*.

7. Johns Hopkins professor David Bell continues, "The scholarly *cordon sanitaire* around his regime should be removed. He is not such a colossus, or such a freak, as to defy rigorous historical analysis." "Collaborators," *The New Republic*, April 2, 2001, 45.

Acknowledgments

Nothing connected with this book gives me more unalloyed pleasure than to thank the many people who contributed, often very importantly, to it. Among fellow historians, I would mention Philippe Minard, Elena Russo, Philip Dwyer, Jacques-Olivier Boudon, Jean Tulard, François Crouzet, Joe Byrnes (and his graduate seminar), Pierre Sorlin, Alain Pillepich, Fernand Beaucour, Lydia Moland, Maurice Agulhon, Jacques Garnier, and Bertrand Joly. A handful of colleagues gave without stinting, no matter how much I asked: Larry Ceplair, Jean-Marc Largeaud, Peter Hicks, Louis Bergeron, Thierry Lentz, and Edward Castleton.

I also had a number of readers from various walks of life who tolerated my "trying out" sections (and wholes) on them: George Kollock, Ian Robertson-Smith, Janet Thorpe, Terry Hankey, Bredo Johnsen, Mary Yost, Stéphan and Apple Guérin, George Englund, Paul Ress, Lawrence Goldman, Marie-France Pochna, David Shaw, and Michel Jacquet.

On the editorial side, I want to thank my old friend Tom O'Brien, whose induplicable ability as an improver of prose has stood me in good stead on this, as on two previous books. Old friends Jack Miles, Vanessa Ochs, and Arlette Ricci gave signal service on "*Frisson*"—indeed I owe its existence to their sighs about the previous tenant of that crucial spot in the book. John Nelson's singular contribution to the lead of Chapter 1 is painful to confess (hell, why couldn't I come up with that?). At Scribner, there are many who helped mightily: Erin Curler, Charlotte Gross, Eva Young, George Wen, Erich Hobbing, and Rodrigo Corral.

This leaves two people—stalwart and loyal friends. One is responsible for there being a book at all: Lisa Drew, my publisher; and Vincent Curcio, who must carry squarely on his broad shoulders the responsibility for almost everything that is any good in the preceding pages.

—Steven Englund
Paris, June 24, 2003

Index

Napoleon I (*cont.*)
　MARRIAGE TO MARIE-LOUISE,
　　516*n*. 15
　birth of a son, 361, 363, 364
　marriage ceremony, 360–61
　Napoleon's renaming from Maria,
　　360
　MILITARY CAREER
　as aide-de-camp with the Army of
　　Italy, 60
　Ajaccio National Guard volunteer
　　battalion, 47, 50, 52, 53, 55, 478*n*.
　　13
　campaign in Egypt, first (1796–1797),
　　126–31
　campaign in Egypt, second (1800),
　　173–77
　campaign in Italy, 97–102
　campaign of 1805, 269–79
　Champagne campaign, 406–9
　as commander of the Army of
　　England, 125
　as commander of the Army of the
　　Interior, 79, 97–98
　crossing of the Alps, 174,. 318–19
　Ecole Royale Militaire (ERM) educa-
　　tion, 21–24
　French Revolution on Corsica and
　　conflicts with superiors, 43, 47,
　　478*n*. 13
　as head of the army's Topographical
　　Bureau, 77–78
　ideological dimension of military suc-
　　cess, 105–6
　invasion of France, 401–6
　Jacobin regime's war against Euro-
　　pean states, 72–74, 480*n*. 11, 480*n*.
　　12
　Le Fère regiment, 25–26, 27, 29, 34,
　　41, 43, 44, 50, 60, 478*n*. 9
　"Little Corporal" diminutive, 108
　myths and legends about Napoleon's
　　battles, 108–9
　Napoleon's attitude toward war,
　　393–94
　Napoleon's leadership with troops,
　　130–31
　Napoleon's command of French lan-
　　guage and accent, 18
　Napoleon's knowledge of the psyches
　　of men in uniform, 104–6
　Napoleon's memory of father, 13–14

Napoleon's reputation, 70, 97, 98, 99,
　100, 108, 480*n*. 12
nobility and caste exclusiveness in the
　armed forces, 23, 28, 477*n*. 12
plans for retaking Toulon from the
　British fleet and Napoleon's
　appointments to the artillery,
　63–65
psychological factors in Napoleon's
　military success, 103–4
recognition as Napoleon rather than
　Bonaparte, 279
recognition of soldiers, 278, 292
Royal Artillery commission, 18, 23, 27
war in Vendée during Thermidor,
　75–79
Waterloo, 439–442, 529*n*. 60
wound at Toulon, 65
PERSONAL LIFE
"court" around Napoleon, 203,
　361–62, 389
Malmaison chateau, 141, 202–3,
　489*n*. 88
relationship with Bonaparte family,
　204–5
residences, 202–3
PERSONALITY AND TRAITS
ability to focus on several things at
　once, 146
acceptance of Corsican identity,
　28–29
anger at British press attacks, 259
approach to money and finances,
　320–21, 509*n*. 76
attitudes toward women, 89
beliefs about humanity, 136, 143–44
beliefs about religion, 30, 31–32, 68,
　479*n*. 22
bequests under will, 21
childhood, 14–15
command of French language and
　accent, 18
comments on Napoleon as head of
　State, 201–2
contemporary awareness of identify-
　ing traits, 196
Corsican influence on Napoleon, 147,
　189, 194, 202, 204, 511*n*. 105
expression of concern for his family,
　20–21, 24, 34
fascination with war, 26
friendships in school, 19, 24